PUBLIC UTILITY
REGULATION

PUBLIC UTILITY REGULATION

BY

G. LLOYD WILSON, Ph.D.

*Professor of Transportation and Public Utilities
and Director of Bureau of Public Affairs,
University of Pennsylvania*

JAMES M. HERRING, Ph.D.

*Assistant Professor of Geography and Public Utilities,
University of Pennsylvania*

ROLAND B. EUTSLER, Ph.D.

*Professor of Economics and Insurance,
University of Florida*

FIRST EDITION

McGRAW-HILL BOOK COMPANY, Inc.

NEW YORK AND LONDON

1938

THE MAPLE PRESS COMPANY, YORK, PA.

To

GROVER GERHARDT HUEBNER, Ph.D.

Professor of Commerce and Transportation
in the Wharton School of Finance and
Commerce of the University of Pennsylvania, this volume is dedicated in appreciation of his distinguished attainments
as teacher, author and research scholar.

PREFACE

The obligation to render adequate service at reasonable and nondiscriminatory rates has long been recognized as a duty of public utility enterprises. This doctrine was established early as a principle of common law. In order to guarantee fulfillment of this obligation, governments have undertaken to regulate and control public utility industries, and today these industries are subject to comprehensive regulatory control in a myriad of forms applicable to many phases of activity. The general acceptance and widespread existence of governmental regulation of public utilities, however, have not resulted in satisfactory solutions of many of the problems arising out of regulatory efforts or complete fulfillment of the obligations of public utility industries. Public utility regulation, therefore, has come to be an acute political, economic, and social issue, upon which public sentiment is divided. It is believed by many that a crisis in public control has been reached wherein the prospect of failure must be faced or regulatory machinery and policies must be extensively and intelligently revised if regulation is to achieve its purposes.

The present volume is an analysis of the nature, extent, and problems of public utility regulation in the United States. The authors approach this subject by considering the historical development of regulation and the emergence of the state public utility commission as the prevailing pattern of regulatory machinery. The problems of state versus local regulation are reviewed, and the state commission, as a regulatory agency, is critically evaluated. The subjects of regulation are then analyzed; regulation of accounting and reporting, rates and valuation for rate-making purposes, rate of return, depreciation, service, security issues, and other aspects are examined from the standpoint of regulatory procedures, techniques, policies, and problems. Issues and conflicts are critically examined. The authors then describe and analyze the expanding role of the Federal Government in respect to the control of public utility industries. The significance and implications of this tendency

are evaluated in terms of the possibilities of more effective
regulation. In this particular, attention is given to the holding
company, the interstate movement of gas and electricity, interstate motor transportation, and communication. Attention is
also given to the activities of the Federal Government in undertaking power projects and in promoting rural electrification.
What these developments portend to the privately owned power
industry and their significance as instances of national economic
planning are indicated. Finally, the issues of government versus
private ownership are evaluated.

A critical viewpoint is followed throughout, the authors
attempting to evaluate the present status of public utility regulation and to show both its strengths and its weaknesses. Controversial issues are examined, and positions, which from the
very nature of the problems are more or less dogmatic, are taken
concerning them. Such viewpoints are not presented with the
purpose of inculcating them into others, but rather to establish
mooring posts in the shifting tides of controversy. In general,
the measuring rod which has been used as the basis upon which
the authors have predicated their acceptance of certain viewpoints and their critical evaluation of regulatory policies has
been the effect upon the public utility companies in the light of
their obligations to render adequate service to the public at
reasonable and nondiscriminatory rates. The point of view that
the authors believe they have presented is a public point of view,
one colored neither by pro-utility nor by anti-utility bias.

The volume is an outgrowth of experience in teaching public
utility economics and regulation. The material is selected,
organized, and presented with the view of giving college students
an understanding of the problems of regulation and an appreciation of the significance of regulation in the present economic and
political organization of society. It is hoped also that laymen,
legislators, governmental officials, and others interested in these
problems will find in the book a well-rounded and complete
analysis.

The authors make no apology for excluding almost entirely a
discussion of railroad, water, and air transportation in this
volume. The size of the transportation industry and its significance to the American people warrant that it be given special and
separate treatment, and this has been done frequently and

adequately by others. The authors wish to point out, however, that many of the problems discussed in this volume are common also to the transportation industries, and thus principles may be made to apply in all cases. Because of the common nature of the problems and because, in many instances, the regulatory policies applicable to the transportation industries are well defined and tested by experience, the authors have felt free to make reference to the regulation of transportation agencies and to draw illustrations from these fields.

It is recognized that an understanding of the problems of regulation and the formulation of sound opinion on controversial issues cannot be obtained without a background knowledge of the economic characteristics and features, organization, functions, services, rate structures, and policies of each of the public utility industries. The authors have not included these features in the present volume, since their earlier volume, "Public Utility Industries," was written specifically for the purpose of serving as an introduction to the broader problems of public utility control and regulation. The two volumes, "Public Utility Industries" and "Public Utility Regulation," are thus companion volumes and together are designed to present a comprehensive survey of public utilities in modern life. The authors believe that jointly they offer data and opinion which will be of value in arriving at sound viewpoints concerning the ever more important questions of public utility regulation.

The documentation throughout the book indicates the sources from which the materials have been drawn, although the authors assume responsibility for their use and interpretation. Grateful acknowledgment is made by the authors to their associates who have read and criticized the manuscripts, and to the many others, including executives of public utility companies and members of federal and state regulatory commissions and their staffs, through whose cooperation and assistance much of the material contained herein has been collected and prepared.

G. Lloyd Wilson,
James M. Herring,
Roland B. Eutsler.

Philadelphia, Pa.,
Gainesville, Fla.,
  June, 1938.

CONTENTS

PUBLIC
UTILITY REGULATION

CHAPTER I

REGULATION BEFORE THE ESTABLISHMENT OF STATE COMMISSIONS

Public utility companies in the United States are subject to detailed, comprehensive regulation by governmental authority. Except for their interstate operations, which are within the exclusive province of federal jurisdiction, these companies are regulated largely by public service commissions established in all states with the exception of Delaware. Why public utilities are so regulated and why the prevailing method is regulation by state bodies are questions we shall answer briefly in this opening chapter.

THE RIGHT TO REGULATE

Regulation of private industry in the interest of the public is not a new feature of American political life. Throughout the history of American governments, and back through centuries of changing economic and political thought in the countries from which most Americans originally came, industry has been subject to sometimes more, sometimes less, governmental regulation. The scope of regulation as well as its intensiveness has varied from time to time in accordance with the prevalence of collectivistic or individualistic ideals. As Prof. Glaeser has pointed out,[1] under the mercantilist philosophy individual initiative was greatly limited; economic wants were viewed from the national instead of the local viewpoint, and industry was regulated in order that it might promote the interests of the state. Royal charters were granted to trading and plantation

[1] GLAESER, M. G., "Outlines of Public Utility Economics," The Macmillan Company, New York, 1931, pp. 156–161.

companies which were thought to be performing extragovern-
mental functions for the achievement of social purposes. On
the other hand, under the laissez-faire philosophy which displaced
mercantilist thought, the state was thought to prosper best
through unrestrained individual effort, the functions of government being merely to prevent the use of force and fraudulent
practices. The history of government regulation of industry
in the United States embraces both these schools of thought.
The colonial governments, influenced by European ideas,
attempted to control the prices of many commodities, but our
early national existence was characterized by a laissez-faire
attitude which came to be modified as time passed only through
recognition of the need for regulation to correct abuses.

While historical concepts throw some light upon the present
problem of deciding what particular industries may properly be
subjected to public regulation, such industries do not fall into
a fixed category with readily distinguishable characteristics
that serve to differentiate them from other industries. The
phrase "clothed with a public interest" is used to describe these
industries; but when and under what circumstances is a business
so clothed with a public interest as to justify public regulation?
Former Chief Justice Taft, in the Wolff Packing Company case,[1]
in seeking an answer to this question, pointed out three classes of
industries said to be clothed with a public interest justifying some
public regulation: (1) those carried on under a public grant of
privileges; (2) certain exceptional callings recognized as public
from earliest times; and (3) businesses not public in their inception
but which have risen to be such and have in consequence been
subjected to some government regulation. The first class
includes most of the industries with which we are here concerned—transportation, water supply, gas and electric service,
and communication. Companies furnishing such services operate under a grant of governmental authority which not only
permits them to operate but also often protects them from competition; or they possess certain special rights and privileges, as
the use of streets and roads and the right of eminent domain.
The second class, which includes such industries as inns, cabs,
and gristmills, occupies no important place in the present
pattern of highly regulated industries.

[1] Wolff Packing Co. v. The Industrial Court of Kan., 262 U.S. 522.

The third of Taft's classes raises a fundamental question as to the conditions that justify public regulation of industries which in the beginning were conceived to be private. Ultimate decision in this matter rests with the Supreme Court of the United States, but this Court has laid down no rules or principles of universal applicability and in a recent decision has held that "there is no closed class or category of businesses affected with a public interest."[1]   On occasion the pressure is strong upon legislative bodies to pass statutes regulating one industry or another, the restraint upon the spread of legislation to the regulation of all industry resting in the courts.   This restraint is exercised by the courts in declaring statutes unreasonable, arbitrary or capricious, or that they deny or abridge constitutional rights of individuals.

Regulation of private property "affected with a public interest" includes both state and federal regulation, the former under retained powers of sovereignty commonly called the police powers, and the latter under a delegated jurisdiction over interstate and foreign commerce. The Supreme Court has dealt with cases involving both sovereignties but with frequently contradictory or inconsistent decisions.   On many occasions the Court has construed the Commerce Clause of the Federal Constitution in a narrow sense which has closely restricted the right of the Federal Government to regulate industry; but on other occasions, notably the recent decisions upholding the constitutionality of the National Labor Relations Act of 1935,[2] it has adopted a broad, liberal interpretation.

Similarly, in construing the right of states to regulate private industry under the police powers, the Supreme Court has vacillated between strict and liberal interpretations. In *Munn v. Illinois*, the Court held that "property does become clothed with a public interest when used in a manner to make it of public consequence, and affect the community at large";[3] but in a later decision, that "a business is not affected with a public interest merely because it is large or because the public are warranted in having a feeling of concern in respect of its main-

---

[1] Nebbia v. New York, 291 U.S. 502, 536, 537.

[2] Nat. Labor Relations Board v. Jones & Laughlin Steel Corp., and other cases, *New York Times*, Apr. 13, 1937.

[3] 94 U.S. 113, 126.

tenance.''[1] In dissenting opinions of the Supreme Court, the widest possible divergence of viewpoints has been presented with respect to the right of states to regulate industry. These range from the dissenting opinion of former Justice Field, in *Munn v. Illinois,* denying the power of any legislature to fix the price which one might receive for his property of any kind, on the ground that if this power may be exercised as to one article it may be as to all articles, to that of Justice Brandeis, dissenting in *New State Ice Co. v. Liebmann*[2] that a state's power extends to every regulation of any business reasonably required and appropriate for the public protection, on the theory that "the business of supplying to others, for compensation, any article or service whatsoever, may become a matter of public concern." This minority view of Justice Brandeis became the majority view in *Nebbia v. New York* in the following statement of Justice Roberts, who wrote the majority opinion:

> There can be no doubt that upon proper occasion and by appropriate measures the state may regulate a business in any of its aspects, including the prices to be charged for the products or commodities it sells. So far as the requirement of due process is concerned, and in the absence of other constitutional restrictions, a state is free to adopt whatever economic policy may be deemed to promote public welfare.[3]

Characteristics of industries affected with a public interest commonly pointed out as distinctive are: (1) the enjoyment of a franchise; (2) the existence of monopoly; and (3) the necessary nature of the services. The Court has specifically declared, however, that the touchstone of public interest in any business is not the enjoyment of a franchise;[4] nor is it the enjoyment of a monopoly.[5] Regulation of prices has been upheld where the business has not depended upon a franchise, and where there was no threat of monopoly.[6] The railroads, for example, which are generally recognized as engaged in a business affected with a public interest, are in competition with each other and

[1] Tyson & Brother v. Banton, 273 U.S. 418, 430.
[2] 285 U.S. 262.
[3] 291 U.S. 502, 537.
[4] Munn v. Illinois, 94 U.S. 113; also Nebbia v. New York, 291 U.S. 502.
[5] Brass v. North Dakota, 153 U.S. 391; and later cases.
[6] German Alliance Ins. Co. v. Lewis, 233 U.S. 389.

with other transportation agencies. The Court has indicated also that the necessary character of the service is not the criterion. Foodstuffs, clothing, ice, and gasoline are not to be regulated as to prices, but milk and insurance contracts may be.[1] Certainly foodstuffs and clothing are necessities, and, because of the development of commercial progress, gasoline and, under some circumstances ice, may be considered to belong to the same category.

The inescapable deduction is that the right of the state to regulate is dependent not alone upon the category to which an industry belongs but also upon the complex of rights and duties imposed upon any industry owing to some peculiar relation to the general public. The Supreme Court has never set up a distinct and separate category of public utilities; in fact, as we have seen, it has held that the concept of a public utility is not static. Always the Court has considered the circumstances of a given case as determinative. With no rule for determining just what types of industries are affected with a public interest it is inevitable that there should be differences of opinion between legislatures and courts, and between members of the Supreme Court itself, with respect to the right of states to regulate particular industries operating under particular sets of conditions. The right of a state to regulate a given industry as a public utility, therefore, is conditioned upon the determination by the Supreme Court of the United States that the business is so "affected with a public interest" as to justify the regulation proposed, a decision that will in no small degree reflect the political and social philosophy of those who make it. That the distinctions between industries affected with a public interest and those not are vague and are breaking down in present thought there is no question. Whether this constitutes an unalterable trend necessitated by changing social and economic conditions only the future will decide.[2]

---

[1] Charles Wolff Packing Co. v. Industrial Court of Kan., 262 U.S. 522; New State Ice Co. v. Liebmann, 285 U.S. 262; Williams v. Standard Oil Co., 278 U.S. 235; Nebbia v. New York, 291 U.S. 502; and German Alliance Ins. Co., v. Lewis, 233 U.S. 389.

[2] For a fuller discussion of this question see G. L. Wilson, J. M. Herring, and R. B. Eutsler, "Public Utility Industries," McGraw-Hill Book Company, Inc., New York, 1936, Chap. I.

REGULATION AND COMPETITION

Although the category of public service industries is not a closed one but expands with changing conditions, the relationship of government to industries recognized as such is clearly distinguishable from its relationship to other industries. In industry generally individuals, within limits, may engage in what industrial activities they choose, serve whom they desire to serve, and charge what they please. In theory at least, reliance is placed upon the competitive activities of self-seeking individuals for an abundance of goods and services at prices fixed by the costs of production. Government, except for the attainment of certain social objectives, is concerned with rules of fair play, with unfair methods of competition, and with practices which may restrain free competition. In the public service industries, however, entry into the field is restricted by the requirement of a license or permit, and those who engage in these industries must provide adequate service, must serve all who apply and are willing to pay the rates fixed by public authority, and may not abandon service without the consent of the government. Reliance is placed chiefly upon regimentation rather than uncontrolled competition for adequate service at reasonable rates.

It is not to be thought, however, that regulation has wholly supplanted, or is designed to supplant, competition. Present attitudes and governmental policies regarding public utility enterprise reflect the influence of an evolutionary history during which the benefits that attach to competitive enterprise have been reluctantly abandoned. In the early history of most utilities called natural monopolies, such as the gas, electric, street railway, water, and telephone utilities, the maxim that "competition is the life of trade" was thought to apply to these as to other industries. Public policy, accordingly, was designed to encourage and promote competition. Thus we find grants of franchises to two or more companies to furnish competing services in the same community. But eventually it came to be recognized that competition in natural monopolies leads to wasteful and uneconomic duplication of plant, facilities, and personnel and to needless congestion of city streets, since real competition implies competing gas mains, electric pole lines or conduits, or street car lines throughout the territory served. Two gas mains or electric lines in a city street, except for the spur that competition affords, cannot serve the consumers more efficiently than one, yet the cost is almost twice as great. In the telephone service, competition results also in an inferior type of service, since the value of a telephone service is directly related to the number of parties interconnected. Competing telephone companies in the same community would need to have duplicate lists of subscribers, in which case all would be paying twice for the same service; or, in the absence of physical connection between the competing companies, the subscribers of one company would have to be content with the service provided by that company. There remain a few instances of competition in natural monopolies, but public policy with respect to such industries is predicated upon regulated monopoly. Noteworthy in this connection is the recent revival of interest in regulation through competition as manifested by the establishment, or the threat of establishment, of publicly owned electric and gas systems. Needless to say, the disadvantages of competition in natural monopolies exist whether the systems be privately or publicly owned.

Public policy regarding other utilities, particularly railroad and motor transportation, telegraph and radio communication, as indicated in federal legislation, is based upon a philosophy of regulated competition. The railroads were organized as competitive enterprises, and regulation by the Federal Government has supplemented rather than replaced competition between the carriers, enforcing competition in some aspects and restraining it in others. The Interstate Commerce Act prohibits certain practices which resulted in the restraint of competition, and the antitrust laws prohibit consolidations or acquisitions of control which would substantially lessen competition between the carriers. While the Transportation Act of 1920 and the Emergency Railroad Transportation Act of 1933 remove some of the earlier prohibitions, the underlying philosophy of regulated competition has not been abandoned. This is clearly indicated in the policy with respect to consolidation. The Interstate Commerce Commission is empowered to permit consolidations or acquisitions of control in harmony with a plan it is directed to prepare, but the law requires that in such a plan competition shall be preserved as fully as possible and that wherever practicable existing routes and channels of trade and commerce shall be maintained.

Similarly, competition has been and remains a marked feature of telegraph and radio communication. Federal policy has stressed the value of competition in these services, and the provisions of the Communications Act of 1934 are designed to insure its continuance. Telegraph consolidation which would restrain competition would run afoul of the antitrust laws, and the Communications Act specifically forbids practices that would unduly restrain competition in or establish a monopoly of radio communication or combinations of radio and wire companies where the effect would be substantially to lessen competition between them.

It is obvious, therefore, that public policy in the United States has not wholly supplanted competition by regulation. Regulation has been undertaken where deemed necessary to eliminate practices not in the public interest or to achieve objectives believed not attainable in a system of unrestrained individual activity. That this should result in inconsistency would normally be expected. For example, almost as good a case could be made against competition in railroad transportation or telegraph communication because of uneconomic duplication as against competition in the so-called natural monopolies. This inconsistency, so far as it may be explained on rational grounds, reflects a reluctance to abandon the benefits of the automatic regulation of competitive forces. The theory of regulated competition has grown out of a recognition of the fact that, while regulation is in large degree incompatible with competition, the ultimate sufferer in unrestrained competition is the public itself.

EARLY FORMS OF REGULATION

1. Judicial Regulation.—Before the advent of legislative or commission regulation, consumers found a certain amount of protection in the courts. They possessed the right to reasonable service at reasonable rates under the common law which had been developed in England and in the United States. However, judicial regulation provided an unsatisfactory recourse to consumers compelled to pay excessive charges. Besides the cost of bringing suit there was the delay which always accompanies judicial proceedings, so that by the time adjudication was completed the relief sought might be of slight avail. Furthermore, courts were not equipped with trained personnel capable of dealing with the technical problems which of necessity must be considered in determining the reasonableness of rates for public utility service. Also, while regulation to be effective must be preventive as well as corrective, it must look to the future and envision change, and it must be continuing; judicial action was sporadic; it was oriented to the past in judicial precedent and was limited to acts already committed. Courts could determine whether a given charge was unreasonable, but they could not fix a rate for the future.

2. Direct Legislative Regulation.—Legislative regulation of public utilities took the form of duties, obligations, and restrictions placed in charters and franchises issued by states or municipalities, and in rare instances by the Federal Government, to public service corporations in exchange for the grant of certain rights and privileges. These rights were: first, the right to be, *i.e.*, the corporate right to exist; second, the right to carry on some business for which the corporation had been organized; and third, the right to use streets and highways in the conduct of their operations. The first two of these, usually referred to as the charter of the corporation, were granted by a special act of the state legislature or under a general incorporation law; the third, commonly called the special franchise, usually was granted by the local government or with its consent, although in some cases by state legislatures.[1]

Historically, legislative regulation of public utilities in the United States came first in attempts to regulate railroads through special charters granted by state legislatures. During the period of early railroad construction the desire for transportation facilities led state governments, and even municipalities, to grant all sorts of direct or indirect subsidies to private corporations, or to build and operate their own railroads. Later the Federal Government granted aid of various kinds to corporations engaged in railroad construction. At first, as was

[1] GLAESER, M. G., *op. cit.*, p. 198; also, JONES, ELIOT, and T. C. BIGHAM, "Principles of Public Utilities," The Macmillan Company, New York, 1931, pp. 105–107.

to be expected, the charters granted railroad corporations were most liberal, but as time passed state legislatures began to insert more restrictive provisions into charters designed to safeguard the interests of consumers. These charters contained provisions regarding the legal and financial organization of the corporation; construction; and, in some cases, details of operation of lines, routes, and rates. With respect to rates, charter provisions usually prescribed fixed maxima or limited the return to given percentages of the capital stock.

Special charters also were granted by legislatures to local utilities at first, even to the extent of granting rights in city streets without the consent of the local authorities. Popular sentiment soon became opposed to such grants, however, and in most states legislation was enacted giving municipalities broader control over local matters.

Regulation by special charters proved to be a most unsatisfactory type. There was the basic defect in that the regulatory program was of necessity incorporated in the charter provisions. This required greater knowledge of utility matters than the legislatures possessed, and accordingly many charters were poorly conceived. Such charters, however, whether or not they adequately protected the public interest, were conceived of as contracts enforceable in the courts. Special charters contained an enormous number of widely varying terms and conditions, resulting in a welter of confusion, although in some states a certain measure of uniformity was achieved by citing previous charters in granting new ones. In addition to the confusion resulting from the multiplicity of charter provisions, reliance early was placed upon the voluntary acts of the corporations for their fulfillment, recourse being had only to the courts in cases of violation. The result was that the companies usually could disregard the terms of their charters when it suited their purposes to do so without being called to account. Some later charters evaded the defects of earlier ones, and in many cases provisions were inserted reserving the right to amend or revoke the charters, but amendments were achieved slowly and with great difficulty.

The generally unsatisfactory experience with special charters led rather early to attempts to control railroads through general incorporation laws, although special charters continued to be granted long after the first of such laws was adopted. These laws included general clauses concerning financial organization, security issues, rates, service, and similar matters applicable to all companies incorporated under them. While general incorporation laws brought a greater measure of uniformity into charter regulation, they added little to the effectiveness of control. Like all forms of legislative regulation, they failed to provide for detailed, continuous administration. Moreover, general laws could not deal with divergent conditions; hence evasion was a simple matter.

The defects of control through general incorporation laws were particularly obvious in connection with attempts to regulate local utilities in this manner. Where a small number of persons could organize a public utility corporation with no more control over their activities than the terms of a general incorporation law it was inevitable that abuses such as fraudulence, overcapitalization, or exorbitant and discriminatory rates should have developed on a broad scale. There was no clear delineation of state and local powers; hence it was always a question as to what conditions, if any, a city might impose upon a utility in addition to those contained in the general laws. Competitive companies sprang into being, cities often granting franchises to competing companies as a means of obtaining service at reasonable rates. The era of competition in local utilities, to which reference has been made, is closely associated with the period of control through general incorporation laws.

In the case of the railroads, legislative regulation took still another form, that of specific laws aimed at specific abuses. The impetus to such legislation sprang from unscrupulous activities of construction rings and directors, the elimination of competition through consolidation and pooling and rate agreements, legislative and official corruption, and unjust discriminations. Characteristic of this type of regulation were laws establishing maximum rates, state-wide classifications of freight and distance tariffs, and other laws designed to prevent unjust discrimination and to control specifically the activities of railroads. However, the inflexible nature of such regulation was quite obvious. It never developed widely in the United States, nor did it last long in railroad regulation. Out of the experience with these earlier forms of regulation grew a firm conviction that regulation is an administrative problem which cannot be handled effectively by courts or legislatures.

3. **Local Regulation.**—State control of public utilities, either by direct legislation or by special or general incorporation laws, was applied mostly to the railroads. Although, as has been intimated, some companies received from the states rights to operate in city streets, in the main the regulation of local utilities was left to local authorities, such regulation taking the form of franchise contracts or city ordinances. This became the prevailing method of regulating local utilities and remained so until the advent of modern public service commissions. On the whole, however, it proved to be ineffectual, as will be shown more fully in the next chapter.

In the beginning, local authorities, as did state and national authorities in the case of the railroads, viewed franchise seekers as public benefactors. Valuable rights were granted, often in perpetuity, without adequate safeguards of the public interest. Even after the value of franchise grants came to be fully appreciated, local officials were poorly qualified to bargain effectively with those who sought the special privileges. They lacked the technical knowledge either to protect the interests of consumers or to deal justly with the utilities, relations between local officials and the utilities too often being characterized by open warfare which resulted neither in justice to consumers nor in stable conditions for the utilities. Frequently the result was supine yielding to the demands of the utilities. In addition, the corruption that frequently has characterized the administration of municipal affairs in the United States was too often reflected in the grants of franchises to public utilities. A further defect of franchise regulation was its inflexibility. A franchise was a contract enforceable in the courts; consequently it had to be drawn with the greatest care. It was impossible, however, to draw up specific provisions which, though equitable at the time, would remain so for any considerable period in the future owing to development and change.

In addition to these defects of franchise regulation, other forces were at work which shifted the emphasis from local to state regulation. Many of the so-called local utilities, in the normal course of development, ceased to remain so. New technological processes and the economies of large-scale operation inevitably expanded utilities formerly operating largely within the confines of a single city into state-wide, even interstate, organizations. The jurisdiction of one municipality was not broad enough to cover the operations of a utility operating in several municipalities. Finally, investigations in New York and Wisconsin, which disclosed the weaknesses and corruption of local regulation and led directly to the establishment of public service commissions in those states, aroused national interest to such a pitch that other states in rapid succession followed the example set by these states.

EARLY RAILROAD COMMISSIONS

Modern public service commissions have developed since 1905, but commissions as agencies of regulation are much older, some being established quite early as adjuncts of legislative regulation of the railroads. Rhode Island created a railroad commission in 1839, New Hampshire in 1844, Connecticut in 1853, Vermont in 1855, Maine in 1858, Ohio in 1867, and Massachusetts in 1869.[1] After the Civil War many southern and western states similarly established railroad commissions.

These early railroad commissions were of the advisory type, being for the most part merely fact-finding arms of the legislatures with no administrative powers. Their duties were confined to the collection of statistics, the receiving of annual and other periodic reports, the appraisal of private property for railroad rights of way, inspection of the roads in the interests of safe operation, and the apportionment of revenues and expenditures to a state to determine whether or not net income exceeded that authorized in charters. With respect to rates, these commissions had no authority, save merely to ascertain whether or not the railroads were observing the rate provisions in their charters, these usually consisting of prescribed maximum rates. Owing to the fact that such maximum rates customarily were set higher than the roads cared to charge, in view of the needs of developing business and the declining costs of transportation which often followed increased volumes of traffic, reliance was placed upon competition, rather than regulation, to insure fair treatment of consumers. Actually, although their members were usually appointed by the governors of the various states,

[1] SPURR, H. C., "Guiding Principles of Public Service Regulation," Public Utility Reports, Inc., Washington, 1924, vol. I, p. 10.

these advisory commissions were merely a part of direct legislative regulation.   State legislatures took the action, whether of a corrective or of a punitive type.

Soon after the Civil War a marked change came to pass in public attitudes toward the railroads.   In the earlier years when railroad promoters were looked upon as public benefactors, and governments furnished all sorts of direct and indirect aid, regulation was superficial and perfunctory.   But many railroad managements belied the public confidence placed in them, and in certain cases the roads came to be regarded as legitimate prey by unscrupulous financial interests concerned more with private profit than with public service.   Rates were too high, and unjust discriminations abounded.   As a result, public dissatisfaction with ineffective legislative control became general, culminating in the Middle West in the Granger movement, backed by the National Grange of the Patrons of Husbandry.   The Grange was an organization of farmers, but they had widespread support among other groups with similar complaints regarding railroad rates and practices.   Out of this agitation grew stricter forms of legislation, the passage of numerous laws fixing maximum transportation rates, and the creation of commissions.

The railroads fought in the courts the wave of rate legislation which ensued, contesting the right of a state legislature to regulate railroad rates.   They based their contentions on the ground that such regulation resulted in the deprivation of property without due process of law, contrary to the Fourteenth Amendment to the Federal Constitution.   The Supreme Court of the United States, however, in the so-called Granger cases,[1] decided in the October term, 1876, upheld the right of a state to regulate railroad rates, taking a position from which it has never receded.

Characteristic of the new legislation was the establishment of commissions of a different type, called mandatory commissions.   The advisory commissions, previously discussed, were a product of the East.   They relied upon publicity and the force of public opinion to accomplish the ends of regulation, their powers being fact finding and advisory.   Mandatory railroad commissions came first in the West and South.   Principal among their powers were those to establish rates and to

[1] Munn v. Illinois, 94 U.S. 113; and other cases.

enforce their rulings in the courts without recourse to legislative action. Illinois was the first state to establish such a commission; in lieu of laws prescribing maximum rates and fares and prohibiting discrimination, the legislature in 1874 conferred mandatory rate powers upon its railroad commission. This was followed by similar action in the same year by the states of Iowa, Wisconsin, and Minnesota. Other states soon set up mandatory commissions.

There was a severe reaction following the panic of 1873, the railroads blaming their difficulties on too strict regulation and succeeding in turning public opinion against mandatory railroad commissions. One after another the states, with the exception of Illinois, stripped their commissions of mandatory powers and reduced them to the advisory type, regulation in their stead being based upon maximum rate laws. In 1887, with the enactment of the Act to Regulate Commerce, the Federal Government entered the field of railroad regulation.

Prior to 1907, few commissions, either state or local, were established with jurisdiction over utilities other than the railroads. Massachusetts created a Board of Gas and Electric Light Commissioners in 1885; and New York, a Commission of Gas and Electricity in 1905. From 1902 to 1907 certain of the railroad commissions had been given jurisdiction over street railways and telephone companies, but for the most part utilities other than railroads were regulated, if at all, by the terms of franchises granted by local authorities.

ESTABLISHMENT OF THE PUBLIC SERVICE COMMISSION IN NEW YORK

The investigation leading to the creation of a public service commission of the modern type in New York State aroused nation-wide interest, chiefly because it was recognized that many of the conditions disclosed prevailed generally. Briefly the facts were these: General dissatisfaction with the rates charged by the companies that had created monopolies of gas and electric service in New York City had developed. Rates were believed to be too high, and it was the general feeling that many practices of public utility managements were inimical to the public interest. Matters were brought to a head by Mayor Seth Low who, in 1902, refused all bids by the private companies for public lighting and, in 1903, instituted suits for the forfeiture of the charters of the Consolidated Telegraph and Electrical Subway Company and the Empire City Subway Company, which controlled all electrical ducts, on the basis of irregularities disclosed by an examination of the books of these companies. A new mayor was elected in 1903 who accepted the terms of the companies, but sufficient interest had been aroused for a popular protest to the state legislature demanding a thorough investigation of the utility situation in New York City. An investigating commission was appointed, with Charles E. Hughes at the head, which disclosed gross abuses of overcapitalization, the manipulation of securities, and various practices which restrained the competition upon which chief reliance was placed for adequate service at reasonable rates. Moreover, this investigation disclosed more than corrupt practices of public utility managements. It brought to light the inadequacies of legislative and franchise regulation with dependence upon advisory commissions and created a demand for a commission with adequate powers to protect the interests of consumers, a state commission free of the corruption of local politics. A Commission of Gas and Electricity was created in 1905, but in 1907 the New York legislature created two commissions with broad mandatory powers. The State was divided into two districts, the Commission for the First District being granted jurisdiction over the utilities in the greater New York area (consisting of the counties of New York, Kings, Queens, and Richmond); and the Commission for the Second District, jurisdiction over utilities in the rest of the State. The Commission for the First District was largely a municipal commission, New York City being required by the law to pay its expenses, except the salaries of the commissioners and those of the Commission's secretary and counsel. However, its powers were prescribed in the State law, and the commissioners were appointed by the governor. The Commission for the Second District corresponded more closely to the commissions that were later set up by other states having state-wide jurisdiction. In 1910 this Commission was given jurisdiction of telephone and telegraph companies, even those operating in the First District.

The developments in New York were not wholly typical of those in other states. Various regulatory authorities had already been established, such as the Board of Railroad Commissioners, the Commission of Gas and Electricity, the Board of Rapid Transit Commissioners, and the Inspector of Gas Meters; and the vast concentration of population in the New York area created problems not to be found elsewhere. The New York experience is recounted here because of the impetus it gave to the state commission movement and because the New York law served as a model for similar laws in other states. In 1921, the commissions of both districts were replaced by a single Public Service Commission with state-wide jurisdiction over all utilities, except that the transportation lines in New York City were placed under a specially created Transit Commission. In 1927 the Public Service Commission and the Transit Commission were made divisions of a Department of Public Service, although their names were not changed.

THE DEVELOPMENT IN WISCONSIN

The development of a state regulatory commission in Wisconsin grew mostly out of the agitation for regulation of railroad rates. During the Granger agitation, to which we have referred previously, Wisconsin had set up a mandatory commission; but in the reaction that followed, the law was repealed. Under the leadership of Governor La Follette, and following a number of investigations which disclosed conditions similar to those which obtained in New York, a Railroad Commission was created in 1905; but in 1907 the powers of this body with respect to railroads were expanded, and its jurisdiction extended to other utilities. The Wisconsin Act of 1907 was more comprehensive than the New York Act, and in some respects it serves better to illustrate the changes effected by the transfer of control of the utilities from local to state authorities.

The railroad statute of 1905 created a commission of three members, appointed by the governor by and with the consent of the state senate and removable by the governor at any time for inefficiency, neglect of duty, or malfeasance in office. By the Act of 1907 the jurisdiction of this Commission was extended to every public utility in the State, including telephone, telegraph, heat, light, water, or power utilities, whether privately or publicly owned. Street railways were defined as railways and thus came under the jurisdiction of the Commission under the railroad statutes. The law required that all public utility rates and charges be reasonable, and the Commission was empowered to establish reasonable rates for the future if, after hearing and investigation, either upon its own motion or upon complaint, it found rates to be unreasonable. Public utilities were required to file schedules of all rates and charges, as well as rules and regulations affecting such rates and charges, and they were forbidden to make charges other than those in the published schedules. These were to be made available for public inspection. No changes in rates could be made without 10 days' notice to the Commission. Unjust discriminations were prohibited, although the utilities were permitted to differentiate between customers in the matter of charges where the use was different.

The Commission was empowered to prescribe the forms of all books, accounts, papers, and records to be kept by the utilities, and they were required to conform to all such directions of the Commission. It was empowered also, after investigation and hearing, to make orders regarding the adequacy of service and was directed to develop and prescribe rules and regulations concerning standards of service. The Commission was authorized to inquire into the management of the business of public utilities and to obtain from them all information necessary to enable it to perform its duties. Without going into further detail, it may be added that the powers of the Wisconsin Railroad Commission embraced practically all aspects of public utility regulation deemed necessary for effective control in the public interest. The 1907 law remained substantially unchanged until 1931, in which year the powers of the Commission were broadened, and its name changed to the Public Service Commission of Wisconsin.

ESTABLISHMENT OF COMMISSIONS IN OTHER STATES

The examples in New York and Wisconsin were quickly followed by other states. In the same year (1907), Georgia extended the jurisdiction of its Railroad Commission to include street railway, telephone, gas, and electric companies. In 1909, Vermont created a Public Service Commission; and in 1910, Maryland and New Jersey, the latter State transforming its Commission from the weak to the strong type the following year. In 1911, California, Connecticut, Kansas, Nevada, New Hampshire, Ohio,

Oregon, and Washington took similar action; and in 1912, Arizona and Rhode Island. In 1913, Colorado, Idaho, Illinois, Indiana, Maine, Massachusetts, Missouri, Montana, North Carolina, Oklahoma, Pennsylvania, and West Virginia created new commissions or broadened the jurisdiction and powers of existing railroad commissions so as to convert them to the modern type. In Massachusetts the jurisdiction of the Commission did not include gas and electric companies, these remaining under the Board of Gas and Electric Light Commissioners; but in 1919 the Board was consolidated with the Public Service Commission into a single body called the Department of Public Utilities. The North Carolina Corporation Commission, which had for some time exercised jurisdiction over street railways and telephones, had its authority extended to gas, electric light, and water companies in 1913. The jurisdiction of the Oklahoma Corporation Commission was similarly broadened; and that of the Pennsylvania Railroad Commission, established in 1907, extended to include street railways and telephones, its name being changed to the Public Service Commission.

So rapid was the growth of the Commission movement that by 1913 half of the states had established commissions of the modern type. It has continued to grow until today every state, with the exception of Delaware, has a commission with jurisdiction over one or more utilities. In 1913, Congress enacted a law creating the District of Columbia Public Utilities Commission. The names of these bodies vary from state to state. In some of the states they retain the old title of railroad commissions, although their jurisdiction generally has been extended; while in other states they are known as public service or public utility commissions. In Illinois the Commission is called the Commerce Commission; in Massachusetts, the Department of Public Utilities; in Minnesota, the Railroad and Warehouse Commission; in Montana, North Dakota, and South Dakota, the Board of Railroad Commissioners; in New Jersey, the Board of Public Utility Commissioners; and in Washington, the Department of Public Works. These names are of no special significance, however. The term "public service commission" may be used intelligently in a generic sense to designate the body in a state having jurisdiction over public utilities.

Though the establishment of state commissions has been universal, no great uniformity exists in the laws defining their jurisdiction, powers, and methods of operation in the various states. This subject will be dealt with more fully in subsequent chapters. In Chap. I we have traced briefly the trend in development of public utility regulation from the legislative control which characterized early attempts at regulation to the modern administrative commission, and a more recent trend from control by local authorities to regulation by state commissions. Chapter II will be devoted to an evaluation of state and local regulation from the viewpoint of effective control in the public interest.

References

COOKE, M. L.: "Public Utility Regulation," Ronald Press Company, New York, 1924.

GLAESER, M. G.: "Outlines of Public Utility Economics," The Macmillan Company, New York, 1931.

JONES, ELIOT, and T. C. BIGHAM: "Principles of Public Utilities," The Macmillan Company, New York, 1931.

KING, C. L.: "The Regulation of Municipal Utilities," D. Appleton-Century Company, Inc., New York, 1912.

MOSHER, W. E., and F. G. CRAWFORD: "Public Utility Regulation," Harper & Brothers, New York, 1933.

NASH, L. R.: "Economics of Public Utilities," McGraw-Hill Book Company, Inc., New York, 1925.

National Civic Federation: "Commission Regulation of Public Utilities," New York, 1913.

SPURR, H. C.: "Guiding Principles of Public Utility Regulation," Public Utilities Reports, Inc., Washington, 1924, vol. I.

WILSON, G. L., J. M. HERRING, and R. B. EUTSLER: "Public Utility Industries," McGraw-Hill Book Company, Inc., New York, 1936.

CHAPTER II

STATE VERSUS LOCAL REGULATION

In Chap. I it was pointed out that in the early period of regulation many state legislatures undertook the direct regulation of local utilities. However, corruption in state politics, unwise legislation, and the disregard of the rights of cities to control the use of their own streets engendered widespread opposition, and control of local utilities quite generally was placed in the hands of local authorities. There ensued a period characterized by local regulation by franchise which lasted until the coming of modern state commissions. Even today in many cities, particularly with respect to certain utilities, franchise regulation constitutes the principal means by which certain utilities are controlled. The essential feature of franchise regulation is that control rests upon a contract between the city and the company, granting specific rights and privileges to, and imposing specific obligations upon, the company in supplying public utility service.

THE NATURE OF FRANCHISES

In a general sense a franchise is any grant of a special right or privilege by a legislative body to persons or corporations, such as the right to exist in a corporate capacity, to carry on a particular business, or to enjoy special privileges. The first two of these rights we have referred to as the charter of a corporation, usually granted by a state legislature by a special act or under a general incorporation law. The third, so far as public utilities are concerned, is a grant of special rights to use streets and highways for poles, wires, tracks, conduits, etc., and to supply service. The term franchise as we shall use it refers to the latter type of grant.

Duration of Franchises.—The duration of a franchise is important alike to the city and the company, since it determines the period during which the special rights and privileges granted in the franchise may be exercised. With respect to duration, franchises are classified as perpetual, limited term, and indeterminate or terminable.

1. *Perpetual Franchises.*—Perpetual franchises are those granted in perpetuity or for extraordinary long terms, such as 999 years. In some cases perpetual franchises have been granted inadvertently where expiration dates have not been set, courts holding such grants to be perpetual. Little will be said here regarding perpetual franchises, although there are such franchises in existence, held principally by street railway companies. Today it is doubtful that any municipality, no matter how blind to its best interests, would grant such rights to public utility companies. No franchise granting a special privilege to a public utility company, especially an exclusive right, should be awarded without adequate safeguards of the public interest; yet to provide proper safeguards for a future that is uncertain, during which revolutionary changes may take place which may not be envisioned at the time the grant is made, is a practical impossibility. The advantages of security to the company and stability of the service which accompany perpetual grants are far outweighed by the fact that, to the extent of the franchise provisions, the city has contracted away its right to control the activities of the company, since perpetual franchises can be terminated only through condemnation under the city's powers of eminent domain. Municipalities have no authority to grant perpetual franchises unless expressly or impliedly authorized to do so by the laws of the state.

2. *Limited-term Franchises.*—Some authorities divide limited-term franchises into short-term and long-term franchises, the distinction being rather artificial, although many objections to franchises running for fifty years do not apply with equal force to franchises the life of which is limited to ten or twenty years. In the interests of brevity our discussion of limited-term franchises will embrace only those with terms up to 50 years. Franchises running for longer periods are of the nature of perpetual franchises.

Limited-term franchises grew out of recognition of the need for periodic readjustments of the relations between the city and the company enjoying special privileges under a franchise, in view of changing technology and economic conditions. This is the chief advantage of such franchises over those issued in perpetuity. There are several disadvantages to limited-term franchises. In the first place, the grant of privileges essential to the performance of public utility service for a limited period of years makes for insecurity of investments and instability of the service. Unless the franchise is for a fairly long term, in which case the advantages of frequent readjustment are lost, it is difficult, or more costly, for the company to secure the necessary capital, since there is a tendency to discourage investment in such enterprises.

In the second place, limited-term franchises do not result in unmixed public benefits so far as service is concerned. Theoretically, the fact that, although the franchise is limited, the company envisions continuous operation and thus must look forward to renewal should constitute a real incentive to the company to extend and improve its service. Nevertheless, if the term is short, a company is not so likely to take a long-term view of its service obligations, and in any case, as the expiration date nears, uncertainty of renewal may well force the management to adopt ultraconservative attitudes toward extensions and new policies and even to skimp maintenance of plant and fixtures. There is also a tendency to evade special provisions in the franchise placing on the company such obligations as street paving, snow removal, and others of like nature.

In the third place, rate provisions, whatever the length of the franchise, may work to the disadvantage of the company or the city. What seems to be a fair rate under a given set of conditions can be manifestly unfair when those conditions change. Public utility companies are in markets not controlled by them for supplies and labor, and the prices they must pay materially affect their costs of operation. A classic illustration of how such franchises may operate to the disadvantage of a utility is the situation in which many street railway systems found themselves in the period of rising prices during the World War. Prices of materials and supplies and wages mounted, yet their rates, and thus their gross revenues, were fixed by inflexible franchise terms. Net earnings were squeezed out between a fixed level of gross earnings and mounting costs of operation. To save the companies, cities often were forced to modify the rate provisions of the franchises, since prolonged operation under fares not sufficiently remunerative would have bankrupted them.

On the other hand, maximum rates in franchises granted gas and electric companies had little influence upon the actual rates. These companies discovered that increased business and profits resulted from lowering rates, so that after a time actual rates bore little relation to the rates prescribed originally in the franchises. City officials becoming aware of these facts, and desiring to insure that economies would be passed on to consumers, found their hands tied by contract. The defect in the system of prescribing rates by contract for a fixed period is that a rate that is reasonable at the time the contract is drawn up may not remain so for the future, yet it cannot be modified without the consent of both parties to the contract. Only when the franchise is silent on rate matters or when the power to alter, amend, or repeal its terms is reserved can local authorities expect to regulate rates so as to keep them in line with changing conditions. Even so, needed changes in franchise terms are made with difficulty in an atmosphere surcharged with accusations and recriminations by those using the utilities either as sources of private gain or for political aggrandisement.

In the fourth place, short-term franchises are likely to increase the political activity of public utility companies. Franchise history in the United States is replete with attempts on the part of utilities to influence municipal legislative bodies and officials as well as the use of utility issues by unscrupulous, demagogic public officials to achieve political ambitions. Such activities are increased where the utilities face periodically the necessity of seeking renewals of franchise grants.

Finally, in the very nature of things, short-term franchises may become long-term or perpetual in effect. Apart from the question of the legal rights of utilities in city streets after franchises have expired are practical considerations which render renewal on some terms almost inevitable, unless the city is in a position to take over the utility and to furnish service itself.

3. *Indeterminate Permits.*—Because of the deficiencies of limited-term franchises there has come into practice in a number of states the use of indeterminate permits. The essential feature of the indeterminate permit is the elimination of a fixed period so that the company may enjoy the privileges granted in the permit continuously during good behavior. While indeterminate permits have been in use for many years in one form or another,

as, for example, the revocable franchises long used in Massachusetts, generally they belong to the period of state commission regulation, and the terms and conditions employed depend largely upon the extent to which the control of local utilities is placed in the hands of state or local authorities. Such permits empower the municipality, in a manner prescribed by law, to purchase the properties of the utility at any time.

The advantages of the indeterminate permit, from the viewpoint of the city, follow from the fact that the company in order to maintain its franchise must be on its metal. Control is continuous, not being dependent upon periodic readjustments of the relationship between the city and the company; hence, rates are likely to be lower with fewer unjust discriminations, and pressure upon the company to extend and improve its service is greater. The company is freer to make costly extensions and improvements knowing that such investments will be secure provided it furnishes a satisfactory service, and it is not under the obligation to amortize its investment within a limited period. The chief advantage to the company is the security granted by a permit essentially permanent in nature. Even where the permit is terminated, the company is protected in that universally the laws require that the city upon terminating the permit must compensate the company adequately for its properties. No such protection exists under a limited-term franchise where the company property would be rendered almost worthless if the franchise were not renewed.

The principal objection raised to the indeterminate permit is that in effect it takes on the nature of a perpetual grant. While a city may have the legal right to terminate a permit, practical considerations might make it impossible or undesirable to do so. Municipal debt limitations and public attitudes unfavorable to municipal ownership and operation might easily constitute insurmountable obstacles. Thus the utilities may be enabled to operate without the restrictions ordinarily made a matter of contract in the other forms of franchises. Other objections to the indeterminate permit are based upon the fact that usually the grant is exclusive. However, in this respect indeterminate permits do not differ from exclusive franchises, the issue being that of public policy regarding the creation of monopolies and not the wisdom of particular types of grants. The effectiveness of the indeterminate permit as a regulatory device depends upon the absence of constitutional and legislative restrictions upon cities in the matter of municipal purchase of utilities and the efficiency of municipal ownership and operation.

DEFECTS OF FRANCHISE REGULATION

Franchise regulation has proved generally to be an ineffective method. The defects have been in part due to the looseness with which franchises were granted by municipal authorities in the early years of development of public utility services. Some reference was made to this in Chap. I, in recounting how valuable rights were granted, often of an exclusive nature and in perpetuity, with few conditions as to their use. Unscrupulous disregard of the public interest was far too common, although few public officials recognized the need for prescribing controlling service standards, and scientific rate making was unknown. Early franchises were short and simple documents, designed merely as enabling acts, with little thought of the need for, or appropriate methods of, regulation. Protection of the public interest was thought to lie in competition, either actual or potential.

The rapid and continuous growth of local public utility services, and the lucrative character of these undertakings, which attracted to them in great number financiers interested primarily in reaping maximum personal profits, led to the inclusion of an increasing number of provisions in franchises in order to safeguard the interests of cities and consumers. Nevertheless, as was indicated previously, for the most part city officials were poorly equipped to cope with franchise seekers. The latter, aided by capable and technically trained representatives, knew what they wanted and how best to obtain it with the least restraint upon themselves and their activities. Also, with corruption in municipal affairs rampant, bribery was a common means employed by franchise seekers to achieve their ends. As a consequence, while franchises became increasingly complex instruments with detailed provisions governing specific rights and obligations, in many cases their terms were written or dictated by those seeking the special privileges.

Adding to this welter of confusion was the fact that franchises were granted by a multiplicity of authorities, ranging from state legislatures to highway commissioners of rural townships. Gradually, however, there appeared widely recognized fundamental principles upon which franchise provisions should be based. Specific provisions embodying these principles generally covered limitation of the term of the franchise, conditions of renewal, option of purchase by the municipality, common-user privileges, street paving requirements, franchise taxes, extensions, and the regulation of rates and service.   Thus, the franchise from a brief, simple grant of powers evolved into an elaborate instrument designed to achieve by contract many of the ends sought today by regulation under commissions.

But it is the very elaborateness of the franchise, the immense detail of matters that must be covered specifically in the contract if control is to be effective, which constitutes the fundamental weakness of franchise regulation.   The more detailed a franchise becomes, the more fixed and inflexible become the relations between the city and the utility, a difficulty not wholly overcome by limiting the terms of franchises so as to provide for periodic readjustment of these relations.   Even with the indeterminate permit, public authorities may not step in to require changes in rates or improvements in service when and as the needs arise. The control of the city under such a document is limited largely to its right to terminate the franchise when service or rates are not satisfactory; and unless the city is able and willing to take over and operate the utility, or a more acceptable private party is available, public clamor for the termination of the franchise is likely to be of little avail.   On occasion such control may be less effective than specific terms in a franchise, despite their inflexibility.

It has been shown previously how attempts to regulate rates by fixed franchise provisions results either in terms that are not controlling or that place utilities in straight jackets.   Similar disadvantages attach to attempts to control service by specific franchise provisions, since no one can foretell when in the future radical changes will be necessary in construction, equipment, or operation.   Consider, for example, the service problems that must be dealt with in drawing up a franchise for a street railway company.   These include specific routes; extensions; joint use of tracks and fixtures; service requirements, such as regularity, frequency, transfer stations, through routing, speed, and carrying capacity; health and convenience, such as cleanliness, ventilation, heating, and lighting; safety requirements, such as location in streets, distance between tracks, brakes, and fenders; construction matters and maintenance of street surface, such as foundations, paving and repair of paving, street widening, strengthening of bridges, cleaning of streets, and snow and ice removal; and many others.[1] To include in a franchise specific provisions regarding such matters, sufficiently detailed to control the service of a street railway company in the public interest yet flexible enough to admit of necessary modifications to suit changing conditions, is a well-nigh impossible task.

Furthermore, there are other matters which must be subject to control if public utility regulation is to be effective, but which are difficult to control by contract. These include the control of capitalization, security issues and the valuation of property, the disposition of earnings, control over operating expenditures, and labor problems, particularly the rights of cities in cases of strike or lockout. A further problem, raised frequently in the past, is that of compensation for franchises. At first, license fees generally were levied, and special obligations, such as street paving, were imposed, but later lump-sum payments were fixed, or a percentage of gross receipts; and as a rule the companies were required to furnish various types of free services to cities. It is worth noting in this connection that often more attention was paid to the compensation for franchises than to conditions necessary to insure reasonable service at fair rates, presumably on the theory that franchises were property rights to be sold by the city on the most advantageous terms.

SLIDING-SCALE FRANCHISES AND AGREEMENTS

Various devices have been developed to escape the inflexible nature of rate provisions in limited-term franchises and to render regulation of rates continuous and automatic. Among these are sliding-scale franchises, developed in Great Britain in the latter part of the nineteenth century and later introduced into the United States. An example of a sliding-scale franchise was that granted to the Boston Consolidated Gas Company in 1906. Its essential feature was an initial standard rate for gas and a stand-

---

[1] WILCOX, D. F., "Municipal Franchises," Gervaise Press, New York, 1910, vol. II, pp. 34–100.

ard dividend rate for the company, with the added provision that the latter could be raised as the price of gas to ultimate consumers was lowered. Provision also was made for the raising or lowering of the standard rate for gas after 10 years on the petition either of the company or of the mayor or selectmen of the cities and towns.

A recent type of sliding-scale plan is the so-called Detroit plan for the control of gas rates in Detroit by contractual agreement between the city and the supplying company. Under this plan a base, or minimum, return of $3,850,000 is allowed the company, plus 7 per cent upon future extensions and improvements. Excess earnings are to be shared by consumers and stockholders on an agreed basis, the consumers to receive their share in the form of a dividend (paid in cash or as a credit on account) at the end of each fiscal year. The first $550,000 of excess earnings is to be divided equally between the consumers and stockholders; and all above this amount, 75 per cent to the consumers and 25 per cent to the stockholders. Only domestic consumers are to share in the dividend on the theory that industrial and commercial gas rates are adjusted in a competitive market, whereas domestic rates are fixed under monopoly conditions.[1]

A modification of the sliding-scale plan which has aroused much comment is the "Washington plan," although in this case representing an agreement between the District of Columbia Commission and an electric utility serving the city of Washington. Its main feature is the adjustment of rates so as to yield an agreed rate of return upon an agreed valuation of the property as the rate base. If rates yield more than the agreed return for a given year they are to be reduced during the next year; if they yield less for a given period they are to be raised. Where earnings yield more than the specified return only a part of the excess is to be used as the basis for rate reductions, the balance to accrue to the company as an incentive to efficient operation. More will be said concerning this plan in Chap. VI.

Sliding-scale schemes of rate regulation have never been employed so widely in the United States as in Great Britain, although interest in them has been revived in recent years. As franchises they provide more flexible rate control than fixed-term franchises, and as a contractual relation between state commis-

---

[1] SMITH, J. W., Our Gas Company, *Public Utilities Fortnightly,* vol. 18, No. 2, pp. 83–88.

sions and utilities they have the distinct advantage of evading many of the delays and the expensive litigation attendant upon the application of the fair-return-upon-fair-value principle of rate regulation, which will be discussed later. However, they have obvious defects. Always there is some base that must be established initially, such as a standard rate, a base return, or a base value, which is difficult to determine with fairness to all parties. In the second place, since the theory of the sliding scale is to reward efficiency in management, reflected in lower price to consumers, by permitting higher dividends, or conversely to penalize inefficiency by lower dividends, it is fundamental that such adjustments reflect only changes for which the management is responsible; yet there are many factors that may influence costs, either to raise or to lower them, which are independent of managerial action. To provide adequate checks upon the management and objective standards for measuring efficiency is difficult; yet without them there is no guarantee of efficiency, since incentives are not likely to extend to all subordinate officials where the rewards go only to the stockholders. Such plans change the nature of, but do not eliminate the need for, administrative supervision.

SERVICE-AT-COST FRANCHISES

Service-at-cost franchises are based on the principle that rates shall be such as to yield sufficient revenues to meet all legitimate costs of providing utility service, including a fair return to the company. The city of Cleveland was the first to introduce a service-at-cost franchise, in 1910, and this example was followed by other cities. For the most part these franchises were adopted during the War and postwar periods, and almost wholly in the street railway industry, to remove from these utilities the crushing burdens occasioned by precipitous rises in costs of operation. However, cost of service is not a new regulatory principle introduced by these franchises; it is a principle fundamental to all regulation of public utilities. Under prevailing interpretations of constitutional rights, public utility rates must yield revenues sufficient to cover expenditures and a fair return upon the fair value of property used and useful in the public service. Cost-of-service franchises merely make this a matter of detailed contractual relationship between cities and public utility companies.

Though the number and variety of detailed provisions in cost-of-service franchises are very great, their principal features are the following: (1) usually the grant of an exclusive monopoly to the company, the right being terminable upon purchase by the city or another designated company under stipulated conditions; (2) detailed service standards, with provision for their enforcement; (3) detailed classification of costs, showing specifically the items included in each classification; (4) the value of the property, or the rate base upon which a return is to be allowed; (5) a stipulated rate of return on the agreed base, and established schedules of rates which will meet the costs; (6) reserves for depreciation and contingencies; and (7) the creation of regulatory machinery.[1] An interesting feature of most of these franchises is a fare-stabilization reserve, the function of which is to reduce the number of changes which otherwise would have to be made in fares. Since revenues may vary from month to month, sometimes less and at other times more than the costs of operation, such changes can be reflected in adjustments in the reserve, fare changes being made only when reserves go below or above prescribed limits.

The principal advantage of service-at-cost franchises is that the control of service conditions is placed in the hands of local authorities, and through them consumers can get at cost the type and quality of service they desire. A further advantage is the stability given to the service, since a company operating under a service-at-cost franchise, although it is not guaranteed a fair return unless it is earned, in the long run is assured of rates that will enable it to meet legitimate costs; hence, its credit standing is improved, and its securities removed from the speculative class.

The main objection to service-at-cost franchises is that, with an assured return, the incentive to efficiency is reduced. Attempts to assure efficient operation have been made in these franchises in the form of detailed regulations concerning service, but there are many details of management quite essential to efficient operation which cannot well be made the subject of contractual relation with the regulatory authority. Such matters include the purchase and utilization of materials and supplies, wages and the efficiency of labor, and the introduction of new

[1] Morgan, C. S., "Regulation and the Management of Public Utilities," Houghton Mifflin Company, Boston, 1923, pp. 190–191.

devices and inventions to improve the quality of the service. For maximum efficiency there must be the will of the management. In recognition of this fact, service-at-cost franchises usually contain provisions designed to promote efficiency similar to those employed in sliding-scale franchises. Such devices have been criticized, as in the case of sliding-scale franchises, on the grounds that higher or lower costs of operation may result from changes in general price levels unrelated to the skill or business acumen of the management; that changes in the rate of return throw the securities of the companies back into the speculative class from which the service-at-cost franchise is supposed to remove them; that increased returns going to the stockholders are not likely to provide spurs to management unless it shares in them; and that if the rate of return varies inversely with the fares charged, pressure will be felt by the management to skimp maintenance and to reduce costs in other ways equally reprehensible.[1]

While the service-at-cost franchise has proved fairly satisfactory in many cases, having resuscitated street railway companies threatened with bankruptcy, as a regulatory device it is not equally adaptable to other types of utility service. It would be much more difficult to adapt this type of franchise to services where schedules are used containing many different rates for different classes of consumers. It is most applicable in the street railway industry because of the uniform fare.

SUPERIORITY OF ADMINISTRATIVE COMMISSIONS

The preceding discussion of franchise regulation should point out its major weaknesses as a method of establishing public control of utilities in their detailed operations. Not only is it difficult to draw up a contract that will provide effective control at any time, but also it is next to impossible to do so for a long period in the future without creating a relationship too inflexible for the modification necessary where conditions change as they do in the supplying of public utility service. Regulation is essentially an administrative matter, and control to be effective must be exercised by a body having powers of continuous supervision. Even with franchises, and especially service-at-cost franchises, there must be some official or board to check continuously the

[1] JONES, ELIOT, and T. C. BIGHAM, "Principles of Public Utilities," The Macmillan Company, New York, 1931, pp. 154–155.

observance of franchise conditions.   In contrast with the inflexibility of franchise provisions, alterable only at the will of both parties or at the expiration of the franchise, a regulatory commission is vested with appropriate powers to act immediately and at any time to bring about changes in rates and service deemed necessary in the public interest.   Franchises are necessary today in order that cities may maintain control over the use of their streets, but it is generally recognized that such franchises should contain only the conditions necessary to safeguard those rights. Regulation of rates and service, and all matters related thereto that require continuous supervision, should not be made a matter of contract but should be the function of an administrative body, whether state or local.

With the coming of state commissions many complex problems have been raised regarding the legal status of franchises and the rights of the parties thereto.   The crucial question is whether or not the state commission can establish and fix rates other than those prescribed in a franchise, a franchise being a contract and inviolable under the contract clause of the Constitution of the United States.   The rule generally applicable is that a state can do so unless the city clearly possesses the power to make such a contract.   Such a power must be expressly conferred, however, since a municipality is merely a creature of the state having only the functions delegated to it; and the legislature under the constitution of the state must have the authority to contract away its right to regulate.

CERTIFICATES OF PUBLIC CONVENIENCE AND NECESSITY

The public utility acts of practically all states provide that no person or corporation shall undertake and engage in the supplying of at least certain types of public utility service without first having obtained from the public service commission a certificate of public convenience and necessity.   The certificate is an order granting to the applicant the right to render a particular service in a given area.   Such a provision applies to all utilities beginning operation after the effective date of the act, and in some states the requirement was made retroactive to all utilities whenever established.   The certificate issued by the state authority does not take the place of a franchise issued by a local authority, however, nor does it dispense with the necessity of the city's taking some form of action.   Most statutes provide that a utility must secure not only a certificate from the state but also a consent from local authorities before beginning construction or operation. Such consent may be given in the form of a local permit or license through the enactment of an ordinance or by the granting of a franchise.   In the case of motor transportation the requirement of local consent, while justified on the ground that a municipality is entitled to control over the use of its streets, often has operated to obstruct the development of routes and the consolidation of routes and companies.   The certificate is an additional requirement designed to achieve specific purposes of state regulation. In addition to its use in state statutes the requirement of a certificate has been incorporated in the federal laws regulating transportation, power, and communication.

REGULATION BY MUNICIPAL COMMISSIONS

As has been pointed out previously, local regulation of utilities by franchise was dependent upon a certain measure of supervision by city officials, at least enough to ascertain whether the terms of franchises were being observed by the utilities.   Some franchises included provisions requiring more or less constant supervision by city officials, particularly with respect to the adequacy and quality of the service.   This was faint recognition of the need for administrative supervision, however.   Municipal commissions came as a counterpart of the state commission movement, an important objective of which was not only to shift the situs of regulation from local to state governments but also to change its nature fundamentally by substituting administrative for legislative control.

In theory the objectives sought through regulation by municipal commissions are the same as those of state commission regulation.   In both, administrative bodies are set up with adequate powers to issue orders with respect to rates and service when and as situations arise that call for them.   The difference is that from the viewpoint of public policy in some jurisdictions, and particularly in the case of certain utilities, it is believed that the interests of consumers and the public generally are best served by local control of utility services.   The history of public utility regulation in the United States holds many instances of swings in popular sentiment back and forth between policies of centralization and decentralization of control. Reaction to ineffective state control of public utilities through charters and legislative enactments brought a change to local control through franchises, but municipal corruption and the inadequacies of local control of utilities that had become state wide in the scope of their operations created the popular sentiment which spurred the state commission movement. Recently there has been some revival of interest in broader local control in the demands of larger cities for home rule powers.

Municipal commissions on a par with state commissions, *i.e.*, having broad powers over most or all utilities operating in a given municipality, have never been a significant feature of public utility regulation in the United States. Few such have been established. Most have had limited jurisdiction with respect to powers and the utilities under their control, *e.g.*, various transit commissions and gas or electric boards or commissions. In some cases administrative duties have been given to committees of city councils, although in most cases separately constituted bodies have been created, or a commissioner has been elected or appointed, these details reflecting for the most part differences in the organization of various city governments. Too often such bodies have been merely advisory ones, dependent for effective action upon city councils.

LOCAL VERSUS STATE REGULATION

In comparing the advantages of state and local regulation it will be advisable, lest our arguments pro and con descend to the level of tenuous generalization, to set up certain postulates of effective regulation in the light of which the relative merits may be weighed. These postulates are: (1) effective regulation requires the establishment of a commission or board with adequate powers, and with sufficient personnel and resources, to collect and analyze vast amounts of utility data; (2) the scope of the jurisdiction of such a commission must be at least as broad as the operations of the utilities it is to regulate; (3) the commission must be as free as possible of political and other influences subversive of the public good; and (4) the exercise of the governmental function of utility regulation must be in consonance with the prevailing centralization or decentralization of governmental functions within the state.

Setting up a commission with adequate staff and resources to carry on the job of regulation is a costly matter. Appropriations for the public service commissions in the different states vary greatly (from less than $50,000 to more than $1,000,000 a year) but in some cases amount to large sums; yet it is generally conceded that even in the states that make relatively the largest appropriations these are inadequate for all the purposes of regulation. While it is true that as a whole, certainly so far as smaller cities are concerned, municipal commissions would not need appropriations comparable with those necessary for state commissions, the cost of maintaining an adequate local commission would be greater than the smaller cities could, or would, afford. This statement, of course, does not apply to our largest cities, since some of these have populations and wealth greater than certain states. Thus, according to the 1930 census, four cities— New York, Chicago, Philadelphia, and Detroit—each had a population greater than the total population of each of 19 states. Only two states—Pennsylvania and Illinois—had a total population greater than New York City. The largest cities, obviously, could as well afford utility commissions as many of the states.

But the cost of local regulation by commissions must be considered from another viewpoint. As will be shown later, local commissions could not wholly supplant state commissions. The latter are necessary to regulate the operations of utilities in communities too small to support commissions and to carry on certain functions of regulation for which municipal jurisdiction is too limited in scope. Too great a multiplicity of local commissions in a state would result in much needless duplication of personnel and effort and could easily lead to an increase in the total costs of regulation out of all proportion to the benefits received. Furthermore, the greater the number of regulatory bodies to which a utility company is subject, the greater the accounting and clerical burden of the utility and the cost of service to the consumers.

The chief advantage of local regulation is that local authorities are in more direct contact with local conditions. Their knowledge is likely to be more thorough and direct than that of a state body having to do with various utilities operating in numerous communities. They are more conversant with the needs and desires of local consumers and are thus better fitted to develop suitable standards of service. Also, local authorities being on the ground know more readily when conditions change and are better able to anticipate the future. These advantages are relative, however, and must be considered in the light of the additional costs incurred to obtain them.

That the territorial scope of the jurisdiction of a regulatory body must be as broad as the operations of the companies it is to regulate is axiomatic in a regulatory system, yet it is in this respect that local control of many utilities is most limited. Utilities formerly considered local are no longer so. Gas companies, as a rule, serve more than one community, and the networks of electric companies and systems spread over numerous communities scattered throughout a state or in many states. Similarly, the bulk of the telephone service of the United States is furnished by the Associated Companies of the Bell System, all of which operate in many cities and most serve communities in more than one state, the Southern Bell Telephone and Telegraph Company operating in nine states.

There are certain utilities, however, which are distinctly local. Water supply is essentially a local enterprise, and though the local company may supply suburban or contiguous areas and may go far afield for sources of water, these do not create insuperable jurisdictional obstacles to local regulation. Urban transportation also is a local problem, and except where the urban systems are incorporated bodily into interurban systems, rates and service may be regulated effectively by local bodies. Even with gas and electric systems, the preponderance in numbers and the concentration of city customers often create problems which lend themselves to at least a measure of local treatment.

Where a utility company serves more than one community, problems arise which call for jurisdiction of a broad scope. Local control of service conditions and standards is possible within limits compatible with the need for state-wide regulation, but local regulation of rates is not feasible. Apart from the difficulties of segregating the property of a state-wide company utilized in a given community, necessary for valuation purposes, and the apportionment of numerous overhead expenses so as to determine the cost of supplying service in a given community, uniform treatment is essential to prevent unjust discriminations as between different communities. Local authorities under pressure from local consumers would seek to obtain as low rates as possible in a particular community, even though "losses" from unduly low rates in one community would have to be recouped by the company by charging higher rates than would be fair and equitable in communities where the pressure would not be so great, or in communities where the company was not regulated locally, if its operations as a whole were to show a profit.

Other aspects of regulation, such as the control of security issues and accounting practices, are state rather than local matters. Control of security issues must be in the hands of authorities having jurisdiction of the company in all its operations. Similarly, nothing but confusion, unnecessary duplication, and waste would result from requiring a company to keep different sets of accounts in accordance with the desires of authorities in the different communities that it serves.

As to political and other subversive influences, pressure has been, and probably always will be, brought to bear upon regulatory bodies. The public nature of the services performed by these industries and the fact that they are regulated by governmental authority inevitably plunge public utilities into the maelstrom of politics. On the one hand are the consumers with real or fancied grievances who furnish the raw material for political demagogues; and on the other hand, the companies who through lobbying activities attempt to control in their interests legislation and the policies of administrative bodies. The issue here is not whether by making regulation state or local we shall be rid of subversive influences, but whether a state body will be better able than a local body to withstand them and to render judgments equitable to all parties concerned, consumers and companies alike.

Those who favor the concentration of regulation of local utilities in state commissions hold that local officials are in too direct contact with the consumers to deal fairly with the companies. Where control is localized, they say, controversial issues over rates and service are more likely to become political issues, and when this happens political officials are prone to side with the larger numerical group, whatever the equities involved. Local political factors affect not at all bodies that are responsible to the state as a whole and not to any particular community. Advocates of local regulation, on the other hand, hold that the direct pressure of consumers on local authorities is not without its advantages. Consumers are notoriously unorganized and as a rule are not able to present a case before a state commission so completely or so effectively as the company. Thus the arguments run on.

Certainly the responsiveness of a state body to the needs and desires of a local community is less direct than that of a local body, but whether or not this is a happy circumstance conditions alone will determine. Direct pressure which results in unfair treatment of utility companies is not to be commended, nor is the yielding of local authorities to such pressure. It does not follow, however, that local regulatory authorities will of necessity be less honest and fair minded than state authorities or that consumers as a whole will be unreasonable and unfair. There are numerous instances in the history of local regulation where a fine cooperation has been developed between local officials and the utilities, in which equitable settlements have been made. Whether or not justice is done will depend largely upon the thoroughness and integrity with which commissioners perform their duties, be they members of state or of local bodies.

The degree of centralization or decentralization of governmental functions in a state is bound to be reflected in the type of control of public utilities, especially where cities have broad home-rule powers. In the case of the electric light and power industry, for example, in most states jurisdiction is with the state commission, local control being limited to regulation of the use of streets and general aspects of service. In some states, however, control is largely local. Thus, in South Dakota regulation of the rates and service of electrical utilities is exercised altogether by municipal authorities; and in several other states, notably Colorado, Kansas, Michigan, and Ohio, state control is limited by home-rule provisions or franchise requirements.

For the many reasons already given, the drift in public utility regulation has been away from the limited jurisdiction of local bodies, but there is much to be said for the decentralization of control so far as this is practicable. The effectiveness of regulation, whether state or local, is dependent in no small degree upon the knowledge and interest of the general public regarding utility matters. Consequently, that system is best, where a rational choice may be made between state and local control, which stimulates and encourages such interest on the part of citizens generally. Because citizens are more conversant with, and more directly interested in, local affairs, the inevitable tendency in centralization is to lessen the incentive of most people to take an active interest in public utility problems and thus to destroy one of the most effective checks upon regulatory authorities.

SUMMARY

From the discussion in this chapter it is clear that the question is not so much whether regulation shall be exclusively state or local but what are the appropriate spheres of each. State commissions are necessary to regulate the rates of companies operating in more than one community; to control the issuance of securities, consolidation, and accounting practices; and to supervise other matters which, depending upon the segregation of other functions in the various states, may properly be deemed state functions. Control of service, on the other hand, is mostly a local matter and should be directly under the control of local authorities. Certainly a city should have the unrestricted right to control the use of its streets and to prescribe the manner in which they shall be used, whether for car lines, bus routes, gas and water mains, or electric and telephone wires. The city should have the right, also, provided it desires to exercise that right, to prescribe standards of service where the problems are local, since the quality of service is a matter that should be determined by those immediately affected.

It is in connection with rate regulation that the difficulties of establishing appropriate spheres of state and local control are greatest. While the problem is not so complex where the utilities are distinctly local, as in the case of the water supply and urban transportation utilities, where utilities serve more than one community local rate problems lose their isolated character and merge into state-wide or regional problems which may be dealt with effectively only by bodies utilizing the broader powers of the state.

Our position is that if the people of a city desire to regulate local utilities that operate within their borders and are willing and able to set up the necessary regulatory machinery, there is no good reason why they should not be empowered to do so. It is obvious, however, that the sphere of local regulation is narrowly circumscribed by the development and organization of public utility services and by the costs of effective regulation. It is limited, also, by the quality of local government; for to place the control of technical utility matters in the hands of corrupt or incapable local officials would not make for effective regulation. While the argument against decentralization based upon the corruption and inefficiency all too characteristic of local regulation during its heyday is not conclusive—for to accept it as such would imply that cities could not so well as states profit by the lessons of history—cleaning up municipal affairs would constitute a proper prelude to the assumption of further governmental functions.

Many feel that local control of public utilities should be considered not solely from the viewpoint of effective regulation but in relation to its effect upon democratic government in general. These view too great centralization of governmental functions as a distinct threat to democracy itself on the ground that centralization leads to remote control of a bureaucratic nature by officials not directly responsible to the citizens. The institutions of democracy, they hold, rest fundamentally upon active interest in and participation in governmental affairs by the great mass of voters, and these are best encouraged and promoted in the direct, intimate relationship between local officials and the voting public. That there is a point to this argument is no more debatable than that local regulation of public utilities might well serve to stimulate such general participation in government. It is our opinion, however, that local regulation must be considered first from the standpoint of efficiency and that for the reasons we have given any broad expansion of local control of public utilities, except in the case of distinctly local utilities, must result either in less effective regulation or in costs out of proportion to the benefits received.

References

BAUER, J. B.: "Standards for Modern Public Utility Franchises," Municipal Administration Service, Publication No. 17, 1930.

BUSSING, I.: "Public Utility Regulation and the So-called Sliding Scale," Columbia University Press, New York, 1936.

CHANTLER, P.: The London Sliding Scale: Incentive and Efficiency in the British Gas Industry, *Journal of Land and Public Utility Economics*, vol. 12, No. 3.

CLARK, H. G.: "Service at Cost Plans," American Electric Railroad Association, New York, 1920.

COOKE, M. L.: "Public Utility Regulation," Ronald Press Company, New York, 1924.

GLAESER, M. G.: "Outlines of Public Utility Economics," The Macmillan Company, New York, 1931.

JONES, ELIOT, and T. C. BIGHAM: "Principles of Public Utilities," The Macmillan Company, New York, 1931.

KING, C. L.: "The Regulation of Municipal Utilities," D. Appleton-Century Company, Inc., New York, 1912.

MORGAN, C. S.: "Regulation and the Management of Public Utilities," Houghton Mifflin Company, Boston, 1923.

WILCOX, D. F.: "Municipal Franchises," Gervaise Press, New York, 1910, vols. I and II.

CHAPTER III

REGULATION BY STATE COMMISSIONS

The discussion in the preceding chapters has been devoted to the background of commission regulation and the appropriate spheres of state and local control. In this chapter we shall deal with the extent and scope of state commission jurisdiction and the source of a state commission's authority, its organization, powers and duties, and procedure. Because of the lack of uniformity in the public utility statutes of the various states few general statements concerning such matters are universally applicable. Nevertheless, there is sufficient uniformity for a certain amount of generalization, and significant exceptions to general practice will be noted on appropriate occasion.

Extent of State Commission Jurisdiction.—Forty-seven states and the District of Columbia now have public service commissions with jurisdiction over some class or classes of public utilities. The District of Columbia Commission has been established by the Congress of the United States, to which it is directly responsible. Delaware is the only state without a public service commission. Many of these bodies were created originally solely for the purpose of regulating steam railroad freight and passenger traffic and rates but, with the growing need for regulation of public services generally, their jurisdiction has been extended to other utilities.

A survey made by Bonbright and Company, as of the year 1930,[1] indicated that all but one of these commissions, the Public Utilities Commission of the District of Columbia, had jurisdiction over steam railroads; all but two over interurban electric railways; all but three over street railways; all but one over motorbuses; all but seven over electric light, heat, and power companies; all but six over natural gas companies; and all but eight over manufactured gas companies. Commissions in 12 states had no juris-

[1] "A Survey of State Laws on Public Utility Commission Regulation in the United States," 2d ed., Bonbright & Co., 1930.

diction over water companies, and those in 20 states had no jurisdiction over oil and gas pipe lines.

A survey of state public utility legislation enacted during the six years following 1930, made by a special committee of the National Association of Railroad and Utilities Commissioners,[1] shows numerous extensions of the jurisdiction of state commissions. In some states, such as Arkansas, Kentucky, and South Carolina, the new legislation effected sweeping changes. In other states the scope of commission jurisdiction over utilities already regulated was extended, and a number of commissions were given broader jurisdiction through redefinition of the term "public utility." In this manner, public heating corporations were placed under the commission in Maine, heat and gas utilities in Michigan, toll roads as well as toll bridges in New Hampshire, and the transportation of gas and electricity in New York. Several states passed laws which specifically provide that certain enterprises are to be regulated. These include aviation and power boats in New Hampshire; public housing corporations in New Jersey and North Carolina; port districts in Michigan; flood control, water carriers, and relief of low-water conditions in Wisconsin; pipe lines in Iowa, North Dakota, and Texas; toll bridges and ferries in Alabama; and oil and gas inspection in Oklahoma and Texas. In all, 19 states dealt with the general jurisdiction of their commissions during the six-year period. Some of the most significant changes have occurred in commission control of motor transportation, three-fourths of the states establishing new or supplemental controls over the operations of motor carriers.

During this period 29 states enacted legislation affecting the organization of their commissions. Some of this legislation was clearly in the interest of economy during the depression years, but in most cases attempt was made to stimulate regulatory activity to new levels of achievement. Of the former type might be mentioned reductions in the size of commissions, although such reductions could have been made for other reasons. In three states (North Carolina, Oregon, and Utah) the number of commissioners was reduced from three to one, although North Carolina and Utah each provided for two part-time commissioners

[1] National Association of Railroad and Utilities Commissioners, *Proceedings*, 1936, pp. 360–402.

paid on a per diem basis. In Illinois and Pennsylvania the number was reduced from seven to five; and in Indiana, from five to three. In other states, however, such as Arkansas, Kansas, and Kentucky, substantial reorganization of the commission, with material changes in or additions to its powers, was accomplished in order to effect greater efficiency. Many changes were wrought in the technical staffs of various commissions. These include the creation of special officers, such as investigators supervisors, legal aides, researchers, statisticians, and others. In a few states the new laws created a special officer, sometimes known as public counselor or prosecutor, to appear before the commission, or the courts in appealed cases, to represent the ratepayers and the general public.

There was a distinct trend in the new legislation to assess against the utilities the costs of regulation. Twenty-five states dealt with this matter, the action in one case being a reversal of the general trend, Massachusetts repealing an old law levying upon electric, gas, and water companies, and municipal plants one-half of the commission's salaries and expenses. Most of the other laws made new assessments which took the form either of providing for payment by the utilities of only a part of the costs of regulation or of providing for the payment of substantially all of the costs. Because of these laws many commissions have been able to secure for their staffs additional experts.

Scope of Commission Powers.—The authority of state public service commissions emanates from the constitutions or legislative enactments of the various states. These laws invariably define more or less specifically the powers that the commissions may exercise, the precise scope of such powers being a matter for court interpretation. Within the boundaries of law and judicial interpretation, regulatory commissions enjoy wide discretionary powers. For example, the laws require that public utility rates be just and reasonable, but the determination of actual rates that are just and reasonable is a matter for the commissions, subject to review by the courts where the constitutional rights of private property are involved. Similarly, grants of authority over service, security issues, certificates of public convenience and necessity, and other regulatory powers are made in broad, general terms in the statutes. Specific application of them in individual cases calls for the employment of discretionary judgment on the part of the commissions.   It is inevitable that this should be so, since attempts to control public utilities by direct legislation result either in laws too detailed and too rigid to admit of flexible control or in toothless laws so loosely drawn as to make of regulation a sham and a farce.

The discretionary powers of public service commissions have been aptly divided into two groups: enabling powers, under which the companies must secure commission approval before specified acts may be committed: and directing powers, by which the commission is authorized to exercise continuous supervision over the operations of utilities and to interfere when necessary in the public interest.[1]   Among the enabling powers are authority to issue, or to refuse to issue, certificates of public convenience and necessity for the inauguration, extension, or abandonment of service; to approve or disapprove the issuance of securities and the assumption of obligations; and to approve or disapprove consolidations. Directing powers include control over accounting practices, rates, valuation, and service standards.

The present public utility laws of the various states have been drafted for the most part in the light of earlier enactments in certain leading states, notably the acts of Wisconsin and New York, which in turn were much influenced by the Interstate Commerce Act.   This has resulted in a certain amount of uniformity of principle with respect to regulation and some uniformity in specific provisions in the various statutes.   Examination of these laws discloses, however, considerable variability in statute phraseology and mechanical detail and in numerous cases the lack of powers generally conceded to be essential to effective regulation.   The Bonbright survey, confined for the most part to the gas and electric utilities, showed that all but five commissions possessed jurisdiction over the rates and service standards of gas and electric utilities.   In two states, however, the statute applied to natural gas rates only; in one other state, to electric rates only; and in three states control over service did not extend to both types of utilities.   All but seven commissions were empowered to determine any question of fact with regard to discrimination, as to both rates and service, and practically all statutes provided that rates must be just and reasonable, that

---

[1] MOSHER, W. E., and F. G. CRAWFORD, "Public Utility Regulation," Harper & Brothers, New York, 1933, pp. 27–28.

rate schedules be filed, that such schedules be adhered to, and that rate changes might be made only after due notice to the commission. All the commissions having jurisdiction over electric and gas utilities were authorized to ascertain and fix valuations, either through specific enactment or as a necessary incident to rate regulation, most statutes providing that valuations be made by the commissions. In 42 states consumers may make complaints about rates or service, and in 36 states commissions possessed authority to initiate complaints and start investigations.

Considerably less uniformity was found in the statutes with respect to other commission powers. In 28 states commissions had authority over the issuance of certificates of public convenience and necessity; in 34 states, authority over accounting practices; in 23 states, varying authority over capitalization and the issuance of securities; in 22 states, authority over consolidations and mergers; and in 31 states the laws required electric and gas companies to make general reports, most statutes adding a requirement for special reports as deemed necessary by the commission.

The survey of the special committee of the National Association of Railroad and Utilities Commissioners indicates that the powers of many state commissions have been broadened materially during the years following 1930. The new legislation in some cases concerns the application of new controls or modifications of old ones, but in many cases the effect is to bring the statutory basis of regulation in certain states more nearly to the level of that in leading states. During this period 24 state commissions received legislative authority which extended their control over affiliated interests. In some cases this represents the grant of such authority for the first time, although in other cases authority formerly granted has been expanded by broadening the definition of affiliated interests or by extending control over specific matters, especially contractual relations. With but a few exceptions the same states also enacted laws extending commission control over securities. Six states (Kentucky, North Carolina, Oregon, South Carolina, Virginia, and Washington) enacted new and fairly complete statutes for the regulation of securities; while several states, including Alabama, Arkansas, Maine, Massachusetts, and Pennsylvania, amended their security laws. In Pennsylvania the change was so great as to make control over securities possible for the first time in that state. In addition to control over the actual issuance of securities, many of the new laws prohibit utilities from extending credit or assuming obligations or liabilities of any other company or person without commission approval. Several states enacted new laws giving their commissions explicit jurisdiction over reorganization of public utility companies and prohibiting, without commission approval, transactions that involve mergers or consolidations or the purchasing, assigning, leasing, mortgaging, or disposing of public utility property. In certain cases states prohibited the declaration and payment of unearned dividends.

Because of the primary importance of regulation of rates and service most commissions already possessed quite complete powers in these matters. Significant new powers have been added in many cases, nevertheless. One of these is the power to issue temporary rate orders, enacted by four states to prevent exorbitant charges to ratepayers during delays in rate proceedings. Others include provisions granting commissions additional authority to suspend proposed increases in rates pending an investigation of their reasonableness and to enter into contractual agreements with utilities, such as sliding-scale agreements. New laws affecting service grant jurisdiction for the first time to certain commissions and in other cases broaden previous jurisdiction, 17 states taking some action. An interesting development is with respect to rural electric service. Several states (including Alabama, Indiana, Mississippi, Montana, New Mexico, North Carolina, South Dakota, Virginia, and Wisconsin) have authorized the creation of public or semipublic bodies, such as power districts, state rural electrification authorities, and cooperatives, for the promotion of rural electric service. However, these laws are separate from those under which the state commissions function, and in most cases the new bodies are independent of the commissions, although a few states make cooperatives subject to their jurisdiction.

As has been stated previously, practically all commissions have authority to make valuations, either by legislative grant or by necessary implication. During the years following 1930 several additional states enacted laws providing that valuations be made by the commissions. In New York and Indiana new laws have given specific mandates as to the methods and principles to be employed by commissions in valuation. The new legislation also has extended commission control over depreciation in certain states.

Comparatively little legislation was enacted regarding accounts and reports, new provisions governing mostly procedural matters. Fifteen states enacted legislation extending commission authority with respect to certificates of public convenience and necessity, franchises, and rights of way.

Exceptional new powers are those in the laws of Oregon and Washington which provide for commission control over excess earnings and the financial budgets of utilities. These laws provide that earnings in excess of a reasonable return must be placed in a reserve fund to be applied in whole or in part against earnings below a reasonable return in subsequent years or to be applied in establishing, replenishing, or maintaining amortization, depreciation, or other contingent funds or for any other purpose beneficial to the consumers. They provide also for the "regulation, restriction and control over the budgets of expenditures of public service companies." In Washington this jurisdiction extends over the entire financial program of a utility, including all estimated revenues and expenditures broken down as the Department may require.

The table on p. 50 summarizes the recent legislation which granted new or supplemental powers to state commissions.[1]

This survey of recent public utility legislation in the various states indicates a decided movement toward strengthening state commission regulation, and incidentally in the direction of greater statute uniformity. That there is still much variance with respect to fundamental powers, however, is evidenced by a recent survey of state commission jurisdiction over and regulation of electric rates and service made by the Federal Power Commission.[2] This survey showed that 38 of the 41 state commissions having jurisdiction over electric utilities possess authority to regulate rates charged by all privately owned utilities, but the scope of jurisdiction varies. In the case of three commissions

[1] National Association of Railroad and Utilities Commissioners, *Proceedings, loc. cit.*

[2] State Commission Jurisdiction and Regulation of Electric Rates and Service, *Rate Series* 6, 1935.

(Connecticut, Missouri, and Pennsylvania) rate powers are limited to the regulation of maximum rates only, the companies being free to promulgate any desired rates below the maximum

Provision	Number of States
Motor carrier regulation	36
Commission organization	29
Assessment of costs of regulation	25
Affiliated interests:	
Definition of affiliated interests	16
Disclosure of interests	9
Control of contracts and/or extension of credit, loans, or guarantees	24
Jurisdiction	11
Securities:	
Control of issuance of securities and/or renewal of indebtedness	21
Control of assumption or guarantee of indebtedness or contracts	9
Provisions on purchases and/or sales by employees	5
Control of reorganizations, mergers, or leases or sales, investments, etc	12
Dividends	7
Rates:	
Temporary rate orders	4
Suspension of proposed rates and/or refunds or overcharges	13
Other powers	15
Service	17
Certificates of convenience and necessity, franchises, rights of way	15
Accounting and reporting	10
Valuation	10
Depreciation	7
General jurisdiction	19
Joint regulation	12
Legal procedure	20
Grade crossings	13
Other legislation	34

level. The jurisdiction of the Ohio Commission does not extend to cases where the utility has a contract with a municipality, the power to regulate electric rates under the state law resting primarily with the municipal council. The Nebraska Commission has jurisdiction over electric rates only in unincorporated territory. In Colorado, Kansas, and Michigan the jurisdiction of the commission is limited also by varying degrees of local control. Twelve commissions have jurisdiction over rates charged by municipally owned electric utilities both within and without the corporate limits; and nine, outside corporate limits only.

Considerable variability exists in the regulation of sales to special classes of customers. Thirty-seven commissions have the right to regulate rates paid privately owned utilities by municipalities for street lighting, water pumping, and other services; and 39 commissions, authority to regulate rates paid such utilities by the Federal Government. Special contracts governing rates to ultimate consumers are prohibited in some states, although in 27 states such contracts are permitted. In 20 of these states commission approval is required, but in the others not. In most states where the commission has jurisdiction over electric rates the power to regulate special contracts between utilities is granted under the authority to regulate rates. Twenty commissions reported that interconnection contracts must be approved by them; and 19 commissions, that they do not require commission approval. In 17 states contracts between operating utilities and management companies, legal firms, and other organizations rendering service to them require commission approval. In 25 other states, although commission approval is not required, such contracts must be filed with the regulatory body. In four of these states (Georgia, New Hampshire, North Dakota, and Pennsylvania) the commissions may disregard such contracts for rate-making purposes if they believe the fees paid are unreasonable.

County or township authorities have first jurisdiction over allocation of rural territory in some states, a franchise from them being a prerequisite to service. In other states, utilities may extend their lines into contiguous unincorporated territory without obtaining permission either of the state commission or of the local authorities. Thirty-five commissions reported that they have authority to require private utilities to make rural extensions, 23 of these commissions having no similar jurisdiction over municipal plants. All commissions having jurisdiction over electric rates have authority to regulate rules governing the financial conditions imposed for rural extensions and connections.

Customer deposits are regulated in some states directly by law, and in others by the commissions. Thirty-five commissions reported that they regulate the amounts of such deposits. Sub-metering is either prohibited or discouraged in most of the states, being prohibited in 18 states and in many others prevented by the prescribing of rate schedules that do not permit energy to be resold. Nineteen commissions reported that they have authority to adopt sliding-scale plans, while 19 other commissions reported no such authority.

The Uniform Public Utilities Act.—The diversity of provision in the public utility laws of the different states reflects not so much varying conditions under which public utility services are rendered as varying degrees of comprehensiveness and effectiveness of regulation. While it is generally recognized that such conditions do vary, as do the political institutions and tradition of the different states, it is believed by many that greater uniformity in public utility statutes would be of distinct public advantage. In the first place, uniformity of regulation in the several states served by one utility would result in decreased operating costs and improved service and would prevent the evasion of regulation by such a utility through the issuance of securities, or the conduct of other operations, in states where such matters would not be subject to commission control. In the second place, comparisons of the effectiveness of regulation in different states could be made more easily and with greater validity, and commissions would have much less opportunity to shift the blame for failures in regulation to defective statutes. Finally, uniform statutes modeled after those of leading states would raise the level of regulation in certain backward states to a marked extent. Public utilities have been regulated for so long a time, and court decisions construing the laws and passing upon the acts of commissions are so voluminous and comprehensive, that tried and true provisions for the basic framework of regulation are well defined.

The movement for uniform public utility legislation among the states dates from a conference of state railroad commissioners, called by the Interstate Commerce Commission in 1889, at which was organized the body now known as the National Association of Railroad and Utilities Commissioners. This organization was at first concerned only with railroad legislation, but with the extension of state commission powers to other utilities a similar need for uniformity in legislation and regulation was recognized. The

National Association eventually set up a special committee to consider the matter of a uniform law, and this committee, in cooperation with the Public Utility Section of the American Bar Association, drew up a Uniform Public Utilities Act. This Act was adopted by the National Conference of Commissioners on Uniform State Laws[1] in 1928 and approved by the American Bar Association in the same year.

The Uniform Public Utilities Act deals with the major aspects of public utility regulation, other than steam railroads, under eight articles, having to do, respectively, with definitions of terms, such as "public utility"; duties and restrictions imposed upon public utilities with respect to rates, service, schedules and adherence to schedules, discrimination, and changes in rates; powers conferred upon the commissions over the fixing of rates, sliding scales of rates, joint use of telephone and telegraph facilities, standards of service, valuations, accounts, reports, and investigations; the utility franchise and certificates of convenience and necessity; procedure before the commission; review and enforcement of commission orders; organization of the commission and office; and miscellaneous provisions. The act was divided into the foregoing separate and distinct articles so that any state so desiring could eliminate any one or more articles and substitute the corresponding provisions of its own laws. It followed closely the provisions of leading statutes which had already been widely copied, and since 1928 many of its provisions have been adopted individually by various states. However, uniformity is still a long way off.

Functions of a Public Service Commission.—A public service commission, in one sense, may be considered as a board of experts having authority, and the duty, to collect, assemble, and interpret facts concerning the operations of the public utilities subject to its jurisdiction. In this respect it is concerned with the analysis of regular and special reports and with a multitude of problems involving the consideration, among other things, of rates and rate structures, accounting practices, and service standards. Much of

[1] The National Conference of Commissioners on Uniform State Laws is an official body composed of representatives appointed by the various states to confer upon, prepare, and propose bills or forms of bills on those subjects upon which it is deemed most desirable that states should act with uniformity.

this is routine work for which the commission may employ a technical staff. However, depending upon the commission and its conception of its duties, it may be an aggressive fact-finding body, initiating investigations of rates and utility practices on its own motion and in this way striving to see to it that utilities fulfill their public service obligations.

In another sense, a public service commission may be looked upon as a semijudicial body, sitting as a court, hearing evidence on both sides in cases of complaint, and rendering decision in accordance with the evidence presented. The procedure of commissions is usually outlined in the acts creating them, and they must conform to such requirements, but commissions are strictly not courts, and they are not bound by the rigid technical rules of evidence that govern court procedure. All interested parties are entitled to be heard, to present evidence, and to cross-examine. Nor is a commission required to decide a case merely on the basis of the evidence presented before it by parties to the dispute. Its duty is to make decision in the light of all facts, and in doing so it may take into consideration the results of its own investigations and all general information upon a given subject within its knowledge.

The different functions of a public service commission thus appear to be somewhat incompatible, since it is difficult for a regulatory commission aggressive in discovering the facts and acting as a prosecutor in the public interest to render decisions upon these facts. In practice it has led to emphasis upon the investigating and prosecuting functions by certain commissions and upon the judicial functions by other commissions. Over-emphasis of the judicial functions by a commission may serve to defeat the primary purpose for which it has been established, *viz.*, the protection of the public interest. It is a recognized part of the duty of a commission to pass judgment upon the rates and practices of public utility companies, but for the commission merely to sit as a court throws burdens of prosecution upon the consumers which they are not able to support. While informal complaints involving minor matters may be handled readily in ordinary administrative routine, the bringing of formal complaints requires the employment of technical and legal assistance which unorganized consumers cannot afford. Even where the city is party to the suit, whether as a consumer or representing the interests of the consuming public under the laws of the state, prosecution is notoriously inadequate. It is to overcome this defect that most commissions have been given authority to initiate investigations on their own motions.

Harmonizing the separate functions of a state commission constitutes a very practical problem, but that it is not impossible of solution is well demonstrated by certain commissions which, while acting in their judicial capacity, have not neglected the investigative functions. One reason for undue emphasis upon the judicial functions is the general inadequacy of state appropriations, which as a rule are too meager to provide personnel for much more than the normal routine work. Where a commission and its staff are fully occupied with routine there is little opportunity for aggressive fact finding and prosecution, and consumers inevitably are left to prosecute their own cases with little or no help in their preparation from the commissions. As has been indicated previously, some states, in order to make up for some of the deficiencies in commission staffs and to provide for more aggressive prosecution, have established public prosecutors or defenders whose functions are to assist consumers in the preparation and prosecution of formal cases. If regulation is to be effective, either this must be done, or state commissions universally must be given full powers to initiate investigations and resources to enable them to carry them on. The creation of a separate office removes an objection frequently raised by commissions to calling upon their own experts to testify in formal cases on the ground that they might have to rule against them and thus undermine the prestige of their staffs.

The functions of a public service commission must be considered from the viewpoint also of their relation to the managements of public utility enterprises. It must not be forgotten that public utilities are privately owned and that the managements, as is true of all private industry, are responsible for the conduct of the enterprises. While the commission as the administrative arm of the state may regulate, neither the state nor the commission is the owner of the property or clothed with the powers of management incident to ownership.[1] Just where the dividing line between regulation and management lies cannot

[1] Missouri *ex rel.* Southwestern Bell Telephone Co. v. Pub. Service Comm., **262** U.S. 289.

be stated with finality, since all regulation constitutes interference with the freedom of management, and the more detailed and intrusive regulation becomes, the more it encroaches upon the general sphere of management. Rates, for example, are fixed in the first instance by the managements, but commissions generally have been given broad powers to modify rate schedules in order to make them reasonable and nondiscriminating. Under the existing system of regulation in the United States reasonable rates are those that will yield a fair return upon a fair value of the property used and useful in the public service. Since this is a net return, the commission besides determining fair return and fair value must inquire into the honesty, efficiency, and economy of management. Just how much latitude shall be given to the judgment of management in these matters is a question difficult to answer, yet one that continually arises.

It cannot be stated specifically and dogmatically how far commissions may go in prescribing methods, techniques, even types of equipment and in penalizing bad or rewarding good management. As a general rule, commissions may interfere with the business policies of a public utility only so far as they affect rates or service or any duty or obligation of the companies in respect thereto.[1] But there are many such matters with respect to which the scope of commission powers is not clear. May a commission dictate the selection of personnel or the salaries to be paid, materials or fuel to be used; may it control the contractual relationships of a utility with other companies, both as to with whom it shall contract and as to the amounts to be paid for supplies and services; and may it decrease or increase rates solely with a view to the effect upon the utility's net revenues? And how far may a commission go in ordering extensions or improvements of service or in prescribing standards of service? Answers to these questions lie in a twilight zone between the clearly defined spheres of management and regulation where court decisions in individual cases provide few general principles as guides. To what extent a commission may substitute its judgment for that of the management is a matter always for the courts to decide, but the circumstances of the individual case have been, and will be, controlling.

[1] Spurr, H. C., "Guiding Principles of Public Utility Regulation," Public Utilities Reports, Inc., Washington, 1924, vol. I, p. 121.

The Role of the Courts in Regulation.—Administrative determinations by regulatory commissions are not final but are subject to review by the courts. Apart from its legality there is sound justification for judicial review, in that commissions often act under ill-conceived legislation, they sometimes are incompetent or lack adequate experience, they are subject to various forms of political pressure, and their acts may be so inconsistent and arbitrary as seriously to threaten the stability of industries in which vast sums have been invested. Appeal from decisions of commissions may be taken to the state courts, in accordance with the laws of the various states, or to the federal courts. As a general rule, the review of a commission order by a court is limited to questions (1) whether the commission has acted within its powers, (2) whether the order is supported by the evidence, and (3) whether the constitutional rights of any party or parties are infringed thereby.

Owing to the dual nature of our government, both state and federal courts have jurisdiction to review commission determinations, appeal to the state courts being provided for in the state laws, and appeal to the federal courts being taken on the grounds that rights guaranteed in the Federal Constitution are being infringed and that property is being taken without due process of law. The result has been a certain amount of clash between reviewing jurisdictions and much delay in the enforcement of commission orders, these usually being restrained by injunction until their validity has been determined. Formerly, much delay was occasioned in rate cases owing to the procedure in review by the federal courts. The utility contesting a rate order of a commission would bring suit in a federal district court, but, since the Judicial Code of the United States made no provision for the certification of the record of the state administrative body, the federal court would have no record upon which to base a decision. In a rate case no final disposition could be made until the court had ascertained the value of the property involved and whether the schedule of charges sought to be set aside would yield a fair return upon that value. Accordingly, the court would appoint a master who would make such a valuation, entirely independent of the commission's previous finding if he chose so to do. Such duplication of work was not only time consuming and wasteful, but it tended to defeat the ends of regulation.

For years there was agitation for reform in the procedure of appeal to federal courts. Most of the important rate cases were taken to the federal courts, with resultant delays of years in passing through federal district and circuit courts before final decision would be rendered by the Supreme Court of the United States. The famous New York Telephone Company case was in the courts for 11 years and cost the company about $5,000,000, which incidentally was paid ultimately by its consumers, not to mention the direct costs to them. The more recent Chicago telephone case was almost as long and costly in litigation. Such delays are expensive, and decisions are rendered under conditions that may have so changed as to render them largely inapplicable.

To reduce delay and to speed up ultimate decision in rate cases, Congress enacted the Johnson Act, approved May 14, 1934.[1] This law deprives the federal district courts of jurisdiction to enjoin, suspend, or restrain the enforcement of an order of a state administrative board or commission

. . . where jurisdiction is based solely upon the ground of diversity of citizenship, or the repugnance of such order to the Constitution of the United States, where such order (1) affects rates chargeable by a public utility, (2) does not interfere with interstate commerce, and (3) has been made after reasonable notice and hearing, and where a plain, speedy and efficient remedy may be had at law or in equity in the courts of such state.

One of the principal advantages of the Johnson Act is the reduction in the delays in appeal procedure, but there are others. As has been pointed out, when a case formerly could be taken to the federal district court a trial *de novo* was had before a master; thus in many instances the lengthy, costly investigation and finding of the commission would be duplicated. Also, it not infrequently happened that in the new trial new evidence would be submitted, and ultimate decision would be rendered on a record different from that upon which the order of the commission originally was issued. Now that appeal must be taken to the state courts the case will be heard upon the record of the commission as certified by it.[2] The district courts

---

[1] 48 Stat. 775.

[2] BALDRIDGE, H., National Association of Railroad and Utilities Commissioners, *Proceedings*, 1934, pp. 71–90.

are not deprived of jurisdiction by the Johnson Act where a "plain, speedy, and efficient remedy" may not be had at law or in equity in the courts of the state. This itself is a matter for judicial interpretation, however, and already the Supreme Court has upheld the assumption of jurisdiction by a district court where such a remedy was deemed not to be available.[1]

Decisions Based on Law and Fact.—While the need for, and the justification of, judicial review of commission decisions is well recognized, and the legal principles governing review may readily be stated, as an actual fact the courts at times have assumed the functions of superadministrative bodies. In principle, courts are concerned with questions of law, not of fact, but clear, objective definition of these terms so as clearly to delimit them and to separate one from the other is impossible. To determine when a commission is or is not acting within its powers, and when its actions are arbitrary or capricious, is clearly a matter for judicial consideration. However, the case is not so clear where the court is called upon to decide whether a commission order is supported by the evidence or whether constitutional rights are being infringed. In such cases is the court to accept the findings of fact by the commission as conclusive, or is it to make separate findings of its own? The question frequently comprehends the extent to which the court will substitute its judgment of fact for that of the commission.

A leading case concerning this point is *Ohio Valley Water Co. v. Ben Avon Borough*, decided June 1, 1920. Acting upon complaint, the Pennsylvania Commission instituted an investigation of the rates of the Ohio Valley Water Company in the Borough of Ben Avon, found the value of the property to be $924,744, and ordered the establishment of a new schedule of rates which would yield a fair return on this value. The company, claiming the Commission's valuation too low, appealed to the Superior Court, which reviewed the certified record, appraised the property at $1,324,621.80, reversed the order, and remanded the proceedings to the Commission with directions to authorize rates that would yield 7 per cent of such value. On appeal, the Supreme Court of Pennsylvania reversed the decree of the Superior Court, holding that there was competent evidence to sustain the Commission's decision and that "in the items

[1] Corp. Comm. of Okla. v. Cary, 296 U.S. 452; and other cases.

wherein the Superior Court differed from the commission upon the question of values, there was merely the substitution of the former's judgment for that of the commission, in determining that the order of the latter was unreasonable."[1]

The case eventually was appealed to the Supreme Court of the United States, which reversed the decision of the Supreme Court of Pennsylvania in a divided opinion. The majority concluded that the state Supreme Court interpreted the Pennsylvania law as "withholding from the courts power to determine the question of confiscation according to their own independent judgment," thus implying that a utility is entitled to an independent judicial review on the law and on the facts. Three dissenting justices held, however, that the question (what amounts should be allowed for several items which entered into the valuation) was one of fact, not of law, and that the commission's determination should be considered conclusive.[2]

Whatever the merits of the Ben Avon case, the Supreme Court did nothing to clarify the distinctions between matters of law and fact, nor have these issues ever been conclusively determined. In a case decided Apr. 27, 1936, the Court reaffirmed its position that courts may make independent judgments of the facts. Chief Justice Hughes, writing the opinion for the Court, made the following statements:

> The fixing of rates is a legislative act. In determining the scope of judicial review of that act, there is a distinction between action within the sphere of legislative authority and action which transcends the limits of legislative power. Exercising its rate-making authority, the legislature has a broad discretion. It may exercise that authority directly, or through the agency it creates or appoints to act for that purpose in accordance with appropriate standards. The court does not sit as a board of revision to substitute its judgment for that of the legislature or its agents as to matters within the province of either [cases cited]. When the legislature itself acts within the broad field of legislative discretion, its determinations are conclusive. When the legislature appoints an agent to act within that sphere of legislative authority, it may endow the agent with power to make findings of fact which are conclusive, provided the requirements of due process which are specially applicable to such an agency are met, as in according a fair hearing and

[1] 260 Pa. 289, quoted in 253 U.S. 287, 289.
[2] 253 U.S. 287, Justices Brandeis, Holmes, and Clarke, dissenting.

acting upon evidence and not arbitrarily [cases cited]. In such cases, the judicial inquiry into the facts goes no further than to ascertain whether there is evidence to support the findings, and the question of the weight of evidence in determining issues of fact lies with the legislative agency acting within its statutory authority.

But the Constitution fixes limits to the rate-making power by prohibiting the deprivation of property without due process of law or the taking of private property for public use without just compensation. When the legislature acts directly, its action is subject to judicial scrutiny and determination in order to prevent the transgression of these limits of power. The legislature cannot preclude that scrutiny or determination by any declaration or legislative finding. *Legislative declaration or finding is necessarily subject to independent judicial review upon the facts and the law by courts of competent jurisdiction* to the end that the Constitution as the supreme law of the land may be maintained. Nor can the legislature escape the constitutional limitation by authorizing its agent to make findings that the agent has kept within that limitation. Legislative agencies, with varying qualifications, work in a field peculiarly exposed to political demands. Some may be expert and impartial, others subservient. It is difficult for them to observe the requirements of law in giving a hearing and receiving evidence. But to say that their findings of fact may be made conclusive where constitutional rights of liberty and property are involved, although the evidence clearly establishes that the findings are wrong and constitutional rights have been invaded, is to place those rights at the mercy of administrative officials and seriously to impair the security inherent in our judicial standards. That prospect, with our multiplication of administrative agencies, is not one to be lightly regarded. . . . Under our system there is no warrant for the view that the judicial power of a competent court can be circumscribed by any legislative arrangement designed to give effect to administrative action going beyond the limits of constitutional authority.[1]

In this same decision the Court held, however, that the judicial duty to exercise an independent judgment does not require or justify disregard of the weight that may properly be attached to findings made by a commission upon hearing and evidence, but on the contrary the judicial decision should be made in the light of such findings. Also, in an earlier case the Court said that "in a question of rate making there is a strong presumption in favor of the conclusions reached by an experienced body after

[1] St. Joseph Stockyards Co. v. United States, 298 U.S. 38, 50–52. Italics ours.

a full hearing."[1] While such statements by the Court imply that considerable weight may be given to commission findings, practically they amount to little but legal verbiage. To say that a presumptive conclusiveness is attached to findings of fact by a regulatory commission means little where such findings may be examined, weighed, and set aside by the courts. Some of the most important findings made by commissions, such as the valuation of public utility property, involve problems that cannot be solved by rule or formula but only through the exercise of judgment. For a court to substitute its judgment for that of the commission in such matters is to imply one of two things: either that the court is in possession of facts not known to the commission or that the former is more capable than the latter of doing justice to all parties. Neither of these assumptions need necessarily hold. As a general rule, commissions are much better equipped than courts to make findings of fact; and if a commission is not an impartial body, or a fair trial has not been granted, these facts may be readily disclosed.

Mr. Justice Brandeis, who concurred in the majority opinion in *St. Joseph Stockyards Co. v. United States*, but, for different reasons, found no good cause for making exceptions in rate cases to the conclusiveness usually attaching to commission findings in other matters of fact bearing upon constitutional rights, said:

Like the lower court, I think no good reason exists for making special issues of fact bearing upon a constitutional right. The inexorable safeguard which the due process clause assures is not that a court may examine whether the findings as to value or income are correct, but that the trier of the facts shall be an impartial tribunal; that no finding shall be made except upon due notice and opportunity to be heard; that the procedure at the hearing shall be consistent with the essentials of a fair trial; and that it shall be conducted in such a way that there will be opportunity to determine whether the applicable rules of law and procedure were observed.[2]

From the preceding discussion it is clear that there is much opportunity for clashes between courts and commissions over findings of fact. In cases involving errors of law or irregularities of procedure, the Supreme Court has set aside an order of a

---

[1] Darnell v. Edwards, 244 U.S. 564, 569.
[2] 298 U.S. 38, 73.

commission for lack of findings necessary to support it; because findings were made without evidence to support them; because evidence was such that it would be impossible for a fair-minded board to come to the result that was reached; because the order was based on evidence not legally cognizable; because facts and circumstances that ought to have been considered were excluded; because facts and circumstances were considered that could not legally influence the conclusion; or because the commission applied a rule thought wrong for determining the value of property.[1]

Weaknesses and Deficiencies of Public Service Commissions. Aside from the lack of essential powers, to which reference already has been made, the chief weaknesses of public service commissions result from certain defects in their constitution and from insufficient appropriations. Most state commissions consist of three members, although in eight states (California, Georgia, Illinois, Massachusetts, Michigan, Missouri, New York, and Pennsylvania) the commissions have five members; and in one state (South Carolina), seven members. Oregon has a single commissioner; North Carolina and Utah, each one commissioner and two part-time commissioners. The statute of each state lays down specific qualifications which must be satisfied before a person may become a member of the public service commission. These include requirements and restrictions concerning age, political status and residence, political affiliation, previous experience, oath of office, bond, and investments in public utility enterprises. However, the requirements vary so much in the different states that we shall not attempt a comprehensive enumeration.[2]

One of the chief criticisms of public service commissions is that their make-up is likely to be influenced unduly by political considerations. In a majority of the states, commissioners are appointed by the governor, usually by and with the consent of the state senate, although in a number of states, especially the southern states, commissioners are elected by popular vote. Appointment by a governor results in most cases in the choice of commissioners from a political viewpoint, whatever the qualifica-

[1] *Op. cit.*, pp. 74–75.
[2] For a fuller treatment of these matters see Mosher and Crawford, *op. cit.*, Chaps. V and VI.

tions for office of individual appointees. This fact is generally recognized, the laws of many states requiring that the commissions be bipartisan bodies so that minority political parties be represented. However, popular election of commissioners does not insure their complete divorcement from untoward political influence. Election to public office in the United States is dependent in no small degree upon the candidate's abilities as a campaigner, and the practice of straight party voting often sweeps into office a complete ticket with slight attention being paid to individuals other than candidates for the leading offices. The unfortunate aspects of this relationship of public service commissions to the political machinery are that political preferment does not insure the selection from available men of those best qualified to perform the duties of the office, and that commissioners so selected are likely to feel obligated to those responsible for their appointment or election.

A few states have attempted to restrict appointment by laying down special requirements for commissioners in the statutes, such as that one be a lawyer or an engineer. However, to make such requirements too restrictive tends to disqualify able men who otherwise would be available for public service, and to make them too broad places few restraints upon the discretion of the appointing authority. Long terms of office for commissioners, and staggered as in the laws of most states so that the terms of not more than one or two commissioners expire in any one year, place helpful restraints upon political domination of public service commissions, in addition to insuring continuity of policy. However, in most states six years is the term of office, and in a number of states the term is four years. These terms are far too short to remove commissions from political control over the membership. New York and Pennsylvania have a 10-year term, but even this is no guarantee against political manipulation, as is shown by the fact that Pennsylvania recently abolished its Public Service Commission, substituting therefor a Public Utility Commission largely for political reasons. In a majority of the states commissioners may be removed by the governors for incompetency, neglect of duty, or malfeasance in office, although in a few states approval of the legislature is required. That the choice of commissioners, and their acts, should be free of political domination is not debatable. How it may be wholly avoided in a democracy in which political power is based upon the control of patronage it is difficult to see. A few states forbid commissioners to participate in political campaigns or party organizations, and such a provision might be adopted more widely. Nevertheless, so long as the present system endures, the appointment and reappointment, or election or reelection, of commissioners will probably be controlled by dominant political interests.

State legislatures generally have attempted, so far as that is possible by statutory provision, to prevent the control of commission policies by the utility companies. All but a few laws provide that commissioners shall have no pecuniary or other interest in any utility subject to their jurisdiction, while other provisions forbid commissioners to hold any other office or engage in any business or occupation inconsistent with their duties or to accept gifts or solicit favors of any kind from utilities. Such attempts to prohibit official or unofficial relations between commissioners and utilities subversive of the public interest are obviously commendatory, but it is impossible to prevent by law a certain amount of fraternizing between commissioners and utility representatives. The success of regulation from this viewpoint is dependent upon the integrity of the individual commissioner and his ability and willingness, whatever his background and interests, to render impartial judgments.

A second defect of public service commissions generally is the rapid turnover of commissioners. In spite of the fact that satisfactory performance of the duties of a commissioner calls for technical and administrative knowledge which must be attained for the most part in actual service, the number of years served by the average commissioner is surprisingly small. A study of the number of years actually served by commissioners retired during the years 1915 to 1929 showed that 199 of 275 appointed commissioners served 4 years or less; and 66 of 115 elected commissioners served 4 years or less. Only 9 of the appointed and 10 of the elected commissioners served 10 years or more. Of 359 appointed commissioners having served or still serving in 1929, only 68 were reappointed for a second term; and only 66 of 177 elective commissioners were reelected for one term or more.[1]

[1] MOSHER and CRAWFORD, *op. cit.*, pp. 61–62.

While this rapid turnover is due in part to the fact that most salaries paid commissioners are low and capable men are apt to find better remuneration for their services in other occupations, it is in large measure due to the vicissitudes of political fortune. The result is a lack of continuity in policy, undue political interference with commission policy, and a regrettable unfamiliarity on the part of commissioners with the tasks they must perform. However, the situation is not so bad as it otherwise might be, owing to the fact that a commission usually has a staff of highly trained personnel who usually are not affected by the changes in the membership of the commission itself and has before it precedents established by it or other commissions on every phase of public utility regulation.

A third weakness is a general lack of adequate appropriations. This results in inability to pay salaries for a technical staff large enough to attract capable men and to employ a sufficiently large staff to carry on effectively the vast detail of work. So great has been the deficiency in some cases that of necessity even statutory duties, such as the valuation of public utility property, have been neglected. Generally, appropriations have been inadequate for the more aggressive work which commissions should undertake. As was intimated previously, there has been far too great a tendency for state commissions to assume a judicial attitude toward their duties, a tendency in no small degree due to inadequate staffs. It must be recognized that if commissions are to be more than judicial bodies hearing complaints inadequately prepared and ineffectively prosecuted by consumers, they must be able to employ enough capable personnel to investigate matters for themselves and to keep pace with technical improvements. In no other way can consumers be assured of good service, improved as progress in the arts makes possible, at reasonable rates.

Attention was called previously to the fact that in recent years a number of states have enacted laws that assess against utilities the cost of regulation. Such laws should enable commissions better to equip themselves, but their constitutionality is questionable. In two states, Louisiana and Washington, special assessment laws were held invalid by the courts, the Louisiana law being declared unconstitutional by a federal district court, and the Washington law by the Supreme Court of that State.[1]   On the other hand, assessment laws have been sustained by the courts in New York and Wisconsin.[2]   A number of state commissions are now operating under such laws.

Organization of a Public Service Commission.—The volume of work handled by an active modern public service commission is enormous.   To carry it on efficiently requires not only a large technical staff but an appropriate division of labor.   The administrative setups in the different states vary too greatly for purposes of generalization, but the student will be able to visualize more clearly the work of a commission by a brief consideration of the organization of a few typical ones.   For purposes of illustration we have chosen the Public Service Commission of Wisconsin and the Public Utility Commission of Pennsylvania.   While these two commissions do not represent decided contrasts with respect to organization, both being organized largely along functional lines, they differ enough to demonstrate the fact that ideas vary as to the most effective ways in which the work of a commission may be divided among the members of the staff.

. To carry on its work the Wisconsin Commission is organized as follows: At the head are the commissioners and the secretary, to whom are directly responsible an assistant secretary in charge of the general office and the general counsel.   The work of regulation is divided among utility, transportation, and securities regulation.   Utility regulation is subdivided into utility rates, concerned with rate analysis and adjustment, informal rate complaints, case investigation, cost analysis, economic investigation, utility statistics, and annual report analysis; accounts and finance, concerned with audits and investigations, utility security issues, and holding-company relations; and engineering, concerned with utility service, utility valuations, continuous inventory, valuations for the securities division, special engineering service, water power, water-pollution investigations, marl, sand and gravel permits, and work for other departments. Transportation regulation is subdivided between motor and

[1] National Association of Railroad and Utilities Commissioners, 1936, *Proceedings*, p. 275.

[2] Wisconsin Telephone Co. v. Pub. Service Comm., P.U.R. 1932B, 195; Kings County Lighting Co. v. Maltbie, 8 P.U.R. (N.S.) 474; and Bronx Gas and Electric Co. v. Maltbie, 10 P.U.R. (N.S.) 1.

railroad transportation, the work being further subdivided among four bureaus concerned with certificates, licenses and permits, case investigations, fees and taxes, tax assessments and collection, field inspection and enforcement; rates and tariffs; statistics and accounts; and case investigations, informal complaints, and Interstate Commerce Commission practice. In addition there is a bureau of railroad engineering concerned with railroad highway crossings; safety measures and devices; track, depot, and miscellaneous inspections. Attached to the engineering bureau of utility regulation are a standards laboratory at the University of Wisconsin, and a division for stream gauging connected with the United States Geological Survey. A total of 285 employees comprised the staff at the end of the fiscal year 1936.

The Pennsylvania Commission represents a simpler type of functional organization. At the head are five commissioners who hold hearings regularly in Harrisburg, Philadelphia, and Pittsburgh. Full sessions are held in Harrisburg. The staff, which normally numbers about 200 persons, is divided among five bureaus: Secretarial Office; Bureau of Engineering; Bureau of Accounts, Rates and Statistics; Bureau of Public Convenience; and Bureau of Law. The Secretarial Office keeps record of all meetings, proceedings, determinations, rulings, and orders of the Commission; acts as executive in charge of the general office, conducting its correspondence and supervising its clerical business; files and preserves all official documents, records, etc.; and acts as disbursing officer. The Bureau of Engineering has a staff of professional engineers in different branches engaged in giving advice; making investigations and reports; and dealing with problems of service facilities, the construction and operation of improvements and extensions thereto, and valuation and rates. It receives accident reports and compiles statistics therefrom for the use of the Commission; makes investigations of accidents and suggests remedial measures; and conducts investigations relative to grade crossing protection. The Bureau of Accounts, Rates, and Statistics prepares, installs, and interprets uniform accounting classifications and reports on field examination of utility accounts; devises, examines, and files annual reports of utilities and compiles statistics; examines into accounting and financial aspects of applications for approval of securities, mergers, sales, leases, etc.; prepares railroad rate data; determines adequacy of compliance with the Commission's rate orders; investigates and approves claims for rate reparation; and receives, analyzes, and files utility tariffs for public inspection. The Bureau of Public Convenience handles correspondence, records, orders, and certificates relating to incorporation, sale, assignment, lease, merger, organization, and renewal of charter of public service companies; applications, etc., to construct, etc., crossings of electric and steam railways over highways; and applications to operate motor vehicles as common carriers, and complaints relevant thereto. It regularly acts as examiner. The Bureau of Law advises the Commission and bureau directors on legal questions; reviews proposed reports; prepares orders, cases, and conducts proceedings instituted by the Commission and to enforce its orders; participates in the conduct of other cases; conducts hearings and holds conferences at the Commission's direction; prepares briefs and argues before courts; and syllabizes and indexes Commission orders.

Summary.—While inadequate in certain states, the legal basis for state commission regulation of public utilities is broader today than ever before. Particularly significant are the many new laws enacted since 1930 by the leading states. Such laws will not only make for more effective regulation in those states but will serve as models for additional legislation in backward states, since it is logical to assume that in the future, as they have in the past, the statutes of leading states will be copied by others. Much of the criticism of state commission regulation is not well founded where statutes are defective and resources inadequate. For effective regulation, commissions must be given the necessary powers; consequently, the first step in the direction of improvement must be the provision of a sufficiently broad and comprehensive legal basis. As to defects in administration, the principal reason for them is the incapacity and inexperience of commissioners, and they are hard to eliminate in a system in which the choice of commissioners depends upon political preferment. Those which are due to insufficient personnel and resources may be corrected, if the states really desire to correct them, by making better provision for regulation or by assessing the costs of regulation directly upon the utilities.

References

CLARK, H. G.: "Service at Cost Plans," American Electric Railway Association, New York, 1920.
DICKINSON, J.: "Administrative Justice and the Supremacy of the Law in the United States," Harvard University Press, Cambridge, 1927.
JONES, ELIOT, and T. C. BIGHAM: "Principles of Public Utilities," The Macmillan Company, New York, 1931.
MORGAN, C. S.: "Regulation and the Management of Public Utilities," Houghton Mifflin Company, Boston, 1923.
MOSHER, W. E., and F. G. CRAWFORD: "Public Utility Regulation," Harper & Brothers, New York, 1933.
National Association of Railroad and Utilities Commissioners: *Proceedings*, 1936.
National Civic Federation: "Commission Regulation of Public Utilities," New York, 1913.
SPURR, H. C.: "Guiding Principles of Public Utility Regulation," Public Utilities Reports, Inc., Washington, 1924, vol. I.
WILCOX, D. F.: "Municipal Franchises," Gervaise Press, New York, 1910, vols. I and II.

CHAPTER IV

REGULATION OF ACCOUNTING AND REPORTING

Commission Control over Accounting.—It was early recognized that the users of a public utility service and the public in general are entitled to a knowledge of the financial status and records of public utility companies. Accordingly, some of the early railroad company charters required that reports be filed with designated state officials. Later, some states required the publication of reports and specified the items to be included. A New York law, passed in 1850, listed over a hundred items. These reports, however, were of little value because they were inaccurate, incomplete, or misleading and not uniform.[1] Experience demonstrated a need for going behind the reports and controlling the accounting system from which data for the reports are obtained. It also became evident that full and accurate information was absolutely essential if the commissions were to carry out the statutory mandates of "reasonable and non-discriminatory" rates. Recognition of this fact lent support to the agitation for commission control over accounting; it has also been one of the main reasons for the development of uniform systems of accounting.

The first exercise of commission control over accounting was made by the Massachusetts Railroad Commission in 1876. The Interstate Commerce Commission, created in 1887, was given limited control over the annual reports of steam railroads; but it was not until later, 1906, that it was given authority over the accounts of railroad companies. About the same time, some state commissions were given control over public utility accounting. New York, in 1905, and Wisconsin, in 1905 and 1907, gave such control to their regulatory commissions; and in the case of the Wisconsin Commission there also was given the right to inspect the accounting records. Other states, subsequently establishing commissions, followed these leads and included con-

[1] GLAESER, M. G., "Outlines of Public Utility Economics," The Macmillan Company, New York, 1931, p. 127.

trol over accounting in their commission powers.[1] All of the 47 state commissions have jurisdiction over railroad accounting; 46 over telephone accounting; 41 over the accounts of gas, electric light, and power companies; and many have control over accounts of other utilities.[2] The Interstate Commerce Commission exercises control over the accounting of railroads and the water, express, and other carriers under its jurisdiction. The Federal Communications Commission has similar authority for the communication utilities. The Federal Power Commission, having jurisdiction over water and electric power companies in interstate commerce and its own licensees, has authority to prescribe regulations for the establishment of a system of accounts, to examine accounts, and to require statements and reports. In practice, the Federal Power Commission has given special attention to capital accounts and the recording of the financial facts of the cost of plant and equipment, though recently it has prescribed a uniform system of accounts for electric utilities engaged in interstate commerce and licensees subject to the provisions of the Federal Power Act.[3] The United States Securities and Exchange Commission has formulated, for use by holding companies registered with it under the Public Utility Act of 1935, uniform classifications of accounts for public utility holding companies and for mutual service and subsidiary service companies.[4] Though the Federal Trade Commission has no jurisdiction over utility accounting, it has collected extensive accounting data in its exhaustive investigation of electrical and gas utilities.[5]

[1] *Op. cit.*, pp. 127–128; American Bar Association, Section of Public Utility Law, "Report on the Standards of Accounting Prescribed for Public Utilities by Federal and State Authorities," Sept. 15–16, 1931, pp. 1–2.

[2] American Bar Association, Section of Public Utility Law, "Report on the Legal Aspects of the Scope and Standards of Accounting Regulations Prescribed for Public Utilities by Public Authority," Oct. 10–11, 1932, pp. 2–3.

[3] *Ibid.* and Federal Power Commission, "Uniform System of Accounts Prescribed for Public Utilities and Licensees Subject to Provisions of the Federal Power Act," Washington, D.C.

[4] U.S. Securities and Exchange Commission, "Uniform System of Accounts for Public Utility Holding Companies" and "Uniform System of Accounts for Mutual Service and Subsidiary Service Companies under the Public Utility Holding Company Act of 1935," Washington, 1936.

[5] Federal Trade Commission, "Utility Corporations," Sen. Doc. 92, 70th Cong., 1st Sess.

Development of Uniform Classifications of Accounts.—The control over accounting exercised by the state commissions and federal regulatory agencies has been directed toward the handling of the accounting records and practices in such a way that the accounts will show (1) the sources of funds flowing into the business, (2) the cost of the property acquired by the business, and (3) the costs of operating the business.   To this end, classifications of accounts have been prescribed and made mandatory for the utilities subject to commission jurisdiction.   The Interstate Commerce Commission has prescribed classifications of accounts for steam and electric railways under its jurisdiction, and the state commissions generally have adopted these classifications of accounts for the intrastate railways.   Accounting systems prescribed for intrastate telephone companies follow generally the classification of accounts for interstate telephone companies originally prescribed by the Interstate Commerce Commission.

The state commissions have tended to use a uniform classification for each type of utility.   The National Electric Light Association, in 1900, appointed a Classification of Accounts Committee which published, in 1914, a standard classification of accounts for electric light and power utilities, which was adopted by a few state commissions.   The National Association of Railroad and Utilities Commissioners, in 1919, instructed its Committee on Statistics and Accounts to formulate uniform systems of accounts for all utilities except railroads and, in 1922, recommended a uniform classification of accounts for gas and electrical utilities as proposed by this committee.   This classification of accounts has been prescribed by the commissions of 28 states.   A uniform classification of accounts for manufactured gas companies, also formulated by the National Association of Railroad and Utilities Commissioners, has been made effective in 22 states.   Standard classifications of accounts for bus companies and natural gas companies have been formulated by this Association, but the extent of their use is not known.   Usually, representatives of utility associations and companies have participated actively in the formulation of these classifications. Utility companies, in states that do not exert control over accounting, often have used voluntarily the standard classification prescribed in another state.   Thus, there has been a tendency for all utilities within a state to use standard classifications of accounts and for standard classifications to become uniformly applicable throughout the United States.   Uniformity will be furthered if the classifications of the Federal Communications Commission and the Federal Power Commission are adopted by the state commissions.

From the standpoint of the regulatory commission and the public, uniform systems of accounts are desirable.   They permit and facilitate comparisons between utilities in providing similar reports and records from each company.   They make possible a valid interpretation of the accounting records and facts, since the content of each account item is known, a circumstance of great value in regulatory practices concerning rates, valuations, and rates of return.   They provide data that may be used to evaluate policies and efficiency of operation and furnish comparable statistical data on investments, capital, and condition of different companies.[1]   The tendency for various states to prescribe the same classification, thereby promoting national uniformity, is likewise desirable.   In addition to enhancing the values of the already mentioned advantages, it would make possible the formation of intelligent opinion concerning combinations and mergers, since the combining units all would have similar records of accounts even though located in different states.

Uniform systems of accounting are of value also to the management and stockholders of utility companies in permitting comparisons of efficiency of operation and costs of service and in keeping the stockholders informed as to the true condition of their companies.   The accounting practices of many of the smaller companies have been placed on a better and sounder basis by the use of classifications of accounts prescribed by commissions.

Relationship of Accounting to Regulation.—Accounting is factual—accounting records the facts of the business unit.   The primary requisite of an accounting system is that there be furnished the necessary facts for a correct analysis of the business. Accordingly, a company's accounts should show the significant events in the life of the enterprise and should provide a complete history of its financial affairs.   This is important for any business, but it is essential for a public utility business.   Obviously it is not to the interest of the rate payers to have current operating

[1] BAILEY, W. G., and D. E. KNOWLES, "Accounting Procedures for Public Utilities," McGraw-Hill Book Company, Inc., New York, 1926, Chap. III.

revenues used to replace worn-out capital equipment or to acquire new capital equipment. The books of the company must show what the facts are, since the rate payers are entitled to know what is the actual amount of the company's investment, what its revenues and operating expenses amount to, and how much return is earned.

Unless these things are known, regulation will be based upon guesswork and, consequently, be ineffective and unsatisfactory. On the other hand, when accounts are scientifically and accurately kept the regulatory agency is furnished with facts upon which its decisions may be based and the knowledge as to exactly what is included in each account. Accounting control is thus an essential part of regulatory procedure not for the sake of regulating accounting practices but as a means of guaranteeing that there will be available the factual data necessary to regulate rates, service, and capitalization.

In this connection it should be emphasized that the accounting system, records, and practices cannot determine any legal and economic facts. Value, depreciation, fair return, working capital, going value, appreciation, etc., are legal and economic in character and are not fixed in the accounting records. However, the accounting records do provide facts upon which determination of these questions may be based. Because of this, it has been stated that

The success of a regulatory statute must depend upon the commission's having full and accurate information of the utility's operations. Thus courts, commissions, and companies alike have recognized that uniform systems of accounts and a broad control over accounting methods are essential to proper commission regulation.[1]

In reviewing the power of the Interstate Commerce Commission over accounting, the United States Supreme Court emphasized in the following words the necessity of accounting facts to regulation:

If the Commission is to successfully perform its duties in respect to reasonable rates, undue discriminations and favoritism, it must be informed as to the business of the carriers by a system of accounting which will not permit the possible concealment of forbidden practices in

[1] American Bar Association, Section of Public Utility Law, "Report by Committee on the Standards of Accounting Prescribed for Public Utilities by Federal and State Authorities," September, 1931, p. 7.

accounts which it is not permitted to see and concerning which it can require no information. It is a mistake to suppose that the requiring of information concerning the business methods of such corporations, as shown in their accounts, is a regulation of business not within the jurisdiction of the Commission, as seems to be argued for the complainants.

The object of requiring such accounts to be kept in a uniform way and to be open to the inspection of the Commission is not to enable it to regulate the affairs of the corporation not within its jurisdiction, but to be informed concerning the business methods of the corporations subject to the act that it may properly regulate such matters as are really within its jurisdiction. Further, the requiring of information concerning a business is not regulation of that business. The necessity of keeping such accounts has been the subject of great consideration. It caused the employment of those skilled in such matters, and has resulted in the adoption of a general form of accounting which will enable the Commission to examine into the affairs of the corporations, with a view to discharging its duties of regulation concerning them.

As we have said, if the Commission is to be informed of the business of the corporation, so far as its bookkeeping and reports are concerned, it must have full knowledge and full disclosures thereof, in order that it may ascertain whether forbidden practices and discriminations are concealed, even unintentionally, in certain amounts and whether charges of expense are made against one part of a business which ought to be made against another.[1]

Complete and accurate accounting records are essential under our system where the reasonableness of rates is determined by their ability to yield a fair return on the fair value of the property. Fair value, while not an accounting figure, is based in part upon the records of investment in plant and equipment; and fair return, which is a net return, means the amount remaining after the legitimate expenses of operation have been paid. That the accounting practices followed materially affect these items is obvious. The relation of depreciation to valuation and the controversies over depreciation versus retirement accounting are illustrations in point. A further illustration is the practice of setting up reserves by charges to operating expense. If the commissions have no control over such reserves, which increase the amount of operating charges and thus affect the rate payers, it is possible that they may be wilfully created as a means of showing

[1] Interstate Commerce Comm. v. Goodrich Transit Co., 224 U.S. 194, 211–212.

greater operating expense than was actually incurred. By later closing out the reserve accounts as credits to surplus, the amounts actually earned are increased without being shown in the profit and loss statement.

These are not the only relationships of accounting to regulation. Almost every utility provides for more than one class of service with a separate and distinct rate schedule for each. If these several classes of service are to be rendered on a nondiscriminatory basis, it is necessary to know what portion of revenue each should yield, and this can be determined only if the costs of rendering each class of service are known.[1] A careful analysis of the costs of each class of service is requisite to the establishment of nondiscriminatory rate schedules for the several classes of service. Regulation of accounting is thus essential not only to questions of reasonableness of rates as a whole but also to the question of fairness of the rates for different classes of service. The validity of the foregoing statements is not weakened by the fact that the principle of joint costs and the difficulties inherent in accounting practices make an absolute cost allocation impossible. Absolute cost analysis is an ideal which, at present, may be only approached in practice.

Regulation of accounting practices is necessary also to prevent the padding of investment accounts where property is bought by utilities from affiliated companies. This was the principal reason for the prescribing by the Federal Communications Commission of several new balance sheet accounts in the system of accounts recently promulgated for telephone companies. These new accounts require telephone companies with respect to telephone plant in service to enter in one account the original cost at the time when the property was first devoted to the public use, and in another account (Telephone Plant Acquisition Adjustment) the difference, if any, between such original cost and the cost to the accounting company, the Telephone Plant Acquisition Adjustment account to be written off or disposed of as the Commission shall direct. These requirements were attacked by the American Telephone and Telegraph Company as arbitrary and tending to destroy real asset values, but they

[1] For an analysis of the relationships of costs of service to the rate schedule, see G. L. Wilson, J. M. Herring, and R. B. Eutsler, "Public Utility Industries," McGraw-Hill Book Company, Inc., New York, 1936, Chap. II.

were upheld by the Supreme Court of the United States. The Court held that belief was widespread that transfers of property between affiliates "complicate the task of rate making for regulatory commissions and impede the search for truth." "Even if the property has been acquired by treaty with an independent utility or a member of a rival system," the Court said, "there is always a possibility that it is nuisance value only, and not market or intrinsic value for the uses of the business, that has dictated the price."[1]

Accounts as Evidence.—In rate cases, investigations, or litigations, accounting records are usually offered to substantiate the claims of the company. That such records may be acceptable evidence, it is necessary that the accounting officers establish the correctness of the accounting principles used and the accuracy of the results obtained. It is generally held that accounting records, kept in accordance with commission regulations and subject to commission supervision, are admissible as evidence. In this connection, it was stated in one decision that:

Books kept in accordance with orders lawfully promulgated by the commission under such powers are on a different footing, in a suit based upon the action of the state and against its officers, from even the same books, if attempted to be used elsewhere. They have a public character, derived from the supervision which can be and is exercised over them. The authorities are not, of course, bound by them in any event; but, prepared as they are, under their direct and constant supervision, they can scarcely be put in the category of the usual ex parte entries about whose admission the cases are concerned. The state, having had so much hand in their creation and such continuous power of examining them, should not be entitled to demand a verification first hand of every item by common-law proof, before they become prima facie competent. The guaranty of their truth is sufficiently established by the scrutiny to which they are always subject, and the penalties which follow upon a disregard of the commission's orders. . . . It would, indeed, be an incredible burden to require every item to be separately established, and even these defendants have not gone so far as that; but, if the books are not prima facie competent, they might call for such proof, nor can I reject them without putting the company upon their mercy.[2]

[1] American Telephone and Telegraph Co. v. United States, 299 U.S. 232.
[2] Cons. Gas Co., v. Newton, 267 Fed. 231, 242, affirmed 258 U.S. 165; see also Mobile Gas Co., v. Patterson, 293 Fed. 208 and cases there cited.

Objective of Accounting Control.—The objective of accounting control is, to restate, to provide factual information and data upon which regulatory decisions may be based. Accounting control is not an end; rather, it is a means for making available data without which regulation cannot be effective. As a means to an end, accounting control does not look toward interference with proper managerial functions. On this point, Judge Learned Hand, of the Southern District of New York, stated:

It is to make the method of accounting by regulated corporations uniform, "so that the accounts could be readily comprehended by those required to examine the same." The object is "not to regulate the management of their finances, but to show what the management was." While the Public Service Commissions in this state are not in any full sense rate-making bodies, they may be described as the eyes of the commonwealth, to keep watch on the public utilities of the state. It is for this purpose that they are authorized and indeed directed to regulate account keeping, to the end that the act of seeing what has been done may be easily performed.[1]

On this same point, the position of the Massachusetts Commission was stated to be:

The Commission realizes that no system of accounts will or should result in absolute uniformity in business practices or policies. The prudence, honesty, and skill with which the different properties are managed are not determined by accounting rules, but if proper accounting rules are faithfully applied, they should be disclosed in the accounts and the public returns. By prescribing this system of accounts, the Department does not undertake to indicate what expenditures it considers should or should not be capitalized. Indeed, in the performance of its duty it cannot do so. Questions of what amounts of new capital may properly be authorized must be determined as they arise, and in their determination many considerations other than those disclosed by the accounts are involved. Consequently, it is to be understood that the department does not commit itself to approve any item set out in any account, either as to the amount or character whether for rate-making purposes or for the approval of the issue of securities. From the facts disclosed by the accounts and the condition, character and financial history of the properties, the commission will, in such

[1] Kings County Lighting Co. v. Nixon, 268 Fed. 143, 146, affirmed 258 U.S. 180.

cases, determine what weight shall be given, if any, to the various items in the several accounts.[1]

Limits to Commission Control over Content of Accounts.— Although the power to prescribe standards of accounting has been fully upheld by the courts,[2] it has been contended by utility companies that this power merely gives the right to systematize the reported results of business and the method of making charges to accounts. The substance of the accounts, *i.e.*, the nature and extent of charges to such accounts, it is claimed, is primarily a managerial function, and, therefore, accounting requirements should not transcend the power to manage by substituting the judgment of a commission for that of the owners. This claim has been frequently upheld. For example, the New Jersey Board of Commissioners was denied the right to enforce an order requiring a utility to rewrite its books as to its capital accounts upon a basis prescribed by the Board in computing a rate of return in a rate case, the New Jersey Court of Errors and Appeals holding that

> The right to regulate a utility does not destroy the rights of private ownership. All the incidents of ownership, except in so far as it may be necessary to curtail them to properly exercise the power of regulation, remain with the corporation. If the order of the Board is arbitrary and unreasonable and beyond the powers given to it by the statute, it is void. It seems to us that one of the rights of private ownership is the keeping of accounts, not solely for the purpose of establishing a basis for fixing rates, but for such other matters as appertain to the ordinary business of a utility corporation. It owes to its stockholders certain rights that may require an entry upon its books of what it determines to be the fair value of its property.[3]

[1] P.U.R., 1921D, 385, 386; see also Southwestern Bell Telephone Co. v. Pub. Service Comm., 262 U.S. 276; Banton v. Belt Line Ry. Corp., 268 U.S. 421; People et cet. New York Rys. Co. v. Pub. Service Comm., 223 N.Y. 373; Havre de Grace and Perryville Bridge Co. v. Towers, P.U.R. 1918D, 490 (Md.).; and Passaic Cons. Water Co. v. Board of Pub. Util. Comm., P.U.R., 1928B, 245 (N.J.).

[2] See, for instance, Interstate Commerce Comm. v. Goodrich Transit Co., 224 U.S. 194, or Kansas City Southern Ry. v. United States 231 U.S. 423.

[3] Passaic Cons. Water Co. v. Pub. Util. Commissioners, P.U.R., 1928B, 242 (N.J.). Concerning limitations upon power of the Commissioners to manage, see also Missouri *ex rel.* Southwestern Bell Telephone Co. v. Pub.

However, absolute limitation of commission authority to the form of the accounts would nullify the efforts of commissions to determine fair value and the reasonableness of rates. This is particularly true with respect to the control of operating expenses. The New York Commission expressed itself on this point, in its report *Re New York Telephone Co.*, as follows:

The question of proper operating expenses is the most difficult one that comes before a regulatory body in a rate proceeding. And yet it is one that in general agitation as to rate matters receives the least prominence. Discussions as to valuation and the different theories sought to be applied in evaluating plant and property have loomed so large in the public mind as to almost preclude consideration of other questions. And the Commission's authority over operating expenses under the statute is narrowly limited. The failure of legislative authority to grasp the materiality of the question, and the failure of the public to appreciate its importance, is doubly unfortunate, since operating expenses have a much greater effect in rate determination than any valuation theory can possibly have.

Lest there be any misunderstanding, it must be emphasized that there is not the slightest doubt but that every cent shown on the books and records of this company as having been expended in the rendering of service, has actually been so expended. This, however, does not cover the question or go to the real difficulty involved. For the criticism is not that the moneys have not been spent, but, rather, if the Commission had authority to enforce some measure of economy in expenditure, the same results could have been secured for less money.

Every effort that this Commission has made in the past to check the steadily mounting expenditures and operating cost have been met by the argument which the courts sustain (citing cases) that the actual determination of what are proper expenses is a function of management, and so long as bad faith or fraud or actual recklessness cannot be shown, such expenditures by a company may not be questioned. The further claim is made that telephone users, especially business subscribers in the larger cities, are constantly demanding a higher quality of service, which costs more to furnish.

Both arguments may be authentic but the fact remains that there ought to be some limitation upon the operating expenses of a public utility.[1]

Service Comm., 262 U.S. 276 (1923;) United Fuel Gas Co. v. R.R. Comm. of Kentucky, 278 U.S. 300 (1928); and Northern Pacific R.R. Co. v. North Dakota, 236 U.S. 585 (1915).

[1] P.U.R., 1930C, 325 (363) (N.Y.).

It is now generally recognized that, in the conduct of rate cases, the reasonableness of charges to particular accounts or the propriety of such charges to particular accounts is a matter that may be reviewed by the regulatory agency and revised for cause.   This right arises not from the power to control accounting practices but from the authority to fix reasonable rates, elements of which are the cost of conducting business and the efficiency and economy with which the enterprise is managed.   Interesting in this connection are recent attempts on the part of certain commissions by regulations to prevent willful padding of charges to accounts.   For example, the Federal Communications Commission has issued instructions along with its system of accounts that all charges to accounts shall be just and reasonable and that payments in excess of such amounts shall be entered in a separate account called Miscellaneous Income Charges. These regulations were upheld by the Supreme Court on the grounds that the prescription of such a standard was not arbitrary but a necessary exercise of regulatory functions to avoid a possible concealment of forbidden practices.[1]   Effective control over accounting must go farther than the prescription of the form of accounts.   It must include direct commission control over the entries.

Needed Revisions in Uniform Classifications.—The testimony before the New York Commission on Revision of the Public Service Commissions Law showed almost unanimous agreement that the present uniform classification of accounts for electrical utilities is inadequate to meet the needs of effective regulation, and the same criticism may be made of the classifications of accounts for other utility services.   In these hearings it was pointed out that the plant account is not adapted to determining the cost of service to various classes of consumers, and it has contributed to maintaining an antiquated rate structure distinctly unfair to the small users of electricity.   In this same connection it was claimed that the present classification of expenses makes it impossible to distinguish between publicity expense aimed at increasing the demand for service and the expenses connected with utility propaganda which is often hostile to the public interest.[2]

[1] American Telephone and Telegraph Co. v. United States, 299 U. S. 232.
[2] New York Commission on Revision of the Public Service Commissions

One witness testified that an ideal system of accounting would (1) positively and accurately reveal the true financial status of the reporting organization; (2) so classify expenditures relating to fixed capital, operation, maintenance, financing, etc., that the costs of the respective functions and of the various classes of service could reasonably be deduced directly without further analysis of original vouchers; and (3) classify revenues as specifically received from the various priced services or other sources.[1]

Report of Counsel for the Commission, Mr. William J. Donovan, emphasized that it is essential:

First, that accounting records shall be prescribed which will record in suitable form all the facts required by the Commission for the exercise of its regulatory powers;

Second, that the Commission shall be fully advised by periodic reports and field audits, as to whether such records are actually being kept in accordance with the requirements; and

Third, that such records, when so kept, shall be utilized by the Commission to the fullest possible extent in the performance of its duties.[2]

The specific recommendations concerning accounting control made by the New York Commission on Revision of the Public Service Commissions Law were:

1. That the burden of proof be placed upon the utility company to justify every accounting entry that may be questioned by the Commission and that any such charge or credit might be suspended pending the submission of such proof.

2. That the annual reports be so revised as to disclose the actual owners of the voting stocks of every public utility company.

3. That there be more frequent field audits of fixed capital and operating expense accounts.

4. That the proposed Research Bureau be given, as one of its principal tasks, the conduct of intensive studies of cost of service, rate structures, and cost accounting.

5. That the Commission be given full authority over the methods of computation and amounts of all charges to operating

---

Law, Report of Commissioners Walsh, Bonbright, and Adie, Albany, 1930, pp. 316 *ff.*

[1] *Ibid.*, p. 318.

[2] "Report of the New York Commission on Revision of the Public Service Commissions Law," Albany, 1930, p. 123.

expense accounts and offsetting credits to reserves for any purpose whatever.

6. That the Commission modify the existing accounting procedure relative to appliance sales and jobbing work.

That putting these proposals into effect would materially enhance the powers of a commission with respect to rate control can be clearly seen. The recommendation giving to the commission the authority to suspend entries until their propriety was approved by the company would place a powerful and necessary weapon in the hands of the commission. That such power might intrude upon the sphere of management is unquestioned, but, in any event, the line of demarcation between regulation and management is difficult to draw and regulation always limits, in one way or another, the powers of management. Public interest in reasonable rates cannot be protected unless the substance and content of the account, as well as its forms, are controlled.

Audits of Utility Accounts.—In connection with the prescribing of uniform classifications of accounts, some of the state commissions have undertaken an audit of the reports submitted by the utilities. Some of the commissions have also set up field audit divisions to make periodic examinations of the records kept by companies under their jurisdiction. In most states, the purpose of these audits is to ascertain if accounts have been kept in accordance with the requirements specified in the uniform classification. Audits looking toward ascertainment of the actual content of the accounts have been limited to valuation cases in which capital accounts are examined and rate cases in which operating expense and revenue accounts are examined.

If the development of accounting control proceeds to the point where the content of accounts becomes subject to commission jurisdiction, frequent audits will become a necessary part of commission activities. Even under the present situation where examination of the propriety of account entries is limited to authority arising from the obligation to establish reasonable rates, field audits are a necessary adjunct to effective control by commissions. Periodic inspections of compliance with the uniform accounting classification regulations are also desirable. In most states, an increase in the size of the commission staffs would be necessary if such audits were to be undertaken.

Accounting for Appliance Sales.—In recent years some public utility companies, especially those in the electrical and gas fields, have undertaken the sale of appliances to customers, and accounting classifications and other regulatory rulings have sanctioned this practice. The utilities have been given the option of selling the appliances at or below cost for the purpose of stimulating the use of the service and charging the loss to operating expense as "New Business Expense" or of conducting jobbing and merchandising operations primarily for profit, with all records segregated and separated from those of the utility service. The independent appliance dealers criticize the former practice on grounds that the sale of appliances at a loss constitutes unfair competition, and the criticism has led to agitation for legislation to prevent the utility companies from engaging in merchandising activities or making it mandatory that their merchandising activities be accounted for separately from utility service activities. On the other hand, the utility companies defend the practice of merchandising appliances, even selling them below cost, on grounds that the customers of a utility company, as well as its investors, benefit from increased utilization of the service. Sales of appliances to promote greater consumption, it is claimed, have the effect of decreasing the unit costs of production and so will be reflected in rate reductions. Such promotional activities, it is further claimed, are legitimately a proper cost of doing business. It can thus be seen that these opposing viewpoints open up a question which is broader than accounting regulations.

There are four schools of thought on this subject.

In the first place, the independent appliance dealers and service agencies feel, not without reason, that they could sell and install more appliances if the public utility companies did not, and they resent the direct competition. The independent dealers believe that the utilities should (1) be deprived of the right to engage in merchandising or jobbing activities or (2) that their merchandising or accounting activities should be conducted under accounting regulations and other restrictions which would make it impracticable for public utilities to sell appliances to customers or make it impossible for the utilities to sell on terms as favorable as could be extended by local dealers. The most insistent demand for antimerchandising laws is to be found in those sections where the utilities have aggressively pushed the sale of appliances, and have not cooperated with local dealers and jobbers, as a means of attaining the objective of increased consumption of the service.

In the second place, persons interested in the lowest possible rates for the utility services have pointed out that a utility's sale of appliances is not conducted on an economic basis. The claim made by this group is that appliance sales are responsible for a volume of operating expenses of advertising, salesmen's salaries, salesrooms, warehouse space, etc., which are not fully covered in the prices charged for the appliances. The appliance sales thus place a burden on the operating expense of the rest of the utility business and so keep the rates for the utility service higher than they otherwise need be. This group advocates a complete segregation of accounts for the appliance business so that the profit or loss would be known. With a segregation of accounts, the regulatory authority would be in a position to determine if a deficit should be allowed as an operating expense or charged against surplus; or if a profit should be credited as a deduction from operating expenses, added to net earnings, or added to surplus. This viewpoint concedes the right of a utility company to sell appliances but denies that such sales are an integral part of the business and so demands a segregation of accounts. Opposed viewpoints claim that such segregation would require an arbitrary allocation of merchandising profits or losses and would be contrary to the economic reasons for the selling of appliances by a utility.

In the third place, there is a belief held by some that public utility companies have become too large, prosperous, and powerful and that any restrictive program, including the prevention of appliance selling, is desirable.

In the fourth place, the utilities have advanced, as the economic justification for appliance selling, the following propositions:

1. Direct or supervised sale is necessary to promote the use of safe appliances and to eliminate or prevent the use of appliances that would create dangerous hazards.

2. A proper and beneficial part of the utility service is to make available or sell to customers appliances that will be safe, efficient, and economical and that will be suited to the purpose for which the appliance is wanted.

3. Appliance sales promote an increase in the use of the service which, as a result of increased volume, greater diversity, and more favorable load factor, reduces the unit cost of production and permits lower rates.

4. The elements of cost and expense which are incurred in the development of increased volume and favorable load factors are properly chargeable as a part of the cost of producing these results.

5. The customer is not properly entitled to receive the benefits of lowered rates unless he defrays through the operating expenses the costs of promoting and securing the increased volume and favorable load factor.

6. The functions of supplying and distributing the utility service, of furnishing safe and adequate service, of promoting new business and increased consumption, and of promoting and preserving volume, diversity, and favorable load factor are integral parts of a going business.

7. No regulatory or accounting procedure is sound that does not consider, as an offset to any deficit arising from appliance sales, the improved service and the reduced unit costs resulting therefrom.

The viewpoint of the utilities emphasizes that appliance selling is an integral part of the utility business and is justified on economic grounds of increased volume of consumption, improved load factor, and greater diversity which, it is assumed, results in lower rates to the consumer. If appliance sales are conducted with this end in view and actually attain it they are as justifiable as any other sound promotional activities. However, opponents of this viewpoint claim that appliance sales are not always conducted on a promotional basis and that even when so conducted the assumed rate reduction may not become an actuality.

In so far as accounting regulations are concerned, the utilities contend that the consumer will be protected if the records are kept so that (1) segregation of accounts between merchandising and utility services are made; (2) the accounts show whether or not the activities as a whole are conducted with a profit or a loss; (3) appliance sales carry, as their share of general expenses, only that portion of general expenses which would not be incurred if the company did not engage in merchandising; and (4) new business expense is not excluded from the appropriate operating

expense accounts or saddled on appliance sales expense accounts
unless such expenses would not be incurred if the company did
not engage in merchandising.[1]

The regulatory trend seems to be toward treating appliance
sales by the utility as an independent and self-contained enterprise. This involves a complete segregation of accounts.[2]
There is, however, an increasing agitation for "antimerchandising" laws, and many bills to that end have been introduced in
state legislatures.[3]

Annual Reports.—Annual reports, standardized and uniform
as to content and form, are now generally required. The
financial records of operation are summarized from the accounts
in the prescribed uniform classifications and are submitted on a
profit and loss statement and a balance sheet. In addition,
other information, not entirely of a fiscal nature, is included in
the annual report. These data are statistical in nature and cover
the results of operation as related to (1) units of service, (2)
units of performance, and (3) units of capital investment. The
purpose of these data is to permit the measurement of efficiency
in construction, operation, and financing. It is from such
statistical data that the relationships between cost of service,
revenues from service, and service output may be determined.
The rates paid for service may also be related to statistical
units, and the whole body of such data may be used in testing
the reasonableness of rates.

Detailed and complete annual reports, therefore, are of great
value to a regulatory agency. All too frequently, however,
annual reports provide the commissions with disconnected,

[1] For an excellent summary of this problem see Section of Public Utility
Law, American Bar Association, "Report of the Committee on the Legal
Aspects of the Scope and Standards of Accounting Regulations Prescribed
for Public Utilities by Public Authority," Oct. 10–11, 1932. A list of cases
dealing with the subject of appliance sales is included in this report at pp.
35–37.

[2] See, for a specific recommendation to this effect, State of New York,
"Report of the Commission on Revision of the Public Service Commissions
Law," Albany, 1930, pp. 34 and 36.

[3] During January and February, 1937, there were introduced antimer-
chandising bills in the legislatures of Texas, New Hampshire, Pennsylvania,
New York, Michigan, Massachusetts, Connecticut, and Ohio. See State
Bills to End Sales of Appliances, *Electrical World* (news issue), vol. 107,
No. 10, Mar. 6, 1937, p. 811.

jumbled, or incomplete data.   In such a condition, the annual reports are misleading to the public who attempt to use them, and they conceal and distort the real picture of a utility's operations and financial status.   When complete, detailed, and comprehensive reports are submitted, they reveal essential facts upon which decisions concerning rates, service, and security issues may be based.   In many instances the data available could establish an informal prima facie case with reference to complaints and petitions made to the commission, and in every instance they should provide the basis for deciding whether or not a general rate case should be initiated.

In addition to the financial and statistical data of the annual reports, statements of the ownership of securities are frequently required.   These data are of little value in indicating the complex security-holding relationships that exist among the securities of many operating companies unless the schedule upon which it is presented is designed to show not only direct ownership interests but also beneficial interests arising from securities held by trustees and others.   In most cases, commission powers will have to be increased before such data can be required.   In so far as holding-company relationships are concerned, state commissions encounter many practical difficulties in collecting data.   This pertinent need may now be met by the federal legislation requiring registration of holding companies with the Securities and Exchange Commission.

Summary.—Without accounting control, effective regulation in the essentials of reasonable and nondiscriminating rates is an impossibility.   Accounting is itself a tool to the end of sound rate regulation.   Many advances have been made with respect to accounting control.   Notable among them are the development and use of uniform classifications within a state and the tendency for the same classifications to be used in many states. National uniformity in accounting practices and control is thus being attained.   To fulfill its function, however, accounting control must look toward the greater development of cost accounting and toward the control of the content of account items as well as control of forms and practices.   Annual reports of financial and operating data are a necessary adjunct to regulation and become the basis for decisions concerning rates, services, and security issues.

References

American Bar Association, Section of Public Utility Law: "Report on the Standards of Accounting Prescribed for Public Utilities by Federal and State Authorities," Sept. 15–16, 1931.
——: "Report on the Legal Aspects of the Scope and Standards of Accounting Regulations Prescribed for Public Utilities by Public Authority," Oct. 10–11, 1932.
American Gas Association: *Proceedings*, annual.
BAILEY, W. G., and D. E. KNOWLES: "Accounting Procedures for Public Utilities," McGraw-Hill Book Company, Inc., New York, 1926, Chap. III.
COOKE, M. L.: "Public Utility Regulation," Ronald Press Company, New York, 1924, Chap. IX.
Federal Power Commission: "Uniform System of Accounts Prescribed for Public Utilities and Licensees Subject Provisions of the Federal Power Act," Washington.
GLAESER, M. G.: "Outlines of Public Utility Economics," The Macmillan Company, New York, 1931, Chap. VI.
HAVERHILL, R. A.: Recent Trends in Utility Appliance Merchandising, *Journal of Land and Public Utility Economics*, vol. 12, pp. 149–160.
HERBERT, F. W.: Uniform System of Accounts for Electric Utilities, National Electric Light Association *Bulletin*, vol. 14.
HENRY, E. G.: Public Utility Operating Property Accounts, *Edison Electric Institute Bulletin*, vol. 4, pp. 335–336.
JONES, ELIOT, and T. C. BIGHAM: "Principles of Public Utilities," The Macmillan Company, New York, 1931, Chap. X.
NASH, L. R.: Fundamentals of Utility Accounting, *Edison Electric Institute Bulletin*, vol. 4, pp. 245–51.
National Association of Railroad and Utilities Commissioners: *Proceedings*, annual.
National Electric Light Association: *Proceedings*, annual (to 1932).
"Report of the New York Commission on Revision of the Public Service Commissions Law," Albany, 1930.
SPURR, H. C.: "Guiding Principles of Public Service Regulation," Public Utilities Reports, Inc., Washington, D. C., 1924, vol. I, Chap. V.
U.S. Securities and Exchange Commission: "Uniform System of Accounts for Public Utility Holding Companies," Washington, 1936.
——: "Uniform System of Accounts for Mutual Service and Subsidiary Service Companies under the Public Utility Holding Company Act of 1935," Washington, 1936.

CHAPTER V

RATE REGULATION

EXTENT AND SCOPE OF COMMISSION JURISDICTION OVER RATES

From the time when the interest of the public in public utility enterprises was first clearly recognized, the common law has embodied obligations of adequate and satisfactory service at reasonable rates. The public interest has continued to demand the enforcement of these obligations, and the establishment and the expansion of the powers of public utility commissions are due specifically to the desire of the public that these obligations be carried out. Legislative standards which reaffirm the common law obligations of adequate service and reasonable rates are stated, and the regulatory commissions are empowered and directed, as administrative agencies, to apply the legislative standards to the facts in each particular case.

Since the question of the reasonableness of rates has tended to be uppermost in the minds of the public, it has been the central problem around which legislative standards have been stated and with which administrative commissions have been concerned. All public utilities are ordered to conform to the legislative standard. At first, some of the state legislatures set up maximum rates as the standard to which the public utilities had to conform, though the general practice today is for the legislative standard to be merely a restatement of the common law obligation of reasonableness. The standard is stated in broad, general terms to the effect that rates and charges must be "just and reasonable" and this broad, general statement is fortified by the further generalization that "unjust and unreasonable" discriminations in rates or charges and "unduly preferential" rates and charges are unlawful and therefore prohibited. Such standards, it should be noted, are not intended to create any new or fundamental rights or to take away any preexisting rights from the public or the utility; for in the absence of legislative standards the public is entitled to just and reasonable rates, and the utility to just and reasonable charges for its service. From time immemorial a public utility has been obligated to make no more than a just and reasonable charge.

The essential feature, then, is that the enforcement of the obligation of reasonable rates is removed from the courts and placed in the hands of administrative commissions which are empowered and directed to see that rates *are* just, reasonable, and nondiscriminatory. This necessitates that constant and continuous control be exercised, and machinery is provided for the enforcement of this obligation, the usual nature of which is that the utilities are authorized to establish and change rates and the commissions are authorized to examine the proposed or existing rates on its own motion, upon the complaint of the consumers or upon the initiative of the utilities. In the event that a commission finds that the rate in question is unlawful for any reason, it is empowered to establish in its place a reasonable rate. The popular idea that the commission laws have taken away the power of the utilities to establish rates is a misconception. Generally, the power of the commissions to make rates arises only where it appears, after a hearing, that the rates made by the utility are for some reason unlawful.

For the protection of the public and in order to permit the commission to carry out its work, it is ordinarily provided that no change in rates or any new rate may be made effective without specified notice being filed. It is also provided that all rates, charges, rate schedules, and tariffs be filed with the commission, and any departure therefrom is prohibited. The commissions generally are given authority, also, to suspend proposed rate changes pending an examination thereof. The necessity for provisions of this sort is obvious. The users of any public utility service are entitled to reasonable notice of any changes to be made in order that business adjustments necessitated thereby may be effected or in order that complaints concerning their unreasonableness may be filed. Also, if the commission is to stand as a protector of the public interest, as it does in many states, it is entitled to a notice of changes in rates in order that it may decide whether an examination into their lawfulness should be made. The power to suspend proposed rates, for periods sufficiently long to permit examination of their reasonableness, is for the purpose of preventing what might be unlawful rates from going into effect.

As was pointed out in Chap. III, not all of the 47 state commissions have control over rates, and many of them have control over the rates of only a single or of a few types of public utilities. However, though no direct regulatory control over rates may be given, practically all state statutes provide that rates shall be just and reasonable and that rate schedules be filed with the commission and that such schedules be strictly adhered to. In the majority of cases the commissions have blanket authority to approve or disapprove rates to be charged and the authority to establish, in lieu of a rate disapproved as unlawful, the actual rate to be charged. In a number of the states, however, the authority of the commission is restricted to the specifying of maximum rates only, although the trend is toward empowering the commissions with authority to establish the absolute or actual rate to be charged; and for the commission, since it is in close touch with the situation, to protect the public interest by taking the initiative in examining proposed rates or rate changes. Effective, satisfactory regulation of rates demands aggressive action of this sort.

The laws require rates, whether made by a utility or prescribed by a commission, to be just, reasonable, and nondiscriminatory. Generally the jurisdiction of the commission in establishing either maximum or absolute rates arises where, after a hearing, the evidence justifies a finding that the rate in question is unjust, unreasonable, discriminatory, or unduly preferential. It is of paramount importance, therefore, to understand clearly what a "just and reasonable" rate is and what a "nondiscriminatory or nonprejudicial" rate is.

THEORY UNDERLYING THE DETERMINATION OF REASONABLE RATES

The theory of rate making provides the basis for arriving at a concept of just and reasonable rates and for understanding why there may be discriminations or preferences in public utility rates.[1] In its broadest aspects and in the absence of regulation,

---

[1] The reader is referred to G. L. Wilson, J. M. Herring, and R. B. Eutsler, "Public Utility Industries," McGraw-Hill Book Company, Inc., New York, 1936, Chap. II, for a more detailed discussion of the theory of rates.

a public utility rate is the equivalent of the economic concept of price. Under conditions of competition, price is the result of the interaction of the forces of supply and demand and, over a period of time, will tend to equal the costs of production. Under conditions of monopoly, where supply is controlled, price tends to be fixed at that point which will yield the maximum profit. The monopolist attempts to determine his costs of production for various quantities of output and to estimate the demand or the price that buyers will pay for these various quantities. Supply will then be controlled at that point which yields the greatest aggregate profit. Since public utilities generally operate under conditions of monopoly, any given public utility is free to fix the rates for its product or service at the point that will yield it the largest net profit. This point is generally referred to as "what-the-traffic-will-bear."

The term what-the-traffic-will-bear is much abused. The popular concept that it means exacting the highest possible charge is erroneous. Rather, it means exacting that charge which, in relationship to the volume of product or service that can be sold, will yield the largest profit. The practice of charging what-the-traffic-will-bear, however, may not result in the similar treatment of all customers. The users of certain services, because that type of service will not stand a high rate, may be asked to pay a comparatively lower rate than other users who, because of their ability to stand a high rate, have comparatively higher rates. Theoretically, therefore, in the absence of regulation, there is nothing that may be described as a just and reasonable rate. Rates are, in the self-interest of the monopolist, determined by the practice of charging what-the-traffic-will-bear, which looks toward providing the largest possible profit.

It is largely because of this situation that the common law obligations of just and reasonable rates were imposed upon those industries affected with a public interest. Without such obligations, of course, the consumer could not be forced to pay more than the value of the service to him, the upper limit beyond which rates cannot go lest customers dispense with the service, since an amount greater than its worth will not be paid. Why, then, it may be asked, are not rates determined on the basis of what-the-traffic-will-bear, since they are usually less than the value of the service, reasonable rates? The reasons for a negative answer to this question are twofold. In the first place, charging what-the-traffic-will-bear is the equivalent of monopoly price and may result in excessive profits. Consumers' surplus is appropriated by the monopolist, and rates that permit this cannot be characterized as reasonable. The rate level, in such a case, is too high to be reasonable. In the second place, the rates for different services may be inequitable. Some services may be charged more than a reasonable rate, and others less than a reasonable rate. Individual rates may be unreasonable or discriminatory.

From a consumer's standpoint, therefore, no rate is reasonable that yields to the utility more than a normal return and that does not assess the costs of producing the service equitably among the various services or classes of customers. On the other hand, the concept of just and reasonable rates embodies protection of the utility as well as the consumer. Costs of production offer the lower limit of rates, and it cannot be demanded that rates be pushed below this point.

Reasonable Rates Defined.—The obligation of charging just and reasonable rates is an obligation to charge rates not above a maximum point set by the value of the service to the user and not below a minimum point set by the cost of producing the service. Within the zone between these two lies the area of reasonableness. Practically, therefore, a just and reasonable rate is one that returns to the utility an amount equal to, and usually greater than, the cost of producing the service and that provides the users a service at an amount not more than, and usually less than, the value of the service.

This concept of just and reasonable rates has been described in a judicial opinion in the following words:

On the one hand a just and reasonable rate can never exceed, perhaps can rarely equal, the value of the service to the consumer. On the other hand, it can never be made by compulsion of public authority so low as to amount to confiscation. A just and reasonable rate must ordinarily fall somewhere between these two extremes so as to allow both sides to profit by the conduct of the business and the improvements of methods and increase of efficiency. Justice to the consumer, ordinarily, would require a rate somewhat less than the full value of the service to him; and justice to the company would, ordinarily, require a rate above the point at which it would become confiscatory. To induce the investment and continuance of capital there must be some hope of gain commensurate with that realizable in other business; the mere assurance that the investment will not be confiscated would not suffice.[1]

Nondiscriminatory Rates.—This concept of a reasonable rate implies that all customers are treated equitably and that no service or class of customers is required to contribute more than its share of the costs of the service. A nondiscriminatory rate is thus one that assesses the costs of production among the customers in proportion to their responsibility for them and that, therefore, places no greater burden on one customer than is placed upon another. Variations or differences in rates based upon differences in cost of service or conditions under which the service is supplied do not constitute unjust discriminations. The essential feature of unjust discrimination is that a burden is placed upon one customer or a class of customers, or a preference is given to one customer or class of customers either by failure to assess equitably and proportionately the costs incurred in producing the service or by arbitrary action.

THE PROBLEM OF RATE REGULATION

The legislative standards of just and reasonable rates and nondiscriminatory rates merely reaffirm the common law obligations of public utilities and therefore provide nothing more than a general rule to be applied to the facts in each particular case. The regulatory commissions are faced with the administrative task of determining the reasonableness of any given rate and, in the event of unreasonableness being found, prescribing the rate that will be reasonable. But in the face of the fact that there are no mathematical criteria or formulas that can be used, the determination of reasonableness and discrimination in rates is no easy task. There are, in every instance, factors influencing the making of rates which cause many complications. Likewise, there are elements of uncertainty in every case which make it impossible to do more than approach an approximation of reasonable and nondiscriminatory rates. These complicating factors and uncertain elements will be discussed in the following portion of this chapter. Attention will first be given, however, to a description of discriminations occurring in public utility rates. The complicating factors of public utility rate making and the

---

[1] Pub. Service Gas Co. v. Board of Pub. Util. Comm., 87 Atl., 651, 95 Atl. 1079.

problems attending the determination of reasonable rates will then be reviewed. This will be followed by an analysis of the judicial rule of reasonableness and its implications in rate regulation.

Types of Discriminations.—The fundamental evil of discrimination is that some customers are treated relatively unfavorably while others are treated relatively favorably. If it so happens that the customers so treated are engaged in businesses which are competitive, one is given an advantage over another.[1] Rebates, departures from published tariffs, and other of the more obvious forms of discrimination are now generally prevented though there still remain many ways, some of which are sanctioned by commissions, in which discriminations in rates take place.

1. *Free services or rates to cities and quasi-public agencies.* Such practices are obviously discriminatory, though they are frequently sanctioned by the commissions and the courts. Their origin seems to be found in the fact that free services were required as compensation paid to a municipality for the right to do business and for the privilege of using the streets. Many franchises still specify that free or reduced-rate services be rendered the city. Free water, electricity (especially for street lighting), street railway service (especially for policemen in uniform), and telephone service have been provided. Recognition of the fact that preferences of this nature necessarily place a burden on other customers is tending to bring about a change in attitude resulting in the elimination of such practices.[2]

2. *Reduced rates or free services for public welfare, charitable, and social agencies.* Services without charge or at less than the full rates frequently have been granted to churches and charitable organizations, and sometimes their employees have been granted similar privileges, the operation of these agencies for the public

[1] This feature is frequently condemned in commission decisions. *E.g.*, see Farmer's Ass'n. v. Chesapeake and Potomac Telephone Co., 5 Ann. Rep. Maryland P.S.C. 167; and Re Pacific Gas and Electric Co., P.U.R. 1920E, 597 (Calif.).

[2] RUGGLES, C. O., Discrimination in Public Utility Rates, *Journal of Political Economy*, vol. 32, No. 2, pp. 191 *ff.* See also: Ellsworth Nichols, "Public Utility Service and Discrimination," Public Utilities Reports, Inc., Washington, D. C., 1928, pp. 856 *ff.* The present authors have drawn extensively upon both these sources in preparing this subsection dealing with discriminations.

good being cited as justification for the practice.[1] It is clear, however, that it results in enforced donations to the charitable agency by those who pay the full rates. It thus becomes a question of public policy, and its continuance can be justified only on grounds of social desirability. Reduced street railway rates for school children present a similar case.

3. *Contract rates.* The establishment of rates by contract with given customers was frequently practiced before the days of commission regulation, and contracts, with rates specified, are still made. The rates specified in the contracts need not be discriminatory or preferential but frequently are. When so found, the commissions ordinarily set them aside.[2] The objection is not to the practice of fixing rates by contract but to the specifying of rates therein that are discriminatory or preferential. In fact, the practice may be essential for the protection of a utility. In those cases where a utility makes a heavy investment to provide a service or to be ready to provide it, as in the case of emergency or breakdown contracts, it must protect itself against possible losses by contracts. Contract rates may, therefore, be desirable, but the commissions should see that the public is protected by having them carry their full share of demand and service charges, *i.e.,* see that they are both reasonable and nondiscriminatory.

4. *Flat rates.* The use of flat rates, regardless of the quantity of service used, makes no assessment of costs except on the per customer basis, none of the costs involved in producing the service being assessed on the basis of the responsibility for them. Discriminations are, therefore, the order of the day when services are rendered on a flat-rate basis. This type of charge is especially common in water services but is sometimes found in other utility services.

5. *Classification of customers.* The classification of service is necessary for administrative reasons and as a means of promoting simplicity in rate structures. If the classification is based upon logical and equitable grounds, no substantial injustice will be done to any person using a given class of service, and the relationships between rates for the several classes of service will not

---

[1] Re Free or Reduced Rate Telephone Service, P.U.R., 1917F, 597, (Mass.); and Re Bangor Gaslight Co., P.U.R., 1915A, 134 (Me.).

[2] For numerous citations to this effect see Nichols, *op. cit.,* p. 950.

involve unjust discriminations. But each rate group must be clearly distinguishable on the basis of the costs of supplying the service and the conditions under which the service is supplied. Thus, factors of quantity of use, time of use, and length of use will serve to differentiate distinct classes of consumers. Frequently, however, the classification is based on arbitrary or unrelated factors and thus results in unjust discriminations and preferences. The use of the product is never a sound basis for classification and frequently has been condemned.[1] Nor can the occupation of the customer be used solely as a basis for classification.

Similarly, preferential rates to a new industry are unsound. Economically they cannot be justified but frequently, on the basis of the "infant industries" argument as used in advocating tariff protection, have been granted. It is true that the resultant increase in business and the resultant progress in the community may warrant an initial and temporary assistance in the form of lowered rates, but a reduction should not be made if there is not reasonable expectation that the new industry will soon carry its full share of costs and unless there are reasonable expectations of a general increase in business. In no case should the reduction permit rates below the amount of the variable or out-of-pocket costs.

6. *Discrimination in rate schedules.* The discriminatory nature of the system of flat rates has already been noted. Many of the other forms of rate schedules commonly in use likewise fail to assess the costs of the service in proportion to the responsibility for them. Rate schedules embodying demand, service, customer, and commodity charges are necessary to distribute costs in relationship to a given customer's responsibility for them. Because of the complicated and complex nature of rate schedules of this type, however, they are in but limited use. Of the simple types of rate schedules, the block rate form, especially if combined with a service charge, is the most likely to minimize unjust discriminations due to the unscientific nature of rate schedules. Flat meter rates assess only the variable costs and therefore, like flat rates, create many discriminations. Step rates may not only be discriminatory but actually promote waste and give lesser charges for greater energy consumption.[2]

[1] *Op. cit.*, pp. 884 *ff.*, for citations.

[2] See WILSON, HERRING, EUTSLER, *loc. cit.*, for a more detailed analysis of

In addition to discriminations inherent in the form of many of the rate schedules in use, there may be practices that create preferences and discriminations. Customers are sometimes allowed to combine the quantities of service consumed at different localities in order to be given the benefit of lower rates per unit accompanying large use. The charging of excessive rentals for certain types of equipment or allowing customers undue amounts for equipment supplied by them are other practices that involve discriminations or preferences and that have, therefore, been condemned.[1]

7. *Discrimination in interutility relationships.* Interutility relationships may give rise to rate discriminations. Instances of this have arisen where a utility operates several different utility services, such as electricity and street railways, and the users of one of the services are charged rates that cover the deficits incurred in furnishing the other service. The overcharge in the rates on the service that is profitable and that makes up the deficit in another service is obviously an unjust burden and therefore discriminatory.

8. *Discriminations resulting from differences in regulatory policies.* Regulatory policies and practices are not uniform between states, and there may be many differences within states arising especially in those cases where municipalities are given "home rule" in the matter of determining public utility rates or where rates are covered in franchises granted by municipalities. Differences in paving-cost provisions, differences in taxes, differences in the granting of free services, and the like may have a marked influence on costs of service. A utility operating in more than one community may find, therefore, that it has to make use of returns from services in a lenient community to meet the greater costs of doing business in a strict community. Rates, of course, should reflect the differences in costs, and any failure to do so constitutes a discrimination.

9. *Discriminations between localities.* An instance of discrimination between localities was cited immediately above where

---

rate schedules and the weaknesses and discriminatory nature of the various rate forms.

[1] See, *e.g.*: Hannibal Trust Co. v. Southwestern Telegraph and Telephone Co., P.U.R. 1916E, 525 (Mo.); Re Bruce Water and Light Comm., 9 Wis. R.C.R. 474; and Currant v. Homer Electric Light and Power Co., P.U.R. 1916A, 917 (Ill.).

it was pointed out that rates that do not take into account differences in the cost of service in several communities served by a single utility are discriminatory. Similarly, the granting of a lower rate in one community than is granted in another community when there are no differences in the cost of service is discriminatory. The general rule is that each community should be given its natural advantages, and the problem is to divide the territory served on the basis of actual differences in conditions rather than upon assumed or arbitrary differences. It is obvious, however, that minute differences in conditions, such as slight differences in distance from the source of supply of the service, cannot be taken into account.[1]

Elimination of Discrimination in Rates.—The complaint of discrimination frequently does not involve the question of reasonableness of rates. The rates at issue may be reasonable per se, but the fact that there are differences between them often creates unjust discriminations or preferences. When this is the case, it is clear that the discrimination can be removed by raising the lower rate, by lowering the higher rate, or by a combination of these two. As a rule, the utility should be allowed the choice of the method to be followed in eliminating the discrimination, a practice that is well established in the matter of place discriminations in railway rates.[2]

Many of the discriminations cited above, however, arise out of the fact that the lower rate does not carry its full share of the costs or the higher rate carries more than its share of the cost. Elimination of the discrimination in such cases involves the determination of the reasonableness of the rates and will therefore depend upon the facts and circumstances in the given case as to whether there should be a lowering or a raising of a rate to eliminate the discrimination. The view has been taken in some cases that the discrimination must be eliminated by lowering the higher rate unless the utility can demonstrate that its elimination by raising the lower rate is justified.[3] A justifiable case would arise,

---

[1] See, for instances of these problems: Re Central Ariz. Light and Power Co., P.U.R. 1922D, 175 (Ariz.); Dallas Power and Light Co. v. Carrington, P.U.R. 1923C, 137 (Tex.); and Ben Avon v. Ohio Valley Water Co., P.U.R., 1917C, 390 (Pa.).

[2] See D. P. Locklin, "Economics of Transportation," Business Publications, Inc., Chicago, 1935, Chap. XXIV, for an analysis to this effect.

[3] Fesler v. Pacific Telephone and Telegraph Co., 4 Cal. R.C.R., 711.

for instance, where the lower rate would result in rendering service at less than cost.[1]

The question of discrimination involves, thus, the determination of the fact as to whether differences in rates are justified by differences in the cost of service or conditions under which the service is supplied. But in determining whether there are differences in cost or conditions of service, the problem of the reasonableness of rates is raised. We now turn, therefore, to an analysis of the complicating factors affecting utility rate making and their effects upon the reasonableness of rates.

COMPLICATING FACTORS IN UTILITY RATE MAKING

It will be recalled that utility rates, in the absence of regulation, will be established on the principle of what-the-traffic-will-bear and that the objective of rate policy, based on this principle, is to provide the utility with the largest possible earnings. Since this may mean a return that is unduly large, we have seen that regulation is necessary to protect consumers against extortionate rates and against unjustifiable differences in rates. Because in the actual practice of establishing rates, the utilities make use of the principle of what-the-traffic-will-bear, the commissions are charged with the responsibility of seeing that, in applying the principle, the interests of the public are not adversely affected. There are, however, many complicating factors in public utility rate making which make the task of determining the reasonableness of rates a difficult one. These are (1) the nature and the amount of the capital investment in public utilities; (2) the tendency to decreasing costs; (3) differences in the conditions under which different customers are served; (4) differences in demand for the service; (5) the problem of joint costs; and (6) competition. These factors tend to commingle in their operation and to complicate further the determination of the reasonableness of rates.

The capital goods used in public utility industries are, to a large extent, specialized in type. This means that they can be used only for this purpose and ordinarily can be used only at the place where they are initially installed. Some of them, of course,

---

[1] *Re* Brookline Petition, 9th Annual Report Massachusetts Gas and Electric Comm., 26.

may be moved, but many are definitely localized at the point of installation, as in the case of hydroelectric dams, gas pipes, water pipes, street railway rails, and the like. In these cases either removal is impossible or the cost of removal would be greater than the value of the property after it was removed. Thus, once the investment is made, the only alternatives are to use it, abandon it immediately, or abandon it gradually as it wears out with use. If the given enterprise is uneconomic, *i.e.*, if it fails to earn a fair return but does earn something more than its out-of-pocket or variable costs, the last alternative is the one likely to be followed. Many of the recent abandonments of interurban electric railway properties are concrete illustrations of this. In so far as rate making is concerned, however, the situation is that the investment is made and therefore must be used. Accordingly, business must be attracted even at the expense of offering service at a rate less than the full costs of production. This accounts for the continued operation of many unprofitable utility enterprises, since it is better to operate and get a small return than it is to abandon the enterprise entirely and lose thereby all or most of the capital investment.

Of even greater significance to rate making is the fact that a large proportion of the capital invested in public utilities is fixed. The returns necessary to be paid for this capital—interest on bonds for borrowed capital; dividends on stock for ownership capital (necessary to be paid if the property is to be maintained in efficient condition); and maintenance costs, which include depreciation to keep the capital investment intact—are largely fixed costs. Thus, a substantial proportion, varying with utilities and with types of utilities, of a utility's total costs are fixed and must be met regardless of the quantity of its output. Almost every utility, therefore, is under pressure to increase its output to the full maximum of its plant, since, by so doing, the costs per unit of output are lowered. This latter statement is another way of saying that public utilities operate under conditions of decreasing costs.

This situation raises significant rate-making problems. Should a utility offer a low rate in order to attract additional business provided the rate yields something in addition to the variable or out-of-pocket costs of the service rendered and thus makes some contribution to the payment of the fixed or overhead costs?

Other businesses make use of this principle, probably the outstanding illustration being cases of "dumping." If it is done by a utility, however, does it result in a low rate which fails to carry its full share of total costs and consequently is an unreasonable rate? And, further, does this practice create unjust discriminations and preferences?

In answer to the last of these questions, it can be shown that the other customers are benefited by lower rates to attract additional business, provided that the total return earned by the utility is kept within reasonable bounds, and provided, further, that the additional business is made to bear all that it can of the total costs. This latter is a question of fact which is difficult to ascertain except in instances of competition where, if a higher rate were quoted, a competitive service would be used, and in instances where a higher charge would cause the service to be dispensed with. Instances of competition are numerous: gas versus electricity for cooking, gas and/or electricity versus coal for power, interurban railways versus motor buses for transportation and so on. Instances of the value of service are more difficult to cite, though railway transportation provides many cases in which, if rates are increased, certain commodities will cease to be shipped. Bulky, low-grade commodities like sand, clay, and brick frequently would be so affected.

On the assumption that the provisos stated above are met, the benefit accruing to existing customers can be shown by an over simplified illustration. Assume in the given case that $30,000 is necessary to cover the fixed costs which include a reasonable return on the capital invested. If it is assumed that 1,000,000 units are produced at a variable cost of 3 cents per unit, the following calculation shows the rate necessary to be paid by the consumers:

Fixed costs.................................	$30,000
Variable cost—1,000,000 units at 3 cents.....	$30,000
Total costs.............................	$60,000
Cost per unit, *i.e.*, rate per unit............	6 cents

Now, if it is further assumed that, without increasing the fixed costs, an additional 500,000 units are sold at 4 cents per unit, the situation and the rate necessary to be paid by the original customers would be:

500,000 units at 4 cents yield.............	$20,000
Variable costs of these units at 3 cents per unit................................	15,000
Balance available for payment of fixed costs.	5,000
Balance of fixed costs necessary to be raised..	25,000
Variable cost of 1,000,000 units at 3 cents....	30,000
Total necessary to be paid by original users of the 1,000,000 units...........	55,000
Cost per unit, *i.e.*, rate per unit............	5.5 cents

Thus, instead of being discriminated against, the original customers have actually been benefited by a lowering of the rate from 6 to 5.5 cents per unit. The caution should be repeated, however, that unjust discrimination would be involved unless the additional business attracted could not, because of competition or the value of the service, pay a rate that would cover its full share of the costs. The practice of making charges made on this basis is sanctioned, and there seems to be a tendency to apply the principle in attracting any new business, though this can not be justified unless the provisos mentioned above have been met. The principle is applied also in the form of promotional rates for the purpose of expanding a company's business. It is assumed here, however, that the expansion in business will ultimately reduce the cost per unit to a point where the promotional rate covers its full share of the costs of production and that any losses in the interim will be assumed by the company and not covered by higher rates to other customers.

However beneficial this practice may be to existing customers in making possible rate reductions to them, it violates our definition of a reasonable rate as one that covers the full share of the costs of producing the service sold at that rate. How, then, can such rates, per se unreasonable, be sanctioned or permitted? There is no theoretical answer to this question. The practical answer is that in considering the reasonableness of rates, as will be described more fully later, it is necessary to consider the rate level as a whole. Thus, where on the whole costs are covered and no unjust discriminations are present, the rates comprising the aggregate of all rates are considered to be reasonable.

The conditions under which a public utility renders its service to different customers also create a situation in which differences in rates may exist. Rates that on their face may appear unreas-

onable or discriminatory may, when these conditions are understood, be reasonable or nondiscriminatory.   In analyzing this
situation the cost conditions in public utilities and the assessment
of costs against the users responsible for them are the factors
to be considered.   It has already been pointed out that fixed or
constant costs comprise a large proportion of the total costs of
producing public utility services.   Operating costs—the costs of
producing and distributing the product or service and the costs
of incidental services to customers—vary with output.

    If the responsibility for the amounts invested in plant and
equipment and their depreciation were directly related to the
quantity of output, it would then be a simple matter to charge
each customer a given amount for each unit of the product or
service used and assess thereby against each customer his full
share of both fixed and variable costs.   But there is no such
direct relationship between the quantity of output taken by
each customer and his responsibility for investment in plant and
equipment and its depreciation.   This arises from the fact that
the public utility plant must be constructed so as to provide a
plant sufficient in size to meet the coincident maximum demands
of all customers.   It is characteristic that this maximum demand
occurs only for a short period each day, week, season, or year.
Most of the time, the capacity of the plant is utilized only to a
smaller extent.

    Thus, if a consumer makes use of the plant during the period
of the "peak of the load," he requires plant facilities proportion-
ate to the rate of the supply at the peak.   During the off-peak
period, this plant capacity might be idle.   On the other hand, a
consumer who makes use of service almost or entirely during
off-peak periods requires little or no additional plant capacity,
and therefore there are no fixed charges attributable directly to
him.   This is particularly important to those utilities such as
electric light and power and street railways which must produce
their services at the moment of consumption and where storage
is not possible.   It becomes evident from a cost standpoint
that differences in the conditions under which service is rendered
justify differences in rates.   Facts incident to this must be
weighed and considered in determining both the reasonableness
of rates and their discriminatory character.   Low rates for
"off-peak" users, entirely or almost free of any share of the

investment costs, are therefore reasonable and nondiscriminatory. The investment costs, in such cases, are properly assessable against those responsible for them—the "peak-load" users.

It is sometimes impossible and frequently difficult to distinguish between peak and off-peak users of service. Reasonable rates, therefore, do not always reflect the differences in conditions under which the service is supplied.[1] Nor is it possible to apply the differences in conditions and costs of service to each individual customer. The number of customers involved would create too great a volume of administrative detail, and the individual differences, in many cases, would be too small for measurement or for practical differentiation in rates. It has, therefore, become common practice to deal with customers in large groups, classified therein on the basis of similarities in conditions and costs of service. Where classification has been done satisfactorily, the ideal individual rate will not differ materially from the actual rate in effect for the customers of that class of service.

But the need for careful scrutiny in determining classes of service is obvious, and there are many factors to be considered. The time of use, because of its relationship to peak costs, is very important. Many utilities make definite off-peak classes, illustrations of which are the low rates offered on some street railways during the off-peak morning and afternoon hours. Quantity of use is also important because of the relationship between per unit cost and volume of output. Customers who make use of large quantities of service during off-peak hours are thus in a very favorable position for low rates, and lower rates for a large volume of use are common. Length or steadiness of use also has a bearing on costs, since steady use reduces costs by eliminating variations in the rate of output. Classification ordinarily reflects also differences in the intensity of the demand for the service and the existence of competition. One usually finds, therefore, that classes of service for which the demand is most intense, such as the domestic users of electricity, tend to have the rate for the class pushed toward the maximum limit of the value of the service. On the other hand, where

---

[1] The problem of peak and off-peak rates for particular utilities is discussed in Wilson, Herring, and Eutsler, *op. cit.*, in the chapters devoted to each type of utility.

there are competitive services available or where the customers can supply themselves, the tendency is for the rate to be pushed toward the minimum limit of the cost of the service.

The very fact that a utility renders several different classes of service adds another complication to rate making and the determination of the reasonableness of rates. Our definition of reasonableness has emphasized, among other things, the assessment of costs among the users in proportion to their responsibility for them. This assumes that costs can be specifically measured. Many of the costs, however, are joint; *i.e.*, the costs are incurred simultaneously or jointly for two, or more, different classes of service. How much, therefore, should be assessed against each service? What share of the salary of the president of the company, for instance, should be assigned on a cost basis to each of the several classes of service rendered by the utility? At best there can be nothing better than an arbitrary allocation of those costs which are not related directly to the volume of the service. Experience and sound judgement permit reasonable approximations of the actual share of costs of each of the services, but the reasonableness of a given rate can never be better than an approximation.

The influence of competition has already been noted in discussing the tendency to decreasing costs and the classification of services for rate-making purposes. Further discussion is not here necessary, though it may be reiterated that competition acts as an inducement for the utility to reduce rates toward the point of cost of service if such a move becomes necessary to get the business.

REASONABLENESS OF THE RATE LEVEL AS A WHOLE AND INDIVIDUAL RATES

Throughout the foregoing analysis of the complicating factors in public utility rate making and the determination of the reasonableness of rates, nothing more than incidental distinction between rates applicable for a particular service and the rates as a whole was made. A moment's reflection reveals, however, that while the complicating factors exert their influence in causing rates for different services to be on different levels, owing to the fact of joint costs, the cost concept cannot be used to measure the reasonableness, except as an approximation, of individual rates.

It was also pointed out in our analysis of differences in rates, due to the factor of decreasing costs, that rates for one class of service might be below the total costs of service but be beneficial to other rate payers in making a contribution to the payment of overhead costs. Justification for this situation was supported if the aggregate of all rates yielded no more than a normal or fair return to the utility. There are, then, standards of reasonableness applicable to rates as a whole—the rate level in general—and other standards applicable to the rates for a given class of service. Analysis of these standards and their application will now be made, and attention called to the uncertain elements or features in them.

THE STANDARD OF REASONABLENESS FOR RATES AS A WHOLE

The costs of producing public utility service have earlier been pointed out to include both fixed and variable costs, which may be classified into three broad groups as follows: (1) return on invested capital, (2) depreciation, and (3) operation. It was also pointed out that reasonable rates must yield the utility sufficient revenue to cover these costs of production. The rates, to be reasonable for the utility, must therefore permit earnings that will yield:

1. The amount of its actual out-of-pocket operating expenses for labor, materials, administration, repairs, taxes, current retirements, and the like.

2. An additional amount to permit it to create and maintain adequate reserve funds for the recurring retirement of large units of property not covered by ordinary maintenance, for contingencies, and for other unforeseeable events.

3. An additional amount to provide for payment on borrowed capital and to provide a return to the owners of the property as compensation for devoting it to public service.

Since on the basis of the what-the-traffic-will-bear principle of rate making, applied in the absence of public regulation, rates will be fixed at that point that yields the greatest return and are the equivalent of monopoly price in economic theory, it was concluded that regulation was necessary in order to keep rates at a level, below the value of service and above the cost of service, that will not yield the utility an excessive return. The return going to a utility thus becomes the standard for measuring the reasonableness of rates as a whole.   As a standard for the level of the rates, it implies the dual obligation of limiting the return to one that is reasonable and of seeing that the return so earned is adequate.

Judicial Statement of the Standard of Reasonableness.— The famous case of *Smyth v. Ames*, decided in 1898, carries the statement of a standard to be used in determining the reasonableness of rates.   The Court there stated:

> What the company is entitled to ask is a fair return upon the value of that which it employs in the public convenience.   On the other hand, what the public is entitled to demand is that no more be exacted from it for the use of a public highway [the case involved railroad rates] than the services rendered by it are reasonably worth.[1]

Actually two standards are here suggested: (1) a fair return on the fair value of the property used and useful in the public utility service and (2) the value of the service to the user.   The latter has received, however, but scant attention and is applied only to limit the maximum point of reasonableness.   The former has come to be the accepted standard for the determination of the reasonableness of the rate level, and it is known as the fair-return-on-a-fair-value rule, or sometimes just simply called the fair value rule.

The fair-return-on-a-fair-value rule stated in *Smyth v. Ames* has been controlling upon public utility commissions in their administrative determination of the reasonableness of rates.   It is, however, replete with uncertain elements and is difficult to apply.   Uncertainties are present in both elements of the rule. What is the fair return to be allowed?   How is it to be measured? Are the costs incurred in rendering the service actual and legitimate?   Is the management efficient and economical?   Can superior efficiency of management be induced and rewarded? Some aspects of the question of fair return will be analyzed in Chap. VII.   Attention has already been given, in Chap. IV, to the control of accounting as a means of insuring the legitimacy of operating and capital charges.

The "fair value" part of the rule is vague, and the whole subject of valuation is controversial.   The major problem centers around the basis to be used in arriving at fair value.

[1] Smyth v. Ames, 169 U.S. 466, 546.

This and other valuation problems will be discussed in Chap. VI. Some aspects of the valuation problems will be discussed below, however, in pointing out some of the problems and implications of the fair value rule, its relationship to confiscatory rates, and the need that has been created for the physical valuation of public utility properties.

Problems of the Fair Value Rule.—Probably the main problem that arises in connection with the fair value rule is concerned with the reasonableness of rates for a given class of service. Applied to the rate level as a whole, it involves the relationship between net income and value of the property. The rate level as a whole must be high enough to yield a fair return, and, if the uncertain elements involved in the rule can be solved, its application to the level of the rates as a whole is clear. However, it cannot be so clearly and definitely related to the rate for a given class of service. We have already seen that under some circumstances a rate that pays its out-of-pocket costs and makes some contribution toward constant costs may be beneficial to the users of the service at the higher rates. Furthermore, the existence of joint costs makes it impossible to determine with certainty the actual costs of rendering any given class of service.

Thus, the mere fact of adjusting rates so that a utility earns a fair return on its fair value does not solve the problem in so far as the rates for the separate classes of service are concerned. In fact, instances occur where the rates on a given class of service are unduly high and the utility is failing to earn a fair return, and, conversely, the rates on a given class of service may be unduly low while the utility is earning more than a fair return.

In spite of these problems, the rule holds that the measure of the reasonableness of the rates for a given class of service is that the full share of costs be covered. It was so stated in 1915 in the case of *Northern Pacific Ry. Co. v. North Dakota* wherein it was held: " . . . outlays that exclusively pertain to a given class of traffic [the case dealt with railroad rates] must be assigned to that class and the other expenses must be fairly apportioned."[1] The principle has subsequently been applied.[2] However, it does

[1] 236 U.S. 585.

[2] Vandalia R. Co. v. Schnell, 255 U.S. 113; and Northern Pacific Ry. Co. v. Dep't. of Pub. Works, 268 U.S. 39.

not mean, as may appear at first glance, that differentiation in rates that is not based on differences in cost is prevented.   The Court apparently was not referring to overhead expenses represented by interest on bonds and return on ownership capital. These two items involve, it will be recalled, a substantial proportion of total costs so that if they are not included in the costs that are required to be distributed substantial differentiation in rates between classes is permissible.[1]

The standard for rates on a given class of service as stated in the Northern Pacific case may be described as an absolute standard.   Actually, owing to the problem of apportioning joint costs, the reasonableness of individual rates in many instances is determined on a comparative basis, and in making comparisons all pertinent factors must be given consideration.   The rates in other communities, the demand characteristics for the service, operating conditions, relative costs of service, and the like are the elements to which consideration is given in measuring rates on a comparative basis.

Another problem arises in those situations in which there is competition between several utility companies, since the fair value rule cannot be applied separately to the companies involved. All competing enterprises must charge the same rate; for, otherwise, up to its capacity of rendering service, use would be made of the one with the lowest rates.   If rates are established so that the most efficient and economical concern makes a fair return, all others will incur deficits.   On the contrary, if rates are established to permit the least efficient and economical concern to make a fair return, all others will make more than a fair return.   This problem is especially acute in railways.   The only solution seems to be to consider the railways as a whole. Congressional sanction was given to this practice in Section 15a of the Transportation Act of 1920, which provided that rates should be prescribed that would give the carriers "as a whole, or as a whole in such rate groups as the Commission shall prescribe" a fair return upon the aggregate value of the properties.[2]   But even though this is the only practical policy to follow, it results in the so-called weaker roads being unable to earn an adequate

[1] For an analysis to this effect see D. P. Locklin, *op. cit.*, pp. 435 *ff.*

[2] For an analysis of this problem as applied to railroads, see *ibid.*, pp. 343 *ff.*

return. The problem of the weak road is serious.[1] In so far as other types of utilities are concerned, the problem of applying the rule to competing enterprises does not arise so often, and in cases where it does arise there are not so many companies involved. Competition is present in some cases in bus and truck line services, in telegraph services, and in infrequent instances in other utilities. Ordinarily, however, franchise grants and the use of certificates of convenience and necessity limit the territory to a given enterprise.

A third problem of the fair value rule arises out of the fact that utility earnings fluctuate. In establishing rates to yield a fair return on a fair value, estimates of future operating expenses, volume of business, and net earnings are necessary. Both operating expenses and volume of business fluctuate, though they do not fluctuate in direct relationship. It is therefore impossible to set rates that do not at times yield the utility more or less than a fair return. For this reason, it is necessary that the concept be considered from a long-run standpoint, and adjustments in rates be made only upon reasonable long-term demonstration that they are too high or too low.

Some Implications of the Fair Value Rule.—It is frequently alleged and sometimes contended in rate cases that the fair-return-upon-a-fair-value rule guarantees to the utilities a specified return. This is an erroneous implication. There are many utility companies which, because of insufficiency in the volume of sales, inefficiency in management, limitations on the maximum rate possible to be charged because of the value of the service, or the fact that a stronger, competing utility charges rates that are lower than are reasonable for the weaker utility, do not make a fair return. No rule of rate making can protect a utility against the operation of economic forces. The purpose and intent of the rule, and this is all that it can do, are to protect the utilities against the arbitrary action of regulatory authorities in setting rates at a level that is unreasonably low.

Conversely, it is sometimes contended that the fair-return-on-a-fair-value rule limits the utility to a specified return. This likewise is an erroneous implication. The right to earn is an

---

[1] For an analysis of this problem and attempts to solve it see *op. cit.*, Chap. XIX; and J. M. Herring, "The Problem of Weak Railroads," University of Pennsylvania Press, Philadelphia, 1929.

incident of ownership.   The fair value rule does not permit regulatory authorities to limit the amount or rate of earnings; rather,
it limits the power of the states to interfere with the right to earn
by prohibiting them from imposing confiscatory rates.   None
of the state laws attempts to limit the amount that a utility may
earn.   The laws regulate rates—they authorize and require just
and reasonable rates and by inference recognize the right of
utilities to earn whatever they can under such rates.   This distinction between the regulation of rates and the regulation of
earnings was pointed out in the opinion in *Cotting v. Kansas City
Stockyards Co.*[1]   To hold that the fair value rule provides for a
limitation on earnings would be tantamount to holding that regulatory authorities are granted the rights of management.   The
cases are legion that hold that the right of management inheres
in the ownership of the property and that there can be no deprivation of this right under the guise of regulation.[2]

Reasonable and Nonconfiscatory Rates.—In discussing
reasonable rates, reference has been made to confiscatory rates.
Confiscatory rates are those which, under the prohibitions of the
Fifth and Fourteenth amendments to the Federal Constitution,
deprive a utility of its property without due process of law.   It is
clear that a rate that deprives the utility of its property by keeping it from making a return is unreasonable as well as confiscatory.   It does not follow, however, that all nonconfiscatory rates
are reasonable.   A rate that returns more than enough to escape
the charge of confiscation does not thereby become extortionate
or unreasonable, since the courts may find that a rate is not so
low as to be confiscatory, but a commission may find it to be so
low as to be unreasonable.   The distinction between a reasonable
and a nonconfiscatory rate was stated, in *Banton v. Belt Line
Ry. Corp.*, to be:

A commission or other legislative body, in its discretion, may determine to be reasonable and just a rate that is substantially higher than
one merely sufficient to justify a judicial finding in a confiscation case
that it is high enough to yield a just and reasonable return on the
value of the property used to perform the service covered by the rate.

[1] 183 U.S. 79., 95.
[2] See, for instances: Banton v. Belt Line Ry. Corp., 268 U.S. 413; Missouri
ex rel v. Southwestern Bell Telephone Co., 262 U.S. 276; and Great Northern
Ry. Co. v. Minnesota, 238 U.S. 340.

The mere fact that a rate is nonconfiscatory does not indicate that it must be deemed to be just and reasonable.[1]

The Need for Valuations of Public Utility Properties.—Since the *Smyth v. Ames* rule of a fair-return-on-a-fair-value has come to be the controlling standard in the determination of the reasonableness of rates, it is apparent that valuations of utility properties are necessary if the rule is to be applied. In actual practice, however, valuations are made only upon the adjudication of rate complaints attacking the reasonableness of the level of the rates. In general, commissions have too small staffs and too little money with which to value the public utility properties under their jurisdiction. Accordingly, valuations are undertaken only when necessity dictates. Even then, because of the uncertainties concerning the basis of valuation, the results are likely to be unsatisfactory for effective rate regulation. The time necessary to make valuations, the costliness of the process, and the variations existing in the valuations made are also reasons why valuations are unsatisfactory. Furthermore, companies are in a better position to make valuations than are commissions or the complainant consumers, and, as a result, the valuations tend to favor the companies.[2] The situation has been aptly described in the following words:

A case is brought before the Commission by complainants who put in such evidence as they can gather. As the public generally has little money available for the hire of experts, the evidence is probably meager. The company replies that it must have time to make a valuation of its plant to determine what it is entitled to earn. They take from two to six months, perhaps more. They present it with experts getting perhaps $200 per day. The public has not the resources to meet such a case but does the best it can. More time elapses while the public representatives attempt to consider and answer the company's evidence. Then the Commission attempts to digest some thousands of pages of evidence and makes its order.

This does not end the case. If the Commission does not grant 8 per cent on what the company claims as its valuation, the company appeals to the Federal Court. Some courts will act like a nickel in a slot machine, the company drops in its nickel and gets its injunction. A

[1] 268 U.S. 413, 422–423 (1925).

[2] For an analysis to this effect see: New York Commission on Revision of the Public Service Commissions Law, Report of Commissioners Walsh, Bonbright, and Adie, pp. 262 *ff.*

Master is appointed to take evidence and it may require months to agree on a Master. Then the Master must try the case *de novo*. The complainants must spend more money to get experts and the company spends more money. The evidence goes to greater length than in the original case. Then the Master must decide the case himself, must review the great volume of evidence without a corps of assistants.

Masters are generally inclined to the belief that if evidence is not contradicted it must be believed. That favors the utilities because they can put on witnesses to testify on matters concerning which the public representatives may have neither the knowledge nor the facts to refute. Probably another year elapses in this process and the Master makes his report. Then the statutory Court passes on the Master's report and renders its decision. All this takes time. Then there is an appeal to the Supreme Court where you take your turn. The case is argued before the Supreme Court and decided. Perhaps five years have elapsed, conditions have changed, new values have been created to be adjudicated and besides, the Supreme Court cannot make rates. Only the Public Service Commission can make rates. So the whole process may start over again.[1]

If this is a true picture of the usual state of affairs concerning valuation as a step in rate regulation, the results necessarily must be unsatisfactory. Further, it is difficult to arrive at a valuation which is acceptable to the parties to a rate dispute. Variations in the valuations made by competent authority are frequent, as instances from New York and Ohio, given as illustrations of conditions existing in other states as well, will show. In the New York Telephone Company case, six estimates of the fair value of the property as of July 1, 1926, varied almost 100 per cent, as follows:

Majority of Commission	$366,915,493
Statutory Court	397,207,925
Minority of Commission	405,502,993
Master's report	518,109,584
Company claims based on:	
Whittemore appraisal	528,753,738
Stone & Webster appraisal	615,000,000

This case, it may be added, was initiated on Aug. 20, 1920, and the new rate schedule, on a temporary basis only, did not go into effect until Feb. 1, 1930.[2] In the Ohio Bell Telephone

---

[1] *Op. cit.*, p. 272.
[2] *Ibid.*, pp. 264–266.

Company case the same inventory was used in arriving at the following fair values:

Company engineers...................	(a)	$157,000,000
	(b)	156,000,000
Appraisers representing the state.......	(a)	127,000,000
	(b)	104,000,000
Commission's valuation...................		104,282,735[1]

There is only one conclusion possible, *viz.*, that present procedure in the making of valuations as a necessary step in applying the fair value rule of rate making has in effect nullified the rule. It is only in those fields in which federal authority has been exercised that valuations offer a promise of availability for regulatory purposes. In the case of the Federal Power Commission, valuations of the property of licensees are maintained currently in connection with the provisions for the recapture of the properties at the expiration of license periods. In the case of the railroads, the Interstate Commerce Commission has undertaken the valuation of railway properties as directed in the Valuation Act of 1913, but this act was modified by the Emergency Transportation Act of 1933 to require, in lieu of the obligation that valuations be kept up to date at all times, that data be kept that would permit the revision and correction of valuations when deemed necessary. Valuations of railroad properties have been made, but the uncertainties as to the bases of valuation to be employed limit their usefulness for rate-making purposes.

Summary.—Control of rates is the heart of the public utility regulatory problem in the United States. Conditions existing in public utility industries dictate, in the absence of regulation, that rates be set on the monopoly profits basis of what-the-traffic-will-bear, a policy that may lead to the establishment of both unreasonable and discriminatory rates. The obligation placed upon regulatory authorities, therefore, is to control the application of the what-the-traffic-will-bear principle to eliminate unreasonable and discriminatory rates. The area of reasonableness of rates lies between the maximum point of value of service and the minimum point of cost of service, and the judicial rule

[1] Ohio Pub. Util. Comm. re Ohio Bell Telephone Co., P.U.R., 1913B, 51, as cited by W. E. Mosher and F. G. Crawford, in "Public Utility Regulation," Harper & Brothers, New York, 1933, p. 204. Other instances are also cited there.

118 PUBLIC UTILITY REGULATION

for the determination of reasonableness within this area, as stated in *Smyth v. Ames*, is that a utility is entitled to a fair return on a fair value. In order to apply this rule, valuation of public utility properties is necessary; but in the present status of regulation, valuation procedure and practices are unsatisfactory. This is due in part to the revaluations made necessary by the practice of judicial review, the length of time necessary to make valuations, the costliness of making valuations, and the lack of funds and personnel on the part of commissions for making valuations. The problem is made difficult by many complicating factors inherent in the nature of the public utility industries; and application of the fair value rule, even though the uncertainties in the elements of the rule itself were eliminated, would be difficult because of these complicating factors. A major cause of the unsatisfactory status of the rule of rate making is found in the uncertainties connected with both fair return and fair value. An analysis of these uncertainties, as well as of other aspects of fair value and fair return, will engage our attention in the chapters immediately following.

References

BARKER, HARRY: "Public Utility Rates," McGraw-Hill Book Company, Inc., New York, 1917.

BAUER, JOHN: "Effective Regulation of Public Utilities," The Macmillan Company, New York, 1925.

——— and NATHANIEL GOLD: "Public Utility Valuation for Purpose of Rate Control," The Macmillan Company, New York, 1934.

Bonbright and Company: "A Survey of State Laws on Public Utility Commission Regulation in the United States," 2d ed., New York, 1930.

GLAESER, M. G.: "Outline of Public Utility Economics," The Macmillan Company, New York, 1931.

GUERNSEY, N. T.: "The Regulation of Public Utilities," outline of address, University of Virginia, 1928 (pamphlet).

JONES, ELIOT, and T. C. BIGHAM: "Principles of Public Utilities," The Macmillan Company, New York, 1931.

LOCKLIN, D. P.: "Economics of Transportation," Business Publications, Inc., Chicago, 1935.

LYNDON, LAMAR: "Rate Making for Public Utilities," McGraw-Hill Book Company, Inc., New York, 1923.

MOSHER, W. E., and F. G. CRAWFORD: "Public Utility Regulation," Harper & Brothers, New York, 1933.

National Association of Railroad and Utilities Commissioners: *Proceedings*, annual (especially Reports of Committees on Public Utility Rates and Valuations).

NICHOLS, ELLSWORTH: "Public Utility Service and Discrimination," Public Utilities Reports, Inc., Syracuse, 1928.

"Report of the New York Commission on Revision of the Public Service Commissions Law," Albany, 1930.

RUGGLES, C. O.: Discrimination in Public Utility Rates, *Journal of Political Economy,* vol. 32, no. 2.

SPURR, H. C.: "Guiding Principles of Public Utility Regulation," Public Utilities Reports, Inc., Washington, 1924.

CHAPTER VI

THE VALUATION OF PUBLIC UTILITIES

One of the most complex and bitterly debated problems in public utility economics and law is that of the valuation of the properties. The importance of valuation, as we have seen, is emphasized because of the wide acceptance of the principle that public utilities are entitled under the law to charge rates for their services that will yield a reasonable return upon the value of the property devoted to and used in the service of the public, after reasonable expenses of operation, depreciation, taxes, and reserves have been met. The right of a utility company to a reasonable return upon the value of the property used in the public service is based upon the Fifth and Fourteenth amendments to the United States Constitution, which provide that neither the federal nor the state governments may deprive any person of property without due process of law.[1] Since the right to a reasonable return upon property used in public service is afforded this protection, neither the federal nor the state governments can so regulate the services or rates of public utility enterprises that the result of regulation is the confiscation of the property. Before undertaking to discuss the economic and legal problems associated with valuation it should be noted that data with respect to the value of public utility properties are required by the companies, by administrative regulatory bodies, and by the courts for a variety of purposes. These include rate making; the issuance of securities; the consolidation of all or part of the properties by consolidation, merger, sale, or lease; awarding compensation to the owners of public utility properties upon condemnation of the properties for public ownership and operation; and the valuation of the assets of the properties in bankruptcy and reorganization proceedings.

Valuation for Rate-making Purposes.—The area of greatest intensity in the storm of controversy over valuation of public

---

[1] United States Constitution, Amendments, Articles V and XIV.

utility property is in the use of conflicting theories of economics, conflicting decisions and orders of administrative regulatory bodies, and conflicting decisions and dicta of courts to support or to refute one or another of the various bases of valuation. It has been well stated that "the 'facts' of the case in hand have opened the way for decisions which have both approved and disapproved every major economic theory of valuation which has yet been advanced."[1]

The discussion of the problems of public utility management and regulation would be less confused if the term "value" were not used in connection with the determination of rate base. The use of the term "value" in rate-base determination leads to confusion because the purpose of the process of "valuation" is to determine the amount of earnings to be allowed and the establishment of rates deemed adequate to produce the earnings. As the term is used in its economic sense, value is determined by the earning power of the property used and useful in producing the earnings. The result is reasoning in a circle, by arriving at the value of the property and then using the valuation so determined as the principal determinant of the earnings to be allowed upon the property which in turn determine the property's value. If the term "rate base" were used instead of "value," the confusion and circular reasoning could be avoided, and the selection of a method of determining the rate base could be considered upon equitable and practical grounds without the difficulties of justifying the use of the term "value."

Measures of Value.—The measures of value most commonly used can be divided into two groups. One of these groups relates to the value of the property at the time of its construction, including:

1. The original cost of the property.
2. The book cost.
3. The historical cost.
4. The prudent investment cost.
5. The investment cost measured by outstanding securities.

The second group of measures of valuation pertain to the value of the property at the time the valuation is made. This group of measures of value include:

[1] BEUTEL, F. K., Valuation as a Requirement of the Process of Law in Rate Cases, *Harvard Law Review*, vol. 43, p. 1262.

1. The reproduction cost value.
2. The reproduction cost value less depreciation.
3. The split inventory value.
4. Taxation value.
5. Market value.
6. Purchase value.[1]

Original or Book Cost.—The original cost of a public utility property is the sum of money that has actually been expended by the company in the acquisition and construction of the property included in the rate base that is used or useful in the service of the public. The amounts expended are determined from the accounts of the corporations, if the books have been kept accurately and completely from the time of organization down to the time of valuation. If the records have not been kept with accuracy and completeness it becomes necessary for those making the valuation to estimate the costs of acquisition at the time of acquisition of the items of property for which actual cost data are lacking. In actual valuation practice it becomes necessary to estimate the cost of many items of property, since the book entries, vouchers, and other direct evidence of the expenditures are lacking from the records. Book cost and original cost should coincide.

Historical Cost.—Historical cost should be the same as original cost, but the expression has been used by the courts in the sense of judging the wisdom and propriety of the expenditures to determine whether or not the amounts actually expended should have been spent. As such it corresponds with prudent investment.

Prudent Investment.—A further refinement in the determination of the rate base, by considering the expenditures that actually have been made in the light of the opinion of the court in particular cases as to whether the expenditures have been made for ill-conceived purposes or otherwise wastefully made, has given rise to what is known as the "prudent investment doctrine." This doctrine attempts to apply the original cost of the property of the utility used and useful in the public service so that the valuation allowed for rate-making purposes coincides with the sum that would reasonably have been expended by a competent and prudent person.

[1] See dissenting opinion of Mr. Justice Brandeis in Missouri, *ex rel.* Southwestern Bell Telephone Co. v. Missouri, 262 U.S. 276 (1923).

This concept has become so completely grafted upon the original and historical cost bases that they have become almost inseparable. In discussing these bases, Mr. Justice Brandeis stated in part in the Southwestern Bell Telephone case:

Historical cost, *i.e.*, the proper cost of the existing plant and business, estimated on the basis of the price levels existing at the respective dates when the plant and the additions were constructed. This is often called prudent investment. Historical cost would, under normal conditions, be equal in amount to the original cost. The phrases are sometimes used to denote the same thing. But they are not the same; and they are often ascertained by different processes. Original cost is the amount actually paid to establish the utility. The amount is ascertained, where possible, by inspection of books and vouchers, and by other direct evidence. If this class of evidence is not complete, it may be necessary to supplement it by evidence as to what was probably paid for some items, by showing prices prevailing for work and materials at the time the same were supplied. But the evidence of these prices is merely circumstantial, or corroborative, evidence of the amount actually paid. In determining actual cost, whatever the evidence, there is no attempt to determine whether the expenditure was wise or foolish, or whether it was useful or wasteful. Historical cost, on the other hand, is the amount which normally should have been paid for all the property which is usefully devoted to the public service. It is, in effect, what is termed the "prudent investment." In enterprises efficiently launched and developed, historical cost and original cost would practically coincide both in items included and in amounts paid. That is, the subjects of expenditure would coincide; and the cost at prices prevailing at the time of installation would substantially coincide with the actual cost.[1]

Investment Cost.—The investment cost of a public utility property represents the amount of securities issued by the company in the acquisition of the property. If all securities were issued upon a basis that would yield to the utility company the par value of the securities without discounts or premiums, or commissions for acquiring the capital, the par value of the outstanding securities should equal the original cost. And if the expenditures for the items of property were wisely and providently expended, the investment cost should equal the prudent investment valuation. Such is an ideal situation seldom achieved in practice. In actuality a large percentage of public

[1] *Op. cit.*

utility capital has been secured through the sale of various kinds
of bonds and preference or preferred stocks.   Estimates as to
the percentage of public utility capital obtained through the
sale of senior securities vary.   Professors Mosher and Crawford
estimate that "the senior securities normally constitute from
one-half to three-fourths of the total claimed investment."[1]
Mr. Justice Brandeis and Prof. Bauer have estimated that
approximately three-quarters of public utility capital has been
secured on a fixed return basis.[2]

A considerable portion of public utility capital has been
obtained by the issuance of capital stock but upon varying bases:
(1) at par value, (2) at prices above par, (3) at prices below par,
(4) without par value, or (5) as bonus stock as inducements to
the sale of bonds or preferred stock.   The difficulties of reconcil-
ing investment value with original cost, historical cost, or
prudent investment are obvious.

**Advantages and Disadvantages of Original Cost as a Rate
Base.**—The most cogent argument of those who support original
cost as a measure of valuation for rate-making purposes is that
this basis compensates the owners of the properties in proportion
to the service that they perform in supplying the capital required
by the enterprises.   They argue that the only reason the owners
of the properties are entitled to a return at all is because they
have invested capital and that, therefore, they should receive a
return on the actual capital invested as shown by the property
investment.

Original cost probably is the most definite measure and the
least conjectural of all bases of valuation.   This does not imply
that original costs are not difficult to discover accurately.   In
many cases records are incomplete, and estimates of the expenditures must be made.   Usually, however, such estimates are less
difficult than the determination of valuation in other ways which
will be discussed later, including the cost of reproducing the
plant and facilities under assumed conditions.

It must not be assumed that original costs are represented
only by the capital invested in physical assets.   As will be

[1] MOSHER, W. E., and F. G. CRAWFORD, "Public Utility Regulation,"
Harper & Brothers, New York, 1933, p. 182.
[2] Southwestern Bell Telephone Co. v. Pub. Service Comm., Missouri, 262
U.S. 307; and BAUER, JOHN, *Public Utility Fortnightly*, May 5, 1929, p. 507.

discussed later, the cost of interest on borrowed funds during construction, promotion and development expenses, and deficits incurred during the pioneer period of development during the initial period of operation must be considered. On the other hand, certain items of expenditure must be excluded, including expenses dishonestly or improperly incurred, or expenditures incurred imprudently or improvidently, when tested by the "prudent investment" doctrine.

However changes in the price level raise difficult problems in the application of the original cost theory of fair value. If 6 per cent is the current rate of return and prices rise to double the former level but the valuation of the property remains constant, the return to the owners in purchasing power is halved. If, on the other hand, the price level falls 50 per cent, the owners of the property receive twice the amount of purchasing power. There is a considerable weight of authority against modifying original costs to allow for changes in the price level. This question will be discussed later.

Reproduction Cost.—The reproduction cost of a public utility is the amount of money that would be expended at the time the valuation is made in the construction or acquisition new of the items of property included in the rate base. The amount required for the reproduction of the property is determined usually by appraisals made by engineers upon the basis of an inventory of the items of property included in the rate base. It is an estimate of present cost and not, as in the case of the original cost bases, a historical cost figure. However, the appraisal of a public utility property, particularly a large and complex system, upon the basis of the cost of reproduction is a complicated, slow, and expensive procedure. Benjamin Franklin once observed that several removals were as costly to a householder as a fire, and it might be observed with equal truth that several valuation appraisals are as costly to a public utility as a similar catastrophe, not to mention the cost to the public in financing the work of appraisal of the public utility regulatory commissions.

Cost of Reproduction Less Depreciation.—In arriving at valuation for rate-base purposes, accrued depreciation is sometimes deducted from the cost of reproduction new in order to arrive at an estimate of the cost of reproducing the property in its actual present condition. The methods of writing off depreciation will be discussed later.

Advantages and Disadvantages of Cost of Reproduction as a Rate Base.—The arguments usually advanced by proponents of the cost-of-reproduction basis of valuation are two in number: first, the owners of regulated enterprises should fare no better or no worse than investors in unregulated competitive enterprises; and, second, the value of a piece of property at any given time tends to correspond to the cost of reproducing it at that time; thus, a plant that cost $100,000,000 and is reproducible for $50,000,000 is worth only $50,000,000 at that time because no more than $50,000,000 would be paid for it if it could be built for $50,000,000. In like manner, a plant that cost $100,000,000 and could be reproduced for not less than $200,000,000 is worth $200,000,000 at that time. The second of these arguments is widely used in support of the first.

There are, however, certain serious defects in the use of the cost of reproduction as a measure of fair value. In exchange-value economics the real value of a plant is not determined by the cost of reproducing the identical plant but by the cost of producing the commodity in a new plant having the most modern equipment required to produce the article. No one would be willing to invest in an obsolete plant if a new one could be built to be operated at much lower operating expenses per unit of product if such a plant could be built for the same cost as the obsolete one. It is the cost of building a modern plant of similar capacity that determines the value of a plant in an unregulated competitive industry, and not the cost of reproduction of a similar plant. Hence, reproduction cost does not cause the owners of a regulated enterprise to fare the same as the investors in unregulated competitive enterprises.

There is, furthermore, a limitation to the concept that the cost of producing the commodity in a new plant regulates the value of an old plant, since, because of technological developments, the value of such a plant would scarcely, if ever, exceed the cost of reproduction and might be considerably less. Reproduction cost, therefore, is a measure of maximum value at best. Even if a new plant of equal capacity were to cost more to construct, it might produce at unit costs so much less than the old plant that the additional cost of construction would be an excellent investment. In such a case it would be unfair to require the consumer to pay rates that would yield enough to pay the high operating expenses of the old plant and produce a return equal to that which would be a fair return upon the greater cost of an up-to-date plant. Yet the courts have held in numerous valuation cases that the plant, the cost of reproduction of which is to be estimated, is a plant identical with that in existence and have declared that the cost of reproduction of the plant must be considered in valuation for rate-making purposes.[1]

In the second place, public utilities often enjoy greater or lesser degrees of monopoly. So long as the industries are protected from competition and allowed to earn a return on the reproduction value of their identical plants, the incentive to build new and more efficient plants which have higher first costs but lower producing costs per unit is lessened.

In the third place, the argument that, since reproduction costs fluctuate widely this basis of valuation is more equitable, in that the fluctuations tend to parallel the fluctuations in the general commodity price level, is partly fallacious. Reproduction costs include a large percentage of labor costs, while the percentage of labor costs in the general price level may be much less. Moreover, the general price level includes the prices of many items that are not included in reproduction estimates. But granting that adjustment of the rate base has merit, there are difficult problems encountered in applying reproduction costs which result directly from fluctuations in the price level. Since a large part of the outstanding securities of public utility companies bear fixed interest or dividend charges, reproduction cost if used as a rate base during a period of low or falling price levels may result in earnings below fixed costs. On the other hand, in a period of high or rising prices the use of reproduction cost may result in earnings on common stocks unreasonably high. Consequently, the owners of public utility properties have often argued strenuously for the theory of reproduction cost when

---

[1] See Smyth v. Ames, 169 U.S. 466 (1890); Wilcox v. Cons. Gas Co., 212 U.S. 19 (1909); Missouri *ex rel.* Southwestern Bell Telephone Co. v. Pub. Service Comm., Missouri, 262 U.S. 276 (1923); Bluefield Water Works and Improvement Co. v. West Virginia Pub. Service Comm., 262 U.S. 679 (1923); McCardle v. Indianapolis Water Co., 272 U.S. 400. 1926; St. Louis and O'Fallon R.R. Co. v. United States, 279 U.S. 461 (1928); and other cases.

prices, particularly building prices, are high and have denounced it with equal vigor as a measure of fair value when prices are low.   The dangers inherent in a rate base which is dependent upon and varies with current costs of reproduction have been pointed out fully by the Interstate Commerce Commission.[1]

In the fourth place, reproduction cost as a basis for valuation is a very difficult measure to apply.   Streets may have been paved since gas mains were laid; the machinery in the plant may be obsolete in type and no longer manufactured; the land may be built up so that if the plant were to be built now, other buildings would have to be torn down; and numerous other factors may have entered in to change the conditions so as to make cost of reproduction an unreal concept.   No general rule has been made as to whether original or present conditions in these matters are to be assumed, commissions and courts having varied interpretations of this problem.

Average Costs of Reproduction.—A variation of the cost of reproduction theory of valuation is the use of average costs computed over a period of time rather than costs at the time of the valuation.   This plan of valuation was used by the Public Service Commission of Indiana in the valuation of the property of the Indianapolis Water Company.   The United States Supreme Court, in striking down this method because it resulted in deprivation of property without due process of law, stated that the Indiana Commission had erred in not giving some recognition to the present cost of reproduction.   The Court did not hold that present cost of reproduction was the sole basis for valuation but that it must be considered as one factor.[2]   One advantage of the use of average cost of reproduction as the basis is that changes in the rate base would not be made frequently, average costs of reproduction being applicable to the period affected and not needing to be changed so frequently to reflect short-range changes in price levels.

The Split Inventory Basis of Valuation.—Regulatory commissions have employed another type of rate base in the valuation of public utility properties particularly useful in times when pronounced and sudden changes have taken place in price levels,

---

[1] Letter from Interstate Commerce Commission to U.S. Senate Committee on Interstate Commerce, Jan. 24, 1930.

[2] McCardle v. Indianapolis Water Co., 272 U.S. 400.

as during the World War period. Under this plan of valuation all of the items of property acquired prior to a given date, known as the "splitting date," are valued at the cost of reproduction as of that date, while all items of property acquired subsequent to the splitting date are included in the valuation at original cost. This plan is the basis for more recent suggestions that public utility properties should be valued by the application of reproduction cost to existing property and of original cost to new property.[1]

Relation of Probable Future Price Levels to Valuation.— In the quest for valuation formulas, regulatory commissions have attempted to relate rate bases to future costs and price levels. The practical value of considering these factors is obvious when one contemplates that the valuation basis will be used not only in the immediate present but in the future and that future rates will be based upon the valuations. But the impracticability of predicting future costs and price levels makes such procedure of uncertain value, although the United States Supreme Court upon several occasions in valuation cases has stated that public utility valuations are not fixed for the present only but also for a reasonable period in the future[2] and that it is essential in valuation that the Commission undertaking the task make an honest and intelligent forecast "of possible future values" upon "a view of all relevant circumstances."[3]

The Reproduction Cost of Service Basis.—Another variation of the cost of reproduction basis for public utility valuation is the cost of reproducing the service, *i.e.*, the use of present costs of reproduction of the most efficient plant that could be constructed at the time the valuation is made to perform the service, rather than the present costs of reproducing the actual plant facilities in the form in which they exist at the time the valuation is made. This basis of valuation places a distinct penalty upon obsolete equipment and inefficient methods of operation, since it tends to recognize as having value only the facilities that would be required to produce the quantity and quality of service

[1] BERNSTEIN, E. M., The Split Inventory: A War Expedient, A Solution in Peace, *Quarterly Journal of Economics*, vol. 44, pp. 493–522.

[2] McCardle v. Indianapolis Water Co., 272 U.S. 400.

[3] Missouri *ex rel.* Southwestern Bell Telephone Co. v. Pub. Service Comm., Mo., 262 U.S. 276.

provided. However, the difficulties in the use of this basis make it of doubtful practical value. Expert judgment would be required and much time and labor expended in appraising not only the facilities of the plants actually evaluated but the hypothetical facilities of the fictitious most efficient plant to perform the services under consideration and in determining the probable differential between the actual costs of operation per unit of service rendered and the hypothetical costs of operation in the nonexistent most efficient plant used as a measuring rod. It would be difficult to obtain substantial agreement among the appraisers as to what would constitute the most efficient property, its costs of operation per unit of service rendered, the physical value of the actual plant, and the differential costs. Even if the time and the money expended in evaluating one property were to be rewarded by a valuation of the actual plant in relation to the most efficient plant in a given case, it would be improbable that different groups of valuation experts would arrive at similar conclusions with respect to another utility property. Disagreements among engineers, accountants, attorneys, and construction, operation, and purchasing experts in the difficult problems of alternative costs would cause delay, expense, uncertainty, and unfairness as among different utility companies and groups of consumers.[1]

Another problem raised by the use of the reproduction cost of service basis is that of the fairness of allowing public service companies to include in the valuation base only such proportion of their actual properties as such properties bear to a theoretical most efficient plant. The march of technological progress in the fields of public utility operation causes rapid obsolescence and depreciation; and if the properties are to keep pace with such progress, provision must be made in the rate structures for return sufficient to enable the properties to be built and rebuilt at a rapid rate. Application of this concept would tend toward high rates per unit for the service and would involve an absurdly rapid amortization of capital. It is questionable, moreover, whether a goal should be set for all types of utilities in all sections

---

[1] See H. G. Brown, *Journal of Political Economy*, vol. 33, pp. 505–530, for a presentation of the advantages of the reproduction cost of service valuation basis; and W. J. Graham, "Public Utility Valuation," University of Chicago Press, Chicago, 1934, pp. 7–8, for summary of disadvantages.

of a large country serving large and small communities under varying conditions based upon a most efficient plant concept. Such procedure would tend to raise standards of service for small properties in areas with sparse population out of proportion to practical requirements. While it is desirable to encourage the reasonable improvement of plant and operating practices where the properties have been allowed to become obviously obsolete and where operating methods are patently inefficient, this can be done, regardless of the basis of valuation employed, by adjusting the rate of return so as to provide a reasonable amount for reconstruction and for an incentive to efficient operation.

The Computation of Physical Values. *Property Used and Useful.*—The rule applied by the courts as indicated by the weight of authority of the decisions concerning property that should, and property that should not, be considered in determining the value of a public utility enterprise for rate-making purposes is that only the property used and useful in the public interest should be included in the valuation base. In *Galveston Electric Co. v. Galveston*, Mr. Justice Brandeis, who wrote the majority opinion, stated that "past losses," *i.e.*, the operating deficits incurred by a utility in building up its operations to a profitable stage, should not be permitted to be included as useful property in ascertaining a subsequent rate base.[1] On the other hand, an argument of the Public Service Commission of Missouri that, because of a decrease in a company's business of a certain percentage, a corresponding reduction should be made in the value of the property on the ground of excess capacity was rejected.[2]

Determination of what property is useful involves the consideration of numerous items from the viewpoint of present and future needs of the company and often brings into opposition the judgment of commissions, courts, and management. The New York Commission, in *Re Elmira Water, Light and R.R. Co.*,[3] distinguished as follows between property that should and that which should not be included in the rate base:

The company seeks to have included in the rate base certain artificial gas mains formerly used in the distribution of artificial gas of the

[1] 258 U.S. 388.
[2] Laclede Gas Light Co., v. Pub. Service Comm., 8 Fed. Supp. 806.
[3] P.U.R. 1922D, 231.

claimed value of $60,385. The city opposes the inclusion of any part
of these artificial gas mains. . . . The company would justify their use
(a portion of the mains) on the theory that it is thereby enabled to
reduce the present gas pressure, these mains being used as a belt-line
or by-pass in which gas is kept at an even flow, and an equal, lower
pressure thereby had; and claims this method will give not only a
more even distribution to all local points, but that gas will be distributed more satisfactorily and economically at greater distances. . . .
The evidence further is, that in every street listed the company has an
artificial gas main paralleling a natural gas main, except Pennsylvania
Avenue. . . .

When duplicated property or parts are found in a utility, the question of inclusion in the rate base depends on:

(a) If used: Is the use necessary from an economical point of view,
to the extent that if the duplicated property were not present the company, in order to furnish sufficient or better service, would add such
duplicated parts to its plant?

(b) If unused: Does reasonable prudence indicate it ought to be
maintained for, (1) probable plant development within a reasonable
future time, or (2) as an insurance of continuity of service?

These old artificial gas mains are not necessary to the distribution of
natural gas in the city of Elmira, and are of doubtful value for service in
the future; although used, they are not necessarily useful from the
economical standpoint.

The utility company cited in its argument to justify the inclu-
sion of this property a decision of the Indiana Public Service
Commission in a case involving the gas rates of Richmond Light,
Heat and Power Company.[1] Commenting upon this case,
Commissioner Blakeslee stated:

In the foregoing case the company maintained in a state of repair
and efficiency its gas manufacturing plant, in the city of Richmond, as
a means of assuring to its patrons an adequate supply of artificial gas
in the event of interruptions in the supply of natural gas. And the
Indiana Commission . . . expressly allowed the inclusion of the gas
manufacturing works, structures and distributing system, on the
ground that such plant may be called into active service at any time.
In the instant case the facts are not the same, and there is nothing,
therefore, in the Richmond decision to support the claim here made.

Although courts and commissions have stated and emphasized
repeatedly that only "property used and useful in the public

[1] P.U.R. 1917B, 300.

service" can be included in the estimate of valuation, the generalization means little. In the final analysis the criterion of usefulness is at best a shifting, unstable standard of judgment determined in each instance by the facts of the individual case. This should be borne in mind throughout analysis of the decisions of the courts and commissions with respect to the inclusion or exclusion of property in valuation cases. It is not possible to state dogmatically, according to any recognizable criteria, that certain kinds of property are to be included, and certain other kinds of property are not to be included, as property "used and useful" in the service of the public.

Whether property is used or useful involves also the consideration of the condition of utility properties at the time the valuation is made. That much useless or obsolete property is included in the rate bases upon which consumers of public utility services must pay a return is well established. Mr. Frank R. McNinch, former chairman of the Federal Power Commission, in a radio address, Mar. 24, 1937, made the following statement regarding this matter:

An expert advises me that while the electric utility fixed capital is reported as being about $13,000,000,000, he is of the opinion, after personal observation of the condition of utility properties in various parts of the country, that its real value is about six and one-half billion dollars. Available data on plant factors and utilization factors throw light on this question. For instance, one large electric system has a plant factor of about 22 per cent, meaning that on the average only 22 per cent of its generating facilities are in use, but the consumers have to pay rates on all of this equipment. This system has a utilization factor of about 56 per cent, meaning there is reserve capacity of 44 per cent at the time of peak load. This would appear to be ample reserve, yet this company is reported as buying new capacity equipment. Why this new equipment unless a portion of the present equipment is ready to be junked? Similar conditions prevail in many other systems to greater or lesser degree.

Inclusion or exclusion of property, depending upon whether the items of property are, or are not, considered to be used and useful property in the service of the public, is made only in valuations for rate-making purposes. In valuations for purposes of approving a sale, for purposes of authorizing the issuance of securities, or for purposes of determining compensation to be paid for condemnation of a utility's plant, the value of *all* of the utility's property must be considered whether or not particular units might be "useful" as devoted to public utility service.

Working Capital as an Item in Valuation.—Working capital has been defined by the Public Utilities Commission of Colorado as the amount of cash, supplies, or other available assets that may be readily converted into cash, reasonably necessary for the purpose of meeting the current obligations of a utility as they arrive, and to enable it to operate economically and efficiently.[1] The purposes of working capital are to enable the utility company to pay its operating expenses in advance of the collection of its outstanding accounts and to allow it to take advantage of cash discounts and such other conditions and circumstances as will increase the efficiency of the service as well as to enable the company to operate economically.[2]

There are three methods of procedure used in determining the amount of working capital. Two of these methods are admittedly less accurate than they are expedient to the particular case at hand. The first and most common method of procedure is that laid down by the Board of Public Utility Commissioners of New Jersey in the case of *Long Branch v. Tintern Manor Water Co.*[3] This method requires consideration of the total amount of business done; the method of collecting, whether monthly, quarterly, or annually; the character of the business done, whether seasonal with a high-season peak or uniform throughout the year; and whether the bills are collectible in advance or at the end of the period during which the service is furnished.

Of the remaining two methods the first is the so-called "lump sum" allowance, based presumably upon the experience or anticipated actual needs of the company without any relation either to the company's rate base or the company's operating expense account; and the second consists of basing the allowance upon a fixed percentage of the utility's rate base or other capital valuation.

[1] *Re* Mountain States Telephone and Telegraph Co., P.U.R. 1917B, 198.
[2] Kings County Lighting Co. v. Lewis, P.U.R. 1920D, 145; 180 N.Y. Supp. 570.
[3] P.U.R. 1918A, 178.

An allowance based on operating expenses is doubtless preferable to an allowance based upon a percentage of the value of the property involved, because the amount of assets of a company are only slightly indicative of the amount of working capital necessary in the conduct of the business. In *Hermann et al. v. Newton Gas Co.*, the New York Public Service Commission, First District, held that the amount of working capital for a gas company is not necessarily indicated by its net current assets of which the chief item is unpaid monthly bills which are figured at the selling price of the gas, and which also include profits and reserves requiring no actual expenditure.[1]

While no rigid method can be employed in computing the working capital allowance, certain obvious variations in the amount of working capital are present in different types of utilities. A utility that does business upon a cash basis, such as an electric railway, and collects each day revenues out of which to meet operating expenses in advance of expenditure requires but little working capital. Gas and electric utilities usually render monthly bills for their services; hence, an allowance of one-twelfth of the amount of the annual operating expenses is a popular but by no means fixed allowance for working capital to such companies. Water and rural telephone companies which often bill for service quarterly, semiannually, and even annually require a proportionately higher allowance with respect to their annual operating expense accounts.

The Computation of Nonphysical Values. *Overhead Values.*— In addition to the estimates of the value of the tangible physical units of a utility's property, allowances are generally made for so-called "overhead costs." These costs are sometimes divided into two categories, which may be designated as specific and general overheads. The Oregon Commission, in *Re Portland Power Co.*,[2] found that overhead expenditures fall into two classes: (1) expenditures that can be said to relate clearly to particular classes of physical property carried in the various primary accounts; and (2) expenditures that do not appear to relate to particular classes of physical property but are more directly applicable to the property as a whole. In the first class are expenditures such as superintendence involved in the

[1] P.U.R. 1916D, 825.
[2] P.U.R. 1916D, 976.

setting up of a telephone pole, which can be directly attributed to that pole. In the second category are such expenditures as the legal or engineering expenses incurred during a whole utility construction job which must be carried as a separate allowance because it covers the entire property. The term "overhead allowance" as generally used in public utility valuation refers to this second class of expenditures.

The nonphysical values represented by overhead costs are considered in the valuation of utility properties for rate making, the sale of securities, the sale of the property, or the determination of compensation to be paid to the owner in condemnation proceedings. Overhead costs must also be considered, whether the valuation of property is in accordance with the reproduction cost theory, the original cost theory, the "prudent investment" theory, or any variations or combinations of these bases.

The method of determining overhead costs is not uniform. The conventional method is to make a separate allowance of an estimated percentage of the physical value for each overhead item. General construction overhead allowance varies from 10 to 20 per cent of the total valuation of the properties—with 15 per cent as a fairly common figure.

Intangible Values.—Up to this point the discussion has been concerned with two steps in the determination of public utility valuation: (1) the computation of the physical values; and (2) the computation of the nonphysical values as represented by overhead costs. The third and final step involves the computation of the intangible values. These values are usually divided into two classes: (a) the special and rather complicated type of intangible value known as "going value"; and (b) other or miscellaneous intangible values, including such things as the value of water rights, franchises, leases, and similar property rights.

"Going Value."—One of the most controversial items in the field of public utility valuation is the subject of "going value." Briefly, going value represents the difference in value between a plant in actual operation and the inventory value of a similar plant assembled but not yet functioning. Courts in valuation proceedings usually permit a separate allowance to be included in the valuation for going value. This allowance is often set

have been incurred in obtaining the franchise or where annual payments in one form or another are made in consideration of the franchise. In a few cases franchise values have been established through consolidations or purchases by legislation or court proceedings, and values so established have been successfully defended.[1]

Water rights, or, as they are sometimes referred to, riparian rights, are in a somewhat different category from other miscellaneous assets. A water right of a power company may in some cases be sold in the open market for a consideration in excess of its cost, and, therefore, it may be said to have a money value. Its value lies in the fact that through this right it is sometimes possible for hydroelectric properties to furnish electric service to customers within the limits of economical transmission at lower cost than from steam or other alternative sources. The most common procedure of determining the value of riparian rights is to determine the total cost of delivering hydroelectric service from the water power in question, exclusive of the value of its riparian rights, and the similar cost of delivery from the most economical substitute source of power. The capitalization of the difference between the two costs represents the value of the riparian rights.[2]

Trends in Court Decisions and Commission Procedure Pertaining to Public Utility Valuation.—It is doubtful that any consistent trends can be traced in the decisions of commissions and courts in public utility valuation because of the changing interests of the regulatory commissions, the public and the utility owners, and because of differences in terminology which have the effect of changing the concepts of value. Mosher and Crawford state that "after . . . years of controversy, of long-drawn-out arguments before the commissions, the state, and federal courts, agreement as to the proper method of determining the investment upon which rewards to management and stockholders are to be computed seems about as remote as it was in 1898, when that basic case, Smyth v. Ames was tried before the Supreme Court."[3]

[1] Cons. Gas Co. v Wilcox, 212 U.S. 19 (1909).

[2] San Joaquin and Kings River Canal and Irrigation Co. v. Stanislaus County, Calif., 233 U.S. 454 (1914).

[3] MOSHER and CRAWFORD, *op. cit.*, p. 182.

The measure of value that the Nebraska Commission contended was the proper basis of valuation in the public interest in *Smyth v. Ames*, the present fair value, and then opposed by the utilities, is the same measure of value that in recent years has been urged by utilities and opposed by the advocates of reduced rates for public utility service who strive to limit the amount allowed the utilities as a basis of valuation for rate making. The measure of value for which the railroads argued in *Smyth v. Ames*, the investment cost as measured by the outstanding capitalization, is similar in some respects to the prudent investment valuation basis which has been generally opposed in recent years by the utilities and urged by many who seek reduced public utility valuation bases. This shifting of positions is explained by the rise in the levels of prices that has taken place since 1898. Valuation based upon present prices when prices are high is attractive to the utilities and unattractive to the rate payers, especially if the properties were constructed during periods of lower prices. Conversely, it is a disadvantageous basis to the utilities but advantageous to those who seek lower utility rates if prevailing prices are low and the properties were built in periods of higher prices. Changes in the price level cause changes in viewpoints.

Similarly, while few public utility valuation experts today argue for valuation based upon capitalization as represented by outstanding securities, many argue for prudent investment as a proper basis of valuation. Yet prudent investment is closely related to capitalization, since it recognizes as the basis for valuation the amount that normally should have been invested in the properties, and this should correspond closely to the securities issued, if "watered stock" is rigidly excluded. The broader powers over the issuance of securities by public utilities granted to regulatory commissions in recent years, if it has done nothing else, has afforded the commissions greater authority to prevent the dilution of the securities of the utility companies and to bring the capital structures closer to the actual investment in the properties.

Valuation Is a Matter of Judgment.—One trend that can be traced is that toward recognition of the principle that valuation is not a matter of formula or formulae but a problem involving the exercise of judgment by a body of qualified experts upon the basis of evidence of value submitted to them in proceedings before them. In *West v. Chesapeake & Potomac Telephone Co.*, Mr. Justice Roberts, writing the opinion of the Court, condemned the substitution of "translators" of dollar value for the application of judgment upon consideration of historical cost and cost of reproduction. The Maryland Public Service Commission in attempting to determine the value of the property took unit costs found for the property in a rate case in 1923, which had been arrived at through the use of commodity prices indices, and brought these unit prices up to date by the further use of commodity indices modified to some extent by the judgment of the Commission. This method of valuation was followed in order to avoid the necessity of a costly appraisal. The company agreed to the use of price indices but insisted that price indices of commodities actually used in the telephone business and not of general commodities be used. However, the Commission refused to use specific commodity indices on the ground that data with respect to such commodities could be obtained only from companies affiliated with the telephone industry so closely, and dominating the field to such an extent, that there was not an open and competitive market to determine the prices of these specific commodities.

The Supreme Court did not find that the formula used by the Maryland Commission would have resulted in confiscation of the utility's property. It merely held that the method of valuation was erroneous and restrained its use for this reason. Three justices, constituting the minority in this case, criticized the majority for not deciding the main issue of confiscation and implied willingness to accept the short-cut method of valuation adopted by the Maryland Commission, so long as the value arrived at did not result in confiscation. The majority opinion stated:

To an extent value must be a matter of sound judgment, involving fact data. To substitute for such factors as historical cost and cost of reproduction, a "translator" of dollar value obtained by the use of price trend indices, serves only to confuse the problem and to increase its difficulty, and may well lead to results anything but equitable and fair. This is not to suggest that price trends are to be disregarded; quite the contrary is true. And evidence of such trends is to be considered with all other relevant factors.[1]

The position of the Supreme Court in this case appears to be consistent with its decision in the O'Fallon case in which the Court expressed its disapproval of valuation by formula.[2]

It would appear, therefore, that despite the ardent quest of economists, engineers, legislators, and jurists for a valuation formula, rule, or guide, pursued for the last quarter century or more, the law of the land, as interpreted by the Supreme Court, is that valuation is not a matter of formula but one of judgment. This means that, except for elements no longer of significance, commissions must continue to evaluate public utility properties in the light of the so-called elements of value, no matter how irreconcilable.

Judgment Must Include Consideration of Certain Factors.— Although valuation has been held to be a matter of judgment the Supreme Court has insisted that consideration be given to certain elements of value, in order that the owners of the properties be protected from confiscation or the deprivation of property without due process of law. These elements of value were enumerated, in *Smyth v. Ames*, in the following words:

We hold, however, that the basis of all calculations as to the reasonableness of rates to be charged by a corporation maintaining a highway under legislative sanction must be the fair value of the property being used by it for the convenience of the public. And in order to ascertain that value, the original cost of construction, the amount expended in permanent improvements, the amount and market value of its bonds and stocks, the present as compared with the original cost of construction, the probable earning capacity of the property under particular rates prescribed by statute, and the sum required to meet operating expenses, are all matters for consideration, and are to be given such weight as may be just and right in each case. We do not say that there may not be other matters to be regarded in estimating the value of the property. What the company is entitled to ask is a fair return upon the value of that which it employs for the public convenience. On the other hand, what the public is entitled to demand is that no more be

[1] West *et al.* v. Chesapeake and Potomac Telephone Co. of Baltimore, 295 U.S. 662 (1935).

[2] St. Louis and O'Fallon R.R. Co. v. United States, 279 U.S. 461 (1929).

exacted from it for the use of a public highway than the services rendered by it are reasonably worth.[1]

That some of the elements mentioned in *Smyth v. Ames* are irreconcilable, since the employment of cost of reproduction invariably produces different results from original cost, matters little, the Supreme Court having held consistently that they must be considered in arriving at a final single-sum value. Thus, in the Minnesota Rate cases, the Court held that it is the property and not the original cost of it that the owner of privately owned property could not lawfully be deprived of without due process of law;[2] and in *Bluefield Water Works and Improvement Co. v. Pub. Service Comm.*, the Court said:

The State Supreme Court of Appeals holds that the valuing of the property of a public utility corporation and prescribing rates are purely legislative acts not subject to judicial review except in so far as may be necessary to determine whether such rates are void on constitutional or other grounds; and that findings of fact by the commission based on evidence to support them will not be reviewed by the court. . . . The record clearly shows that the Commission in arriving at its final figure did not accord proper, if any, weight to the greatly enhanced costs of construction in 1920 over those prevailing about 1915 and before the war, as established by uncontradicted evidence; and the company's detailed estimate cost of reproduction new, less depreciation, at 1920 prices, appears to have been wholly disregarded. This was erroneous. Plaintiff in error is entitled under the due process clause of the Fourteenth Amendment to the independent judgment of the court as to both law and facts.[3]

Again in the O'Fallon R.R. case, the Court held:

Paragraph 4, of Section 15 A of the Transportation Act of 1920 states: that in determining values of railway property for purposes of recapture the Commission shall give due consideration to all the elements of value recognized by the law of the land for rate-making purposes, and shall give to the property investment account of the carriers only that consideration which, under such law, it is entitled to in establishing values for rate-making purposes. . . . This is an express command; and the carrier has clear right to demand compliance therewith.[4]

[1] Smyth v. Ames, 169 U.S. 466, 546–547.
[2] Simpson *et al.* v. Shephard, 230 U.S. 352 (1913).
[3] 262 U.S. 679 (1923).
[4] St. Louis and O'Fallon R.R. Co. v. United States, 279 U. S. 461 (1929).

Accordingly, in exercising judgment in the valuation of public utility properties the regulatory commissions must consider all items and elements of value and all methods of determining value, including cost of reproduction, original cost, and present cost in particular.

Judicial Review of Valuation Is Not a Matter of Revision.— A third trend that appears to be indicated by Supreme Court decisions is the inclination to the view that the place of courts in valuation proceedings is not that of boards of revision but of judicial bodies for the protection of constitutional rights of the parties.   The Court has held that it is not the function of courts to inquire into valuation methods used by regulatory commissions unless the results of the application of the methods in particular cases are confiscatory, the burden of proof in such cases to show that confiscation results from the application of particular valuation methods being upon the utility.   This was stated directly in *San Diego Land and Town Co. v. Jasper,*[1] and more than thirty years later the Court reaffirmed its position in the West Ohio Gas Co. case.[2]   In practice, however, court determinations necessarily have involved consideration of methods of valuation.   In the Los Angeles Gas and Electric Co. case neither the commission's estimate of valuation nor its methods of arriving at the valuation were upset by the Supreme Court,[3] but those of the Maryland commission in *West v. Chesapeake and Potomac Telephone Co.*[4] were.   It would appear upon casual observation that the position of the Court in these two cases was not altogether consistent, but a more careful reading of the decision in the Maryland Telephone case indicates some basis for the difference in attitudes.   In the Maryland case the Commission appears to have exercised judgment in selecting and modifying some of the commodity indices but to have relied upon these indexes to such an extent that the method approached a mathematical formula and did not constitute a judgment on the basis of factual data, as was the case in the San Diego, the West Ohio, and Los Angeles Gas cases.

[1] San Diego Land and Town Co. v. Jasper, 189 U.S. 439 (1903).

[2] West Ohio Gas Co. v. Pub. Util. Comm. Ohio (No. 2), 294 U.S. 79 (1935).

[3] Los Angeles Gas and Electric Co. v. R. R. Comm. of Calif., 289 U.S. 287 (1933).

[4] 295 U.S. 662.

Concerning this apparent inconsistency, Mr. Justice Roberts, in the Maryland Telephone case, said:

. . . It is not the function of a tribunal inquiring into the question of confiscation to set aside the legislative finding for mere errors of procedure. The duty of a court is merely to ascertain whether the legislative process has resulted in confiscation. In *Los Angeles Gas and Electric Corp. v. R.R. Comm., supra,* this Court said:

"The legislative discretion implied in the rate making power necessarily extends to the entire legislative process, embracing the method used in reaching the legislative determination as well as that determination itself. We are not concerned with either, so long as constitutional limitations are not transgressed. When the legislative method is disclosed, it may have a definite bearing upon the validity of the result reached, but the judicial function does not go beyond the decision of the constitutional question. That question is whether the rates as fixed are confiscatory."

The language was used in respect of the claim that values of various elements had been ignored by the Commission. It was found, however, that though error might have been committed in respect of the items specified, other allowances neutralized the possible error. . . . Nothing said in either of these cases justifies the claim that this court has departed from the principles announced in earlier cases as to the value upon which a utility is entitled to earn a reasonable return or the character of evidence relevant to that issue. It is apparent from what has been said that *here the entire method of the Commission was erroneous and its use necessarily involved unjust and inaccurate results.* In such a case it is not the function of a court, upon a claim of confiscation, to make a new valuation upon some different theory in an effort to sustain a procedure which is fundamentally faulty.[1]

The Trend toward Agreed or Contract Valuation Bases.—A final trend which should be noted in the plans and methods of public utility valuation is that toward the adoption of rate bases fixed by agreement or contract between the regulatory commissions and the public utility companies. A typical plan of this sort is the so-called "Washington plan" which became effective Jan. 1, 1925. Another is the contract valuation plan proposed in New York.

The Washington Plan.—In 1917 the District of Columbia Commission, after a study of the properties of the Potomac Electric Power Company, operating in Washington, established

---

[1] West v. Chesapeake and Potomac Telephone Co., 295 U.S. 662, 674–675, italics ours.

a rate base and schedules of rates estimated to yield the company a return of 7 per cent upon the valuation of the property based upon the total investment account reported to the Commission.[1] The Potomac Electric Company sought and obtained a temporary injunction restraining the Commission from the enforcement of its order upon condition that the utility company keep special accounts of the amounts paid by consumers and post bond to guarantee the repayment of the difference between the charges collected and the charges as they would have been under the Commission's order. In March, 1920, the Supreme Court of the District of Columbia sustained the valuation and rate order of the District Commission and dissolved the injunction. Appeal was taken by the Electric Company to the Court of Appeals of the District of Columbia alleging that the valuation was inadequate as a result of use by the Commission of 1914 prices in its order despite higher prices in effect on the date of the Commission's order, Dec. 31, 1916. The decision of the Court of Appeals sustained the position of the Potomac Electric Company, and the case was remanded to the Supreme Court of the District for further hearing. The United States Supreme Court declined to take jurisdiction upon appeal upon the ground that no showing that a constitutional question was involved had been made.[2] As a result of this litigation it became necessary to revise the rate base. A sliding-scale rate was worked out jointly by the Commission and the company and sanctioned by a consent decree of the Supreme Court of the District of Columbia handed down Dec. 31, 1924. Under the first plan, the valuation of the utility property was fixed at a figure agreed to be fair and just by the utility company and the Commission, and approved by the court, as a fair value as of Dec. 31, 1916. It was agreed that the prior order of the Commission fixing the valuation of the property should be modified to the agreed basis and that a revised schedule of rates agreed upon by the parties and included in the Court's decree should be charged as the lawful rates until modified or set aside by the Commission in accordance with the agreement.

The first plan became effective Jan. 1, 1925. The valuation base, depreciation-reserve requirements, and sliding scale of

[1] District of Columbia Commission, Order No. 223, Dec. 31, 1916.
[2] Keller *et al.* v. Potomac Electric Power Co. *et al.*, 261 U.S. 428 (1923).

rates were fixed by the agreement and subject to the provision that the rate base for any subsequent year should be determined by the addition of all additions and betterments, undepreciated but weighted, to the rate base. Depreciation was based upon a modified straight-line basis. Additions to reserve were permitted in amounts such as to make the total reserves not more than 20 per cent of the value plus additions. Interest was permitted at the rate of 4 per cent per year to accrue upon the reserve account, and it was provided that the amount of interest should lessen the amount of depreciation to be included as an operating expense. If the rates established for any year yielded the company a return of more than $7\frac{1}{2}$ per cent upon the value of the property, one-half of the excess above the $7\frac{1}{2}$ per cent was required to be used as a basis for the reduction of rates for the succeeding year. If the rates established yielded less than $7\frac{1}{2}$ per cent for any period of five consecutive years, or less than 7 per cent for any period of three consecutive years, or less than $6\frac{1}{2}$ per cent for any year, rates were to be increased to a level necessary to yield $7\frac{1}{2}$ per cent. Provision was made for the division of the funds impounded during the rate dispute between the consumers and the company.

The first agreement continued in effect from 1925 to 1931. During this period, the increase in the number of consumers and in the average per consumer consumption of electricity caused the rate of return consistently to exceed the agreed fair return of $7\frac{1}{2}$ per cent despite rate reductions in each of the six years 1926 to 1931, inclusive. The number of consumers increased steadily each year from 82,700 in 1925 to 145,600 in 1931. The average consumption per residential customer increased from 456 kw.-hr. in 1925 to 714 kw.-hr. in 1931, and average commercial-retail consumption increased from 4,494 kw.-hr. in 1925 to 6,936 kw.-hr. in 1931. The rate of return ranged from a low of 9.22 per cent in 1927 to a high of 10.70 per cent in 1930. Rates for residential consumers were reduced from 7 cents for the first 60 kw.-hr. in 1926 to 4.2 cents in 1931.

In 1930 an attempt was made by the District of Columbia Commission to reach an agreement with the company for revision of the agreement so as to reduce earnings, but, failing, the Commission, by order of June 8, 1931, modified the rate scale. The company sought an injunction in the Supreme Court of the

District of Columbia which was denied, the Court embodying in its decree a revised sliding scale of earnings. Appeal was taken to the District of Columbia Court of Appeals, but while the appeal was pending the Commission and the company reached an agreement, and the case was remanded to the Supreme Court of the District. This court sanctioned the new agreement in a consent decree, in 1933.[1]

Under the revised agreement the rate of return was reduced from 7½ to 7 per cent, and the excess earnings over 7 per cent were required to be used as a basis for reductions in rates for subsequent years, as follows: If the rate of return should be between 7 and 8¼ per cent, one-half of the excess was to be used as basis for reduction of rates for the following year; if the earnings should be over 8¼ per cent and less than 9 per cent, an additional three-fifths of the excess above 8¼ per cent were to be so used; if the rate of return should be over 9 per cent, a further additional three-fourths of the excess above 9 per cent was to be used as the basis for rate reductions. If earnings should fall below 6¾ per cent for any two consecutive years, or below 6½ per cent for any single year, the rates were to be increased to yield 7 per cent. Between 1932 and 1935, the rate of return declined from 8.81 per cent in the former year to 7.40 per cent in the latter. Reductions in rates were made in 1933, 1934, and 1935, although they were small.

In 1936 a further modification was made in the sliding scale by order of the Commission.[2] Under this order the rate of fair return was fixed at 6½ per cent with the following scale of excess earnings to be used as the basis of rate reductions for the following years:

Earnings	Amounts of Excess to Be Used for Rate Reductions
6½ to 7¾ per cent..	One-half of excess
7¾ to 8½ per cent..	Additional three-fifths of excess above 7¾ per cent
8½ per cent or over.	Additional three-fourths of excess above 8½ per cent

If the earnings fall below 6½ per cent for any two consecutive years, or below 6 per cent for any year, the rates are to be raised

---

[1] District of Columbia Public Utilities Commission, Order No. 919, June 8, 1931. Potomac Electric Power Co. v. Pub. Util. Comm., D.C. Equity No. 53475, July 27, and Nov. 16, 1931 (Supreme Court, District of Columbia). Potomac Electric Power Co. v. Pub. Util. Comm., D.C. (Supreme Court, District of Columbia, Feb. 7, 1933).

[2] Order No. 1476, Pub. Util. Comm., D.C., Feb. 5, 1936.

so as to yield 6½ per cent. Four results may fairly be said to have been achieved by the "Washington sliding scale" plan:

1. The Commission and the company have been spared the expense of a valuation.
2. The rates to consumers have been steadily and materially reduced.
3. Cooperation between the Public Utility Commission and the company has been promoted and encouraged.
4. The delays and expense of litigation have been minimized.

Although not entirely satisfactory to all parties at interest, the plan is an interesting and valuable contribution to valuation technique and to the improvement of relationships between utility companies and regulatory commissions.

Findings of the New York Commission on Revision of the Public Service Commissions Law.—The Commission appointed to study the whole question of public utility regulation in New York State, after careful consideration of the valuation cases decided by the United States Supreme Court, the findings of the New York State Public Service Commissions, and plans of valuation submitted by experts in this field, recommended a contract valuation plan based upon five principles:

1. Valuation of all public utility properties in the State, excepting only steam railroads and street railways, would be made by the Public Service Commissions according to the factors prescribed by the "law of the land." Steam railroads were omitted because of the jurisdiction of the Interstate Commerce Commission, and electric railways were excluded because these properties had experienced difficulty in earning a return even upon the book costs of the properties. In the valuation of other public utility properties, book costs, present day costs, and other factors of valuation prescribed by the law of the land were to be taken into account.

2. The Public Service Commissions would be authorized to enter into contracts with the utility companies, excepting steam railroads and electric railways, under which initial valuations made by the Public Service Commissions would be used as the rate bases for the existing properties of the contracting companies for specified periods up to 10 years. During the contract period the initial valuations, arrived at by appraisals made by the

Commissions with the aid and cooperation of the public utility companies, would remain unchanged excepting for provision for depreciation and obsolescence.

3. The initial contract valuation, determined as stated above, would be subject to modification by the addition of investments in the properties made during the period of the contracts. The investments permitted to be added were to be based upon the amounts actually expended by the companies and approved by the Public Service Commission. Rate regulation during the contract period would be exercised through accounting control. The new investments made subsequent to the beginning of the agreements, after having been approved as to nature and amount, controlled by accounting procedure, would be added to the amount of the initial or contract valuation with allowance duly made for depreciation and other approved reserves. In order to avoid the necessity of too frequent rate changes, a rate adjustment reserve would be provided to be set up by the utility companies.

4. At the end of the contract period, the valuation of the public utility property would be revised, and a new contract arranged between the company and the Public Service Commission. At the time when the new contracts would be made it was contemplated that the then existing properties of the companies would be reappraised in the same manner as used in the initial valuation. Consideration was to be given in the reappraisal to changes in the price level and to any modifications in the law of the land governing the factors to be considered as factors entering into valuation.

5. In cases where the public utility companies were unwilling to enter into valuation contracts, the Public Service Commission would be authorized to make initial valuations of the companies' properties and to keep these valuations revised according to accepted valuation and accounting methods.

The virtues of the "New York" plan of valuation are that it tends to achieve certainty and definiteness and to displace the vagueness and chaos in public utility valuation. A definite rate basis subject at all times to accounting control is provided upon which the rate of return may be applied.[1]

---

[1] "Report of the Commission on Revision of the Public Service Commissions Law," J. R. Lyon Co., Albany, 1930, vol. I, Part III, pp. 16–22.

The Bonbright Plan.—Another method of public utility valuation for rate-making purposes was recommended to the New York Commission on Revision of the Public Service Commissions Law by Dr. James C. Bonbright, of Columbia University, a member of the Commission. Dr. Bonbright proposed that the rate base should be determined for all utilities excepting steam and electric railway properties by a legislative mandate requiring the valuation of existing public utility properties and subsequent investments in public utility property according to the following methods of procedure: Initial valuations would be made of all properties as of the date of the adoption of the Act. These valuations were to take into account every element properly considered under the law of the land, including actual cost, reproduction cost, general expenditures, depreciation, going value, and any other relevant factors, and when once determined would remain unchanged in the future without regard to price fluctuations, costs of construction, or other conditions. With respect to the valuation of subsequent investments it was proposed that the amounts of the reasonable and actual cost of the new properties acquired should be entered into the accounts of the companies and added to the initial valuations, determined as described above. By this method the Public Service Commission would have always available through accounting control the actual rate base. Provision was made for maintenance, depreciation, and the retirement of any unit of property.

Summary.—In concluding this discussion of the valuation problems that have confronted, and still confront, regulatory commissions, public utility enterprises, and the courts, a few conclusions may be hazarded in spite of the welter of conflicting opinions. The conclusion seems to be justified that, because of the futility of attempting to find "present value," as interpreted by the Supreme Court, every time that rates are at issue, agreed or contract bases of valuation, arrived at by agreement between the regulatory commissions and the companies, are practical solutions of the problem. Such procedure results in rate bases that are fixed and can readily be brought down to date through accounting control, thus avoiding the wasteful and time-consuming process of duplicating the work done in the original valuations. Over against the argument that contract valuations are likely to be favorable to the utilities, which is based upon the premise that otherwise the utilities would fare better in the courts, it may be asserted that the consumers are probably better off where such contracts are made than under the prevailing costly and ineffective methods of rate regulation. Furthermore, as time goes on and the properties change and grow, contract valuations tend more and more nearly to represent actual prudent investment.

At the present writing, the prudent investment principle of valuation seems destined to become the accepted rule. As we have pointed out, this principle has long been popular with regulatory commissions, both state and federal, and it is now receiving much public attention. President Franklin D. Roosevelt has thrown the weight of his influence back of the prudent investment principle, and a prominent spokesman for the utilities, Mr. Wendell L. Willkie, president of the Commonwealth and Southern Corporation, has publicly stated the willingness of utility executives to accept it, if given assurance that the federal power policy is not designed to destroy the private power industry. This issue also came before the Supreme Court of the United States in a case involving an order of the California Railroad Commission requiring the Pacific Gas and Electric Company to reduce its gas rates. The enforcement of this order, issued in 1933, was stopped by a federal district court on the ground that proper evidence of the cost of reproduction had not been considered, and the lower court was upheld by a 4 to 4 decision of the Supreme Court of the United States, Mr. Justice Sutherland not participating. Recently, the Court, in reconsidering its action, remanded the case to the lower court for findings as to confiscation. It is to be hoped that the Supreme Court will uphold the prudent investment principle and will set aside the concept of "present value" which for nearly 40 years has done much to render rate regulation ineffective. Prudent investment is a fixed, nonfluctuating rate base, fair to all parties concerned. It can readily be ascertained and can be kept current merely through accounting procedure. Adjustments because of changes in price levels can be made, as they should be, in the rate of return.

References

BAUER, J.: "Effective Regulation of Public Utilities," The Macmillan Company, New York, 1925.

BONBRIGHT, J. C.: "Public Utility Valuation," McGraw-Hill Book Company, Inc., 1937.

COOKE, M. L.: "Public Utility Regulation," Ronald Press Company, New York, 1924.

FLOY, H.: "Value for Rate-making," McGraw-Hill Book Company, Inc., New York, 1916.

GLAESER, M. G.: "Outlines of Public Utility Economics," The Macmillan Company, New York, 1931, Chaps. XIV, XV, XVI, XX, XXI, and XXII.

GRAHAM, W. J.: "Public Utility Valuation," University of Chicago Press, Chicago, 1934.

GRAY, J. H., and J. LEVIN: "The Valuation and Regulation of Public Utilities," Harper & Brothers, New York, 1933.

GRUNSKY, C. E., and C. E. GRUNSKY, JR.: "Valuation, Depreciation and the Rate Base," John Wiley & Sons, Inc., New York, 1927.

HARTMAN, H. H.: "Fair Value," Houghton Mifflin Company, Boston, 1920.

HAYES, H. V.: "Public Utilities: Fair Present Value and Return," D. Van Nostrand Company, Inc., New York, 1915.

JONES, ELIOT, and T. C. BIGHAM: "Principles of Public Utilities," The Macmillan Company, New York, 1913, Chap. V.

MOSHER, W. E., and F. G. CRAWFORD: "Public Utility Regulation," Harper & Brothers, New York, 1933, Chaps. XIII, XIV, and XV.

NASH, L. R.: "Public Utility Rate Structures," McGraw-Hill Book Company, Inc., New York, 1933, Chaps. XII and XIII.

———: "Economics of Public Utilities," 2d ed., McGraw-Hill Book Company, Inc., New York, 1931, Chap. VII.

PATRICK, M. M.: How the Sliding Scale Basis of Rate Making Works, *Public Utilities Fortnightly*, vol. 11, No. 9, pp. 506–514.

POND, O. L.: "The Law of Public Utilities," Bobbs-Merrill Company, Indianapolis, 1913, Chap. XXIV.

RAYMOND, W. G.: "The Public and Its Utilities," John Wiley & Sons, Inc., New York, 1925, Chap. XXI.

"Report of the New York Commission on Revision of the Public Service Commissions Law," Albany, 1930, vols. I, II, III, and IV.

RUGGLES, C. O.: "Problems in Public Utility Management," McGraw-Hill Book Company, Inc., New York, 1933, Sec. VI.

ULM, A. H.: A Unique Experiment in Rate Regulation, *Public Utilities Fortnightly*, vol. 6, No. 11, pp. 656–662.

WELCH, F. X.: The Fall of a Short-cut Valuation Method, *Public Utilities Fortnightly*, vol. 16, No. 5, pp. 253–259.

——— and collaborators: "Cases on Public Utility Regulation," Public Utility Reports, Inc., Washington, 1936, Part V.

WHITTEN, R. H., and D. F. WILCOX: "Valuation of Public Service Corporations," 2d ed., Banks Law Publishing Co., New York, 1928, 2 vols.

WU, S. T.: "Railroad Valuation and Fair Return," University of Pennsylvania Press, Philadelphia, 1930.

WYMAN, BRUCE: "Public Service Corporations," Baker, Vorhees and Co., New York, 1921, 2 vols.

CHAPTER VII

FAIR RETURN

Fair return, as the term is used in public utility economics and regulation, is the amount that a utility is entitled to earn upon its property after all reasonable operating expenses, including annual depreciation expense, have been met. The sum or amount of revenue permitted to be earned over and above operating expenses is a return upon the capital employed as a reward or compensation for the employment of the capital. Interest upon bonded or funded indebtedness is not considered as an operating expense, so that the fair return should be sufficient to pay interest charges upon funded debt as well as to yield an amount sufficient to pay reasonable dividends upon the capital invested in the enterprise in the form of unfunded debt and capital stock.

The elements or component parts of fair return are (1) pure interest upon capital employed, (2) a premium or compensation for the risk to which capital is exposed by investment in the enterprise, and (3) a reward for the management of the property to the extent that such reward or compensation is considered to be due those who have invested funds in the property.

Fair value, or valuation, and fair return, or the rate of return, are entirely separate and distinct terms, but they are closely related. The purpose of valuation or the determination of a fair value is to arrive at a sum in relation to which the utility company is to be permitted to fix reasonable rates which will yield reasonable operating expenses and a fair return or yield annually upon the value of the property used in public service. Thus, fair return is based upon the value of the property used in public service and not upon the capitalization or outstanding securities of the companies. Obviously it does not correspond to corporate interest payments or to dividend payments. If the outstanding securities equal the valuation of the property used in the service of the public, the rate of return will tend to equal the rate of payment by the corporation for capital in dividends and interest charges, with due account being given to surplus and reserves.

Some writers upon public utility economics, including Prof. Glaeser, have likened fair return or the rate of return to wages of capital.[1] As such, the rate of return includes the interest or dividend rate necessary to attract the funds of investors to the enterprise, compensation for the risks involved in investment in the industry, the cost of obtaining capital funds, and provision for reserves and surplus.

The difference between the rate of return and the distribution of the earnings of a public utility corporation among various classes of bondholders, preferred stockholders, and common stockholders can best be shown by a simple example of a public utility company valued for rate-making purposes at $50,000,000. If it is assumed that the fair return allowed the company is 7 per cent, the earnings based upon this rate of return will be $3,500,000 per year. Let us assume that this company has outstanding $50,000,000, par value of securities divided among the following classes in the following proportions:

Mortgage bonds: $20,000,000, par value; paying 4 per cent
    interest; annual interest charges............................$800,000
Income bonds; $10,000,000, par value; paying 5 per cent interest;
    annual interest charges...................................$500,000
Preferred stock: $10,000,000, par value; paying 6 per cent dividend
    rate; annual dividends....................................$600,000
Common stock: $10,000,000, par value

The interest charges upon the $20,000,000 of mortgage bonds, and $10,000,000 of income bonds, aggregate $1,300,000 leaving $2,200,000 available for dividends for the preferred and common stockholders. If the preferred stock dividend rate is 6 per cent, the dividend payments to this class of security owners will require an additional $600,000, leaving $1,600,000 to be distributed as earnings among the holders of the $10,000,000 of common stock, or a yield of 16 per cent. Of course, not all of this amount should be distributed annually in the form of dividends since part should be set aside as surplus.

In this illustration it is clearly seen that the use by a utility company of borrowed capital upon which interest is paid, as

[1] GLAESER, M. G., "Outlines of Public Utility Economics," The Macmillan Company, New York, 1931, p. 408.

well as ownership capital upon which dividends are paid if earned, results in high earnings on common stocks in periods of relatively good earnings, provided the amount of securities outstanding is approximately equal to the valuation, or rate base, and provided the interest rate upon the bonds is relatively low. For this reason public utility corporations in times of low money rates endeavor to refinance the funded debt so as to reduce interest rates, or fixed charges, and thus to increase the amount of earnings available for dividends upon common stocks. However, one of the unfavorable aspects of public utility enterprise in times of depression, or of adverse conditions within or without the industry, is the inability of the utility companies at such times to refinance their outstanding bonds at lower interest rates because of the uncertainty as to the future of many public utility enterprises. Fear of the possibility of public ownership and operation, and of the adverse effects of possible restrictive regulation, are also obstacles to the free investment of capital in utility industries at favorable rates in times when such uncertainties are felt to exist.

STATUTORY BASES OF FAIR RETURN

The principle of allowing public utility companies to earn a fair rate of return upon a fair valuation of the properties devoted to public use, as well as the converse of the idea, that of preventing a rate of return in excess of a fair return, is by no means a recent idea in public utility regulation. In the "Granger laws" and other state laws enacted during the period between the close of the Civil War and the opening of the twentieth century, state statutes attempted to limit the earnings of public utilities usually through maximum rate or maximum fare laws. In *ex parte Young,* however, the United States Supreme Court held that although the determination of whether or not a railway rate prescribed by a state statute was so low as to be confiscatory was a question of fact, the solution of the problem raised a federal question under the Constitution in which the sufficiency of the rates became a judicial question over which the federal courts had jurisdiction.[1]

In *Smyth v. Ames,* 10 years before, the Supreme Court had held that the adequacy or inadequacy of a remedy at law for

[1] *Ex parte* Young, 209 U.S. 123 (1908).

the protection of rights of one entitled to invoke the powers of a federal court is not to be conclusively determined by statutes of the particular state in which suit may be brought, but the party entitled to sue in the federal court may invoke its jurisdiction in equity whenever the established principles and rules of equity permit. Such parties may not be deprived of right to sue in the federal courts because the right also exists to sue in a state court on the same course of action.[1] It may be said with respect to statutory rates of return, therefore, that while their use is not contrary to the Constitution of the United States, they cannot have the effect of barring the rights of those affected by their use to appeal to the courts for adjudication of the legal results of their use or of confiscating the properties of the utility companies without due process of law.

One of the foremost instances of the use of a statutory rate of fair return is found in the provisions of the Interstate Commerce Act, added to the Act by the Transportation Act of 1920.[2] This rule of rate making and recapture was added in the hope that the provisions would be of substantial assistance in building up an effective system of railroad transportation. Congress directed the Interstate Commerce Commission, in exercising its power to prescribe just and reasonable rates, to adjust rates of the carriers as a whole, or as a whole in rate groups or territories designated from time to time by the Commission, which would earn, as nearly as may be, a fair return upon the property of the carriers used in transportation service. In adjusting rates to earn a fair return, the Commission was directed to initiate or adjust rates that would earn a fair return in net railway-operating income upon the fair value of the property under "honest, efficient and economical management" and with reasonable expenditures for maintenance of way, structures and equipment. For the first two years, the Act set the fair return at $5\frac{1}{2}$ per cent of the fair value with the provision that the Commission might, in its discretion, add not over one-half of 1 per cent for improvements, betterments, or equipment chargeable to capital account.

After the expiration of the period of two years stipulated in the Act the Commission was directed to determine and publish

[1] Smyth v. Ames, 169 U.S. 466 (1898).

[2] Interstate Commerce Act, Section 15A, added by Transportation Act, 1920 (41 Stat. La. 488).

a uniform fair rate of return.   In fixing the fair return the Commission was directed to give "due consideration among other things" to: (1) the transportation needs of the country; and (2) the necessity, under honest, efficient, and economical management of existing transportation facilities, of enlarging the facilities in order to provide the people of the United States with adequate transportation.

In exercising its discretionary power, the Commission, in 1922, fixed $5\frac{3}{4}$ per cent as a uniform rate of return for all rate groups or territories, giving as a reason for the increase that courts and state regulatory bodies had recognized that public utilities, including railroads, may be permitted individually to earn 6 per cent, or more, upon the fair value of their properties. In this case the Commission was dealing with the aggregate of the properties of a number of railroads and not with the return upon any one railroad.   The Commission felt bound to interpret the Act as the expression of the intent of Congress to create a steady and reliable flow of money for maintaining adequate transportation, which might be disturbed if a substantial reduction were made in the rate of return.   "The fact that a utility may reach financial success only in time, or not at all, is a reason for allowing a liberal return on the money invested in the enterprise," the Commission said.[1]

Recapture of Excess Earnings.—The rule of rate making of the Interstate Commerce Act provided that any individual carrier that received net railway operating income for any year in excess of 6 per cent of the value of its property, as determined by the valuation provisions of the Interstate Commerce Act, should place one-half of the excess of income in a reserve fund of its own and that the other half should be paid to the Interstate Commerce Commission to be placed in a general railroad revolving contingent fund administered by the Commission either by making loans to carriers to make expenditures for capital account, such as for the purchase of new equipment, or to refund their maturing securities, or by purchasing equipment or facilities and leasing them to the carriers.   Loans to railroads from the contingent fund were to be made by the Commission upon application by the carriers and upon approval by the Commission upon a showing by the carriers that they were financially able to repay

[1] Reduced Rates, 68 I.C.C. 676 (1922).

the loans and that the purpose of the loans was to enable the applicant carriers better to meet the transportation needs of the public. The Act required the carriers who borrowed from the railroad contingent fund to pay 6 per cent interest upon the loans, the interest payments and payments of the principal to be placed in the contingent fund so as to keep it replenished. In like manner, the rentals upon equipment bought with the proceeds of the fund and leased by the carriers from the Commission, and the proceeds from the sale of equipment, were directed by the Act to be placed in the contingent fund.

A carrier was permitted and directed to retain the other half of any amounts earned in excess of a fair return to be placed in a reserve fund for the payment of interest or dividends upon its securities, or for rentals for leased property, until the reserve fund should amount to 5 per cent of the value of the railroad's property as determined under the valuation provisions of the Interstate Commerce Act. After the carrier's reserve fund had reached that amount the carrier was authorized to use its share of excess income for any lawful purpose.[1] Carriers were authorized to retain any part or all of the excess earnings upon any new lines for a period not exceeding 10 years upon approval of applications for such authority by the Interstate Commerce Commission.[2]

The principles of fixing rates to yield a predetermined rate of return, and the recapture of part of the excess earnings beyond a fair return, embodied in the Transportation Act of 1920, as interpreted and applied by the Interstate Commerce Commission, involved the following significant features:

1. The recognition of the responsibility of public regulatory authority to fix rates for railroad transportation carriers as a whole or by groups so as to afford an opportunity to earn a fair return upon the valuation of the properties.

2. The ignoring of individual carrier requirements in the first instance by fixing rates for the carriers as a whole or by groups.

3. The recognition of valuation of the carriers' properties by public authority as the base upon which earnings were to be computed.

4. The fixing of a temporary fair return by statute, and the statutory mandate given the Interstate Commerce Commission

[1] Interstate Commerce Act, Section 15A, Paragraphs (5) to (16), inclusive.
[2] *Ibid.*, Section 15A, Paragraph (18).

to assume the responsibility for determining fair return for the future.

5. The assertion of the right of public authority to fix rates designed to yield a fair return to carriers as a whole or by groups and to compel carriers earning in excess of the fair return to return part of the excess to the government.

6. The assertion of the right of government to direct carriers in the disposal of their respective shares of earnings in excess of the fair return.

7. The assertion by the government of the power to use part of the earnings in excess of the fair return earned by certain carriers as funds to be used in making loans to carriers in less favorable financial circumstances or to use the funds to purchase equipment to be leased to such carriers.

The United States Supreme Court upheld the constitutionality of the recapture clause of the rule of rate making,[1] but the efforts of the carriers to have the obnoxious recapture clause repealed by Congress did not end with this decision. Meanwhile the desperate financial plight of a number of railroads during depression years added new force to the opposition to recapture, and the rule of rate making and the recapture clause, which had been woven into the Interstate Commerce Act by the Transportation Act of 1920, were repealed by the Emergency Railroad Transportation Act of 1933. The rule of rate making and the provisions with respect to a fair return in terms of a percentage return upon the fair valuation of the railroads' properties were stricken from the Act. The Interstate Commerce Commission was directed in prescribing just and reasonable rates to consider three factors, among other unnamed ones: (1) the effect of rates upon the movement of traffic; (2) the need of adequate and efficient railroad transportation service at the lowest rates consistent with supplying the service in the public interest; and (3) the need of revenues sufficient to enable the carriers to provide such service under honest, efficient, and economical management.[2]

Thus, the recapture of excess earnings by the government from carriers earning more than a fair return was completely abolished, and the provision of the Act with respect to the

[1] Dayton and Goose Creek R. R. Co. v. United States, 263 U.S. 456.

[2] Emergency Railroad Transportation Act, 1933, Section 205, amending Interstate Commerce Act, Part I, Section 15A, Paragraphs (1) and (2).

recovery of the excess earnings from the carriers was terminated. The general railway contingent revolving fund was liquidated, and the funds on hand were distributed among the carriers in proportion to the amounts each carrier had paid into the fund. The taxes of the carriers were directed to be computed as though the recapture clause had never been in existence.[1] The termination of this statutory basis of determining a fair return upon fair value placed upon the Interstate Commerce Commission the responsibility of making rates for interstate carriers so as to yield revenues sufficient to provide adequate and efficient railroad transportation service under honest, efficient, and economical management, without benefit, or limitation, of a statutory measuring rod to determine a fair rate of return.

PROCEDURE IN FIXING RATE OF RETURN IN ABSENCE OF STATUTORY RATE

Where there is no statutory basis of return the state regulatory commissions must proceed to fix the rate of return to be earned by utility companies by consideration of the economic problems to be discussed later, including an examination of the elements to be considered in the fair return. Generally, the determination of the rate of return is left by the regulatory statutes to the discretion of the state commissions subject to court review.

Elements to Be Considered in Fixing a Fair Return.—Much of the confusion that is to be found in economic treatises upon the subject of fair return and in discussions of the subject in legal treatises and in court decisions is due to the tendency to consider fair return as a constant rather than as a variable. The conclusion appears justified that fair return varies from time to time, from one type of public utility industry to another and among individual public utilities of the same type. If we accept the definition that a fair rate of return is the rate required to attract the amount of investors' funds needed for the development of a given public utility industry, under honest accounting and competent and responsible management,[2] it follows that the amount must be a variable sum.

[1] *Op. cit.*, Section 206, amending Section 15A, Paragraph (6) of the Interstate Commerce Act, Part I.

[2] JONES, ELIOT, and T. C. BIGHAM, "Principles of Public Utilities," The Macmillan Company, New York, Chap. VI, p. 253.

Considering only the element of time, experience has adequately demonstrated that within a single type of utility, and even in the history of one utility company, the amount of return upon invested capital required to insure a free flow of capital to the industry or company depends upon the earnings at different times of other industries; and upon the risks of the enterprise, which vary from time to time. Changing price levels, changes in the interest rate paid by financial institutions upon savings accounts, and changes in the financial condition and management of the companies are factors that enter into the consideration of the rate of return to be allowed in comparison with the rates allowed in other industries.

As among groups of utilities, changes in the rate of return must be made from one group to another, as changes occur in the attitude of the public toward different groups of utilities; as technological changes occur which add to or detract from the apparent prospects of different groups of utilities; as changes occur in the risk to which money invested in one group of utilities is subjected in comparison with funds invested in another group of utilities; and according to the financial records of different groups of utilities.

Within single types of public utility enterprises the same rate of return will not always attract adequate supplies of capital to particular utility companies at a particular time because of differences among utilities of the same type with respect to their reputations for honesty and efficiency of management; their respective records of losses or surplus earnings from past operations; their relationships with management, holding, or subsidiary operating companies; the simplicity or complexity of their financial structures; and their respective records of public relations. For these reasons it is not wise to determine a fair rate of return mathematically identical for all public utility industries of all types and for all times. On the other hand, it is not practicable to allow the rate of return to be fixed at any given time for any particular public utility within a group of public utility enterprises without definite criteria by which to judge what rate is fair.

The fair rate of return for any given public utility at any given time must be determined by giving adequate consideration to all of the following elements together with the application of impartial judgment to each of these elements viewed in the light of relative conditions as among groups of utilities and for utilities within each group. These factors, which are pertinent in so far as they affect the rate of return allowed a utility enterprise in comparison with the rate of return earned by other industries with which the utility company'competes for funds, are:

1. The earnings of comparable or related industries.
2. The prevailing rate of interest.
3. The price levels prevailing at any given time as measured by price indexes.
4. The risk entailed in investment in the industry.
5. Technological standards and probable effects of technological changes upon the industry.
6. The effects of taxation upon earnings of the industry.
7. The record of the industry with respect to profitable or unprofitable operation as reflected in the accumulation of surplus or deficit.
8. The record of honesty, efficiency, and progressiveness of management.
9. The amount deemed necessary to supply an incentive to efficiency and economy in management.
10. The fear of adverse or restrictive regulatory policies and attitudes.
11. The size of the utility enterprise, small local utilities often being required to pay more for the use of capital than companies that because of their size have access to national or even international money markets.

The Rate of Return and Investors and Consumers.—Investors in public utilities should receive approximately the same rate of return as investors in comparable unregulated enterprises. This rate of return must be high enough to give the investor a fair return and the consumers good service but low enough to give the consumers reasonable rates. If the rates are too high it may result in a marked curtailment of use, for the demand for public utility services and commodities is not absolutely inelastic. Moreover, since a high rate of return facilitates the sale of securities, with overexpansion resulting, fixed charges are increased, and, in depression years, the rates must necessarily be raised to meet these fixed charges, with a further curtailment of use as the consequence. On the other hand, if the rate of return is too low, the utility will probably cut down on the quality of its service by trying to save on maintenance and other operating expenses. Capital will not be invested in the enterprise, and the industry will not grow along with the community that it serves. Thus it is very important to both the utility and the consumer that the rate be fixed accurately. As stated by one writer on public utility problems

. . . the earnings of the public service property should be such that, within the life of the property, there will be returned to the owner of the property the capital which he has properly invested in it, and, in addition thereto, interest at a reasonable rate upon such amount of capital as from time to time actually and properly remains as an investment in the property.[1]

A further point is that since procedure for estimating the required earnings of public utilities, which may be correct if consistently and continuously applied, may be unfair to either the owner or the rate payer if introduced at a later period, it should be regarded as imperative that consideration be given to past history when the rates of an operating concern are to be fixed. Such consideration, however, is best given in fixing the original rate base.

Mosher and Crawford have suggested that adequate administration of the rate of return should aim at six things:

1. Stabilizing profits to eliminate speculation from the conduct of utilities.

2. Enabling utilities to compete in the money market for funds at low rates for the expansion and progressive development of their services.

3. Reducing the element of risk.

4. Providing an adequate reserve or surplus for contingencies and for the reward of capital in lean years.

5. Promoting efficient and economical management and penalizing extravagance, poor planning, and unprogressive management.

[1] GRUNSKY, C. E., "Valuation, Depreciation and the Rate Base," John Wiley & Sons, Inc., New York, 1917.

6. Providing good service to the public at the least possible cost consistent with the foregoing.[1]

The stabilization of profits and speculation are mutually exclusive. At present, though, stabilization is difficult because of the lack of a workable basis for determining base values; the organization of vast holding companies; the lack of control, in some states, over security issues and the subsequent "writing up" of properties; the absence of interstate regulation; and the failure to place checks upon the rate of return, thus permitting the accumulation and capitalization of huge surpluses.

Favorable competition for investors' funds must be made possible if expansion is to continue parallel to the growth of communities served. This involves comparisons between the earnings of utilities and other companies in the same locality and comparison between the utilities and companies elsewhere as well as in the same locality where access is had to national or international money markets. It has been maintained by some that the net earnings of a public utility should in some measure exceed the return from ordinary safe investments.[2] Judging from the returns allowed in the past, that seems to be the general attitude, although there are some who maintain that it should be lower. Professor Sumner Slichter reaches the conclusion that the rate of return should be lower because of three things: in the first place, supervision of accounts and finances reduces the risk to investors by making it more difficult for insiders to exploit the corporation; in the second place, the risks of competition are either removed or much reduced; in the third place, the sales of some types of public utilities, such as electric power and light companies, decline less in times of depression than do those of many other businesses.[3]

The risk factor must be taken into consideration in fixing the rate of return, and an alert regulatory body will do everything in its power to cut down the occurrence of possible risks. Risks vary in different localities and in different companies, and the

[1] MOSHER, W. E., and F. G. CRAWFORD, "Public Utility Regulation," Harper & Brothers, New York, 1933, p. 228.

[2] GRUNSKY, C. E., and C. E. GRUNSKY, JR., "Valuation, Depreciation, and the Rate Base," John Wiley & Sons, Inc., New York, 1927.

[3] SLICHTER, SUMNER, "Modern Economic Society," Henry Holt & Company, New York, 1931, pp. 419–420.

rate of return for each locality or company should reflect this variation.

The building up of reserves for known and unforeseen contingencies, and to produce a regular flow of dividends, should be permitted in the rate of return. Adequate provision should be made in operating expenses for the depreciation of plant and equipment, since it is manifestly equitable that the investor is entitled either to have his capital returned to him or to have his equity maintained.

Many writers upon public utility economics and law have expressed the conviction that efficient management should be rewarded and that adequate and constructive public utility regulation should stimulate management through reprimands and possibly penalties on the one hand and rewards on the other. Others hold only that inefficient managements should be penalized. For the purpose of rewarding efficient management the rate of return is a useful device, but its administration requires the setting up of standards of service and efficiency and the fixing of a rate of return that a utility will receive from a certain rate if those standards are met. This requires the measuring of the quality of service as well as the cost, for it is not advantageous to lower cost and sacrifice quality. Quality and costs have been measured, with more or less success, in several states including Wisconsin, Massachusetts, and Illinois. This is done by naming the several factors, grading each, and then getting a composite grade. Suggested factors are (1) lowness of rates, (2) continuity of service, (3) security of service or reserve services available, (4) excellence of public relations, and (5) adequacy of employees and their compensation. A company, then, that just meets the standards will receive the standard return; one that more than meets them will receive a higher return; and one that fails to meet them will not be allowed to charge rates sufficiently high to produce the standard return. The reward should be earmarked and divided between management and stockholders. However, since it is primarily a reward for efficient management, it should go mostly to the former.

In administering the foregoing factors it must always be remembered that rates cannot be higher than the value of the service nor so high as to produce marked curtailment in the use of the service. In the pioneer stages of the development of many utilities the number of rate payers will be small, and it is advisable to have the utility operate at a loss, for rates that would cover the cost of service would undoubtedly be higher than the value of the service. If this loss is included in the rate base, the burden is shifted to later consumers from the investors or consumers in the early stages of the development of the properties.

Varying the rate of return according to an index number so as to keep it constant in purchasing power is necessary with a fixed rate base. This, we believe, is the only practical way of reflecting changes in the price level. The problem of finding a suitable index number is then much simplified. It, in itself, makes the administration of the rate of return a more precise process and eliminates speculation. In addition, it is much more easily administered than an adjustment in the rate base. A further advantage of applying an index number to the rate of return rather than to the rate base is a psychological one. Investors would object less to receiving a lower return in dollars during depression years if the rate-base value were kept up than they would to receiving the lower return at the same time the publicly fixed value of the property was reduced. Since any change in the rate of return, provided it is still high enough to earn fixed charges, affects only common stockholders, it becomes a relatively simple matter to regulate the rate of return so that the common stockholders receive a more nearly constant return in purchasing power. It should be borne in mind, however, that if the rate of return is increased beyond what is popularly believed to be adequate there is apt to be strong popular reaction against it.

It has been suggested that common stock, in the future, be given a definite return and that equalization reserves be set up in order to make this possible. Mosher and Crawford, however, point out that in times of severe depression these equalization reserves might be wiped out, which would be serious if the dividend had been guaranteed as suggested.[1] This difficulty may be avoided, it is claimed, by giving bond-holders and preferred stockholders a fixed return in purchasing power for the future, using a definite index number. This would allow the total return to be adjusted according to an

[1] MOSHER and CRAWFORD, *op. cit.*, pp. 242–243.

index number and do much to eliminate speculation. It would also allow rates to be lowered in times of depression and raised in times of active business prosperity and high price levels.

The Rate of Return as an Incentive.—Various plans have been devised under which the rate of return is made flexible so that, as the operation of the property is made more efficient and more economical, progressive increases are allowed in the rate of return. Plans of this sort require that standards of service and rates be regulated as well as the rate of return. A standard or a set of standards are set up insuring the consumers high quality of service. Rates are allowed for service at several different standards of service, and a series of rates of return are provided so as to permit the utility company successively higher rates of return as higher quality of service is rendered and rates per unit of service are decreased. A simple example will suffice to illustrate the operation of plans of this sort. An electric light and power utility valued at $100,000,000 is allowed rates that will yield a rate of return of 5 per cent upon the valuation of $100,000,000, or $5,000,000 per year, provided electric service is afforded within certain prescribed areas with a small percentage of interruption of service, at rates scaled upon a domestic consumption rate of 7 cents per kilowatt-hour for the first block. As service is provided by the utility over wider areas and with higher standards of service, at base rates starting with $6\frac{1}{2}$ cents per kilowatt-hour, an increase of $\frac{1}{4}$ per cent is allowed in the rate of return. The higher the standard of service and the lower the rate, the higher the rate of return allowed.

The Report of the Commission on Revision of the Public Service Commissions Law of the State of New York is constructive and suggestive in this connection. This Commission recommended:

First, that in the case of a contract, a rate of return on the initial valuation should be agreed upon by the Public Service Commission and the companies concerned;

Second, that for future investments the rate of return should be fixed for bonds and preferred stocks at the market price received from the purchaser and that for common stocks the Public Service Commission and the companies should agree upon a reasonable rate of return necessary to attract new capital, with proper allowance for amortization of discount and premiums; and

Third, that the Commission should use this method as far as possible as a guide for determining rates of return for companies that do not enter into a contract.[1]

The Commission found that there had been a preponderant tendency to permit an 8 per cent return, despite various circumstances surrounding each utility. It was conceded, also, that 8 per cent return was a settled policy or guiding principle with the New York Public Service Commissions, apparently acceptable both to utility managements and to the public.

Under the contract plan, it was recommended that an agreed rate of return should be earned on the total initial valuation, taking into account the cost of securing capital by the company in recent periods, the financial status of the company, and other pertinent factors. Provision should be made that, with the retirement of any indebtedness, bonds or stocks, the amount of return would be diminished by the amount of reduction in the fixed-charge or dividend requirements resulting from such retirement. With regard to additional investments, made following the initial valuations, the rate on each addition would be fixed by the Public Service Commissions in accordance with actual and reasonable cost of capital of the company, whether in the form of notes, bonds, or preferred stocks, proper allowance being made for amortization of discounts and premiums. In regard to the additions paid for through the issuance of common stock or out of earnings distributable as interest or dividends, an agreed rate of return fixed in the contract would be applied to the total amount of such equity investment. It was assumed by the investigating commission that such a rate would not exceed 8 per cent.

One of the features of the Commission's proposal was the recommendation that the Public Service Commissions consider ways and means of stimulating more efficient management, through the valuation and research staff, (1) by developing standard measurements of efficiency and (2) by devising a scheme of rewards and penalties. The investigating commission expressed fear that in the case of the adoption of a more rigid scheme of regulations there would be the danger of the companies' showing less initiative in introducing economies and more efficient

[1] "Report of the New York Commission on Revision of the Public Service Commissions Law," vol. I, p. 22.

methods of organization and administration and that this danger would increase as regulation became more effective. Therefore, it was recommended that it would be very desirable to consider means by which the management of the utility companies might be stimulated to constantly improve operating and managerial practices. Although not a matter for legislation, the investigating commission recommended that the Public Service Commission, through its research division, should consider the possibilities of improving utility management by offering rewards for maintenance and improvement of standards of operation, something that would necessitate the development of measurements of efficiency. No such measurements had been worked out and tested in actual experience, but it was believed by the investigating commission that this is a proper function of regulation and that criteria of efficiency might successfully be devised. The most feasible method of rewarding efficiency recommended by the investigating commission was the provision for variation in the rate of return upward where standards higher than the established standards were maintained and downward in case a given utility company should fall below what was recognized as a normal standard.[1]

In the course of the hearings, Prof. Livingston, of Columbia University, suggested the following five criteria to be used:

1. Lowness of rates.
2. Continuity of service.
3. Security of service.
4. Excellence of public relations.
5. Qualifications and training of employees, and reasonableness of wages of employees.[2]

The investigating commission did not adopt this suggestion in its recommendation. Instead, it expressed the opinion that much further study would be required before any set of criteria of this character could be standardized and applied with reasonable precision, with fairness to all concerned, and before an effective plan of apportioning the benefits of efficiency between

[1] "Report of the New York Commission on Revision of the Public Service Commissions Law," vol. 1, pp. 24–25.
[2] *Ibid.*, p. 108.

the stockholders, the consumers, and management could be devised. The investigating commission expressed its belief, however, that as regulation becomes more effective and as earnings are more stringently limited to a fair return, the problem of incentives tends to become increasingly important.

Before leaving this question of rewards for efficiency in the form of an increase in the rate of return, it should be repeated that those who disapprove of this method of rewarding efficiency urge that efficiency can be encouraged by excluding unreasonable operating expenses in the process of fixing rates. They hold that there is a practical difficulty in allowing utilities of the same type, different rates of return depending upon the relative efficiency or inefficiency of the management.

The Courts and the Rate of Return.—It has been suggested in several connections that the rate of return is a question of fact subject to review by the courts and not a matter to be determined by the use of any mathematical, economic, engineering, or legal formulae. It is appropriate, therefore, to review briefly some of the leading decisions in cases where the question of confiscation has come before the courts for adjudication. In order to determine whether or not the rates allowed the utilities produce earnings that yield a rate of return upon the value of the properties so low as to be confiscatory, the courts must consider not only legal problems but the basic economic facts considered by administrative bodies charged with this responsibility. The decisions and orders of public utilities regulatory commissions involving as they should these economic problems must be reviewed by the courts to protect the owners from confiscatory rates of return and consumers and the public from unduly high rates and exploitation.

In *United Rys. v. West,* the Supreme Court stated:

What will constitute a fair return in a given case is not capable of exact mathematical demonstration. It is a matter more or less of approximation about which conclusions may differ. The court in the discharge of its constitutional duty on the issue of confiscation must determine the amount to the best of its ability in the exercise of a fair, enlightened and independent judgment as to both law and facts.[1]

[1] 280 U.S. 234 (1929); see also Ohio Valley Water Co. v. Ben Avon Borough, 253 U.S. 287 (1919); Bluefield Co. v. Pub. Service Comm., W. Va.,

What compensation is reasonable in a given case is a question of fact to be determined in the light of the evidence in each particular case. No court of last resort has undertaken to say what percentage on the value such an investment should yield its owners in all cases. The courts have found it difficult to define the terms "reasonable" and "rate" with any exactness. Thus, Mr. Justice Steers, in *Lenaswee County Gas and Electric Co. v. Adrian,* remarked: "Both 'reasonable' and 'rate,' while words of frequent use, are relative terms of such varied and shaded meaning, not only in the abstract, but often in the particular connections used, as to be difficult of exact definition and afford a broad field for controversy."[1]

The question of the maximum return a utility is entitled to earn for its services as a general principle also has not been judicially defined. Federal and state tribunals have been reluctant to announce even a range of percentages of return upon property accepted as constituting fair return. On at least one occasion the United States Supreme Court refused to state that a return of 6 per cent upon valuation was so low as to deprive the utility owner of his property without due process of law,[2] although in a subsequent opinion the same tribunal stated that "a reasonable rate of return is not less than seven per cent."[3] The upper limit of reasonable return, the point at which the public can successfully assert that charges are excessive, has likewise not been definitely determined by judicial interpretation.

A study of leading decisions indicates that the Supreme Court of the United States has never declared rates confiscatory where they brought as much as 6 or 7 per cent return upon the actual net investment. In his minority opinion in the Southwestern Bell Telephone Company case, Mr. Justice Brandeis presented an analysis of all the rate cases passed upon by the Supreme Court since *Smyth v. Ames.* There had been only 25 cases in which the question of fair return on fair value was involved, and in no case were the rates declared void because the valuation determined by the commission was too low or the assumed rate of return

---

262 U.S. 619 (1923); and Lehigh Valley R. R. Co. v. Pub. Util. Comm., 278 U.S. 24 (1928).

[1] 209 Michigan 52, 176 N.W. 590 (1920).

[2] Wilcox v. Cons. Gas Co., 212 U.S. 19, 49–50 (1909).

[3] McCardle v. Indianapolis Water Co., 272 U.S. 400 (1926).

insufficient. In *New York Telephone Co. v. Prendergast,* however, a lower court held that a rate of return of less than 6 per cent to the telephone company was confiscatory, constituted denial of equal protection of law, and amounted to the depriving of the company of property without due process in violation of the Fourteenth Amendment and of denying to it equal protection of the laws.[1]

Rate of Return and the Reasonableness of Rates.—Whether or not existing or prescribed rates and charges in given instances afford reasonable compensation is, therefore, a judicial question.[2] For this reason a statute that provides that the rates fixed shall be final and conclusive as to their reasonableness is invalid, since it deprives the corporation of its property without due process of law.

It is an established principle, however, that the sufficiency of the rate prescribed to produce a fair profit upon the value of the property employed in the business is to be strongly presumed. The rates must be plainly unreasonable to the extent that their enforcement would be equivalent to the taking of property for public use without such compensation as under the circumstances is just both to the owner and to the public. The burden of showing the confiscatory character of such rates rests upon the complaining company.[3] Where the statutory rate to be charged indicates a very narrow line of division between possible confiscation and proper regulation, as based upon the value of the company's property, and the division depends upon the varying opinions of witnesses as to such value and upon the apprehended result of operating under such rate, a court of equity should not restrain the enforcement of such a rate until a fair trial has been made of continuing the business thereunder.[4]

In decisions of the state courts and of the lower federal courts, reasonable rates have been defined as those which yield a fair return on the investment coupled with the right of the consumer to have no more exacted from him than the service is worth to him. Thus, in *Kennebeck Water District v. Waterville,* where the

[1] 36 Fed. (2d) 56 (1929).

[2] Lincoln Gas, etc., Co. v. Lincoln, 223 U.S. 349 (1919).

[3] See Peoria Gas, etc., Co. v. Peoria, 200 U.S. 48 (1906).

[4] See Wilcox v. Cons. Gas Co., 212 U.S. 19 (1909); and Lincoln, etc., Gas Co. v. Lincoln, 223 U.S. 349 (1919).

reasonableness of the rates to be charged the consumers of water
was involved, a Maine court held that "while the company is
entitled so far as this case shows to a fair return upon the value
of the property used for the public at the time it is being used, the
public, that is, the consumers, may demand that the rates shall
be no higher than the services are worth to them, not in the
aggregate but as individuals."[1]

The Value of the Service and Rate of Return.—In *Bruns-
wick Water District v. Maine Water Co.* the Court stated that
"reasonableness relates both to the company and the customer
. . . A public service company cannot lawfully charge in any
event more than the services are reasonably worth to the public
as individuals, even if charges so limited would fail to produce
a fair return to the company upon the value of its property or
investment."[2]

This same rule was early announced by the Interstate Commerce Commission in cases within its jurisdiction, although in
later decisions this Commission has paid much greater attention
to the costs of performing transportation than in the earlier years
of regulation. In *Imperial Coal Co. v. Pittsburgh and Lake
Erie Railroad Co.* the Commission said: "The value of the
service is generally regarded as the most important factor in
fixing rates."[3]

The Utah Public Utility Commission in deciding a rate case
contended that the effects of the economic depression after 1929
warranted reductions in rates because the present rates exceeded
the value of the service and would, if continued, result in the
loss of consumers to the company. But upon appeal of this
decision of the Utah Commission, the United States District
Court held:

> We cannot agree that any opinion of the United States Supreme
> Court sustains the proposition that in fixing fair and reasonable rates
> the customers' ability to pay and the value of the service to him are
> paramount and controlling. If rates are so low as to be confiscatory
> of the utility's property, they are condemned by the Fourteenth
> Amendment. If they are so high as to yield a greater return on the
> value of the property used and useful in the service than other invest-

[1] 97 Maine 185 (1902); 54 Atl. 6, 13.
[2] 99 Maine 386 (1904); 59 Atl. 537.
[3] 2 I.C.C. 436 (1889).

ments made with equal risk, they are unfair to the customer and should be reduced.[1]

Also, in a decision of the Supreme Court of the State of Washington, in *Puget Sound Power and Light Co. v. Dept. of Pub. Works of the State of Washington*, the Court stated: "It is true, perhaps, that the abandoning of the farms will affect the future demands for power, but if enlightened self-interest does not lead the respondents to go as far as they can or may in maintaining a market, the law may not compel it."[2]

Similarly, the Supreme Court has been cautious in allowing public utility regulatory commissions to order utilities to adopt scales of rates made purposely low in order to develop volume business and seek to earn a fair return in this way. Such an attempt was made by the Ohio Commission in connection with "developmental" rates prescribed for the West Ohio Gas Company. In its decision on appeal from the order of the Ohio Commission the United States Supreme Court, Mr. Justice Cardozo, writing the opinion of the Court, stated:

We are not unmindful of the argument urged by counsel for the commission that the effect of lower prices may be to swell the volume of the business, and by thus increasing revenues enhance the ultimate return. Upon the record as it comes to us, this is guesswork, and no more. There has been no attempt to measure the possible enhancement by appeal to the experience of other companies similarly situated or by any other line of proof. Present confiscation is not atoned for by merely holding out the hope of a better life to come.[3]

The question as to whether a rate can be unreasonably low without being confiscatory, which has been suggested by students of the problem, including Prof. Ernst Freund, appears to be a purely legalistic one which is of little practical significance. The real question is whether a rate will result in sufficient return to attract the necessary investment. If it is sufficient for that purpose, then the rate is nonconfiscatory; if insufficient, it is confiscatory. The phrase "unreasonably low" ordinarily can

[1] Telluride Co. v. Pub. Util. Comm. Utah, 5 P.U.R. (N.S.) 199, 8 Fed. Supp. 341 (1934).

[2] 7 P.U.R. (N.S.) 14 (1935).

[3] West Ohio Gas Co. v. Pub. Util. Comm. Ohio, No. 2, 294 U.S. 79 (1935).

sensibly be applied only to an insufficient rate which therefore will be confiscatory.[1]

Whatever the finding of a regulatory commission, the established rule is that the courts must exercise independent judgment on the law and the facts in all cases in which the issue of confiscation is raised, as was pointed out in Chap. III. This rule has been stated by the United States Supreme Court, in *Crowell v. Benson,* as follows:

> In cases brought to enforce constitutional rights, the judicial power of the United States necessarily extends to the independent determination of all questions, both of fact and law, necessary to the performance of the supreme function. The case of confiscation is illustrative, the ultimate conclusion almost invariably depending upon the decisions of questions of fact. This court has held the owner to be entitled to "a fair opportunity for submitting that issue to a judicial tribunal for determination upon its own independent judgment as to both law and facts."[2]

References

BAUER, JOHN: "Effective Regulation of Public Utilities," The Macmillan Company, New York, 1925, Chap. X.

COOK, M. L.: Editor, "Public Utility Regulation," Ronald Press Company, New York, 1924, Chap. III, by Milo R. Maltbie.

DORAN, H. B.: "Materials for the Study of Public Utility Economics," The Macmillan Company, New York, 1930, Chaps. XIII and XIV.

FREUND, ERNST: "Administrative Powers over Persons and Property," University of Chicago Press, Chicago, 1928.

GLAESER, M. G.: "Outlines of Public Utility Economics," The Macmillan Company, New York, 1931, Chap. XIX.

GRUNSKY, C. E., "Valuation, Depreciation and the Rate Base," John Wiley & Sons, Inc., New York, 1917.

GRUNSKY, C. E., and C. E. GRUNSKY, JR.: "Valuation, Depreciation and the Rate Base," John Wiley & Sons, Inc., New York, 1927.

JONES, ELIOT, and T. C. BIGHAM: "Principles of Public Utilities," The Macmillan Company, New York, 1931, Chap. VI.

MOSHER, W. E., and F. G. CRAWFORD: "Public Utility Regulation," Harper & Brothers, New York, 1933, Chaps. XVI and XVII.

NASH, L. R.: "Economics of Public Utilities," McGraw-Hill Book Company, Inc., New York, 1933, Chap. IX.

National Association of Railroad and Public Utility Commissioners: "Proceedings of Conventions," New York, annual.

[1] See FREUND, ERNST, "Administrative Powers over Persons and Property," University of Chicago Press, Chicago, 1928, p. 298.

[2] Crowell v. Benson, 285 U.S. 22, 60 (1931).

New York: "Report of the New York Commission on Revision of the Public
Service Commissions Law," Albany, 1930, vols. I, II, III, and IV.

PARKER, FRANK: "Elements in the Cost of Money to Public Utilities, 1914–
1922, *Journal of Land and Public Utility Economics*, vol. 2, pp. 73–93.

RAYMOND, W. G.: "The Public and Its Utilities," John Wiley & Sons, Inc.,
New York, 1925, Chap. XXIV.

RUGGLES, C. O.: "Problems in Public Utility Management," McGraw-Hill
Book Company, Inc., New York, 1933, Sec. XI, Part 7.

SMITH, Y. B., and N. T. DOWLING: "Cases on the Law of Public Utilities,"
West Publishing Company, St. Paul, 1926, Chap. V, Part 3.

SMITH, N. L.: "The Fair Rate of Return in Public Utility Regulation,"
Houghton Mifflin Company, Boston, 1931.

WELCH, F. X., and collaborators: "Cases on Public Utility Regulation,"
2d ed., Public Utility Reports, Inc., Washington, 1932, Chap. XI.

WU, S. T.: "Railroad Valuation and Fair Return," University of Pennsylvania Press, Philadelphia, 1930, Chaps. V, VI, and VII.

CHAPTER VIII

DEPRECIATION

DEFINITION AND CAUSES OF DEPRECIATION

The fact that physical properties deteriorate and wear out is generally recognized. Deterioration and wearing out begin when physical properties are brought into use and continue until the property can render no further service. This process of wearing out and ultimate loss of service value is called depreciation, which may be defined as a loss in service life or a decline in value in use of physical property. The loss in value in use resulting from the expiration of the service life of property may also be conceived of as a decline or diminution in the value of the property. Loss of service life and lessening in value are caused by both physical and functional factors. Physical depreciation takes place as the unit of property disintegrates and ultimately becomes unfit for further service. Functional depreciation takes place when the unit of property is no longer adapted to the use to which it is being put. There are several causes for each of these types of depreciation:

1. Physical depreciation arises from:
    a. Wear and tear incidental to use, caused by friction, vibration, etc.
    b. Natural phenomena as rust, rot, decay, and other natural processes which occur with the passage of time.
2. Functional depreciation arises from:
    a. Obsolescence—when a unit of property can be replaced by one that renders a better service or the same service at a lower cost. Obsolescence is common in dynamic industries in which many changes in the arts are occurring.
    b. Inadequacy—where an otherwise serviceable unit becomes inadequate to meet the demands placed upon it. This frequently occurs in rapidly growing communities.
    c. Governmental requirements necessitating the replacement of serviceable property, illustrated by the removal of grade crossings, placing trolley wires underground, etc.

Depreciation is separate and distinct from repairs and maintenance, although the rate of depreciation is affected by the extent of repairs and maintenance, since no unit of property will likely remain long in serviceable condition without necessary repairs and without being properly maintained. But even with repairs and maintenance, which are ordinarily made as recurring costs of operation to maintain operating and service efficiency, depreciation will take place, and the property unit will ultimately reach a point where its service efficiency can no longer be maintained. It is a misconception frequently made to assume that repairs and maintenance offset or prevent depreciation.

CONTROVERSIAL DEPRECIATION PROBLEMS

In spite of the general recognition of the meaning and causes of depreciation, the subject is replete with controversial issues. The chief moot points are:

1. What is the nature of depreciation charges?
2. Is it desirable that there be regulatory control of depreciation practices and allowances?
3. What is the method of accounting for it? Should a depreciation reserve be set up, and, if so, how should the amount of depreciation be measured and how should the reserve be accumulated?
4. What is its effect upon the valuation of property for rate-making purposes?
5. Should the amount of the depreciation allowance be computed on the basis of original or reproduction costs?
6. What is the relationship between the depreciation reserve and the actual deterioration of the property?

Because of these many disputed points, the whole subject is full of complexities and uncertainties. It is one of the uncertain elements in regulation, and a clarification of the issues will do much toward promoting effective regulatory control of public utilities.

NATURE OF DEPRECIATION CHARGES

Depreciation charges are necessary only for those classes of property whose life is longer than the interval of time in the fiscal accounting period, usually a year. For those classes of property which are entirely used up during such an interval, no annual depreciation charge is necessary—the cost of such property is clearly an expense of operation and is ordinarily charged as an operating expense at the time it is used or acquired. In order that a proper recording of all the expenses of operation may be shown for each accounting period, however, it is necessary that the loss in value arising from the wearing out of units of property whose service life is longer than the accounting period likewise be shown as an expense of operation during the given accounting period. This is the reason why annual depreciation charges are necessary, for without them the full costs of the year's operation would not be shown. The depreciation charge allocates, as a cost of operation, the loss in value of fixed capital used up in the process of production during a given accounting period. Depreciation charges thus are a means and measure of the distribution of capital charges to the operating accounts during each of the accounting periods over which the service life of physical property extends and is an important element of operating costs. The amount of depreciation occurring or the amount of the cost of fixed property to be allocated is equivalent to the portion of the property's life used up during the interval. Measured on a "straight-line" basis, one-tenth of the cost of property with a normal service life of 10 years would be the depreciation charge for 1 year.

A confusion frequently enters here. The term "service life" is sometimes interpreted to mean "service efficiency." It is, under such an interpretation, claimed that a unit of property kept properly repaired will operate as efficiently as a new one and that service efficiency remains unimpaired by wear, tear, or other causes when offset by proper repairs. It is then stated that since the property is operating efficiently, there could be no diminution in service value and that therefore no depreciation charge has been incurred. It is not here denied that a unit of property 10 years in service and in perfect repair may not have a service efficiency of 90 per cent or more as compared to a new unit. It is pointed out, however, that, if the normal life of such units of property is 20 years, the 10-year-old unit has used up 50 per cent of its service life and has lost 50 per cent of its service value; or, in other words, it has depreciated 50 per cent. This distinction between service life and service efficiency is necessary in analyzing the nature of depreciation charges, since the use of the term service efficiency frequently leads to erroneous reasoning.

BASIS OF COMMISSION REGULATION

The regulation of depreciation, both as to methods of accounting for it and as to its amount, has generally been brought under commission jurisdiction, usually through the regulation of accounting and the establishment of uniform accounting systems. Depreciation must be given consideration as one of the elements involved in rate making, since the amount of depreciation affects the rate base. Also, effective rate regulation depends upon control by the regulatory body of operating expenses, and depreciation is one of the more important of these. Undoubtedly, the intent of legislative enactments creating regulatory agencies has been that these agencies would exert control over accounting practices and would consider the amount of operating expenses in arriving at the level of rates. An illustration of this intent is found in the Transportation Act of 1920 which specifically authorized the Interstate Commerce Commission to

. . . prescribe for carriers subject to this act, the classes of property for which depreciation charges may properly be included under operating expense, and the percentages of depreciation which shall be charged with respect to each of such classes of property. . . . The carriers subject to this chapter shall not charge to operating expenses any depreciation charges on classes of property other than those prescribed by the Commission or charge with respect to any class of property a percentage other than that prescribed therefor by the Commission. . . . [1]

Though commission control of depreciation practices is now generally accepted, some utility representatives take an extreme view and contend that the amount of the depreciation charge should be left entirely to the discretion of the utility's management. The claim is made that the management should be left free to vary the amount of the annual depreciation charges in order that the amount of the depreciation allowance may be made to conform to the company's financial needs, reducing it in times of stress and increasing it when earnings are large.[2]

[1] Transportation Act of 1920, Section 20, Paragraph 5.

[2] See, *e.g.*, testimony of Sidney L. Mitchell in Interstate Commerce Commission Docket No. 14,700, Depreciation Charges of Telephone Companies; and Docket No. 15,100, Depreciation Charges of Steam Railroads.

Such a practice would be in conformity with that of some private businesses which consider depreciation not as an operating expense but as a reserve set up as a part of surplus from net earnings. Properly conceived as an operating charge, however, the depreciation allowance is intended to record an actual expense which is the spreading of the cost of fixed assets over the accounting periods during the useful life of such assets.

DEPRECIATION ACCOUNTING METHODS

The problem of accounting for depreciation is one of the most controversial of the depreciation issues.   Solution of this problem is important because the accounting method used appears later in the crux of the controversy, *viz.*, the relationship between depreciation and valuation.

The methods of charging for depreciation are two: the replacement method and the reserve method. The replacement method is based upon the theory or assumption that the only obligation upon the users of the service is to pay for the service and the cost of replacements as needed.   It is then pointed out that in a large, complex public utility property, the cost of replacements tends to be practically uniform from year to year so that no depreciation charge or reserve is necessary.   All replacements, it is contended, should be a charge against current operating expenses.   Allocation of the cost of fixed assets is thus made only as replacements take place.   The only reserve involved is a small "replacement reserve" which need be large enough only to equalize the differences in cost of replacements from year to year.   In essence, this method provides for a Replacement Reserve account which is created out of surplus. Later debits to or credits from surplus maintain this account at the desired level.   Actual replacements, handled through the replacement reserve account, are charged to operating expenses for the cost of the new item; the proper capital account is credited with the cost of the replaced items and debited with the cost of the new item.   In this way, the capital accounts of the company show any addition or decrease in value for replaced items.   Since replacements are all charged to the current year's operating accounts, there is no need for a "depreciation reserve." The replacement method of accounting for depreciation was adopted by the National Association of Railroad and Utility

Commissioners in 1920, revised in 1922, and is extensively used for utilities under their jurisdiction.

A practice similar to replacement accounting for depreciation is what is called "retirement accounting." The latter is a refinement of the replacement method designed to show at all times the cost of the fixed assets. This is achieved by capitalizing all units of fixed property, including replacements, at the time of their acquisition and charging to operation the costs of any units that are eliminated, replaced, or withdrawn from service.

The depreciation reserve method of accounting for depreciation assumes either that the periodic depreciation allowance, which as an operating expense is a part of the rate charged for the service, is a partial return of the capital invested or that the value of capital equipment is equal to the value of all the service that it will render so that as units of service are given off, the value of the capital equipment becomes less and less. When this method is followed, an annual depreciation allowance is considered as a part of the year's operating expenses and a balance sheet account "Reserve for Depreciation" is shown as a deduction from, or as an offset to, the fixed capital accounts. Whenever a fixed unit of property is retired from service, the Reserve for Depreciation is debited with the amount of its cost and is thereby reduced by that amount. The proper fixed capital account is credited with the cost of the retired unit, thereby taking it out of the capital accounts, and is debited with the cost of the new item, thereby showing it as a part of fixed capital.

The effect of a depreciation reserve on the balance sheet record of the status of the company is shown in the following simplified illustrations:

1. Balance sheet at the beginning of business:

Fixed Assets	$100,000	Capital Stock	$110,000
Current Assets	10,000		
	$110,000		$110,000

2. At the end of one year of operation, assuming (*a*) that a depreciation reserve account is set up on a straight-line basis; (*b*) that fixed property has a service life of 20 years and there is credited to this account, as a charge against the year's operation, 5 per cent of the cost of the fixed assets; and (*c*) that, in order to

keep the illustration simplified, all net profits are distributed as dividends and therefore no surplus is created, the balance sheet would show:

Original Fixed Assets.....	$100,000	Capital Stock...........	$110,000
Original Current Assets..	10,000	Reserve for Depreciation	5,000
Other Assets...........	5,000		
	$115,000		$115,000

3. The asset account Other Assets shown above was entered to indicate that the credit to the depreciation reserve released from the year's operating income the amount of the depreciation charges. The company could use the amount so released either to increase its assets or to decrease its liabilities. In a growing business, it is likely that the company would acquire fixed assets to take the place of those worn out. In such a case, the balance sheet would show:

Fixed Assets...........	$105,000	Capital Stock...........	$110,000
Current Assets.........	10,000	Reserve for Depreciation	5,000
	$115,000		$115,000

4. It is not necessary that the company use the funds released from the year's income to increase its assets or to decrease its liabilities. It could, if it desired, set these funds aside and specifically save them for use in replacing property at a later date: In this case, the balance sheet would show:

Fixed Assets...........	$100,000	Capital Stock...........	$110,000
Current Assets.........	10,000	Reserve for Depreciation	5,000
Depreciation Reserve Fund	5,000		
	$115,000		$115,000

Attention should be drawn to several points brought out in these illustrations. In the first place, a special depreciation reserve fund does not exist unless it is specifically set up. When such a reserve fund is created, it is often invested in some assets outside the business which are expected to yield an income. Ordinarily, however, it is believed that the funds released through the medium of a depreciation reserve charge can be invested to greatest advantage in the business itself, and this, especially in a growing business, is the usual procedure. Secondly, the existence of the depreciation reserve account shows that a part of the costs of the fixed assets have been allocated to operating costs.

From these illustrations, it can readily be seen that the reserve method, provided the amount of the depreciation allowance is sufficient to cover the loss in service life, shows the extent to which the property has been used up in rendering service and the status of the property at the end of any accounting period. In the replacement method, on the other hand, the status of the property is not shown in the balance sheet records, and the actual charge for retiring the property does not appear in the operating expenses until the unit of property reaches the end of its useful life. This weakness, however, is defended on the practical grounds that once replacements start, they will be practically uniform from year to year and therefore place approximately the same charge against each year's operations.

The depreciation method is prescribed by the Interstate Commerce Commission for steam railroads under its jurisdiction with respect to equipment and is optional for other classes of property. Depreciation reserve accounting was also required by the Interstate Commerce Commission for telephone companies, and this practice has been continued by the Federal Communications Commission. Most of the state commissions have followed the Interstate Commerce Commission in requiring depreciation reserve accounting for railroads and telephone companies. In addition, some of the state commissions, *e.g.*, that of Pennsylvania, require depreciation reserve accounting for all utilities, though, as has previously been mentioned, most of the state commissions specify replacement accounting for all utilities other than railroads and telephone companies.

In the long run, the replacement method and the depreciation reserve method give identical results, since both methods account for the total cost of property used up in providing the service. Any difference between them resolves itself into the question of when the charge will be made; *i.e.*, will it be made at the time of replacement, or will it be made in annual installments throughout the life of the property. The question also is raised as to the effect of depreciation on the rate base.

In so far as the first of these questions is concerned, it is claimed that the replacement method is the more satisfactory because the charges appearing in the operating accounts in any

year are the actual charges of that year except as they may be
modified by the replacement reserve to provide uniformity.
The depreciation reserve method is denounced as being unsound
because it is based upon estimates of "service life" which, it is
claimed, cannot be established with any reasonable accuracy.
Even though the annual reserve allowance is based upon observation rather than estimate, it is claimed, the functional causes will
operate to make the observation an invalid measure of depreciation.   It is also claimed that the depreciation reserve method
places undue burdens on the consumers by requiring large
annual charges against consumers which are unnecessary to
provide for replacements.

On their face these contentions seem to have some merit, but
upon analysis it becomes apparent that there is failure to understand the purpose and nature of the annual depreciation charge.
It should be recalled that the fundamental purpose of a depreciation charge is to allocate against the consumers the cost of
property that is equivalent to the proportion of its service life
used up during an accounting period.   Thereby the capital
fund of the business will be maintained intact.   The replacement method fails to do this, since there is no relationship
between replacements in any one year and the amount of the
fixed capital used up during that year.   Sound public policy
recognizes the validity and desirability of safeguarding the
investor's interests by making periodic charges to maintain the
capital fund intact.   The consumer's interest is in harmony
with this view because depreciation charges are likewise a means
of maintaining continuity of service by making provision for
replacing property that has reached the end of its service life.
It is not clear how, in the long run, depreciation charges can be
more burdensome than replacement charges, since both methods,
as has earlier been indicated, account for the cost of property
used in rendering service.   A simple illustration will clarify
this point.   Assume that a unit of property which cost $5,000
is replaced at the end of its five years of service life.   Its cost
would be accounted for as shown on page 187.

Those who favor the replacement method further contend
that the primary cause of depreciation, in most of the fields
of public utility service, is functional and arises from either
obsolescence or inadequacy.   Neither of these can be satis-

Year	Charges under replacement method	Charges under depreciation reserve method
1	0	$1,000
2	0	1,000
3	0	1,000
4	0	1,000
5	$5,000	1,000
Total charges	$5,000	$5,000

factorily anticipated by a depreciation reserve charge, and therefore, it is claimed, the replacement method is necessary in order that replacements may be made for depreciation of this nature.

The factor of obsolescence, unless its economic implications are clearly understood, tends to becloud the issue of the relative desirability of these two methods. Though at the present time the Supreme Court recognizes obsolescence as a factor to be included in the annual depreciation allowance,[1] it is considered contrary to economic reasoning to attempt to assess the cost of obsolescence against past users of the service. The past users of the service receive no benefits from the new unit installed to render better or cheaper service, and, since they receive no benefits, they should have none of the cost assessed against them. It is only physical depreciation that the past users are obligated to cover in the rates paid by them. When the cause of the depreciation is functional, the future consumers are the ones who benefit by having either a cheaper service or a better service, and it should be an obligation upon these consumers to pay for the costs of such property. Therefore, its cost should be charged to the future, not the past, service and amortized from the savings (or increased rates necessary) in the future. Therefore, if functional depreciation be ruled out of the annual depreciation allowance, the charge that the depreciation reserve method cannot anticipate it is no longer applicable. Also, if obsolescence is expected to occur, a company may wisely anticipate it by setting up contingency reserves out of surplus, such reserves not to be a part of and to have no effect upon the depreciation allowance.

[1] *Infra*, p. 194.

The Measurement of Depreciation.—When the depreciation reserve method is used, there arises a further controversy as to the best measure of the amount of annual depreciation. It is true that the determination of depreciation involves a large degree of judgment and that no fixed rules can be laid down and followed. However, when persons with experience and understanding make the appraisal, there is no reason why, with a reasonable amount of adjustment permitted by the regulatory agencies from time to time, the measured depreciation will not be fair to all parties concerned.

The methods for measuring the annual depreciation allowance are (1) the "observation" method, (2) the "service-output" method, and (3) the "life-table" or estimated-life method.

The observation method involves personal inspection of the property and relies upon the judgment of the appraiser. It is obvious that this method can be no better than the judgment of the appraiser and that no two appraisers are likely to arrive at the same result. Furthermore, some property, as gas and water mains, cannot be inspected, and annual inspections of large properties for the purpose of making depreciation allowances are not feasible. As a consequence, the observation method is not extensively used. It is, however, valid as a check against estimates of service life and for making adjustments in the reserve accumulated from estimates.

Under the service-output method, the life of the asset is reckoned in terms of its probable quantity of output, the depreciation allowance being in proportion to the output during a given period of time. This would measure depreciation in terms of kilowatt-hours of electricity, M.C.F. of gas, gallons of water, and so on, during the accounting period. Because of widely fluctuating production schedules, it is more frequently recommended for manufacturing industries than for public utilities.

The life-table method relies upon past experience and attempts, on the basis of such experience, to predict the length of time that various classes of property will last. On the basis of such estimates, the "average life" is used to determine the amount of the depreciation charge for each class of property. The validity of the estimates will depend upon the amount of experience upon which they are based and the extent to which past experiences recur in the future. This method involves exactly the same principles as does the use of mortality tables in life insurance. With reasonable adjustments, past experience can be used as a basis for predicting the future.

RELATION BETWEEN DEPRECIATION AND VALUATION

We now come to the other basic difference between the replacement method and the depreciation reserve method. This is the most crucial aspect of the depreciation problem and relates to the valuation of the rate base. In question form, it may be asked: Is the proper rate base to be determined without respect to depreciation, or is it to be considered as the cost, original or reproduction, less depreciation?

The advocates of the depreciation reserve method are in favor of deducting depreciation from the cost, original or reproduction, of the property in arriving at the rate base. The Interstate Commerce Commission has consistently followed this practice in the valuation of railroad properties carried on by its Bureau of Valuation. On the other hand, the proponents of the replacement method deny that there is any diminution of value for rate-making purposes in a property that is well maintained and where replacement has taken place for all units of property whose useful life has expired. The only depreciation that they admit is that which is due to deferred maintenance or repairs and is called "accrued depreciation." This viewpoint is based upon the concept of service efficiency rather than service value. The replacement method assumes that a utility plant has a perpetual or indefinite life and that its value therefore never depreciates when it is properly repaired and maintained. Such an assumption precludes the deduction of depreciation from cost to arrive at the rate base. The existence of a depreciation reserve and its deduction from the cost of the plant, it is further claimed, result in the confiscation of property.

The depreciation reserve advocates contend, on the contrary, that the measure of actual depreciation is the balance in the Reserve for Depreciation account and that this balance should be deducted from the cost of the property to arrive at the true rate base. Rather than causing confiscation of property, it is pointed out, the purpose of this method of depreciation and valuation is to maintain the investment. If properly followed, the net investment is always shown as the total cost of the property less the depreciation reserve. Making a depreciation allowance annually, which as earlier noted releases funds from operating income which may be used for an increase in the company's own assets or for investment in a special fund, safeguards the property from confiscation.

These differences in viewpoint were strikingly brought out in the hearings on depreciation charges for railroads and telephone companies before the Interstate Commerce Commission. They were reported by the Commission as follows:

The hearings developed a wide and striking difference of opinion upon a basic question partly of fact and partly of theory. This question is of such controlling importance that we shall discuss it at the outset. It must be determined before the numerous questions of law to which the proceedings have given rise can profitably be discussed. Representative of the opposing views are the position of the telephone companies, on the one hand, and the position of the railroad, gas, and electric light companies, on the other hand.

The Telephone View.—The position of the telephone companies, briefly stated, is that the ultimate expense of furnishing service includes the cost of everything used up in the process, whatever it may be. It includes the cost of things that are used up slowly, such as automobiles, switchboards, buildings, pole lines, and other items of plant, just as inevitably as it includes the cost of things that are used up rapidly, such as labor, gasoline, coal, lead pencils, paper, and the like. As we understand the view of these companies, depreciation expense represents the cost incurred during an accounting period in the process of using up in service items of physical property whose lives extend over more than one such period, regardless of how they are used up. This cost is a part of, and should be shown in, operating expense; it should be shown when it is incurred, and it is incurred throughout the life of the property in service. It should, therefore, be charged to operating expense in periodical installments throughout this service life. Replacements, these companies say, do not measure depreciation expense, for it is determined by the amount and cost of the property used up. It exists whether or not the property is replaced, and is incurred regardless of whether depreciation charges are accrued. Such charges should be made in order that the accounts may properly record the facts. As the result of making them, a reserve will be created which will, if the charges have been accurately estimated, at any time, equal the loss in existing property due to the process of consumption in service. This reserve protects the integrity of the investment.

The Railroad View.—The position of the steam railroad, gas, and electric light companies, stated briefly, is that a railroad or public utility property is a composite of many separate units and should be so considered with respect to depreciation. While most of these separate units have terminable lives and are worn out in service or abandoned from time to time for better substitutes, there is no depreciation in the composite property so long as it is well maintained. Maintenance is the making of needed repairs and replacements. If properly maintained, the railroads say, the composite property does not depreciate or lessen in value or service ability. In fact it may be worth more to a prospective purchaser when seasoned by long-continued operation than when new. No reserve is needed to protect the integrity of the investment, but the creation of such a reserve may be desirable to spread the cost of retiring certain large units of property and prevent a disproportionate burden upon the operating expenses of any one year. In the case of a large, composite property which has "struck its gait," it is claimed that retirements of most property units are about the same in amount from year to year, so that there is no need for such an equalizing reserve. In the case of the larger units, there may be such need, but the reserve should be called a "retirement" rather than a "depreciation" reserve. Its amount is not a matter of mathematical computation from theoretical service lives, but rather a matter of judgment. Where property is unexpectedly retired, not because it has been worn out, but because some more efficient substitute has been developed, the cost of retirement should be spread, not over the past, but over the future, so that the burden may fall upon those who gain the benefit from the enhanced efficiency. The ascertainment of service lives, upon which what the gas and electric companies call "theoretical depreciation charges" are dependent, is, they say, a wholly impracticable undertaking requiring a knowledge of the future which no one has. It is contended that the making of such depreciation charges merely results in the accumulation of a huge reserve which will in time fluctuate around 50 per cent of the recorded investment; that such a reserve serves no useful purpose; and that it is a burden both upon the patrons of the company and upon the investors in its securities. If it were to be assumed that the composite property would at a certain time come to the end of its life, there might be need for such a reserve, but in most cases such properties may for all practical purposes, it is asserted, be regarded as perpetual.

The question raised by this divergence of opinion merits the most careful consideration. There is general agreement that, with the exception of land and grading, most of the property units which make up the plant of a railroad or telephone company are gradually worn out

in operation or are abandoned from time to time in favor of better substitutes.   There also can be no doubt that the cost of such worn-out
or abandoned property units is a part of operating expense to be charged
against the service.   The basic question is whether such cost should be
charged in bulk at the time when each unit is retired, or should be
anticipated by periodical installments spread over its service life.[1]

The Supreme Court on Depreciation.—The problem of the
relationship between depreciation and valuation has been
brought before the courts frequently.   In tracing the trend of
court decisions, this problem will be given attention, and findings
concerning other depreciation issues will be indicated.   It
should be noted at the outset, however, that issues have not
always been presented in a clear-cut way and that the findings
of the courts have been directed not only toward principles
but also toward particular facts and the application of principles by commissions and lower courts.   In many instances,
therefore, there are conflicting opinions concerning most of the
moot depreciation questions.[2]

The United States Supreme Court did not deal extensively with
the subject of depreciation before its opinion in the Knoxville
Water Company case in 1909.   Prior to that time, only incidental
reference was made to depreciation, but it was recognized by the
courts that a utility was obligated to keep its property in good
operating condition.[3]   In at least one opinion, however, it was
specifically denied that the utility had a right to accumulate
an unspent reserve by making charges against operation on the
grounds that only such expenditures as are actually made can
be considered as deductions from earnings.[4]

[1] 118 I.C.C. 301–303.

[2] For more complete selection of cases and decisions concerning deprecia-
tion, see: MASON, PERRY, The U.S. Supreme Court on Public Utility
Depreciation, *Accounting Review*, vol. 11, No. 3; SPURR, H. C., "Guiding
Principles of Public Service Regulation," Public Utilities Reports, Inc.,
Rochester, 1925, vol. 2, Chaps. XVIII–XLIV (cites many of the state com-
mission decisions and state court decisions as well as federal court cases);
and WHITTEN, R. H., and D. F. WILCOX, "Valuation of Public Service
Corporations," The Banks Law Publishing Co., New York, 1928, vol. 2,
Chaps. XXXI–XXXIII.

[3] See, *e.g.*, Union Pacific R. R. Co., v. United States, 99 U.S. 420 (1878);
and Reagan v. Farmers Loan and Trust Co., 154 U.S. 362 (1894).

[4] United States v. Kansas Pacific Ry. Co., 99 U.S. 455 (1878).

In the first leading case on public utility valuation, *Smyth v. Ames*, the Court presented a series of factors to be considered but made no direct reference to depreciation. Though the Court did mention "present value," most subsequent commentators believe that this meant undepreciated reproduction cost.[1] Decisions following that in *Smyth v. Ames*, usually based directly on the reasoning there, sometimes did mention depreciation as an element to be considered in arriving at the rate base.[2]

The Knoxville Case.—The Knoxville Water Company case, decided in 1909, was the first in which there appeared an extended discussion of depreciation. In this case, the master in the lower court fixed the valuation on the basis of reproduction cost new without a deduction for depreciation, and the Circuit Court had sustained this valuation. In reversing this ruling, the Supreme Court held that "some substantial allowance for depreciation ought to have been made in this case."[3] The ruling in the Knoxville case established (1) that deduction must be made for depreciation in order to determine present fair value; (2) that the depreciation which is to be deducted is the result of age and use and begins with the use of the property; and (3) that depreciation determines net income rather than being an allocation of net income.

With the statement of these principles as a precedent, subsequent valuation opinions have considered the problem of depreciation both as a periodic charge to operations and as a deductible item in determining the rate base. In the Minnesota Rate cases the Court held that depreciation must be deducted from the cost of reproduction new, stating that "the depreciation in question is not that which has been overcome by repairs and replacements, but is the actual existing depreciation in the plant as compared with a new one."[4] Depreciation accounting rules of the Interstate Commerce Commission were upheld and

[1] 169 U.S. 466 (1898); see *supra*, p. 142 for a more extended discussion of this case.

[2] See, *e.g.*, San Diego Land and Town Co., v. Nat. City, 174 U.S. 739 (1899); San Diego Land and Town Co., v. Jasper, 189 U.S. 439 (1903); and Stanislaus County v. San Joaquin and Kings River Canal and Irrigation Co., 192 U.S. 201 (1904).

[3] Knoxville Water Co. v. Knoxville, 212 U.S. 1. 10.

[4] Simpson v. Shepard, 230 U.S. 352 (1913).

sanctioned in *Kansas City Southern Ry. Co. v. United States;*[1] and in *Pacific Gas and Electric Co. v. San Francisco* the Court indicated that if obsolescence is predictable it should be included in the depreciation allowance and deducted from the cost of the property.[2]

New York Telephone Company Case.—The question of handling excessive depreciation charges was involved in *Publ. Util. Comm. v. New York Telephone Co.* The specific point at issue concerned a finding of the Board of Public Utility Commissioners of New Jersey that the balance in the depreciation reserve was excessive, and it therefore refused to allow rates that would permit the utility to cover its operating expenses, continue to build up depreciation reserves at the same rate, and earn a fair return.   Instead, it directed that a portion of the depreciation reserve be set aside to absorb the deficits in future years when the earnings should be less than a reasonable return.   This finding was not sustained, thus contradicting the opinion held by many state commissions that the depreciation reserve is contributed by consumers and that they have an equitable interest in it.   The Court stated:

It may be assumed, as found by the Board, that in prior years the company charged excessive amounts to depreciation expense and so created in the reserve account balances greater than required adequately to maintain the property. It remains to be considered whether the company may be compelled to apply any part of the property or money represented by such balances to overcome deficits in present or future earnings and to sustain rates which otherwise could not be sustained.

The just compensation safeguarded to the utility by the Fourteenth Amendment is a reasonable return on the value of the property used at the time that it is being used for the public service, and rates not sufficient to yield that return are confiscatory. . . . Constitutional protection against confiscation does not depend on the source of the money used to purchase the property. It is enough that it is used to render the service. . . . The customers are entitled to demand service and the company must comply. The company is entitled to just compensation and, to have the service, the customers must pay for it. The relation between the company and its customers is not that of partners, agent and principal, or trustee and beneficiary. . . . The

[1] 231 U.S. 423, 447 (1913).
[2] 265 U.S. 403 (1924).

revenue paid by the customers for service belongs to the company. The amount, if any, remaining after paying taxes and operating expenses including the expense of depreciation is the company's compensation for the use of its property. If there is no return, or if the amount is less than a reasonable return, the company must bear the loss. Past losses cannot be used to enhance the value of the property or to support a claim that rates for the future are confiscatory. . . . And the law does not require the company to give up for the benefit of future sub- scribers any part of its accumulations from past operations. Profits from the past cannot be used to sustain confiscatory rates for the future. . . .

Customers pay for service, not for the property used to render it. Their payments are not contributions to depreciation or other operating expenses or to capital of the company. By paying bills for service they do not acquire any interest, legal or equitable, in the property used for their convenience or in the funds of the company. Property paid out of moneys received for service belongs to the company just as does that purchased out of proceeds for its bonds and stock. It is conceded that the exchange rates complained of are not sufficient to yield a just return after paying taxes and operating expenses, includ- ing a proper allowance for current depreciation. The property or money of the company represented by the credit balance in the reserve for depreciation cannot be used to make up the deficiency.[1]

For the Court to have continued to hold to this view would have created difficulties in effective rate regulation, since both the rate of depreciation and the rate of return are necessarily based upon judgment, and adjustments are necessary to correct errors of over- and underestimates. If the depreciation reserve were to be considered as a closed subject and no adjustments therein were to be permitted, it would necessitate that both the commissions and the utilities advocate extreme views. Appa- rently, the opinion in this case failed to consider the depreciation reserve as a means of providing for replacement of capital but rather considered it as a part of the utility's earnings.[2] Fortu- nately, this view was slightly modified in *Smith v. Ill. Bell Telephone Co.*, wherein the Court indicated that there was no intention as above stated to prevent the determination of correct future allowances for depreciation.[3]

[1] 271 U.S. 23 (1926).

[2] For a similar analysis, see M. G. Glaeser, "Outlines of Public Utility Economics," pp. 358 *ff*.

[3] 282 U.S. 133 (1930).

The Baltimore Railways Case.—Probably the most extensive treatment of the subject of depreciation by the U. S. Supreme Court is to be found in *United Ry. and Electric Co. v. West.* The majority opinion, contrary to any previous opinions and contrary to business, accounting, and regulatory practices generally, held that the amount of the depreciation charge should be based upon present value or reproduction cost rather than upon original cost.   It was stated:

The allowance for annual depreciation made by the Commission was based upon cost. The court of appeals held that this was erroneous and that it should have been based upon the present value. The court's view of the matter was plainly right. One of the items of expense to be ascertained and deducted is the amount necessary to restore property worn out or impaired, so as continuously to maintain it as nearly as practicable at the same level of efficiency for the public service. The amount set aside periodically for this purpose is the so-called depreciation allowance. Manifestly, this allowance cannot be limited by the original cost, because, if values have advanced, the allowance is not sufficient to maintain the level of efficiency. The utility "is entitled to see that from earnings the value of the property invested is kept unimpaired, so that at the end of any given term of years the original investment remains as it was at the beginning." . . . This naturally calls for expenditures equal to the cost of the worn-out equipment at the time of replacement; and this, for all practical purposes, means present value. It is the settled rule of this court that the rate base is present value, and it would be wholly illogical to adopt a different rule for depreciation.[1]

The effect of this decision has been most disturbing upon public utility accountants as well as upon regulatory commissions. Its most unfortunate feature is that if applied in practice the result will be the substitution of variable opinion for computations based upon actual fact. The most scathing criticism of the theory underlying the decision in the Baltimore case is found in a lengthy dissenting opinion written by Mr. Justice Brandeis, excerpts from which are quoted below:

It is urged by the Railways that if the base used in determining what is a fair return on the use of its property is the present value, then logically the base to be used in determining the depreciation charge—a charge for the consumption of plant in service—must also be the present

[1] 280 U.S. 234, 253–254 (1930).

value of the property consumed. . . . But acceptance of the doctrine of *Smyth v. Ames* does not require that the depreciation charge be based on present value of plant. For an annual depreciation charge is not a measure of the actual consumption of plant during the year. No such measure has yet been invented. There is no regularity in the development of depreciation. It does not proceed in accordance with any mathematical law. There is nothing in business experience, or in the training of experts, which enables man to say to what extent service life will be impaired by the operations of a single year, or of a series of years less than the service life.

Where a plant intended, like a street railway, for continuing operation is maintained at a constant level of efficiency, it is rarely possible to determine definitely whether or not its service life has in fact lessened within a particular year. The life expectancy of a plant, like that of an individual, may be in fact greater, because of unusual repairs or other causes, at the end of a particular year than it was at the beginning. And even where it is known that there has been some lessening of service life within the year, it is never possible to determine with accuracy what percentage of the unit's service life has, in fact, been so consumed. Nor is it essential to the aims of the charge that this fact should be known. The main purpose of the charge is that irrespective of the rate of depreciation there shall be produced, through annual contributions, by the end of the service life of the depreciable plant, an amount equal to the total net expense of its retirement. To that end it is necessary only that some reasonable plan of distribution be adopted. Since it is impossible to ascertain what percentage of the service life is consumed in any year, it is either assumed that depreciation proceeds at some average rate (thus accepting the approximation to fact customarily obtained through the process of averaging) or the annual charge is fixed without any regard to the rate of depreciation. . . .

The business device known as the depreciation charge appears not to have been widely adopted in America until after the beginning of this century. Its use is still stoutly resisted by many concerns. Wherever adopted, the depreciation charge is based on the original cost of the plant to the owner. When the great changes in price levels incident to the World War led some to question the wisdom of the practice of basing the charge on original cost, the Chamber of Commerce of the United States warned businessmen against the fallacy of departing from the accepted basis. And that warning has been recently repeated: "When the cost of an asset, less any salvage value, has been recovered, the process of depreciation stops—the consumer has paid for that particular item of service. There are those who maintain that the obligation of the consumer is one rather of replacement—building for building, machine for machine. According to this view depreciation should be based on replacement cost rather than actual cost. The replacement theory substitutes for something certain and definite, the actual cost, a cost of reproduction which is highly speculative and conjectural and requiring frequent revision. It, moreover, seeks to establish for one expense a basis of computation fundamentally different from that used for the other expenses of doing business. Insurance is charged on a basis of actual premiums paid, not on the basis of probable premiums three years hence; rent on the amount actually paid, not on the problematical rate of the next lease, salaries, light, heat, power, supplies are all charged at actual, not upon a future contingent cost. As one writer has expressed it, 'The fact that the plant cannot be replaced at the same cost, but only at much more, has nothing to do with the cost of its product, but only with the cost of future product turned out by the subsequent plant.' As the product goes through your factory it should be burdened with expired, not anticipated, costs. *Charge depreciation upon actual cost less any salvage.*"

Such is today, and ever has been, the practice of public accountants. Their statements are prepared in accordance with principles of accounting which are well established, generally accepted and uniformly applied. By those accustomed to read the language of accounting a depreciation charge is understood as meaning the appropriate contribution for that year to the amount required to make good the cost of the plant which ultimately must be retired. On that basis, public accountants certify to investors and bankers the results of operation, whether of public utilities, or manufacturing or mercantile concerns. Corporate securities are issued, bought, and sold, and vast loans are made daily, in reliance upon statements so prepared. The compelling logic of facts which led businessmen to introduce a depreciation charge has led them to continue to base it on the original cost of the plant despite the great changes in the price level incident to the World War. Basing the depreciation charge on cost is a rule prescribed or recommended by those associations of businessmen who have had occasion since the World War to consider the subject.

Businessmen naturally took the plant at cost, as that is how they treat other articles consumed in operation. The plant, undepreciated, is commonly carried on the books at cost; and it is retired at cost. The net profit or loss of a business transaction is commonly ascertained by deducting from the gross receipts the expenditures incurred in producing them. Businessmen realized fully that the requirements for replacement might be more or less than the original cost. But they realized also that to attempt to make the depreciation account reflect economic conditions and changes would entail entry upon new fields of conjecture and prophecy which would defeat its purposes. For there is no basis in experience which can justify predicting whether a replacement, renewal, or substitution falling in some future year will cost more or less than it would at present, or more or less than the unit cost when it was acquired.[1]

The Lindheimer Case.—In *Lindheimer et al. v. Ill. Bell Telephone Co.*, issue was joined over deduction of the accrued depreciation reserve from the rate base. The Illinois Commission, as many commissions have done, contended that in so far as the depreciation reserve was accumulated out of charges to annual operating expenses based upon estimates of service life, the accrued depreciation reserve at any time would represent the actual depreciation of the property and should be deducted in ascertaining the rate base. The telephone company, on the other hand, claimed that the depreciation was measured by the "actual," or "observed," depreciation. The company said that the depreciation reserve in a given year

. . . does not purport to measure the actual depreciation at that time; that there is no regularity in the development of depreciation; that it does not proceed in accordance with any fixed rule; that as to a very large part of the property there is no way of predicting the extent to which there will be impairment in a particular year. Many different causes operating differently at different times with respect to different sorts of property produce the ultimate loss against which protection is sought. As the accruals to the depreciation reserve are the result of calculations which are designed evenly to distribute the loss over estimated service life, the accounting reserve will ordinarily be in excess of the actual depreciation. Further, there are the special conditions of a growing plant—"there are new plant groups in operation on which depreciation is accruing but which are not yet represented, or are but slightly represented, in the retirement losses." Where, as in this instance, there has been a rapid growth, retirements at one point of time will relate for the most part to the smaller preceding plant, while the depreciation reserve account is currently building up to meet the "increased eventual retirement liability" of the enlarged plant.[2]

That there may be substantial differences between "observed" depreciation and the depreciation reserve is shown by the fact that in this case the latter amounted to two or three times the

[1] *Ibid.*, pp. 261–270.
[2] 292 U.S. 151, p. 171.

former as estimated. The Supreme Court agreed with the company's counsel that "the reserve balance and the actual depreciation at any time can be compared only after examining the property to ascertain its condition" but held that the annual allowances for depreciation were excessive, in the light of expenditures for current maintenance and in the face of the disparity between "actual" depreciation, as ascertained by the company, and the amount of the depreciation reserve. Confiscation being the issue, the Court said, the burden was upon the company to show that the rates would not yield a fair return after all legitimate expenses were met, and this the company had not done in view of excessive charges for depreciation. With respect to the company's method of accounting for depreciation, and the significance of excessive charges, the Court said:

While property remains in the plant, the estimated depreciation rate is applied to the book cost and the resulting amounts are charged currently as expenses of operation. The same amounts are credited to the account for depreciation reserve, the "Reserve for Accrued Depreciation." When property is retired, its cost is taken out of the capital accounts, and its cost, less salvage, is taken out of the depreciation reserve account. According to the practice of the company, the depreciation reserve is not held as a separate fund but is invested in plant and equipment. As the allowances for depreciation, credited to the depreciation reserve account, are charged to operating expenses, the depreciation reserve invested in property thus represents, at a given time, the amount of the investment which has been made out of the proceeds of telephone rates for the ostensible purpose of replacing capital consumed. If the predictions of service life were entirely accurate and retirements were made when and as these predictions were precisely fulfilled, the depreciation reserve would represent the consumption of capital, on a cost basis, according to the method which spreads that loss over the respective service periods. But if the amounts charged to operating expenses and credited to the account for depreciation reserve are excessive, to that extent subscribers for the telephone service are required to provide, in effect, capital contributions, not to make good losses incurred by the utility in the service rendered, and thus to keep its investment unimpaired, but to secure additional plant and equipment upon which the utility expects a return.[1]

Summary of Court Concepts.—While the Supreme Court has not passed upon all theories concerning public utility depre-

[1] *Ibid.*, pp. 168–169.

ciation, and while it has not been fully consistent in some of its findings, the following conclusions seem to be justified:

1. Depreciation is rightfully to be considered as an operating cost, the principal purposes of which are to provide for the financing of replacements and to prevent the impairment of capital invested.

2. It is both a right and a duty of the utility to provide adequately for depreciation and for functional as well as physical depreciation. However, because of the impossibility of predicting functional depreciation, and because such depreciation is rightfully a charge on future consumers, a clear presentation of the nature of functional depreciation and the method of treating it is necessary.

3. Some deduction for depreciation is required in fixing the rate base.

4. Apparently still an issue is the question of whether the amount of depreciation is to be based upon reproduction cost of the retired unit or its original cost. Though the majority opinion of the Court supported the former view in the Baltimore Railways case, the dissenting opinion has behind it the weight of prestige and the authority of experience.

SUMMARY

The cost of furnishing public utility service includes as one of its elements the value of the service life of the physical plant and equipment used up in rendering the service. This is the true measure of the annual depreciation and is properly a charge to be assessed against and paid by the consumers of the service. When property is retired and replaced before the end of its normal service life on account of functional causes, the future consumers are the ones to bear the cost, since in no way can the past consumers receive service from or benefit by the new equipment. In order to provide for replacements, to maintain intact the capital investment, and to show as accurately as possible the proper charges for each period's depreciation, the depreciation reserve method is an economically sound method. The most practical and satisfactory method of accumulating this reserve is on the straight-line basis, although experience and observation may indicate the desirability of modifying the rate of accumulation from time to time. It follows, therefore, that depreciation as a current cost of operation must be included in the return received, or a utility will operate at a loss. Whatever the basis of valuation, the depreciation reserve should be deducted in determining the rate base; for, if the utility has been under regulation for a long time, the amount of the depreciation reserve is likely to be a good measure of the actual depreciation. The deduction of depreciation does not result in confiscation of a utility's property because, if the reserve is accompanied by a reserve fund invested in outside property or cash, the utility has no right to expect the consumers of the service to pay a return on it, since it is not used for rendering the service. If, as is now usually the case, the amount shown in the depreciation reserve is invested in additions and betterments in the utility's own property, such investment will be shown as assets and included in the rate base. To fail to deduct the depreciation reserve in such a case would mean giving the utility a double return, and the depreciation reserve would thereby become a basis for it to demand higher rates and a larger return.

The present authors believe that the foregoing statement of principles is sound and that their application in accounting procedures, rate regulation, and valuation will result in fair dealing to all parties. They recognize, however, that the problem has become complicated by inconsistencies in utility accounting practices and vacillation in court decisions. Though not in sympathy with the replacement method, they recognize that effective regulation can result from consistency in the application of this method, and that, for existing properties without adequate depreciation reserves and because many state commissions have followed this method, it can be continued without materially injuring the utility's stockholders or its customers. However, since the federal regulatory agencies and taxing authorities have established depreciation reserve standards, it would indeed be desirable if these could be adopted and uniformly applied by state commissions. Most important is that a given theory be consistently applied, since otherwise there will exist a loophole through which earnings may be unjustifiably increased and diverted to stockholders.

References

BAUER, JOHN: "Effective Regulation of Public Utilities," The Macmillan Company, New York, 1925, Chap. VII.

BENEDICT, LOUIS: Depreciation: What It Is and How It Is Computed, *Public Utilities Fortnightly*, vol. 6, No. 5.

BRENNAN, J. F.: Depreciation by the Insurance Method, *Journal of Land and Public Utility Economics*, vol. 9, No. 1.

CARTER, R. A., and W. L. RANSOM: "Depreciation Charges of Railroads and Public Utilities," a memorandum filed with the Depreciation Section of the Bureau of Accounts, of the Interstate Commerce Commission, privately printed, New York, 1921.

DORAU, H. B.: "Materials For the Study of Public Utility Economics," The Macmillan Company, New York, 1930, Chap. XI.

GLAESER, M. G.: "Outline of Public Utility Economics," The Macmillan Company, New York, 1931, Chap. XV.

GRAHAM, W. J.: "Public Utility Valuation—Reproduction Cost as a Basis for Depreciation and Rate-base Determination," Ph. D. thesis, private edition distributed by University of Chicago Libraries, Chicago, 1934.

GRANT, E. L.: Depreciation: An Operating Expense or an Appropriation of Earnings, *Journal of Land and Public Utility Economics*, vol. 4, No. 3.

HAYES, H. V.: "Public Utilities—Their Cost New and Depreciation," 2d ed., D. Van Nostrand Company, Inc., New York, 1916, Chaps. IX, X, and XI.

JONES, ELIOT, and T. C. BIGHAM: "Principles of Public Utilities," The Macmillan Company, New York, 1931, Chap. X.

MALTBIE, W. H.: "Theory and Practice of Public Utility Valuation," 1st ed., McGraw-Hill Book Company, Inc., New York, 1924, Chaps. XII–XVII.

MASON, PERRY: The Supreme Court on Public Utility Depreciation, *Accounting Review*, vol. 11, No. 3.

MILES, L. P.: "Relation of Depreciation or Retirement Reserve to Value," address before American Bar Association, Chicago, 1930, quoted in part in *Public Utilities Fortnightly*, vol. 6, No. 9.

MOSHER, W. E., and F. G. CRAWFORD: "Public Utility Regulation," Harper & Brothers, New York, 1933, Chap. XI.

NASH, L. R.: "Depreciation Accounting Methods for Public Utilities," address before International Congress on Accounting, 1929, quoted in part in *Public Utilities Fortnightly*, vol. 4, No. 9.

———: Public Utility Depreciation Accounting, *Journal of Land and Public Utility Economics*, vol. 2, No. 4.

RAYMOND, W. G.: "The Public and Its Utilities," John Wiley & Sons, Inc., New York, 1925, Chaps. IV–VIII, and XXIII.

RIGGS, H. E.: Facts and Fallacies about Straight Line Depreciation Methods, *Public Utilities Fortnightly*, vol. 12, No. 7.

SPURR, H. C.: "Guiding Principles of Public Service Regulation," Public Utilities Reports, Inc., Rochester, 1925, vol. II., Chaps. XXVIII–XLIV.

WHITTEN, R. H., and D. F. WILCOX: "Valuation of Public Service Corporations," The Banks Law Publishing Company, New York, 1928, vol. II, Chaps. XXXI–XXXIII.

CHAPTER IX

REGULATION OF SERVICE

Commission Jurisdiction over Service.—Consumers judge a public utility according to the quality and quantity of service as well as according to the amount of the rates. These two criteria are mutually dependent because service and rates are related in terms of cause and effect. If rates are lowered without specifying the quality of the service to be given, it is easy for the utility to make up the difference between the old and the new rates by comparably lowering the quality of its service. Similarly, a high standard of service cannot be maintained unless rates are high enough reasonably to compensate the utility for supplying such service. Since low rates place pressure upon a public utility to lower service standards or to postpone extensions and improvements, the reasonableness of rates, from the standpoint of the consumer, cannot be measured without considering the quality of the service. Service standards and regulations concerning the quality of the service, setting forth the duties, responsibilities, obligations, and privileges of a public utility in the conduct of its business, are among the essentials of effective regulatory control. Protection of the consumer's interest in adequate, safe, and sufficient service is a responsibility of the regulatory agency.

All states, except Kentucky and Delaware, have authorized their state commissions to exercise control over standards of service for railways. In all but five of the states, the commissions exercise control and supervision of service standards for privately owned and operated light, heat, power, and gas utilities, many of these commissions also having authority over the service standards of municipally owned and operated utilities. In some cases, the municipalities are given the right to determine the standards for the utilities operating within their boundaries. Where there is no state control over municipally owned and operated services, the municipality establishes and maintains, as it deems desirable, its own service standards.[1]

Because of differences in technology and because of problems peculiar to a given public utility service, it is necessary to establish separate service standards and regulations for each kind of public utility service, although some problems do not lend themselves to control by a set rule. Problems of the latter type are those concerning the establishment, extension and abandonment of service, and those concerning certain practices such as connections with long-distance telephone lines, common carrier connections at junction points, and the times at which service will be available. Construction of general principles to be used as guides in formulating specific requirements is the most that can be done for such matters.

The Need for Regulation of Service.—The regulation of service is not so critical a problem today as it has been in the past. Many improvements in the arts and technologies of the public utility services, the rendering of service on a larger scale as communities have grown in size, and recognition on the part of the utilities that it is good business policy to provide adequate and suitable service have resulted in progressive improvement in the quality of service, the utilities in many cases having taken the initiative in developing standards. There is usually a "service standards section" in each of the national utility associations, and at least one association, the American Gas Association, has established a laboratory. The standards established by regulatory agencies are considered by some utilities to be minimum requirements.

The state commissions have given much attention to the problems of developing and determining fair standards. Investigations have been made directly by them or in conjunction with technical and professional associations, educational institutions, utility associations or companies, and the Bureau of Standards. This last agency has made extensive studies for determining standards for gas, electrical, and telephone utilities. The National Association of Railroad and Utilities Commissioners has a committee on "Service of Public Utilities." Such attention to service indicates full appreciation of the fact that even though service standards generally may be satisfactory, there

[1] *Supra*, pp. 49 *ff.*

are certain service problems that present important questions to given consumers or to a given utility. Moreover, most of the public utility industries are continuing to make improvements in service. To settle these important questions and to revise service standards to keep them abreast with changes in the arts necessitates continued attention and control by the commissions. It is also necessary, at times, to force particular utilities to maintain the required standards.

The importance of satisfactory service standards for gas utilities, equally true of any utility, has been summarized by the Bureau of Standards as follows:

In the formulation of service rules and in the enforcement of such requirements, it should always be borne in mind that these regulations are really a technical specification covering the quality of the commodity and service to be supplied under a franchise which is in effect a contract with the people. These specifications should not be looked upon as police regulations of the State or the city, but rather as a part of a business arrangement between purveyor and users of gas; and if properly drawn they will protect the interests of both parties to the contract. To do this, they must not only be fair and equitable, but also clear and comprehensive, defining precisely and without ambiguity all the important conditions which it is expected the gas company shall meet in furnishing gas service. The fact that the company is likely without requirement to fulfill certain important conditions is not sufficient reason for the omission of these conditions from the rules or ordinance. And, on the other hand, it is not reasonable or fair to the gas company to omit rules which afford it protection against unreasonable demands or unjust criticism.[1]

Obligations of Utilities with Respect to Service.—The common law recognized that certain callings were pervaded with a public interest that placed upon them certain obligations. In addition to the obligation to serve at reasonable rates, the common callings were obligated to serve without discrimination and to provide reasonably adequate facilities and service. Statutory enactments establishing regulation of public utilities have continued these common law obligations. In addition, there have been some statutory provisions affecting special items of service. Regulatory commissions may thus enforce specific requirements

[1] Bureau of Standards, Standards for Gas Service, *Circular* 405, p. 2, November, 1934.

as well as apply the common law principles of adequate service. In order to carry out the application of these principles, some commissions have been authorized and directed to establish standards of service, the right of a commission to establish, supervise, and control standards having been frequently upheld. This right has been sustained even though the standards established have conflicted with franchise provisions, municipal ordinances, or contracts already made by the utility.[1]

Uniform versus Local Standards.—Standards of service for uniform application throughout a state have much to commend them. The operations of the companies under a state-wide standard can be controlled with a minimum of difficulty; comparisons of operation and rates are possible; appliances may be moved from one locality to another; and interconnection and consolidation of systems can be more readily accomplished. However, despite the recognized advantages of a state-wide standard, many commissions have recognized the desirability of making exceptions in certain localities, although this has its limitations. If the principle of making exceptions were applied generally, it would mean an individual standard for each locality, and this would require an enormous volume of detailed work, especially in checking upon the maintenance of the standards. Nevertheless, economic and engineering factors differ from plant to plant, and these should be considered. Such problems as the availability of fuels, age and condition of the plant, magnitude of the demand, the load curve, and ability of the company to finance improvements will affect a company's operations and might be justification for exceptions from uniform standards. Fairness to the public demands that only demonstrably desirable exceptions be permitted so that so far as possible the standards for service can be applied uniformly throughout a state.

There has been some criticism of the establishment of service standards on the ground that standards measuring quality must be stated in terms of existing technological developments and, therefore, have a tendency to fix technical efficiency at that

[1] See, for illustration, *Re* Midway Gas Co., P.U.R., 1920C, 624 (Calif.); *Re* Pub. Service Co., P.U.R., 1918D, 240 (Ill.); Lortz v. Union Electric Light and Power Co., P.U.R. 1918F, 223 (Mo.); and *Re* Interurban Telephone Co., P.U.R., 1919D, 800 (Wis.).

point.[1] The validity of this criticism appears to be in terms of specific standard requirements and failure to revise them as technological improvements take place rather than against the practice of prescribing service standards. It is well, however, to keep this criticism in mind during the following analysis of service standards.

Our analysis of service standards will first deal with certain problems that are common to all public utilities, *viz.*, the establishment, extension, and abandonment of service. Following these, the standards for particular utility services will be described in so far as the standards are affected by technology and special conditions in a given industry. The standards for electric service and gas service will be analyzed as illustrative of the nature of service standard regulations. However, some of the major problems found in other services will be noted. The portions of the service standard regulations dealing with the measurement of service, relations with the public, maintenance of standards, and the like will then be discussed without reference to particular utilities, since these problems are generally common to any utility service. The analysis will be closed with a description of methods used to grade utility services.

Establishment of Service.—Under common law, entrance into a business undertaking was made simply by providing facilities and offering to render the service, anyone being permitted to enter into a public calling. However, expansion in the size of the unit providing service, expansion in the sphere of operation, and the desirability of obtaining special rights, such as eminent domain for a toll-road company, resulted in the general practice of incorporating the enterprises providing public utility services. Thus, original exercise of control over the establishment of public utility enterprises came with the granting, by legislative enactment, of special charters. This practice, in turn, was modified when the enterprises became incorporated under general incorporation laws and received the right to provide service by a franchise issued by municipal or state authorities. Later, control over the establishment of public utilities was placed under commission jurisdiction. This was provided in 1892

---

[1] See, *e.g.*, quotations from L. H. Kinnard, president of the Bell Telephone Company of Pennsylvania, in M. L. Cooke, "Public Utility Regulation," Ronald Press Company, New York, 1924, pp. 133–136.

in New York for steam railways and in 1895 for street railways. Since then, other states have added this authority so that now practically all state commissions exercise it to a greater or lesser extent. The regulatory device most commonly used to control the establishment of service is a "certificate of convenience and necessity" which may be described as a formal notification or permit to render service.

The fundamental purpose of the certificate of convenience and necessity is to protect the consumers from the ill effects of injurious competition, effects that have been well summarized by the Colorado Commission, as follows:

Under this theory (of unregulated competition), public utility corporations were led into rate wars in which each company endeavored to obtain an advantage over the other by temporarily reducing rates, which ordinarily had the effect of destroying one or both of the utilities, resulting in inadequate service, and generally in a consolidation of these public utilities operating in the same field, with the result to the public of being compelled to pay the losses of one or both companies brought about by this ruinous competition, this generally taking the form of increased rates which the consumers are compelled to pay.[1]

Secondary purposes of certificates of convenience and necessity are: (1) to protect existing utilities from unnecessary and undesirable competition; (2) to protect the general public by preventing unnecessary congestion of public property such as too many taxis or motorbuses on city streets or duplicating sets of telephone poles, street railway tracks, and the like; (3) to protect the consuming public through consideration of the financial responsibility, experience, and reliability of applicants; (4) to protect investors by refusing certificates when the proposed enterprise appears financially hazardous; and (5) to protect consumers by coercing utilities to give proper rates and service under the threat of revocation or the issuance of a permit to a competing company.[2] The use of certificates of convenience and necessity in conformity with these objectives has resulted in promoting the public interest through reasonable rates and satisfactory

[1] Western Light and Power Co. v. City of Loveland, P.U.R., 1918B, 644 (Colo.).

[2] HALL, F. P., Certificates of Convenience and Necessity, *Michigan Law Review*, vol. 28, p. 107.

service and the protection of the public utilities in their right to freedom from unnecessary competition.[1]

The problems and questions arising in the administration of certificates of convenience and necessity, and the determination of whether a certificate will be issued or not, center around the following points:

1. If the community is not already served by this kind of utility, is there sufficient demand to justify inauguration of the service?

2. If the kind of service to be supplied is in the experimental stage, is the experiment safe? Is the proposed venture financially feasible?

3. If the community is already served by a similar-type utility, should it permit a competing service, or should absolute monopoly be encouraged?

4. If the community is being served unsatisfactorily or inadequately, should the existing company be given the opportunity to improve its service, or should a new company be allowed to operate?

5. What should be done with utilities already operating? Should certificates be required of them?

6. What factors should be considered in issuing certificates?

7. Can the holders of a certificate transfer it without the consent of the commission?

8. Under what conditions, if any, should certificates be revoked?

Statutory requirements and commission policies and practices vary with respect to each of these administrative questions. Practices are, however, becoming more standardized and uniform, and certificates of convenience and necessity are proving to be effective devices in giving public control over the establishment of service, maintenance of satisfactory service, and protection of the utilities already providing service.[2]

Extension of Service.—In some states, the problem of extension of service is handled similarly to the establishment of service

---

[1] LILIENTHAL, D. E., and I. S. ROSENBAUM, Motor Carriers and the State, *Journal of Land and Public Utility Economies*, vol. 2, No. 3, pp. 258 *ff*.

[2] See F. P. Hall, *op. cit.*, for a discussion of practices; and H. C. Spurr, "Guiding Principles of Public Service Regulations," Public Utilities Reports, Inc., Rochester, 1925, vol. I, Chap. III, for a collection of decisions concerning certificates of public convenience and necessity.

by requiring certificates of convenience and necessity. In most instances, however, no certificate is required when the utility merely wishes to expand its services within territory already served by it or to extend its services into adjacent territory provided the new territory is not already served. No existing competing service is likely to be encountered in the extension of electricity, telephone, gas, or water services; but motorbus and truck lines, on the contrary, are likely to enter into an already served territory when service is expanded to contiguous regions. Because of this, motor carriers ordinarily are required to have their certificates of convenience and necessity altered or modified before being allowed to make extensions of service.

The real problem concerning extensions of service arises not out of voluntarily requested or undertaken extensions but out of inducing or requiring a utility to extend its service to adjacent areas. Requests for extensions into new suburban residential areas are often made to all kinds of local utilities, many commissions being given authority to require such extensions as shall be reasonably necessary and proper for the accommodation, convenience, and service of patrons and the public.[1] It is hardly feasible or wise, however, to order extensions into sparsely settled territory which for some time, and perhaps for a long time, will not provide sufficient revenue to pay a return on the additional investment required. To handle problems of this nature, commissions usually set up requirements as to the conditions and circumstances under which extensions will be ordered. Such regulations frequently specify that the new customers pay part, or all, of the capital costs or specify conditions for amortizing the costs by specific annual charges or by higher rates. Thus, prospective customers can determine the conditions necessary to be met in order to have an extension made for them. Development of residential areas surrounding a community are directly affected by a utility's policy in making extensions, since inability to get water, light, telephone, gas, and transportation service will retard development and tend to

---

[1] This has been interpreted to mean that the utility cannot be forced to enter territory not included in its charter or franchise. See, *e.g.*, *Re* Union R.R. Co. P.U.R., 1916F, 773 (N.Y.); Towers v. United R.R. and Electric Co., P.U.R., 1915F, 474, 126 Md. 478, 95 Atl. 170; and Prest-O-Lite Co., Inc., v. Indianapolis Street R.R. Co., P.U.R., 1920B, 577 (Ind.).

keep property values low. Potential customers in rural areas also are interested in the requirements and regulations affecting extensions. Establishment of definite rules and conditions under which extensions will be made is therefore desirable.

Abandonment of Service.—Discontinuance of service by a public utility presents an important problem. On the one hand, the customers deprived of the service are affected and may be seriously inconvenienced and damaged. On the other hand, the utility is probably operating the service at a loss and will find its financial position vastly improved by discontinuing such unprofitable operation. This question assumed importance for the steam railways in the 1920's as expansions of bus and truck services made inroads upon railway traffic, especially on branch lines; and for other utilities during the exigencies of a downward swing in business activity in the 1930's. These utilities, realizing that some parts of their service were being operated at a loss, have attempted to discontinue unprofitable branches in order to ease the difficulties being caused by declines in revenues.

Most states now have laws concerning abandonment, and in some others control has been implied from the statutes providing for reasonable service. The Interstate Commerce Commission is given authority over abandonments of railways under its jurisdiction by the Transportation Act of 1920, and it has had to rule upon many requests made to it by the steam railways. Total abandonment and complete withdrawal from service can be made as a matter of right, though some statutes require that Commission permission be received. Most requests for abandonment, however, involve the discontinuance of specific services or services in specified areas. In deciding on these requests, the commissions usually refuse to permit abandonment of unprofitable parts when the service as a whole is making a fair return and to safeguard the public interest require that some provision be made to supply those who would be deprived of service. This latter often means curtailment rather than abandonment of existing services or the provision of a substitute service such as a bus service for a streetcar service. It is generally required that there be sound justification before abandonment will be permitted, operation at a loss, absence of a need for continuation of the service, shifts in population, and exhaustion of resources being the chief reasons given for making abandonments.

The right to control abandonments and the application of these principles in deciding upon permitting discontinuance of service have been frequently upheld. In *United Fuel Gas Co. v. R.R. Comm. of Ky.*, the Supreme Court said:

The primary duty of a public utility is to serve on reasonable terms all those who desire the service it renders. This duty does not permit it to pick and choose and to serve only those portions of the territory which it finds most profitable, leaving the remainder to get along without the service which it alone is in a position to give. An important purpose of state supervision is to prevent such discriminations [case cited], and if a public service company may not refuse to serve a territory where the return is reasonable, or even in some circumstances where the return is inadequate, but that on its total related business is sufficient [cases cited], it goes without saying that it may not use its privileged position, in conjunction with the demand which it has created, as a weapon to control rates by threatening to discontinue that part of its service if it does not receive the rate demanded. The powers of the state, so far as the Federal Constitution is concerned, were not exceeded by the action of the commission, in compelling appellants to continue their service in the cities named so long as they continued to do business in other parts of the state, and to there avail of the extraordinary privileges extended to public utilities.[1]

Standards of Service for Specified Utilities. 1. *Electric Light and Power Services.*—Because the determination of safe, adequate, and proper electric service involves engineering as well as economic questions, which are highly technical in nature, the present discussion will be limited to pointing out the requirements of satisfactory service and to indicating the nature of the standards that have been set up. Central stations encounter varied conditions of operation and possess different facilities for providing service. Though very small plants are becoming fewer in number, the sizes of central stations vary in capacity from 100 to hundreds of thousands of kilowatts. The operating conditions that affect adequacy and efficiency of service relate to (1) central station operation, (2) the transmission and distribution system, and (3) the energy measuring and utilization devices. From the viewpoint of the consumer, the continuity of service and the

---

[1] 278 U.S. 300, 309 (1928); see, also, Hall, F. P. Discontinuance of Service by Public Utilities, 13 *Minnesota Law Review*, 181–215 and 325–347; and O. P. Field, The Withdrawal from Service of Public Utility Companies, *Yale Law Journal*, vol. 35, p. 169, for a collection of cases and discussion of principles and problems.

regularity of voltage are the two most important requisites of a satisfactory service, although the time, place, and nature of the use also must be considered.

Continuity of service is likely to be affected by accidents and breakdown of boilers, engines, turbines, generators, transformers, and distribution lines. This may result in interruptions to service which, in the absence of stand-by units, duplicate lines, or connection with other sources of supply, may last for a considerable interval of time. To prevent such contingencies, commissions sometimes require that emergency equipment be installed. The utility is under obligation to prevent as far as possible interruptions to service and to restore service as soon as possible after an interruption; and a record of the time, duration, and causes of all interruptions to service ordinarily must be filed with the commission.[1]

Irregular voltage is a source of annoyance and dissatisfaction with electric service, since it affects lighting and lasting qualities of lamps and the speed, temperature, and starting torque of motors. Uniformity of voltage is attained through control of generating equipment and switchboards. For this latter, voltmeters and ammeters are used, and, on alternating-current circuits, wattmeters and frequency meters also are used. Voltage regulation of the distribution system, both feeders and mains, is necessary in order that the station control of voltage may be carried through the bus bar to the consumers' outlets. It is now common for the commissions to establish a standard voltage and specify the allowable variation therein. The Bureau of Standards states that "circuits used primarily for lighting should be designed for a maximum voltage variation at the company's main service-terminals of not more than 5 per cent plus or minus from the standard average service voltage for any considerable time, while 10 per cent plus or minus may be allowed on power lines."[2]

Records of station loads and outputs are usually required to be kept and submitted to the commission. On the basis of these records, the efficiency of the distribution system may be

[1] Unless otherwise noted, this discussion of electric service standards is adopted from Bureau of Standards, Standards for Electric Service, *Circular* 56, September, 1923, 2d ed.

[2] *Ibid.*, p. 16.

judged. These records show the amount of energy loss; *i.e.*, they permit the determination of the ratio of energy sold at customers' service terminals to the energy delivered to the bus bars. Losses arise from leakage, transformers, meters, lines, meter errors, and unaccounted-for causes. Excessive losses indicate a need for improving the equipment and operations of the distribution system.

The subjects usually included in the standards of service rules for electric service are presented in outline form below. Some of the items listed are self-explanatory; those dealing with voltage and regularity of service have already been mentioned; others, marked by an asterisk, will be discussed later along with similar rules for other utility services. The outline follows:

I. Statutory requirements and general provisions.
    1. Definition of commission, utility, and customers.
    2. Reservation by the commission of rights to alter, amend, and revise rules.
    3. Privileges of a utility to establish reasonable rules and regulations to which customers must comply as a requisite to receiving service.
II. Operation and maintenance.
    1. Maintaining adequate service and making reports thereof to the commission.
    2. Construction, installation, etc., to be in accordance with accepted practices and approved engineering standards.
    3. Identification and inspection of poles.
    4. Grounding of low-potential circuits.
III. Meters.*
    1. Location, specifying accepted and nonaccepted locations of meters.
    2. Meter testing facilities, equipment, and standards.
    3. Accuracy requirements of watt-hour meters and demand meters.
    4. Places, methods, and time of testing meters.
    5. Tests upon request of customer.
    6. Test by commission.
    7. Meter records and reports.
IV. Information to customers.*
    1. Information concerning reading of meters, bills and billing, lighting, and services.
    2. Files of rate schedules, rules and regulations.
V. Voltage and frequency.
    1. Standard nominal voltage and permissible variations in
       a. Lighting service.
       b. Power service.
    2. Standard frequency.
    3. Voltage surveys and records.

VI. Records.*
   1. Station instruments and meters.
   2. Station operating records and interruptions of service.
   3. Service complaints.
VII. Charges, deposits, and refunds.*
   1. Meter rentals.
   2. Refunds and prorated bills for inaccurate meters.
   3. Deposits
      a. Conditions upon which they may be demanded.
      b. Records.
      c. Conditions for return.
VIII. Accidents.*
   1. Record.
   2. Reasonable care to be exercised.
  IX. Extension of lines.
   1. Conditions upon which they will be made.[1]

2. *Gas Utilities.*—The usefulness of a gas supply, due to the
use of gas almost exclusively for cooking, water and house heating, gas engines, and industrial purposes, is best measured in
terms of its heating value. It is characteristic of the present-
day gas supply to consist of mixtures, natural gas ordinarily
containing methane with some ethane, propane, butane, etc.,
and manufactured gas usually containing hydrogen, carbon
monoxide, methane, small quantities of other hydrocarbons,
and some nitrogen and carbon dioxide. Consequently, a given
quantity of gas may have any heating value within a wide
range.[2]

Heating value is ordinarily measured in terms of British
thermal units[3] per cubic foot of gas. In nontechnical terms,
heating value represents the heat units contained in a given
volume of gas. Since gas is now seldom used for lighting purposes, the consumer is no longer interested in its illuminating
quality (which was early specified as "candle power") and is
concerned almost solely with quantity of heat units delivered.
Nor is the consumer directly interested in the quantity of
gas necessary to provide any desired quantity of heat units,

---

[1] *Op. cit.,* pp. 218 *ff.*

[2] Unless otherwise noted, this discussion of standards for gas service is
based upon Bureau of Standards, Standards for Gas Service, *Circular* 405,
Nov. 8, 1934, which is an exhaustive study of the subject.

[3] A B.t.u. is defined as the quantity of heat necessary to raise 1 pound of
water 1°F.

although indirectly he is interested in the quantity factor because of the fact that his appliances have an "input rating" which indicates the nearly highest rate at which heat can be safely and satisfactorily liberated within the appliance. If the heat of combustion of the gas supply is much less than the rating, *i.e.*, the B.t.u. content per cubic foot is small, too much time for heating or inability to get the desired heat results. On the contrary, if the B.t.u. content provides more heat than the input rating specifies, there is incomplete combustion, and the likelihood of the liberation of poisonous gases, such as carbon monoxide.

There is a reasonably wide range of heat supply on either side of the rating within which the appliance will give satisfactory service. The adjustment of the burner, *i.e.*, the control of the size of the orifice for gas and the air shutter, permits the burner of most appliances to be adapted to varied conditions of heat value of gas. Once adjusted, however, changes in heat value require a new adjustment to be made. Accordingly, it is desirable that the heat value standard be maintained.

Heating value differs according to the type and composition of the gas. The most usual heating values are about 550 to 600 B.t.u. per cubic foot for coal gas, about 525 to 650 B.t.u. per cubic foot for carbureted water gas depending upon the quantity of oil gas included, and from less than 800 to as much as 3350 B.t.u. per cubic foot for natural gas. The standard established, therefore, will depend upon the gas supplied. Uniformity or lack of variation in heating value is generally specified at about 5 per cent above or below the average stated in the standard. Variations greater than this proportion provide an unsatisfactory service. Testing requirements, to insure maintenance of the heating value, are ordinarily specified. The standard fixed for a natural gas supply must necessarily be related to the composition of the supply, its mixture with other natural gases, its mixture with manufactured gas, and the practice of "reforming" it to a gas of lower heating value. Maintenance of uniformity should be specified for natural gas as for manufactured gas. A change in the heating value standard should not be permitted unless there is a corresponding change in the rates, and it should carry with it the obligation to readjust consumers' appliances.

Heating value depends upon the composition of the gas. No special composition problems are created so long as a natural gas supply comes from a field of limited extent or so long as variations in composition are no more than would be accidentally produced under the usual methods of manufacture. In the case of mixtures, however, it is necessary to control specific gravity and the percentage of inerts. From a chemical standpoint, composition determines the purity of the gas and the extent to which substances with a harmful effect are present. At present, there are no rules limiting the quantity of inert constituents, carbon dioxide, oxygen, and nitrogen, because of the wide variety of methods of producing gas. Limitation by rule would either be unduly restrictive or be so liberal as to be ineffective. Because of the general undesirability of inerts, however, their amounts should not be increased without good cause.

Carbon monoxide is the only constituent that is poisonous in the amounts ordinarily present in gas. Coal gas contains from 5 to 10 per cent, and water gas from 25 to 30 per cent carbon monoxide. To limit its quantity, therefore, would seriously affect the production of water gas, which is the major type of manufactured gas. No limitations on carbon monoxide are now made anywhere in the United States. A large proportion of the deaths caused by gas are suicidal or are due to irresponsible conditions such as drunkenness or gross ignorance. Moreover, many of the remaining cases of gas poisoning result not from the carbon monoxide content of the gas itself but from carbon monoxide formed by the combustion of gas with insufficient air. Protection of the consumers thus lies more in the regulation of the construction and adjustment of appliances and education in the use of gas rather than limiting its carbon monoxide content.

Other "impurities" are present. Sulphur compounds, when burned, form sulphur dioxide. This, in turn, can form sulphuric acid and corrode metal parts and attack cement or mortar in chimneys. The sulphur content arises from the coal or oil used in producing the gas. A limitation on sulphur, therefore, limits the fuel which may be used. The Bureau of Standards recommends a limit of 20 grains of sulphur per 100 cubic foot of gas, pointing out that such a limit, though reducing the most common present state standards of 30 grains, will not materially restrict the choice of fuels and brings the gas well below the point where it produces a disagreeable odor when burned. It is also recommended that no more than a trace (0.1 grain per 100 cubic foot of gas) of hydrogen sulphide be permitted, since this sulphur compound can be removed at relatively small cost. The removal will prevent the ill effects of hydrogen sulphide in attacking the copper and brass tubing of appliances and in corroding silverware, paint with lead bases, and so on. Though the adverse effects of considerable quantities of ammonia in gas are disputed, the Bureau of Standards finds that it can be kept below 5 grains per 100 cubic feet in all cases except small plants which could not operate economically ammonia-removal apparatus. The Bureau recommends that this amount be set as the maximum.

The pressure at which gas is supplied to the user is an important factor in determining the quality of the service rendered. Satisfactory service in this respect demands sufficient pressure at all times, an excess of pressure at no time, and as uniform pressure as possible at all times. Excess pressure causes leaks and inability to control temperatures; deficient pressure causes an inefficient heating service. Lack of uniformity of pressure affects control of temperature. Minimum pressures and variations therein have long been specified by most commissions. Measured by inches in a water column, a typical standard is:

Minimum Pressure, Inches	Greatest Variation Possible, Inches
2 to 3	2
3 to 4	$2\frac{1}{2}$
Over 4	3

To promote economy in distribution and better service, the Bureau of Standards recommends the establishment of a maximum pressure standard, of not over 12 inches, with the requirement that the pressure at the customer's meter outlet shall never be less than one-half the established maximum.

Other features of standards for gas are concerned largely with records, meters, tests, etc. These will be discussed later with similar regulations for other utility services.

3. *Telephone Service.*—Telephone service involves a considerable number of factors and should be related to individual community needs. These latter vary widely with the size of the community and with the nature of its business and social interests. There exists also a wide variety of facilities for rendering the service. Furthermore, rapid and frequent technological

changes have occurred in the telephone industry. Because of this fact, telephone service has become progressively better. These factors, however, make the formulation of service standards for telephone communication difficult and but few commissions have attempted to establish them.[1]

The recommendations of the Bureau of Standards with respect to standards for telephone service were as follows:

1. Adequacy of service development.
    a. Adequacy of classes of service: the classification of services in each locality should be related to the needs of the users, and each community should have such classes of service as will cover all reasonable needs.
    b. Adequacy of plant facilities: plant facilities may be inadequate: first, with respect to rendering any service at certain points or to certain points; second, with respect to rendering any desired class of service and, third, with respect to rendering the required amount of service. To provide and maintain a uniform grade of service necessitates careful study and anticipation of the traffic to be offered because an increase in traffic without a corresponding increase in facilities results in overloading and the lowering of the grade of service provided.
    c. Adequacy of operations: if service is not to be lowered by receiving calls faster than they can be handled, it is necessary that the force of operators be large enough and competent enough to handle the traffic offered.
2. Quality of speech transmission.
    a. The quality of speech transmission is dependent upon the degree of loudness in its reproduction, the accuracy of its reproduction, and the degree of uniformity with respect to both. The attainment of satisfactory service in these respects is dependent upon the development of the telephone arts, the physical equipment used, and the conditions of the plant.
3. Dependability of speech transmission.
    a. Dependability of speech transmission is directly related to the plant design, its construction and installation, and its conditions. The details of the relations here involved are many.
4. Quality of operation.
    a. Speed of operation: the handling of calls on a manual system involves time for answering the call on the part of the operator, time to connect the called and the calling lines, time to ring the station called, and time to effect a disconnection after the call is completed and a disconnect signal is given. Type of equipment affects the speed of these operations, though the adequacy and competency of the operators and the

[1] HERRING, J. M., and G. C. GROSS, "Telecommunications: Economics and Regulation," McGraw-Hill Book Company, Inc., New York, 1936, pp. 350–351.

rate at which they work are also important factors. The training, experience, and supervision of operators are important to keep the average time to each of these operations to a minimum. Automatic equipment fixes the time involved for each operation for which it serves. Delays in effecting any of these operations cause annoyances to the user and give rise to many complaints.

b. Accuracy of operation: the achievement of accuracy depends upon the accuracy of the directory, of the calling party, and of the operators and upon certain features of the plant. Operating errors result in delay, inconvenience, and annoyance.

c. Secrecy: the information that may be passed over telephone lines is unquestionably the property of the users of the telephone. It is difficult to trespass on telephone lines, since access to lines is generally difficult, and the trespasser must be provided with necessary apparatus and know how to use it. Company employees, however, must have access to lines. Double connections and cross talk sometimes permit conversations to be overheard. Listening by subscribers on party lines is not under control of the company. Probably the main preventative of secrecy violation is in the laws that have made it illegal for employees to divulge the telephone conversations that they have overheard.

d. Uniformity of operation: the average time required for each of the elements involved in the speed of service is the measure of uniformity in service, and the criterion of lack of uniformity is the degree of variation from these averages.

5. Dependability of operation.

a. Reliability of switching equipment: the design, manufacture, and installation of the switching equipment affect its operation, but equally important are its inspection and testing and the promptness and thoroughness with which it is restored to normal operating efficiency.

b. Reliability of the operating force: the individual characteristics of each member of the operating force is a direct factor affecting reliability. Over-all reliability is, however, dependent upon the *esprit de corps* of the force as a whole.

6. Degree of safety.

a. The element of safety is not only of importance to the user of the service and the company's employees but also to the general public. Plant design and construction must consider this element to a high degree.[1]

But few state commissions have attempted to establish rules governing telephone service as suggested in the foregoing findings of the Bureau of Standards. However, many of the states have rules concerning one or another of these points. In general,

[1] Bureau of Standards, Telephone Service, *Circular* 112, June 24, 1921, pp. 159 *ff.*

most of the commissions have prescribed that construction be in accordance with recognized standards and practices, such as those stated in the Bureau of Standards National Electrical Safety Code. This is usually supplemented by a requirement specifying proper upkeep and repair, including tests and inspections. Adequacy of service is covered by regulations affecting the switchboard capacity, size of the operating force, and the number of subscribers on party lines. Some regulations concerning average speed have been made, as have also requirements covering phraseology and methods to be employed by operators to facilitate the handling of traffic. Regulations concerning the publication and revision of directories have sometimes been made.[1]

4. *Street Railway and Motorbus Services.*—Variation in local conditions and needs makes standards for street railway and motorbus services difficult to formulate. Many and diverse factors affect every feature of these services. Patrons are in close contact with the agency rendering the service, and criticism and complaints may be made easily. Thus, even though commission attention long has been focused upon the problems of standards for these services, little has been done beyond formulating very general regulations or stating specific requirements for given local conditions.

The elements and factors involved in adequate and satisfactory service for street railways and motorbuses are (1) speed, (2) frequency and regularity of service, (3) convenience and comfort, (4) safety, and (5) courtesy. As previously noted, with the exception of specific requirements, such as the frequency of nonrush-hour service and the frequency of owl-car service, and the establishment of general rules concerning the number of cars per a specified unit number of passengers, the number of seats per a specified unit number of passengers, the maximum load for types of cars, etc., the commissions have not specified elaborate and detailed standards for these services.[2]

---

[1] *Op. cit.*, pp. 192 *ff.*; see also M. E. Atwater, "Telephone Standards," in M. L. Cooke, "Public Utility Regulation," Ronald Press Company, New York, 1925, pp. 122 *ff.*

[2] The reader is again referred to G. L. Wilson, J. M. Herring, and R. B. Eutsler, "Public Utility Industries," McGraw-Hill Book Company, Inc., New York, 1936, for a study of the characteristic features and practices of the particular utility in question.

5. *Water Supply Utilities.*—Like street railway and bus service, water supply utilities operate under a variety of conditions. Moreover, the bulk of the service is rendered by municipally owned and operated plants which frequently are not under commission supervision. Little has been done, therefore, in regard to general standards except for establishing regulations concerning construction and maintenance, metering and tests of meters, and pressure. The highly important factor of purity and pollution is sometimes under the jurisdiction of health authorities,[1] though a few commissions have authority to establish regulations for this and have formulated purity standards.

Service Standards Common to Many Utilities.—Certain service requirements are applicable to many types of public utility service. These include matters affecting measurement of the service, relations with the public, information to be furnished, maintenance of standards, and the like. Though of necessity the rules for each utility service must be related to the distinctive characteristics of that service, and thereby likely to be found in the standard code set up for a given service, they are discussed here as being common to all utilities in order to avoid duplication.

1. *Meters and Measurement of Service.*—The measurement of service for gas, electricity, and water is done by meters. Since accuracy of the meter is a prime requisite, requirements regarding frequency, standards, equipment, etc., for testing the accuracy of meters are usually specified. The initiation of tests by customers or the commission is sometimes included in the regulations. Rules for adjusting rates for inaccurate meters are sometimes stated.

2. *Information and Records.*—Most public utilities are required to furnish customers or keep on public file information concerning rates and service and the rules and regulations required of the patrons by the utility. Records of complaints and their disposition, station operation, interruptions to service, tests of customers' meters and appliances, and tests of station instruments and meters are required by commissions. On the basis of such records, commissions know the extent to which service standards are maintained and when and where improvements in operation are necessary.

---

[1] See, *e.g.*, Pool v. Mokelumne River Power and Water Co., P.U.R., 1918C, 572 (Calif.).

3. *Payment of Bills, Deposits, Refunds, Etc.*—The setting of a time limit for payment of bills, the requiring of deposits to insure payment of bills, the nature of refunds that may be made, and the like are conditions usually set forth by a utility as a requisite to obtaining and continuing to obtain service. The commissions may either approve the rules and regulations of a given company or, as is now generally coming to be the case, set up regulations to which company rules must conform. As a part of these rules, other conditions affecting the furnishing or discontinuance of service are stated.

4. *Safety and Continuity of Service.*—Safety and continuity of service are promoted by rules covering inspections. Many technical standards for construction and maintenance must be followed in making inspections. Accidents ordinarily must be reported in full to the commissions.

Grading Utility Services.—The establishment of service standards and the requiring of reports from the utility (and inspections thereof by commission inspectors) do little more than give information that rules have been violated or that service has been rendered in compliance with rules. Such data are valuable for use in making decisions concerning certificates of convenience and necessity, abandonment, revision of standards, and adjustment of complaints and in getting given utilities to maintain service standards. However, they do not provide a picture of the service as a whole by a given utility or a basis for comparing the service rendered by different utilities or for determining whether or not there is improvement in compliance with service standards from year to year. The great problem with respect to service standards is their enforcement.

Most commissions, chiefly because of inadequate resources and personnel, make little effort to enforce compliance with the service standards that they set up, although a few commissions pay considerable heed to this important matter. The methods employed fall into two categories: (1) routine inspections by the commission staff and (2) grading public utility services. Routine inspection, if carried on adequately, is a great and continuing burden upon a commission, requiring a considerable staff of inspectors regularly making rounds, since infrequent and spasmodic inspections accomplish little. Some commissions, notably the Wisconsin commission, have been able to carry on the work of inspection economically by employing capable engineers and combining this work with other duties, such as valuations or special investigations of utility matters, including rates.[1] However, the detail and expense involved explain readily why such work is confined to the larger and better staffed commissions.

Grading of public utility service is done by setting up a rating scale with various aspects of service weighted in accordance with a grading point system. The service of each utility company is then graded periodically on the basis of the weights fixed in the standard scale. A 100-point scale used by the Wisconsin Commission for grading gas and electric service is shown in the following table:[2]

Rule		Subject	Credit			
Gas	Electric		Gas, per cent	Rank	Electric, per cent	Rank
	14	Creeping meters	. . .	. .	4	6
1	15	Accuracy of meters	7	4	7	3
	16	Installation tests	. . .	. .	5	5
2	17	Periodic tests	14	3	14	2
3	18	Meter-testing records	5	6	5	5
4	19	Meter-testing equipment	5	6	5	5
5	20	Request tests	4	7	4	6
6	21	Referee tests				
7	22	Meter readings on bills	4	7	4	6
8	. .	Heating value	21	1		
9	. .	Calorimeter equipment	7	4		
	23	Interruptions	. . .	. .	18	1
	24	Station records	. . .	. .	6	4
10	25	Pressure and voltage variation	18	2	18	1
11	26	Pressure and voltage surveys	6	5	6	4
12	. .	Purity	4	7		
13	. .	Complaint records	5	6		
	27	Information	. . .	. .	4	6
		Total..................	100		100	

[1] MOSHER, W. E., and F. G. CRAWFORD, "Public Utility Regulation," Harper & Brothers, New York, 1933, p. 176.

[2] Bureau of Standards, "Technical Conference of State Utility Commission Engineers," 1923, p. 8. See Chap. VII for a more complete discussion of graded utility services and their relation to the rate of return.

Summary.—It has now become the general practice for the regulatory commissions to establish rules and standards for service. Compliance with these standards is the test of the adequacy and efficiency of the utility's service. Service standards are a necessary part of regulation because of the interrelationship between service and rates. Some specific items, such as establishment of service, are more widely and strictly controlled than others, and some services, such as electricity and gas, are more extensively controlled than others. Variations in operating conditions and the nature of the service make the formulation of standards for some utilities, such as street railways, difficult. Differences in facilities and variations in operating conditions also limit the establishment and application of a service standard code uniformly throughout a state, though the tendency is toward uniform standards. In general, service standards attempt to insure that the utility's service will provide the customers with service that is efficient, regular, adequate, safe, courteous, comfortable, and prompt. Control over service is one of the best criteria of the effectiveness of public utility regulation.

References

American Gas Association: *Proceedings*, annual.
Bureau of Standards: Standards for Electric Service, *Circular* 56, Washington, 1923.
———: Standards for Gas Service, *Circular* 405, Washington, 1934.
———: Technical Conference of State Utility Commission Engineers, *Miscellaneous Publication* 58, Washington, 1923.
———: Telephone Service, *Circular* 112, Washington, 1921.
COOKE, M. L.: "Public Utility Regulation," Ronald Press Company, New York, 1924, Chap. VI.
FIELD, O. P.: The Withdrawal from Service of Public Utility Companies, *Yale Law Journal*, vol. 35.
GLAESER, M. G.: "Outlines of Public Utility Economics," The Macmillan Company, New York, 1931, Chap. XXVII.
HALL, F. P.: Certificates of Convenience and Necessity, *Michigan Law Review*, vol. 28.
———: Discontinuance of Service by Public Utilities, *Minnesota Law Review*, vol. 43.
HERRING, J. M., and G. C. GROSS: "Telecommunications: Economics and Regulation," McGraw-Hill Book Company, Inc., New York, 1936.
JONES, ELIOT, and T. C. BIGHAM: "Principles of Public Utilities," The Macmillan Company, 1931, Chap. IX.

LILIENTHAL, D. E., and I. S. ROSENBAUM: Motor Carriers and the State, *Journal of Land and Public Utility Economics*, vol. 2.

MOSHER, W. E., and F. G. CRAWFORD: "Public Utility Regulation," Harper & Brothers, New York, 1933, Chaps. VIII and XII.

National Association of Railroad and Utilities Commissioners: *Proceedings*, annual.

National Electric Light Association: *Proceedings*, annual (to 1932).

"Report of the New York Commission on Revision of the Public Service Commissions Law," Albany, 1930.

Service Standard Rules: as issued by some of the state commissions.

SPURR, H. C.: "Guiding Principles of Public Service Regulation," Public Utilities Reports, Inc., Rochester, 1924, vol. I, Chaps. III and VII.

CHAPTER X

REGULATION OF SECURITY ISSUES

The Background of Commission Regulation of Security Issues.
American corporations, and those in the field of public utility
services have not been exceptions, frequently have been
organized and promoted on a basis of overcapitalization. In
many enterprises, the amount of capitalization was much in
excess of and bore little relationship to the cost or value of the
company's assets, a situation that resulted from unregulated
financing and promotion of corporate enterprises. Even though
this may have encouraged and stimulated the rapid development of business enterprises in all fields of economic activity,
it was accomplished at the expense of top-heavy and cumbersome
capital structures which, in the field of public utilities, have come
to be a serious problem in satisfactory regulation. The placing
of emphasis upon the making of profits from the sale of securities
rather than from the operation of the enterprise encouraged this
tendency to overcapitalization. Although the practices causing
overcapitalization were many, chief among them may be mentioned the giving of stock as a bonus with bonds sold and the
paying for franchises, promoter's services, legal services, and
financing and other services with securities the amount of which
would be determined solely by the promoters. Also, operating
practices of many enterprises tended to increase the amount of
overcapitalization. There would be a failure to distinguish
between capital and income, thus necessitating the issuance of
additional securities in order to pay for replacements for which
no depreciation had been provided, although in many cases
rapid technological advances made it necessary to issue additional
securities in order to replace obsolete equipment before its costs
could be written off as operating expenses. It was common,
also, as consolidations were effected, for the consolidated units
to issue securities in excessive amounts. Finally, there were

many fraudulent issues through the use of construction companies and other devices.[1]

Grievances against stock watering by the railroads were early expressed. The Windom Committee, reporting to Congress in 1874, declared that no other abuse had "contributed so much to the general discontent and indignation as the increase of railway capital by '*stock watering*' and '*capitalization of surplus earnings.*'" The Cullom Committee, reporting to Congress in 1886, decried the practice of stock watering in even stronger terms and declared that it had "imposed a serious and continous illegitimate burden upon commerce." It was recommended that the states take action to control this abuse. The states, however, then made no direct attempts to limit or control railway capitalization, feeling that if overcapitalization adversely affected rates the remedy would lie in regulating the rates rather than in controlling financial practices.[2]

Extent of Commission Control over Security Issues.—The impetus to Commission control over security issues came in 1888 when rates fixed by a state commission were enjoined as confiscatory on grounds that they were not high enough to yield the railroad sufficient revenue to permit it to pay interest on its bonds and dividends on its stocks.[3] Though subsequent decisions established value of property instead of capitalization as the rate base, it then appeared that security regulation was necessary in order to regulate rates. Thus, a number of states soon passed laws designed to restrict the issuance of securities by railroads and public utilities, such laws being passed in New York in 1889; Texas, 1893; Massachusetts, 1894 (making more drastic laws controlling security issues passed earlier); and Maine and New Hampshire, 1897. State regulation of security issues has been added in other states. As was shown in Chap. III, 23 state commissions were reported as having control over securities and capitalization by 1930; since then 6 states

[1] See, *e.g.*: RIPLEY, W. Z., "Railway Problems," Ginn and Company (Athenæum Press), Boston, 1913, Chaps. I, IV, XXI; Federal Trade Commission, "Utility Corporations," Sen. Doc. 92, 70th Cong., 1st Sess., Part 73-A, Appendix L-3.

[2] LOCKLIN, D. P., "Regulation of Security Issues by the Interstate Commerce Commission," University of Illinois Studies in the Social Sciences, Urbana, 1925, pp. 9–11.

[3] Chicago and Northwestern Ry. Co. v. Day, 35 Fed. 866 (1888).

have enacted fairly complete laws regarding these matters, and several other states have amended previous laws. The extent of control varies from mere publicity to practically complete and unlimited control. Agitation for federal control of security issues by interstate railway carriers was opposed by the railway and banking interests and was not given to the Interstate Commerce Commission until 1920. Public utility holding-company security issues became subject to control by the United States Securities and Exchange Commission by provision of the Public Utility Holding Company Act of 1935.

The Need for Security Regulation.—The consequences of unrestricted freedom in financing, with overcapitalization and other abuses arising, made it imperative that security issues be controlled. The Committee on Railway Capitalization of the National Association of Railway Commissioners in its report of 1915 stated that those in control of railroads had too frequently directed their activities to the speculative manipulation of securities rather than to the legitimate operation of the railroad. It was declared that those who were directly concerned with and interested in the improvement of operations were often thwarted by a speculating board of managers who had no interest beyond that of exploitation through security issues.[1] The New York Court of Appeals long ago pointed out that the public had been fraudulently imposed upon by public utility corporations which issued securities for improper purposes designed to result in the personal enrichment of the company's officers and that public control, looking toward prevention of the issuance of stocks and bonds not needed for corporate purposes, was one of the reasons for giving commissions power over security issues.[2]

One state commission stated that the need for public control was found in the fact of overcapitalization, the consequences of which

. . . were far-reaching and disastrous in their effect, and it was only a comparatively short time before the state found it necessary to intervene on behalf of the general public, which too often was misled, and

[1] National Association of Railway Commissioners, *Proceedings*, 1915, p. 337.

[2] People *ex rel.* Delaware and Hudson Co., v. Stevens, 197 New York 1, 90 N.E. 60.

in fact in many cases actually defrauded by such fictitious issues of stocks, and the securities of such corporations. The first intervention by the state was through the courts, which many years ago set up a trust fund doctrine, the effect of which was to declare the difference between the par value of the stock and the amount which had actually been paid for it in money or property, a trust fund in the hands of the holders of such stock for the benefit of the creditors of the corporation, available in the event of the insolvency of the corporation by suit at the instance of the receivers thereof. Such suits frequently resulted in a great injustice to holders of the stocks of such corporations who purchased the same with actual knowledge of the facts relating to the issue of such stocks, but without any conception or idea of the legal consequences attached to such purchase. The great majority of these cases arose where the stock had been issued in large amounts for property or services for the use of the corporation. Then it was that the state stepped in and declared that henceforth no stock should be issued in exchange for property or services unless the latter were worth the amount of the par value of such stock, the determination of this question being left in many instances to the directors of the corporation, whose decision was made final in the absence of actual fraud or bad faith. Later many of the states enacted additional provisions prohibiting the issue of stock for cash less than the whole par value thereof. So great was the demand of the public for state intervention along this line, that in many of the states such provisions were placed directly in the Constitution thereof. In nearly all of the states in the union there are today such provisions on the statute books, where they do not appear in the Constitution.[1]

The regulation and control of security issues thus arose out of financial practices leading to unwarranted, and sometimes fraudulent, overissuance of securities, the consequences of which affected adversely the ability of the company to raise capital, the rates and services offered, and the investor in its securities.

Capital, Capitalization, and Financial Structure.—The economist uses the term "capital" to mean goods that have been produced and that are used to produce other goods or services. This concept distinguishes man-made goods from nature-made goods such as land and other natural resources. But both these types of goods as well as property rights and intangible items are used by businessmen in the operation of a business enterprise; hence, the businessman generally uses the term capital to refer

[1] *Re* United Rys. and Electric Co., P.U.R. 1917D, 820 (Md.).

to all these kinds of goods, and, for convenience sake, they are likely to be expressed in terms of money. In the business sense, therefore, capital refers to the investment in the business.

Capitalization is a term used to mean the valuation assigned to the capital used in the business. That part of the capitalization which represents ownership interests is shown as stock, and that part which is borrowed is shown as bonds. Since capitalization refers to values, it is possible that the actual or real values of the capital will be increased or decreased to conform to the capitalization of the company. When capitalization is greater than the actual value of the capital of the business, overcapitalization is said to exist. Undercapitalization is the contrary situation. Owing to the dynamic nature of economic phenomena and consequent fluctuation in value, it is seldom that the value of a business' capital and its capitalization actually coincide. Over- and undercapitalization are deemed to exist, then, when there is an unwarranted difference between the value of the capital and the capitalization.

It is sometimes considered, especially for competitive businesses, that any capitalization that will earn the usual or market rate of return is proper. When this concept is used, overcapitalization is said to exist when the rate of earnings falls below the market rate. This concept is not applicable, as has been noted, in public utilities because of the control of rates by regulatory authority with the consequent possibility of fixing rates at such a level as will yield earnings on any desired capitalization.

Overcapitalization is likely to be accompanied by "watered stock," a term used to describe the condition of issuing stock in greater amount than its real value. In order to hide the existence of overcapitalization and watered stock, the balance sheet of a company in this status is likely to contain fictitious assets, assets arbitrarily overvalued, or liabilities arbitrarily undervalued. Because of the fact that watered stock is frequently found in cases of overcapitalization, the terms are loosely used as being synonymous.

Financial plan refers to the amount and relationship of assets, liabilities, and net worth in the business. Capital structure is that part of the financial plan which has to do with the proportion of stocks and bonds represented in the capitalization of the business.[1] These terms were explained because of the fact that security regulation grew out of, and is concerned directly with, these matters. Since there are no general definitions of them, and since they are used in various ways by others, the authors have explained them with a view also to defining their meaning as used in this volume.

Relationship of Capitalization and Capital Structures to Ability to Raise Capital.—The ability of the enterprise to raise new capital for expansion, extension, or betterment of its service or to provide from its earnings for proper maintenance and depreciation looking toward replacements of worn-out or obsolete equipment is affected by the amount and nature of its capital structure. It has frequently been pointed out that the utility industries have been rapidly growing industries and have pressure against them to expand and enlarge their services. Likewise, the utility industries have been characterized by rapid technological advances, and capital is needed for betterments if a given utility is to offer the most up-to-date services to its patrons. In cases where a given company is overcapitalized, with consequent low dividends on its stocks, and is constantly having difficulty in meeting its fixed charges, its ability to raise new capital is doubtful. Nor will such a company likely have sufficient earnings to provide for expansion, extensions, or replacements due to obsolescence by means of reinvesting earnings. Similarly, the company with a top-heavy financial structure, *i.e.*, one with an unduly large proportion of bonds and preferred stock and consequently heavy and burdensome fixed charges, will not be in position to raise capital on economical terms nor will it be in a position to reinvest earnings. Security control, if it is to promote effective regulation, must take cognizance of overcapitalization and must take steps to correct and prevent it. It must also look toward sanctioning the issuance of securities in accordance with sound financial practices so that fixed charges will not exact too great a proportion of a company's earnings.

[1] For a further discussion of these various terms and their meaning, see any text on corporation finance. Suggested references are: DEWING, A. S., "Financial Policies of Corporations," Ronald Press Company, New York, 1921; HOAGLAND, H. E., "Corporation Finance," McGraw-Hill Book Company, Inc., New York, 1933; or BURTCHETT, F. F., "Corporation Finance," Harper & Brothers, New York, 1934.

There are no standard criteria as to either the amount or the proportion of the various types of securities which should be represented in the capital structure. Experience has demonstrated, however, that there are sound principles that should be followed. In so far as amount of capital is concerned, private businesses consider that the maximum limit is earnings capitalized at the normal rate of return and the minimum is the cost of the assets. Because of difficulties in forecasting the earnings, the more conservative practice is to capitalize on the basis of costs of assets. In the public utility field, capitalization on the basis of earnings is not justifiable, since an unregulated monopoly, such as a public utility, could command earnings as high as the traffic would bear, which might result in a capitalization much in excess of cost of assets. Under public regulation, earnings must be related to cost (or value) of the assets. To fix rates at a point that would yield a return on a capitalization in excess of cost (or value) of the assets would be to ask the consumers of the service to pay unreasonably and unjustifiably high rates. The various proportions of bonds, preferred, and common stock represented in the capital structure will depend upon the regularity as well as the volume of earnings and the nature of the assets used in the business. With a relatively large proportion of fixed assets and with comparatively regular earnings, public utilities have found it safe to issue large proportions of bonds and preferred stock, the two together often comprising as much as two-thirds to three-fourths of the total capitalization.[1]

Overcapitalized concerns frequently find it impossible to pay a return on outstanding securities. In such cases, if the capital structure contains a large proportion of bonds and preferred stocks, it is likely that all the earnings allowed by regulatory commissions limiting rate levels so as to yield a fair-return-on-a-fair-value would be required to meet the fixed charges on the bonds and the fixed commitment on the preferred stock. Common stocks would receive little or no dividend, and their prices

---

[1] DEWING, *op. cit.*, in vol. II, Chaps. III–VI, discusses the principles underlying the financial plan. Chapter V, The Financial Plans of the New Public Utility, describes the relationship between rates and earnings and the effect of earnings on the kind and volume of securities to be included in the capital structure.

would probably be so low as to make it practically impossible to sell more common stock. It would be difficult, also to sell additional preferred stock or bonds in the event that more capital were needed in the business. Viewing such an impending status with alarm, a utility would be likely to defer needed maintenance, to lower the quality of its service, to neglect depreciation and other reserves, or to follow other practices in order to make available funds with which to pay dividends, no matter how reprehensible these practices may be. Where overcapitalization exists the only alternative short of commission sanction of rates high enough to pay a return on the excess capitalization is to effect complete capital reorganization, a process that is both slow and difficult and that does not reflect credit upon the managers of the concern.

The problems before a regulatory commission in such an event are serious, and any action is likely to meet criticism from one source or another. If the commission allows the utility rates which yield a return on the watered stock involved in the over-capitalization, it is criticized for sanctioning unreasonably high rates. If it keeps rates down to the reasonable level of yielding a fair-return-on-a-fair-value, the utility is likely to defer maintenance and depreciation and to let the quality of its service become impaired, continuation of these policies possibly making conditions eventually worse and forcing a reorganization. Immediately, however, criticism arises from lowering the quality of service rendered. If rates are kept down to a low level and the utility attempts to correct its weak financial position through reorganization, the investors voice criticism because of the losses that they must take. The question is also raised: What can and should a commission do about a request to issue new securities in the case of an already overcapitalized concern? Failure to grant authority for the issue keeps needed capital out of the business, and service necessarily suffers. Permission to make the issue carries with it the recognition of the fact of overcapitalization and the tacit assumption that rates permitted will be high enough to pay a return thereon.

Relation of Overcapitalization to Rates and Quality of Service.— Overcapitalization and top-heavy capital structures, it has been indicated, affect the ability of a company to raise capital. From the standpoint of the public, however, the real seriousness of overcapitalization lies in its effects upon rates and service, tending to cause rates to be higher and the quality of the service to be poorer. The relationship between overcapitalization and the level of rates arises indirectly from the effect of capitalization on the value of the rate base. In *Smyth v. Ames*, one of the elements of value was declared to be the amount and market value of a company's bonds and stocks, although the burden of increased rates to pay a return on fictitious capitalization was not sanctioned.[1] Subsequent court and commission decisions and statutory provisions have emphasized value of the property as the rate base, so that theoretically no consideration is given to capitalization in determining the value of the rate base. On practical grounds, however, capitalization is likely to have a marked influence on valuation and therefore on rate levels. Many have contended that the commissions, in determining value and rate levels, cannot ignore the facts of a company's capitalization.[2] In any event, it is characteristic of rate cases that the utility company will present its capitalization, its fixed charges, and the amounts available and needed for a return on the company's stock. Even though it may be admitted that the capitalization is excessive and contains watered stock, it is pointed out that it was issued legally and that failure to allow the company earnings sufficiently large to pay a return on it penalizes both the present investor in the security and the company's credit standing.

If a commission does not recognize overcapitalization and let it influence the value of the rate base, and thereby holds rates down to a level where the watered stock receives no return, the utility company is placed in a trying predicament. Stockholders demand, and exert pressure upon the company for, the payment of dividends, and the burden of fixed charges is likely to be pressing; consequently, even though the company may be successful in maintaining service without deterioration in quality, it most probably cannot make needed improvements, betterments, and extensions in service.

[1] 169 U.S. 466, 544.

[2] See address of Joseph B. Eastman, as quoted in J. M. Herring and G. C. Gross, "Telecommunications: Economics and Regulation," McGraw-Hill Book Company, Inc., New York, 1936, pp. 324–325.

The results in many cases of overcapitalization, then, are that the investors pay for it by suffering losses in receiverships or reorganizations, or the consumers pay for it in higher rates or poorer quality of service. A practical problem is thus presented in rate cases where overcapitalization is a factor. It is doubtful if the commissions possess the necessary statutory authority to correct directly the maladjustments arising out of past over-capitalizations or even that such authority is available because of constitutional limitations upon the impairment of contracts. As a practical matter it must be recognized that though the practices in accordance with which the securities were issued are not now sanctioned, they were not then unlawful and that drastically to disrupt the capital structures now might impair the credit of the industry and might preclude, even for a long time, the ability of the industry to attract capital needed to continue and to expand service. Encouragement has been given to "squeezing out the water" so that, with present control looking toward prevention of overcapitalization and with many of the previously overcapitalized companies gradually correcting this situation, the problem of overcapitalization of operating companies and its effect upon rates and service is becoming less serious. However, the complications added by holding-company securities, as will be noted more fully later, continues over-capitalization as an important regulatory problem.

Scope of Commission Jurisdiction over Security Issues.— All commissions, as was pointed out earlier, have not been given control over security issues, and some have very limited power, such as requiring publicity of the issue. In those states which have strict control, new securities (stocks, bonds, notes, and other evidences of indebtedness payable more than 12 months after their issue date) must be approved by the commission before they can be issued. The commissions are charged to approve security issues only for specified purposes and only in amounts reasonably necessary to accomplish these purposes. The purposes usually specified are (1) acquisition of property; (2) construction, completion, extension, or improvement of facilities; (3) improvement or maintenance of service; (4) refunding of existing securities; and (5) reimbursement of moneys actually expended from income.[1]

[1] JONES, ELIOT, and T. C. BIGHAM, "Principles of Public Utilities," The Macmillan Company, New York, 1931, p. 512.

The use of the receipts from the sale of the security, to insure that they were used for the purposes intended, usually must be reported to the commission.

The procedure generally followed is for the utility to make application to the commission for authority to issue the securities. The commission's approval, if granted, specifies the type of security to be issued, the amount of the issue, the purposes of the issue, and the price at which the issue is to be sold. If the utility is not satisfied with the conditions and terms specified in the certificate of authority, it may withdraw the application or fail to act upon it. The fact that capital is needed, however, effectively gives the commissions control of the terms and conditions upon which it may be raised. It is also necessary, if the securities are offered for sale in interstate commerce, that they be registered with the United States Securities Exchange Commission in compliance with the Securities Act of 1933 and amendments thereto.

In deciding upon applications for the issuance of securities, many problems come before the commissions. Some of the more significant of these problems are:

1. *Treatment of Overcapitalized Corporations.*—The needs for capital for legitimate purposes may be as great for an overcapitalized corporation as for one that is not overcapitalized. A refusal to sanction the issue may result in curtailment or cessation of service or prevent betterments necessary to satisfactory service. Because of these facts, the commissions seldom refuse to grant the authority if the proposed securities are to be issued in reasonable amounts and in accordance with sound financial practices and if they are for a lawful and necessary purpose.[1] This policy contemplates the maintenance of satisfactory service and is generally accompanied by policies looking toward eliminating gradually the excess of capitalization originating in the past.

2. *Prevention of Overcapitalization.*—Though it may not be practical to eliminate suddenly past overcapitalization, care can be exercised to prevent it from occurring in the future. Overcapitalization may result through capitalization of replacements and through placing values upon new property, additions, improvements, and betterments in excess of the actual value of

[1] For a more detailed discussion on these points, see *op. cit.*, pp. 513–518.

such property. The commissions are here obligated to determine (1) that the expenditure is properly capitalizable; (2) that the new property, additions, or betterments are for proper corporate services and thereby justifiable as part of the utility's operating property; and (3) that costs of the capitalizable expenditures are reasonable.

Increase of capitalization may take place when outstanding securities are converted or refunded by the issuance of a larger amount of securities than the par value of those refunded or converted; but if the excess represents capitalization of reinvested earnings or acquisition of additional assets, overcapitalization has not taken place. On the other hand, if the company's capital liabilities are increased without increases in assets, overcapitalization has taken place. Thus, if the funding issue is for a larger par value than the original and the difference is covered up by a fictitious increase in the value of assets, the excess represents overcapitalization.

Similarly, capitalization of operating expenses must be prevented or overcapitalization results. This, unless guarded against, may arise in the funding of short-term notes, the proceeds of which were used to pay operating expenses.

3. *Funding of Short-term Obligations.*—Under present security control statutes, the utilities usually are left free to issue short-term obligations, with maturities of one year or less, without commission approval, since it is necessary that a utility company be free to act in cases of emergency, complete deprivation of freedom in financing being unwise. However, it is possible, as mentioned above, that short-term obligations may become the basis of an application for a funding issue which, if authorized, would cause overcapitalization.

The New York Commission on the Revision of the Public Service Commissions Law pointed to another danger of uncontrolled issuance of short-term obligations when it stated:

It is apparent that unrestricted issue of short term notes, without notice to the Commission, except through the medium of annual reports might bring a utility corporation into a financial situation threatening the maintenance of service, without opportunity for the application of remedial measures which might otherwise be involved.[1]

[1] P. 39.

To prevent this contingency from occurring, it was recommended that all short-term notes be reported within 10 days after their issuance and that their amount be limited to a maximum of 5 per cent of the stated value of the company's outstanding securities.

4. *Capitalization of Bond Discount.*—There are only a few court decisions on the subject of capitalization of bond discount, but the trend of these decisions seems to be against the practice.[1] The state commissions usually have ruled that bond discounts are not to be capitalized, though this has been permitted in Rhode Island.[2] The general practice is to consider that the amount of this discount is a deferred debit to be amortized by periodic charges to income along with other interest accruals and is to be completely amortized upon the maturity of the bonds. Since the discount could have been prevented, theoretically, by having the bonds bear a higher interest rate, it is tantamount to prepaid interest and should be so handled. This is the practice followed by the Interstate Commerce Commission which, under its accounting classification, has prescribed that the discount on bonds be charged to an account denominated Discount on Funded Debt and amortized over the life of that debt. The excess of capital liabilities over the assets received in return for bonds sold at a discount is therefore eliminated upon the maturity of the obligations.[3]

5. *The Problem of Stock Discounts.*—The issuance of stock at a discount results in the inflation of capitalization, since the par value of the securities issued exceeds the value of the assets received in exchange; but because of the nature of the securities market and the financial status of the issuing corporation, it is frequently impossible for stock to be sold at par. The alternatives to sale below par, in such cases, are financing by means of writing up the value of the property received in exchange for the stock or by issuing bonds. The choice of the former alternative causes overcapitalization, while the choice of the latter results in an increase in fixed charges. Overcapitalization hidden by fictitious values of assets or excessive fixed charges may create a worse condition than that created by the sale of

[1] See, *e.g.*, Streator Aqueduct Co. v. Smith, 295 Fed. 391.
[2] *Re* United Electric Power Co., P.U.R., 1928B, 646 (R.I.).
[3] Locklin, *op. cit.*, p. 82.

stock below par. In some states, where "antistockwatering" laws prevent the issuance of stock below par, there is a noticeable tendency to finance through bond issues, causing thereby unduly high fixed charges. There are conditions that justify the sale of stock below par. The danger of such sales lies in the deceptions that frequently accompany the practice, *viz.*, entering fictitious assets or fictitious values of existing assets rather than showing the fact of a discount in an asset account denominated Discount on Stock. If these questionable practices are adequately provided against, the sale of stock below par can be sanctioned. The regulations of the Interstate Commerce Commission provide such safeguards by prescribing that the difference between the par value of the stock issued and the value of the assets received therefor must be charged to Discount on Capital Stock. Entries in this account remain there until offset by (1) premiums received on the subsequent sale of the same class of stock, (2) assessments on stockholders, (3) specific appropriations from income or surplus for that purpose, or (4) charges to Profit or Loss upon reacquirement of the stock. In this way, the excess of capitalization over assets caused by the issuance of stock below par is always evident.[1]

6. *Stock of No-par Value.*—Stock cannot always be sold at par. If attempts are made to enforce the sale at par or above, it has already been noted that resort will be had to financing through bond issues with a consequent increase in fixed charges, or the values of the property acquired with the proceeds of the stock sold will be inflated. If sales below par are permitted, technical overcapitalization results and, though surrounded by safeguards of being clearly shown in a Discount on Stock account, is not understood by many. It is therefore suggested that no-par value stock be sold for whatever it will bring. By this means it is pointed out there would be no excess of par values over assets upon which dividends would be expected, and the situation of technical overcapitalization would be eliminated.

Though no-par value stock has much to commend it, it is not a panacea, and it should not be assumed that restrictions upon its issuance are not needed. In substituting the sale of no-par value stock for the sale of par value stock below par, the problem is not solved. If the proposed new shares are sold for a lesser

[1] *Op. cit.*

price than was received for earlier shares, the earnings on the older shares may be lessened to pay a return upon the newer ones; and if the company attempts to maintain a dividend scale of x upon both old and new issues, it is in exactly the same situation as if it attempted to pay x per cent dividends on stock with a par value of $100 per share, part of which had been sold below par.

It has been advocated that no-par value stock should be used exclusively in public utility industries on the ground that it will solve the problem of overcapitalization and make security regulation unnecessary. If par values are eliminated, it is pointed out, there is no par value existing to set up in comparison with the assets, and, consequently, overcapitalization could not exist. It is further claimed that there is no implication of an intrinsic value, as is frequently assumed in the case of par value stock. Instead of making such an assumption, the investor in the security can look only to value of the company's property in order to determine the value of his fractional interest therein, and to earnings of the company to estimate the probable dividends to be paid on his fractional interest in the company.

On the other hand, there are those who believe that no-par value stock is unwise and undesirable, pointing out that (1) even though overcapitalization is no longer possible, the results of excessive issuance of no-par value stock may be equally as serious as overcapitalization; (2) stockholders are released from liability to creditors for payment of the stated par value of shares, a situation contrary to public interest; (3) restrictions against impairment of capital and payment of unearned dividends are removed in those instances where stated capital is less than the amount received for the stock, the balance being credited to Surplus which may then be used to pay dividends; (4) it makes it easy for the corporation to pay excessive amounts for property or services acquired in direct exchange for securities, thereby causing a situation identical with overcapitalization which would not show on the company's books; and (5) a single stock account, Capital Stock, does not show the actual conditions under which stock was sold, as is the case where Premium and Discount accounts are carried.

The summary of arguments against no-par stock indicates that its use would not provide a cure for the evils of overcapitalization, although it is possible, by careful regulation, to avoid any of the abuses of no-par value stock. The conclusion is inevitable, therefore, that abuses are likely to exist with either form of stock and that regulation is necessary in either case.[1]

7. *Stock Dividends.*—Applications for the issuance of stock dividends must be considered in relationship to the sources of surplus that is to be distributed in this manner, the capitalization problems differing in each case. A common source of surplus is that arising from writing up the value of assets to correspond to a higher reproduction cost of the property. The problem of a surplus originating in this manner arises in those cases where the reproduction cost theory is used in determining the rate base. Only by distributing such a surplus as a stock dividend can the amount of capitalization be made to equal the rate-making value. If such values are used for rate making, it seems logical that capitalization should be related thereto; but if the logic of this reasoning is followed, a serious problem would be raised in a period of falling prices, since there is no easy method of reducing capitalization. The conservative view is to refuse to permit the capitalization of such surpluses.[2]

A second source of surplus is the inclusion in assets of intangibles such as good will, franchise value, or going value. Since market value finds no acceptance as a rate base, there is no argument upon which to justify the capitalization of a surplus represented by intangible values of this nature. This argument was used by the New Jersey Commission in refusing to authorize the capitalization of a book surplus of this sort.[3]

A third source of surplus lies in the write-up of appreciation in land values. Though the reproduction cost theory of valuation permits the capitalization of appreciation in the value of assets, increments in land values generally have been considered as not capitalizable. The basis for this view is found in the nature of the "unearned increment" included in appreciation of land values. The Interstate Commerce Commission, as early as 1911, in considering an application by the Chicago, Burlington, and Quincy Railroad Company for an increase in rates in order to pay a return on the appreciation of land values, stated:

[1] See *op. cit.*, Chap. XII, for a summary of the problems and arguments of no-par value stock.

[2] See, *e.g.*, *Re* Toms River Water Co., P.U.R. 1932C, 230.

[3] Riverton and Palmyra Water Co., N.J. Pub. Util. Comm. R., V, 586.

In a very real sense these added land values do not come to the railroad as a railroad, but as an investor in land which has been dedicated to a public use; and, being so dedicated, it may be strongly urged that the increment added thereto from year to year by communal growth should not necessitate an imposition of additional rate burdens upon the public.[1]

Similarly, the Indiana Commission held

Appreciation of land values represents no investment, no expenditure, no outlay by the company. It is an additional value which usually occurs by reason of the expenditure of others, the improvement of neighboring or adjacent real estate, the growth of a city, etc. It is a contribution by the public and surely the public should not be penalized for it.[2]

Surplus due to reserves accumulated to meet depreciation, obsolescence, or unforeseen contingencies constitutes a fourth source. Surplus accumulated as the result of reserves usually represents a direct charge upon the consumer, and as an operating charge the amount of such accumulations should be limited to the amount necessary for these purposes. If more than necessary is accumulated, the consumer is paying more in rates than is reasonable; and if such surpluses were capitalized, the consumer would be asked also to pay a return on that which would necessitate still higher rates.[3] Under the depreciation reserve method of accounting, the reserve set aside for depreciation is not included in the fair value of the property, and no return is allowed on it. If this view is accepted, it follows that surpluses that represent such reserves should not be capitalized and that stock dividends based thereon should not be permitted.

A fifth source of surplus is that arising from reinvested earnings. It is surplus from this source that causes the greatest controversy in regard to stock dividends. From a legal standpoint, it is argued that if the property is used in rendering the service, it is immaterial whence it came and the utility is entitled to a return on it. Being entitled to a return, it can, it is claimed, legitimately be capitalized. This viewpoint has been upheld by some of

[1] 20 I.C.C., 307, 344.

[2] *Re* Indianapolis Water Co., P.U.R., 1919A, 448, 469.

[3] See, for a statement to this effect, the Massachusetts Gas and Electric Light Commission 9th Annual Report, p. 8; also Lindheimer v. Ill. Bell Telephone Co., 292 U.S. 151.

the state courts and the lower federal courts.[1] A further contention is that reinvested earnings represent dividends withheld
from stockholders and that the stockholders are entitled to stock
dividends as an acknowledgment of the withholding of such
earnings.

On the other hand, it is contended that surpluses that represent
reinvested earnings should be held in trust for the benefit of the
public which has built up the surplus. As an implied trust, it is
argued, such surpluses should not be capitalized, and property
acquired therewith should not be included in the value of the
rate base.[2]

A compromise between these extreme viewpoints has been
supported by some state commissions. The viewpoint here
expressed is that if the earnings that are reinvested represent
earnings in excess of a fair return, they are clearly a capital
contribution made by the consumers; but that if the reinvested
earnings are earnings that were no more than a fair return and
were withheld from the stockholders for the purpose of reinvestment, it is clear that the contribution was made by the stockholders, and in no way can it be considered as a contribution
by the consumers. In instances of the former, to capitalize
the surplus and issue stock dividends would be denied; whereas
in instances of the latter, such permission would be granted.[3]
This compromise view can be justified on the ground of equitable
treatment of both consumers and stockholders. From a practical
standpoint, however, it may be difficult to distinguish between
surpluses arising out of excessive earnings and those arising out
of reasonable earnings withheld from stockholders. It should
also be noted that excess earnings might have been distributed
as dividends at the time they were earned and hence would not
be recoverable by the consumers who made them possible in
the high rates paid. Thus the company that did not distribute

[1] See, *e. g.*, Fall River Gas Works Co. v. Board of Gas and Electric Light
Comm., 214 Mass. 529 (1913); Brymer v. Butler Water Co., 179 Pa. 231,
(1897); Grafton County Electric Light and Power Co. v. State, P.U.R.,
1915C, 1064 (N.H.); Garden City v. Garden City Telephone, Light and
Manufacturing Co., 236 Fed. 693 (1916).

[2] See, *e.g.*, statements of Commissioner Eastman in "Chicago, Burlington,
and Quincy Railroad, Stock Of," 67 I.C.C. 156 (1927).

[3] See, *e.g.*, New Hampshire Public Service Commission, "Report on an
Investigation of Railroads, 1912," pp. 340 *ff.*

its excess earnings but reinvested them in operating plant and equipment, would be penalized if not allowed a return thereon.

Because of the legal question of property rights, it seems that surpluses from reinvested earnings, whether reasonable earnings withheld from the stockholders or excess earnings, are the property of the company and hence the property of the stockholders. Property rights therein can be exercised, such a surplus can be capitalized, and a stock dividend issued. The regulatory commissions are justified in refusing permission to issue stock dividends to capitalize an earned surplus only if the property acquired therewith does not increase the company's earning power.

8. *Guarantee of the Soundness of the Security.*—The commissions have never assumed that their approval of a security issue is in any sense a guarantee of the soundness of the investment, the soundness of the enterprise, or the quality of management of the enterprise, although the investing public often assumes that commission approval is equivalent to such a guarantee. The certification made by the commission actually covers only the fact that the property or service to be acquired is reasonably required for the purposes specified in the application and that such purposes are properly capital charges and not charges to operating expenses. To prevent investors from assuming a guarantee of the issue, the Transportation Act of 1920 and some state laws specifically provide that the approval of securities shall not be considered as a guarantee of their soundness.[1]

However, a commission is obligated to examine the financial status of the company requesting permission to issue securities, since the consumers are entitled to protection against the issuance of securities that do not have behind them the prospect of reasonable earnings or that are likely to burden the company with heavy fixed charges. Approval given after determining the effect of the proposed securities and the earnings of the company will

---

[1] The states with such laws are Arizona, California, Illinois, Indiana, and Missouri. Pennsylvania, which formerly required only publicity of the issue, specified that filing is not to be considered as a guarantee. These data are taken from Section of Public Utility Law, American Bar Association, "Report on the Legal Aspects of the Scope and Standards of Accounting Regulations Prescribed for Public Utilities by Public Authority," Oct. 10–11, 1932.

incidentally, at least, offer a sort of guarantee to the investor. And certainly the investor is safeguarded by the commission which prevents the issuance of securities that would cause over-capitalization. Also, the approval of a security issue carries with it the implication that rates will be sanctioned that permit a return on the security, and the investor is thus benefited. Protection of the investor, however, is an incidental benefit and not a primary purpose of security regulation. It would be unwise and contrary to the general public interest to place a commission in the position of assuming to guarantee securities as to soundness and return. In fact, it could do this only if it managed the operation of the enterprise and controlled completely its financial affairs.

9. *Capitalization in Consolidations and Mergers.*—It is claimed by many that consolidations and mergers of public utility properties have been made on the basis of prices and values in excess of the actual value of the combining properties. Hence, it is pointed out, the consolidated company is likely to issue securities to an aggregate amount greater than had been issued by the constituent companies. In this way, the excess values paid for properties will be capitalized, and the consolidated company will be overcapitalized.[1] Does a regulatory commission, in such an instance, have the right to prevent the consolidation? If not, how can it prevent the establishment of rates based on the excess values paid for the consolidating properties? On this point, the Missouri Commission said:

While the purchase price is considerably more than the appraisal shows the property to be worth, the Commission feels that it "should not arbitrarily interfere with the transfer of these properties, nor intervene as to the price paid by parties competent to contract, who desire to pay excess prices for what they purchase, or deny to the seller the benefit of this contract, and its chief function is the exercise of its lawful power to cause good service and reasonable rates to be given to the public so that efficient service will be rendered by the utility and a fair and reasonable return will be made the investor in the rate authorized for this service.

[1] See, for an analysis of this situation, National Association of Railroad and Utilities Commissioners, Report of Committee on Capitalization and Intercorporate Relations, *Proceedings*, 37th Annual Convention, 1925, pp. 363–364.

However, purchasers of these plants paying an excessive value should not be allowed to charge this excess to plant account, nor should they be allowed as against the public in a valuation of the system, a return upon these excess investments.[1]

Recognizing the effect of overcapitalization on rates, service, and credit standing of the company, some commissions hold that the consolidation should be denied if it is likely to increase rates or impair the service.[2] Certainly there is no reason to expect the regulatory agencies effectively to control security issues if the control that they exercise can be circumvented by the device of assigning property values of any amount to companies involved in consolidation and mergers. Control over securities, if over-capitalization is to be prevented, is necessary.

The Massachusetts Plan of Security Regulation.—The development of regulation in Massachusetts has followed a different course from that in the other states. The emphasis in Massachusetts has been upon the control of securities, and control over rates has been effected by controlling security issues. As early as 1861, railroad securities were regulated, and it was prescribed that no additional stock could be issued for less than the par value of outstanding shares. It applied this principle to all public utilities, and the Massachusetts law now provides that gas, electric, and water utilities can issue securities at no less than par and at prices no lower than are consistent with the public interest, as approved or fixed by the Commission or by sale at auction.[3] Legislation and control in Massachusetts have been founded on the assumption that the return to investors in public utility companies should be based upon the capitalization of the company, which should be kept as low as possible. As a result of this regulation, there exists virtually no overcapitalization of public utility companies in Massachusetts, and

[1] *Re* Mountain Grove Creamery, Ice, and Electric Co., *et al.*, P.U.R., 1926B, 346, 351.

[2] See, *e.g.*, Electric Pub. Util. Co. v. Pub. Service Comm., P.U.R., 1928E, 862 (Md.); *Re* Palmyra Gas and Electric Co., P.U.R., 1917E, 505 (N.Y.); and *Re* Southern Illinois Light and Power Co., P.U.R., 1919D, 489 (Ill.).

[3] Section of Public Utility Law, American Bar Association, "Report of the Committee on the Legal Aspects of the Scope and Standards of Accounting Regulations Prescribed for Public Utilities by Public Authority," Oct. 10–11, 1932, p. 23.

the amounts actually invested in the utilities are definitely known.[1]

The Massachusetts plan, as explained by Chairman Atwill and Commissioner Goldberg to the New York Commission on the Revision of the Public Service Commissions Law, provides that

. . . the relation between the state and the utilities is mutually fair when the state approves the issue and the issue price of every share of capital stock; and when rates are so fixed as to permit dividends on the stock that will attract new capital as required, and will maintain an open market price for the stock at least equal to the price at which it was issued. . . . This is accomplished by fixing rates so as to yield, on the capital stock and premium, a rate of return which is varied according to the judgment of the Commission, taking into account "the efficiency of the company, the efficiency of its management, the question whether it has placed back earnings into additions to the plant, the amount of depreciation it has taken, the amount of its surplus." . . . Under this system of regulation . . . "the only issues that can arise in a rate case are whether the operating expenses are too large or too small, whether the company is taking too much depreciation or too little, whether there are improper or improvident contracts or management fees, or whether the rate of return in the particular case shall be so much or so much."[2]

Consistent with the view of keeping capitalization as low as possible, the utilities are ordinarily denied a right to earn a return on reinvested earnings which were in excess of a fair rate of return. Illustrative of the viewpoint of the Department of Public Utilities is the statement

Much of the property of this company has been built up out of earnings. So far as we are aware, it has never been definitely established that in determining the rate base for the fixing of rates, consideration cannot be given to the fact that the value of the property employed has been largely developed at the expense of the public by the expenditure of past earnings, exceeding a fair return upon the capital invested.[3]

[1] BARNES, I. R., The Challenge of the Massachusetts Commission, *Public Utilities Fortnightly*, vol. 4, No. 9, pp. 545–546,

[2] "Report of the Commission on Revision of the Public Service Commissions Law of New York," summary of testimony of Chairman Atwill and Commissioner Goldberg of the Massachusetts Department of Public Utilities in the Report of William J. Donovan, counsel, pp. 98–99.

[3] Customer v. Worcester Electric Light Co., P.U.R., 1927C, 708.

The right to a return on reinvested earnings has been recognized, however, when the reinvestment arose from earnings not in excess of fair return which, in lieu of dividends being paid, were reinvested.[1]

The stringent control over security issues in Massachusetts has caused varying comment.[2] It is interesting to note that while other states have found their attempts to limit rates to reasonable amounts frequently nullified by the fact of overcapitalization and the practical necessity of allowing a return thereon, Massachusetts early controlled security issues, practically wiped out overcapitalization, and fixed rates at a level that would yield a return on the controlled capitalization. The Massachusetts Department of Public Utilities has deviated but slightly from this policy. After being given absolute control over rates in 1913, it held in several cases that utilities were entitled to a fair return on the capital prudently and honestly invested. In following this rule, prudent investment has not been defined but usually has been considered to be the same as the company's capitalization.[3] The policy followed seems to have worked satisfactorily and is attractive in many ways. Its success is due to the consistency of its application and to the fact that from the beginning of regulation, which came comparatively early in Massachusetts, strict control was exerted over security issues. Other states, without this 50-year old tradition and practice of regulating security issues and basing rates thereon, could not suddenly adopt and follow this plan. However, as further experience with control of security issues succeeds in eliminating overcapitalization, the policy of basing rates on capitalization could be applied more widely.

The Massachusetts record is remarkable in the limited amount of litigation that has taken place. It has been reported that in 50 years of regulation, there have been only four appeals to

[1] See, *e.g.*, Federated Civic Clubs v. Springfield Street R.R. Co., P.U.R., 1925A, 127.

[2] In addition to citations already made, see: JACKSON, C. D., Will The Commission Regulate Stock Exchange Prices? *Public Utilities Fortnightly*, vol. 4, No. 11, p. 652; MOREHOUSE, E. W., The Regulatory Rebellion in the Bay State, *Public Utilities Fortnightly*, vol. 5, No. 13, p. 814; and Paid-in Investment as a Public Utility Rate Base in Massachusetts, *Harvard Business Review*, vol. 6, p. 499.

[3] BARNES, *op. cit.*, pp. 547 *ff.*

the courts in rate cases—one to the state court, which was decided against the company, and three to Federal Courts—all of which were withdrawn before coming to actual adjudication. This achievement, according to Commissioner Atwill, has resulted in no small degree from the recognition of the fact that

. . . the people of Massachusetts would quickly go into the business themselves, take the whole undertaking over themselves, rather than pay much more than they have been paying under our system of regulation. . . . So the problem really in our State is, are the utilities going to force public ownership and public operation by demanding what they claim are their constitutional rights, or had they rather go along as they have in the past, undertaking what we visualize as a public function and getting a reasonably fair return for the undertaking.[1]

The Problem of Holding-company Security Issues.—Holding companies operate extensively in the United States, but in spite of their extensive holdings little has been done by the states to regulate them. In 24 states there is no provision for regulatory control, and in the rest there is but limited authority vested in the commissions. Several states, like New York and Wisconsin, have given their commissions authority to look into transactions between operating and holding companies, although the most usual limitation is that an out-of-state holding company cannot own more than a small proportion, say 10 per cent, of the stock of an operating company in the state. Many ingenious devices to circumvent this limitation have developed, *e.g.*, pyramiding of the holding-company structures or domiciling the holding company in another state so as to avoid regulation.[2]

The existence of the holding company is the direct result of the policy of several states of permitting one corporation to hold stock in another. This policy represents an abandonment of the common law principle prohibiting intercorporate stock-holding. Legalization of the practice seems to have been based in part upon the desire to obtain incorporation fees and franchise taxes. As more and more states successively permitted cor-

[1] "Report of the Commission on the Revision of the Public Service Commissions Law of New York," testimony of Chairman Atwill of the Massachusetts Department of Public Utilities as quoted in Report of William J. Donovan, counsel, p. 98.

[2] TAYLOR, HORACE, and associates, "Contemporary Problems in the United States," Harcourt, Brace & Company, New York, 1936–1937 ed., vol. II, pp. 188–189.

porations to acquire stock ownership in other corporations, the inducements thus held out lost much of their value in attracting incorporation in a given state. In order to regain an advantage, there arose a form of competition to grant or permit other privileges so as to induce selection of that state for incorporation. Incorporation regulations thereby became more and more lax, and companies desiring to function as a holding company could easily find a haven of lax incorporation laws permitting them to engage in almost any conceivable practice.[1]

This state of affairs, coupled with the ineffectiveness and lack of state regulation, resulted in many abuses, which fall principally into two classes:

1. Unsound and needless financial structures and practices which are a detriment and frequently a menace to the investor or the consumer or both.

2. The milking of operating companies through the devices of numerous forms of contracts, arrangements, and loans.

The Federal Trade Commission summarized the unsound practices of holding companies, involving financial measures and security issues, as follows:

  a. Pyramiding companies owning or controlling the operating companies for the purpose of enabling a minimum of investment to control a maximum of operating facilities, involving a greedy and highly speculative type of organization detrimental to the financial and economic welfare of the Nation.

  b. Loading the fixed capital account of public utilities with arbitrary or imaginary amounts in order to establish a base for excessive rates.

  c. Writing up the fixed assets without regard to the cost thereof, with the result of watering the stocks or creating a fictitious surplus.

  d. Gross disregard of prudent financing in excessive issue of obligations, imperiling the solvency of the company and involving excessive charges for interest, discount, commissions, redemption, etc.

  e. Manipulation of the security markets to deceive stockholders, bondholders, or potential purchasers of securities.

  f. Misstatement of earned surplus, or failure to distinguish earned from capital surplus, and making payment of dividends from the latter.

[1] Federal Trade Commission, "Utility Corporations," Sen. Doc. 92, 70th Cong., 1st Sess., Part 73-A, pp. 8–10.

g. Deceptive or unsound methods of accounting for assets and liabilities, costs, operating results and earnings, including write-ups, unrealized or fictitious profits, stock dividends, etc.

h. Evasion of State laws in effecting sales of security issues.[1]

The existence of holding companies with resulting concentration of control has produced a vast superimposed structure of corporations which must, each in turn, derive their revenues from underlying operating companies. The holding companies and their associated companies generally have issued securities of great variety and grade of preference and frequently in excessive amounts, the latter circumstance inevitably creating pressure to derive the desired revenues from the operating companies and therefore substantially affecting rates. Effective control of holding-company issues is necessary to remedy these abuses if the holding company is to be allowed to exist.

Federal Control of Holding-company Securities.—The Securities Act of 1933 required of holding companies, as it required of all other corporations, the registration of securities to be offered for sale. In so far as interstate holding companies in the field of public utilities is concerned, the powers granted the Securities Exchange Commission by the Act of 1933 were made more sweeping and positive by the Public Utility Act of 1935. The regulations imposed by Congress on public utility holding companies cover many topics: (1) definition and description of companies subject to the act; (2) provision of registration with the Securities Exchange Commission; (3) simplification of holding-company structures from the standpoint of territory covered and corporate structure, abolishing any pyramiding beyond the second degree; (4) acquisition of securities, utility assets, and other interests; (5) protection of operating companies; (6) control over service, sales, and construction contracts; and (7) regulation of security issues. The first six of these topics are discussed in Chap. XI.

Concerning security issues, the Public Utility Act of 1935 provides that no registered holding company or subsidiary thereof may issue a security unless the Securities Exchange Commission has ordered effective a "declaration" regarding the proposed issue as filed by the corporation. Declaration of a proposed issue need not be filed if (1) it is an issue or renewal

[1] *Op. cit.*, pp. 62–64; for other abuses of holding companies, see Chap. XI.

of a limited amount of short-term obligations; (2) it consists of securities issued by a subsidiary operating company to finance operations and expressly approved by the proper state commission; (3) it consists of securities issued by a nonutility subsidiary; and (4) it consists of securities issued pursuant to conversion or subscription rights already outstanding. However, notification of proposed issues of such exempted securities must be filed.

The declaration to be filed must contain information similar to that required for security issues under the Securities Act of 1933 plus any additional data required by the Securities Exchange Commission. The Commission cannot approve a proposed issue unless the securities are of one of three specified types, *viz.:*

1. Securities that are (*a*) par value common stock, without preference; (*b*) secured bonds; (*c*) a guaranty or assumption of liability on the security of another company; (*d*) receiver's certificates; or (*e*) trustee's certificates. By this provision, stock without par value, stock with preference, and income or debenture bonds are, in effect, prohibited from being issued by holding companies.

2. Securities of operating companies and securities issued in reorganizations. This provision recognizes that preferred stocks and income bonds can be issued by the companies operating the service properties. It is also recognized that in the course of readjustments it is sometimes necessary to issue the kind or type of security already outstanding.

3. Securities of any kind authorized under the Securities Act of 1933 prior to Jan. 1, 1935, and regarded by the Securities Exchange Commission as appropriate in the public interest or for the protection of consumers and investors.

It is also provided that the securities must bear a sound relationship to the corporate structure; the contemplated financing must be appropriate and necessary to efficient operation of the enterprise; the fees and commissions must be reasonable; and the conditions of sale must not be detrimental to the interests of the public, investors, or consumers.

These provisions look to national control of the security issues of public utility holding companies and their subsidiaries so as to protect the purchasers of the securities and the consumers of utility service. Elimination and prevention of the abuses found by the Federal Trade Commission are expected to result from federal control of securities, as well as the lifting of the pressure of unnecessary capital liabilities upon the underlying operating companies and the consumers of their services.

An amendment to the Federal Power Act, contained in Title II of the Public Utility Act of 1935, provides that interstate electrical utilities, not subject to control by a state commission, may issue securities only upon approval of the Federal Power Commission. To secure approval by the Federal Power Commission, proposed issues must be for a lawful and necessary corporate purpose and in the public interest.

Summary.—Unregulated and uncontrolled issuance of securities by public utility corporations has resulted in many cases of overcapitalization. Regulation of rates, where overcapitalization exists, is made difficult, and consumers are affected adversely by high rates or poor service or both. In their control of security issues, which is now recognized as an essential part of regulation, the commissions have encountered many problems, but, in general, security control has come to be effective, and recognized principles of sound financing are being applied. One thing the Massachusetts plan of regulation demonstrates is that control of securities and capitalization can lead to effective and satisfactory regulation. Probably the presence of unregulated and uncontrolled holding companies has done more than any other single factor to nullify the good results of control of operating-company securities. This problem has grown in seriousness and magnitude because of practical limitations upon the attempts of states to control holding companies. Control of holding-company securities by the Securities Exchange Commission should do much toward strengthening this weak point in regulatory practices and machinery.

References

American Bar Association, Section on Public Utility Law; "Report of the Committee on the Legal Aspects of the Scope and Standards of Accounting Regulations Prescribed for Public Utilities by Public Authority," Oct. 10–11, 1932.

BARNES, I. R.: The Challenge of the Massachusetts Commission, *Public Utilities Fortnightly*, vol. 4, No. 9.

BEARD, C. A., and G. H. E. SMITH: "Current Problems of Public Policy," The Macmillan Company, New York, 1936, Chaps. XIV and XV.

BONBRIGHT, J. C.: "Railroad Capitalization," Chaps. I, II, and IV, Columbia University Studies in History, Economies, and Public Law, vol. XCV, No. 1, Longmans, Green & Company, New York, 1920.

Bonbright and Company: "A Survey of State Laws on Public Utility Commission Regulations in the United States," revision of 1930, New York.

BURTCHETT, F. F.: "Corporation Finance," Harper & Brothers, New York, 1934.

COOKE, M. L.: "Public Utility Regulation," Ronald Press Company, New York, 1924, Chap. VIII.

DEWING, A. S.: "Financial Policies of Corporations," Ronald Press Company, New York, 1921.

Federal Trade Commission: Utility Corporations, 70th Cong., 1st Sess., Doc. 92, Part 69-A (contains an extensive bibliography), and Part 73-A.

FULLERTON, F. C.: Appraising Individual Public Utility Issues under the New Law, *Magazine of Wall Street*, vol. 56, pp. 590–593.

GLAESER, M. G.: "Outlines of Public Utility Economics," The Macmillan Company, New York, 1931, Chaps. XVII and XVIII.

HOAGLAND, H. E.: "Corporation Finance," McGraw-Hill Book Company, Inc., New York, 1933.

JACKSON, C. D.: Will The Commission Regulate Stock Exchange Prices?, *Pub. Utilities Fortnightly*, vol. 4, No. 11.

JONES, ELIOT, and T. C. BIGHAM: "Principles of Public Utilities," The Macmillan Company, New York, 1931, Chap. XI.

LAGERQUIST, W. E.: "Public Utility Finance," McGraw-Hill Book Company, Inc., New York, 1927.

LOCKLIN, D. P.: "Regulation of Security Issues by the Interstate Commerce Commission," University of Illinois Studies in the Social Sciences, Urbana, 1925.

MOREHOUSE, E. W.: The Regulatory Rebellion in the Bay State, *Public Utilities Fortnightly*, vol. 5, No. 13.

MOSHER, W. E., and F. G. CRAWFORD: "Public Utility Regulation," Harper & Brothers, New York, 1933, Chap. IX.

National Association of Railroad and Utility Commissioners (formerly National Association of Railway Commissioners): *Proceedings*, annual.

"Report of the New York Commission on Revision of the Public Service Commissions Law," Albany, 1930.

SPURR, H. C.: "Guiding Principles of Public Service Regulation," Public Utilities Reports, Inc., Rochester, 1924, vol. I, Chap. IV.

TAYLOR, HORACE, and associates: "Contemporary Problems in the United States," Harcourt, Brace & Company, New York, 1936–1937 ed., vol. II.

U.S. Congress, House of Representatives, Committee on Interstate and Foreign Commerce, Hearing on House Report 5423, Parts 1, 2, and 3, Government Printing Office, 1935.

WHITTEN, R. H., and D. F. WILCOX: "Valuation of Public Service Corporations," 2d ed., Banks Law Publishing Company, New York, 1928, vol. II, Chap. XI.

CHAPTER XI

REGULATION OF HOLDING COMPANIES

THE EXTENT OF HOLDING-COMPANY CONTROL

Investigations by the Federal Trade Commission have disclosed two important facts: (1) that holding-company domination of the electric light and power industry is one of its salient features, and (2) that recent years have witnessed a marked increase in the concentration of control into fewer hands. In 1914, large local corporations and management companies dominated the industry, but by 1924, holding companies had become a prominent feature. In that year the most important single group was the General Electric Company group (including the Electric Bond and Share companies), with 13 per cent of the total energy generated by private companies. Six other large holding-company groups controlled 28 per cent, and other holding companies about 24 per cent of the total. Altogether about 65 per cent of the privately owned electric utility industry was controlled by holding-company groups.

During the period 1925 to 1930 there were still further acquisitions of large and then independent operating companies by holding-company groups and further consolidations of two or more holding companies into larger holding-company groups. The results were that during the years 1929, 1930, and 1932 the United Corporation group controlled about 20 per cent, the Electric Bond and Share Company group approximately 14 per cent, and the Insull interests over 10 per cent of the total electric energy generated by private utility companies. Add to these the totals controlled by other holding companies, and we find that for those three years 82.3, 77.9, and 78.8 per cent, respectively, of the totals were controlled by holding-company groups. Even this understates the importance of holding companies, since the United Corporation owned a minority interest (2.8 per cent) in the voting stock of Consolidated Gas, Electric Light & Power

257

Company of Baltimore, Niagara Hudson Power Corporation owned 29.7 per cent of the voting stock of Central Hudson Gas and Electric Company, The North American Company and Standard Gas and Electric Company each owned an interest in Pacific Gas and Electric Company (the former 25.8 per cent, and the latter 10 per cent of the voting stock), and The North American Company owned 17.9 per cent of the voting stock of Detroit Edison Company. Together these companies generated 6.2, 7.5, and 6.8 per cent, respectively, of the total electric energy generated in the United States by private companies for the years 1929, 1930, and 1932.[1]

Surveys show that holding-company control also is an important feature of the organization of the gas industry. Reports to the Federal Trade Commission for 1930 from gas-operating companies controlled by 44 holding-company groups show that these groups controlled 66.4 per cent of the gas manufactured and 23.3 per cent of the natural gas produced in the United States. The United Corporation group, with 12.1 per cent of the United States' total, was the most important group in the manufactured gas industry, the Insull group being next with 10.5. The Electric Bond and Share Company group was the most important controlling group in the natural gas industry with 7.4 per cent of the United States total, the United Corporation group being next with 4.2 per cent. Cities Service Company ranked third as a producer of natural gas, with 3.7 per cent of the United States total.

In railroad transportation the holding-company device has been used frequently and on a large scale to effect control of separate railroad properties, and the problems thus raised have added to the difficulties of regulation and have complicated the task of consolidating the railroads into a limited number of systems. However, in this volume we do not deal exhaustively with railroad problems. In the other transportation utilities trends toward and away from consolidation have been conflicting and confusing. Early tendencies to combine electric railway properties with the generation and distribution of electric energy for other uses have tended to disappear, many electric light and power companies having disposed of their transportation proper-

[1] Utility Corporations, Sen. Doc. 92, 70th Cong., 1st Sess., Part 72-A, pp. 36–39.

ties. Recently there have been marked tendencies toward the combination of electric railways with bus systems, and the holding company has been an efficient means of effecting common control, but holding companies have presented no regulatory problem in this field of the magnitude found in the gas and electric utilities. Nor has the regulation of water-service utilities been complicated to any marked degree by holding companies. Because of the wide prevalence of public ownership of water utilities, among other factors, holding companies do not dominate this industry.

Holding companies are a marked feature of the organization of the communication utilities, notably the telephone industry, the bulk of which is controlled by the American Telephone and Telegraph Company. However, while there has been a great deal of integration of communication operating companies in the interests of efficient and economical service, there has not been the same degree of pyramiding of holding company upon holding company, chiefly for financial reasons, that is observed in the gas and electric utilities. Moreover, what regulatory problems have been created by holding companies in these fields are akin to those in other fields. It is clear, therefore, that the need for regulation of holding companies has been most acute in the gas and electric utilities, and the discussion in this chapter, accordingly, will be confined for the most part to the regulation of gas and electric holding companies.

THE ECONOMIC BASES FOR HOLDING COMPANIES

The bases for holding companies in the gas and electric utilities rest primarily upon three foundations: (1) the operating economies and increased operating efficiency which can be achieved through common control of the management of several small operating companies; (2) the saving in the cost of and the superior quality of financial, engineering, and managerial services furnished many operating companies by a single headquarters staff; and (3) the larger possibilities of developing different kinds of service and of broadening consumption.

Advantages of Combining Small Plants into One System.— The advantages of bringing many small operating gas or electric plants under common managerial control are for the most part economies of large-scale operation. These may be summarized briefly as follows:[1]

1. The replacing of small, obsolete, inefficient production units by larger and more efficient units.

2. The interchange of equipment and facilities among the various companies.

3. Standardization of equipment and facilities.

4. Improved load, diversity and capacity factors.

5. Centralized purchasing of supplies and materials.

6. Centralization of the placement of insurance and the handling of claims.

7. More expert mobilization and use of labor.

8. More economical use of specialists and executives.

9. Economies in the use of fuel.

10. More uniform, continuous, dependable, and high-quality service.

Improvement in Technical and Financial Management. *Financial Services.*—The main financial function of a holding company is to assist in securing necessary capital for operating companies that serve relatively small cities or rural communities. This is done principally through the furnishing of common stock funds to the operating companies, the remaining funds needed by them being secured for the most part by the sale of their own preferred stocks and bonds directly to the investing public. It is claimed that a holding company, because of its size, its contacts with money markets, and the size of the issue where the needs of various companies must be met, can obtain the necessary funds from the investing public more readily and at lower cost than the individual companies working separately.

A second financial function of a holding company is that of temporarily financing the current capital needs of its subsidiaries pending permanent financing. This is usually done through the process of the holding company's paying the bills for materials and supplies of the subsidiaries and leaving in their treasuries the funds representing earned surplus available for dividends on their common stocks which are owned by the holding company. The effect of this procedure is to build up a tempo-

[1] WILSON, G. L., J. M. HERRING, and R. B. EUTSLER, "Public Utility Industries," McGraw-Hill Book Company, Inc., New York, 1936, pp. 385–387.

rary open-account indebtedness of the subsidiary to the holding company.

A third financial function of a holding company is to furnish, more or less temporarily, funds needed in senior security financing of operating companies when market conditions are not favorable for the sale of such securities to the investing public. In several cases holding companies have invested considerable sums in the preferred stocks and bonds of subsidiaries whose earning power was weak and whose securities accordingly were not in favor with investors. With improvement in earning power the holding companies later were enabled to dispose of such investments on acceptable terms.

Centralization of Engineering, Construction, and Managerial Functions.—One of the principal advantages of the holding-company setup is the facility and economy with which engineering, construction, and managerial functions which require for their performance a staff of highly paid specialists may be performed for a group of operating companies by a single headquarters organization, or through some controlled subsidiary. Operating companies separately could not furnish themselves with comparable staffs of technical experts. Historically these service arrangements have their origin in the sale or underwriting of securities and in construction contracts with provisions for the upkeep and maintenance of the plants built.[1] In some holding-company groups there are neither service arrangements nor the service function, but these are exceptions, the general rule being a well-rounded and perfected service system within each holding-company organization.

There is a wide diversity among holding-company groups as to the bases upon which rest the obligations involved in service arrangements and as to the manner in which the services are performed. In some cases the head companies have no contracts with the subsidiaries but merely allocate arbitrarily to them certain charges for services rendered or have working arrangements with the subsidiaries. Managerial supervision is sometimes carried on directly by a staff in the employ of the holding company, although generally managerial and engineering services are performed by a separate organization. In such cases

[1] Relation of Holding Companies to Operating Companies in Power and Gas Affecting Control, House Report 827, Part 6, 73d Cong., 2d Sess., p. 1.

formal contracts are drawn up covering the services to be rendered and the compensation to be received. Such formal contracts prescribe relations and define obligations in minute detail, the contracts being variously called construction, engineering, management, operating, or supervision contracts.

The development of specialized servicing organizations is one of the outstanding aspects of present-day holding-company organization. In the beginning some of these were not affiliated with the operating companies serviced, and even today some servicing is done by organizations not affiliated with the companies serviced. It is the general rule, however, that the servicing organization is a part of the holding-company organization, although it may perform services for unaffiliated or municipal companies. The separate service organization may consist of the staff of an engineering and management corporation which is controlled by the chief holding company; it may be controlled by individuals or interests who are in managerial control of the holding company and its subsidiaries; or it may consist of the individuals, and their staffs, who founded the chief holding company and who exercise managerial control over it. In some cases the servicing organization may have no other function than servicing, although in other cases it may own the voting stocks of the utilities serviced and will thus combine the holding-company function with that of servicing.

Types of Services. *Management Services.*—The activities commonly included under management contracts between holding or servicing and operating companies cover a wide range. In some cases the servicing organization may be made the actual operating manager of the client company's properties, with authority to supervise and direct the management and operation of such properties for a term of years. Construction design, construction, and supervision of construction are usually not included under the managerial fee, but often the servicing company that furnishes the management will pass upon the advisability of construction, furnish plans and specifications, supply all preliminary engineering, and furnish consulting engineering service. Management service generally includes responsibility for organization and personnel; employment and discharge of employees and the fixing of their compensation; advice regarding financial needs; the placing of insurance; plans for extending business; supervision of the preparation, analysis, and presentation of statistics; assistance in the formulation of rate schedules; and public relations service. Other services which may be included under the management contract, but which in some cases are covered by separate contracts with separate compensation, are:

1. Purchasing. This service may include merely giving advice regarding the needs of the client company and the best sources of supply, but often the management company may furnish a buying organization to effect economies through quantity purchases skillfully made.

2. Appliance Merchandising. This service includes advice in the buying and selling of public utility appliances, from the standpoint both of profit from sales and of the increase in local consumption of the utility service. Compensation for the service may be a part of the management fee, although the servicing company may take over the appliance merchandising business and operate it for its own profit.

3. Legal Service. This service usually involves on the part of the management company the keeping in touch with all legal problems, recommending such legal assistance as may be necessary, and conferring with and aiding outside legal firms in connection with financing, organization of new companies, reorganization, consolidation, and like activities. Such legal work may be performed under the management fee, or the management company may maintain a special legal department and charge a special fee for legal service.

4. Accounting Service. This service may include anything from complete accounting systems to the development of uniform accounting for an entire holding-company organization. It usually includes also services in connection with periodic audits, certificates, reports, taxes, insurance, and rate cases. The charge is almost always a part of the management fee, but in some cases the service is separated and a special fee charged.

5. Advertising. This service usually involves the supervision of the advertising and publicity for operating companies, and the compensation is as a rule a part of the management fee.

6. Sale of Subsidiary Stocks and Securities. This service may include the sale of the serviced company's stocks and securities, the supervision of consumers' campaigns for such sales, and the

preparation of all reports and advertising material in promotion of sales. Where this service is covered by the management fee it is usually restricted to local sales. Where it is more extended it is covered by special provisions with separate compensation.

Engineering and Construction Services.—The services covered by engineering and construction contracts are many in number and vary widely with the different servicing companies. As a general rule, however, these contracts include construction and supervision of construction and usually the designing for construction. On the other hand, the general practice is to class all consultative engineering, engineering that can be performed at the head office, and engineering that pertains to utility operations as management services covered by the management fee. A few engineering services are frequently compensated for on a separate basis. Among these are field engineering, engineering for construction, estimates of construction work, appraisals, inspections, and a few others.[1]

Bases for Determining Charges for Services.—Fees received by the various holding or servicing companies may be divided into three broad classes: (1) management and supervision fees, which include fees for management, consultation, and supervision; (2) departmental supervision and special service fees, which include services by holding-company departments as distinguished from management fees where the entire operations of the subsidiary are managed and supervised; and (3) construction or engineering fees. Some holding companies rendering service collect the fees directly from the companies serviced; other holding companies divide the fees with the servicing company or, where they own the servicing companies, receive payment in the form of dividends paid by the servicing companies.

Fees may be divided according to the basis used to determine the amount into five groups: (1) fixed, or lump-sum, fees; (2) percentage of gross revenues; (3) percentage of capital expenditures; (4) special fees; and (5) allocation of expenses. A fee for management and supervision services is frequently a lump sum or a percentage of the gross revenues of the company serviced. Fees for construction and engineering services are assessed usually on the basis of a percentage of the capital expenditures. Special fees are related to the type and the extent of the service

---

[1] Utility Corporations, *op. cit.*, Part 72-A, pp. 599–602.

performed. Where the fee is based upon the allocation of expenses, a portion of the general expenses or a portion of the specific departmental expenses of certain holding companies is allocated to and collected from subsidiary operating companies, in lieu of fees for management or other services.[1]

Larger Possibilities of Developing Service and Broadening Consumption.—It is claimed also that holding-company managements, because of broader familiarity with developments among various companies, if not because of superior talent, are likely to be less shortsighted than local managements in the adoption of methods to develop the service and to broaden consumption. The Federal Trade Commission lists a number of benefits that have accrued to consumers during the period of holding-company development, although the Commission does not imply that they are wholly due to the activities of holding companies, nor does it attempt to measure their influence. These benefits are:

1. Widely extended service, especially in electric power and natural gas, to reach many small communities, suburban areas, farms, and isolated industrial operations, particularly paper mills, quarries, gravel pits, etc.

2. Much improved service in dependability, regulation of voltage, adequacy to meet growing demands with little or no delay, all results of new investments and greater skill in construction and operation.

3. Intensive methods designed primarily to sell appliances and increase the customers' total consumption but having the effect also of improving the service or reducing its cost to consumers.

4. Steadily declining price to consumers during the past 25 years, with the possible exception of the war and immediate postwar periods.[2]

Measuring the benefits of holding companies to the consumers of utility service in these matters, as in others, is at best a difficult task. All holding companies have not adopted equally enlightened or honest policies in their management of controlled operating companies, as will be shown later in this chapter, and speculation as to what might have taken place in the absence of holding-company control is quite bootless. Nevertheless, it is due the managements of the better holding-company groups to

[1] *Op. cit.*, pp. 462–465.
[2] *Ibid.*, pp. 840–841.

say that even though they have not been wholly responsible for
the initiation of policies that have redounded to the benefit of
ultimate consumers, at least they have not stood in the way of
their adoption.   That there has been exploitation, and at times
in a broad and unscrupulous manner, no one familiar with the
facts will deny.   It is also true that many of the claimed advantages of holding companies are unreal.   But this does not deny
the existence of real advantages, nor does it relieve legislatures
and regulatory commissions of the twofold duty of preserving
these advantages while adopting measures to wipe out practices
that result in exploitation.

TYPES OF HOLDING-COMPANY GROUPS

Most of the holding-company groups in existence today have
been created for the performance of one or more of the economic
functions outlined in the preceding section, but the attainment
of other objectives at times has been an important motivating
force.   Holding-company groups may be classified roughly
according to their major objectives into the following types: (1)
the diversified investment type, (2) the large connected type,
(3) the large-city type, and (4) superholding companies.   The
utilities controlled by a holding company of the diversified
investment type do not constitute one continuous chain or network in contiguous territory but often are widely separated
geographically.   Examples of this type are the groups of the
Electric Bond and Share Company, the Standard Gas and
Electric Company, Commonwealth and Southern Corporation,
Utilities Power and Light Corporation, Cities Service Company,
and those that were controlled by Middle West Utilities Company and Central Public Service Company.

Utilities controlled by a holding company of the large connected type lie wholly, or largely, in a contiguous network.
Examples of this type are the Niagara Hudson Power Corporation group, the Associated Gas and Electric Company group,
the United Gas Improvement Company group, and the New
England Power Association group.   The diversified investment
and large connected types are not sharply divided, and as a
result of expansion many groups that formerly were of the
diversified investment type have approached more and more
closely the large connected type, *e.g.*, the group headed by the

United Gas Improvement Company. These two groups contain utilities that primarily serve communities of small or medium size, although some may serve large cities.

Holding companies of the large-city type control utilities that for the most part serve large cities. The most notable example of this type is the group controlled by the North American Company. The American Cities Company was formerly of this type, but it became insolvent. The principal reasons for the scarcity of this type of holding-company group are that the opportunities for service by holding companies lie chiefly in the financing of utilities in smaller communities and in providing them with high-grade managerial, engineering, purchasing, legal, and other services. In addition, as has been pointed out, many holding-company groups beginning with the control of utilities serving smaller communities have come to embrace in their systems utilities serving large cities.

Superholding companies represent a recent trend toward grouping under common control of formerly independent holding-company groups. The outstanding illustration of this type is the group controlled by The United Corporation. Organized in 1929 by J. P. Morgan & Company, in association with Bonbright & Company, Inc., this corporation grew by the acquisition of control of holding companies until it came into practical control of a network of utilities extending, with only one important break, from the Great Lakes and the St. Lawrence River to the Gulf of Mexico. According to the Federal Trade Commission, the formation of this combination was foreshadowed by the earlier discussion of "superpower" grouping or connection of all electric power utilities in the northeastern part of the United States and discussions of former Governor Pinchot's "giant power plan," which would involve the construction of huge generating plants at the mouths of coal mines to be connected with the local utilities by a network of transmission lines. The groups and companies substantially under the control of The United Corporation include Public Service Company of New Jersey, the United Gas Improvement Company, Niagara Hudson Power Corporation, Columbia Gas and Electric Corporation, the Commonwealth and Southern Corporation, and Consolidated Gas Company of New York.[1]

[1] *Op. cit.*, pp. 111–116.

UNDESIRABLE FEATURES OF HOLDING-COMPANY DEVELOPMENT AND CONTROL

1. **Pyramiding.**—One of the most undesirable features of holding-company development has been the practice of pyramiding, by which is meant the interposition between a holding company and the operating companies of one or more subholding companies. There are two main objectives to be accomplished through pyramiding. In the first place, it provides a way of reducing the amount of funds required by the interests concerned in obtaining control of operating utility companies, since control of only the voting stocks is necessary. In the second place, a greatly increased amount of income will accrue to the dominating interests if the operating companies prosper. This can be demonstrated readily by a hypothetical illustration: Assume an operating company with a capitalization of $1,000,000, divided into 50 per cent of 5 per cent bonds, 25 per cent of 6 per cent preferred stock, and 25 per cent common stock. To control this company a first-degree holding company purchases the $250,000 in common stock, but it raises the funds by selling $125,000 of its own 7 per cent preferred stock to the investing public and $125,000 of common stock to a second-degree holding company. The second-degree holding company raises the $125,000 by selling $62,500 of its own 7 per cent preferred stock to the investing public and $62,500 of common stock to a third-degree holding company. The third-degree holding company raises the $62,500 by selling $31,250 of its own 7 per cent preferred stock to the investing public and $31,250 of common stock to a fourth-degree holding company, which in turn sells $15,625 of its own 7 per cent preferred stock to the investing public. If the operating company earns 7 per cent on its total investment, or $70,000, there remains, after interest and preferred dividends, $30,000 of income for the common stockholders, or 12 per cent on the investment. This $30,000 goes to the first-degree holding company which must pay $8,750 in preferred dividends, which leaves $21,250 income on its common stock, or 17 per cent. This $21,250 goes to the second-degree holding company, and so on. On the basis of these assumed facts the return to the second-degree holding company would be 27 per cent on $62,500; to the third-degree holding company, 47 per

cent on $31,250; and to the fourth-degree holding company, 87 per cent on $15,625. Examples of pyramiding in actual practice have often exceeded the extent of this hypothetical case. Thus, in the Associated Gas and Electric System there were 12 companies in one line of control from top to bottom of the pyramid.[1]

It must be quite obvious to the reader, however, that any considerable falling off in the earnings of operating companies may have serious, even disastrous, effects upon the superstructure of holding and subholding companies. The unsoundness of such pyramiding was amply illustrated after the financial panic of 1929, when within a few years more than 90 electric and gas systems were placed in receivership or declared bankrupt. These included such large companies and systems as Corporation Securities Company of Chicago; Insull Utilities Investments, Inc.; National Public Service Company; Mississippi Valley Utilities Investment Company; Seaboard Public Service Company; Central Public Service Company; Central Public Service Corporation; Tri-Utilities Corporation; American Community Power Company; Appalachian Gas Corporation; Duquesne Gas Corporation; and Texas-Louisiana Power Company.

Not all subholding companies represent a pyramiding of equities and control, however. In some cases there is merely the substitution in the hands of investors of the securities of the holding company for those of the operating company. Also, pyramiding often results merely through the acquisition by one holding company of the control of a previously independent holding company, and a pyramid so created is often removed subsequently by the dissolution of the acquired holding companies.

From the viewpoint of the public interest, pyramiding results not only in the sale of securities of little or no value to the investing public but in complicated superstructures which defy analysis except by experts and which militate against effective regulation of operating companies. A highly pyramided structure enables the dominant interests to contrive means of exacting from operating companies excessive fees for management, engineering, and construction and to present appearances of income where real income does not exist through the capitalization of excessive expenditures for construction, interest, and general overhead applicable to construction; by the neglect of adequate

[1] *Op. cit.*, pp. 157–159.

provision for depreciation; by inter-company profits on the sales of properties, securities, and other assets; and by the creation of inflated and fictitious values for purposes of capitalization, the burden of all of which must be borne by the operating companies. The truth of the matter is that holding-company superstructures have been used directly by certain unscrupulous interests to evade regulation in the public interest by state commissions. So complete is the domination of public utility operating companies by holding companies that effective regulation requires not only the regulation of holding companies but, as a preliminary, the simplification of holding-company structures so as to make such regulation intelligent and equitable to all parties concerned.

2. Write-ups and Inflation in Capital Assets.—As was suggested in the preceding section, the pyramiding of a holding company permits, even invites, the creation of fictitious values for capitalization purposes. The Federal Trade Commission in its investigation of 18 top holding companies, 42 subholding companies, and 91 operating companies, the combined assets of which amounted to $3,116,207,926 for the top holding companies, $2,186,302,222 for the subholding companies, and $3,306,893,610 for the operating companies, determined that the amount by which the capital assets of all the companies examined were written up in value over cost totaled $1,491,031,823. Of this amount, $273,420,165 was included in the 18 top holding companies, equal to 9.6 per cent of the total capital assets of these companies, excluding the write-ups; $309,495,058 was included in the 42 subholding companies, or 16.5 per cent of the total capital assets; and $599,329,206 was included in the 91 operating companies, or 22.1 per cent of the total capital assets.[1]

The nature of these write-ups of capital assets and the methods by which they have been accomplished have been summarized by the Federal Trade Commission as follows:

1. Large profits taken by some companies for construction work included in the fixed-capital accounts of the companies for whom the work was performed; also, capital stock and bond discounts, excessive and erroneous amounts for overhead expenses, and intangibles included as elements of construction cost;

2. Write-ups in the value of properties or securities to reflect profits in the transfer of such properties or securities between members of the

[1] *Op. cit.*, pp. 298–299.

same system; also write-ups accompanying the transfer of servicing or other contracts; and

3. Write-ups of the values of fixed assets of a consolidated company resulting from the combination of two or more companies, based upon optimistic judgments of the economies to be achieved by the consolidated company, or mere superficial inspection of the properties by their engineering staffs, with a view to capitalizing to the utmost the potential earning power of the consolidated company. In some cases revaluations were undertaken for purposes other than to justify issues of stocks and bonds in consolidations, mergers, or reorganizations, or upon orders from regulatory commissions. Appraisals were made also of water rights, going-concern value, and other intangibles as a basis for revaluation. In such cases of revaluation of tangible or intangible property, however, amounts added to fixed capital were for the most part credited to capital surplus or retirement reserve.

All of the various forms of write-ups were for the most part capitalized by security issues, of which those not required for purposes of control were sold to the investing public. In this way those initiating the transactions, the dominant interests, were enabled to recover in cash, or in securities of the issuing companies, a substantial portion, if not the whole, of their investments, without relinquishing control. The effect of write-ups that reflect no real value upon investors is obvious. They possess securities which at best have back of them questionable earning power or asset value. As to ratepayers, the significance is that book value, if only unconsciously, is likely to influence determinations of property values for rate-making purposes. Most of the write-ups on the books of operating companies were, in effect, concealed, the result being that net earnings on the obscured actual investment might constitute an unreasonable return although appearing quite reasonable when compared with written-up book values. That they have created real obstacles to effective regulation there is little doubt. In cases of informal requests for lowered rates the showing of a moderate return on book value has often been sufficient to damp the ardor of complainants, and in formal rate cases it has been difficult, if not impossible, for those demanding lower rates to prove that the book value was incorrect and unfair. The Federal Trade Commission gives as its general conclusion that "write-ups have been used to capitalize hoped-for and often realized earnings at rates of return in excess of what might have been considered as reasonable by public authority and to that extent have influenced the maintenance, or establishment, of rates which would bring such higher rates of return."[1]

3. Abuses in Intercompany Financial Practices.—It has been pointed out that one of the claimed economic functions of holding companies is their ability to obtain capital more readily and cheaply for their controlled subsidiaries than they could for themselves. There have been many occasions in the past, however, especially during the first year or two after the financial panic of 1929, when holding companies instead of being a financial prop and stay to operating companies have been real burdens, and at times when the operation companies have needed them most. Members of the various state commissions have reported instance upon instance where holding companies leaned upon the superior credit of operating companies to bolster up their own tottering empires.[2]

This was usually accomplished by having the operating utility borrow from banks on short-term notes, which were not subject to the jurisdiction of a state commission, and to lend part or the whole of the proceeds to the holding company on the latter's unsecured note. Later, application would be made to the state commission by the operating company for authority to refund these short-term obligations by the sale of securities to the public. Loans of this type also have been made between subsidiaries in the same holding-company group. These "upstream" loans in many cases have wrought serious hardships upon the operating companies, jeopardizing their credit and financial soundness.

Many other financial practices have been carried on by holding companies that have been burdensome to operating companies. Among these are the refunding of outstanding short-term obligations at higher interest rates and the lending of money to subsidiaries at rates higher than these companies could obtain in a free money market. Holding companies also through their control of the boards of directors have forced the payment of unearned dividends by operating companies. To such an extent was this done in some cases that the surplus, and even the capital stock, of operating companies was seriously impaired. A further

[1] *Op. cit.*, p. 848.
[2] See National Association of Railroad and Utility Commissioners, *Proceedings*, 1932 and 1933.

practice consisted of the utilization of the employees of operating companies in the solicitation of utility customers during working hours for the purpose of selling holding-company securities. All these abuses of intercompany financial relationships ultimately affected the consumers of the service. In so far as they made the securing of capital and other funds more costly, and especially where operating companies were called upon to sustain by their credit the holding-company superstructure, the inevitable results were that the cost of the service would be unduly high or that maintenance and depreciation costs would be slighted with consequent deterioration in the quality of the service.

4. Abuses in Connection with Fees for Service.—It is generally conceded that many of the services rendered operating companies by holding companies or servicing companies controlled by holding companies are valuable services and that they should be adequately compensated for them. However, it has been well argued that if the economic basis for the holding company is economy and efficiency in the performance of services of a type and quality that individual operating companies cannot furnish so well for themselves, such services should be furnished by the holding company at cost or cost plus a reasonable profit, the economies being passed on to the ultimate consumer. In support of this view it is pointed out that some holding companies make no charges for services rendered or do not employ affiliated servicing companies.

That the charges for services rendered operating companies by holding or affiliated servicing companies should at most not exceed cost and a fair margin of profit is elementary in a regulatory system based upon the principle of limiting rates to levels that will return operating expenses and taxes and yield a fair return upon the fair value of the property used in the public service. However, the investigations of the Federal Trade Commission have established beyond doubt or argument that in the past many payments for services rendered have been exorbitant when judged by this standard. Thus, during the period from 1907 to 1928, inclusive, the American Gas and Electric Company received from subsidiary companies as fees for engineering and supervision 173 per cent of the total salaries and expenses for the same period; during 1931, Electric Bond and

Share Company received in fees for services 177 per cent of the expenses allocated to services; in 1928, North American Light and Power Company received in fees 136 per cent of the total expense of the company; and in 1930, income from servicing fees to W. S. Barstow & Company (Delaware), in the Associated Gas and Electric Company group, were eight times as great as the expenses of rendering the services.[1] These illustrations are not presented as typical of holding-company charges, but they do indicate that in some of the largest systems payments have far exceeded the cost to the company furnishing the services.

The Supreme Court of the United States has taken the attitude recently that fees charged operating companies for services should bear a definite relationship to the cost to the servicing company of furnishing them. In a case involving the rates of the Illinois Bell Telephone Company there were at issue the charges made by the American Telephone and Telegraph Company to the Illinois Bell Company. These charges are made under the license contract which the American Telephone and Telegraph Company has with its subsidiaries in payment for certain rights and privileges granted and certain services furnished by the parent company. This fee, which originally was $4\frac{1}{2}$ per cent but is now $1\frac{1}{2}$ per cent of the gross earnings of each subsidiary operating company, had been attacked frequently by state commissions, but the Supreme Court had laid down the rule that in the absence of proof of fraud, bad faith, or the abuse of discretion the charges must be allowed as legitimate operating expenses.[2] In *Smith v. Ill. Bell Telephone Co.*,[3] decided in 1930, the Court reversed its position in this matter by saying that where the power of stock ownership is so exercised as to "commingle the affairs of the corporations and make them practically one" the courts must not be deceived by "mere forms of law" but must deal with the "substance of the transaction." As for the license fees, the Court said that while there was no reason to doubt that valuable services were rendered to the subsidiaries by the parent company, "specific findings" should be made with respect to "the cost of such services to the American Company and the

[1] Utility Corporations, *op. cit.*, Part 72-A, pp. 466–467.

[2] State *ex rel.* Southwestern Bell Telephone Co. v. Mo. Pub. Service Comm., 262 U.S. 276.

[3] 282 U.S. 133.

reasonable amount which should be allocated in this respect to the operating expenses of the intrastate business." On this basis, among others, the case was remanded to the District Court for further findings.

In arriving at its findings of fact with respect to the cost to the American Telephone and Telegraph Company of furnishing services to the Illinois Bell Telephone Company under the license contract, the District Court considered, first, the evidence as to the work performed by the 12 departments of the American Company, each of which furnished license-contract services, and the reasonable amount of the costs of operating these departments that should be allocated to the Illinois Company;[1] second, the Illinois Company's proper share of the cost to the American company incurred in maintaining the receivers, transmitters, and induction coils (these were formerly owned by the American Company but in 1928 were sold to the operating companies) plus 6 per cent for depreciation and an annual return of 6 per cent on the fair value of these instruments; third, the Illinois Company's share of the cost to the American Company under its obligation to insure and hold harmless the licensees against loss or damage from suits or judgments for infringements of any patents; and, fourth, the Illinois Company's share of the cost of office space and office furniture and fixtures for the 12 departments. An amount claimed by the American Company as the cost of maintaining, in the form of cash or short-term, nonfluctuating, low-yield securities, adequate funds to meet any reasonable demands of the licensees the Court disallowed, as it did also an amount claimed for taxes paid by the American Company, as expenses which were included under the license contract.

From a consideration of these facts the Court arrived at the sums shown in the table on p. 276, as the cost to the American Company of furnishing license services to the Illinois Company.

In determining the reasonable operating expense that should be allowed for license contract services to the Illinois Company, the Court took "the amounts found to be the costs to the Ameri-

---

[1] These 12 departments are (1) operation and engineering, (2) development and research, (3) information, (4) personnel, (5) public relations, (6) treasurer, (7) controller, (8) secretary, (9) administration (including sundry items), (10) general service bureau, (11) operation (general), and (12) legal. Ill. Bell Telephone Co. v. Gilbert, P.U.R. 1933E, 301, 303.

can Company of those services, unless such amount for a given year is larger than the amount charged on the books of the company." In the latter case, it allowed as an operating expense the smaller amount charged on the books of the company.[1] When this case was finally adjudicated the Supreme Court found the depreciation charges of the Illinois Bell Company to be so excessive as to remove any doubt that the rates

Year	Cost to the American Telephone and Telegraph Company	Amounts actually paid by the Illinois Bell Telephone Company
1923	$1,088,195	$1,662,014
1924	1,156,046	1,787,095
1925	1,369,836	1,901,069
1926	1,412,867	1,845,571
1927	1,422,869	1,980,880
1928	1,005,063	1,036,616
1929	1,040,529	834,276
1930	1,191,882	864,131
1931	1,068,303	834,199

were not confiscatory.[2] Thus, there was in this case no decision with respect to the license fees, nor has there been in any case decided since that time any final decision as to methods of determining reasonable fees for service. The matter still awaits final decision.

The importance to consumers of exorbitant fees for supervision and management services is that these are charges to the operating expenses of the operating companies and must be covered by the rates. In so far as the fees constitute bona fide and fair payments for services rendered they provide an indirect source of income to the companies that hold the stocks of the operating companies and are of direct benefit to the consumers in the form of more efficient and economical management and superior service. But too often such fees have been exploited as a source of direct income to holding companies, or the dominant interests, and, without regulatory control to bring them in line with the cost of rendering the services, consumer interests cannot

[1] Ill. Bell Telephone Co. v. Gilbert, P.U.R. 1933E, 301, 316.
[2] Lindheimer *et al.* v. Ill. Bell Telephone Co., 292 U.S. 151.

be adequately protected. A further factor is that the profit element in fees furnishes a temptation to increase the number of special services so rendered beyond the needs of operating companies at the expense of other security holders of the operating companies and the rate payers. Engineering fees in connection with the formulation of plans for additions and betterments to properties, fees for financing, and cost-plus fees on construction are generally not charged directly against operating expenses but are capitalized, thus increasing the rate base and becoming a part of the depreciable property. In either case the fees ultimately are recouped from the consumers.

It may be objected even further that no profit on service fees by holding companies is justified, since the holding company, having assumed ownership and direct management, in substance has become a part of the operating company organization and as such has no right to profits from management except those derived from dividends. This principle has been recognized in the formation recently by certain holding-company groups of servicing companies organized on a mutual basis. In the Commonwealth and Southern Corporation group, for example, the stock of the mutualized service company is owned by the operating companies in the ratio of the gross earnings of each to the total gross earnings of all. This company renders service without profit to the operating companies at fees based upon the gross earnings of the group approximately sufficient to cover the estimated cost. If any excess of fee remains at the end of the year, this is returned to the operating companies. Among the services rendered are supervision of operations, financing, issue and sale of securities, accounting and reporting, tax matters, insurance, rates, commercial and merchandising activity, statistical information, technical and engineering development and design, operating analysis, cost records, purchasing, and others.[1] In the absence of a mutualized service company, regulation in the public interest is necessary. But such regulation to be intelligent and efficient must be undertaken by the Federal Government, since while under existing laws some state commissions may question the propriety of engineering and management fees paid by the operating companies, the holding companies, as a rule, are not under their jurisdiction, and they

[1] Edison Electric Institute *Bulletin*, March, 1935, Part 2, p. 7.

generally lack adequate powers of access to the books and records of holding or management companies.

5. Competition among Holding Companies.—Not the least important of the unfavorable features of holding-company activity has been the competition of holding companies for the control of strategic operating companies and of holding-company groups. In the early stages of holding-company development opportunities abounded for the acquisition of operating companies, and consolidations were brought about for the most part in order to create larger operating properties to take advantage of the efficiencies made possible by improvements in the art. As more and more operating companies came under the control of holding-company groups, however, the problem changed largely to one of competition for the control of holding companies as well as operating companies. The motives underlying such activities consisted of the desire to add to growing systems already integrated operating-company groups, to accomplish greater security for the dominant interests through territorial and other forms of diversification of investment, to create super-power systems or power zones where properties were contiguous, or to build up control for promotional or management purposes over great power combinations consisting of properties widely separated territorially. The net effect of such activities too often has been the paying of exorbitant prices for operating- or holding-company stocks, thus creating inflated values which have appeared in the capitalization of the top companies and the creation of unwieldy, uneconomic organizations bearing little relationship to the economy and efficiency of the service, which after all constitute the principal economic justification of holding companies.

In pursuing policies of territorial expansion it was inevitable that in many cases no single holding company should obtain control of all the companies operating in a market area; hence, it often happened that several unaffiliated holding companies controlled adjoining properties, and there developed sharp competition, especially among the rapidly expanding holding companies, to bring them under common control. Destructive competition was avoided in many instances, however, by cooperation in control rather than competition between interested holding-company groups, or by the joint use of generating, transmitting, and other electric facilities by unassociated companies. In some instances there would develop a certain degree of comity in the division of territory between holding-company groups, under which each would develop and consolidate its own system and make advantageous inter-connections for the purchase, sale, or exchange of energy. The advantages of this type of cooperation over competition are obvious, although the effect was merely to reduce the amount of inflation of values and to lessen the complication of holding-company structures.

At this point mention should be made of the influence of investment bankers upon holding-company structures. As the Federal Trade Commission has said, no large holding-company structure has grown to its present size without the aid of investment bankers, and it is probably true that not many of the existing holding-company structures have developed entirely without competition among more or less powerful competitive banking groups. Through this relationship with bankers, holding companies have been enabled to perform what truly economic function there has been in the substitution of their securities for those of operating companies by tapping broader and cheaper sources of capital. But out of this situation grew much grave abuse. Investment bankers not only furnished necessary capital, but they solicited the flotation of additional securities, relying principally upon the holding companies for business. The resulting evils consisted of the unnecessary pyramiding of holding-company structures and the exertion of great pressure on holding-company managements to give attention to the desires and alignments of investment bankers in the formation and operation of holding-company groups. It was inevitable in such a situation that many holding-company alignments should reflect primarily the competition of banking groups rather than operating economies and efficiencies.[1]

A further significant influence of investment bankers is reflected in the formation of superholding companies like The United Corporation group. This has been well stated by the Federal Trade Commission, as follows:

> The financial profit of the operating utility as such depends upon the prosperity of the industries and commerce of the communities served.

[1] Utility Corporations, *op. cit.*, Part 72-A, pp. 75–81.

Beyond this, the prosperity of many individual industrial units is dependent on efficient, adequate, and low-cost service from the utilities. If the banking interests should become interested in any particular industry in a given locality, it is conceivable that their influence might be exerted in favor of that interest and to the possible detriment of conflicting interests. Through the joining of such large financial and public-utility holding and operating interests, it would seem possible that machinery might be set up by which dominating interests within the organization might reach out to specific industries and communities over a vast area to influence important factors in the economic progress of such areas and industries. Economic history usually indicates that wherever such situations exist, regulation in the public interest becomes necessary in order so to control concentrated power as to prevent its abuse, and by the same token regulation becomes increasingly difficult.[1]

The effect upon consumers of the competition between holding companies for properties, which resulted in the payment of inordinately high prices, is that such imprudent purchases had to be financed, and the earnings of the operating companies increased to sustain the top-heavy structures. Building up the gross earnings of operating companies, however, proved to be too slow and painstaking a process, so that many holding-company managements were driven to serious straits. Asset write-ups in corporate mergers and consolidation were employed, as was the device of failure to include in operating expense adequate provision for depreciation. The inevitable consequence of such practice was an overstatement of the net income of operating companies and the resultant payment of dividends that represented not actual earnings but funds that should have been reserved for the purpose of replacing worn-out plant and equipment.

STATE REGULATION OF HOLDING COMPANIES

Legislation bearing upon the regulation of holding companies has been enacted by a number of states since 1930, although before that time not much had been attempted. In 1930, statutes were enacted in Massachusetts and New York; in 1931, in Kansas, Michigan, North Carolina, Oregon, and Wisconsin; and in 1932, in Alabama. In 1933, the laws in several of these states were modified or expanded, and laws were enacted in Illinois, Indiana, Maine, New Hampshire, Pennsylvania, Ver-

[1] *Op. cit.*, pp. 115–116.

mont, and Washington. From 1930 to 1936, 24 states enacted laws extending commission control over affiliated interests.

The laws of the different states vary widely in their provisions and the methods by which they seek to attain similar objectives. All, however, embrace one or more of the following subjects:

(1) Definition of affiliated company or affiliated interests, prescribing a percentage of voting stock as a measure of affiliation;

(2) Attempted authority on the part of the commission to examine books, contracts and records of affiliated companies, and to require such companies to file reports of certain transactions;

(3) Reports of utilities to the commission to disclose holders of stocks;

(4) Approval of contracts between utilities and affiliated companies;

(5) Approval by the commission of loans of money or securities or extension of credit by utilities to affiliated companies;

(6) Restrictions on payment of dividends by utilities;

(7) Power to exclude from accounts of utilities payments to affiliated companies;

(8) Requirement of proof by utilities of cost to affiliated companies of services, material or commodities furnished to utilities; and

(9) Prohibition against acquisition of stock of one utility by another utility or by another corporation, thus preventing establishment of affiliated relationship.[1]

In several states, extension of jurisdiction over foreign holding or affiliated companies has been attempted by a variety of methods. These embrace statutory declarations that affiliated interests are public utilities; that a foreign corporation shall be deemed to be doing business within the state if it furnishes to an affiliated utility for intrastate operations any service, equipment, facilities, or commodities; that a foreign corporation that owns a majority of voting stock of a corporation organized by or licensed to do business in the state shall be deemed to be represented in the state by any officer of such foreign corporation coming into the state, thus rendering him subject to service of process; and that a foreign holding company shall be prohibited from acquiring stock or control of a local operating utility unless it enters into an agreement to inform the commission of transactions between the utility and the holding company and to submit to jurisdiction of

[1] "Report of the Special Committee on the Regulation of Holding Companies and of the Relations between Such Companies and Affiliated Operating Companies," American Bar Association, Section of Public Utility Law, 1933.

the commission in so far as such transactions affect rates or charges of the utility.

While it is clear that the states are not altogether helpless to protect public utility consumers from unscrupulous holding-company interests, it is equally apparent that state powers must be supplemented if such protection is to be complete. It is axiomatic in a regulatory system that the scope of regulatory powers must be as broad as the activities to be regulated, yet if public utility operating companies following the lines of economic advantage, or if holding companies, cross state lines they create interstate problems with which states cannot successfully cope. A single state cannot deal adequately with a holding company whose operations cover several states, nor can its regulation of the operating companies under its jurisdiction be effective without full access to the books and records of the controlling holding companies. Control over the accounting practices of holding companies, together with authority to examine books and records and to require meaningful reports, is fundamental to the disclosure of facts essential to a proper determination of the reasonableness of payments by operating companies to holding companies, and this for the most part lies beyond the jurisdiction of the states, especially with respect to foreign corporations. Furthermore, the unnecessary complication of holding-company structures, which it is generally conceded presents insuperable obstacles to effective regulation, is a matter with which state governments have not adequate authority to deal. For the solution of these problems, as well as of others, students of the situation have long contended that direct regulation of holding companies by the Federal Government is essential.

This viewpoint, at least in part, became officially that of the National Association of Railroad and Utility Commissioners when at the annual meeting of that body in 1932 the following resolution was adopted:

WHEREAS, this Association is not convinced that general Federal regulation of relations between utilities and their affiliated companies is necessary or desirable but recognizes that State regulation may be greatly helped if the powers of the Federal Government can be utilized in determining facts as to relationships and business arrangements between utilities and affiliated interests: Now, therefore, be it

RESOLVED, that this Association deems it desirable and necessary that the facts as to the corporate and business relationships between holding companies or their affiliated interests and affiliated public utilities as to matters affecting the reasonableness of rates and charges made to the utilities for services or commodities or other purposes by a holding company or other affiliated interest be made available to the regulatory bodies of the several States, and that the Executive Committee and the Committee on Legislation be directed to support appropriate legislation to obtain these results.[1]

Since the National Association of Railroad and Utility Commissioners, a body composed for the most part of members of state commissions, has been zealous and aggressive in its opposition to further encroachment of the Federal Government upon the powers of the states, it is logical to assume that this action sprang from thorough knowledge of the inadequacies of state powers in the regulation of operating companies controlled by holding companies beyond their jurisdiction. In 1935, Congress enacted a law, called the Public Utility Act of 1935, which in Title I provides for broad and detailed regulation of gas and electric holding companies by the Securities and Exchange Commission of the Federal Government. However, because of the uncertainty regarding the constitutionality of this law, and various legal actions, little attempt has been made up to this time to enforce its provisions.

FEDERAL REGULATION OF HOLDING COMPANIES UNDER THE PUBLIC UTILITY ACT OF 1935—TITLE I

The Public Utility Act of 1935 is in reality two acts in one. Title I deals with the regulation of holding companies, while Title II amends the Federal Water Power Act and broadens the powers of the Federal Power Commission to include jurisdiction over interstate movements of electric energy. In this chapter our attention will be confined to Title I.

1. The Need for Federal Regulation of Holding Companies.— The need for federal regulation of holding companies is stated by Congress in Section 1, Title I, in the following words:

Public utility holding companies and their subsidiary companies are affected with a national public interest in that, among other things, (1)

---

[1] National Association of Railroad and Utility Commissioners, *Proceedings*, 1932, pp. 467–468.

their securities are widely marketed and distributed by means of the mails and instrumentalities of interstate commerce and are sold to a large number of investors in different States; (2) their service, sales, construction, and other contracts and arrangements are often made and performed by means of the mails and instrumentalities of interstate commerce; (3) their subsidiary public-utility companies often sell and transport gas and electric energy by the use of means and instrumentalities of interstate commerce; (4) their practices in respect of and control over subsidiary companies often materially affect the interstate commerce in which those companies engage; (5) their activities extending over many States are not susceptible of effective control by any State and make difficult, if not impossible, effective State regulation of public-utility companies.[1]

2. The Companies Affected.—Title I is made applicable only to gas and electric holding companies. A "public utility company" is defined as an electric utility company or a gas utility company, and a holding company as

(A) any company which directly or indirectly owns, controls, or holds with power to vote, 10 per centum or more of the outstanding voting securities of a public-utility company or of a company which is a holding company by virtue of this clause or clause (B), unless the Commission, as hereinafter provided, by order declares such company not to be a holding company; and

(B) any person which the Commission determines, after notice and opportunity for hearing, directly or indirectly to exercise (either alone or pursuant to an arrangement or understanding with one or more other persons) such a-controlling influence over the management or policies of any public-utility or holding company as to make it necessary or appropriate in the public interest or for the protection of investors or consumers that such person be subject to the obligations, duties, and liabilities imposed in this title upon holding companies.[2]

---

[1] Section 1 (a).

[2] The Securities and Exchange Commission is bound by law to declare that a company is not a holding company under clause (A), if it finds that the applicant "(i) does not, either alone or pursuant to an arrangement or understanding with one or more other persons, directly or indirectly control a public-utility or holding company either through one or more intermediary persons or by any means or device whatsoever, (ii) is not an intermediary company through which such control is exercised, and (iii) does not, directly or indirectly, exercise (either alone or pursuant to an arrangement or understanding with one or more other persons) such a controlling influence over the management or policies of any public-utility or holding company as to

A "subsidiary company" of a specified holding company is defined as "any company 10 per centum or more of the outstanding voting securities of which are directly or indirectly owned, controlled, or held with power to vote" by a holding company, or by a company that is a subsidiary company of a holding company. Thus, although to be a holding company under the law a company must have at least one or more gas or electric subsidiaries, any company may be a subsidiary of a holding company, whether it be a gas, electric, water, telephone, industrial, financial, or other company, if it be subsidiary to a holding company as defined.

An "affiliate" of a specified company means "(A) any person that directly or indirectly owns, controls, or holds with power to vote, 5 per cent or more of the outstanding voting securities of such specified company; (B) any company 5 per cent or more of whose outstanding voting securities are owned, controlled, or held with power to vote, directly or indirectly, by such specified company; (C) any individual who is an officer or director of such specified company, or of any company which is an affiliate thereof"; and (D) any person or class of persons deemed by the Securities and Exchange Commission to be in such relation to such specified company that there is liable to be an absence of arm's-length bargaining in transactions between them which would require regulation in the public interest or for the protection of investors or consumers.

A gas utility company means "any company which owns or operates facilities used for the distribution at retail (other than distribution only in enclosed portable containers, or distribution to tenants or employees of the company operating such facilities for their own use and not for resale) of natural or manufactured gas for heat, light, or power." Thus gas companies engaged in the production and/or sale of gas at wholesale are excluded. An electric utility company means "any company which owns or operates facilities used for the generation, transmission, or distribution of electric energy for sale, other than sale to tenants or employees of the company operating such facilities for their

---

make it necessary or appropriate in the public interest or for the protection of investors or consumers that the applicant be subject to the obligations, duties, and liabilities imposed in this title upon holding companies." Section 2 (a), (7).

own use and not for resale." The Securities and Exchange Commission is directed to declare a company not an electric utility company if its business is primarily other than that of an electric utility or if it operates within a single state and substantially all of its outstanding securities are owned directly or indirectly by another company to which such operating company sells or furnishes electric energy for its own use and not for resale, provided that the purchasing company is primarily engaged in manufacturing (except the manufacturing of gas and electricity), and provided further that the operating company furnish so small an amount of energy to others that regulation is not necessary. The Commission shall declare a company not to be a gas utility company if it is primarily engaged in business other than that of a gas utility company or if the small amount of gas distributed makes regulation unnecessary. No company shall be deemed to be a holding company or subsidiary company unless the Commission shall have issued an order declaring it so.

Section 3 empowers the Commission to exempt any holding company, and every subsidiary company thereof as such, from any provision or provisions of Title I, unless and except in so far as it finds the exemption detrimental to the public interest or the interest of investors or consumers, if

(1) The holding company and every subsidiary company thereof which is a public utility company from which the holding company derives, directly or indirectly, any material part of its income are predominantly intrastate in character, and carry on their business substantially in the State in which the holding company and every subsidiary company thereof are organized;

(2) The holding company is predominantly a public utility company operating only in the State in which it is organized and in States contiguous thereto;

(3) The holding company is only incidentally a holding company, primarily engaged in business other than that of a public utility company, and not deriving, directly or indirectly, any material part of its income from subsidiaries which are public utility companies, or deriving a material part of its income from such subsidiaries if substantially all the outstanding securities of such companies are owned by the holding company;

(4) The holding company is temporarily a holding company solely by reason of the acquisition of securities in the liquidation of debt

previously contracted or in connection with the underwriting or distribution of securities; and

(5) The holding company is not, and derives no material part of its income from subsidiaries which are, a company or companies the principal business of which within the United States is that of a public utility holding company.[1]

3. Registration of Holding Companies.

3. **Registration of Holding Companies.**—The first step in the regulation of holding companies is the requirement of registration. On or after Oct. 1, 1935, but not later than Dec. 1, 1935, any holding company may register by filing with the Commission a notification of registration in such form as the Commission by rules and regulations may prescribe. The Act declares that unless a holding company shall have registered within the specified time, it shall be unlawful for it, directly or indirectly,

(1) to sell, transport, transmit, or distribute, or own or operate any utility assets for the transportation, transmission, or distribution of, natural or manufactured gas or electric energy in interstate commerce;

(2) by the use of the mails or any means or instrumentality of interstate commerce, to negotiate, enter into, or take any step in the performance of, any service, sales, or construction contract undertaking to perform services or construction work for, or sell goods to, any public-utility company or holding company;

(3) to distribute or make any public offering for sale or exchange of any security of such holding company, any subsidiary company or affiliate of such holding company, any public-utility company, or any holding company, by use of the mails or any means or instrumentality of interstate commerce, or to sell any such security having reason to believe that such security, by use of the mails or any means or instrumentality of interstate commerce, will be distributed or made the subject of a public offering;

(4) by use of the mails or any means or instrumentality of interstate commerce, to acquire or negotiate for the acquisition of any security or utility assets of any subsidiary company or affiliate of such holding company, any public-utility company, or any holding company;

(5) to engage in any business in interstate commerce; or

(6) to own, control, or hold with power to vote, any security of any subsidiary company thereof that does any of the acts enumerated in Paragraphs (1) to (5), inclusive, of this subsection.[2]

[1] Section 3 (a).
[2] Section 4 (a).

4. Regulation of Security Issues.—The law specifies that it shall be unlawful for any registered holding company or subsidiary thereof (1) to issue or sell any security of such company or (2) to exercise any privilege or right to alter the priorities, preferences, voting power, or other rights of the holders of an outstanding security of such company until it shall have filed a declaration with the Commission and shall have received an order permitting such declaration to become effective. These provisions do not apply to the issuance, renewal, or guaranty of notes or drafts not part of a public offering, which mature or are renewed for not more than nine months, and which together with other such notes or drafts outstanding do not exceed 5 per cent of the par value (market value where there is no par value) of the outstanding securities. The Commission is empowered to exempt from the foregoing provisions issues by a subsidiary that have been approved by the state commission of the state in which the subsidiary is organized and is operating. This provision evades duplication of regulation by state and federal commissions in respect to security issues. The Commission may exempt also securities issued to finance the business of a subsidiary that is not a holding company, a public utility company, an investment company, or a fiscal or financing agent of such companies. Certain restrictions are imposed under which the Commission shall not permit a declaration to become effective. In addition, registered holding companies and their subsidiaries are forbidden to sell securities of a holding company from house to house and to sell securities of a holding company through officers or employees of a subsidiary.[1]

5. Regulation of Holding-company Corporate Structures.— To eliminate the abuses that have arisen through the creation of unduly complex, overlapping, pyramided, illogical, and uneconomic holding-company structures, the Commission, in Section 11, is directed to

. . . examine the corporate structure of every registered holding company and subsidiary company thereof, the relationships among the companies in the holding-company system of every such company and the character of the interests thereof and the properties owned or controlled thereby to determine the extent to which the corporate structure of such holding-company system and the companies therein may be

[1] Section 6. See Chap. X for a fuller discussion.

simplified, unnecessary complexities therein eliminated, voting power fairly and equitably distributed among the holders of securities thereof, and the properties and business thereof confined to those necessary or appropriate to the operations of an integrated public-utility system.[1]

The operations of a holding-company system, as soon as practicable after Jan. 1, 1938, are to be limited to a "single integrated public utility system," although the Commission may permit a holding company to continue control over one or more additional integrated systems if (1) such additional systems cannot be operated as independent systems without the loss of substantial economies which may be achieved under common control; (2) if such additional systems are located in one state or in adjoining states or in a contiguous foreign country; or (3) if the continued combination of such systems under common control is not so large (considering the state of the art and the area or region affected) as to impair the advantages of localized management, efficient operation, or the effectiveness of regulation. These provisions limit the holding-company structure ultimately to operating companies, a holding company controlling them, and a holding company over the first holding company.

An "integrated public utility system" in the case of electric utilities is defined as

. . . a system consisting of one or more units of generating plants and/or transmission lines and/or distributing facilities, whose utility assets, whether owned by one or more electric utility companies, are physically interconnected or capable of physical interconnection and which under normal conditions may be economically operated as a single interconnected and coordinated system confined in its operations to a single area or region, in one or more States, not so large as to impair (considering the state of the art and the area or region affected) the advantages of localized management, efficient operation, and the effectiveness of regulation.

and in the case of gas utilities as

. . . a system consisting of one or more gas utility companies which are so located and related that substantial economies may be effectuated by being operated as a single coordinated system confined in its operations to a single area or region, in one or more States, not so large as to impair (considering the state of the art and the area or region affected)

[1] Section 11 (a).

the advantages of localized management, efficient operation, and the effectiveness of regulation: *Provided,* That gas utility companies deriving natural gas from a common source of supply may be deemed to be included in a single area or region.[1]

It should be noted that the term integrated public utility system is defined first as to electric and then as to gas utilities. There is no express provision as to the application of the term to a combination of gas and electric utilities.

To render the control over the corporate structures of holding companies more complete, the Commission is given power to supervise the further growth of holding companies. Section 9 provides that it shall be unlawful, without the approval of the Commission, for any registered holding company or any subsidiary company thereof to acquire, directly or indirectly, any securities or utility assets or any other interest in any business; or for any person to do so if such person is an affiliate or will by virtue of such acquisition become such an affiliate. The provisions of this section do not apply to acquisitions that have been expressly authorized by a state commission or to acquisitions where such public utility companies and all other public utility companies in the same holding-company system are organized in the same state, where the business of each such company is substantially confined to such state, and the acquisition has been expressly authorized by the state commission of that state. The provisions of this section also do not apply to the acquisition of government securities or to readily marketable securities, commercial paper, and other securities acquired through the investment of current funds or appropriate in the ordinary course of business within the limits of rules and regulations prescribed by the Commission. Section 10 prescribes the manner of obtaining approval of acquisitions from the Commission. Section 8 provides that whenever a state law prohibits, or requires approval by the state commission of the ownership or operation by a single company of a gas and an electric utility serving substantially the same territory, no holding company shall take a step that would result in its having a direct or indirect interest in both types of companies serving the same territory without express approval of the commission of the state

[1] Section 2 (a) (29).

or, if it already has any such interest, to acquire, without the express approval of the state commission, any direct or indirect interest in an electric or gas utility company serving substantially the same territory as that served by the companies in which it already has an interest.

6. Regulation of Intercompany Loans and Transactions.— It has been pointed out that some of the gravest abuses of holding-company control have arisen in connection with the financial and other transactions between holding and operating companies. To prevent the recurrence of such abuses in the future, Section 12 provides, in part, that

(1) No registered holding company in the future shall borrow or receive any extension of credit or indemnity from any public utility company in the same holding-company system, or from any subsidiary company of such holding company.

(2) No other intercompany loans ("downstream" as well as "upstream") shall be made except in accordance with such rules and regulations as the Commission may prescribe.

(3) No registered holding company or subsidiary thereof shall declare or pay any dividend on any security of such company, or acquire, retire, or redeem any security of such company, in contravention of such rules and regulations or orders as the Commission may deem necessary or appropriate to protect the financial integrity of companies in holding-company systems, to safeguard the working capital of public utility companies, to prevent the payment of dividends out of capital or unearned surplus, or to prevent the circumvention of the provisions of the law or the rules and regulations of the Commission.

(4) No registered holding company shall, in contravention of rules, regulations and orders of the Commission, sell any security which it owns of any public utility company, or any utility assets; and no person shall solicit any proxy, power of attorney, consent, or authorization regarding any security of a registered holding company or subsidiary thereof in contravention of rules, regulations and orders of the Commission.

7. Regulation of Service, Sales, and Construction Contracts.— Section 13 provides that no registered holding company shall enter into or take any step in the performance of any service, sales, or construction contract by which such company undertakes to perform services or construction work for, or sell goods to, any associate company thereof which is a public utility or mutual

service company, except in the case of transactions conditionally or unconditionally exempted by the Commission as being
necessary in the public interest. It provides also, that no subsidiary of a registered holding company, and no mutual service
company, shall perform such services for, or sell goods to, any
associate company except in accordance with rules and regulations prescribed by the Commission. The latter provision does
not apply to transactions conditionally or unconditionally
exempted by the Commission "if such transactions (1) are with
any associate company which does not derive, directly or
indirectly, any material part of its income from sources within
the United States and which is not a public-utility company
operating within the United States, or (2) involve special or
unusual circumstances or are not in the ordinary course of business." The rules and regulations of the Commission regarding
such transactions may prescribe, among other things,

. . . such terms and conditions regarding the determination of costs
and the allocation thereof among specified classes of companies and for
specified classes of service, sales, and construction contracts, the duration of such contracts, the making and keeping of accounts and cost-
accounting procedures, the filing of annual and other periodic and
special reports, the maintenance of competitive conditions, the disclosure of interests, and similar matters.

With respect to mutual service companies, which under the law
must be approved by the Commission, Section 13 empowers the
Commission to prescribe rules and regulations regarding the
manner of application for approval. It provides, further, that
the Commission shall not approve, or continue the approval of,
any company as a mutual service company unless the Commission
finds that such company

. . . is so organized as to ownership, costs, revenues, and the sharing
thereof as reasonably to insure the efficient and economical performance
of service, sales, or construction contracts by such company for member
companies, at cost fairly and equitably allocated among such member
companies, at a reasonable saving to member companies over the cost
to such companies of comparable contracts performed by independent
persons.

This section also makes it unlawful for any person whose
principal business is the performance of service, sales, or con-

struction contracts for public utility or holding companies to enter into or take any step in the performance of such contracts with any public utility company engaged in interstate commerce, or with any registered holding company or subsidiary thereof, in contravention of rules and regulations prescribed by the Commission to govern such matters.

8. **Accounts and Records; Reports.**—The Commission is empowered to require registered holding companies, subsidiaries and affiliates, and mutual service companies to make, keep, and preserve such accounts, cost-accounting procedures, correspondence, memoranda, papers, books, and other records as it deems necessary in the public interest or for the protection of investors or consumers or the enforcement of its rules, regulations, or orders. The Commission is given authority also to require every registered holding company and every mutual service company to file such annual, quarterly, and other periodic and special reports as it deems necessary and appropriate.

9. **Miscellaneous Provisions.**—In addition to the provisions aforementioned the Act contains many other clauses which in some instances introduce new regulatory features designed to outlaw practices formerly engaged in by holding companies that clearly have not been in the public interest. In Section 12, Paragraph (*h*), it is provided that no registered holding company, or any subsidiary thereof, shall (1) make any contribution whatsoever in connection with the candidacy, nomination, election, or appointment of any person for or to any office or position in the Government of the United States, a state, or any political subdivision of a state or any agency, authority, or instrumentality of any one or more of the foregoing or (2) make any contribution to or in support of any political party or any committee or agency thereof. The term "contribution" as defined includes "any gift, subscription, loan, advance, or deposit of money or anything of value, and includes any contract, agreement, or promise, whether or not legally enforceable, to make a contribution." By Paragraph (*i*) of the same section it is made unlawful for any person employed or retained by any registered holding company, or any subsidiary thereof, to present, advocate, or oppose any matter affecting any registered holding company, or any subsidiary thereof, before the Congress or any member or committee thereof, or before the Securities

and Exchange Commission or the Federal Power Commission, unless first such person has properly filed with the Commission a statement of the subject matter in respect of which the person is retained or employed, the nature and character of such retainer or employment, and the amount of compensation to be received.

In order to prevent officers and directors of a registered holding company from making unfair or improper use of information received through their intimate connection with the affairs of the companies in financial dealings, every such person is required to file with the Commission, each month in case of change of ownership, a statement of the securities of such registered holding company, or any subsidiary company thereof, of which he is, directly or indirectly, the beneficial owner. Where any profit is realized by such officer or director from the sale and purchase or purchase and sale of any security of a registered holding company, or subsidiary thereof, within any period of less than six months, such profit shall inure to and be recoverable by the holding company or subsidiary company in respect of the security of which such profit was realized "irrespective of any intention on the part of such officer or director in entering into such transaction to hold the security purchased or not to repurchase the security sold for a period of more than six months."[1]

To eliminate banking control contrary to the public interest, Section 17, Paragraph (c), provides that after one year from the effective date of Title I, no registered holding company, or any subsidiary thereof, shall have as an officer or director thereof any executive officer, director, partner, appointee, or representative of any bank, trust company, investment banker, or banking association or firm, or any such officer or representative of any corporation a majority of whose voting stock is owned by any bank, trust company, investment banker, or banking association or firm, except as may be permitted by the Commission.

Other provisions enable the Commission to make studies and investigations, to hold hearings and subpoena witnesses, and to prosecute offenses. Provision is made for the court review of Commission orders, and jurisdiction of offenses and suits is ascribed to appropriate courts.

[1] Section 17 (a) and (b).

SUMMARY

In this chapter we have pointed out first the economic bases of public utility holding companies in order that the student may have some facts upon which to separate the good from the bad. That holding companies can, and do, perform economic functions in view of technological developments, especially in the gas and electric utilities, and the general organization of large-scale enterprise there is no doubt. But this does not condone the abuses that we have discussed in detail, and which must be condemned by all fair-minded people, nor does it justify the existence of holding-company superstructures erected primarily by those interested in the utility industries not from the viewpoint of service to the public but as a source of private gain. That regulation of holding companies in the interest of investors, rate payers, and the general public is necessary is no longer debatable, nor that regulation must employ federal powers because of the inadequacies of state control. The task of regulation will consist not only of the elimination of specific abuses but in the revamping and simplification of holding-company structures so as to make holding-company systems conform to economic functions. The Public Utility Act of 1935, for the first time, grants to public authorities the powers necessary to accomplish these purposes, although so far there has been no real attempt to put this law into effect, it apparently being the purpose of federal authorities to await final decision on its constitutionality.

Recently, in a case involving the Electric Bond and Share Company the Supreme Court upheld the registration provisions of the Public Utility Act of 1935.[1] The Court made no attempt, however, to state the limits of permissible regulation in the execution of the declared policy of Title I, hence many vital matters may still be brought before the Court for final adjudication. At the present writing movements are afoot which eventually may test more fundamentally the Act and the policies of the Securities and Exchange Commission in carrying out its provisions. The decision requires registration, but even before it was handed down holding companies owning about 44 per cent of the total assets of the companies believed to be subject

[1] New York Times, March 28, 1938.

to the Act had registered with the Commission. Also, a number of the companies which had registered, notably the American Waterworks and Electric Company, had taken steps to simplify their corporate structures in conformity with the provisions of the Act.

References

BERLE, A. A., and G. C. MEANS: "The Modern Corporation and Private Property," Commerce Clearing House, Inc., New York, 1932.

BONBRIGHT, J. C., and G. C. MEANS: "The Holding Company," McGraw-Hill Book Company, Inc., New York, 1932.

LILIENTHAL, D. E.: "The Regulation of Public Utility Holding Companies," *Columbia Law Review*, Vol. 29, April, 1929, pp. 404–440.

National Association of Railroad and Utility Commissioners: *Proceedings*, 1932–1936.

Relation of Holding Companies to Operating Companies in Power and Gas Affecting Control, House Report 827, 73d Cong., 2d Sess., Part 6.

Report of the Special Committee on the Regulation of Holding Companies and of the Relations between Such Companies and Affiliated Operating Companies, American Bar Association, 1933.

Utility Corporations, Sen. Doc. 92, 70th Cong., 1st Sess., Parts 72-A and 73-A.

WILSON, G. L., J. M. HERRING, and R. B. EUTSLER: "Public Utility Industries," McGraw-Hill Book Company, Inc., New York, 1936.

CHAPTER XII

THE FEDERAL GOVERNMENT AND THE PUBLIC UTILITIES

The problems of public utility regulation in the United States are complicated by the existence of two sovereignties, state and federal, the powers of which are mutually exclusive, each being predominant in its appropriate sphere. When the Federal Constitution was adopted, the individual sovereign states delegated therein to the Federal Government certain powers, but all powers not expressly delegated, or necessarily implied in the carrying out of the express powers, were reserved to the states, unless specifically prohibited to them, and to the people. Among the powers delegated to the Federal Government were the power to regulate commerce among the various states and with foreign countries, the power to create and maintain a postal system, and the power to levy and collect taxes. It is under such powers as these, which have been more or less specifically defined and limited in court interpretations, that the Federal Government, if at all, may exercise regulatory control over public utilities. The scope of federal jurisdiction thus stands in contrast with that of the states, which under their police powers may regulate public utilities in the interest of the general welfare.

The need for federal regulation of public utilities is greater today than ever before, owing to the increasing volume of interstate operations which tend to place these companies farther and farther beyond the limits of state jurisdiction. However, the expansion of federal activities in this field intensifies two long-standing problems: the development of coordinate, cohesive federal policies; and the determination of the proper spheres of federal and state control where interstate and intrastate operations are intermingled. In this chapter we shall sketch in broad outlines the major aspects of these problems, some of which will be discussed in more detail in subsequent chapters.

The Federal Government and the Transportation Utilities.—
The Federal Government first undertook the regulation of
railroads, to which were soon added, by broadening the definition
of the terms "railroad" and "transportation," express and sleep-
ing car companies, industrial railways, private car facilities,
terminal facilities of every kind, and pipe lines.   In railroad
transportation, where interstate operations predominate, there
has been a clearly marked tendency for the scope of federal
jurisdiction to broaden and for that of the states to constrict.
This tendency has been manifest not alone in the legislation of
Congress but in the interpretations of Congressional powers
by the courts.

Before the passage of the Interstate Commerce Act in 1887,
which marked the advent of the Federal Government into the
field of railroad regulation, there was a certain tendency on the
part of states to usurp authority over matters interstate.   This
encroachment was clearly reflected in the so-called Granger
laws, adopted by many states to regulate railroad rates and
practices, and the courts were sympathetic with state needs
in upholding the right of a state, in the absence of federal legislation, to legislate in the interests of those within the state even
though it might indirectly affect those without.[1]   Under such
an interpretation it was inevitable that the attempts of various
states to regulate interstate commerce should go farther and
farther afield and that the courts would eventually lay a restraining hand upon state powers.   This was done in the Wabash
case, in which the Supreme Court held that the right of continuous transportation from one end of the country to the other
free from the restraints that states might choose to place upon
it is the right that the commerce clause of the Federal Constitution was intended to secure.[2]

Under federal regulation the tendency has been for Congress
and the courts to broaden the scope of the jurisdiction of the
Interstate Commerce Commission.   The growth of interstate
railroad transportation brought about such a commingling of
interstate and intrastate operations that distinctions between
them became more and more arbitrary.   One after another the
powers of the states have been restricted or modified until the

[1] Peik v. Chicago and Northwestern Ry., 94 U.S. 164.
[2] Wabash, St. Louis and Pacific Ry. Co. v. Illinois, 118 U.S. 557.

dominance of the Federal Government in the twilight zone between powers clearly state and those clearly federal is well established. This is the significance of the decisions in the Minnesota rate cases[1] and the Shreveport case.[2] In the latter case, the Supreme Court held that

> . . . wherever the interstate and intrastate transactions of carriers are so related that the government of the one involves the control of the other, it is Congress, and not the State, that is entitled to prescribe the final and dominant rule, for otherwise Congress would be denied the exercise of its constitutional authority and the State, and not the Nation, would be supreme within the national field.

Under this decision the Federal Government may regulate intrastate matters, including intrastate rates, if necessary to prevent discrimination against interstate commerce.

In the past, federal regulation of transportation has been confined for the most part to railroad transportation, although interstate pipe-line transportation has been subject to the jurisdiction of the Interstate Commerce Commission since 1906. However, pipe lines enjoy great inherent advantages in the transportation of petroleum, and they are largely plant facilities of huge integrated oil systems, so that their regulation has not presented many difficult or urgent problems. Common carriers by water, both on the inland waterways and coastwise, largely have been unregulated by any federal agency, although the Interstate Commerce Commission now regulates all joint rail-water rates of interstate water carriers and the port-to-port rates of such water carriers as are owned by railroads. The United States Shipping Board Bureau formerly regulated to a considerable extent common carriers by water in foreign commerce, except ocean tramp ships and contract water carriers on the Great Lakes, and had rather complete regulatory authority over common and contract carriers in the intercoastal trade through the Panama Canal. The Merchant Marine Act of 1936, however, created the United States Maritime Commission and transferred to it all the powers and duties of the Shipping Board Bureau, providing further that after the expiration of two years the President of the United States was authorized to

[1] 230 U.S. 352.
[2] 234 U.S. 342.

transfer to the Interstate Commerce Commission, by executive order, any or all regulatory powers vested in the Maritime Commission.

In recent years the coming of sturdy new competitive transportation agencies, motor and air transportation, has added to the old a host of new problems and has forced us as a nation to reexamine the entire structure of the relationship of the Federal Government to transportation. More and more widely appreciated is the fact that our whole transportation system must be viewed as a unit and our transportation problems treated as aspects merely of a "single, unified problem." The nature of this problem has well been stated by Mr. Joseph B. Eastman, former Federal Coordinator of Transportation, in the following words:

> The ideal is plainly a national transportation system which will utilize each means of transport to the best advantage, encouraging its use in the service to which it is best fitted, discouraging its use in service to which it is not well adapted, promoting cooperation and the utmost coordination which will be of advantage, establishing order in the place of disorder, preventing competition from assuming wasteful and destructive forms, and in short, attempting to build up a system which will be sound economically and financially, be able to supply the best service at the lowest reasonable cost, and keep up with the march of the times.[1]

The achievement of such an ideal, however, would involve a reconsideration of the fundamental policies underlying our regulatory system. Historically, as we pointed out earlier, federal regulation of the railroads has been predicated upon regulated competition, *i.e.*, the enforcement of competition in some respects, and its restraint in others. Some of the earlier requirements of law with respect to competition, such as the prohibition in the original Act to Regulate Commerce against the pooling of freights by the railroads and the prohibitions in the antitrust laws against combinations that would suppress or materially reduce the free and normal flow of goods in the channels of interstate trade, have been relaxed by the provisions of the Transportation Act of 1920 and the Emergency Railroad Transportation Act of 1933, but the philosophy of competition

---

[1] Report of the Federal Coordinator of Transportation, 1934, House Doc. 89, 74th Cong., 1st Sess., p. 14.

has not been discarded. While present thought seems to favor a coordinated transportation system, it is widely felt that the appropriate place of each agency in such a system should be determined through the operation of the forces of competition.

But the effective development and application of the philosophy of competition presuppose that each agency will be free and untrammeled in the conduct of its operations, a condition that cannot obtain if one of the agencies is subject to regulatory supervision and its competitors are not. To equalize competitive conditions, as well as for other reasons which will be discussed more fully in a succeeding chapter, Congress enacted the Motor Transportation Act of 1935. The situation still remains unsatisfactory, however, with water carriers partly unregulated, and air carriers regulated by the Interstate Commerce Commission only with respect to rates for the carriage of mail, there being no regulation of their charges for common carrier services.

A further reason for the extension of federal control over the interstate operations of motor transport carriers should be mentioned here because of its kinship to problems involved in the relationship of the Federal Government to other utilities. With the growing importance of motor transportation it was inevitable that most states should have enacted laws placing the intrastate operations of motor common carriers under the jurisdiction of state commissions. However, an outstanding aspect of motor transportation is the volume of interstate carriage by common carriers, a part of thich was originally made interstate to avoid state regulation. Because such commerce is beyond the jurisdiction of the states, federal regulation is necessary to supplement state regulation for effective control of motor transportation.

Federal Regulation of Air Transportation.—The development of civil aviation has given rise to new and somewhat different problems in the regulation of transportation. From small beginnings civil aviation has grown to an industry of considerable economic importance. This growth has been particularly rapid during the past ten years. From 1926 to 1936 the total number of firms in the industry nearly doubled; airplanes in operation trebled in number; miles flown by miscellaneous commercial and private flyers increased 4 times; annual air-mail poundage increased 17 times; and the total number of passengers carried per year by scheduled air lines increased 149 times.   A significant fact regarding air passenger transportation is that the length of individual air trips has increased, a trend reflected in the statistics of passenger miles flown.   Passengers carried in domestic sched-uled air-line operations increased from 374,935 in 1930 to 1,020,-931 in 1936, but during the same period domestic passenger miles flown increased from 84,014,572 to 435,740,253.   It should be noted, however, that this divergence in trends may be traced partially to the effect of consolidations of air lines, since a long journey which now may be taken over one line formerly was taken over the routes of two or more companies, thus adding to the passenger totals of each but not affecting the passenger-mile total.   Air express increased in each successive year from 3,555 pounds in 1926 to 8,350,010 pounds in 1936.[1]   Selected statistics of the growth of civil aviation are presented in the table on p. 303.

A large proportion of air transport operations are interstate, and regulation, accordingly, must be federal to the extent of these operations.   Nevertheless, intrastate operations, which are not within the scope of federal jurisdiction, are of considerable importance, and there are many matters concerning safety of operation and the protection of property rights in which the states may, and do, take great interest.   Thus, there arise here, as in so many other fields, problems of determining the proper spheres of federal and state control and of effecting necessary cooperation between federal and state authorities.

Prior to 1926 the interest of the Federal Government in commercial aviation was expressed largely through the activities of the National Advisory Committee for Aeronautics, created by act of Congress, Mar. 3, 1915, and the Post Office Department. The principal duties of the National Advisory Committee for Aeronautics were the supervision and direction of the study of flight problems with a view to their practical solution, the determination and description of problems for scientific experi-mentation, and the application of the results of scientific studies to practical problems.   The Post Office Department, through contracts for mail carriage, did much to encourage and support civil aviation.   Attempts to set up a basic law that would give the Federal Government fairly complete control over air trans-

[1] *Aeronautics Bulletin* 1, Aug. 1, 1937, pp. 37–39.

PROGRESS OF CIVIL AERONAUTICS IN THE UNITED STATES

Scheduled air-line operations	1926	1927	1928	1929	1930	1931	1932	1933	1934	1935	1936
Airways, domestic and foreign:*											
Services in operation	18	23	63	97	122	126	136	112	98	109	110
Express mileage	4,434	7,233	8,379	11,775	20,445	21,348	46,821	46,120	50,652	60,377	61,458
Mail mileage	8,039	8,223	14,561	26,597	41,501	43,735	45,436	44,665	46,003	51,428	51,740
Passenger mileage	3,715	7,557	11,455	19,730	36,136	45,704	47,358	47,321	49,353	52,387	61,458
Total mileage, domestic and foreign	8,404	9,122	16,667	36,321	49,549	50,398	48,530	47,687	50,801	60,451	61,532
Express and freight carried, pounds:											
Domestic	3,555	45,859	210,404	249,634	359,523	788,059	1,033,970	1,510,215	2,133,191	3,882,397	6,958,777
Foreign	0	0	6,240	7,809	109,048	363,289	566,851	942,597	1,316,484	1,689,340	1,391,233
Total	3,555	45,859	216,644	257,443	468,571	1,151,348	1,600,821	2,452,812	3,449,675	5,511,737	8,350,010
Mail, carried by contractors, pounds:											
Domestic	269,671	1,065,498	3,545,525	7,099,581	7,985,010	9,097,411	7,393,257	7,362,180	7,411,004	13,276,023	17,706,159
Foreign	107,535	204,801	517,648	672,433	528,665	545,800	515,466	454,352	460,880	503,585	617,853
Total	377,206	1,270,299	4,063,173	7,772,014	8,513,675	9,643,211	7,908,723	7,816,532	7,871,884	13,779,608	18,324,012
Miles flown:											
Daily average, domestic and foreign	11,830	16,083	29,242	68,881	101,220	129,825	139,542	149,706	133,662	174,084	201,017
Mail, domestic and foreign†	4,240,407	5,543,578	7,846,296	14,869,166	19,904,185	33,113,720	36,053,067	41,671,490	27,340,293	39,977,189	44,027,794
Domestic routes	4,258,771	5,779,863	10,400,239	22,380,020	31,992,634	42,755,417	45,606,354	48,771,553	40,955,396	55,380,353	63,777,794
Foreign routes	59,316	90,626	273,211	2,761,479	4,952,569	4,630,570	5,326,613	5,870,992	7,831,155	8,159,880	9,526,610
Passengers carried:											
Domestic	5,782	8,661	47,840	159,751	374,935	469,981	474,279	493,141	461,743	746,946	1,020,931
Foreign	0	18	1,873	13,654	42,570	52,364	66,402	75,799	99,627	113,815	127,038
Total	5,782	8,679	49,713	173,405	417,505	522,345	540,681	568,940	561,370	860,761	1,147,969
Passenger miles flown:‡											
Domestic					84,014,572	106,442,375	127,038,798	173,492,119	187,858,629	313,905,508	435,740,253
Foreign					19,732,677	13,526,202	19,513,789	25,307,960	37,408,930	46,663,923	56,003,800
Total					103,747,249	119,968,577	146,552,587	198,800,079	225,267,559	360,569,431	491,744,053

* Domestic scheduled air lines operate within the continental limits of the United States. Foreign operations cover activities of American air lines in foreign countries.
† Includes Post Office Department operations.   ‡ One passenger carried one mile.
Source: *Air Commerce Bulletin*, vol. 7, No. 12, pp. 280–284; and vol. 8, No. 12, pp. 262–264.

portation came to naught because of disputes over the methods to be employed in regulation and questions as to the constitutionality of such legislation.

Air Commerce Act of 1926.—Federal regulation of air transportation was established on a firm basis by the Air Commerce Act of 1926. This Act announced a twofold purpose on the part of the Federal Government—to encourage and promote, as well as to regulate, air commerce. Seven different departments or agencies of the Federal Government were given functions or duties relative to the carrying out of the provisions of the Act. To the Department of Commerce was assigned the duty of administering and enforcing the major provisions of the law; to the President, authority to make necessary airspace reservations; to the Secretary of the Treasury, the duty of providing rules for the entry and clearance and customs regulation for aircraft engaged in foreign commerce; to the Secretary of Labor, authority to deal with all immigration problems relative to aircraft; to the Secretary of Agriculture, the duty of supplying meteorological information; to the Secretary of War, authority to designate military airways; and to the Bureau of Standards, the duty to carry on such research and development work as would tend to create improved air navigation facilities.[1]

By the principal regulatory provisions of the Act, the Secretary of Commerce was authorized:

1. To grant registration to aircraft.

2. To provide for the rating of aircraft as to their airworthiness.

3. To subject such aircraft to periodical examination.

4. To examine and rate airmen serving with aircraft of the United States as to their qualifications for service.

5. To examine and rate air navigation facilities.

6. To issue, suspend, or revoke registration of aircraft and certificates of airmen.

7. To establish air traffic rules for the navigation, protection, and identification of aircraft, including rules as to safe altitudes of flight and rules for the prevention of collisions between vessels and aircraft.

8. To establish airways.

9. To encourage civil aeronautics in various ways.

[1] ROHLFING, C. C., "National Regulation of Aeronautics," University of Pennsylvania Press, Philadelphia, 1931, p. 35.

In addition to the foregoing provisions of the basic law, the Secretary of Commerce was empowered to announce rules and regulations of a technical nature to govern detailed operations and the development of the industry. The Air Commerce Act was designed to foster and govern the safe and technical growth of aeronautics and not to provide for the regulation of the financial and economic aspects of air commerce. The Act has been amended from time to time in minor matters, but the original purpose and the framework of legislation have remained unaltered. One important amendment is that contained in the Air Mail Act of 1935 which authorizes the Postmaster General to award air-mail contracts for three years to the lowest responsible bidder, to permit extensions of routes up to 250 miles, to designate primary and secondary routes, and to prescribe the number and frequency of schedules. The Interstate Commerce Commission is given power to raise or lower air-mail rates within limits set by the Act and to make annual examinations of the entire business records of air-mail contract holders in order that no unreasonable profits may be realized. Other clauses prohibit the merging of competing carriers on parallel routes, but cutthroat competition between two contract carriers is prohibited if the effect would be adversely to affect the service and the carrying of mail.

There has been, and is now, much criticism of the federal law with respect to aviation on the ground that federal activities in this field are not properly coordinated and that the various agencies to a certain extent work at cross purposes. There are those who believe that federal regulation of aviation should be placed almost wholly under the control of the Interstate Commerce Commission on the theory that the Federal Government should consolidate its methods of supervision over all forms of transportation into one agency. Others hold, however, that the Department of Commerce has been in such close touch with the aviation industry for a number of years that it is more conversant with the problems. Moreover, they claim, what the industry needs is not so much regulation as sympathetic understanding and assistance. These controversies led to the provision, in the Air Mail Act of 1934, for a Federal Aviation Commission of five men to make a broad investigation into all phases of aviation.

Report of the Federal Aviation Commission.—The Federal Aviation Commission in its report to Congress, January, 1935, recommended that an Air Commerce Commission be created to coordinate many functions of the Federal Government which seemed essential to a sound development of aviation and to the protection of the public interest and to which could be transferred powers necessary in a field where the government must, on the one hand, exercise minute and extended regulation and, on the other hand, supply a variety of direct and indirect aids. The Commission's reasons for not recommending that these functions be placed in the Interstate Commerce Commission were stated as follows:

The need for such a commission to deal with certain problems of aviation seems to us clear. The work that it would have to do is so specialized and so extensive that we make strong recommendation that it should be either a separate and wholly independent body or a quasi-independent division of an over-all commission or group of commissions dealing with all phases of transportation. We do not believe that all of the manifold functions of regulation and of assistance which the government should exercise with respect to civil aeronautics can be properly assigned to any existing body that already has other duties of the most pressing and arduous nature, even though it be possessed of as splendid a reputation and tradition as those of the present Interstate Commerce Commission. Speed of regulatory action seems an essential in dealing with an art that undergoes such constant and rapid change. Speed can only be attained through placing authority with a group that will specialize in this particular field until they acquire an understanding of its problems that will make repeated preliminary explanation of the fundamentals unnecessary. It cannot be attained by piling a new and highly specialized group of questions on top of an already crowded docket of quite a different order. . . . [1]

The Federal Aviation Commission recommended that the functions of the proposed commission should include the following:

1. The issuance of certificates of convenience and necessity to air lines;
2. The approval of the conditions of service and the charges of air lines;

[1] Report of the Federal Aviation Commission, Sen. Doc. 15, 74th Cong., 1st Sess., p. 53.

3. The supervision of the financial structure of air lines and of their ownership, in so far as that may be necessary to preserve proper competition;

4. The fixing of the payments to be made by the Post Office for the transport of mail upon air lines, both domestic and foreign;

5. The allocation of such direct aids to air transport, both domestic and foreign, as may be appropriated by the Congress;

6. The approval of applications for Reconstruction Finance Corporation loans by air lines or other aeronautical enterprises;

7. The approval of the proposals of the Department of Commerce for new federally maintained airways;

8. The approval of recommendations by the Department of Commerce or any other federal agency for the establishment of new air transportation services on selected world trade routes;

9. The collection and the making of public record of financial and operating data in suitably comparable form for all air-transport enterprises;

10. The fostering of the orderly development of collective bargaining in air-line labor disputes;

11. The examination and licensing of aircraft, aeronautical equipment, and airmen;

12. The rating of air-navigation facilities;

13. The specification of minimum standards of equipment and of the operating methods and organizations and ground facilities of air lines;

14. The approval of proposed trade and traffic agreements between American air-transport lines operating outside the United States and their competitors;

15. The approval of applications from airports to be recognized as qualified for the installation and maintenance of lights and other air-navigation facilities at government expense;

16. The approval of any arrangements which may be made for the lease or charter by government to a commercial operator of any government-owned airship or airship base;

17. The approval of all applications to purchase governmentally produced helium gas or to export helium;

18. The acceptance of the role of arbitrator in cases arising under aeronautical patents;

19. The making of a further study of the bearing of international agreements upon the development of American air navigation and the protection of American interests in the air, and the presentation of recommendations relative to American participation in such agreements;

20. The reporting, both annually in regular form and at intervals as special communications may be requested by the Congress or the

President, upon the state of civil aviation at home and abroad, the apparent trend of its development, and the apparent relation of that development to government policy; and

21. The presenting to the Congress at intervals its recommendations for such changes in the laws relating to civil aeronautics as are necessary to keep abreast of progress and to take advantage of experience.[1]

Though the Federal Aviation Commission recommended the establishment of a new administrative body with the broad powers over civil aviation above enumerated, it realized that the responsibilities of the Department of Commerce in the aeronautical field would remain diversified and important after the transfer of such powers. Among these responsibilities would be the construction and management of the national airway system, with its hundreds of isolated beacon and landing-field sites; the general development and encouragement of air commerce and the special advocacy of those air routes appearing most important to American commerce; and the general promotion of private flying through the support of pioneer experimental work, the collection and dissemination of information, and otherwise. The Commission believed that these mixed duties of administration and promotion called for special representation in the inner councils of the Department of Commerce, and it recommended that an Assistant Secretaryship of Commerce be created to supervise and to coordinate all the aeronautical interests of the Department. Such an assistant secretaryship, the Commission believed, might be extended to cover all the Department's work with respect to transportation, especially because of the importance of coordinating aerial and marine activities in respect of trade-route development and of the improvement of aids to navigation. The Committee recommended also the transfer of the Weather Bureau to the Department of Commerce in the interests of more complete coordination. So far no action has been taken on these or other proposals to coordinate federal control of aviation.

State Regulation of Aviation.—Because of the limitations upon federal licensing authority it is essential that the individual states enact laws to insure at least the safe operation of aircraft, and there has been a great deal of state activity in this matter,

[1] *Op. cit.*, pp. 245–246.

practically every state having some law having to do with aeronautics. These laws for the most part have dealt with the licensing of aircraft and airmen and the establishment and operation of airports, but numerous miscellaneous matters are covered by them, *e.g.*, the definition of common carriers by air and the requirement of a license, the inspection of aircraft for plant pests, and the prohibition of the use of aircraft in hunting and in the transportation of narcotics or intoxicating liquors. Some states have set up commissions with comprehensive powers for the regulation of intrastate aviation, including economic and financial phases. The great defect in the existing system of aviation regulation is the lack of uniformity in state and federal requirements.

The need for uniformity throughout the United States in the requirements regarding the airworthiness of aircraft, the competency of airmen, and most particularly the operation of aircraft in the air is quite obvious. It must be recognized that there can be but one standard of airworthiness, that there is a limited range of piloting ability, and that there should be no variation in operating rules. As early as 1922, the Aeronautical Committee of the American Bar Association proposed that the various states enact a Uniform State Aeronautics Act, a Uniform Air Licensing Act, and a Uniform Airport Act, and this body has maintained continued interest in the matter of uniformity.

The proposed Uniform State Aeronautics Act contains, among others, provisions declaring state sovereignty in the airspace above its territory, except where granted to the United States; vesting ownership of the airspace in the owner of the land underneath, subject to the right of flight at a reasonable altitude; the fixing of absolute liability upon the owner or lessee of the aircraft for ground damage; and prohibiting dangerous flying and hunting by aircraft. To date, less than half of the states have adopted the Uniform Aeronautics Act, and most of these have repudiated the provision making the owner or lessee of aircraft absolutely liable for ground damage.[1] The Uniform Air Licensing Act would create a commission to issue licenses to aircraft and airmen, setting up the federal requirements in these matters;

[1] McCormick, J. F., Aviation Law—Its Scope and Development, *Air Law Review*, vol. 6, No. 4, p. 292.

while the Uniform Airport Act would authorize municipalities to acquire, equip, and regulate airports, to condemn land for this purpose, to issue bonds, and to enact tax measures.

In May, 1934, the Committee on Aeronautical Law of the American Bar Association again recommended the uniform aeronautical regulatory act for state adoption. This action gave further impetus to the work already done by this Committee and by the Committee on Aeronautical Acts of the National Conference of Commissioners on Uniform State Laws, the Federal Bureau of Air Commerce, and the National Association of State Aviation Officials, work that has resulted in steady and rapid progress toward uniformity. If aviation is to escape the harmful effects of conflicting state regulation such as troubled the railroads in their early history and hampered the development of uniform control of highway transportation, uniform state regulation must be achieved. The attainment of this objective was deemed by the Federal Aviation Commission so necessary and so urgent that it recommended that "if the several states do not adopt substantially uniform aeronautical regulatory laws within a reasonably early time, a Federal constitutional amendment should be adopted which will give to the Federal Government exclusive control of all phases of civil aeronautics within the United States."[1]

The Federal Government and the Electrical Utilities.— Historically, the gas and electric utilities have been considered local utilities, but probably the most pronounced recent trend in the regulation of electrical utilities has been the increasingly important role played by the Federal Government. This has been due primarily to the fact that while the distribution of electric energy to ultimate consumers still remains a local industry, the techniques of production and interconnection have so broadened the scope of operations that transmission networks cross the borders of many states. The local distributing system, subject to the jurisdiction of a state commission, may purchase its energy from, or be part of, an integrated interconnected system the operations of which reach far beyond the jurisdiction of a single state. In Chap. XI we have dealt with the necessity for federal regulation of holding companies in this field, but the large and increasing volume of interstate movements of electric energy

[1] Report of the Federal Aviation Commission, *op. cit.*, p. 237.

has created the need for federal regulation to supplement state regulation if the interests of ultimate consumers are to be adequately protected.

Prior to 1935, federal regulation of the electric light and power industry was confined almost wholly to the control of licensees of hydroelectric projects in the navigable waters of the United States. By the Rivers and Harbors Act of 1890,[1] Congress had prohibited the creation of any obstruction, not affirmatively approved by law, to the navigable capacity of any waters under the jurisdiction of the United States, so that with the recognition of the value of hydroelectric sites private industry found it necessary to secure Congressional approval for their development and exploitation. Such approval was not obtained readily, however, and the attitude of our Chief Executives, notably Presidents Theodore Roosevelt and Taft, prevented what otherwise might have been unrestrained exploitation of the nation's water power resources. Congress and the Presidents refused to permit the development of these resources except within the bounds of regulatory provisions designed to protect the public interest. The power industry was unwilling for the most part to submit to the regulatory measures proposed, and as a consequence the development of power projects in navigable streams proceeded slowly until the enactment of the Federal Water Power Act of 1920. Since that time the number of private power projects in navigable streams has grown apace but always subject to the requirements of law and of the Federal Power Commission, created to administer the Federal Water Power Act. Federal regulation of interstate commerce in electricity, other than that of the licensees under the Federal Water Power Act, was undertaken for the first time by passage of the Public Utility Act of 1935.

Of another sort are the activities of the Federal Government that involve the initiation and construction of power projects in various sections of the United States. Among these the one that has aroused most comment is the Tennessee Valley project. Begun as a program designed to rehabilitate a vast region drained by the Tennessee River, it had as primary objectives the improvement of navigation, the control of flood waters of the Tennessee and the Mississippi rivers, and the prevention of

[1] 26 Stat. 454.

soil erosion. It was proposed also to produce electric power at the dams to be built in this region and thus to aid in the rehabilitation by bringing cheap power to homes, farms, and factories. But the power aspects of this program extended far beyond the mere rehabilitation of a backward region. From the beginning the sponsors of the project and those entrusted with carrying it out have spoken of establishing in the Tennessee Valley a government-owned power system which would serve as a "yardstick" by which to measure the efficiency of private production and the reasonableness of the rates charged by private electric companies. They proposed to encourage municipalities to purchase or set up distribution systems of their own and to purchase power at wholesale from the government system. To insure reasonable rates to the ultimate consumers the Tennessee Valley Authority retained by contract a measure of control over the retail rates.

Two aspects of the power policy of the Federal Government as thus far developed are clear: (1) stimulation of the use of electric energy on a much broader scale than has been the case, especially by domestic and rural consumers; and (2) the direct provision of electric generation facilities and the encouragement of government ownership and operation as a means both of supplying additional cheap electric energy and of providing a check upon the effectiveness of public regulation of the private industry. Illustrative of the latter are the federal generation and transmission projects and loans and grants by the Public Works Administration to municipalities for the purpose of constructing or purchasing their own distribution systems. Illustrative of the former, in addition to these projects, is the inauguration of a broad program of rural electrification sponsored, and partially supported, by the Federal Government.

But the activities of the Federal Government in the development and utilization of hydroelectric power constitute only a part of its interests in the use and control of the navigable waters of the United States. No less than 34 individual agencies of the Federal Government have to do, directly or indirectly, with matters involved in the conservation and utilization of water resources. Many are not concerned directly with the development of electric power, but their activities are a part of the total picture and bear a significant relationship to those of other agencies so concerned. A summary of these agencies and their principal activities is contained in the chart on pp. 314 and 315.

That some central planning agency should be set up to develop a sound, adequate, cohesive federal power policy, and particularly to coordinate the activities of so many agencies, each of which has some functions with respect to the control and utilization of our water resources, is a matter beyond dispute. A mere enumeration of the agencies indicates the breadth and magnitude of federal interests, but in the light of the fact that each agency is a vested interest jealous of its powers and not averse to the use of obstructive tactics if it may enhance its individual importance thereby, the need for a coordinating body with adequate powers is imperative. Furthermore, the various objectives of flood control, irrigation, improvement of navigation, control of soil erosion, generation of electric power, and even the protection of wild life and the preservation of scenic beauty can be attained most economically through broad coordinated programs. Efforts of the Federal Government to develop the generation and utilization of electric energy do not, and should not, constitute an isolated program but part of a comprehensive policy designed to achieve all these common objectives.

The National Resources Committee, created June 7, 1935, to succeed the National Resources Board, established by President Roosevelt, June 30, 1934, is a body having many of the research functions of such a central planning agency. It is established to collect, prepare, and make available to the President, with recommendations, such plans, data, and information as may be helpful to a planned development and use of land, water, and other national resources. The water-resources work of this Committee is carried on through the Water Resources Committee, composed of eight representatives of federal agencies (Public Health Service, Corps of Engineers, Biological Survey, Soil Conservation Service, United States Geological Survey, Bureau of Reclamation, Federal Power Commission, and Tennessee Valley Authority) and four members outside the federal service. The Water Resources Committee makes investigations of the collection of, utility of, and standards for basic hydrologic data; the past and proposed construction programs of federal agencies; and such national problems of water use and control as water pollution and land drainage.

TABULAR INDEX OF FEDERAL AGENCIES CONCERNED WITH WATER USE AND CONTROL

Agency	Basic hydrologic data						Problems of water use and control								
	Precipitation	Evaporation	Stream flow and coastal waters	Ground water	Quality of water (including silt)	Dam-site and river survey	Flood protection	Hydro-electric power	Irrigation	Land drainage	Navigation	Waste disposal and pollution	Water supply —urban	Water supply —rural	Wild-life conservation
Department of Agriculture:															
Bureau of Agricultural Engineering	S	DS	DS	DS	DS				DS	DS				DS	
Bureau of Biological Survey			S			S									DSC
Bureau of Entomology and Plant Quarantine										SC					
Bureau of Plant Industry	DS	DS			DS				DS					DSC	DSC
Forest Service	D	D	DS	DS	DS	DS	DSC	DSR						DSC	
Soil Conservation Service	DS	DS	DS		DS	DS	DSC								
Weather Bureau	DS	DS	DS				D								
Department of Commerce:															
Bureau of the Census									D	D					
Bureau of Fisheries												DS			DSC
National Hydraulic Laboratory			S												
U.S. Coast and Geodetic Survey			DS												
Department of the Interior:															
Bureau of Mines				DS	DS							DS			
Bureau of Reclamation	DS	DS	DS	DS	DS	DS		DSC	DSC	DSC				DSC	
Division of Grazing									DSR					DSR	
General Land Office								DSC	DSR			DSC	DSR		
National Park Service												SC	DSC		DSC
Office of Indian Affairs			S	D		DS	D	DSC	DSC					DSC	
U.S. Geological Survey—Water Resources Branch	S	S	DS	DS				D	D				DS	DS	
U.S. Geological Survey—Conservation Branch			DS			DS		DSR	R						

TABULAR INDEX OF FEDERAL AGENCIES CONCERNED WITH WATER USE AND CONTROL.—(Continued)

Agency	Basic hydrologic data						Problems of water use and control								
	Precipitation	Evaporation	Stream flow and coastal waters	Ground water	Quality of water (including silt)	Dam-site and river survey	Flood protection	Hydro-electric power	Irrigation	Land drainage	Navigation	Waste disposal and pollution	Water supply —urban	Water supply —rural	Wild-life conservation
State Department:															
International Boundary Commission—United States and Mexico	DS	DS	DS		DS	DS	DSCR	DSR	DSCR			SCR	SCR		
International Joint Commission							SR	SR	SR		SR	SR	SR		
Treasury Department:															
Public Health Service					DS					S		S	SR		
War Department:															
Corps of Engineers	DS	DS	DS	S	DS	DS	DSC	DSC	DSC		DSCR	S	S		
Independent agencies:															
Emergency Conservation Work							C		C	C			C	C	C
Farm Credit Administration									DS	DS					
Federal Power Commission								DSR							
National Resources Committee	S	S	S	S	S	S	S	S	S	S	S	S	S	S	S
Panama Canal	DS	DS	DS		DS	DS		DSC		DSC	DSC	DSC	DSC		
Public Works Administration							C	C	C	C	C	C	C	C	C
Reconstruction Finance Corporation							C	C	SC	SC	C	C	C	C	C
Rural Electrification Administration								S							
Tennessee Valley Authority	DS	DS	DS		DS	DS	DSC	DSC	C		DSC	DS	C		DSC
Works Progress Administration							C	C	C	C	C	C	C	C	C

Legend
D—Collects data.
S—Carries on studies and research.
C—Supervises construction.
R—Regulates nonfederal activity.
Source: National Resources Committee, Water Resources Committee.

It maintains an information service concerning impending construction work and study programs for federal and state planning agencies.

The National Resources Committee has recognized that the broad scope and the magnitude of the work of this character already undertaken by the Federal Government, and that which must be done in the future to bring the major programs to successful conclusion, require adequate provision for planning of a comprehensive, permanent nature. It has recommended, therefore, the establishment of a permanent advisory National Planning Board responsible directly to the President and charged with the duty of preparing plans and general policies, stimulating and encouraging regional and state planning, and advising the President on the progress and development of planned proposals. This Committee has recommended also the establishment of a permanent National Development Administration to be based upon the powers, duties, and functions of various temporary or emergency bodies, *e.g.*, the Emergency Administration of Public Works, the Works Progress Administration, the Allotment Committee, and the Federal Employment Stabilization Office.

While recommending the establishment of national planning on a solid, permanent basis, the Committee has advised that full advantage be taken of the demonstrated usefulness of state planning boards and that regional planning commissions of the general type of those set up in the Pacific Northwest and in New England be established as advisory bodies for planning purposes in their respective areas. Such regional planning commissions have consisted of representatives of state planning boards and of a federal district chairman representing the National Resources Committee. The Committee has recommended also the encouragement of interstate compacts as a means of solving regional problems wherever this procedure is found to be feasible, federal participation in some classes of compacts requiring continuous administration to take the form of participation in the personnel of an interstate commission, in the administration of an interstate agreement, or in the financing of an interstate agreement. The objectives that it is hoped would be accomplished by cooperation with state bodies are the utilization of state as well as federal constitutional powers and local participation and interest in the projects themselves.

The National Resources Committee has recommended further that serious consideration be given to federal authorities of a regional-functional nature, such as the Tennessee Valley Authority, as a means of dealing with subnational problems. Such government-owned corporations, the Committee believes, would provide flexible agencies for dealing with special sets of regional problems, would avoid the necessity of setting up new units of government, and would combine in unique fashion some of the strongest advantages of public and private business. As a result of investigation, the Committee found that the Tennessee Valley Authority had shown facility in adjusting itself to local situations: (1) by contractual arrangements with local authorities; (2) by administrative and financial arrangements; (3) by coordination of planning agencies, local, state, and national; and (4) by serious attention to the social and economic possibilities of public-works development.[1] The influence of this recommendation is reflected in President Roosevelt's recent proposal to set up such agencies.

These recommendations of the National Resources Committee present an ambitious program of national planning but no more broad or ambitious than the activities already undertaken by the Federal Government. If we are to spend hundreds of millions, even billions, of dollars on public works of this nature it would seem the part of wisdom to plan such expenditures so as to achieve the maximum public good. Certainly careful advance planning is necessary to avoid waste and to prevent costly antagonisms where the problems are regional or national in scope and the units of government involved various. Planning in connection with water utilization should begin with the proper organization and coordination of the various federal bureaus, but it should involve also proper coordination of state, regional, and national activities. Recently certain steps have been taken looking forward to the establishment of a permanent power policy. These will be discussed fully in subsequent chapters.

The Federal Government and the Communication Utilities.— The need for federal regulation of communications, as of other

[1] National Resources Committee, Regional Factors in National Planning, December, 1935, pp. x–xi.

utility services, springs from their interstate character. The courts have held that all radio communications, even though intended only for intrastate transmission, because of inter-ference effects, are interstate commerce. Telegraph com-munication is largely interstate, only about 25 per cent being intrastate. And while the bulk of telephone communication is intrastate, the interstate toll business is important in volume, and the interstate and intrastate operations are inextricably commingled owing to the fact that the same telephones and much of the same equipment and personnel are utilized in furnishing both services.

Until 1934 federal policy with respect to communications was characterized by the same lack of coordination we have pointed out in the case of transportation and power. The Interstate Commerce Commission had jurisdiction over the rates and practices of wire and wireless companies engaged in interstate and foreign commerce, except that rates for government telegraph messages were fixed by the Postmaster General. The executive branch of the Federal Government had jurisdiction over the granting of licenses for the landing of cables on the shores of the United States and the right to reserve for, and assign to, strictly governmental agencies bands of radio frequencies and particular frequencies. The Federal Radio Commission possessed author-ity to license and to regulate the operation, but not the rates and charges, of radio communication companies. No federal agency existed to deal comprehensively with communication problems as such.

The enactment of the Communications Act of 1934 rationalized the relationship of the Federal Government to the communication utilities. All jurisdiction over interstate and foreign communica-tions was placed in a new body, the Federal Communications Commission, except that authority to grant cable-landing licenses and to set aside and assign to governmental agencies radio frequencies was retained in the executive branch of the Federal Government. The Act provides, further, that nothing in the Submarine Cable Act of 1921, which gave to the Chief Executive authority over cable-landing licenses, shall be con-strued to limit the power and jurisdiction of the Communications Commission with respect to the transmission of cable messages. In addition, the Act grants to the Commission jurisdiction over many communication matters not formerly subject to regulation by any federal agency. Unified federal control of communications should make for greater clarity and soundness of policy, since the communication services, while in many respects competitive, are in others intimately coordinated. Intelligent regulation of one agency calls for complete knowledge and control over the activities of other agencies, whether competitive or coordinative.

References

Air Commerce Bulletin, vols. 5–7.

HERRING, J. M., and G. C. GROSS: "Telecommunications: Economics and Regulation," McGraw-Hill Book Company, Inc., New York, 1936.

McCORMICK, J. F.: Aviation Law—Its Scope and Development, *Air Law Review*, vol. 6, No. 4.

National Resources Committee: Regional Factors in National Planning, December, 1935.

————: Federal Agencies Concerned with Water Use and Control, January, 1936.

Report of the Federal Aviation Commission, Sen. Doc. 15, 74th Cong., 1st Sess.

Report of the Federal Coordinator of Transportation, 1934, House Doc. 89, 74th Cong., 1st Sess.

"Report of the Special Committee Appointed to Survey and Report on Competition as a Factor and Motif in Transportation Regulation, American Bar Association," 1936.

ROHLFING, C. C.: "National Regulation of Aeronautics," University of Pennsylvania Press, Philadelphia, 1931.

CHAPTER XIII

REGULATION OF MOTOR TRANSPORTATION

MUNICIPAL OR LOCAL REGULATION
OF MOTOR TRANSPORTATION

Motor transportation generally, as well as the operation of motor vehicles for hire in the United States, is subject to the regulation of several different jurisdictions. First, regulation is exercised by municipalities or local governments through the ordinances of municipal councils and the administrative regulations of local administrative bodies, including departments of public safety and police departments. (The term local governments is used here broadly to include cities, boroughs, villages, towns, or townships.) Second, counties exercise jurisdiction, where the county governments are distinct from the municipalities, through the regulations of state governments usually administered by county commissioners or other bodies. Third, regulation is exercised by the state governments through the acts of state legislatures or assemblies and the rulings and orders of state administrative bodies, including public utility commissions, highway boards or departments, highway patrols or police, or other state agencies. Finally, the Federal Government regulates motor transportation through an Act of Congress, the Motor Carrier Act of 1935, and the administrative orders, rulings, and decisions of the Interstate Commerce Commission and of its Bureau of Motor Carriers. We shall first discuss the regulation of motor transportation and motor carriers by local and county governments. State and federal regulation will be discussed later.

Municipal Regulations.—The local governments, cities, boroughs, villages, and towns are the governmental subdivisions directly interested in the regulation of motor vehicles and the transportation of passengers and merchandise over the highways, whether the transportation service is performed by private motor vehicles, by contract carriers, or by common carriers. The municipal governments are directly concerned with the intimate details of regulating the use of local streets and roads, with the construction and maintenance of highways, and, to some extent, with the conduct of the business of freight and passenger transportation over the streets of the local communities.

Restrictions upon the Use of Highways.—The regulations of municipalities with respect to the use of streets and roads apply to private and public vehicles. They vary considerably from municipality to municipality so that generalization is difficult, if not impossible. Typical regulations of this sort include: (1) traffic control through systems of light coordination or synchronization, by other mechanical devices, by hand semiphores, or by police control; (2) speed restrictions and regulations; (3) parking regulations; (4) restrictions upon use of streets, such as one-way street regulations, prohibition of left-hand turns, crossing regulations and establishment of quiet zones, and special regulations governing traffic on boulevards and other special streets; (5) restrictions upon the size and weight of vehicles using certain municipal streets or bridges, based usually upon the dimensions and weights of the vehicles or upon the weights per unit of tire surface; (6) restrictions upon maximum load weight per vehicle; and (7) general police regulations governing the use of streets.

Authority over Highway Construction and Maintenance.— Local governments are concerned, also, with the financing, planning, and supervision of the construction of new streets and roadways and with the repair of highways already in use. Regulations of this type affect the whole field of motor transportation, private as well as public, and citizens and taxpayers generally, as well as motor-vehicle owners and operators. Typical of this sort of local governmental regulation are the municipal ordinances and regulations pertaining to: (1) the authorization, issuance, and marketing of bond issues; (2) the planning of new streets; (3) the opening and paving of streets; (4) the formulation of paving standards and specifications; (5) the awarding of contracts for construction or the direct construction by municipal construction departments; (6) the supervision of local street and highway construction; (7) the formulation of standards of maintenance and the letting of contracts for maintenance work; (8) the provision of municipal organizations to supervise highway maintenance; (9) the amortization of street bond issues; and (10) the taxing of property and persons to defray expenses of road construction and maintenance.

Regulation of Motor Carriers for Hire.—In addition to the two types of municipal regulations applying to the construction and maintenance of streets and to the use of municipal thoroughfares by all types of motor and horse-drawn vehicles, another important group of local regulations applies to vehicles operated in the public service for hire.   Regulations of this nature include: (1) the designation of taxicab stands; (2) the prohibition of operation of public vehicles upon certain streets; (3) the designation of bus stops, waiting time, and regulations governing the receiving and discharging of passengers; (4) the issuance of licenses for garages, gasoline stations, and other vending establishments; (5) the requirement of licenses and the collection of special fees for vehicles used in various types of public service; (6) the special registration of vehicles used by carriers of passengers and merchandise in for-hire services; (7) the promulgation of regulations requiring that each passenger be given a seat in common carrier buses; (8) the requirement of bonds and other surety for performance of common-carrier services; (9) the promulgation of regulations affecting the conduct of common-carrier freight business, including station or warehouse facility locations, use of streets to and from stations, size and weight of trucks and loads, and other regulations of this nature; and (10) the regulation of rates and fares, usually exercised concurrently with state regulatory bodies.

Identification of Carriers for Hire.—One of the most important groups of municipal regulations affecting motor transportation requires that motor carriers for hire be identified and registered. In cases where individuals or partnerships are engaged in the operation of motor transportation services for hire under names other than their own, state laws or municipal ordinances sometimes require that the names under which the businesses are conducted be registered with the office of the prothonotary of the common pleas court of the district in which the business maintains its principal place of business.[1]

Another type of municipal ordinance requires that motor vehicles used in the service of the public for hire be registered

[1] Fictitious Names Act, Pennsylvania, June 28, 1917, as amended.

with the Department of Public Safety. The owners and operators of such vehicles are required to submit proof that the applicants for such registration have complied with all federal, state, and municipal regulations applicable to carriers of the class to which the applicants belong. The vehicles registered under ordinances of this kind are required to show the names and addresses of the owners and the Department of Safety registration numbers, in addition to the registration numbers assigned the operators by the state regulatory commissions or by the Interstate Commerce Commission. Ordinances of this type make it a misdemeanor, punishable by fine, to fail to register vehicles subject to the ordinance and prohibit the operation of vehicles that fail to display identification numbers.[1]

Sources of Municipal Power to Regulate Motor Transportation.—Local governments in the United States derive their authority to regulate motor and highway transportation from either one of two sources. In a number of states, the state constitutions grant "home rule" to municipalities of certain classes. This gives the local governments authority to exercise a number of functions of government which otherwise would come within the jurisdiction of the states, including the regulation of motor and highway transportation within the cities. In other states, the power to regulate motor and highway transportation is delegated to local governments by state legislatures in the form of incorporation laws, charters, or specific statutes giving the municipalities the power to regulate highway and vehicle transportation within the municipal limits.

The powers of the municipalities are either the results of reservations or of grants of power by which the states and local governments arrange for the regulation of the highways and motor and other vehicle transportation. Whatever the source of the power of the municipalities, the courts have held that the ordinances of the local governments may not exceed the state constitutions, that they may not conflict with the laws of the several states in which the municipalities are located, and that the regulations must be reasonable in their requirements. In *Fifth Avenue Coach Co. v. the City of New York*, for example, the United States Supreme Court held that common-carrier motor transportation companies may not engage in any services not provided

---

[1] Ordinance of Council, City of Philadelphia, Aug. 6, 1936.

for in their charter privileges and that municipal ordinances providing reasonable regulations for the benefit of all motor vehicle operators and in the interests of public safety are constitutional.[1] But municipal ordinances that are contrary to the Constitution, state or federal, are invalid. Also, the courts of some states have held that when city ordinances and state laws conflict the former are void.[2] The principle that local ordinances regulating highway and motor transportation must be reasonable has been stated by the courts of several states, including, among others, the courts of Illinois and Ohio.[3]

Intracity and Intercity Regulations.—The powers of municipalities to regulate transportation over city streets and highways are for the most part confined to intracity transportation between points within the corporate limits of the local governments, although this is not true in all cases. In many states intercity highway transportation is under the jurisdiction and control of the state public service commissions or, as in the case of several states, of administrative bodies which have jurisdiction only over motor transportation. In several states, including notably Oregon, Washington, and Wisconsin, the state regulatory bodies have exclusive jurisdiction, also, over all matters pertaining to intracity highway transport. A larger number of state legislatures have given the state regulatory commissions, or other state bodies, control over state-wide motor and highway transportation but have granted to the municipalities certain powers to regulate traffic over the highways that lead through the cities or towns and to control common-carrier highway transportation between the towns and contiguous localities. This amounts to a system of state control with local consent and cooperation. However, the courts of several states and district federal courts have held that municipal ordinances may not interfere to a material degree with intrastate or with interstate commerce. The scope of the powers of local governments, limited in this important respect, is otherwise very broad. The municipalities, in general, are empowered to exercise the same degree of regulation, restriction, and control over highway and motor transporta-

[1] Fifth Avenue Motor Coach Co. v. City of New York, 221 U.S. 467.

[2] State of W. Va. v. City of Charleston, 92 W. Va. 611.

[3] See City of Chicago v. Shaw, 258 Ill. 409; Perryville v. Ridgway, 108 Ohio St. 245; and, Murphy v. Toledo, 108 Ohio St. 343.

tion as the state authorities, provided the powers have been properly delegated by the state legislatures to the local governments.

Administration by Municipalities.—Municipalities, as a rule, define the policies of regulating and controlling highway and motor transportation by ordinances of city or borough councils or other local legislative bodies. In many cases, broad powers are stated and delegated to a local administrative department or body. These ordinances provide the legal basis upon which automobiles, buses, and trucks may use the local streets; the plans of financing, constructing, and maintaining the streets; and the regulations affecting the common-carrier motor freight and passenger businesses.[1] If the ordinances are lawfully made and are reasonable, they are valid as within the police powers of the local governments.

A recent federal court decision with respect to the powers of municipalities to regulate common-carrier motorbus operation is indicative of the probable future trend in municipal regulation. The city of Philadelphia levied an annual fee of $50 per vehicle on buses operating in Philadelphia engaged in local or interstate transportation and established other regulations governing the operation of buses in the city. The collection of the fee by the city upon the buses owned and operated by a Delaware corporation was enjoined by a temporary injunction. In dismissing the plea for a permanent injunction the federal court held that buses wherever owned would become a menace to the city unless proper regulations were made upon their operation. It was held to be essential to the orderly supervision of traffic that the routes as well as the stopping and starting points of buses should be designated and that the buses should be required to bear a plate showing the city license number and pay a reasonable fee for the privilege of operation over the city streets. Vehicles using municipal highways may reasonably be required to be subject to the control of local governments which also control the highways within their jurisdiction, provided always that the regulations are reasonable and as nearly uniform with respect to various types of service as is possible under the circumstances.[2]

[1] See Sprout v. City of South Bend, Ind., 153 N.E. 504; Packard v. Banton, 264 U.S. 140; and Hodge v. Cincinnati, 284 U.S. 335.

[2] American Transit Co. v. City of Philadelphia *et al.;* and American Motor Coach Co. v. City of Philadelphia, 18 Fed. (2d) 991.

Enforcement of Local Regulations.—The general enforcement of these ordinances is delegated to the local police departments, departments of public safety, highway commissions, or other administrative departments of the cities or towns, subject of course to the control of councils and to the restrictions with respect to intercity and interstate traffic. The regulation of certain phases of motor and highway transportation, particularly with reference to vehicular traffic in certain parks, boulevards, or other districts, is delegated by the municipal governments to special county, park, or other commissions. Park commissions sometimes are given jurisdiction over the direction of traffic, roads, and highway construction and maintenance, restriction of types of vehicles using the roads, and other regulations affecting the use of roads in public parks within city limits.

Lack of Uniformity.—The delegation of powers to regulate motor and highway transportation by state legislatures to local units of government has gone through many changes and has resulted in a welter of confusion, which at present is still very great. Particularly in the regulation of intercity business over the highways have the policies varied from state to state and from year to year. Complete control by municipalities has been replaced largely by state control of intercity traffic by state administrative bodies with local consent of the municipalities interested in the operation of the carriers passing into, out of, or through their jurisdictions. This has been done by requiring the carriers to obtain certificates of public convenience and necessity before beginning operations. Division of powers between the state and municipal governments has been superseded, in certain states, by complete and exclusive control of state-wide motor and highway transportation by the state commissions, the municipalities being bereft of power to regulate intercity transportation. A most unfortunate feature has been the changing back and forth from one policy to another, to the confusion of the owners and operators of private as well as common-carrier motor vehicles. The changes have made motor vehicle operation an uncertainty, and the variations in municipal regulating ordinances in the same state have made municipal regulation unduly burdensome.

Recently, however, highway codes have been worked out in a number of states which have tended to bring about uniformity in the regulations of motor and highway transportation among the cities of one state. These codes as a rule have standardized certain phases of regulation in state-wide and intercity transportation on the highways while leaving with the municipalities a considerable degree of control over purely local highway and vehicular traffic matters. This trend toward uniformity is greatly to be desired; for, although the owners and drivers of private motor cars, industries and their fleets of private carrier trucks, contract carriers, and common carriers of merchandise and passengers are protected by the courts against unreasonable municipal regulations, the variations in regulations from city to city and state to state can, and do, cause hardship and confusion whether the respective regulations are reasonable in themselves or not.

Also, various national organizations, including associations of motor vehicle manufacturers; local, state, and national trucking and bus associations; associations of automobile owners and automobile clubs; city and state highway departments; bar associations; insurance underwriters' organizations; safety councils; and individual experts have been engaged in constructive efforts seeking to achieve greater uniformity in highway regulation. A National Conference on Street and Highway Safety has drafted the text of four uniform motor vehicle acts, and this Conference has drafted, also, revisions of the uniform vehicle code, a model municipal traffic ordinance, and a manual on street traffic signs. The work of these organizations is slowly but surely bearing fruit.[1]

STATE REGULATION OF MOTOR TRANSPORTATION

The rapid and steady increase in the number of motor vehicles, the development of highways, and the ease of entry into the motor transportation business have conspired to increase the number of operators of motor vehicles for hire engaged in the transportation of passengers or property and have made regulation of motor and

---

[1] National Conference on Street and Highway Safety, texts of Uniform Motor Vehicle Act, Uniform Motor Vehicle Anti-theft Act, Uniform Motor Vehicle Operators' and Chauffeurs' License Act, Uniform Act Regulating the Operation of Vehicles on Highways, Model Municipal Traffic Ordinance, Manual on Street Traffic Signs, etc.

highway transportation a necessity in order to protect the public generally, all users of the highways, shippers and receivers of freight, all types of transport carriers, and motor carriers. However, the increase in the number of motor vehicles of all types using the highways, in the number and variety of motor carriers transporting passengers and property for hire, and in the number and variety of vehicles owned and operated by industrial and commercial concerns has created perplexing problems in regulation. The problems of regulation are further complicated by the relatively small scale upon which the average motor transport business, particularly in the field of freight transportation, is conducted and by the intensity of competition between motor carriers and other forms of transportation, the keen rivalry among motor carriers of various types, and the struggle between motor carriers and privately owned and operated freight vehicles.

In many other fields of public utility regulation, the problem is the control of large-scale industries, often partial or complete monopolies relatively immune from competition, excepting indirect competition between the utilities and alternative services. But in the regulation of the motor transportation industry the primary problems have been to conserve the motor transportation industry in the interests of the public generally and to bring order out of the chaos of competition among the numerous large and even more numerous small operators in the field. It is impossible to gain a perspective of the problems of motor-vehicle regulation by the states unless it is borne in mind that there are more than 24,000,000 automobiles, over 4,000,000 freight-carrying vehicles, and nearly 124,000 motorbuses in service in the United States. The United States Bureau of the Census estimates that in the field of motor truck transportation the average number of vehicles operated per concern is about three and that in the field of bus transportation the average number of vehicles operated is less than 11 per operating company. We shall survey first the regulations applicable to all motor vehicles and operators and, second, the regulations that apply to vehicles operated in the service of the public for hire.

General State Regulations.—Regulations imposed by states upon motor vehicles generally vary widely from state to state with respect to the nature of the regulations as well as to the bases upon which the regulations, licenses, and fees are imposed. Generally, state regulations of this character may be divided into the following classes:

1. Vehicular license or registration requirements and fees.
2. Operators' or chauffeurs' licenses and fees.
3. Insurance of certificates of title to the vehicles.
4. The taxation of motor vehicular operation, particularly through gasoline or fuel taxes.
5. Regulation of size and weights of vehicles and loads.
6. Regulation of speed and safety in operation.
7. The assumption of liability of motor-vehicle operators.
8. "Port-of-entry" regulations.
9. Miscellaneous regulations.

These regulations are for the purposes of raising revenue, particularly for the construction and maintenance of highways and for highway policing and administration; for the protection of the users of highways generally; for the conservation of highways; and for the protection of the public against fraud, theft, and irresponsible operation.

Automotive Vehicle Licenses.—Soon after the advent of motor vehicles upon the highways, the states one after another adopted policies requiring that the motor vehicles be registered with the states in the names of the owners and that license tags be issued to identify the vehicles using the highways. State registration laws are inspired partly by the desire to identify the vehicles and partly to raise revenues. All states in the United States and the District of Columbia have motor-vehicle registration fees, assessed upon a number of different bases, including a flat fee basis; horsepower; weight of vehicle; weight of vehicle and load; cost or valuation of the vehicle; piston displacement; horsepower and gross weight; horsepower and cost or valuation; weight and cost; weight, horsepower, and value; and flat fee and weight.

State motor-vehicle registration fees in 1936 amounted to nearly $360,000,000. Federal excise taxes in the same year exceeded $314,000,000, and personal property taxes upon motor vehicles were $87,500,000, including about $12,500,000 state motor carrier taxes. If the latter are excluded, the net personal property tax imposed by cities and counties upon motor vehicles

in 1936 was about $75,000,000.   Dealers, who are required in
most states to have special licenses and plates, paid over $2,000,-
000 additional in dealers' licenses and fees for dealers' motor-
vehicle plates or tags in 1936.

Operators' and Chauffeurs' Licenses.—State regulations
requiring the licensing of operators or chauffeurs of motor vehicles
are in force in 41 states and the District of Columbia.   These
laws require all persons operating motor vehicles of their own, or
for others, to be licensed and set the minimum age at which
persons will be licensed.   Operators' and chauffeurs' licenses in
1936 yielded the states over $23,500,000 in receipts.

Title Certificates, Transfer, and Reregistration.—Twenty-
three states and the district of Columbia require that owners'
titles to motor vehicles be registered with the state registrar
of motor vehicles, or other state officer, as proof of ownership.
In the states where regulations of this sort are in effect, a deed
of title is required of each owner of a motor vehicle for each
vehicle owned.   This title instrument identifies the vehicle and
is registered with the state in the same way as deeds to real
property are registered with the county authorities.   The title
papers establishing the ownership of motor vehicles must be
transferred from owner to owner when a transfer is made in the
ownership of the vehicle.   This form of regulation benefits motor
vehicle owners greatly, as it aids in tracing stolen motor vehicles
and tends to deter motor thieves by making the disposal of stolen
vehicles more difficult than would be the case if evidences of title
were not required.   In 1936, state receipts from registration of
certificates of title to motor vehicles were $8,211,000.   The
revenues derived from transfer or reregistration fees in the same
year in the 33 states and the District of Columbia which impose
these types of fees amounted to nearly $8,000,000, in addition to
the title certificate fee receipts.

Gasoline or Motor-fuel Taxes.—The most important source
of state tax revenues applicable to motor vehicles and operation
is the gasoline or motor-fuel tax.   All 48 states and the District
of Columbia impose such taxes, and, in addition, the Federal
Government and some counties and cities also impose gasoline
taxes.   In 1937, the state gasoline taxes ranged from 2 to 7 cents
per gallon.   The average total gasoline state and federal tax

collected in 50 representative cities in 1936 was 5.35 cents per gallon.[1] The United States Bureau of Public Roads estimated that the net total receipts of the states and the District of Columbia from gasoline taxes in 1936 amounted to $606,631,000. In addition, some states require license fees of motor-fuel distributors and dealers, and some impose inspection fees, fines and penalties, and miscellaneous fees or taxes related to motor fuel, making the total net motor-fuel or gasoline tax fees $691,420,000.[2] The tendency in motor-fuel tax collection has been for the states to make the distributors responsible for the payment of the tax to the state and require the distributors to collect the tax from the consumers.

Size and Weight Regulations.—All of the state governments in the United States have enacted laws regulating the size of individual motor vehicles, the number of vehicles that may be included in tractor or truck and trailer combinations, and the gross weights of the vehicles and loads. The laws regulating size govern the maximum width of the motor vehicles; their maximum weight; the maximum length of any single motor-vehicle unit (truck, tractor-and-trailer, tractor-and-semitrailer, or truck-and-trailer); and, in some states, the minimum tandem axle spacing. Gross weights are usually regulated in terms of a maximum allowed weight per inch of tire width or per axle. In some states different gross weight limits are provided for vehicles equipped with solid and pneumatic tires.

State laws governing maximum size and gross weights of motor vehicles vary greatly. Fortunately, however, there is a discernible trend toward uniformity, although progress in this direction is very slow. Many individuals and organizations have worked toward uniformity for many years, and their efforts are achieving some success. The American Association of State Highway Officials has recommended a uniform set of maximum size and weight limits which have been approved by a number of national associations of automobile owners and manufacturers, petroleum producers, rubber manufacturers, shippers,

---

[1] Estimate of American Petroleum Industries Committee, "Automobile Facts and Figures," 1937 ed., Automobile Manufacturers Association, New York, p. 32.

[2] *Ibid.*, p. 30.

farmers, and business concerns.[1]   The uniform maximum size and weight limits are recommended to:

1. Establish one of the fundamental prerequisites of highway design;

2. Promote efficiency in the interstate operation of motor vehicles, by eliminating the restricting influences of lack of uniformity;

3. Secure safety in highway operation;

4. Remove undesirable equipment and operations from the highway; and

5. Stabilize on a definite basis the many relationships between the highway and the motor vehicle.

The Association recommends a maximum width for motor vehicles of 8 feet and a maximum height of 12 feet 6 inches.   The maximum length recommended for single vehicles is 35 feet; and for combinations of two units, 45 feet.   Truck tractors and semi-trailers operated together are considered as single vehicles in applying the maximum length regulations.

A maximum axle load of 16,000 pounds per axle is recommended for motor vehicles equipped with solid, cushion, or high-pressure pneumatic tires.   A wheel load of 8,000 pounds with a maximum of 9,000 pounds for vehicles equipped with low-pressure pneumatic tires is recommended.

A formula is recommended for the determination of gross weights of vehicle and load, the maximum gross weight to be determined by adding 40 to the distance between the first, or front, and last, or rear, axles of the vehicle or combination of vehicles and multiplying this sum by a coefficient to be determined by the individual states.   It is recommended that this coefficient be not lower than 700.   If 700 is used as the coefficient, the maximum gross weight of a vehicle, the front and rear axles of which are 25 feet apart, would be determined as follows:

---

[1] Including the American Automobile Association, the American Farm Bureau Federation, the American Motorists Association, the American Petroleum Institute, the Automobile Manufacturers Association, the Detroit Board of Commerce, the National Association of Motor Bus Operators, the National Grange, the National Highway Users Conference, the National Industrial Traffic League, the National Transportation Committee, and the Rubber Manufacturers Association.

Length between axles = 25 feet = L.

Coefficient = 700 = C.

Gross weight = $G.W.$

$(L + 40) \times C. = G.W.$, or,

$(25 + 40) = 65 \times 700 = 45,500$ pounds, or $22\frac{3}{4}$ tons, gross
weight of the vehicle and load.

It is urged that the gross weight recommendations are particularly applicable to bridges, since axle loads and length limitations are determinative in their practical applications. It is recommended also that special permits be obtained for occasional movements of commodities requiring equipment exceeding these recommended maximum dimensions.

A comparison of these recommended maximum size and axle load limits with the regulations of the states having size and axle load regulations shows the extent to which the recommendations coincide with the state laws in effect.[1]

Item	Number of states with maximum regulations		
	Larger	Same	Smaller
Width......................................	2	45	2
Height.....................................	13	26	10
Length, single unit........................	10	16	23
Length, combination........................	23	15	11
Length, tractor and semitrailer............	38	8	3
Axle load.................................	27	16	6

The Regulation of Speed and Safety Equipment Regulations.— The regulation of motor-vehicle speeds has been one of the important aspects of state regulation, and a phase of regulation in which there have been, and still are, wide variations in the maximum legal speed limits. There has been a tendency to provide different rates of speed for operation of vehicles of different types—automobiles, buses and trucks—and for operation in congested districts and in the open country. Generally, the states that have enacted maximum speed laws recently have put the maximum limits at speeds between 40 and 50 miles per hour. In some states there is no maximum speed limit, but

[1] "Automobile Facts and Figures," 1937 ed., p. 59.

vehicles must be operated at all times at safe and reasonable speeds, and operation at excessive speed is deemed prima-facie evidence of unsafe operation. In recent years the operation of vehicles at unreasonably low speeds has become a safety hazard, and state regulatory efforts are directed toward the elimination of unduly slow operation, as well as toward the elimination of unduly fast operation.

The American Association of State Highway Officials has recommended that state laws should require that no motor vehicle should be operated at so slow a speed as to impede or block normal and reasonable highway traffic movement, excepting where reduced speeds are necessary for safe operation, or where vehicles are proceeding at reduced speeds necessarily or in compliance with the law. The Association recommends that maximum speeds for buses or trucks should be fixed by law at 45 miles per hour and that passenger automobiles should be operated at such speeds as are consistent at all times with safety and the proper use of the roads. These standards place the regulation of speeds, both maximum and minimum, upon the flexible basis of judgment rather than upon the more rigid basis of maximum and minimum speeds in miles per hour. The Association recommends that vehicles equipped with solid rubber tires or cushion tires should be operated at a speed not in excess of 10 miles per hour.[1]

In addition to speed regulations the states regulate the equipment required in the interests of safe operation of motor vehicles. However, the regulations apply with such variations in the different states as to make coherent description impracticable. The regulations cover:

1. Brakes.
2. Flares and fuses.
3. Directional signaling devices.
4. Speedometers.
5. Stop lights.
6. Clearance lights.
7. Reflectors.

State laws and commission regulations placing limits upon the maximum consecutive hours on duty, maximum working

[1] Uniform Standards adopted by the American Association of Highway Officials, Nov. 17, 1932.

hours in any period of time, and minimum hours off duty before again going on duty, applicable to drivers of motor vehicles, come within the category of safety regulations, as do state laws requiring insurance to protect the public, employees or patrons. Another group of regulations that are designed to promote safety are the state laws providing for penalties and, in some cases, the revocation of licenses of drivers who are convicted of operating with gross negligence or while under the influence of intoxicating liquors.

A trend toward greater uniformity in safety and equipment requirements among state laws and state regulatory bodies has been marked in recent years. This trend has been greatly accentuated by the safety and equipment regulations adopted by the Interstate Commerce Commission. In addition, the motor transportation industry generally has adopted safety glass and other equipment designed to reduce the hazard of accidents or to mitigate the severe effects of accidents upon human life and property.

Compulsory Assumption of Liability.—In one state, Massachusetts, the law requires, as a condition precedent to the operation of motor vehicles, that the owner-operator establish his financial responsibility to liquidate judgments against him by posting cash, securities, bond, or insurance policy. This state law, which attracted nation-wide attention and comment when it was enacted, has since been modified in minor details several times. A law of this type is usually referred to as a "compulsory insurance law," but this is a misnomer because it is a law requiring the compulsory assumption of financial responsibility by means of funds or securities and not compulsory insurance. The state of Montana has a uniform financial responsibility act. During the past few years in several other states, legislative committee investigations have been conducted, or bills have been introduced into the legislatures, affecting the compulsory assumption of motor-vehicle operator liability, New York and Illinois being two states in which such action has been taken.

The trend toward requiring motor-vehicle operators to assume financial responsibility for the operation of the vehicles is particularly pronounced in the regulations imposed upon commercial vehicles. This tendency has been toward requirements identical with or similar to the regulations in this respect of the

Interstate Commerce Commission applicable to interstate operators.

A few states require nonresident vehicle operators to designate residents of the states upon whom process can be served in event of accidents. One state, Delaware, requires nonresident motor-vehicle operators to post bond in the amount of twice the esti-mated damage before there may take place the removal of the nonresidents' vehicles from the places where accidents in which they are involved have occurred.

Port-of-entry Regulations.—In 1933, the State of Kansas enacted the first of the so-called port-of-entry laws. Following the enactment of this law, nine other western states passed similar laws. Generally, these laws require all motor trucks and buses to enter the states upon designated highways. At or close to the state boundaries the vehicles are required to stop, submit to safety inspection of the vehicle, pay a tax, and obtain clearance papers before proceeding to the destinations within the states. One of the purposes of the port-of-entry laws is to check the bootlegging of gasoline. Another purpose is to assist in the collection of ton-mileage taxes upon trucks and buses, which had been levied upon the intrastate truckers in these states but had sometimes been evaded by irresponsible operators who crossed state lines. A third purpose is to enforce the state highway safety and equipment laws upon all vehicles using the state highways, including vehicles used in both intrastate and interstate services. A fourth purpose is to assist in the enforce-ment of other inspection and tax laws of the state.

Ports of entry are located along the borders of the states where the principal interstate highways cross the state lines. The vehicles are stopped at the ports where inspectors of the states inspect them for the condition of headlights, clearance lights, brakes, connections between tractors and trailers, and other equipment to establish the roadworthiness of the vehicles. Drivers are examined for intoxication or other inability to operate the vehicles properly. They are required to produce evidence that the vehicles are insured to cover public liability and property damage, as required by the state laws, with insurance companies authorized to write insurance in the respective states.

At the time of entrance the driver is required to fill in a form, provided for the purpose, identifying the vehicle as to ownership, make of vehicle, state of registry, amount and kinds of insurance carried, nature and weight of goods carried, and destination. A copy of the manifest of the cargo carried by the vehicle also is required.

Freight vehicles subject to the state motor carrier acts are taxed by the states through the assessment of a lump sum deposit or minimum fee from which ton-mile taxes are deducted as they are reported monthly by the operators. Foreign motor-vehicle owners may elect either to pay the taxes upon the same basis as intrastate operators or pay a special tax graduated according to the weight of the vehicle and load and the distance the vehicle is operated in the state. This tax, which is payable at the port of entry, is imposed only upon the inbound movement into the state. The outbound movement is tax exempt in order to promote the exportation of products of the state to other states on the return movements of the out-of-state trucks. At the ports, vehicles and contents are inspected also to assist in the enforcement of the state's agricultural products and live-stock inspection laws, cigarette tax laws, and other miscellaneous state regulations.

The larger motor freight companies and motorbus companies usually provide their drivers with the forms for entry drawn up in the companies' offices and arrange for the payment of the taxes by the companies so as to reduce the time required for clearance of the vehicles at the ports. Bus companies usually notify the inspectors at the ports in advance of the arrival of the buses so that clearance papers may be ready when the buses arrive. Smaller operators and those entering the states only occasionally are required to complete these formalities and pay the taxes at the ports. A study made of the operation of the system at Kansas ports of entry gives an estimate of the average time required for clearance of between 3 and 5 minutes per vehicle, although delays at the ports, caused usually by conges-tion, are in some cases as much as 15 or 20 minutes.[1]

Although serious opposition to the port-of-entry laws has not been expressed generally by motor-vehicle operators or other interested persons, objections have been raised upon several grounds. First, the ratio of collection costs to taxes collected

[1] "The Kansas Port of Entry Law," *Highway Users Series* No. R1, National Highway Users Conference, Washington, D.C., November, 1934.

is relatively high.   Second, the regulations affect only interstate and not intrastate operators.   Third, if the safety inspections are thorough, there are congestion and delay; and if the inspections are not thorough, they are of doubtful value.   Fourth, the existence of port-of-entry regulations causes motor vehicles to by-pass the states where the regulations are in force in favor of routes through other states and tends to cause goods to be sent to markets in states where no such regulations are in force.   Fifth, laws of this sort tend to break down reciprocity in motor-vehicle regulation as between states where port-of-entry laws are operative and states that have no such regulations.   Finally, if every state in the United States had port-of-entry laws the system would become intolerably cumbersome and burdensome upon highway traffic between the states.   In 1937, port-of-entry bills were introduced, or considered, in a dozen or more states but were either defeated in legislature or failed to be reported out of the legislative committees to which they had been assigned. The popularity of laws of this sort in the United States appears to have passed its zenith and to be declining.

Miscellaneous State Regulations.—In addition to state laws and administrative regulations pertaining to the several phases of motor-vehicle operation discussed above, many states have regulations upon a number of aspects of vehicle operation and highway use that cannot conveniently be placed in any of these categories.   The rapid increase in the number of house trailers used by tourists, vacationists, and "rolling residents" has caused the states to require licenses for trailers of this type. In addition to licenses, special state regulations have been made in a number of states governing the use and operation of house trailers.   In a number of states the motor vehicles—automobiles, trucks, and tractor-trailer units—operated by farmers, and by farm cooperative associations, are partially, or wholly, exempt from certain taxes and regulations, including gasoline taxes and many carrier regulations which will be discussed later in this chapter.

Reciprocity.—Many states grant to the owners and operators of motor vehicles registered and licensed in other states privileges of operation without requiring the licensing of the vehicles in both states, in exchange for similar privileges extended to owners and vehicles registered in the reciprocating states.   The need for reciprocity arrangements is particularly pressing between states where trading areas are partly in one state and partly in one or several other states, and where motor vehicles must pass over the highways of one state to reach markets or centers of production in others. In some cases the number of trips permitted to be made by vehicles registered and licensed in other states is limited to a fixed number of trips per month, while in other cases full reciprocity is granted. The recent trend has been toward the liberalization of state registration and license laws to accord greater reciprocity between adjoining states.

STATE REGULATION OF MOTOR CARRIERS

Motor carriers, as the term is used in most state regulatory statutes, include common carriers and contract carriers. In addition to these two categories of motor operators, both of which serve others for hire, there are two other classifications of those engaged in highway services: the private operators of commercial vehicles and brokers.

The definitions of these classifications in the various state regulatory statutes vary, but generally a common carrier is understood to be an operator who holds himself out to serve the public generally for hire up to the limit of his facilities, for reasonable compensation, and without unjust discrimination among his patrons. Motor common carriers recognized by state legislation may be carriers of either passengers or property, or both, operating over either regular or irregular routes.

Contract carriers, as defined by representative state statutes, are carriers who arrange, upon the basis of either oral or written contracts, with a limited number of patrons to provide defined motor transportation services for hire. Contract carriers may be carriers of either persons or goods and may engage in either fixed-route or irregular-route services.

Private operators generally are those engaged in the transportation of goods in connection with the businesses of proprietary industries which own or operate the vehicles.

Brokers, under the state statutes, are intermediaries in the field of highway transportation, whose function it is to bring together travelers or shippers and consignees who require transportation services and carriers who provide the services.

Every state and the District of Columbia now has a statute regulating motor carriers. All 49 jurisdictions in the United States regulate common carriers, 30 states placing motor common carriers under general public utility regulatory laws, and 19 jurisdictions placing motor common carriers under laws relating exclusively to motor transportation regulation. Many of these laws have been enacted during the past five years. A number of state statutes regulating common-carrier motor vehicles have been revised by the state legislatures since 1935 in order to reconcile state regulation with interstate regulation under the Federal Motor Carrier Act of 1935.

A composite résumé of three studies of the status of common-carrier regulation by the states, based upon a study made by the Federal Coordinator of Transportation in 1933, revised by experts of the Department of Public Service of the State of Washington in 1936, revised by one of the authors to reflect known changes up to 1937, is believed to indicate the present situation.[1] All of the statistical data used in this discussion have been derived in this way. The term "states," as used in this discussion, includes the District of Columbia.

States in which common carriers are subject to state public utility laws. 30
States in which common carriers are subject to motor carrier laws...... 19
States in which common carriers are subject to state regulation........ 49
States in which common carriers of passengers are regulated:
    In regular-route services.. 49
    In irregular-route services...................................... 38
States in which common carriers of property are regulated:
    In regular-route services.. 47
    In irregular-route services...................................... 43

Contract carriers are not so generally regulated by the states as are common carriers, although contract carriers of passengers in regular-route and in irregular-route services are regulated in 26 states, and contract carriers of property in regular-route and irregular-route services are regulated in 37 states. Twelve states regulate private motor-vehicle operators engaged in the

[1] See Table VII, Federal Coordinator of Transportation, *Report*, Regulation of Transportation Agencies, Sen. Doc. 152, 73d Congress, 2d Sess., Mar. 10, 1934; and Appendix A, "Summary of State Regulation of Motor Carriers," in Reply Brief of Appellants in Prater *et al.* v. Dept. of Pub. Service, State of Washington *et al.*, Supreme Court, State of Washington, No. 26251, 1936.

transportation of property, and a few states regulate brokers in the field of motor transportation. The trend apparently is definitely toward the enactment of laws regulating common and contract carriers, private operators, and brokers.

Exemptions from Regulation.—Certain types of motor-vehicle operations are exempt from the state regulatory statutes or, if not exempt, are subject to less stringent regulations. The state laws vary widely with respect to exemptions. In some cases common and contract carriers and private operators engaged in services of certain kinds are exempt from regulation, while in other cases private or contract carriers may be exempt when engaged in these services, but common carriers engaged in the same services are not.

Among the types of motor-vehicle operation exempt under the provisions of representative state laws are:

1. Motor vehicles engaged in operation within corporate limits of local governments;

2. Those engaged in operation in suburbs or contiguous zones around municipalities;

3. School buses;

4. Mail and government-owned vehicles;

5. Vehicles carrying products or property of the owners of the vehicles;

6. Vehicles used only in occasional operations;

7. Vehicles transporting agricultural products; and

8. Other miscellaneous exempted classes of operation.

Certificates and Permits.—State laws usually require common carriers by motor vehicle to apply to the state regulatory body— public utility or public service commission, motor carrier commission, state department, or other administrative body— and receive from it a certificate of public convenience and necessity as a prerequisite to lawful operation. Forty-three states require common carriers to obtain certificates of public convenience and necessity. Permits, licenses, or special certifications, variously designated in different states, are required as conditions precedent to contract operation in 33 states. In a few states, applicants for the privilege of engaging in service as a broker must apply for and obtain licenses from the regulatory body in the state in which they conduct operations. In several states private operators are required to apply for and obtain certificates, permits, or licenses. In 45 states, certificated, permitted, or licensed motor vehicles must display identification plates or numbers placed in conspicuous places upon the vehicles.

The issuance of certificates of public convenience and necessity to applicants by the state regulatory commissions is conditioned, in virtually every state, upon a showing by the applicants that the service is reasonably necessary and for the convenience of the public. The laws of 40 states specifically provide for such a showing, and in 3 states, although no specific provision is found in the law, such a showing is to be reasonably inferred. The state commissions in administering the laws, and in exercising judgment in the granting or denying of applications for certificates of public convenience and necessity or applications for permits or licenses, consider: (1) the character of the services proposed to be rendered; (2) the nature of the applicants' facilities; (3) the effects of the proposed services upon the highways and other highway users; (4) the nature and facilities of existing transportation agencies, including railroads, and the probable effects of the proposed services upon existing services; (5) the financial responsibility of the applicants; and (6) the fitness, willingness, and ability of the applicants to begin operation at the time specified and to continue to render the authorized services until relieved of their obligations to do so by the regulatory bodies. Generally, the number of states in which all of these matters are considered in connection with the applications of contract carriers for permits is less than the states considering these factors in common-carrier applications for certificates; and, as a rule, the states are less exacting in their standards in considering contract-carrier applications than in dealing with those of prospective common carriers. However, in the past several years, there has been a well-defined tendency to raise the requirements in case of contract carriers. This is due partly to the regulation of contract carriers in interstate commerce by the Interstate Commerce Commission under the Motor Carrier Act of 1935, and partly to the growing appreciation of the effects of contract-carrier operation upon common carriers.

The state commissions are given either express or implied authority to fix the terms and conditions to be attached to certificates or permits. In 35 states specific authority is given the regulatory bodies to fix terms and conditions in connection with certificates of public convenience and necessity, and in 23 states similar powers are granted in connection with contract-carrier permits. The regulatory commissions are given powers in connection with the certificates of public convenience and necessity to require: (1) the filing or approval of schedules; (2) the filing or approval of rates and charges; and (3) the observance of schedules. The commissions, usually, may: (1) amend, suspend, or revoke the certificates for cause; (2) fix the term of the certificates; (3) prohibit unauthorized abandonment of the service; and (4) prohibit the unauthorized transfer or sale of the properties of the motor carriers.

State laws defining the powers of regulatory commissions do not, as a rule, give the commissions such broad bases of power in connection with the permits of contract carriers as with the certificates of common carriers. In some states, the state commissions may require contract carriers to file their schedules or contracts with the commissions, and the commissions may attach terms and conditions to the permits. In a smaller number of states than the number in which the commissions are authorized by law to act in these matters in the case of common-carrier certificates, the regulatory bodies may control the permits of contract carriers by: (1) prohibiting the unauthorized abandonment of the services; (2) prohibiting the sale or transfer of the permits; (3) amending, suspending, or revoking the permits; and (4) specifying the terms of the permits.

In several states the legislatures have declared in the regulatory statutes that certificates of public convenience and necessity and permits are not to be considered as franchise or property rights. In others, although the laws do not specifically make this declaration, there is a well-defined tendency to consider certificates and permits merely as authority to operate, not as franchises. In 35 states the laws provide that existing common carriers shall have preference or priority in the granting of applications for certificates, and in 23 states similar preference is required by law to be given to the applications of existing contract carriers. In a number of states dual operation as a common carrier and as a contract carrier either is prohibited or allowed only upon specific approval of the regulatory commission.

State Commission Powers in Regulating Common Carriers.— In the regulation of common carriers by motor vehicle the state regulatory commissions exercise broad powers. Representative powers exercised by state commissions in connection with motor carriers and the number of states exercising each power are listed below:

Powers	States Exercising Jurisdiction
1. General supervision and regulation	49
2. Compelling obedience to the law and observance of the commissions' orders	46
3. Adjustment of complaints against motor carriers	47
4. Conduct of investigations upon motion of the commissions	46
5. Making of general rules and regulations	49
6. Inspections and investigations	47
7. Regulation of facilities, safety, and services	49
8. Requiring of observance of common-carrier schedules	42
9. Prescription and regulation of uniform accounts and records of motor common carriers	48
10. Requiring of issuance and regulating of terms and conditions of bills of lading and receipts	25
11. Requiring of annual reports of motor carriers	47
12. Requiring of accident reports	48
13. Requiring of special reports	43
14. Requiring of public liability and property damage insurance or bond	48
15. Requiring of fidelity bond to be posted	16
16. Requiring of carriers to carry cargo insurance or bond to insure payment of claims	32
17. Regulation of capitalization, mergers, and acquisition of control by and of motor carriers	20

Common-carrier Rate Regulation.—The rates and charges of motor common carriers are usually subject to regulation by state public utility commissions or by other regulatory bodies. In almost every state the commissions are given power to fix or prescribe reasonable motor common-carrier rates, fares, and charges or to approve or disapprove the carriers' rates. In a few states the commissions are either given the power to fix minimum rates, fares, or charges or specifically directed to set minimum rates or charges. In 45 states motor common-carrier rates are required to be just and reasonable; in 44 states unjust and unreasonable discrimination is specifically prohibited; and in 43 states rebates are prohibited by statute. Common carriers' tariffs of rates and charges are required to be published, posted, and filed with the respective state commissions; and in 45 states the statutes require the carriers to adhere strictly to their tariffs. In 43 states the carriers must give public notice to the commissions of intention to make changes in rates, fares, or charges. State commissions have power to suspend the proposed rates, fares, or charges of motor common carriers in 31 states.

In one state, Louisiana, the law requires that motor common-carrier rates may not be lower than corresponding railroad rates, while in several other states the corresponding rates of rail carriers must be considered in making motor rates or charges. Joint motor-rail rates are permitted in 9 states, and joint motor rates are allowed by statute in 23 states.

Generally, the trends in state regulation of the rates, fares, and charges of motor common carriers are toward broader and more stringent regulation by state commissions; closer relationship between the regulation of interstate motor-carrier rates by the Interstate Commerce Commission and of intrastate rates by the state commissions; closer harmony between the rates of competing carriers; and the extension of the use of joint rates via routes embracing motor and rail carriers.

Contract-carrier Regulation.—In the regulation of contract carriers by motor vehicle, state commissions generally have more limited jurisdiction than that which they are empowered, or directed, to exercise in the regulation of motor common carriers. In 10 states the laws require that contract carriers file their contracts with the regulatory commissions; and in 13 states, that they file minimum rates. Other typical state regulations of contract carriers include:

Powers	States Exercising Jurisdiction
1. Regulation of facilities and safety	28
2. Observance of schedules	9
3. Regulation of accounts and records	33
4. Requirement of bills of lading or contracts	14
5. Requirement of annual reports	22
6. Requirement of accident reports	33
7. Public liability and property damage insurance required	36
8. Cargo insurance or bond required	14
9. Control of capitalization, securities, mergers, or acquisition of control	7

Regulation of Private Operations.—As a rule the states do not undertake the regulation of private operators of motor vehicles beyond regulations affecting safety, equipment, insurance, and the maximum hours of service of drivers and helpers engaged in the operation of the vehicles. In some states, however, regulation has gone beyond such matters; and, either by legislative enactment or by decisions of the state courts or of the public service commissions, many of the regulations applicable to common and contract carriers have been applied to private operators. In Texas, where a comprehensive motor-carrier act is in effect, an attempt was made to relieve private carriers of certain regulations to which they had been held to be subject by decision of the State Supreme Court, and a bill was passed by the Texas Legislature specifically relieving private operators of the regulations. The bill was vetoed by the Governor, however, and the veto was sustained by a narrow margin. The Legislature then passed a resolution stating that it was not the intention of the Legislature in enacting the Motor Carrier Act of the State to include the regulation of motor vehicles operated in the transportation of goods, wares, and merchandise owned by the owners of the vehicles. The effect of the resolution is that a seller of merchandise who transports the merchandise from one place to another in motor trucks owned by the seller, who adds to the sale price of the goods at point of delivery a charge to cover a part or all of the cost of transportation, is not engaged in transportation for hire and is not subject to the Texas Motor Carrier Act or to any rule or regulation promulgated pursuant to the Act.

Procedure in Applying for Right to Operate Motor Services for Hire.—The procedure required to be followed by applicants for certificates of public convenience and necessity, permits to conduct contract-carrier services, or licenses as transportation brokers is not uniform among the states. Usually, however, the applications are made to the regulatory commissions, and the following data with respect to the applicants and the proposed services must be shown:

1. The name and address of the petitioner and of the attorney of the petitioner;

2. The nature and character of the service to be rendered;

3. The powers, rights, franchises, and privileges of the petitioner under ordinances, municipal contracts, or other authorization;

4. The style, manufacturer, maker's number, capacity, and state motor-vehicle license of each motor vehicle owned by the petitioner that he wishes to operate in the public service;

5. A complete statement of the petitioner's financial ability to furnish adequate public service;

6. The persons, partnerships, or corporations furnishing or having the right to furnish similar service, including steam railroads, electric railways, express companies, and other motor operators;

7. A statement that the service proposed to be rendered is necessary and proper for the service, accommodation, and convenience of the public; and

8. A statement that the petitioner proposes to begin furnishing service immediately upon the receipt of a certificate of public convenience and necessity.

Applications are executed before a notary public, and several copies are filed with the public service commissions. Usually the applications are heard at public hearings scheduled by the commission and decided by majority vote of the members of the commissions. A nominal filing fee must usually accompany the applications.

Applications of substantially similar form are required to be made by those seeking the privilege of engaging in service as transportation brokers. The applicant must state the nature and extent of the service proposed to be rendered, prove the ability of the applicant to render it, and indicate the carriers whose services are to be used.

The provisions of a representative state public utility law and the regulations of a typical state commission with respect to the procedure necessary to obtain a certificate of public convenience and necessity, or a permit as a contract carrier, or a license as a broker, may be summarized as follows:

1. The filing of an application for certificate, permit, or license in the prescribed form, praying for a certificate or for the renewal of a certificate, permit, or license;

2. The payment of the filing fee;

3. The fixing of a time and place of hearing at which the petition may be heard before the commission, a commissioner, or an examiner of the commission;

4. The publication by the applicant of the time and place of hearing in a newspaper having general circulation in the territory to be served or the docketing of the hearing by the commission;

5. The service of a copy of the petition, with notice of hearing, upon all competitive carriers furnishing service in the district covered by the application;

6. At the hearing, establishing by the applicant, by competent testimony, that the proposed service is necessary for the service, accommodation, and convenience of the public; and that the applicant's financial responsibility and general character are satisfactory; and

7. If the application is approved, the issuance of a certificate of public convenience, with such limitations and conditions as, in the judgment of the commission, are warranted and required under the evidence.

Typical Regulations Governing Certificated Carriers.—The holders of certificates in intrastate commerce are required, under the provisions of typical laws, to observe many regulations provided for in the law or by administrative orders of the state commissions. The certificates of public convenience and necessity of common carriers and permits of contract carriers are limited to the routes or territories for which the certificates or permits are granted. The number of vehicles that may be operated by certificate or permit holders is specified in the certificates or permits; and if the carriers wish to operate additional equipment, permission must be obtained from the public service commission to do so. The certificates and permits are not transferable excepting under the conditions prescribed by the public service commission and with its approval.

The vehicles authorized to be used in common- or contract-carrier services must show the name of the certificate holder and his certificate or permit number. All vehicles operated by certificated or permitted carriers must be licensed by the state and the drivers must be similarly licensed. The holders of certificates or permits are required to file the numbers of the license tags of the vehicles with the public service commission immediately upon receipt of the license from the state highway department. The vehicles operated by certificated or permitted bus transportation companies, as a rule, are not permitted to carry a greater number of passengers than the number specified in the certificate or permit.

Certificates and permits in many states are issued initially for a limited period of time, usually for a few years, and at the expiration of that period applications must be made for renewal. In some states, if the operators have had the certificates or permits renewed several times, subsequent renewals are made for longer periods, or permanent certificates are granted which continue in effect until surrendered or cancelled for cause. The holders of certificates or permits are required to give to the businesses conducted under these authorizations the personal attention and supervision required to insure that all rules and regulations of the public service commission are complied with. In some states the employment or retention of incompetent or unfit persons to operate vehicles is deemed sufficient grounds for the revocation of certificates or permits or for the refusal to grant renewals. Applicants for the privilege of conducting common- or contract-carrier services are usually required to demonstrate their financial responsibility and to maintain adequate liability and indemnity insurance coverage. The amount of insurance required is either fixed by the state statutes or determined by the public service commission.

All accidents encountered by the vehicles of certificate or permit holders that result in injury to persons or damage to property are required to be reported promptly to the public service commission.

Taxicab operators are required to have their vehicles equipped with taximeters in plain sight of the passengers and to post a schedule of rates in a conspicuous position on the inside of the body of each taxicab. Similar regulations with respect to the conspicuous posting of a schedule of rates are found in connection with the requirements pertaining to the operators of motorbuses, "jitneys," and automobiles used in public service.

Common carriers engaged in freight or passenger service are required to publish, post, and file schedules of rates and charges with the public service commission and to keep copies of their tariff schedules available for public inspection in the form and manner prescribed by the public service commission. Contract carriers are often required to file copies of the contracts and schedules of their minimum rates. The public service commissions usually reserve the right to cancel or revoke certificates or permits at any time, after notice and hearing, for violation of the law or of the commissions' administrative rulings or for failure to operate vehicles in a safe manner.

Motor-carrier Taxes.—In all but a few states special licenses or tax fees are placed upon motor vehicles used in services for hire. In some states special taxes are levied upon carrier vehicles in lieu of the regular automotive license fees and taxes. Other states levy fees of one kind or another upon carrier motor vehicles in addition to the ordinary motor-vehicle licenses. These special levies take the form of taxes based upon the seating capacity of the vehicles; taxes upon for-hire operators' permits; ton-mileage taxes; taxes upon unladen weight of the vehicles or mileage operated; and occupational or privilege taxes. Other taxes are based on gross weight or width of vehicles or other units of size. In 1936, the special truck taxes amounted to $383,563,000, or $95.60 per motor truck operated. This figure includes all trucks without regard to the services in which they are employed. Separate figures for trucks used in carrier services are not available. In the same year, motorbuses operated in revenue services paid $38,475,500 in special taxes, or $785.22 per bus operated.[1]

FEDERAL REGULATION OF MOTOR TRANSPORTATION

In the decade between 1925 and 1935 numerous bills were introduced into Congress providing for Federal regulation of interstate motor transportation. These bills failed, however, to become law. In 1933 Congress enacted the Emergency Railroad Transportation Act of 1933, which, among other things, provided for the creation of the office of the Federal Coordinator of Transportation; and, subsequently, studies were made by the Coordinator's staff of the services and rates of motor carriers and the effects of motor transportation upon other forms of transportation. The earlier bills, the studies of the Coordinator, and the cooperation of various groups of motor carriers may be said to have accelerated the passage of the Motor Carrier Act,

[1] "Automobile Facts and Figures," Automobile Manufacturers Association, New York, 1937 ed., pp. 34–36. Bus figures are compiled by the National Association of Motor Bus Operators.

the first federal law regulating motor transportation, which was approved on Aug. 9, 1935.

The bill that became, after amendments and modifications, the Motor Carrier Act was based largely upon the legislation recommended by the staff of the Federal Coordinator of Transportation after intensive study of the needs of the motor transportation industry for regulation, and after consultation with spokesmen for the motor truckers and shippers. Extended hearings were held upon the Senate and House Bills by the Senate and House Committees. The Act became effective, generally, on Oct. 15, 1935, although postponement of certain sections of the Act postponed the effective date of these portions of the law. These provisions will be discussed later.

The Policy of Regulation.—One of the many distinctive features of the Act is the declaration of the policy of Congress with respect to the regulation of motor transportation. This policy is declared to be that regulation shall take place in such ways as to recognize and preserve the inherent advantages of motor transportation and to promote sound economic conditions within the industry and among carriers in the public interest by promoting efficient service, reasonable charges, improved relationships within the industry, the coordination of transportation, and the improved regulaton of motor and other types of carriers. The declaration of policy specifically forbids unjust discrimination, undue preferences or advantages, and unfair or destructive competitive practices.[1]

The whole background of interstate regulation, developed since the passage of the Act to Regulate Commerce of 1887 in connection with railroads and other carriers subject to the Interstate Commerce Act, is made applicable, in so far as these regulations are appropriate to motor transportation, by making the Interstate Commerce Act, as amended down to the present time, Part I of this Act. The provisions of the Motor Carrier Act of 1935, specifically applicable to motor transportation, are made Part II of the Interstate Commerce Act.

The Act applies to all interstate or foreign transportation of persons or property by motor carriers. Interstate commerce includes transportation between places in one state and those in another or between places in the same state which passes through

[1] Motor Carrier Act, 1935, Section 202 (a).

another state, when the transportation is performed wholly by motor vehicles or partly by motor vehicles and partly by railroad, express, or water carriers. Foreign commerce includes transportation between places in the United States and those in foreign countries or between points in the United States when the movement is through foreign territory.[1] These broad definitions of interstate and foreign commerce are susceptible of interpretation so as to include many movements of goods by motor vehicles entirely within a single state, city, or metropolitan area, when the freight hauled by the motor vehicles is to move, or has moved, in interstate or foreign commerce. However, the exact status of many of these movements must be determined by decisions of the courts in applying the law to particular cases and by administrative rulings of the Interstate Commerce Commission.

Types of Carriers.—The Act recognizes four types of motor-vehicle operators and business arrangements in interstate commerce. The first type—common carriers—is defined as motor carriers that "undertake, directly or by lease or any other arrangement," to transport for the general public for hire over regular or irregular routes. This classification includes also the motor-vehicle operations of railroads, steamship companies, express companies, forwarding companies, and other carriers engaged in common-carrier interstate service by motor vehicle.[2]

The second category—contract carriers—includes those which conduct motor transport services for compensation "under special and individual contracts or agreements," whether the operations are conducted directly or by lease or by other arrangements.[3]

A third classification—private carriers of property by motor vehicle—includes those which transport goods by motor vehicle as owners, lessees, or bailees, when the transportation is in the furtherance of any commercial enterprise, including the sale, lease, rental, or bailment of the goods.[4]

The fourth division of those subject to the Motor Carrier Act includes brokers—those who as principals or agents, and not as

[1] *Op. cit.*, Section 202 (b).
[2] *Ibid.*, Section 203 (a), (14).
[3] *Ibid.*, Section 203 (a), (15).
[4] *Ibid.*, Section 203 (a), (17).

the bona fide agents or employees of any motor carrier, undertake to sell any type of transportation services subject to the Act or who hold out "by solicitation, advertisement or otherwise as one who sells, provides, furnishes, contracts or arranges for such transportation."[1]

Common carriers, contract carriers, and brokers are required to obtain authority to operate their services from the Interstate Commerce Commission. In the case of common carriers the authorization documents are known as certificates of public convenience and necessity. Contract carriers must obtain corresponding documents known as permits; and brokers must apply for licenses to conduct or continue their operations.

The "Grandfather Clause" of the Act.—All common carriers who were in bona fide operation on June 1, 1935, and all contract carriers who were in operation on July 1, 1935, were entitled as a matter of right under the so-called "grandfather clause" of the Act to have the Interstate Commerce Commission issue certificates or permits to them without requiring further proof that public convenience and necessity would be served by their operations, and without further proceedings before the Commission, provided the carriers should have applied to the Commission for certificates or permits within 120 days from the effective date of the Act, Oct. 15, 1935. The period of grace for filing applications under the grandfather clause expired on Feb. 12, 1936. During the grace period, the Bureau of Motor Carriers of the Interstate Commerce Commission was deluged with work in counseling and assisting motor operators in preparing and filing these vitally important applications and in caring for the applications after they were filed. Carriers who were in operation prior to the statutory dates—June 1 or July 1, 1935— were permitted to operate for 120 days after Oct. 15, 1935, without certificates or permits; but after Feb. 12, 1936, those who had not filed applications no longer had the privilege or right of continuing in business unless prior to Feb. 12 they had filed their applications. Since Oct. 15, 1935, any new motor transport operator has been required to obtain a certificate, if a common carrier; a permit, if a contract carrier; and a license, if a broker before engaging in service over any public highway in interstate or foreign commerce. Operation without having

[1] *Op. cit.*, Section 203 (a), (18).

obtained a certificate or permit in willful violation of the Act is subject to fine of $100 for the first offense and $500 for each subsequent offense. Each day of violation is considered a separate punishable offense.[1]

Carriers Exempt from Regulation.—The provisions of the Motor Carrier Act give the Interstate Commerce Commission authority to establish and enforce reasonable requirements for the promotion of safety of operation by prescribing the qualifications and hours of service of employees and the standards of equipment applicable to all motor carriers—private, contract, and common carriers alike. These provisions, but not the rest of the Act, apply to school buses; taxicabs; hotel buses; motor buses operated under the control of the Secretary of the Interior of the United States in the national parks; motor vehicles operated and controlled by any farmer and used in the transportation of his agricultural commodities or products or in the transportation of supplies for his farm; trucks operated and controlled by cooperative associations, as defined in the Agricultural Marketing Act; trolley buses operated by overhead electric wires; motor vehicles used exclusively in the transportation of livestock, fish, including shellfish, or agricultural commodities but not including the manufactured products of agriculture; and trucks used exclusively in the transportation of newspapers.

The provisions of the Act, except those pertaining to employees and safety which, as has been previously stated, apply to all interstate motor operations, do not apply to the transportation by motor of passengers or goods wholly within single municipalities or between contiguous municipalities or zones that are physically adjacent to and commercially parts of the municipalities, unless the Interstate Commerce Commission shall find that the application of the Act is necessary to carry out the policy of Congress. If, however, the motor carriers engaged in such local transportation are under common control or management or are working under arrangements for continuous carriage or shipment to, or from, points outside the municipal areas, they are subject to all the provisions of the Act. Thus, purely local movement of freight by truck to or from consignees or shippers, both of whom are located within the same municipal area, such as movements of goods from the places of business of sellers to

[1] *Op. cit.*, Section 206 (a), 209 (a), and 211 (a).

those of buyers, would appear not to be subject to the law, although movements within the same areas that are integral parts of through interstate movements by motor, rail and motor, or water and motor would appear to be subject to regulation. Certainty on this score, however, is impossible until the Interstate Commerce Commission shall have undertaken to determine the status of such movements by decisions or orders interpreting the Act, and until the courts shall have handed down judicial interpretations of the application of the law to specific cases.

The Act also exempts, until such time as the Commission finds it expedient to apply the Act, the "casual, occasional or reciprocal" transportation of passengers or commodities for compensation by persons not engaged in motor transportation as a regular business.[1]

The General Regulatory Jurisdiction of the Interstate Commerce Commission.—The Interstate Commerce Commission is granted the power and charged with the responsibility of regulating common-carrier motor transport operators by establishing reasonable requirements for continuous and adequate service, uniform accounts and reports, preservation of records, qualifications and maximum hours of service of employees, safety of operation, and equipment. In the case of contract carriers, the Commission's jurisdiction is the same as in the case of the common carriers, except that no provision is made to give the Commission jurisdiction over, or responsibility for, standards of continuous and adequate service of contract carriers, and the Interstate Commerce Commission has jurisdiction over only the minimum rates of contract carriers and not over maximum or actual rates, as in the case of common carriers. The jurisdiction of the Commission is still more restricted in the case of private carriers, extending only to matters pertaining to safety of operation, qualifications of employees, hours of service, and standards of equipment.

Brokers in the field of motor freight transportation are subject to the authority of the Interstate Commerce Commission to the extent of being required to apply to the Commission for licenses and of establishing their financial responsibility. The Commission also has authority to regulate their accounts, records,

[1] *Op. cit.*, Section 203 (b).

and reports as well as to determine the nature of their operations and business practices.[1]

Certificates of Public Convenience and Necessity.—Applications for the certificates of public convenience and necessity required of all common carriers, except those qualifying under the grandfather clause of the Motor Carrier Act, must be made in writing in the form prescribed by the Commission and verified under oath. The applicants must demonstrate that they are "fit, willing and able" to perform the proposed services and to conform to the provisions of the Act and the rules and regulations made by the Interstate Commerce Commission. It must be shown that the proposed services are required by the present or future public convenience and necessity. The certificates granted to the successful applicants do not confer any proprietary or property rights in the use of the public highways but only the privilege of their proper use in the conduct of the business of the certified carriers.[2] Permits for contract carriers must be applied for in the same manner, and the applicants must prove to the Commission that the proposed contract services are consistent with the public interest and with the declared policy of Congress with respect to motor transportation.[3]

When the applications for certificates or permits involve not more than three states, the Commission is directed by the Act to refer the applications to joint boards composed of one representative of each public utility commission in the states in which operations are conducted by the applicants. If more than three states are involved, the Commission may in its discretion refer the applications to joint boards constituted in the same way. Matters involving the supervision, change, or revocation of certificates, permits or licenses, and other matters may also be submitted to these joint boards. The recommended orders of the joint boards are filed with the Interstate Commerce Commission and become orders of the Commission according to the same procedure as in cases heard by members of the Commission or its attorney examiners who act in cases not referred to the joint boards.[4]

[1] *Op. cit.*, Section 204 (a).
[2] *Ibid.*, Section 206 (a).
[3] *Ibid.*, Section 209 (a).
[4] *Ibid.*, Section 205.

The certificates, permits, or licenses granted by the Commission indicate tle terms and conditions upon which the privileges are granted, including:

1. The routes to be served;
2. The termini between which operations may be conducted or the territories within which the operations may be carried on;
3. Limitations upon the exercise of the privilege; and
4. Restrictions or limitations upon the extension of routes or territories.

An important provision stipulates that no terms, conditions, or limitations shall restrict the right of motor carriers to add to their equipment and facilities over the routes, between the termini, or within the territories specified in the certificates, as the development of their business and the demands of the public require. Common carriers who operate over regular routes may occasionally deviate from their routes or the regular termini between which they are authorized to operate under general or special rules that the Interstate Commerce Commission may prescribe. Common carriers engaged in passenger service over regular routes may operate special or charter-bus service under similar regulations. Certificates for passenger service may include also authority to transport newspapers, baggage, express, or mail in the same vehicles with the passengers or to transport the baggage of passengers in separate vehicles.[1]

Dual operation as a common and contract carrier in the transportation of freight is prohibited over the same routes or within identical territories unless the Commission finds that such services by the same carriers may be performed consistently with the public interest and policy of Congress.[2]

The Regulation of Rates and Charges.—It is not feasible to discuss all of the matters over which the Interstate Commerce Commission has jurisdiction and for which it has responsibility in the regulation of the affairs of motor carriers. Of outstanding importance, however, is the regulation of the rates and charges of the carriers. The Commission has power to require motor carriers to establish, observe, and enforce just and reasonable rates over their own individual lines and over joint routes. This includes the obligation of using proper classifications of freight;

[1] *Op. cit.*, Section 208.
[2] *Ibid.*, Section 210.

packing, marking, and shipping regulations; tariffs of rates and charges, with initial tariffs, which were required to be filed, to become effective Apr. 1, 1936, and which might not be increased or decreased thereafter except upon 30 days' notice to the Interstate Commerce Commission, and to the public; and proper bills of lading or freight receipts.[1]

Contract carriers are not required to publish and file with the Commission tariffs containing their complete rates and charges but only their minimum rates. In the discretion of the Commission, they may be required to file copies of their contracts with those for whom they perform the trucking services, indicating the minimum charges, and any rules, regulations, or practices affecting the services and the charges for them.[2]

It is important to note that in determining the reasonableness of the rates or charges of motor carriers, the Commission is directed by the Act not to give any consideration, in valuation proceedings, to good will, earning power, or the certificates of public convenience and necessity under which the carriers operate. The Commission is specifically directed to give consideration among other factors, to the inherent advantages of motor transportation; the effect of the rates upon the movement of traffic; the public need of adequate and efficient motor transportation service at the lowest rates consistent with furnishing such service; and the needs of the carriers for revenues sufficient to enable the carriers, under honest, economical, and efficient management, to provide service up to this standard.[3]

The charges of motor carriers must either be paid before the goods are delivered at destination, or arrangements must be made for the weekly or monthly settlement of charges, under regulations prescribed by the Interstate Commerce Commission, to insure freedom from unjust discrimination or undue preference or prejudice among shippers or consignees.[4] All of the business affairs of the motor carriers subject to regulation must be conducted subject to uniform sets of accounts and records to be prescribed and enforced by the I.C.C. Failure to keep such accounts, or the falsification, destruction, mutilation, or altera-

[1] *Op. cit.*, Sections 216, 217, and 219.
[2] *Ibid.*, Section 218.
[3] *Ibid.*, Section 216 (h) and (i).
[4] *Ibid.*, Section 223.

tion of records, when done knowingly and willingly, is punishable by fines ranging from $100 to $5,000.[1]

Motor-carrier Finances and Securities.—The Interstate Commerce Commission has the authority and the duty imposed upon it by the Act to require motor carriers to post insurance and surety bonds to indemnify the public and the passengers and owners of the goods transported by the carriers for loss of life or injury and damage to the vehicles or property of others.[2]

The Commission is given authority over the consolidation, merger, and acquisition of motor carriers subject to the Act and over the issuance of securities of all motor carriers where the par value of the outstanding securities and those proposed to be issued is $500,000 or more.[3]

The Administration of the Act.—The commission has designated Division 5 of the Interstate Commerce Commission composed of Commissioner Joseph B. Eastman, as chairman of the division, and Commissioners Lee and Rogers, as the division for motor-carrier administration. Subordinate to Division 5 of the Commission is the Bureau of Motor Carriers. The Bureau of Motor Carriers has two assistant directors, one having general supervision over the sections comprising the headquarters organization, and the other having jurisdiction over the field organization. There is also an assistant to the director who has responsibility for the administrative section supervising the dockets, mails and files, and stenographic staff of the Bureau.

The headquarters organization of the Bureau of Motor Carriers is as follows: The Section of Certificates has jurisdiction over certificates, permits, licenses, surety bonds, and insurance; the Section of Finance, the responsibility for the securities of motor carriers and mergers in which they are concerned; and the Section of Traffic, the supervision of the rates, classifications, charges, tariffs, the concurrence of carriers in the tariffs of others, the suspension of tariffs, and the division of rates and charges. The Section of Accounts has jurisdiction over the uniform systems of accounts for motor carriers. These must be devised, prescribed, and enforced. A Section of Complaints is provided to

[1] *Op. cit.*, Section 220.
[2] *Ibid.*, Section 215.
[3] *Ibid.*, Sections 213 and 214.

attend to the formal and informal complaints involving motor carriers and services affecting them.   The Section of Safety has responsibility for and jurisdiction over matters pertaining to hours of service of motor-carrier employees and motor vehicular safety regulations.   The Section of Law and Enforcement has responsibility for the enforcement of the provisions of the Motor Carrier Act and the interpretation of legal questions involving the Bureau and regulated motor carriers.   Plans have been made also for a Section of Statistics and a Section of Research, but these have not yet been organized.

The field staff of the Bureau of Motor Carriers consists of 16 district offices under the direction of district directors.   Each district staff has a force of supervisors, rate agents, accountants, and examiners.   Joint-board agents act as liaison agents between the Bureau of Motor Carriers of the Interstate Commerce Commission and the state regulatory commissions.   The district directors have jurisdiction over the district supervisors, who act as contact representatives between the Bureau and the motor carriers in the field.

Shippers and the Motor Carrier Act.—Shippers and consignees in interstate commerce by motor service are directly affected by the Act, since they, as well as carriers, are subject to fine or imprisonment, or both, for violations of the Act in which they knowingly and wilfully participate.   However, they are assured that information concerning their shipments and business arrangements will be kept strictly confidential, since the Act imposes penalties for the unauthorized disclosure by motor carriers of information concerning shipments or shippers or consignees.   Of great benefit to shippers and consignees is the fact that the rates they pay for their transportation services, and those paid by their competitors, will tend to be stabilized and made matters of public information available to all, through the publication and filing of the carriers' tariffs of rates and charges.   Furthermore, shippers and consignees, large and small, are given necessary protection against unjust and unreasonable discrimination and other unfairly prejudicial arrangements. These have been all too common in motor transportation, as they had been in other transportation industries before the advent of effective public regulation.   Under the Motor Carrier Act they are made punishable offenses.

References

Automobile Manufacturers Association: "Automobile Facts and Figures," New York, annual.

Bureau of Railway Economics: An Economic Survey of Motor Vehicle Transportation in the United States, *Special Series* No. 60, Washington, D.C., 1933, Chaps. XV to XVIII.

EDWARDS, F. K.: "Principles of Motor Transportation," McGraw-Hill Book Company, Inc., New York, 1933, Chaps. XV and XVI.

Federal Coordinator of Transportation: Regulation of Transportation Agencies, Sen. Doc. 152, 73rd Cong., 2nd Sess., 1934.

JOHNSON, E. R., G. G. HUEBNER, and G. L. WILSON: "Principles of Transportation," D. Appleton-Century Company, Inc., New York, 1928, Part V, Chap. XL.

McCOLLESTER, PARKER, and F. J. CLARK: "Federal Motor Carrier Regulation," Traffic Publishing Co., New York, 1935.

MILLER, S. L.: "Inland Transportation—Principles and Policies," McGraw-Hill Book Company Inc., New York, 1933, Chaps. XXXIII and XXXIV.

Motor Carrier Act, 1935, Public No. 255, 74th Cong., S. 1629.

National Association of Railroad and Public Utility Commissioners, *Proceedings of Annual Conventions*, 1929 to 1937.

National Conference on Street and Highway Safety.: "Uniform Motor Vehicle Code."

National Highway Users' Conference: "The Kansas Port of Entry Law," Washington, D.C., 1934.

Prater *et al.* v. Dept. of Pub. Service, State of Washington *et al.*, Supreme Court, State of Washington, No. 26251, Reply Brief of Appellants, Appendix A, 1936.

United States Department of Commerce, Bureau of the Census, Census of Business, 1935, "Motor Trucking for Hire," Washington, D.C., May, 1937.

WAGNER, W. H.: "A Legislative History of the Motor Carrier Act, 1935," H. C. Cecil, Washington, D.C., 1935.

WILSON, G. L.: "Motor Traffic Management," D. Appleton-Century Company, Inc., New York, 1928, Chaps. XIV to XVI.

CHAPTER XIV

FEDERAL REGULATION OF INTERSTATE COMMERCE IN GAS AND ELECTRICITY

INTERSTATE MOVEMENT OF ELECTRICITY

Statistical compilations of the volume of interstate movements of electricity differ greatly, recent surveys producing a figure in the neighborhood of 17 per cent of the total quantity generated in the United States. The Federal Trade Commission found interstate movements in 1929 to amount to 14.7 per cent of the total quantity generated by all privately owned companies, and 15.3 per cent in 1930. In the latter year electric transmission lines crossed 8 of the 14 boundaries between border states and Canada or Mexico, and, out of a possible total of 105 boundaries between different states, transmission lines of 20 holding-company groups reporting to the Commission crossed 88 boundaries.[1] A more recent study shows that interstate movements of electric energy in recent years have increased materially in volume and in the ratio to total production; *i.e.*, the total amount of interstate electric power has increased more rapidly than the total generation. This survey gives the following figures[2]:

Year	Kilowatt-hours generated	Interstate movement	Percentage of total generated
1928	80,453,498,000	9,314,288,000	11.7
1929	90,084,428,000	11,134,284,000	12.5
1930	88,591,736,000	11,901,681,000	13.5
1931	85,575,307,000	12,488,401,000	14.6
1932	76,885,248,000	12,595,460,000	16.4
1933	79,259,087,000	14,146,000,000	17.8
1934	84,532,153,000	14,800,000,000	17.5

[1] Utility Corporations, Sen. Doc. 92, 70th Cong., 1st Sess., Part 72-A, pp. 42–43.

[2] Edison Electric Institute *Bulletin*, vol. 3, No. 3, p. 70.

The growth in interstate movements reflects in part the completion of interconnection programs, although a large proportion results from the construction and operation of large plants across state boundaries from large city markets. Thus, the State Line steam plant of East Chicago, supplying the Chicago market, is located in Indiana; the Conowingo hydro-electric plant, supplying Philadelphia, is located in Maryland; and the Cahokia steam plant, supplying St. Louis, Mo., is located in Illinois. Two of these, the Conowingo and the State Line plants, contribute almost 20 per cent of the total interstate movement. Practically all interstate sales of power are at wholesale rates, and transfers between divisions of the same operating company constitute about one-half of the total. Only about 6 per cent of the total interstate movements are between non-affiliated companies.

Whether or not large plants like those mentioned have been located as they are because those locations are most suitable, as the companies contend, or to evade state regulation, as others contend, it is pretty generally conceded that state regulation cannot be wholly effective while so large a part of the total operations lie beyond the control of state commissions. This point is further substantiated when we consider the situation in individual states. In 1933, there were generated in the state of Delaware 6 million kilowatt-hours, but 4 million were exported and 133 million imported; Illinois generated 6,205 million, exported 985 million, and imported 1,088 million; Indiana generated 2,446 million, exported 1,045 million, and imported 423 million; Maryland generated 1,742 million, exported 1,691 million, and imported 1,095 million; New Hampshire generated 585 million and exported 342 million; while Vermont generated 464 million and exported 294 million kilowatt-hours.[1]

INTERSTATE MOVEMENT OF NATURAL AND MANUFACTURED GAS

No statistics are available for the total quantity of manufactured gas transmitted across state lines, but all estimates indicate that it is a very small proportion of the total manufactured. A different situation exists, however, in the natural

[1] McNinch, F. R., The Evolution of Federal Control of Electric Power, *Journal of Land and Public Utilities Economics*, vol. 12, No. 2, p. 116.

gas industry. Out of a total of 1,770,721 million cubic feet
produced in the United States in 1934, 414,183 million cubic
feet, more than 23 per cent, moved in interstate or foreign
commerce, including exports to Canada and Mexico. The
largest movements were 139,564 million cubic feet from Texas
to 13 other states and Mexico; 93,346 million cubic feet from
Louisiana to 8 other states; and 63,688 million cubic feet from
West Virginia to 5 other states and the District of Columbia.
Other large shipments were from Pennsylvania, Kentucky,
Kansas, and Oklahoma. In all, natural gas was transported
from 17 to 31 states, the District of Columbia, Canada, and
Mexico.[1] It is estimated that in 1934 roughly 50 per cent of
natural gas sales by public utilities was transported interstate.[2]
Natural gas pipe-line mileage increased roughly 50 to 60 per cent
from July, 1929, to December, 1933; and while there was not
much new construction during the years following, it is anticipated that much new mileage will be constructed in the immediate future.[3]

LIMITS ON STATE REGULATION OF GAS AND ELECTRICITY

The development of interstate commerce in gas and electricity
raises the question of the adequacy of state powers to protect
ultimate consumers from unreasonable charges. It has been
established by decisions of the United States Supreme Court that
the transmission of gas or electricity produced in one state to
another state for distribution to ultimate consumers is interstate commerce, although the Court has held that the retailing
of gas (and the same is true for electricity) by the local companies
to their consumers is intrastate commerce, even though the mains
of the local companies are connected permanently with those
of the transmitting company.[4] With respect to state regulation
of interstate commerce, the rule, as laid down by the Supreme
Court, is that while in the absence of federal regulation individual
states may regulate matters in interstate commerce admitting of

[1] Bureau of Mines, Statistical Appendix to "Minerals Yearbook," 1935,
pp. 40–42.

[2] Bureau of Mines, *Mineral Market Reports*, No. 414, Oct. 29, 1935.

[3] TROXEL, C. E., Long-distance Natural Gas Pipe Lines, *Journal of Land
and Public Utility Economics*, vol. 12, No. 4, pp. 344–345.

[4] Pennsylvania Gas Co. v. Pub. Service Comm., 252 U.S. 23; Pub. Util.
Comm. v. Landon, 249 U.S. 236; and other cases.

diversity of treatment according to the special requirements of local conditions, a state may not directly regulate or burden interstate commerce.[1] Certainly no state may regulate interstate rates. The issues involved and the limitations upon the jurisdiction of state commissions where gas and electricity move in interstate commerce can best be presented by the analysis of a few cases decided by the Supreme Court.

1. The Pennsylvania Gas Case.—In this case the rates of a single company which produced gas in one state, transmitted it over a state line, and sold it to ultimate consumers in another state were involved. The Pennsylvania Gas Company, a corporation, from wells located in Pennsylvania, transmitted and sold natural gas to ultimate consumers in Warren, Corry, and Erie, Pa., and, also, through pipe lines some 50 miles in length, to consumers in Jamestown, Ellicott, and Falconer, N. Y. Consumers of gas in Jamestown filed a complaint with the New York Public Service Commission demanding a reduction in rates. The Commission assumed jurisdiction over these rates and was sustained by the Court of Appeals of New York. The case was then appealed to the Supreme Court of the United States.

The Supreme Court held that the transmission from the wells in Pennsylvania to the consumers in New York was interstate commerce and that the states were prevented by constitutional limitations from directly regulating or burdening interstate commerce. However, the Court said that it was not an infringement upon the authority delegated to Congress for the states, in the absence of action by Congress, to pass laws indirectly affecting interstate commerce when needed to protect or regulate matters of local interest.

Where the subject is peculiarly one of local concern [the Court held], and from its nature belongs to the class with which the state appropriately deals in making reasonable provision for local needs, it cannot be regarded as left to the unrestrained will of individuals because Congress has not acted, although it may have such a relation to interstate commerce as to be within the reach of the Federal power.[2]

As to this particular matter, in upholding the jurisdiction of the New York Commission, the Court said:

[1] Port Richmond and Bergen Point Ferry Co. v. Board of Chosen Freeholders, 234 U.S. 317; Pa. Gas Co. v. Pub. Service Comm., 252 U.S. 23.

[2] Pa. Gas Co. v. Pub. Service Comm., 252 U.S. 23.

The thing which the state commission has undertaken to regulate, while part of an interstate transmission, is local in its nature, and pertains to the furnishing of natural gas to local consumers within the city of Jamestown, in the state of New York. The pipes which reach the customers served are supplied with gas directly from the main of the company which brings it into the state; nevertheless, the service rendered is essentially local, and the sale of gas is by the company to local consumers, who are reached by the use of the streets of the city in which the pipes are laid, and through which the gas is conducted to factories and residences as it is required for use. The service is similar to that of a local plant furnishing gas to consumers in a city.[1]

2. **The Kansas Natural Gas Company Case.**—In this case the question of a state's jurisdiction over the wholesale rate charged a local distributing company by an interstate company engaged in producing and transmitting natural gas, but not in distribution to ultimate consumers, was at issue. The Kansas Natural Gas Company, a Delaware Corporation, produced and bought natural gas mostly in Oklahoma, but some in Kansas, gas from both sources being mingled for transportation in pipe lines. The gas was transported by the company to towns and cities in Kansas and Missouri, where it was sold at wholesale rates to local distributing companies. The Kansas Natural Gas Company increased its wholesale rate from 35 to 40 cents per MCF, an action undertaken without the approval of the commissions in Kansas and Missouri, the company challenging the jurisdiction of these bodies over rates for gas transported in interstate commerce. Three cases were grouped for decision, each one presenting the single question as to whether the business of the interstate company was interstate commerce free from state interference.

In its decision the Supreme Court, while pointing out that the dividing line between cases in which the state may or may not regulate in the absence of congressional action is not always clearly marked, again declared that the commerce clause of the Federal Constitution restrains states from imposing a direct burden upon interstate commerce. This case was distinguished from the Pennsylvania Gas Company case, in that whereas in the latter the transaction was distinctly local in character, in the Kansas Natural Gas Company case the sale and delivery were an inseparable part of a transaction in interstate commerce.

[1] Pa. Gas Co. v. Pub. Service Comm., 252 U.S. 23.

"Enforcement of a selling price in such a transaction," the Court said, "places a direct burden upon such commerce inconsistent with that freedom of interstate trade which it was the purpose of the commerce clause to secure and preserve." The Court also distinguished this case from an earlier one[1] in which it was held that the business of supplying local consumers is a local business, even though the gas be brought from another state. Here, the Court said, the sale of gas is in wholesale quantities to distributing companies for resale to ultimate consumers, the transportation, sale, and delivery constituting an unbroken chain, fundamentally interstate from beginning to end.[2] By this decision the wholesale rate was placed beyond the jurisdiction of the state commission having jurisdiction over the distributing company.

3. The Attleboro Case.—This case involved an order of a state commission affecting the wholesale rate for the sale of electric energy in interstate commerce. The Narragansett Electric Lighting Company, a Rhode Island corporation, was engaged in the generation of electric energy at its plant in Providence, R. I., which it sold to ultimate consumers in Rhode Island and also at wholesale to the Attleboro Steam and Electric Company, a Massachusetts corporation, for distribution to consumers in Attleboro and vicinity, the current being delivered at the state line. This rate was approved by the Rhode Island Public Utilities Commission, and the generating plant of the Attleboro company was dismantled. After the contract rate had been in effect for several years the Rhode Island Commission found that, owing principally to the increased cost of generating electricity, the Narragansett Company, in serving the Attleboro Company, was suffering an operating loss without any return on the investment devoted to such service. The Commission, therefore, issued an order putting into effect a new schedule which raised the rate to the Attleboro Company. The case was finally appealed to the Supreme Court, which held that the rate to the Attleboro Company was beyond the jurisdiction of the Rhode Island Commission.

In this case it was contended that the Rhode Island Commission could not effectively regulate the rates for ultimate con-

[1] Pub. Util. Comm. v. Landon, 249 U.S. 236.
[2] Missouri v. Kan. Natural Gas Co., 265 U.S. 298.

sumers in Rhode Island if the rate to the Attleboro Company were not under its control; that if the Narragansett Company were to continue to supply the Attleboro Company at a loss, this would tend to increase the burden on the local consumers and impair the ability of the Narragansett Company to give them good service at reasonable prices; and that the fixing of the rate by the Rhode Island Commission should be sustained as being essentially a local regulation, necessary to the protection of matters of local interest as under the ruling in *Pennsylvania Gas Co. v. Pub. Service Comm.* The Court held, however, that this case was controlled by the Kansas Gas Company case. Regulation by the Rhode Island Commission of the rates charged the Attleboro Company by the Narragansett Company, the Court said, places a direct burden upon interstate commerce from which the state is restrained by the force of the commerce clause. The Court went on to say that it was immaterial that Rhode Island was the state from which the current was transmitted and not that in which it was received, as in the Kansas Gas Company case, since the forwarding state obviously had no more authority than the receiving state.[1]

Mr. Justice Brandeis dissented from the majority opinion of the Court on the ground that the business of the Narragansett Company was essentially intrastate, the only current sold outside the state of Rhode Island being that delivered under contract to the Attleboro Company, and that the problem was local in character. The order of the Rhode Island Commission, he said, was a valid exercise of the police power of the state to protect the consumers of approximately 97 per cent of the power sold by this company from unjust discrimination and that the silence of Congress with respect to the regulation of interstate commerce in electricity did not imply that the company should remain free from public regulation. The majority decision stated, however, that

. . . the test of the validity of a state regulation is not the character of the general business of the company but whether the particular business which is regulated is essentially local or national in character; and if the regulation places a direct burden upon its interstate business it is none the less beyond the power of the state because this may be the smaller part of its general business.[2]

[1] Pub. Util. Comm. v. Attleboro Steam and Electric Co., 273 U.S. 83.
[2] *Ibid.*

4. The Western Distributing Company Case.—In this case was involved the authority of a state commission to inquire into the reasonableness of the wholesale rate charged a local distributing company under its jurisdiction where the wholesale company, although engaged in interstate commerce in gas, was affiliated with the distributing company. The Western Distributing Company, incorporated in West Virginia, owned and operated a distributing system for natural gas in Eldorado, Kan., and purchased its gas at wholesale from an interstate company, Cities Service Gas Company, which owned and operated a number of interstate pipe lines and sold natural gas to various distributing companies. The Western Distributing Company applied to the Kansas Public Utilities Commission for authority to increase its rates on the ground that the existing rates did not yield a fair return on the fair value of its property. The Kansas Commission insisted that in order to determine the reasonableness of the local rates it would be necessary to inquire into the reasonableness of the wholesale rate, since out of total expenses of operation and maintenance for the year ending Nov. 30, 1930, amounting to $283,049.07, the Western Company paid $176,-260.32 for the gas purchased from Cities Service Gas Company. The Western Company, however, refused to make a showing with respect to the wholesale rate, and the Commission dismissed the proceeding. The case was appealed eventually to the Supreme Court of the United States. At the time of the appeal the corporate relationship between the Western Distributing Company and Cities Service Gas Company was as follows: the common stock of Western Distributing Company was owned by the Gas Service Company, the stock of which in turn was owned by the Cities Service Company; while the common stock of Cities Service Gas Company was owned by the Empire Gas and Fuel Company, the controlling interest in the common stock of which also was owned by the Cities Service Company.

In its decision the Supreme Court held that while the rate charged by the pipe-line company for gas delivered at the city gate was an interstate rate not subject to regulation by any state authority, it did not follow that any inquiry by the state commission into the reasonableness of the wholesale charge, in view of the relationship between the companies, constituted an attempt upon the part of the state to circumvent federal authority and to

accomplish by indirection what the Federal Constitution forbade
it to do directly.   In its bill of complaint the company included
a number of averments which were not denied by the Commission,
and which it was contended constituted a prima facie case for
the reasonableness of the wholesale rate charged.   In brief,
these were that the Western Company did not own or produce
any natural gas; that the only source of supply for the city of
Eldorado was the main of the Cities Service Gas Company; that
no supply at a lower price could be obtained from any other
source; that the same rate was being charged to other distributing
companies along the lines of the Cities Service Gas Company
and was being charged by another independent pipe line to
another city; that an ineffectual effort had been made to find local
gas available to Eldorado; and that the Western Company had
attempted to get a lower rate from Cities Service Gas Company
but had failed.   The Court held, however, that the averment of
negotiation and effort to procure a reduction in the wholesale
rate meant little in the light of the fact that the negotiators were
both acting in the same interest.   Regarding the right of a state
to inquire into the reasonableness of such a wholesale rate between
affiliated companies, the Court made the following significant
statement:

Having in mind the affiliation of buyer and seller and the unity of
control thus engendered, we think the position of the appellees is sound,
and that the Court below was right in holding that if appellant desired
an increase of rates it was bound to offer satisfactory evidence with
respect to all the costs which entered into the ascertainment of a reasonable rate.   Those in control of the situation have combined the
interstate carriage of the commodity with its local distribution in what
is in practical effect one organization.   There is an absence of arms'-
length bargaining between the two corporate entities involved, and of
all the elements which ordinarily go to fix market value.   The opportunity exists for one member of the combination to charge the other
an unreasonable rate for the gas furnished and thus to make such unfair
charge in part the basis of the retail rate.   The state authority whose
powers are invoked to fix a reasonable rate is certainly entitled to be
informed whether advantage has been taken of the situation to put an
unreasonable burden upon the distributing company and the mere fact
that the charge is made for an interstate service does not constrain the
commission to desist from all inquiry as to its fairness.   Any other rule
would make possible the gravest injustice, and would tie the hands of

the state authority in such fashion that it could not effectively regulate the intra-state service which unquestionably lies within its jurisdiction.[1]

The effect of these decisions of the Supreme Court is to place beyond the jurisdiction of state commissions interstate wholesale rates for gas and electricity charged local distributing companies. State commissions may take action only with respect to transactions in interstate commerce which are conceived to be of local rather than national significance, or where inquiry into the reasonableness of transactions between affiliated companies is essential to the determination of reasonable rates to ultimate consumers. Except in such cases, where a distributing company purchases gas or electricity under an interstate wholesale rate, the state commission having jurisdiction over the rates of the distributing company must accept as fixed and beyond its control the cost of the gas or electricity, although this may represent the principal element of cost for the distributing company. Nor has the commission in the state where production or generation takes place any control over the rate, whatever the effect on the company under its jurisdiction or on its consumers. The authors believe that the only effective way by which to stop up this gap in regulation is through federal regulation of interstate commerce in gas and electricity. There are those, however, who contend that this problem could be solved without federal regulation by cooperative action on the part of the various states involved in an interstate transmission.

Interstate Compacts.—The principal argument in favor of reliance upon cooperation between states for the regulation of interstate matters is that, since the bulk of the operations of gas and electric utilities are intrastate in character and since the character of regulation is bound to reflect local conditions, regulation of these services should remain in the hands of the state authorities who are most conversant with the needs of the consumers as well as the problems of the companies that serve them. Over against these advantages, however, must be placed the difficulties of obtaining effective cooperation between states and the question as to the adequacy of state powers to deal with interstate problems. Certainly little confidence could be placed in cooperation on a voluntary basis where there is such differential

[1] Western Distributing Co. v. Pub. Service Comm. of Kan., 285 U.S. 119.

treatment of the multitude of common problems that face the state commissions. Moreover, in view of the decisions of the Supreme Court, the states could not regulate the wholesale rates charged the distributing companies under their jurisdiction if such rates were interstate rates. Nor could the states obtain the access to the books and records of holding companies essential to the determination of reasonable intercompany charges if the operations of such companies cover more than one state.

A proposal frequently made which is designed to retain complete control of gas and electric service in the hands of state bodies, while broadening such control to include interstate matters beyond the jurisdiction of a single state, is through more extensive use of interstate compacts. The interstate compact is a legal device for interstate cooperation resting on a negative provision in Article I, Section 10, of the Federal Constitution to the effect that no state shall enter into any agreement or compact with another state without the consent of Congress, it having been assumed that with such consent it may do so. The compact has been used rather widely by states to effect necessary cooperation for the solution of common problems. By December, 1935, 57 interstate compacts had been authorized by Congress, 30 of them having been approved since 1918. Of these, 34 have finally become effective through ratification by the states involved. In addition, 13 compacts have been authorized by one or more states without congressional approval or authority yet being made.[1]

The interstate compact has been employed to solve eight types of interstate problems, *viz.*, boundaries and cessions of territory, interstate debt settlement, criminal jurisdiction over boundary waters, taxation of common resources, uniform legislation for improving industrial conditions, utility regulation, control and improvement of navigable streams, and the conservation of natural resources. In the settlement of boundary disputes and in a few other matters the compact method has had a fair degree of success, but in other cases it has proved to be an unwieldy, cumbersome device. Its principal defects are the circumscribed, straight-jacketed administration that results and the problem of obtaining compliances. These defects will best appear from

[1] National Resources Committee, "Regional Factors in National Planning," December, 1935, p. 36.

a consideration of two types of compacts, frequently referred to as successful ones—the agreement between New York and New Jersey creating the Port of New York Authority, and the Colorado River compact.

The Port of New York Authority is a self-sustaining public corporation, the central body being a board of commissioners representing both states, with staffs for engineering and other phases of the planning of the port of New York. It has the power to borrow and has built and operates bridges, tunnels, and a freight station. As a business enterprise the Port of New York Authority has been a success, but it has not been successful in carrying out any "comprehensive plan" for the development of the port of New York, which was the primary purpose for its creation. The Port of New York Authority has been hampered by limitations and insufficient grants of power, defects that seem to be inherent in the compact method. For example, it has no power of condemnation, this power having to be granted in all statutes authorizing construction by the Authority; it is forbidden to pledge the credit of either state without the state's consent; and the compact reserves the right of each state to enact legislation giving the state governors authority to veto official acts of commissioners from their respective states, a right that both states have exercised. As a result, whenever valuable interests such as water rights and transportation facilities have been the subject matter of distribution or development, the Authority has found itself hampered by clashes of interest and all manner of interferences and obstructions.[1] Other agencies of this type are the Delaware River Bridge Commission, organized by the states of New Jersey and Pennsylvania, for building and operating a bridge over the Delaware River between Philadelphia and Camden; and the Lake Champlain Bridge Commission, organized to construct and operate a bridge over Lake Champlain between New York and Vermont.

The Colorado River compact is in many respects the most important of the compacts yet entered into between states. In this region, where the maintenance of an adequate water supply is a primary objective of public policy, the allocation of the waters of the Colorado River is such a constant and pressing issue that interstate cooperation is fundamental to the welfare

[1] *Ibid.*, pp. 40–41.

of the region. But in this very situation lie the elements of discord and conflicts of vital interests which militate against such cooperation, since this river makes possible the irrigation of hundreds of thousands of acres of land otherwise untillable, and upon the development and use of its waters the well-being of millions of people in seven states is dependent. Flood control is necessary for the protection of the lives and property of many people in these regions, and the Federal Government, through the Boulder Dam and related projects, is attempting to control the flood menace and to develop the generation of hydroelectric power.

A compact was drawn up which was ratified by the legislatures of six of the seven states affected in 1923, but was never ratified by Arizona. Eventually a six-state compact was drawn up and ratified eight years after the first steps were taken to initiate the compact. Every provision in the compact represented a compromise between seriously conflicting interests, and the final result was not wholly satisfactory to any group. The compact was designed to achieve the following major purposes:

1. To provide for an equitable apportionment of the use of the waters of the Colorado River system.

2. To establish the relative importance of different beneficial uses of water.

3. To promote interstate comity.

4. To remove causes of present and future controversies.

5. To secure the expeditious agricultural and industrial development of the Colorado River Basin.

6. To store water for use as needed.

7. To protect life and property from floods.[1]

It is the opinion of the National Resources Committee, arrived at after considerable study, that the Colorado River Compact is a disappointment to proponents of the compact method. When the commissioners first met, there were two factors that practically precluded any final and mutual agreement. None of the states knew or was willing to say with exactness what its future needs for water might be, and each state was interested in driving the most favorable bargain. The compact has not accomplished its original purpose: the division of water between each of the states; nor has anything been done, except to initiate basic

[1] *Ibid.*, p. 69.

resource studies, to promote the expeditious agricultural and industrial development of the Colorado River Basin, to store water for use as needed, or to protect life and property from floods. The only matter really provided for by the compact was the protection of one group of states from future encroachments by other states. So far as the compact method as applied in this particular case is concerned, the National Resources Committee found it to be impractical when there is not sufficient knowledge at hand upon which to base decisions; when the subject of the compact is so related to extraneous factors that the problem requires continuous consideration in the light of changing conditions; and when its purpose is to encourage the development of an area, and the compacting parties are unwilling to relinquish to an agency of the compact the authority necessary to accomplish the purpose.[1]

We have considered here two examples of the compact method: one between two states only and dealing with relatively simple problems requiring continuous administration; the other involving fundamental issues of policy of several states. These are not cited as illustrative of all types of interstate compacts or especially of compacts that would have to be developed to deal with the regulation of interstate commerce in gas or electricity. They do illustrate, however, defects in the compact method that we believe render it an unsatisfactory device for the solution of such problems. If obstacles are encountered that render the drawing up of compacts to govern such matters of interstate policy or planning difficult, even impossible, how much more difficult it would be to draw up a compact to provide the administrative flexibility necessary to meet conditions that change rapidly and continuously.

Aside from the fact that a compact must be agreed upon and ratified by the individual states and by Congress, which renders initial adoption and amendment slow and difficult, it must be drawn up to meet an uncertain future. In fields of human activity where changes are rapid and continuous, by the time a compact was drawn up or amended, conditions might have so changed as to render its provisions largely inapplicable unless broad administrative powers were granted. The recent history of the gas and electric utility industries has been replete with

[1] *Ibid.*, p. 70.

changes that have modified radically techniques of production
and have broadened the scope of operations of individual units.
On top of this have come holding companies which have spread
networks of control over operating units covering wide areas,
the patterns of which have continually changed. In fact, these
very developments have created the problems for which a solution
is sought. Regulation to be effective must keep pace with
such changes, and the powers and duties of regulatory bodies
must be broadened or modified to meet new problems as they
arise.

The main purposes sought to be accomplished by interstate
compacts for the regulation of interstate commerce in gas and
electric energy would be the determination of costs and the
reasonableness of the wholesale rates charged companies engaged
in distribution to ultimate consumers, as well as the reasonableness of intercompany payments for services, supplies, etc.
How these ends could be achieved under changing conditions by a
device as inflexible as the compact it is difficult to see. Changes
in ownership or control, as well as in the organization of the
services, could be utilized readily by those interested in obstruct-
ing regulation, where the scope of regulatory powers would of
necessity be defined in the compact. This device is most likely
to be successful in cases where autonomous administration is
possible, not where successful administration requires adequate
authority, opportunity for initiative, and flexibility. It has
been suggested that Congress might delegate broad administrative authority under the compact scheme[1] and in this way retain
the advantages of regional control, but the ramifications of
interconnection and the widespread activities of holding companies cross so many state boundaries that for the most part
these problems have become national in scope and importance.
It seems logical, therefore, since the powers of the Federal
Government must be invoked in any case, that the regulation
of interstate commerce in gas and electricity should be placed
in the hands of a federal commission. This Congress has done
with respect to interstate commerce in electricity, although for
some illogical reason such authority was not extended to the

[1] *Cf.*, DONOVAN, W. J., "Regulation of Interstate Transmission of Gas
and Electricity," an address before the American Bar Association, September, 1931.

interstate transmission of gas.   We shall turn now to an analysis of the powers of the Federal Power Commission over the interstate transmission of electric energy as provided in the public Utility Act of 1935.

PROVISIONS OF THE PUBLIC UTILITY ACT OF 1935 WITH RESPECT TO FEDERAL REGULATION OF ELECTRIC UTILITY COMPANIES ENGAGED IN INTERSTATE COMMERCE

As has been said, the Public Utility Act of 1935 is in fact two acts in one.   Title I, discussed in Chap. XI, applies to gas and electric holding companies, while Title II deals with the regulation of interstate transmission of electric energy.   Title II is divided further into three parts.   Part I amends and broadens the powers of the Federal Power Commission over licensees of the Federal Government under the Federal Water Power Act (these amendments are discussed more fully in Chap. XV).   Part II contains the provisions regarding the regulation of electric companies engaged in interstate commerce; and Part III, various procedural and administrative provisions applicable both to licensees under the Federal Water Power Act and to electric utility companies engaged in interstate commerce.   The provisions of Part II of Title II apply to the transmission of electric energy in interstate commerce and to the sale of electric energy at wholesale but not to any other sale of electric energy, nor do they deprive any state or state commission of its lawful authority now exercised over the exportation of hydroelectric energy transmitted across a state line.

The Federal Power Commission is given jurisdiction over all facilities for the interstate transmission or sale of electric energy but, unless expressly provided for in Parts II and III of Title II, not over facilities used for the generation of electric energy, or over facilities used in local distribution only or for the transmission of electric energy in intrastate commerce, or over facilities for the transmission of electric energy consumed wholly by the transmitter.   Electric energy is held to be transmitted in interstate commerce if transmitted from a state and consumed at any point outside thereof but only in so far as such transmission takes place within the United States.   "Sale of electric energy at wholesale" means sale to any person for resale.   The provisions of Part II do not apply to publicly owned plants; any agency, authority, or instrumentality of the United States; a state or any political subdivision of a state; or any corporation that is wholly owned, directly or indirectly, by any such governmental authority.[1]

1. Interconnection and Coordination of Facilities.—In order to insure an abundant supply of electric energy throughout the United States with the greatest possible economy and with regard to the proper utilization and conservation of natural resources, the Federal Power Commission is given authority to divide the country into regional districts, each of which shall embrace an area that in the judgment of the Commission can economically be served by properly interconnected and coordinated electric facilities. This shall be done, however, only after the Commission shall have given each state situated wholly or in part within such a district reasonable opportunity to present its views and recommendations and shall have received and considered such views and recommendations. The Commission is to encourage and promote voluntary interconnection and coordination of facilities for the generation, transmission, and sale of electric energy; and it is given authority, upon application by any state commission or by any person engaged in the transmission or sale of electric energy, by order to direct a public utility to establish physical connection of its facilities with one or more other persons engaged in the transmission or sale of electric energy or to sell energy to or exchange energy with such persons, if it finds such action necessary or appropriate in the public interest and that no undue burden will be placed upon such public utility thereby. The Commission is given no authority to compel the enlargement of generating facilities for such purposes, however, or to compel a public utility to sell or exchange energy if to do so would impair its ability to render adequate service to its customers. The Commission may prescribe the terms and conditions of such arrangements, including the apportionment of cost between the companies and the compensation or reimbursement reasonably due to any of them.[2]

In the case of any war in which the United States is engaged, or whenever the Commission determines that an emergency exists by reason of a sudden increase in the demand for electric energy

[1] Section 201.
[2] Section 202 (a) and (b).

or a shortage of electric energy or of facilities for generation and transmission or of fuel or water or other causes, the Commission may, upon its own motion or upon complaint, require such temporary connections and such generation, delivery, interchange, or transportation as it deems necessary to meet such emergency. After six months from the effective date of the Act no person is permitted to transmit any electric energy from the United States to a foreign country without first having secured an order of the Commission authorizing it to do so. The Commission may deny an application for such authority if it finds that the proposed transmission would impair the sufficiency of electric supply within the United States or would impede the coordination in the public interest of facilities subject to the jurisdiction of the Commission; or it may grant the authority in whole or in part or upon such terms as it deems necessary or appropriate.[1]

These clauses give to the Commission broad powers over the organization and interconnection of electric power systems both under normal circumstances and during an emergency. They are designed to bring the networks more nearly into conformity with the requirements of economy and efficiency than many competent observers contend has been achieved in certain cases under holding-company control and to provide a national system which will not break down in war or other emergency. The voluntary feature is an important one in that it sets up a procedure designed to employ first and primarily those whose interests are directly affected in bringing about changes in existing interconnection networks. Such changes as are necessary in the public interest can best be effected by cooperation between the Commission and the companies, since in this way many obstructive practices can be avoided. Compulsion may be necessary, but it should be employed only as a last resort.

2. **Disposition of Property; Consolidations; Security Issues.**—Section 203 provides that no public utility shall sell, lease, or otherwise dispose of the whole of its facilities subject to the jurisdiction of the Federal Power Commission, or any part thereof of a value in excess of $50,000, or by any means whatsoever, directly or indirectly, merge or consolidate such facilities with those of any other person, without the consent of the

[1] Section 202 (c) and (e).

Commission. It is provided also that the Federal Power Commission shall give reasonable notice of applications for authority under this section to the governor and state commission of each state in which physical property affected is situated, thus providing for consultation with state authorities in matters that may be of interest or importance to them.

The provisions of Section 204 give to the Commission full authority over the issuance of securities and assumption of obligations by public utilities owning or operating facilities subject to the jurisdiction of the Commission. However, to avoid duplication of regulation these provisions are not made applicable to a public utility organized and operating in a state under the laws of which its security issues are regulated by a state commission. A further provision designed to avoid duplication of regulation as well as unnecessary labor and expense on the part of the companies enables any public utility whose securities have been approved by the Commission to file with the Securities and Exchange Commission duplicate copies of reports filed with the Federal Power Commission in lieu of the reports, information, and documents required under Section 7 of the Securities Act of 1933 and Sections 12 and 13 of the Securities and Exchange Act of 1934. The specific provisions with regard to security issues are similar to those in state laws which have been discussed previously (see Chap. X). They do not apply to notes or other obligations of a maturity of not more than one year, aggregating together with all other such notes or obligations outstanding not more than 5 per cent of the par value of the other securities of the public utility then outstanding. The Commission may not authorize the capitalization of the right to be a corporation or of any franchise, permit, or contract for consolidation, merger, or lease in excess of the amount (exclusive of any tax or annual charge) actually paid as the consideration for such right, franchise, permit, or contract.

3. **Rates and Charges.**—All rates and charges, and all rules and regulations affecting or pertaining thereto, in connection with the transmission or sale of electric energy subject to the jurisdiction of the Commission shall be just and reasonable. There shall be no undue preference or advantage, nor any unreasonable difference in rates, charges, service, or facilities, either as between localities or as between classes of service.

Schedules of all rates and charges for any transmission or sale, subject to the jurisdiction of the Commission, shall be filed with the Commission and kept open in convenient form and place for public inspection. Unless the Commission otherwise orders, no change may be made in any such rate, charge, classification, or service or in any rule, regulation, or contract relating thereto, except after 30 days' notice to the Commission. The Commission, either upon complaint or upon its own initiative, may suspend the operation of any new schedule pending a hearing and decision as to its reasonableness. Such suspension may not be for a longer period than five months beyond the time such schedule otherwise would go into effect. If the proceeding shall not have been concluded within the specified time, the new schedule will go into effect, but the Commission may require the utility to keep a separate accounting to the end that if later the schedule is found to be unreasonable, appropriate restitution may be made to the rate payers. The burden of proof to show that an increased rate or charge is just and reasonable rests upon the public utility. The Commission has full authority to determine and fix just and reasonable rates and charges.[1] Section 206 provides also that the Commission, upon its own motion or upon request by any state commission, may investigate and determine the cost of the production or transmission of electric energy by means of facilities under the jurisdiction of the Commission in cases where the Commission has no authority to establish a rate governing the sale of such energy.

Section 208 provides that the Commission may investigate and ascertain the actual legitimate cost of the property of every public utility subject to its jurisdiction; the depreciation therein; and, when necessary for rate-making purposes, other facts that bear upon the determination of such cost or depreciation and the fair value of such property. To facilitate such determinations the Commission may require every public utility subject to its jurisdiction to file an inventory of all or any part of its property, together with a statement of the original cost thereof, and to keep the Commission informed regarding the cost of all additions, betterments, extensions, and new construction.

4. Adequate Service.—Section 207 empowers the Commission, but only upon complaint of a state commission and after notice

[1] Section 205, and Section 206 (a).

to each state commission and public utility affected and after opportunity for hearing, if it finds that any interstate service of any public utility subject to its jurisdiction is inadequate or insufficient, to determine the proper, adequate, or sufficient service to be furnished and to fix the same by its order, rule, or regulation. The Commission's jurisdiction over service, however, does not include authority to compel the enlargement of generating facilities for such purposes or to compel a public utility to sell or exchange energy when to do so would impair its ability to render adequate service to its customers.

5. **Cooperation with State Commissions.**—As has been pointed out, much of the opposition by state commissions to federal regulation of interstate commerce in gas and electricity grew out of a real fear that the Federal Commission would usurp some of their functions or that its regulations and requirements would conflict with those promulgated by themselves. That there is the possibility of duplicate, even conflicting, requirements by state and federal commissions with respect to accounting practices, security issues, service, and many practices of public utilities subject to both jurisdictions is clear. An important feature of Title II, Part II, of the Public Utility Act of 1935, therefore, is the extent to which Congress has attempted to demarcate the appropriate spheres of federal and state jurisdiction. However, the border lines of these spheres cannot be sharply delineated, and reliance must often be placed upon cooperation between federal and state bodies in dealing with common problems. No better illustration of this can be found than in the field of railroad regulation. Here the Interstate Commerce Commission has developed a system of cooperation with state commissions in railroad matters which other federal commissions facing similar problems may well use as a model. Fortunately the Public Utility Act of 1935 provides the legal basis for such cooperation in the regulation of interstate commerce in electric energy.

Section 209 provides that the Federal Power Commission may refer any matter arising in the administration of Part II to a board composed of a member or members, as determined by the Commission, from the state or from each of the states affected by such matter. Any such board is vested with the same power and is subject to the same duties and liabilities as in the case of a member of the Commission when designated by the Commission to hold any hearings, and the action of such board shall have such force and effect as the Commission shall prescribe. The board shall be appointed by the Commission from persons nominated by the commission of each state affected or by the governor if there is no state commission, and each state affected is entitled to the same number of representatives on the board, unless it waives such right. The Commission may, however, revoke any reference to such a board whenever it believes sufficient reason exists therefor. The practical value of such joint boards is that full advantage may be taken of the superior knowledge of local conditions possessed by the state commissions in arriving at decisions, and in formulating orders that can be made effective where interstate matters are involved only by authority of the Federal Commission.

The Commission also is authorized to confer with any state commission regarding the relationship between rate structures, costs, accounts, charges, practices, classifications, and regulations of public utilities subject to both federal and state jurisdiction and to hold joint hearings with any state commission concerning any matter with respect to which the Commission is authorized to act. The Commission may make available to state commissions such information and reports as may be of assistance in state regulation of public utilities and may make available, upon request from a state, to such state as witnesses any of its trained rate, valuation, or other experts. Thus is provided a broad legal basis for cooperation between the Federal Power Commission and state commissions in the regulation of the interstate transmission of electric energy. It remains for the commissions themselves to develop the details of procedure necessary to make such cooperation effective.

6. **Accounts; Records; Depreciation.**—In Part III of Title II the Federal Power Commission is authorized to require all licensees under the Federal Water Power Act and all electric utilities subject to its jurisdiction to make and keep such accounts, records of cost-accounting procedures, correspondence, memo-randa, papers, books, and other records as it may deem necessary or appropriate for purposes of administration of the Act, including accounts, records, and memoranda of the generation, trans-mission, distribution, delivery, or sale of electric energy; the

furnishing of services or facilities in connection therewith; and receipts and expenditures. The Commission may prescribe a system of accounts to be kept by licensees and public utilities subject to its jurisdiction and may classify such licensees and public utilities and prescribe a system of accounts for each class. In addition, it is empowered to determine the accounts in which particular outlays and receipts shall be entered, charged, or credited; and the burden of proof to justify every accounting entry questioned by the Commission is placed upon the person making, authorizing, or requiring such entry. The Commission is granted, at all times, access to and the right to inspect and examine all accounts, records, and memoranda of licensees and public utilities subject to its jurisdiction and is authorized to require by order any information with respect thereto. Similar authority is granted the Commission with respect to the books, accounts, memoranda, and records of any person who controls, directly or indirectly, a licensee or public utility subject to its jurisdiction and of any other company controlled by such person, in so far as they relate to transactions with or the business of such licensee or public utility.[1]

The Commission is authorized also to require licensees and public utilities subject to its jurisdiction to carry proper and adequate depreciation accounts; and from time to time to ascertain, determine, and by order fix the proper and adequate rates of depreciation of the several classes of property. No such licensee or public utility shall charge to operating expenses any depreciation charges on classes of property or any percentage of depreciation, other than those prescribed by the Commission.[2]

These clauses give the Federal Power Commission the necessary authority to obtain from licensees and public utilities subject to its jurisdiction the facts essential to intelligent and effective regulation, but they raise important questions of overlapping jurisdiction. The law specifically states, and it would be true without such statement, that nothing in the Act shall relieve any public utility from keeping any accounts, memoranda, or records that it may be required to keep by or under the laws of any state, nor does the Act limit the power of a state commission in the exercise of its jurisdiction over such utilities to

[1] Section 301 (a), (b), and (c).
[2] Section 302.

determine the percentage rate of depreciation to be allowed as to any class of property, or the composite depreciation rate, for the purpose of determining rates or charges. The Act provides that before prescribing rates of depreciation the Commission shall notify each state commission having jurisdiction with respect to the public utility involved and shall receive and consider such views and recommendations as may be presented by such state commissions; but the authority for separate action by the Federal Power Commission with respect to accounts, records, and depreciation is clear, and in this situation lie possibilities of duplicate or conflicting requirements not in the public interest. That this is not solely an academic matter is evidenced by the recent conflict between the Federal Communications Commission and the New York Public Service Commission with respect to accounting systems for telephone companies and the difficulties experienced by the Interstate Commerce Commission in determining depreciation charges for railroad and telephone property. For the Federal Commission to require a utility to keep a different system of accounts than that required of the same utility by a state commission is to impose needless burdens upon the utility for the attainment of little, if any, public good; and the determination of different rates of depreciation by two such authorities for similar property operated under the same or similar conditions would create a situation in which fair and equitable regulation from the viewpoint both of the consumers and of the companies would be difficult to achieve. Effective regulation requires that the Federal Commission have such powers, but equitable treatment of all concerned demands that these common problems be dealt with by the federal and state commissions in a spirit of wholehearted cooperation.

7. **Miscellaneous Provisions.**—Part III contains many other procedural and administrative provisions defining the nature and scope of the authority of the Federal Power Commission over its licensees and the public utilities subject to its jurisdiction, a few of which we shall briefly mention. It is made unlawful for the officers or directors of a public utility subject to the jurisdiction of the Commission to receive money or anything of value in respect of the negotiation, hypothecation, or sale of the securities of such utility or to participate in the making or paying of any dividends of such utility from any funds properly included

in capital accounts. Interlocking directorates are prohibited, except as permitted by the Commission. Provision is made by which complaints may be brought against utilities not observing the law and for the investigation of the matters complained of by the Commission if the complaint shall not have been satisfied by the utility after due notice and the lapse of a reasonable time. The Commission is authorized to make investigations and in so doing to hold hearings, call witnesses, and take depositions. Provision is made for rehearings and court review of commission orders and for the enforcement of the Act and the regulations and orders of the Commission.

The chief benefits to be expected from federal regulation of interstate commerce in electric energy may be summarized as follows:

1. It should prevent rate discriminations which companies sometimes have perpetuated in one state at the expense of consumers in another state, as in the Attleboro case.

2. It should prevent the charging of exorbitant wholesale rates to intrastate distributing companies by interstate generating and transmission companies formerly not subject to rate regulation, since the Federal Power Commission is authorized, upon the request of any state commission, to investigate the cost of the production and transmission of electric energy in interstate commerce.

3. It should assist the fact-finding function of regulation by the requirement of uniform accounting procedure on the part of interstate utilities, since different and conflicting accounting systems have militated against the full disclosure of facts essential to effective regulation.

Title II of the Public Utility Act of 1935 is designed to supplement and to make more effective state regulation of electric utilities and to provide the basis of cooperation where cooperation between state and federal commissions is necessary. Rate control by the Federal Power Commission is limited to control over interstate wholesale rates, which are constitutionally beyond the powers of states to regulate. This Commission may not regulate local rates, and the Act confers upon it no authority to regulate intrastate rates under the doctrine of the Shreveport case, *i.e.*, to regulate intrastate rates which adversely affect interstate rates. The clauses providing for the fullest measure of cooperation between the federal and the state commissions should accomplish much by way of eliminating jurisdictional controversies.

THE NEED FOR REGULATION OF INTERSTATE COMMERCE IN NATURAL GAS

It has been pointed out that while the manufactured gas industry has remained essentially local and intrastate in character, with a few important exceptions, the interstate operations of natural gas companies are widespread and of great volume, owing principally to the discovery of huge deposits in limited areas and the transmission through long pipe lines of natural gas to many and widely scattered consuming areas. In this industry there are many illustrations of complete corporate differentiation of the functions of (1) gas recovery from the ground, (2) transmission from the fields to centers of consumption, and (3) local distribution to ultimate consumers; but it is significant from the standpoint of regulation that the same holding company may, and often does, control all three types of corporations, operating them as a single system. The opportunity thus created for exorbitant or unfair profits from intercompany transactions is clear, and it is one that unscrupulous holding companies have not been loath to utilize. The Federal Trade Commission found it characteristic of the natural gas holding companies which it examined that strictly distribution subsidiaries showed small returns, while producing and transmission pipe-line companies, selling gas at wholesale to the local utilities and to industries, showed good profits.[1]

The importance of this matter to ultimate consumers of natural gas is that reasonable rates are dependent upon reasonable "gate" or wholesale rates, since it is axiomatic under our system of regulation that rates must cover all legitimate costs and yield a fair return on the fair value of the property. But since the cost of the gas is the principal element of cost for a natural gas distributing company, it is equally true that protection of the consumers cannot be complete or effective without control of the wholesale rate by the same authority or by authorities with competent jurisdiction working in cooperation with each other. So far as affiliated transmission and distributing natural

[1] Utility Corporations, *op. cit.*, p. 853.

gas companies are concerned, under the decision of the Supreme Court in the Western Distributing Company case, a state commission having jurisdiction over the distributing company may inquire into all costs, including the cost of the gas. But a state commission may not fix a reasonable interstate rate; and although it may not allow the full charges made by the wholesale company in its calculations of allowable deductions before fair return, such procedure could not do otherwise than to raise problems for the distributing company, unless the wholesale company were to reduce its rate in conformity with the findings of the state commission. To earn a fair return where a commission should find the wholesale rate too high, but the wholesale company would refuse to lower it, the distributing company would be forced to reduce costs somehow, either by neglect of maintenance or depreciation or by other practices which eventually would result in inferior service.

A further complicating problem is created where a transmission company supplies distributing companies in two or more states. Two or more state commissions inquiring independently into the cost of gas delivered to the different distributing companies under their jurisdictions would in all likelihood arrive at confusing and inequitable determinations, since, in addition to the costs that could be directly allocated, it would be necessary also to include a proper proportion of the joint costs incurred in the performance of all services in determining the total cost of supplying a given utility with gas. The confusion that might result from the application of different theories of cost allocation and varying opinions as to the amounts to be allocated in each individual case would be most unfortunate. Uniformity is required for equitable treatment of all parties concerned, and this can be attained only by placing the wholesale rate under the jurisdiction of a single authority, which, of necessity, in the absence of a compact or similar means of cooperation between state commission, would have to be a federal authority.

In cases where there is no affiliation between transmission and distribution companies, it is established by Supreme Court decisions that neither the state in which the natural gas is produced nor the state in which it is distributed to the ultimate consumers has jurisdiction over the interstate rate. Certainly it must be conceded that in such cases, regulation of the interstate rate by the Federal Government is an essential concomitant of effective regulation to protect the ultimate consumers.

The necessity for federal regulation of interstate commerce in gas, manufactured and natural, is fully appreciated by the state commissioners themselves. At the annual convention of the National Association of Railroad and Utilities Commissioners, in 1935, a resolution was unanimously adopted endorsing legislation to this effect. This resolution pointed out, whereas the business of the transmission and sale of gas in interstate commerce at wholesale for resale, under the decisions of the Supreme Court, was not subject to regulation by the states, that, in the absence of federal legislation, it was wholly unregulated and there was no way for public authorities to determine whether or not such gas was being obtained by distributing companies at just and reasonable prices.[1] For Congress to set up machinery to regulate interstate commerce in electricity and to leave interstate commerce in natural gas unregulated is inconsistent and incongruous. Early drafts of the Public Utility Act of 1935 contained a third title which would have provided federal regulation of interstate transmission of gas, but this title was eliminated when the law was enacted. It is to be hoped that Congress will soon correct this deficiency in regulatory machinery.

References

JONES, ELIOT, and T. C. BIGHAM: "Principles of Public Utilities," The Macmillan Company, New York, 1931.

McNINCH, F. R.: The Evolution of Federal Control of Electric Power, *Journal of Land and Public Utility Economics*, vol. 12, No. 2.

MOSHER, W. E., and F. G. CRAWFORD: "Public Utility Regulation," Harper & Brothers, New York, 1933.

National Resources Committee: Regional Factors in National Planning, 1935.

TROXEL, C. E.: Long-Distance Natural Gas Pipe Lines, *Journal of Land and Public Utility Economics*, vol. 12, No. 4.

————: Regulation of Interstate Gas Transmission, *Journal of Land and Public Utilities Economics*, vol. 13, No. 1.

Utility Corporations, Sen. Doc. 92, 70th Cong., 1st Sess., Part 72-A.

[1] National Association of Railroad and Utilities Commissioners, *Proceedings*, 1935, pp. 417–418.

CHAPTER XV

NATIONAL POWER POLICY AND THE FEDERAL POWER COMMISSION

The Problem and Nature of Conservation.—The conservation of water power resources is a challenging problem. Water has been a major factor in giving us a high order of economic development. There exists a twofold problem of adjusting water resources to the use and convenience of man and of adjusting man's activities to the limitations imposed by these same resources. "Planning for the use and control of water," states the National Resources Board, "is planning for most of the basic functions of the life of the nation. We cannot plan intelligently for water unless we consider the relevant problems of the land. We cannot plan intelligently for water and land together unless we plan in terms of collective interests."[1]

The National Resources Board has also pointed out that the key to the beneficial use and control of the waters of the country is to be found in recognition of four unities, viz.:

1. *Unity of physical factors* which involves the relationship between precipitation and drainage and the relationship between water and other physical factors created in the functioning of the hydrologic cycle.

2. *Unity of man's interests* which involves the collective interest of society in the use and control of water systems.

3. *Unity of responsibility* which involves protection of the common interests in the multiple uses of water.

4. *Unity of action* which involves the formulation and carrying through of a plan designed for the greatest good of all.[2]

The utilization, development, and control of water resources thus present complicated problems, much of the complexity being due to the multiplicity of uses of water resources. Until recently, it has been the common practice to approach a water

[1] National Resources Board, *Report*, Dec. 1, 1934, p. 260.
[2] *Ibid.*, pp. 260 *ff.*

resource with a view to utilizing it for one specific purpose such as the elimination of a flood hazard, the improvement of navigation, the provision of irrigation, or the generation of hydroelectric power. Frequently, however, the achievement of some one given objective could be promoted by combining other objectives with it. Such combinations, however, may present many difficulties and involve conflicts between private and public interests.

The full conservation of water resources thus involves consideration of all the potential uses of the resource and the inclusion of all such uses in the development for the purpose of securing the greatest total benefit and of making the cost of each component part less than it otherwise would be. Involved also in the problem of conservation of water resources is the peculiar factor that to conserve means to use. Every pound of coal or every barrel of petroleum used means the exhaustion by just that much of a nonreplaceable resource. But, because of the hydrologic cycle, water resources are generally recurring. To fail to make use of them today means just that much potential use irrevocably lost. This applies particularly to the generation of electricity from the force of running water—unless the force of the fall of the water is used today, that particular force is lost forever.

The scope of this volume will not permit the discussion of the conservation of water resources other than the conservation of water power. Attention will be given to other problems of water resources only in so far as they are directly related to water power. The present chapter discusses water power resources from the standpoint of the development of a national power policy and the creation of the Federal Power Commission as an administrative agency to carry out the national power policy. The following chapter will develop the water power resources from the standpoint of government projects designed to make use of them.

Federal Authority over Water Resources.—In the delegation of powers to the Federal Government, the Constitution provides that the Congress shall have power "to regulate commerce with foreign Nations and among the several states."[1] This provision vests control over navigable streams in Congress. In so far as power sites on the public domain are concerned, they fall

[1] Article I, Section 8.

under the jurisdiction of Congress in the power granted it "to dispose of and make all needful rules and regulations respecting the territory or other property belonging to the United States."[1]

Exercise of Federal Control over Water Resources.—Albert Gallatin, while Secretary of the Treasury, in 1808, prepared a report in which it was recommended that Congress construct, as a part of a comprehensive plan of internal improvements, a series of canals and turnpikes along the Atlantic Coast. From that time on, Congress has acted in various ways concerning the navigable and public domain waters of the United States. Surveys of the tributaries of the Mississippi were authorized in 1819, and surveys for canals in various parts of the country were authorized in 1824. Because of the great importance of transportation to the scattered populations in the then United States and because of the recognized need for improved and cheap agencies of transportation, the factor of navigation was given sole consideration during this early period. Other uses were not then important. Abundant rainfall in the seaboard states made irrigation an unimportant need; and because of the heavy vegetation which held the waters back, as well as the fact that there were no concentrated urban populations as exist today, the dangers of floods were minimized, and flood control was scarcely necessary. Electricity was unknown so that the only water power problems were those of utilizing direct power from water wheels. In view of these situations, it is not surprising that Congress emphasized transportation developments and made grants of public lands and loans from the Treasury to aid in the vast waterway and canal development of the period from about 1825 to 1840. Congress itself carried out none of these projects; it was done by the states or state-chartered corporations.[2]

---

[1] Article IV, Section 3.

[2] For a summary of the Congressional enactments covering water power, see *Congressional Digest*, "The Federal Government and Water Power, 1788–1930," vol. 15, No. 10, pp. 227 *ff.* The present discussion has made extensive use of this summary, and, unless otherwise noted, the quotations in this and the following subsection of this chapter are from legislation, etc., as there quoted. A similar summary is contained in the first *Annual Report* of the Federal Power Commission at pp. 44 *ff.* An extensive study of legislation on this subject is that of J. G. Kerwin, "Federal Water Power Legislation," Columbia University Press, New York, 1926. A survey of the development of the national power policy is contained in F. R. McNinch,

After a more general settlement of the western states, other water uses became important. Farmers and miners in the west had appropriated waters, used streams, and built ditches much as they pleased for mining and irrigation needs. Many conflicting claims arose which were settled by local custom and by local courts and laws. Congressional recognition of these uses of water in so far as navigable streams were involved was contained in an act passed in 1866 which confirmed the rights to water thus settled and authorized further acquisition of water rights by individuals for "mining, agricultural, manufacturing, and other purposes." Further recognition of these rights was made in 1870 when Congress declared that vested rights in public lands for irrigation ditches and canals would be effective against subsequent patentees.

It was not until 1884 and afterward that the Federal Government exercised extensively its authority over navigable streams. In that year, the Secretary of War was directed to report whether bridges or structures over or in navigable streams were interfering with navigation. This step was followed in 1890 with the enactment of a law providing that "the creation of any obstruction, not affirmatively authorized by law, to the navigable capacity of any waters, in respect of which the United States has jurisdiction, is hereby prohibited." Pursuant to the provisions of this law, an Act of Congress is required to authorize the construction of a bridge, dam, or other structure on navigable streams.

Recording of claims to water rights on the public domain was required in an act passed in 1891 and amended in 1895. These two acts authorized the Secretary of the Interior to grant rights of way on the public domain for ditches, canals, and reservoirs, primarily for irrigation and incidentally for power. These acts officially recognized the hydroelectric developments that had been started in the early 1890's and which presented many new problems. Lands acquired for hydroelectric dams were held by trespass or under statutes not designed for this purpose, and power companies were active in getting possession of power sites by homestead claims, purchase, or

Federal Control of Electric Power, *Journal of Land and Public Utility Economics*, vol. 12, No. 2, pp. 111 *ff*.

otherwise. To bring some order out of the chaos then developing, the Secretary of the Interior was authorized, in 1896, under general regulations to be fixed by him, "to permit the use of a right of way, not exceeding 40 acres, upon public lands and forest reservations, for the purpose of generating, manufacturing, and distributing electric power." This, in turn, was superseded, in 1901, by an act that clarified the powers of the Secretary of the Interior and authorized him to grant rights of way for "electrical plants, poles, and lines for the generation and distribution of electrical power." From the standpoint of the electrical industry, this legislation was unsatisfactory because the permits issued thereunder were revocable at will. The Agricultural Appropriation Act of 1911 changed this condition by authorizing the Secretary to grant easements or rights of way, for a period not exceeding 50 years, for electrical poles and lines over federal public lands, forests, and reservations.

Congress, in the General Dam Act of 1906, enacted its first general legislation fixing the conditions attaching to power authorizations on navigable streams. In each such authorization, plans and specifications were to be approved by the Chief of Engineers and the Secretary of War, who could at any time require the grantee to construct, maintain, and operate, without expense to the United States, locks and other navigation facilities or to grant any land needed and free power for the operation of such facilities if constructed by the Government. Authority was reserved to the Government to construct locks in the dam and to control water discharges and pool levels. Grantees were required to maintain, at their own expense, lights, signals, and fishways. Construction must be started in one year and completed within three years. No time limit was placed on the duration of grants, but they could be repealed by Congress, and, in the case of refusal to comply with orders of the Chief of Engineers or the Secretary of War, any dam could be removed by the Government at the expense of the grantee and without compensation.

Thus, Congress had, by this time, declared the nature of its control over water power sites. Actually, however, but few restrictions were placed upon grantees, and the policy was not well defined, in that the Secretaries of War, Interior, and Agriculture each had been given some control over power sites.

At the same time, there were many who were demanding more definite control on the part of the Federal Government.

Emergence of a Water Power Policy.—In compliance with the Act of 1906, many special acts were passed by Congress authorizing the construction of water power dams on navigable streams. One such act, providing for an extension of time for completion of the Rainey River Power Company's dam and power plant, came before President Theodore Roosevelt in 1908. Shortly before, the President had notified the Senate Committee on Interstate Commerce that no water power bills would be approved unless they provided for a government charge and a time limit for completion. Since this special Act contained no such provision, it was vetoed.[1] President Theodore Roosevelt, in his veto message, voiced his opinion as to the need for and principles of a national power policy as follows:

We are now at the beginning of a great development in water power. Its use in electrical transmission is entering more and more largely in every element of the daily life of the people. Already the evils of monopoly are becoming manifest; already the spirit of the past shows the necessity of caution in making unrestricted grants of power.

The present policy pursued in making these grants is unwise in giving away the property of the people in the flowing waters to individuals or organizations practically unknown, and granting in perpetuity these valuable privileges in advance of the formulation of definite plans as to their use. In some cases, the grantees apparently have little or no financial or other ability to utilize the gift and have sought it merely because it could be had for the asking.

In place of the present haphazard policy of permanently alienating valuable public property, we should substitute a definite policy along the following lines:

First, there should be a limited or carefully guarded grant in the nature of an option or opportunity afforded within reasonable time for development of the plant and for execution of the project.

Second, such a grant or concession should be accompanied, in the act making the grant, by a provision expressly making it the duty of the designated official to annul the grant if the grant is not begun or plans are not carried out in accordance with the authority granted.

---

[1] Subsequent to this veto, it was disclosed that the Rainey River Power Company had started construction prior to 1906 but had voluntarily accepted the provisions of the Act of 1906, had made heavy investments in the dam, and had suffered delays due to forces beyond its control. The Act was passed over the veto at the request of the President.

Third, it should also be the duty of some designated official to see to it that in approving the plans the maximum development of the navigation and power is assured, or at least that in making the plans these may not be so developed as ultimately to interfere with the better utilization of the water or complete development of the power.

Fourth, there should be a license fee or charge which, though small or nominal at the outset, can in the future be adjusted so as to secure a control in the interest of the public.

Fifth, provision should be made for the termination of the grant or privilege at a definite time, leaving to future generations the power or authority to renew or extend the concession in accordance with the conditions which may prevail at the time.

The demand for definite, restrictive control by the Government was beginning to receive more general support. It was not accepted, however, until after a bitter struggle. President Theodore Roosevelt continued to demand governmental restrictions and, as a leading exponent of conservation, restated his demands for the formulation and execution of a power policy. He believed that disastrous consequences would result from the failure to adopt regulatory control over water power developments. In his veto message, in 1909, of a measure to authorize the erection of a dam on the James River, Missouri, these consequences were stated to be:

The great corporations are acting with foresight, singleness of purpose, and vigor to control the water powers of the country. They pay no attention to State boundaries and are not interested in the constitutional law affecting navigable streams except as it affords what has aptly been called a "twilight zone," where they may find a convenient refuge from any regulation whatever. . . . They are demanding legislation for unconditional grants in perpetuity of land for reservoirs, conduits, powerhouses, and transmission lines to replace the existing statute which authorizes the administrative officers of the Government to impose conditions to protect the public when any permit is issued. Several bills for that purpose are now pending in both Houses. . . .

The new legislation sought in their own interest by some companies in the West, and the opposition of other companies in the East to proposed legislation in the public interest, have a common source and a common purpose. Their source is the rapidly growing water-power combination. Their purpose is centralized monopoly of hydroelectric power developments free of all public control. It is obvious that a monopoly of power in any community calls for strict public supervision and regulation.

I esteem it my duty to use every endeavor to prevent the growing monopoly, the most threatening which has ever appeared, from being fastened upon the people of this nation.

The power issue was now before the public and was receiving much attention. After the inauguration of President Taft, Congress again considered water power legislation and, in 1910, enacted a second General Dam Act which, in the nature of a compromise, amended the Act of 1906. The issue was argued during the presidential campaign of 1912, at which time Congress was considering a number of water power bills. After much partisan and intense debate, one of these bills authorizing the Alabama Power Company to build a dam across the Coosa River was passed. In vetoing it, President Taft stated:

If the Federal Government chooses to build this dam itself as an aid to navigation, its right to the water power incidentally created would be beyond question. When, instead of building the dam itself, it builds it by an agent, as proposed by this bill, I believe it to be equally clear that the dam and all its incidents, including the water power created, is within the regulative power of the Federal Government in respect to navigation.

The issues thus brought into the open took two directions of settlement. On the one hand, the Federal Government itself went into power production, the development of which is discussed in the next chapter. On the other hand, legislation looking toward federal control of water power projects by private companies was enacted. The struggle over this legislation, its content, changes, and present status is the subject of the remainder of this chapter.

The Issues Involved.—There are three major concepts as to the best method for developing the water power resources in the United States. These are:

1. The waters should be impounded, the power stations built, and the current generated and sold by the Government, either to consumers or to private companies which will distribute it to consumers. This concept, supported by those who believe generally in public ownership and operation of public utilities, also holds that irrigation, flood control, and navigation should be developed in coordination with power.

2. The development of water power should be left wholly to private industry which should be given a free hand to construct and operate generating plants and distribution lines. The only control necessary or desirable, this group believes, should be that exercised by the existing state regulatory commissions.

3. The title to the water power sites should be retained by the Government. Private companies should be permitted to develop them under lease. In this way, ownership and ultimate control are retained in the people.

The fight, during the first two decades of the twentieth century, was largely between those advocating private development and those advocating development by private interests under leases. Some agitation for public ownership and operation, engendered in connection with the Muscle Shoals project in Alabama, appeared on the horizon, but it did not have extensive support. This viewpoint came into prominence later, after support was given it by the Democratic Administration which came into office in 1933.

The demand for the retention of ownership of power sites in the public came largely from representatives of the Department of Interior, the Forest Service of the Department of Agriculture, and some congressional committees. The general nature of the demands of this group was expressed in the statements of Presidents Theodore Roosevelt and Taft, in their veto messages concerning several water power acts. On the other hand, opposition to governmental control and the demand for a free hand in the development of water power by private companies came from the states' rights advocates in the Far West and the South—both of which wanted rapid development of water power —and the electrical industry.

A bitter and protracted struggle took place, and, although the centering of interest in the World War detracted general public attention from the power issue, both interested groups continued to voice their demands. The United States Chamber of Commerce recognized the importance of the problem and, in 1918, held a referendum among its membership. The principles established thereby as being those which it believed should be embodied in legislation covering this subject follow:

1. That federal legislation to encourage the development of water powers should at once be enacted.

2. That authority to grant permits should be vested in an administrative department or commission.

3. That the permits should be at least 50 years in duration, any shorter period being at the applicant's option.

4. That tolls should attach only to use of public lands or benefits derived from headwater improvements.

5. That permittees should be entitled to acquire the right to use public lands forming only a small and incidental part of the development.

6. That recapture be exercised only upon payment of fair and just compensation.

7. That, if recapture is not exercised, the investment of the permittee should be adequately protected.

8. That rates and service should be regulated by state commissions where the service is intrastate, with federal regulation only where several states are directly concerned and do not agree, or where there is no state commission.

9. That if any jurisdiction to regulate the issuance of securities is exercised, it should be solely by the states.

10. That no preference should be granted as among applicants amounting to a subsidy from the government creating unequal competition.[1]

The Federal Water Power Act of 1920.—The proper control of water power resources means both the conservation of a valuable natural resource and the development of the electrical power latent in the streams and rivers. Congress recognized that regulation was necessary if these objectives were to be obtained. The problem was to reconcile the conflicting views of the conservationists and the water power interests. The resulting legislation on this subject, the Federal Water Power Act of 1920, which created the Federal Power Commission, was a compromise measure. It was, however, considered as marking "the end of the period of discussion and controversy which for more than a decade had been waged both in Congress and outside over national power policy with respect to water power under Federal control."[2] The act provided for privileges to be extended to private interests in the development of water

---

[1] BUTTERWORTH, WILLIAM, Business Regards a National Water Power Policy, *Public Utilities Fortnightly*, vol. 3, No. 6, pp. 322 *ff*.

[2] Federal Power Commission, *Annual Report*, 1920, p. 5.

power but at the same time hedged these privileges with restrictions designed to protect conservation of water resources and to protect the consumers of the generated power against exorbitant charges.

Provisions of the Act of 1920.—The Federal Water Power Act of 1920 provided for the creation of the Federal Power Commission to be composed of three ex-officio members: the Secretary of Agriculture, the Secretary of War, and the Secretary of the Interior. A full-time executive secretary, at a salary of $5,000 per year, was also provided. Each of the governmental departments whose secretaries composed the Commission, it will be recalled, had previously been given some jurisdiction and control over federal water power sites. It was provided, therefore, that the work of the Commission was to be performed by the engineering, technical, and clerical personnel of these departments.

The duties of the Commission were to collect data on the utilization of water-power resources and the power industry and to issue licenses for the development of water power on navigable streams or waters on the public lands of the United States. Licenses could be granted to either private or governmental agencies. The policy to be followed in granting licenses was stated in broad, general terms to be that the Commission should give preference to applications from states and municipalities if their plans were as well adapted as those of private applicants for conserving and utilizing the navigation and water resources of the region. As between private applicants, the Commission was directed to consider the relative ability of the applicants to carry out plans best suited to utilize water power resources in the public interest.

The duration of licenses to be granted for the construction of power projects on waters subject to federal jurisdiction could not be more than 50 years. At the expiration of the license period, the United States Government could take over the properties of a licensee, could permit them to be taken over by another, or could issue a new license to the original licensee. In the event that the property should be taken over at the expiration of the license period, the licensee must be paid his actual, legitimate net investment in the properties. The net investment was defined as the actual original cost plus additions and betterments and "severance damages" minus such unappropriated surplus or depreciation, amortization, and sinking fund reserves as had been accumulated during the license period in excess of a fair return on the investment.

The licensee was required to plan his project in conformity with a plan of development providing for the fullest reasonable utilization of the stream's resources. The plant was to be maintained in good operating condition, and replacements of worn-out or obsolete equipment made. Reasonable annual charges were to be assessed as the licensee's share in the cost of administration of the act and as a payment for the use of public land and property. A prescribed uniform system of accounting was to be kept.

The Federal Power Commission, though having sole authority concerning authorization of licenses and types of structures to be built, was given only conditional authority over the regulation of rates, services, and security issues of licensees. Only in the event that the state in which the project should be located did not regulate it or in the event that the several interested states could not agree was the Federal Power Commission given regulatory jurisdiction.

Administration of the Act of 1920.—Within several months after its creation, the Federal Power Commission had formulated and promulgated rules and regulations concerning forms of applications, permits, licenses, etc. It is interesting to note that from the beginning the cooperation and advice of the electrical industry were sought, and series of conferences were held preliminary to the adoption of rules and regulations. Subsequent conferences were held concerning questions of finance, and rules therefor were adopted early in 1921. With the new administration on Mar. 4, 1921, a new set of cabinet officers was installed as the ex-officio Federal Power Commission, and representatives of the electrical industry succeeded in reopening the question of requirements for accounting systems.

The Federal Power Commission apparently held a very conciliatory attitude. Its first *Annual Report* stated:

The cooperation which has been effected between the Commission and other agencies, such as the American Engineering Council, the National Electric Light Association and the National Association of Public Utility Commissioners, is the expression of a definite policy on the part of the Commission. It is charged under the law with the protection of the

public interest in the great national water power resources, and this is
its first duty. It is also its duty to encourage by every means the
development of these resources for public use and enjoyment and in the
interest of the country's economic progress. It believes that this
development can best be hastened through united action; and it stands
ready to cooperate with every agency, public or private, that is willing
to approach mutual problems in a spirit of cooperation.[1]

Private power interests advocated a very liberal interpretation
of the Act, and there is some evidence that the policy of seeking
their advice did not always result in complete protection of the
public interest. The Chief Accountant of the Federal Power
Commission stated:

While the rules and regulations of the commission were being considered, it was repeatedly asserted by representatives of the power
interests that they had a part in the preparation and passage of the
Federal Water Power Act; that they knew what was meant by certain
passages and provisions of the act and that Congress never intended
that the act should be construed and administered as proposed by
the commission's staff.[2]

The heart of the Federal Power Commission's authority hinged
on its control of the accounts of licensees. The auditing of the
records of investment had a twofold purpose: first, to aid the
Federal Power Commission and the state commissions in regulating rates and charges and, second, to fix the "net investment"
that the Government would have to pay if it were to take over the
property at the expiration dates of licenses. It is obvious that
it would be to the advantage of licensees to have liberal provisions
in the accounting rules. During the reopened conference
on this subject, the representatives of the private utilities
questioned the desirability of the policies previously determined
and attacked the law governing the Federal Power Commission.
At this juncture, the Federal Power Commission had prepared
an opinion interpreting the Water Power Act. The solicitors
of the Departments of War, Agriculture, and Interior reviewed
and approved this opinion, whereupon it was adopted by the
Federal Power Commission. Since the earlier adopted account-

---

[1] At pp. 19–20.
[2] Hearings, S. 3619 and Sen. Res. 80, 71st Cong., 2d Sess., 1930, p. 6.
Testimony of W. V. King.

ing regulations were in conformity with this interpretation, no changes in them were made. Further close harmony and cooperation with the electrical industry were deterred by these events.[1]

The work of the Federal Power Commission was hampered by administrative problems and difficulties. An ex-officio commission of cabinet members meant that the Commission itself was composed of political leaders unfamiliar with the problems presented and unable to give but little time to them. The shortness of their tenure in office and the impermanency of the commission membership made it practically impossible to formulate and carry out any consistent policy. These difficulties were magnified by the facts that the Federal Power Commission could employ directly only a few key employees and that its work had to be carried out by personnel loaned by the War, Agriculture, and Interior Departments, provisions to this effect being specified in the Act, and the Comptroller General ruling that assistance could not be procured elsewhere. The personnel assigned to the Federal Power Commission by these departments was inadequate to carry out the engineering and accounting work required, so that actually much of the work had to be "farmed out" to personnel in the several departments whose secretaries composed the Commission. There seems to have been no general cooperation among them, nor were they equipped to do the technically specialized work involved.[2]

Since the administrative difficulties were largely the result of defects in the law establishing the Commission and providing for its organization, requests for amendatory legislation and additional assistance were frequently made.[3]

Reorganization of the Commission, 1930.—President Hoover, in a message to Congress in December, 1929, recommended that the Federal Power Commission be reorganized and that its

[1] HERRING, E. P., "Public Administration and the Public Interest," McGraw-Hill Book Company, Inc., New York, 1936, Chap. IX; this is an excellent summary of the problems of administration of the Federal Water Power Act of 1920 and is drawn upon extensively by the present authors. See also by the same author, The Federal Power Commission and the Power of Politics, *Public Utilities Fortnightly*, vol. 15, No. 5, pp. 223 *ff.*, and vol. 15, No. 6, pp. 292 *ff.*

[2] *Ibid.*

[3] See, for instance, Federal Power Commission, *Annual Report*, 1928, p. 2.

powers be extended.   Sometime earlier there had been a change
in the executive secretaryship which was followed by changes
in the solicitorship and chief counselorship.   There was some
evidence that laxity in carrying out the provisions of the Act
had taken place; charges and countercharges began to be aired;
and the Senate undertook an investigation which disclosed
many weaknesses and demonstrated the ineffectiveness of
regulation by the Federal Power Commission as then constituted and organized.[1]

There followed a further step in strengthening federal power
regulation.   An amendment to the Federal Water Power Act
provided for the appointment by the President of an independent commission composed of five full-time commissioners.
No additional authority was given except that the Federal
Power Commission was now empowered to employ directly
its own staff, and an appropriation for that purpose was made.

The new Commission was from the outset embroiled in the
hotbed of politics.   Immediately upon entering office, the Commissioners dismissed the Chief Accountant, Solicitor, and
Executive Secretary.   The Senate was enraged at this action
and attempted to recall the name of Commissioner George Otis
Smith whom they had just confirmed.   President Hoover refused
this request, and much bickering took place.   There was some
tendency to criticize the entire Commission.[2]

In spite of an inauspicious start, however, the revised Federal
Power Commission took a positive view toward the problems of
regulation.   Data upon which to formulate and carry forward
the work of regulation were collected.   Through several changes
in the membership of the Commission and through support
accorded by the Democratic Administration since 1933, the
Federal Power Commission has been active in formulating and
carrying out a national power policy.   The former vice chairman, Basil Manly, expressed the new viewpoint in the following
language:

That act clearly contemplated not only the formulation of a national
power program after a thorough survey of the nation's power resources,

[1] Hearings, S. 3619 and Sen. Res. 80, 71st Cong., 2d Sess., 1930.
[2] HERRING, *op. cit.*

but specifically provided that the commission should make recommendations to Congress whenever it deemed that any project should be developed by the federal government itself.[1]

Broadening the Powers of the Federal Power Commission.— Title II of the Public Utility Act of 1935 provides for a broadening of the powers of the Federal Power Commission. This part of the Act makes a declaration of policy to the effect that the interstate transmission of electricity, which hitherto had been in a "twilight zone" and practically unregulated, is subject to federal regulation. As in the Act of 1920, however, Congress provided that federal jurisdiction should apply only to those matters not subject to regulation by the state or states concerned. The licensing power was continued to be vested in the Federal Power Commission, and new or revised powers were provided. The powers over electricity in interstate commerce were discussed in the preceding chapter. They are summarized briefly here, along with other new powers, as follows:

1. Division of the country into regional districts for the voluntary interconnection of generating and transmission facilities to assure an abundant supply of electricity throughout the United States with the utmost economy. Promotion and encouragement of interconnections both within and between districts is ordered. In time of war or other emergency, the Commission is empowered to require temporary interconnections.

2. Denial to public utilities subject to the Federal Water Power Commission of the privilege of selling, leasing, or otherwise disposing of property whose value is in excess of $50,000 or of merging or consolidating without first getting an authorization from the Federal Power Commission to the effect that the proposed action is consistent with the public interest.

3. Exercise of jurisdiction over security issues and assumption of corporate liabilities of public utilities that are engaged in the interstate transmission and sale of electric energy and that are not regulated by a state commission.

4. Supervision over rates and charges for electric energy transmitted across state lines and sold wholesale for resale by utilities under the jurisdiction of the Federal Power Commission.

[1] Address before the City Club of Boston, Mar. 9, 1934. Quoted in *Congressional Record*, Mar. 26, 1934.

5. Cooperation with state commissions in investigating the cost of production and transmission by means of interstate facilities beyond jurisdiction of the requesting state.

6. Provision of a plan for cooperation with state commissions, including procedure for joint hearings and the creation of joint boards, to consider matters of mutual interest arising under the Federal Water Power Act.

7. Revision of the uniform system of accounts for public utilities and licensees subject to the jurisdiction of the Federal Power Commission. In so far as is practicable, federal agencies engaged in the generation and sale of electric energy for ultimate distribution to the public are to be subject to these accounting rules.

8. Requiring public utilities to carry adequate and proper depreciation accounts and giving the Federal Power Commission authority to determine and fix the rates of depreciation to be charged against the property of licensees.

9. Provisions against interlocking directorates in utilities and financial or other institutions handling their securities.[1]

Studies and Reports of the Federal Power Commission.—Two series of studies have been undertaken by the Federal Power Commission. These studies are providing for the first time much needed data and information. With the exception of the five-year census of electrical industries, the data collected by the Geological Survey (now collected by the Federal Power Commission), special studies undertaken from time to time by governmental agencies, and reports of trade associations and trade journals, there has been a paucity of information concerning the electrical industry. There is no doubt that clearer and sounder public policies may be formulated on the basis of the data now being made available. These studies include:

A. *Power series:*

No. 1, Interim Report, covers power development, requirements, dependable capacity, undeveloped water power, fuel resources, relation of water and fuel power, interstate transfers, and other phases of power development.

---

[1] Title II, Public Utility Act of 1935. The Federal Power Commission *Annual Report* 1936 carries a summary of these changes and the work of the Commission in administering them.

No. 2, Principal Electric Utility Systems in the United States, covers those companies which have 90 per cent of the installed capacity of the United States. The utility holding companies involved are listed along with their intermediate companies and subsidiaries. Their chief characteristics—financial, physical, and electrical operations—are described.

No. 3, The Cost of Distribution of Electricity, covers the cost of retail distribution of electric energy from the substation to the customer's meter. The costs of distribution are an important factor in the cost of service, and hitherto but few definite data concerning them have been available.

No. 4, The Use of Electric Power in Transportation, analyzes the past and potential uses of electrical power in the major power-using industry in the country.

B. *Rate series:*

No. 1, Preliminary Report, lists the domestic and residential rates in effect in cities of 50,000 population and over.

No. 2, State Reports, consists of 48 separate reports of domestic and residential rates in effect in communities, large and small, in each state.

No. 3, Average Typical Residential Bills, is a summary of average charges by states, geographic subdivisions, and the United States.

No. 4, Rates for Electrical Service to Commercial and Industrial Customers, lists and describes light and power, commercial, and industrial class rates.

No. 5, Comparative Study of Publicly and Privately Owned Electric Utilities, considers, in addition to rates, data on taxes paid by private utilities, data on taxes and cash contributions of municipalities and "free services" rendered, as essential elements in the comparison of rates.

No. 6, State Commission Jurisdiction and Regulation of Electric Rates and Service, presents detailed data of state regulatory agencies as they affect both publicly and privately owned electric utilities. The specific authority of each state commission is shown, and the most important features are graphically presented.

No. 7, Electric Rate Uniformity, describes the present extent
and trends toward uniformity in rates schedules and forces
promoting uniformity.

No. 8, Rural Electric Service, covers the rate schedules,
extension policies, construction practices, costs, and
mileage of rural lines and services.

In addition to these studies, the Federal Power Commission
has prepared a "Glossary of Important Power and Rate Terms,
Abbreviations, and Units of Measurement" and several large
maps of service areas and generating plants and transmission
lines in the United States.[1]

Litigation Concerning the Federal Water Power Act.—Both
the legality of the Federal Power Commission and the legality of
certain of the powers conferred upon it have been attacked in
the courts. The constitutional authority of Congress to vest
the Federal Power Commission with authority over the navigable
streams and public waters was challenged in a suit filed by the
State of New York in 1923. Conferences were held between the
Federal Power Commission and the New York State Water
Power Commission, however, and the suit was withdrawn. The
State of New Jersey filed that same year a similar suit which was
decided by the Supreme Court. The decision pointed out
that the bill of complaint had for its purpose the obtaining of a
judicial declaration that Congress had exceeded its authority in
enacting the Federal Water Power Act. The complaint was
dismissed on grounds that it failed to show that any right of a
state was prejudicially affected and that Congress clearly had
authority over navigable waters and the waters on public lands.[2]

The right of the Federal Power Commission to enforce the
accounting provisions of the Federal Water Power Act and its
power to hold hearings in connection with the ascertainment of
actual, legitimate costs was questioned in a suit brought by the
Clarion River Power Company. Had these contentions been
upheld, it is apparent that the reservation of the authority to
recapture properties at a fair price would in effect be nullified
by the resulting possibility of inflation in valuations. The
authority of the Federal Power Commission was sustained by

[1] The content of these studies and reports is summarized more extensively
in the Federal Power Commission *Annual Report*, 1936.

[2] New Jersey v. John G. Sargent, 70 L. ed. 289.

the Circuit Court, and the Supreme Court denied a writ of certiorari in 1932.[1]

There has been long-drawn-out, and as yet unsettled, litigation concerning the Commission's authority over waters formerly navigable and now nonnavigable and over the nonnavigable headwaters of navigable streams. The importance of this question lies in the effect of headwater dams on navigation below them. This question originated in connection with the matter of a license for the Appalachian Power Company to build a dam on the New River, Virginia, which the Federal Power Commission denied on grounds that it would affect adversely navigation on the Kanawha below. The subsequent claim that the Federal Power Commission had no jurisdiction was denied in a decision by the Supreme Court. In spite of the judicial determination of the jurisdiction of the Federal Power Commission, the Appalachian Power Company announced its intention of proceeding with the construction of a power dam without a license. Similarly, the Union Carbide and Carbon Corporation started construction of a dam on the same river without first securing a license. The Federal Power Commission has instituted injunction proceedings in both cases which are now before the courts.[2]

Significance of Water Power.—In the 16 years since its creation, the Federal Power Commission has issued 575 major and minor licenses. Including applications pending and preliminary permits, there are 714 active projects under the jurisdiction of the Federal Power Commission. These projects have a total primary capacity of 4,082,274 horsepower with an estimated ultimate installation of 12,325,913 horsepower. Actually, therefore, the Federal Power Commission exercises jurisdiction over only a small proportion of the electric power capacity of the United States; and many contend that the importance of the Federal Power Commission is diminishing, since, in addition to its limited jurisdiction, it is pointed out that hydroelectric energy is declining in relative importance. The latter claim is made in spite of the fact that approximately 40 per cent of the output of electric energy in the United States is hydrogenerated. The

[1] Clarion River Power Co. v. Federal Power Comm., 77 L. ed. 554; 61 App. D.C. 186; 59 F. (2d) 861.

[2] Federal Power Commission, *Annual Report*, 1935, pp. 7–8; 1936, p. 26.

Federal Power Commission, in discussing this matter, has stated:

Another factor of far-reaching importance affecting water-power development is the improvement of steam plant design. In recent years substantial advances have been made in the design of hydro-electric projects. The great expansion of the market has permitted larger and larger units to be installed and vast water power projects to be constructed. These have resulted in much higher efficiency in the extraction of the potential energy from the falling water and lower operating costs. During the same period, however, the improvement of the efficiencies of the steam electric stations has been even more remarkable. By use of higher pressures, higher temperatures, larger units, improved types of boilers, and other mechanical improvements the thermal efficiency of the modern steam station has been so increased as to produce twice as much useful energy from a fuel unit as was possible a decade ago. Modern water power machinery is now so close to the theoretical limit that there is little room for improvement. This is not true, however, in the case of steam electric plants, and further gains within economic limits are authoritatively predicted for the immediate future. The substantial reduction in the cost of steam generation by stations of modern construction has greatly narrowed, if not overcome, the margin hitherto enjoyed by water power in many localities. With the most favorable water-power sites already in service, it is obvious that new projects must undergo the most critical comparison with the equivalent steam capacity, particularly in regions where cheap fuel supplies are available.

The altered conditions have led to frequent expressions to the effect that henceforth hydraulic power will be of diminishing importance, and development of most of the remaining sites will be found economically impracticable. The facts available do not warrant any such general conclusion. Admittedly water power is faced with much keener competition than it has ever had to meet in the past, but in many situations it will be found to be clearly advantageous. The problem is complex, and the solution which will produce the lowest cost coupled with the most reliable service may be found only by searching analysis of each individual situation. Systems depending primarily on hydro power are finding it desirable to provide a substantial proportion of the needed generating capacity in steam plants as a protection against periods of abnormally low water supply. On the other hand, the systems deriving the major part of their requirements from fuel power discover that the most economic arrangement includes some water-power capacity, particularly for use on the peak of the system load. A system served with generating capacity properly balanced between steam and hydro in most cases offers more favorable costs than if the dependence is placed entirely on one source or the other. In other words, a combination of steam and hydro is more economical as a general rule than either one alone.[1]

Summary. *The National Power Policy and the Place of the Federal Power Commission.*—The Federal Power Commission has been strengthened and is now receiving the administration support necessary to permit it to function as an effective regulatory agency. It is collecting factual data upon which it can build a program for the protection of the public interest and which can serve as a basis in guiding and formulating governmental policy concerning power. In the formulation of national power policy, as voiced and carried out under the leadership of President Franklin D. Roosevelt, it is not intended that the Federal Power Commission shall become the only agency of execution and administration. To bring coordination among the several agencies dealing with power, President Roosevelt established, July, 1934, a National Power Policy Committee. Its purpose is stated to be:

Its duty will be to develop a plan for the closer cooperation of the several factors in our electrical power supply—both public and private—whereby national policy in power matters may be unified and electricity be made more broadly available at cheaper rates to industry, to domestic and, particularly, to agricultural consumers.

Several agencies of the government, such as the Federal Power and Trade Commissions, have in process surveys and reports useful in this connection. The Mississippi Valley Committee of Public Works is making studies of the feasibility of power in connection with water storage, flood control and navigation projects. The War Department and Bureau of Reclamation have under construction great hydroelectric plants. Representatives of these agencies have been asked to serve on the committee. It is not to be merely a fact-finding body, but rather one for the development and unification of national power policy.[2]

The National Power Policy Committee, though without authority to administer power policies, is constituted as a policy

[1] Federal Power Commission, *Annual Report*, 1929, pp. 3–4; see also for a comparison of steam and hydrogeneration, *Power Series* No. 1, Interim Report.

[2] Taken from the President's letter authorizing creation of the Committee as quoted in E. P. Herring, *op. cit.*, p. 154.

forming body, and its findings and recommendations are likely to be those receiving administration support.   Thus, though the Federal Power Commission is strengthened in its power over navigable streams and public waters, it represents but one feature in the enlarged national power policy, and it is likely to be guided in its administrative tasks by policies created, at least in part, by another agency.   Its work is, in turn, to be coordinated with the policies of all other governmental agencies dealing with power. The objectives of the national power policy, relying upon the twin foundation stones of stricter regulation and control and the direct provision of electrical facilities, are the broadening of the use of electricity and the making of cheaper rates.   As was pointed out in Chap. XII, however, there still remains the problem of setting up an effective coordinating agency equipped with adequate powers to formulate and apply a coordinated, cohesive national power policy.

References

BUTTERWORTH, WILLIAM: Business Regards a National Water Power Policy, *Public Utilities Fortnightly*, vol. 3, No. 6.
CARLISLE, FLOYD: "National Power and Resources Policies," paper presented before World Power Conference, Washington, 1936.
Congressional Digest, The Federal Government and Water Power—1788–1930, vol. 15, No. 10.
DuPuy, W. A., Facts and Fallacies about the Power Commission, *Public Utilities Fortnightly*, vol. 6, No. 2.
Federal Power Commission, *Annual Reports*.
———: *Rate Series*, Nos. 1–8.
———: *Power Series*, Nos. 1–4.
HERRING, E. P.: "Public Administration and the Public Interest," McGraw-Hill Book Company, Inc., New York, 1936.
———: The Federal Power Commission and the Power of Politics, *Public Utilities Fortnightly*, vol. 15, No. 5.
KERWIN, J. G.: "Federal Water Power Legislation," Columbia University Press, New York, 1926.
LEWIS, E. A., compiler: "Federal Power Commission Laws," Government Printing Office, 1935.
MANLY, BASIL: "The Federal Government and the Public Utilities," address before the Institute of Public Affairs, Charlottesville, July 15, 1936, (mimeographed).
McNINCH, F. R.: Federal Control of Electric Power, *Journal of Land and Public Utility Economics*, vol. 12, No. 2.
National Association of Railroad and Utilities Commissioners, *Proceedings*, annual (especially Reports of the Committees on Water Power).

National Resources Board, *Report,* Dec. 1, 1934, Washington.
National Resources Committee: "Federal Agencies Concerned with Water
   Use and Control," Washington, 1936.
Soil Conservation Service: "Little Waters," Washington, 1936.
United States Congress: Reorganization of the Federal Power Commission,
   Hearings, S. 3619, 71st Cong., 2d Sess., 1930.

CHAPTER XVI

FEDERAL POWER PROJECTS

The national power policy fostered and carried out by the Democratic Administration under the leadership of President Franklin D. Roosevelt centers around the provision of cheap electric energy to all classes of customers, and the program looking toward the attainment of that goal involves many features. These are: elimination of uneconomic holding companies; control of accounting and security issues of holding companies; promotion of extensive rural electrification; cheapening of electrical appliances; strengthening of the Federal Power Commission for the purpose of more effective control and regulation of power sites on navigable streams and waters on public lands, and the regulation of interstate commerce in electricity; collection of factual data to be used for the formulation of power policies and the coordination of agencies engaged in the administration of power policies and programs; and the generation of power by the Federal Government. Coordination of these various phases of the power programs was contemplated by the establishment, in July, 1934, of the National Power Policy Committee which, as earlier noted,[1] was charged with the responsibility of developing a plan for the cooperation of all the factors in the electrical power supply and coordination and unification of the national power policy.

This national power policy and the various programs undertaken thereunder did not come into existence overnight. Much of it had to be shaped in terms of what had gone before. Its genesis is found in the earlier history of the country, and its prevailing principles are the result of long intense struggles on the part of conflicting interests. In its earliest aspects, development of power resources by private interests was favored; but, gradually, there entered the view that there should be public control and retention of ownership in the power sites under federal jurisdiction. This phase of the power issue confronted

[1] See p. 411.

the American people during the first decades of the present century, and its development was traced in the preceding chapter.

Agitation for governmental participation in the development of power projects received little attention during this early period, the prevailing philosophy of laissez faire and the emphasis upon private initiative militating against direct governmental action. Some irrigation projects involved an incidental production of hydroelectric power, but the amount so produced was usually small, and it was not generally considered that the Federal Government was engaged in power production. A small group of persons, however, spurred on by the Government investments in Muscle Shoals, on the Tennessee River in Alabama, were urging expansion of governmental activity looking toward power production. The movement for direct governmental participation in the development of power resources came into prominence when support was accorded it by President Franklin D. Roosevelt. Both before and after his inauguration in 1933, President Roosevelt frequently asserted that the provision of electric energy on a broadened scale and at cheaper rates was socially desirable and that positive steps must be taken by the Federal Government if that objective were to be obtained.[1] The possibilities were envisioned in the following words:

I have strengthened the belief that I have had for a long time . . . that the question of power, of electrical development and distribution is primarily a national problem.

Here then you have the clear picture of four great government power developments in the United States, the St. Lawrence River in the Northeast, Muscle Shoals in the Southeast, the Boulder Dam project in the Southwest, and finally, but by no means the least of them, the Columbia River in the Northwest. Each of these will be forever a national yardstick to prevent extortion against the public and to encourage the wider use of that servant of the people—electricity.[2]

With the support and backing thus granted, federal development of power projects has proceeded rapidly. The initial step was to develop, with these revised ends in view, projects in which governmental participation had already occurred. New projects also have been undertaken, and many others have

---

[1] See, *e.g.*, WOLFSON, J. D., "Power Views of Franklin D. Roosevelt," National Power Policy Committee, 1934.

[2] *Ibid.;* taken from a campaign speech in Portland, Ore., Sept. 21, 1932.

been proposed.   Federal power developments are thus becoming a major factor in the electrical power situation in the United States.   To show their place, significance, and influence, this chapter is devoted to a description and analysis of the major projects.

DEVELOPMENT OF THE TENNESSEE RIVER

Governmental interest in the Tennessee River originated in the early 1800's when consideration was given to the possibility of improving navigation thereon to provide a waterway route to the then developing Southwest territory.   Secretary of War John C. Calhoun, in 1824, had a survey made of the Muscle Shoals section, and Congress, in 1827, authorized an expenditure of approximately $700,000 for certain navigation improvements there.[1]

Many years later, further attention was given to navigation on the Tennessee when, in 1872, the United States Army Engineers recommended additional improvements in the open channel of the river.   In 1875, construction of a canal around Elk River Shoals was begun.   By 1900, further improvements involving expenditures of about $3,000,000 had been made.   Until this time consideration had been given only to navigation, but the possibilities of combining power developments with the navigation improvements were suggested in reports made between 1905 and 1912.   With this end in view, a detailed survey was made in 1915.

After passage of the National Defense Act, June 3, 1916, Muscle Shoals was selected as the site for a power dam to provide power for the experimental manufacture of nitrates.   Two nitrate plants, one to use a modified Haber process and the other to use the cyanamide process, were constructed.   The power dam to supply the needed energy, known as Wilson Dam, was started in 1917.   Construction was halted in 1921 with the

---

[1] For more extensive summaries of the development of the Tennessee River see: GLAESER, M. G., The Federal Government's Tennessee Valley Power Project—No. 1, Its Genesis, *Public Utilities Fortnightly*, vol. 13, No. 6, pp. 319 *ff.*; and KIMBLE, ELLIS, The Tennessee Valley Project, *Journal of Land and Public Utility Economics*, vol. 9, No. 4, pp. 325 *ff.*   The present authors have drawn extensively on both these sources, and, unless otherwise noted, the material included in this subsection of the chapter is adapted from these discussions.

dam about one-third complete. In 1922, Congress appropriated funds for its completion which occurred three years later. Complete surveys of the area were made while the dam was being completed. The total cost of Wilson Dam and its power plants amounted to $45,000,000. The total investment in the project, including the nitrate plants, auxiliary steam generation plants, a limestone quarry, and a connecting railroad, amounted to $80,000,000.

Once completed, the Muscle Shoals project became a political football. Farm interests, typified by the American Farm Bureau Federation, advocated private operation under a long-term lease providing for the manufacture of fertilizer. The electrical industry advocated private operation with a view to power generation. One congressional committee supported the latter view and recommended to Congress, in 1926, that it be leased for a period of 50 years to 13 allied power companies, but the proponents of public operation, under the leadership of Senator George W. Norris, were strong enough to block any efforts to effect leases with private interests. This group also succeeded in getting two bills through Congress providing for governmental operation. Both were vetoed; the first received a pocket veto by President Coolidge in 1928, and the second was vetoed by President Hoover in 1931. The question of the use to be made of Muscle Shoals thus became the major battleground for the issue of private versus public operation.

In its final form, however, the project involved more than the issue of private versus public operation of power resources. It was conceived that irrigation, navigation, flood control, and reforestation, combined with power production, could effect a social and economic rehabilitation of the area. Thus, the project became one for the unified, coordinated development of a whole area with social objectives in view. It was also conceived that the power produced could be used as a "yardstick" to measure the reasonableness of the rates of private utilities. These are the elements that became embodied in the Tennessee Valley Authority project.

The Tennessee Valley Authority. 1. *Its Fundamental Purpose.*—The Tennessee Valley Authority was among the first of the activities included in the New Deal legislation initiated under the guidance of the Democratic Administration in 1933.

As enacted in 1933 and amended in 1935, the Tennessee Valley Authority Act specifies that the primary purposes of the program are the conservation and development of the resources of the Tennessee Valley; flood control and navigation improvements are emphasized. The possibilities of power production were recognized, and the Act specifically provided:

Section 9a. The board is hereby directed in the operation of any dam or reservoir in its possession and control to regulate the stream flow primarily for the purposes of promoting navigation and controlling floods. So far as may be consistent with such purposes, the board is authorized to provide and operate facilities for the generation of electric energy at any such dam for the use of the Corporation and for the use of the United States or any agency thereof; and the board is further authorized, whenever an opportunity is afforded, to provide and operate facilities for the generation of electric energy in order to avoid the waste of water power, to transmit and market such power as in this act is provided, and thereby, so far as may be practicable, to assist in liquidating the cost or aid in the maintenance of the projects of the Authority.

Authorization to generate and distribute power is, by the provision of this section of the Act, contingent upon and supplementary to the primary objectives of flood control and navigation. These are the controlling elements, and priority must be given to them in carrying out the purposes for which the Tennessee Valley Authority was created. A reading of the act, however, indicates that there should be a unified and coordinated development of all phases of the program, and power production thus becomes one of the integral parts of the project. From the public point of view, attention has been focused upon the power developments, and in many respects they present the most spectacular features of the undertaking. In order to understand and evaluate the power activities, however, it is necessary to consider all phases of the coordinated program and the elements involved in the ultimate objectives.

2. *The Area Affected.*—In its broadest aspects, the Tennessee Valley Authority is charged with the responsibility of the complete regulation of the Tennessee River system looking toward an orderly physical, economic, and social development and rehabilitation of the entire area. The accompanying map shows

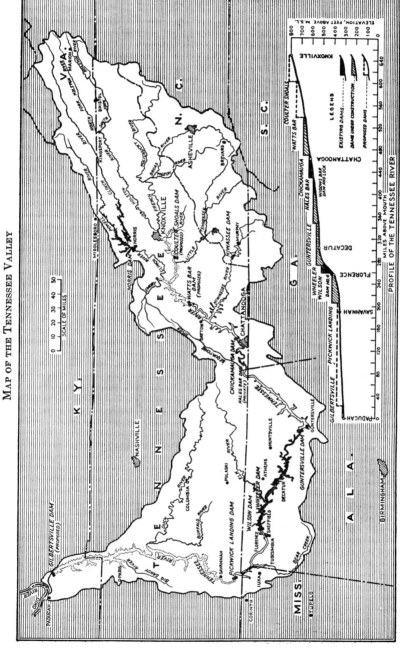

Map of the Tennessee Valley

Source: Tennessee Valley Authority, *Annual Report*, 1936.

the area affected by the Tennessee Valley Authority program as well as the major construction projects undertaken and proposed. The major physical feature of the area is the Tennessee River whose headwaters are in eastern Tennessee, western Virginia, and northern Georgia. The Tennessee itself begins just above Knoxville and flows in a southwesterly direction across Tennessee, crosses northern Alabama, thence flows northward through western Tennessee and Kentucky, and empties into the Ohio at Paducah, Ky. It is about 650 miles long and drains an area of approximately 40,000 square miles. The drainage area is populated by about two and a half million persons, of whom about one-half are farm dwellers. There are a variety of mineral and metal resources. About one-half the area is covered with forests from which most of the merchantable timber has been cut.

3. *Navigation Improvements.*—The Tennessee Valley Authority is directed to construct a 9-foot channel from the mouth of the Tennessee to Knoxville. This undertaking accounts for the chief expenditures made up to the present time and is likely to be a major expenditure for some time. This purpose is to be accomplished by a series of 10 large dams, of which three—Wilson Dam at Muscle Shoals, Dam No. 4 below Muscle Shoals, and a privately owned power dam at Hales Bar—were already in existence. There will also be many small dams, canals, and locks. Since the natural flow of the Tennessee is extremely variable, storage of water for release during the dry season necessitates a series of dams on the tributary streams. The Wheeler and Norris dams have been completed; projects at Pickwick Landing, Guntersville, Chickamauga, and Hiwassee are under way; and projects at Gilbertsville, Watts Bar, Coulter Shoals, and Little Fontana are being studied.[1]

The proposed navigation improvements will add 642 miles to the inland waterway network of the Mississippi Valley and the Gulf Coast. When this network is completed, it will consist of more than 5,000 miles of waterways with modernized channels of 9-foot draft and over 1,000 miles with 6-foot draft. It will then be the largest improved inland waterway system in the world. The United States Corps of Engineers estimates that the traffic on the Tennessee will be over 17,000,000 tons by 1950,

[1] Tennessee Valley Authority, *Annual Report*, 1936, pp. 11 *ff*.

with an annual savings of over $22,000,000 in transportation costs.[1]

4. *Flood Control.*—The Tennessee Valley Authority Act directed that the dams constructed on the main streams be of a type to produce the maximum benefit for navigation and at the same time contribute to the control of flood waters in the Tennessee and Mississippi basins. Flood losses on the Tennessee have been estimated to amount to approximately $1,750,000 annually.[2] The navigation improvement dams are designed to provide storage for flood control. To carry their cost economically, flood control and navigation can advantageously be combined with power production projects. Storage reservoirs are necessary on the tributaries of the Tennessee as well as on the main river, since the tributaries—the Clinch, Holston, French, Broad, Little Tennessee, and Hiwassee rivers—are the primary source of the flood waters of the Tennessee. The immediate construction program of the Tennessee Valley Authority involves projects for the control of flood waters on three of these tributary rivers. These flood control projects have been considered in relationship to the flood problems of the Mississippi River and have been designed with the objective of exerting substantial control of the Mississippi River floods.[3]

5. *Production of Fertilizer.*—The fertilizer program authorized was twofold in nature: (1) conducting experiments looking toward a reduction in the cost of plant foods; and (2) conducting large-scale tests to determine their economic worth under practical farm conditions. In carrying out this phase of the program, nitrate plant No. 2, already constructed, was remodeled to carry on experiments in phosphate production. Though originally constructed to produce nitrates, phosphate production was undertaken because it was felt that adequate sources of nitrates for plant foods would otherwise be made available and that phosphates were more likely to become the limiting factor in soil improvement. Processes for transforming insoluble natural phosphates into a form available for growing crops have

[1] *Ibid.*

[2] United States Corps of Engineers made this estimate; see House Doc. 328, 71st Cong., 2d Sess., Mar. 24, 1930, p. 734.

[3] Tennessee Valley Authority, "The Unified Development of the Tennessee River System," March, 1936, pp. 16 *ff.*

been discovered, and initial demonstrations of the use of the phosphates so produced have been undertaken.[1]

6. *National Defense.*—Activities in this category were provided for as follows: (1) maintenance and operation of government properties at Muscle Shoals in the interest of national defense; (2) operation of laboratories and experimental plants and undertaking of experiments to furnish products for military purposes; and (3) turning over, in the event of national emergency, any or all of the properties belonging to the Federal Government for war purposes. These ends have been kept in view in connection with the remodeling of the nitrate plants, the conduct of chemical experiments and research, and the provision of electrical power.[2]

7. *Social and Economic Rehabilitation.*—The Tennessee Valley Authority is directed to consider the effect of its development of the resources of the area upon the economic well-being of the people and to foster an orderly and proper social and economic development. Problems of far-reaching consequence are raised. Studies are being conducted to determine the effect of changed transportation conditions, problems of public health, problems of electric power utilization, recreational opportunities, economic development and use of the natural resources of the area, the economic balance between market and subsistence crops, the availability of commercial credit, and others. Because of the importance of forests in the area and because of their effect on stream flow, much attention has been given to the problems of reforestation and forest management. In order to determine the possibilities of industrial development, studies of mineral resources and experiments in their refining, extraction, and utilization have been undertaken.[3]

8. *The Unified Program.*—The unified program for the development of the Tennessee Valley involves a coincidental production of electric power, but the power policy, which will be discussed more fully below, must necessarily be coordinated with the other phases of the program. The common objective is an integrated development of the whole area looking toward the proper use, conservation, and development of resources to provide for the

---

[1] Tennessee Valley Authority, *Annual Report*, 1936, pp. 35 *ff*.

[2] *Ibid.*, pp. 49 *ff*.

[3] *Ibid.*, pp. 55 *ff*.

common welfare. Control of flood waters and improvement of navigation are the keystone of the arch, although agricultural, industrial, and social developments, as well as national defense, are important stones in the arch. Even though power production is authorized as a supplement to flood control and navigation improvements, it is an important stone in the arch in its own right. The Tennessee Valley Authority, on this point, states:

> The same works which are useful for navigation and flood control can be employed to generate a very large amount of electric power, and the three purposes can be achieved by a single coordinated program much more economically than though each purpose were pursued without relation to the others. Thus it is proving to be possible to work out a single plan for an economical development of the Tennessee River system so that floods will be tamed, a great system of navigation made possible, and the natural power of the river rendered available.[1]

Power Policy of the Tennessee Valley Authority.—Power production is carried on under a grant of authority to generate and sell electric energy in quantities consistent with stream flow regulation for the purpose of promoting navigation and controlling floods. Congress specified that it should be the policy, in so far as practicable, to distribute and sell power

> . . . equitably among the States, counties, and municipalities within transmission distance. This policy is further declared to be that the projects . . . shall be considered primarily for the benefit of the people of the section as a whole and particularly the domestic and rural consumers to whom the power can economically be made available, and accordingly that sale to and use by industry shall be a secondary purpose, to be utilized principally to secure a sufficiently high load factor and revenue returns which will permit domestic and rural use at the lowest possible rates and in such manner as to encourage increased domestic and rural use of electricity.

Consistent with this declaration of policies, the Tennessee Valley Authority is directed to give preference to public agencies and cooperative organizations in the sale of power, though it is authorized to make sales to corporations, partnerships, and individuals.[2]

---

[1] *Ibid.*, p. 2.

[2] An analysis of the strengths and weaknesses of the power program is found in R. W. Harbeson, The Power Program of T.V.A., *Journal of Land and Public Utility Economics*, vol. 12, No. 1, pp. 19 *ff*.

Contracts for the sale of power cannot be for longer than 20 years. In cases where the purchased power is to be resold for a profit, the contract is cancellable on five years' notice if the Tennessee Valley Authority needs the power thus sold to supply nonprofit agencies. For publicly owned transmission systems which are connected at the generating plant and buying power wholesale, however, contracts may be for 30 years.

In order to carry out the mandates and policies expressed in the Act, the Tennessee Valley Authority announced the principles of its power policy as follows:

1. The business of generating and distributing electric power is a public business.

2. Private and public interests in the business of power are of a different kind and quality and should not be confused.

3. The interest of the public in the widest possible use of power is superior to any private interest. Where the private interest and this public interest conflict, the public interest must prevail.

4. Where there is a conflict between public interest and private interest in power which can be reconciled without injury to the public interest, such reconciliation should be made.

5. The right of a community to own and operate its own electric plant is undeniable. This is one of the measures that the people may properly take to protect themselves against unreasonable rates. Such a course of action may take the form of acquiring the existing plant or setting up a competing plant, as circumstances may dictate.

6. The fact that action by the Authority may have an adverse economic effect upon a privately owned utility should be a matter for the serious consideration of the Board in framing and executing its power program. But it is not the determining factor. The most important considerations are the furthering of the public interest in making power available at the lowest rate consistent with sound financial policy, and the accomplishments of the social objectives which low-cost power makes possible. The Authority cannot decline to take action solely upon the ground that to do so would injure a privately owned utility.

7. To provide a workable and economic basis of operations, the Authority plans initially to serve certain definite regions and to develop its program in those areas before going outside.

8. The initial areas selected by the Authority may be roughly described as (a) the region immediately proximate to the route of the transmission line soon to be constructed by the Authority between Muscle Shoals and the site of the Norris Dam; (b) the region in proximity

to Muscle Shoals, including northern Alabama and northeastern Mississippi; and (c) the region in the proximity of Norris Dam.

. . . .

9. Every effort will be made by the Authority to avoid the construction of duplicate physical facilities, or wasteful competitive practices. Accordingly, where existing lines of privately owned utilities are required to accomplish the Authority's objectives, as outlined above, a genuine effort will be made to purchase such facilities from the private utilities on an equitable basis.[1]

Construction of power-producing facilities has gone forward. The generating plants at the Wilson Dam were taken over, and generating plants were constructed at the Wheeler and Norris dams. Additional generating facilities are planned in connection with dam construction now underway and proposed for the future. Transmission lines of two types have been constructed, *viz.:* (1) lines to connect the existing and authorized power installations so that they may supplement one another; and (2) lines that carry power to municipal or cooperative distribution systems or to supply the industries with which the Tennessee Valley Authority has contracts.[2]

In order to be in a position to dispose of its power, the Tennessee Valley Authority entered into a contract, Jan. 4, 1934, with the Commonwealth and Southern Corporation, the chief holding company with properties in the area, and its subsidiaries, the Alabama Power Company, the Mississippi Power Company, and the Tennessee Electric Power Company. This contract provided for options for the purchase of electric properties, the sale of distribution systems to municipalities in certain counties, restrictions on territorial expansion by the contracting parties, and interchange of power. Later, the eastern Tennessee properties, including the distribution system in Knoxville, of the Tennessee Public Service Company were acquired by purchase from the National Power and Light Company, a holding company.[3]

[1] Tennessee Valley Authority, *Annual Report*, 1934, pp. 22, 23.

[2] Tennessee Valley Authority, *Annual Report*, 1936, p. 28. Contracts to supply industries with power came to the Tennessee Valley Authority by assignment in connection with the purchase of property from private utilities.

[3] Tennessee Valley Authority, *Annual Report*, 1934, pp. 24 *ff.*

The Tennessee Valley Authority is not engaged in the distribution of electricity to the ultimate consumer. Its functions terminate with the delivery of power to the lines of distribution agencies, both public and private. Since the Act directs the Tennessee Valley Authority to encourage the widest possible use of the power thus sold wholesale, the terms of resale are a matter of importance and are covered in the contract providing for the purchase of power by a distributing agency. Power generated by the Tennessee Valley Authority is distributed through four principal types of distribution agencies, as follows:

1. *Municipalities*—these are cities which own their own distribution systems and which have contracted for the purchase of power wholesale.

2. *County electric power associations*—these agencies are private, non-profit membership corporations which are organized on a county-wide basis for the purpose of acquiring and operating distribution systems. Members of the associations are supplied with power purchased wholesale from the Tennessee Valley Authority.

3. *Interim power districts*—these are distribution systems temporarily operated by the Tennessee Valley Authority. It was found that, in the purchase of farm lines and adjoining small distribution systems and in the construction of rural lines, direct operation was necessary pending organization of farmers' organizations or negotiations with adjacent municipalities or associations to take them over.

4. *Private power companies*—these are companies to which power is delivered under the interchange agreement previously mentioned.[1]

At the end of the fiscal year 1936 there were 16 municipalities and eight electric power associations buying power from the Tennessee Valley Authority. The private utilities, however, were the largest buyers of Tennessee Valley Authority power. Out of gross revenues of $1,170,000, interchange of power to private utilities yielded $588,801.[2]

The production of power has shown a great increase. An output for the fiscal year of 1934–1935 amounting to 122,000,-000 kw.-hr. was increased for the next fiscal year to 476,000,000 kw.-hr. This, it was believed, was due largely to the reduction in rates that had been made. The combination of lowered

---

[1] Tennessee Valley Authority, *Annual Report*, 1935, pp. 26 *ff.*; 1936, pp. 31 *ff.*

[2] Tennessee Valley Authority, *Annual Report*, 1936, p. 34.

rates and expanding production indicates that the stalemate of high rates limiting consumption and limited consumption causing high rates has been broken.[1] In commenting upon this situation, as well as upon the question of the market for power, the Tennessee Valley Authority stated:

> One of the effects of such low rates . . . is to expand existing markets and to create new markets. That this expansion is not a mere transfer of customers from one wholesaler to another is shown by the fact that the privately owned utilities in the Tennessee Valley region have greatly expanded their gross sales since the inauguration of the TVA. Electricity has been made available to those who did not use it before and has been made available in larger quantities to those whose purchases were formerly limited. The Tennessee Valley region is beginning the development of a power economy which will unquestionably demand a large additional supply of electricity. There will soon be a market for all the available publicly produced prime power. The TVA did not create this market, but it has helped to discover it.[2]

Power Contracts and Rate Policies of the Tennessee Valley Authority.—A standard form of contract to apply to the sale of power to municipalities was devised. The first contract signed was with Tupelo, Miss., on Oct. 27, 1933, and the first power was delivered under this contract on Feb. 7, 1934. The essential provisions of these standard contracts are:

1. The contractor agrees to purchase its entire power requirements from the Tennessee Valley Authority unless exceptions are specified.

2. The contractor agrees to pay for power at standard wholesale rates which are:

> *a.* Demand charge: 90 cents per kilowatt of demand per month. Demand is defined as the highest integrated load during any 60-minute period during the month for which determination is made.
>
> *b.* Energy charge:

---

[1] Some private utilities have initiated rate programs designed to accomplish this objective. For the nature of such policies and references to instances where they have been applied, see G. L. Wilson, J. M. Herring, and R. B. Eutsler, "Public Utility Industries," McGraw-Hill Book Company, Inc., New York, 1936, p. 127.

[2] Tennessee Valley Authority, *Annual Report*, 1936, p. 8.

Kilowatt-hours per Month	Charge per Kilowatt-hour, Mills
First 100,000	4
Next 200,000	3
Next 700,000	2.5
Additional	2

Charges for energy in excess of 360 times the demand shall be subject to a reduction of 0.5 mill per kilowatt-hour from the otherwise applicable rate.

3. Electricity resold by the contractor is at retail rates established in the contract. Standard resale retail rates for residential service are:

Kilowatt-hours per Month	Cents per Kilowatt-hour
First 50	3.00
Next 150	2.00
Next 200	1.00
Next 1,000	0.40
Additional	0.75

4. The contractor agrees to apply its electric system revenues against the following items in the order named:

  a. Operating expenses.

  b. Interest on electric system bonds.

  c. Amortization of electric system bonds.

  d. Reasonable reserves for new construction and contingencies.

  e. Payments in lieu of taxes at rates equivalent to taxes assessed against other property of a similar nature.

  f. A return on the equity of not more than 6 per cent per annum.

  g. Reduction in rates.

5. The contractor also agrees to administer its electric system as a separate department, not to mingle funds or accounts with those of its other operations, to keep its electric system accounts in accordance with a uniform system of accounting as prescribed by the Tennessee Valley Authority, and to furnish operating and financial data as requested.

6. Rate adjustments will be made in the event of major increases or decreases in the general price and wage levels as

measured by the cost-of-living index of the Department of Labor. The Tennessee Valley Authority further agrees to reduce its wholesale rates if, in its opinion, reductions in the cost of generating and transmitting energy make reductions feasible.[1]

The resale rates for Tennessee Valley Authority power are materially lower than are the rates of private utilities. Studies indicate that the savings per customer range from about 50 to 60 per cent.[2] It is significant that in every case of the use of Tennessee Valley Authority power, there has been a greatly increased consumption of current, amounting in many communities to over 200 per cent. Also, every contractor reselling Tennessee Valley Authority power has made a margin, in several cases very substantial margins, over aggregate costs which include payments in lieu of but equivalent to taxes, depreciation, interest, and operating expenses.[3]

The costs of power production by the Tennessee Valley Authority are not yet known. The law provides that there be shown a segregation of the cost of properties (or value of properties taken over) among (1) flood control, (2) navigation, (3) fertilizer production, (4) national defense, and (5) power development; but since these cost allocations are in the process of being made, the actual investment made for power production is yet undetermined. As of June 30, 1936, the net investment in all the programs amounted to over $96,000,000 with $7,391,649 being charged to the direct investment in power plants and electricity facilities. Operating costs for electricity production, without including a return on the investment or depreciation, amounted to 0.000306 cent per kilowatt-hour generation.[4]

Tennessee Valley Authority Rates as Yardsticks.—In formulating its rate policies, the Tennessee Valley Authority declared that the details of costs should be shown so as to "permit a comparison of operation with privately owned plants, to supply a 'yardstick' and an incentive to both private and public man-

---

[1] Copies of power contracts are printed as appendices to the *Annual Reports* of the Tennessee Valley Authority.

[2] Tennessee Valley Authority, Economics of Electric Distribution—Effects of Reduced Rates in TVA Service Areas, *Statistical Bulletin* 8, May, 1936.

[3] Tennessee Valley Authority, *Annual Report*, 1936, p. 30.

[4] *Ibid.*, p. 130.

agers." Director David E. Lilienthal clarified the yardstick concept by stating:

> The power policy written into the Tennessee Valley Authority Act represents an attempt to regulate public utilities not by quasi-judicial commissions but by competition. The Act definitely puts the Federal Government into the business of rendering electric service. The Authority is required to acquire a market and to set up an area in which to conduct its operations. The results of these operations in this limited area are intended to serve as a "yardstick" by which to measure the fairness of the rates of private utilities, and to prevent destructive financial practices by the latter.[1]

The ideals involved in the yardstick policy were stated by Director A. E. Morgan to be:

> The President wishes that somewhere in America there should be a case of public generation, distribution and sale of power. He is of the opinion that power developed in this country ought not everywhere to be a public project, that private development of power has decided advantages and ought not to be abandoned. But he feels there ought to be here and there cases of public ownership which can serve as comparisons. And if they are to serve as comparisons, they must be open and aboveboard with nothing hidden. They must be fair with no special arbitrary advantage. They must pay taxes just as private utility companies must do, and every other reasonable charge if they are to provide us with a fair comparison.[2]

Private Utility Attitude toward the Tennessee Valley Authority.—There have been many criticisms voiced against the Tennessee Valley Authority power program and activities by private utilities. These, in general, may be summarized under four headings.

1. *Destruction of Private Property.*—In a bill of complaint for an injunction against the Tennessee Valley Authority, the Tennessee Electric Power Company, joined by 18 other companies, declared that the Tennessee Valley Authority, in cooperation with the Federal Administration of Public Works, had carried on a systematic campaign to coerce and intimidate the power companies to sell their distribution systems and

[1] LILIENTHAL, D. E., Business and Government in the Tennessee Valley, *Annals of the American Academy of Political and Social Science*, vol. 172, p. 46.

[2] MORGAN, A. E., Power and the New Deal, *Forum*, vol. 93, No. 3, p. 132.

transmission lines at prices arbitrarily fixed by the Tennessee Valley Authority at a value far below the fair value of the property sought to be taken.[1] Other claims of the destruction of property values include the adverse effects of the Tennessee Valley Authority on the value of securities of private companies operating in the area and their inability to refinance maturing obligations.[2]

The validity of these contentions is open to doubt. One commentator, in discussing the agreement made with the Commonwealth and Southern Corporation and its subsidiaries early in 1934, concluded: " . . . this agreement demonstrates that TVA is minded to carry out the congressional mandate without destroying the prudent investment in privately owned utilities and without inaugurating a policy of national economic waste in the duplication of power facilities."[3]

The policy and attitude of the Tennessee Valley Authority concerning this question were expressed by Director A. E. Morgan, as follows:

The Authority has determined, if possible, to buy existing facilities at fair prices, and though hundreds of communities have asked for its service, and a considerable number have voted to buy power from the Authority, yet not a single competitive line has been built. Negotiations with private companies have been entered into in good faith, and contracts have been made for the purchase of transmission and distribution facilities. In case of the purchase of the Knoxville power system, some very unfair and misleading criticism has been leveled at the Authority. The critics have not told the public that the utility company involved, at one stroke of the pen, increased its capitalization from

[1] Tennessee Electric Power Co. *et al. v.* Tenn. Valley Authority *et al.*, Bill of Complaint, in Equity No. 904, filed in the District Court of the United States for the Northern District of Alabama, May 29, 1936.

[2] See, *e.g.*, GUILD, J. C., JR., How the T.V.A. Really Hurts Private Companies, *Public Utilities Fortnightly*, July 2, 1936; and WILKIE, W. L., Lessons of the T.V.A., *The Financial World*, June 3, 1936. These articles, together with several others, are reprinted in "The TVA," *Edison Electric Institute, Publication* S10, 1936; see also, on this same point, Commonwealth and Southern Corporation, "Analysis of the Annual Report of the Tennessee Valley Authority," Feb. 15, 1937, p. 51.

[3] GLAESER, M. G., The Federal Government's Tennessee Valley Project: No. 3, Power Policy of TVA, *Public Utilities Fortnightly*, vol. 12, No. 8, p. 461.

$12,000,000 to $17,000,000 without adding one cent to its actual properties.   Neither did these critics disclose the fact that the utility
company had been using high power rates to pay eight per cent dividends
on an almost obsolete street car system which was not even paying its
operating expenses.   Over half the capitalization of the company was
made up of water and of a nonproductive street car system.   The price
offered by the Tennessee Valley Authority and accepted by the company is full payment of all the actual useful investment.[1]

2. *Additional Power Not Needed.*—It has also been claimed
by the privately owned utilities in the area that the present
demand for power is being supplied and the private companies
can supply any increased demand for power for a reasonable
period in the future.   It is further claimed that the Tennessee
Valley Authority is cognizant of this fact.   In support of this
latter contention, reference is made to the minutes of a meeting
of the Board of Directors of the Tennessee Valley Authority
on Oct. 13, 1933, which states, among other things, that:

We know the existing demand is being adequately supplied by the
privately owned utilities.   There are only two ways whereby the
Authority can dispose of this additional block of power: (1) Sale in
bulk to private utilities. Since these utilities have now adequate supplies, this alternative implies the creation of additional demand consequent upon either a substantial industrial development, or substantial
increases in domestic and farm use, rendering existing privately owned
facilities inadequate.   Distribution would continue to be through the
facilities of existing companies.   Rates to the ultimate consumer of
power purchased from the Authority would be regulated by the
Authority, under the terms of the contract of purchase.   (2) By sale
of such power to municipalities or to the public agencies which are now
being served by private utilities.   The Authority might dispose of its
power by taking part of the field now occupied and served by the
existing utilities.   A typical case is sale at wholesale to a municipality
which owns its own distribution system, now purchasing at wholesale
from a private utility.   Since there are few municipalities in the area
which own their distribution systems, such a method of disposing of the
Authority's power would involve the acquisition by such municipalities

---

[1] Tennessee Valley Authority *News-Release*, Oct. 2, 1934, of the text of an
address by Dr. A. E. Morgan before the Technical Club of Madison, Wis.,
Oct. 1, 1934; see, also, *News-Release*, Apr. 25, 1934, of the text of an address
by David E. Lilienthal before the League of Women Voters, Boston, Massachusetts, Apr. 24, 1934.

of distribution facilities now owned by the utilities, or the construction of competing facilities.[1]

One analysis of the existing generating capacity and the demand for power in the area concludes that the private utilities have an excess capacity of 35 per cent over the normal sales in the Tennessee Valley.[2] The Tennessee Valley Authority and other governmental agencies, on the contrary, conclude that an expansion in the use of power is creating a need for all the power that will be produced. In this connection it is stated:

> There is every indication that the market for power will continue to grow steadily, and the problems in the Tennessee Valley region will not be to find a demand for power but to produce power to meet the demand. The increase of 19 per cent in power production by all agencies in the region between May, 1935, and May, 1936, is an indication of what may be expected.

This conclusion, expressed in the last report to Congress, is confirmed by the findings of the National Power Survey of the Federal Power Commission. The power demands in the Tennessee Valley will soon exceed the existing dependable supply.[3]

3. *Subsidization of Purchasers of Tennessee Valley Authority Power.*—This claim hinges upon several points. In the first place, it is claimed, the Public Works Administration subsidizes the purchase or construction of retail distribution facilities in making a grant for 45 per cent of their cost and a loan, on very favorable terms, for the remaining 55 per cent. Another form of subsidy is claimed to be found in the fact that the Tennessee Valley Authority absorbs expenditures for new business and other sales-promotional activities which otherwise would have to be made by the agencies buying the power from the Tennessee Valley Authority.[4]

[1] Excerpt from minutes of a meeting of the Board of Directors of the Tennessee Valley Authority, Oct. 13, 1933, quoted in Tenn. Electric Power Co. *et al.* v. Tenn. Valley Authority *et al.*, Bill of Complaint, in Equity, No. 904, filed in the District Court of the United States, for the Northern District of Alabama, May 29, 1936, pp. 122 *ff.*

[2] DOYING, G. E., Millions for Kilowatts, *Public Utilities Fortnightly*, vol. 15, No. 9, p. 445.

[3] Tennessee Valley Authority, *Annual Report*, 1936, p. 33; see, also, the quotation *supra*, p. 427.

[4] See, for instances of these claims, BENNION, H. S., Subsidies from the Federal Taxpayer to Communities Served by the TVA, *Edison Electric*

4. *Unfairness of the Yardstick.*—The major critical attacks against the Tennessee Valley Authority are made on this score. The arguments usually advanced are summarized by the Commonwealth and Southern Corporation in its "Analysis of the Annual Report of the Tennessee Valley Authority," which points out that the resale rates imposed by contract on municipalities distributing Tennessee Valley Authority power were arbitrarily established long before its costs of electric service could have been known. The specific instances of unfairness in the yardstick were summarized as follows:

1. Thus far, practically none of the expenditures made by TVA for dam construction have been shown in their financial statements as an investment in power facilities. Instead, such investment is charged to navigation and flood control, with an explanation that allocation to power will not be made until completion of the projects. In the meantime, the casual readers of the TVA report get a false impression of power investment.

Doubtless such an allocation will ultimately be made, charging the investment in the various projects to navigation and power. It should be remembered, however, that in many cases dams built by private utilities also make possible navigation, as for example, the Hales Bar Dam on the Tennessee River, where no part of the capital investment can be charged to navigation. Rates of the Tennessee Electric Power Company must yield a return upon all of the investment.

2. TVA financial statements show no interest on funds invested in power-producing facilities.

3. TVA financial statements do not include any allowance for depreciation on power-producing facilities.

4. Certain items of operating expense, such as power furnished the War Department for the operation of navigation locks, and expenditures for reservoir maintenance, all of which would be charged to operating expense by a private utility, are not shown in the TVA statement as operating expense. Instead they are classified as capital investment.

5. During the fiscal year 1936, TVA paid a total tax of $45,347. At the end of the fiscal year its total investment, excluding properties turned over to it, namely Wilson Dam, Sheffield Steam Plant, etc., amounted to about $100,000,000. Including the properties turned over to it its total investment at the end of the year exceeded $220,-

---

Institute, Publication S10, p. 7; and Commonwealth and Southern Corporation, "Analysis of the Annual Report of the Tennessee Valley Authority," Feb. 15, 1937, pp. 46–47.

000,000. Upon such an investment the private utilities would pay a tax of $2,750,000. These figures speak for themselves.

6. TVA enjoys subsidies through the franking privilege for mail, printing at government expense, reduced freight rates, and many other items, none of which are available to private utilities.[1]

Tennessee Valley Authority Relations with Private Utilities.— Though there were conflicting interests concerning Muscle Shoals long before the Tennessee Valley Authority was conceived and created, and though there were immediate criticisms voiced against it, the Tennessee Valley Authority inaugurated a policy of attempting to cooperate with the private utilities in the region affected. The contract with the Commonwealth and Southern Corporation and some of its subsidiaries is illustrative of the policy adopted. Apparently, there was no intention of setting out ruthlessly to take over the properties of the private companies, although there were some differences of opinion among the Directors of the Tennessee Valley Authority. Director A. E. Morgan consistently advocated and promoted close cooperation, while Director David E. Lilienthal demanded a militant invasion of the power field in order to supply cheap energy.[2] At times the former view tended to prevail, since, at

[1] Commonwealth and Southern Corporation, "Analysis of the Annual Report of the Tennessee Valley Authority," Feb. 15, 1937, pp. 39–40.

Articles pro and con on the Tennessee Valley Authority are numerous. In addition to those already cited which criticize the Tennessee Valley Authority, the reader is referred to other illustrative criticisms such as: ZIMMERMAN, J. E., Private vs. Government Ownership and Operation of Public Utilities, *Edison Electric Institute, Publication* S 6, pp. 44 *ff.*; WILKIE, W. L., Government and the Public Utilities, *ibid.*, pp. 34 *ff.*; PORTER, J. H., Yardsticks, *ibid.*, pp. 53 *ff.* (reprinted from *Public Utilities Fortnightly*, vol. 15, No. 2, pp. 74 *ff.*); IRWIN, WILL, The Great Tennessee Bubble, *Public Utilities Fortnightly*, vol. 11, No. 8, pp. 439 *ff.*; ELY, OWEN, The Yardstick Experiments, *ibid.*, No. 6, pp. 285 *ff.*; COREY, HERBERT, Is TVA Telling the Truth?, *ibid.*, vol. 15, No. 8, pp. 391 *ff.*; Trying to Pry into TVA, *ibid.*, vol. 16, No. 13, pp. 801 *ff.*; A Yardstick That Is Not Air Conditioned, *ibid.*, vol. 18, No. 7, pp. 341 *ff.*, 1936; and CARPENTER, W. M., Hidden Costs at Muscle Shoals, *Edison Electric Institute Bulletin*, July, 1936.

[2] Since this chapter was written, the conflict in viewpoints among the directors of the Tennessee Valley Authority gave rise to charges and counter-charges made in public. President Roosevelt called a conference of the directors and later removed Dr. A. E. Morgan from the Board. Congress took cognizance of the situation and in March, 1938, authorized an extensive

the request of President Franklin Roosevelt, in the fall of 1936, a conference with power officials of private companies was held for the purpose of considering a system by which the Tennessee Valley Authority and the private utilities in the South would pool power to supply electric current on an economical basis without crushing the private utilities.

A pooling arrangement has much to commend it. Commenting upon this possibility, Basil Manly, former Vice-chairman of the Federal Power Commission, has stated:

. . . the establishment of a system of regional pooling would appear to present the best solution of the numerous problems created by the development of large blocks of hydroelectric power as an incident to the construction of Federal public works projects. From the standpoint of the Federal Government it would afford an orderly method of disposing of electrical energy in large quantities and would thus provide an assured source of revenue for the liquidation of the expenditures involved in such projects. It would minimize the conflict with privately owned utilities and avoid the duplication of transmission facilities which will be necessary if the power from the Federal projects is to be marketed at the existing load centers. It would make power available to communities and agricultural areas throughout large regions at rates as low as, if not lower than, the rates which must be charged if the Federal agency seeks to find a market for all its power by selling directly to industries and communities located within reasonable transmission radius of the project.

To the private utilities which are directly affected, the adoption of such a plan of regional pooling would create a condition of security which would enable them to proceed immediately with the refunding of outstanding securities at the low interest rates which are now available. Investors in their securities would be protected not only from possible losses arising from direct competition but also from severance damages that otherwise would be created if municipalities should acquire local distribution systems. Power generation and transmission costs would be substantially equalized throughout large regions. The utilities participating in the pool, as well as the consumers within the territory affected, would be benefited by the incidental development of power in connection with the construction of Federal public works projects.[1]

investigation of the Tennessee Valley Authority by a joint congressional committee.

[1] MANLY, BASIL, "Regional Coordination and Integration of Electric Utilities—the Federal Point of View," paper presented before the World Power Conference, Washington, D.C., Sept. 10, 1936.

The essential elements of such a pool, according to this same authority, are as follows:

1. An effective Federal agency must be created to operate the pool. Such agency should preferably have a board of directors in which the national interest would be preponderantly represented but which would also afford an opportunity for regional and local interests to have an effective voice.

2. The agency must possess adequate power and financial resources to acquire control of or construct a transmission network which will ultimately cover the entire area of the region in which the pool is to operate. In the opinion of the writer it would not be desirable for this agency to purchase transmission facilities or construct them except where it is necessary. All the practical objectives of the pool can be attained as effectively by lease of transmission facilities as by purchase.

3. All participants in the pool must commit themselves to place their generating facilities, transmission lines and substations under the control of the managers of the pool, subject to such agreements as may be necessary with reference to the basis upon which power is to be taken from the generating stations and delivered to distribution systems and the compensation that is to be paid for the use of transmission lines.

4. There must be agreement that all distribution systems, whether publicly or privately owned, shall be supplied from the transmission network at rates which shall be uniform for communities which possess the same characteristics and are similarly situated.

5. The central agency must possess adequate powers to construct additional transmission lines and interconnections wherever necessary and to plan and, if necessary, finance and procure the construction of such additions to generating facilities as may be required by the pool to meet the present and future requirements of the region served.[1]

The immediate possibilities of forming such a pool, however, were brought to an end when a group of private utilities were granted an injunction which temporarily restrained the Tennessee Valley Authority from carrying out its power program.[2] In requesting that the conferences on pooling be discontinued, President Roosevelt stated: "The securing of an injunction of this broad character, under the circumstances, precludes a joint transmission facility arrangement and makes it advisable to discontinue these conferences."[3]

[1] *Ibid.*

[2] See *infra*, p. 439, for further reference to this injunction.

[3] Text of letter to members of the power pooling conference as quoted in the Jacksonville, Fla., *Times-Union*, Jan. 27, 1937.

The pooling conference was discontinued while negotiations were underway for a renewal of the interchange of power contract with the Commonwealth and Southern Corporation. No agreement could be reached, and the existing contract terminated. Further cooperation at this time between the Tennessee Valley Authority and the private utility companies seems doubtful, since the Commonwealth and Southern Corporation refuses to contract for the further interchange of power unless the Tennessee Valley Authority agrees to refrain from the construction of competing lines. At present, negotiations are under way for the purchase by governmental authorities on a comprehensive basis of certain properties of the private utilities in the Tennessee Valley.

Litigation concerning the Tennessee Valley Authority.— The first major litigation involving the Tennessee Valley Authority originated in the Ashwander case in which a small group of preferred stockholders of the Alabama Power Company attacked the validity of the contract of Jan. 4, 1934, between the Tennessee Valley Authority and the Alabama Power Company and others. These stockholders demanded that the Board of Directors of the Alabama Power Company cancel the contract. Refusal of this demand resulted in a suit against the Tennessee Valley Authority requesting that the contract be declared invalid and that the Tennessee Valley Authority be restrained from further power sales. The Supreme Court of the United States upheld the right of the Tennessee Valley Authority to sell power but declined to discuss the validity of the Tennessee Valley Authority Act as a whole, the decision of the Court being limited to the question of the sale of power generated at Wilson Dam. The Court stated:

The Wilson Dam and its power plant must be taken to have been constructed in the exercise of the constitutional functions of the Federal Government.

.   .   .   .

That the water power and the electric energy generated at the dam are susceptible of disposition as property belonging to the United States is well established.

.   .   .   .

We know of no constitutional ground upon which the Federal Government can be denied the right to seek a wider market. We suppose that in the early days of mining in the West, if the government had undertaken to operate a silver mine on its domain, it could have acquired the mules and horses and equipment to carry its silver to market. And the transmission lines for electric energy are but a facility for conveying to market that particular sort of property, and the acquisition of these lines raises no different constitutional question, unless in some way there is an invasion of the rights reserved to the State or to the people. We find no basis for concluding that the limited undertaking with the Alabama Power Company amounts to such an invasion. Certainly, the Alabama Power Company has no constitutional right to insist that it shall be the sole purchaser of the energy generated at the Wilson Dam; that the energy shall be sold to it or go to waste.[1]

Since the broader issue of the constitutionality of the power program of the Tennessee Valley Authority was not ruled upon in the Ashwander case, the Tennessee Electric Power Company, joined by 18 other companies, filed suits in equity in both the Chancery Court of Knox County, Tennessee, and the District Court of the United States for the Northern District of Alabama. Both these suits sought to enjoin the Tennessee Valley Authority from carrying out its power program on grounds that the activity is in violation of constitutional restrictions upon federal authority. The filing of the actions in these two suits followed the failure of the Georgia Power Company to obtain an interlocutory injunction in the District Court of the United States for the Northern District of Georgia. The decision in this case was later upheld by the Circuit Court of Appeals.[2] In the meantime the case in the Knox County Chancery Court was removed to the Federal District Court for Eastern Tennessee where an injunction was granted. Appeals were taken and the United States Circuit Court of Appeals reversed the interlocutory injunction granted the utilities and remanded the case for further proceedings.[3] On further hearing, the District Court denied the request for a permanent injunction and, in so doing, declared that the Tennessee Valley Authority is a valid exercise of Federal

[1] Ashwander v. Tenn. Valley Authority *et al.*, 297 U.S. 288 (1936).
[2] Georgia Power Co. v. Tenn. Valley Authority, 14 Fed. Sup. 673; 17 Fed. Sup. 769; 89 Fed. (2d) 218.
[3] Alabama Power Co. v. Tenn. Valley Authority, 92 Fed. Rep. (2d) 412.

powers.[1] It was this litigation that brought to an end the
pooling conferences earlier mentioned.

Results of Tennessee Valley Authority Operations.—The
Tennessee Valley Authority program is far from completion.
In the plans for the unified development of the Tennessee
River system, it is proposed to extend the construction period
for the proposed major dams through 1943. From a power
standpoint, several of the main generating stations and intertie
transmission lines have been built, the Wilson, Wheeler, and
Norris dams now providing an installation of 205,000 kw.
When installations are made at Pickwick, Guntersville, Chickamauga, and Fowler Bend, the proposed installations will be
225,000 kw. with a potential installation of 400,000 kw. This
is about one-fourth of the capacity of the private utilities in the
region. From a quantity standpoint, therefore, the Tennessee
Valley Authority is in a position to push forward in providing
power. In its power policy thus far developed, the Tennessee
Valley Authority also has carried out the congressional mandate
to make electricity available more cheaply to domestic and rural
consumers. What the ultimate effect upon the private utilities
will be is impossible to predetermine. The final evaluation of
the program, however, must give weight to the fact that significant rate reductions have been made and that there has been
a marked increase in the consumption of electric power. As a
demonstration of the costs of producing power on a large scale in
publicly owned plants, it will shed much light on the moot question of public ownership. Its primary significance, however,
lies in the fact that it represents the development of natural
resources on the basis of planning with broad social objectives
as the goal to be attained. Similar possibilities exist in other
areas in the United States, and we now turn to a description of the
developments and proposals for other power projects.

THE COLUMBIA RIVER PROJECTS

In 1925, Congress provided for a survey of the Columbia River
for the purpose of formulating plans for the development of the
River for navigation, irrigation, and power production. Pursu-

[1] Tennessee Electric Power Co. *et al.* v. T.V.A. *et al.*, 82 L. Ed. Ad. Op.
643.

ant to this action there was made a report[1] which proposed a series of 10 dams to utilize the 1,300-foot fall of the Columbia River in its 750-mile course from the Canadian border to the sea. It was reported that power plants could be constructed in connection therewith to provide an aggregate installed capacity of more than 10,000,000 horsepower. The proposed system of dams also would provide, with associated channel improvements, for seagoing ships to Dallas, 190 miles inland, and for barges to Priest Rapids, 400 miles inland.[2]

Data on the possibilities of developing the Columbia River were thus available when attention was directed toward water resources conservation and construction of hydroelectric facilities as public works projects to provide for employment and to stimulate industrial activity. An initial allotment of Public Works Administration funds, in an amount not to exceed $63,000,000, was made for Grand Coulee, the uppermost of the proposed dams. Shortly thereafter, an initial allotment of $20,000,000 was made for Bonneville, the lowermost of the proposed dams.

The Grand Coulee, which is being constructed under the supervision of the Bureau of Reclamation, is the largest single project of this nature that has been undertaken. When completed, the dam will have over 11,000,000 cubic yards of concrete. It will be equipped with the world's largest pumping plant, the capacity of which will be 16,000 cubic feet of water per second against a head of more than 300 feet. This plant is to provide water for the extensive irrigation proposed. The original dam was started as a low-power dam, but its plans were recast to a high dam to provide also for irrigation.[3] The Bonneville Dam, under supervision of the United States Corps of Engineers, was completed in 1937. In addition to power production, Bonneville will extend navigation for a distance of 50 miles up the River.

The potentialities of power production from Bonneville and Grand Coulee, together with the other proposed dams, are

[1] Printed as House Doc. 103, 73d Cong., 1st Sess., March, 1932.

[2] National Resources Committee, "Public Works Planning," December, 1936, p. 127.

[3] RIGGS, H. E., Economic Aspects of Grand Coulee, *Electrical World*, vol. 106, pp. 3143 *ff*.

stupendous and challenge the imagination. The region is favorable for the development of hydroelectric power, and the rates for electricity in this section, in general, are already as low as anywhere in the United States. The most pressing problem, from the standpoint of power, is the stimulating of power-consuming industries to serve as markets for the potential power output. The National Resources Committee suggests that construction of further units in the proposed development be postponed until the power produced at Bonneville and Grand Coulee is absorbed and the regional requirements for power make additional facilities necessary.[1]

Owing to the nearing of completion of the Bonneville Dam, a Committee on National Power Policy was asked by President Franklin Roosevelt, on Jan. 18, 1937, to submit a plan for the administration and operation of the project. Many persons saw in the recommendations of this Committee a hint as to the probable administration of other federal power projects under construction. However, because of the fact that Bonneville and Grand Coulee will necessarily be complementary to one another, and to the further fact that all proposed projects in the Columbia River basin should be under a single administration, the recommendations suggested a provisional form of administration for Bonneville pending the establishment of a permanent administrative agency for the entire development. It was recommended that an administrator be appointed to operate the power project with the advice of a board of advisors representing the War and Interior Departments and the Federal Power Commission. The administrator would be authorized to build transmission lines and to sell surplus power (*i.e.*, power not needed for navigation purposes) at rates approved by the Federal Power Commission. It was also recommended that rates should be fixed with a view to encouraging the widest possible use of power, having regard to recovery of the cost of production and amortization of the capital investment. In the sale of power, as in the case of the Tennessee Valley Authority, it was recommended that preference should be given to public or cooperative agencies in order to extend the use of electricity by domestic and rural customers. Contracts for the sale of power, it was further recommended, should not be for more than 20 years in duration,

[1] National Resources Committee, *loc. cit.*, p. 127.

should be adjustable at five-year intervals, and should, if deemed desirable, contain a schedule of rates for current resold by the contractor to consumers.[1]

BOULDER DAM

Flood and irrigation problems on the Colorado River have long received attention. Diversion of water for irrigation purposes began with the first settlers, and extensive irrigation works were later provided by private interests and, after 1902, by the Bureau of Reclamation. The danger of floods, especially to Imperial Valley which is below sea level, made control of the Colorado River a necessity. The question was not whether to build a dam but where to build it and what additional uses to make of it. The matter of constructing a dam was complicated by the fact that the portion of the drainage basin affected covered parts of seven states, and there existed numerous conflicting claims for the use of the Colorado's waters.

Solution of these problems was made possible by the Colorado River Commission, composed of representatives from the states of Arizona, California, Colorado, Nevada, New Mexico, Utah, and Wyoming, under the leadership of Herbert Hoover while Secretary of Commerce. This Commission proposed and drew up the interstate compact under which the present development had taken place and which provides for the division and apportionment of the impounded waters. The federal act ratifying the compact provided that electrical power developments should be subservient to the agricultural and industrial uses of the water but required that flood control and irrigation costs be repaid from revenues derived from the sale of power.[2] It was further provided that construction could not be begun until the Secretary of the Interior had made contracts for the sale of

[1] Sen. Doc. 21, 75th Cong., 1st Sess., Feb. 24, 1937.

[2] It is interesting to note that Article IV of the Compact specified that inasmuch as the Colorado River had ceased to be navigable for commerce, reservation of its waters for navigation would seriously limit the development of the basin. Congress, on the other hand, specified in the Boulder Canyon Act that improvement of navigation was one of the major purposes. That purpose was subsequently held by the Supreme Court to be a valid one to make constitutional the act authorizing the construction of the dam.

water and power which would insure the repayment of the costs of construction, operation, and maintenance of the project.[1]

The project involved the construction of a dam in Boulder Canyon for which a contract was let on Apr. 30, 1931. It was completed in about five years, and the first energy went to the lines in October, 1936. The impounded waters, forming Lake Meade, have a volume of 30,000,000 acre-feet which provides ample storage volume for flood control in addition to the storage needed for power production and irrigation. The All-America Canal, below the dam, will carry irrigation water to the Imperial Valley and solve some of the international problems arising from the fact that the earlier canal was routed in part through Mexico. Though not a part of the project proper, the Upper Parker Canyon Dam, 155 miles below Boulder Dam, has been identified with it. An aqueduct from this dam will carry water 239 miles to Los Angeles and 12 neighboring cities.[2]

Contracts for the disposal of power from the initial installation of 1,835,000 horsepower provide that firm or primary power will be sold at 1.63 mills per kilowatt-hour at transmission voltage and that secondary, or dump power, will be sold at 0.5 mill per kilowatt-hour. The power contracts provide for the purchase of power by the Metropolitan Water District, Los Angeles and other cities, the Southern California Edison Company, and other power companies.[3] It is estimated that the

. . . gross power revenue over a 50-year period is $361,000,000. This will repay the government for the cost of the dam and powerhouse (but not power equipment), interest on the investment, depreciation, and all maintenance and operating charges and leave in addition the handsome profit of $166,500,000. Of this profit, 18.75 per cent ($31,200,000) goes to the State of Nevada and a like amount to Arizona in lieu of taxes they would receive from a private company. The remainder, 62.5 per cent, goes to Uncle Sam.[4]

[1] For an analysis of the Compact and the Boulder Canyon Act of 1927, see National Resources Committee, "Regional Factors in National Planning," December, 1935, pp. 61 *ff.*; or Ray Lyman Wilbur, and Northcutt Ely, The Hoover Dam, U. S. Department of the Interior, Washington, 1933.

[2] The Boulder Canyon Project, *Electric Journal*, vol. 33, No. 11, pp. 478 *ff.*

[3] WILBUR and ELY, *op. cit.*, pp. 23 *ff.*

[4] The Boulder Canyon Project, *Electric Journal*, vol. 33, No. 11, p. 478.

THE MISSISSIPPI VALLEY BILL

The Mississippi River and its tributaries present problems of great magnitude. Property damage from recurring floods is large, and, though much has been done in the way of flood control, it is generally conceded that more effective control of floods is a dire necessity. From a navigation standpoint, the Mississippi offers a valuable resource, and many navigation improvements have been made. Provision of a nine-foot channel north to Minneapolis and west on the Missouri River is now underway, and the Federal Government sponsors the operation of a barge line by the Inland Waterways Corporation.

It was conceived by the sponsors of the Tennessee Valley Authority, therefore, that a similar development for the Mississippi Valley would provide the potentialities of more effective flood control, assist in the further improvement of navigation, and provide facilities for the generation of hydroelectric energy. Accordingly, Senator George W. Norris introduced into the United States Senate a bill to create a Mississippi Valley Authority. The nature of this measure was substantially the same as the Tennessee Valley Authority Act except that some broader powers would be granted. The bill proposed to establish a commission of three persons to be given general authority over flood control, navigation, irrigation, soil erosion prevention, and power production activities. With the exception of the Ohio River Valley, which would be turned over to the Tennessee Valley Authority, it was proposed that jurisdiction by the commission be exercised over the entire drainage basin of the Mississippi River.[1] The area affected would thus comprise about two-thirds of the area of the United States.

While the Mississippi Valley Authority bill was under consideration by a subcommittee of the Senate Committee on Agriculture, the private utility interests raised the same type of objections and criticisms as were voiced against the Tennessee Valley Authority. The claim was made that the proposed Mississippi Valley Authority would mean the extravagant use of public funds for a general federal electric power program under the guise of fostering flood control but worked out on an

[1] S. 3524, 74th Cong., 2d Sess., 1936.

accounting basis which would make unfair and ruinous competition for the privately owned electric utilities in the area.[1]

The group that had supported the Tennessee Valley Authority gave support to the proposed Mississippi Valley Authority, emphasizing the possibilities of effective flood control and the desirable social and economic results to be attained. However, the bill did not receive active administration support and was not enacted into law.

THE PROPOSED CONSERVATION AUTHORITIES ACT

Experience with efforts directed toward the development of the nation's water resources has demonstrated conclusively that for effective, sound development it is necessary to approach an entire river system to coordinate all phases of the water's uses. The National Resources Committee repeatedly has emphasized this view in its various planning reports, and it is generally recognized that the need for comprehensive planning and development is becoming more pertinent. It is not surprising, therefore, that President Franklin Roosevelt recommended a comprehensive plan for development of the water resources in the United States. In his message to Congress on June 3, 1937, he proposed that the country be blanketed with regional authorities to be in charge of the conservation of water resources and protection against dust storms, floods, and soil erosion. Declaring that dust storms, floods, and droughts are nature's warning that action is imperative, the President stated that "Prudent management demands not merely works which will guard against these calamities but carefully formulated plans to prevent their occurrence. Such plans require coordination of many related activities."[2]

Senator Norris and Representative Mansfield introduced in the United States Senate and House of Representatives, respectively, bills to make this proposal effective. The bills differed in several essentials, the major point of difference being

---

[1] Hearings, on S. 3524, 74th Cong., 2d Sess. For a summary of the arguments against the proposed bill, see The Committee of Utility Executives, "The Case against the Mississippi Valley Bill," Washington, D.C., 1936.

[2] Text of Presidential Message to Congress, June 3, 1937, as quoted in the *New York Times*, June 4, 1937.

that the Mansfield bill proposed to separate power production from the other activities contemplated and would provide for separate power authorities to manage the electric power output. For purposes of analysis, the Norris bill will be summarized. The proposals of this bill are:

1. Creation of seven corporate conservation authorities as agencies and instrumentalities of the United States Government to carry out the provisions of the Act. The authorities proposed and the territories of each are:

a. *Atlantic Seaboard Authority.*—Drainage basins of the rivers flowing into the Atlantic Ocean and of the rivers flowing into the Gulf of Mexico, from the east, below the basin of the Suwannee River.

b. *Great-Lakes Ohio Valley Authority.*—Drainage basins of rivers flowing into the Great Lakes and the Ohio River, except those of the Tennessee and Cumberland rivers, and the rivers flowing into the Mississippi River above Cairo, Ill., from the east.

c. *Tennessee Valley Authority.*—Drainage basins of the Tennessee and Cumberland rivers, of the rivers flowing into the Mississippi River below Cairo, Ill., from the east, and of the rivers flowing into the Gulf of Mexico east of the Mississippi River, except the rivers below the basin of the Suwannee River.

d. *Missouri Valley Authority.*—Drainage basins of the Missouri and Red River of the North and of the rivers flowing into the Mississippi River above Cairo, Ill., from the west.

e. *Arkansas Valley Authority.*—Drainage basins of the Arkansas, Red, and Rio Grande rivers, of the rivers flowing into the Mississippi River below Cairo, Ill., from the west and of the rivers flowing into the Gulf of Mexico west of the Mississippi River.

f. *Southwestern Authority.*—Drainage basins of the Colorado River, of the rivers flowing into the Pacific Ocean south of the California-Oregon line, and of the rivers in the Great Basin.

g. *Columbia Valley Authority.*—Drainage basins of the Columbia River and of the rivers flowing into the Pacific Ocean north of the California-Oregon line.

2. The Columbia River Authority is directed to take over the Bonneville project from whatever administration is provided therefor.

3. The Tennessee Valley Authority is to be the Tennessee Valley Authority as now constituted except that its jurisdiction is extended. All present Tennessee Valley Authority powers would remain in force and be transferred to the Authority as created in this Act.

4. The board of directors for each authority, consisting of three members, is to be appointed by the President with the approval of the Senate. Terms of office are for nine years, and the salary proposed is $10,000 per annum.

5. For the purpose of coordination and integration of plans, projects, and activities, the authorities are to be placed under the supervision of the President.

6. The authorities are to submit each year a plan for construction and other activities for the ensuing year. The plans are to consider the integrated development of water, soil, and forest resources for the purposes of navigation, prevention and control of floods, and soil reclamation.

7. In the event that any projects involve the generation of electric energy, the appropriate authority is empowered to take steps to dispose of any of it not needed for the operation of dams, lifts, locks, etc.

8. In the disposal of power, preference is to be given to states, subdivisions thereof, and nonprofit agencies. To make this possible, as well as to provide adequate markets and outlets and to prevent monopolization, authority to build and operate transmission lines, rural distribution lines, etc., is vested in each authority.

9. Rate contracts would be limited to periods of not longer than 20 years, and those made with agencies reselling the bulk of the power purchased by them could be canceled on 5-years' notice.

10. Rate schedules for the sale of energy should be constructed so as to encourage the widest possible use of energy, having regard to the recovery of the cost of generation and transmission of electric energy, including reserves for maintenance and upkeep and the amortization of the capital investment over a reasonable period of years.

11. States would be given power to form compacts to cooperate with the authority in the areas in which they are located.[1]

As in the case of the Tennessee Valley Authority, the proposed Mississippi Valley Authority, and other federal projects, flood control, navigation, and irrigation are specified as major purposes of the proposed undertaking. Production of power coincidental to the carrying out of the other purposes is significant, and there seems to be no doubt that power production is considered by the sponsors of the various projects to be just as important as, or even greater in importance than, any of the other objectives. The far-reaching consequences and possibilities involved in this proposal are of such magnitude that their visualization and appraisal in advance are difficult. The potential beneficial results of a planned development on a national scale for a basic resource, however, are worthy of careful consideration. The hit-and-miss results arising out of the lack of planning which has characterized previous developments would be eliminated in favor of planning to achieve predetermined objectives. The national power policy of making electricity "more broadly available at cheaper rates to industry, to domestic, and particularly to agricultural consumers" would undoubtedly be carried out as one of the objectives of the planned developments. That

[1] S. 2555, 75th Cong., 1 Sess., June 3, 1937.

such a result would promote the general welfare of the people as a whole is hardly questionable. At the same time, the magnitude of the potential power developments imply that there will be nation-wide power services and possibly nation-wide power systems under governmental operation. The consequent effects upon the privately owned electrical industries cannot be definitely stated, but the problems of government cooperation with them would be many and complex. The Federal Government would become a significant, if not a dominant, factor in the electrical power industry. In such a case one's own beliefs as to the desirability of public ownership and operation must necessarily become the standard for evaluating the power proposals of the bill to create regional conservation authorities for the whole of the United States.

SUMMARY

If the Conservation Authorities bill becomes enacted into law, it will be a long time before the extent of the power developments will be known. Without them, however, the Federal Government already has gone forward in undertaking many large power producing projects. The extent and status of these projects, as of Jan. 1, 1937, are summarized in the table on p. 450. The extent of these developments indicates that federal power policy is definitely committed to the utilization of hydro-power sites to generate electric power by the Federal Government. This may in time, as proposed in the Conservation Authorities bill, be extended to blanket the United States. Certainly the formulation and execution of the present developments are on a sufficiently large scale to enable us to conclude that the days of uncontrolled power developments are over. A much strengthened Federal Power Commission, effective regulation of holding companies, and the elimination of "twilight" zones in which no regulation exists are the handmaidens linked to the providing of electrical power by federal agencies. The foundations upon which the present power policy and program are based, and the criterion upon which it asks to be evaluated, is the making of power more broadly available at cheaper rates. Coupled with this are the conservation and unified development of one of the nation's basic resources—water.

FEDERAL AND FEDERALLY AIDED POWER PROJECTS
(As of Dec. 31, 1937)

Project	Initial power installation, hp.	Appropriated to date	Initial cost
Part A—Tennessee Valley Authority Projects			
Wilson Dam.............	261,400	....	$46,950,748
Norris Dam..............	132,000	....	36,310,370
Wheeler Dam............	90,000	....	35,217,964
Pickwick Dam...........	96,000	....	33,119,497
Guntersville.............	102,000	....	34,123,660
Chickamauga............	108,000	....	40,435,645
Hiwassee................	80,000	....	17,000,000
Gilbertsville.............	*	....	112,000,000
Total................	869,400	$191,066,270†	$355,237,884
Part B—Corps of Engineers			
Fort Peck...............	*	$ 96,337,000	$108,600,000
Bonneville..............	86,000	51,248,700	51,000,000
Passamaquoddy‡........	*	7,000,000‡	6,500,000‡
Bluestone Reservation§...	*	649,850	11,684,800
Total................	86,000	$155,235,550	$177,784,800
Part C—Bureau of Reclamation			
Boulder Dam............	515,000	$113,810,000‖	$126,500,000
Grand Coulee............	478,000	35,750,000‖	186,000,000
Kendrick (Seminoe).......	30,000	13,857,000¶	20,000,000
Central Valley...........	375,000	23,600,000**	170,000,000
Colorado—Big Thompson.	40,000	900,000	7,036,693
Total................	1,438,000	$187,917,000	$509,536,693
Part D—Summary			
Tennessee Valley Authority............		$191,066,270	$355,237,884
Corps of Engineers....................		155,235,550	177,784,800
Bureau of Reclamation...............		187,917,000	509,536,693
Total		$534,218,820	$1,042,559,377

* Undetermined.

† TVA appropriation not allocated to specific projects.

‡ Project now suspended; unexpended balance of $500,000 will be returned to Treasury, making total cost $6,500,000.

§ Project now suspended.

‖ Includes PWA financing.

¶ Includes PWA and ERA financing.

**Includes ERA financing.

Source: *Electrical World*, vol. 107, No. 1, pp. 98–99, and vol. 109, No. 3, pp. 102–103.

It is too early to evaluate these huge national programs, which are for the most part in their development stages. At the present writing the constitutionality of the entire power program of the Tennessee Valley Authority is being attacked in the federal courts. If sustained, the legal path will be opened to power developments by public authority on a scale without precedent in the United States. So far as the energy generated in these projects meets real needs, there is economic justification for them. If, however, these projects can be developed only at the expense of private industry, either through the loss of existing markets or of opportunities for the development of new markets, the issue becomes one of private versus public enterprise. This issue should be placed for decision squarely before the American people.

References

BROWN, HARRISON: A Great American Experiment, London *Fortnightly Review*, July, 1935. (Reprinted in *Congressional Record*, July 24, 1935.)

CARPENTER, WILLIAM: Hidden Costs at Muscle Shoals, *Edison Electric Institute Bulletin*, July, 1936.

Committee of Utility Executives: "The Case Against the Mississippi Valley Authority Bill," Washington (pamphlet).

Commonwealth and Southern Corporation: "Analysis of the Annual Report of the Tennessee Valley Authority," New York, Feb. 15, 1937.

COREY, HERBERT: Is T.V.A. Telling the Truth?, *Public Utilities Fortnightly*, vol. 15, No. 8.

———: Trying to Pry into T.V.A., *Public Utilities Fortnightly*, vol. 16, No. 13.

———: A Yardstick That Is Not Air Conditioned, *Public Utilities Fortnightly*, vol. 18, No. 7.

DOYING, G. E.: Millions for Kilowatts, *Public Utilities Fortnightly*, vol. 15, No. 9.

Edison Electric Institute: Government and Business, *Publication* S6, 1936.

———: The TVA, *Publication* S10, 1936.

Electric Journal, Boulder Canyon Project, vol. 33, No. 11.

ELY, OWEN: The Yardstick Experiment, *Public Utilities Fortnightly*, vol. 15, No. 6.

GLAESER, M. G.: The Federal Government's Tennessee Valley Project, *Public Utilities Fortnightly*, vol. 13, Nos. 6, 7, and 8; and vol. 15, No. 1.

HARBESON, R. W.: The Power Program of T.V.A., *Journal of Land and Public Utility Economics*, vol. 12, No. 1.

IRWIN, WILL: The Great Tennessee Bubble, *Public Utilities Fortnightly*, vol. 11, No. 8.

JONES, D. M.: Background Factors Leading to the Boulder Dam Development, *General Electric Review*, vol. 39.

KIMBLE, ELLIS: The Tennessee Valley Project, *Journal of Land and Public Utility Economics*, vol. 9, No. 4.

LILIENTHAL, D. E.: Business and Government in the Tennessee Valley, *Annals of the American Academy of Political and Social Science*, vol. 172.

MANLY, BASIL: "Regional Coordination and Integration of Electric Utilities," paper presented before World Power Conference, Washington, Sept. 10, 1936.

Mississippi Valley Committee of the P.W.A.; *Report*, Oct. 1, 1934.

MORGAN, A. E.: Power and the New Deal, *Forum*, vol. 93, No. 3.

National Resources Committee: "Public Works Planning," December, 1936.

———: "Regional Factors in National Planning," December, 1935.

NELSON, W. R.: The Boulder Canyon Project, *Smithsonian Institution Annual Report*, 1935.

NORRIS, G. W.: Politics and Muscle Shoals, *Congressional Record*, Dec. 19, 1927.

RIGGS, H. E.: Economic Aspects of Grand Coulee, *Electrical World*, vol. 106, Apr. 22, 1937.

Tennessee Valley Authority: *Annual Reports*.

———: *News Releases*.

———: *Statistical Bulletins*.

———: Tennessee Valley Authority, 1933–1937.

———: The Unified Development of the Tennessee River System, 1936.

U. S. Congress: Hearings, S. 3524, Control of Flood Waters in the Mississippi Valley, 74th Cong., 2d Sess., 1936.

———: Columbia River and Tributaries, House Doc. 103, 73d Cong., 1st Sess., 1932.

———: Development of the Rivers of the United States, House Doc. 395, 73d Cong., 2d Sess., 1934.

———: Tennessee River and Tributaries, House Doc. 328, 71st Cong., 2d Sess., 1930.

———: Bonneville Electric Power Project, Sen. Doc. 21, 75th Cong., 1st Sess., 1937.

———: Colorado River Development, Sen. Doc. 186, 70th Cong., 2d Sess., 1929.

WILBUR, R. L., and NORTHCUTT ELY: "The Hoover Dam," U. S. Department of the Interior, 1933.

WOLFSON, J. D.: "Power Views of Franklin D. Roosevelt," National Power Policy Committee, 1934.

CHAPTER XVII

RURAL ELECTRIFICATION

The national power policy holds as its main objective the broadened use of electricity at lower rates. Rural electrification on an extensive scale is necessary if that objective is to be attained. The need for electricity on the farm and the anticipated desirable social results of rural electrification are, in the opinion of many, justification for carrying out this phase of the national power policy. In many respects, electric energy is of more importance to farm families than it is to urban families, although the use of electric energy has revolutionized and made possible the present-day large-sized cities, and electric current for the operation of transportation agencies, elevators, and for other purposes is essential to the well-being of the residents of cities. As direct consumers, however, the urban dwellers use electricity only for domestic purposes. The farm consumers, on the other hand, include in their domestic services such things as water pumping, woodcutting, milking, churning, and other daily chores. These uses, combined with the ordinary domestic uses of electricity for washing, ironing, refrigeration, cooking, water heating, and cleaning, immeasurably lighten and ease the burdens of farm housekeeping. In addition, the farm makes use of electricity for power and other productive purposes. The benefits of farm electrification arise from making the farm a better place to live and from the provision of machinery and appliances to improve or cheapen productive processes, the social values of improved living conditions on the farm resulting from the electrification of farms being many.[1] A need for the improve-

[1] See, for comments to this effect: Howard, J. R., Rural Electrification, National Electric Light Association, *Proceedings*, 1929, vol. 86, pp. 77 *ff.*; Winder, M. S., Saving the Farm For the Family, National Electric Light Association, *Proceedings*, 1930, vol. 87, pp. 61 *ff.*; Zinder, Hanina, Problems of Rural Electric Service, *Journal of Land and Public Utility Economics*, November, 1928, p. 338; and Coyle, D. C., "Electric Power on the Farm," pp. 11 *ff.*, Rural Electrification Administration, Washington, 1936.

ment in rural living conditions is indicated by the fact that most farm families are without many of the basic comforts of the home. The Rural Electrification Administration reports that of the persons living on farms:

> 73 per cent must carry water from wells or other sources of supply.
> 77 per cent must put up with unsanitary, inconvenient outdoor toilets.
> 93 per cent have neither bathtub nor shower.
> 76 per cent must depend upon kerosene or gasoline lamps and apparently 10 per cent use candles or are entirely without light.
> 33 per cent heat their homes partially or entirely with fireplaces.
> 54 per cent with stoves.
> 48 per cent are compelled to do their laundry work out of doors.[1]

Extent of Rural Electrification.—Rural electrification has been, until recently, left almost entirely to the initiative of private utilities. Their efforts, with but few exceptions, were concentrated on the development of services in urban communities so that the extension of lines into rural areas proceeded slowly. Since 1935, however, rural electrification has come to be considered as an essential part of the national power policy and recognized as a matter of national concern. Federal, state, and local governmental bodies are cooperating with private utilities in extending electrical services to rural areas, and the number of electrified farms is now being rapidly increased.

Practically all of the development of rural electric service has taken place since 1920. The impetus given to rural electrification by several pioneering companies and the centering of attention on this problem by the National Electric Light Association in the early 1920's resulted in an extension of rural lines until 1929 when there occurred a decrease in the number of farms added to electric lines. There was again an increase in the number of farms electrified in 1930, followed by large decreases through 1933. An increase in the number of farms electrified again occurred in 1934, and the activities of federal agencies resulted in large increases in the number of farms added each year since 1934. By the beginning of 1937, there were almost 900,000 farms served by central stations. This number represents slightly more than 14 per cent of the farms in the United States; and for farms with dwellings valued at $500 or more,

---

[1] Rural Electrification Administration, "Light and Power for the Farm," p. 1.

33 per cent are electrified. In addition to those served by central stations, it is estimated that approximately 250,000 farms are served by individual lighting plants. The following table presents the number of farms served by central stations, the percentage of all farms thus served, and the increase in the number served each year for the period from 1923 to 1936.

FARMS SERVED BY CENTRAL STATIONS

Year	Number of farms served	Percentage of total farms served	Increase in number of farms served
1923	177,561	2.8	
1924	204,780	3.2	27,219
1925	246,150	3.9	41,370
1926	309,125	4.9	62,975
1927	393,221	6.2	84,096
1928	506,242	8.0	113,021
1929	576,168	9.2	69,926
1930	649,919	10.4	73,751
1931	698,786	11.1	48,867
1932	709,449	11.3	10,663
1933	713,558	11.4	4,109
1934	743,954	11.8	30,396
1935	788,795*	12.5*	44,841*
1936	897,873	14.3	109,078

* These figures represent corrections of those previously reported in *Electrical World*, vol. 106, No. 1, p. 62.

Source: *Electrical World*, vol. 107, No. 1, p. 73.

The expansion in rural electrification since 1935 is due in some part to improved business conditions but undoubtedly is due mostly to the activities of various federal agencies in carrying out the phase of the national power program which looks toward the furtherance of a more extensively electrified rural America. The Tennessee Valley Authority has built several hundred miles of lines into rural areas and sells power there to cooperative groups which have built their own distribution lines. The Electric Home and Farm Authority formerly made loans to individuals for the purpose of wiring homes or purchasing appliances. It also standardized certain appliances which are now being sold at prices lower than formerly. The Federal Housing Administration makes loans for installing pressure water systems and for modernizing bathrooms and kitchens, and the Rural Electrification Administration was created to promote the construction of rural electric lines, to extend electric services to as many farms as possible, and to encourage the use of electrical energy in quantities sufficient to improve living conditions on the farm.[1] Cooperation by state agencies and utility companies has enhanced the work of these federal agencies, but the accelerating rate of growth of recent years will have to continue if farm electrification is to become general. Continued participation, encouragement, and assistance by the Federal Government is probably necessary if further rapid advancement is to be expected. Private companies, though laying the groundwork for rural electrification, encounter obstacles which make it difficult for them to carry out extensive rural electrification programs. These obstacles can be removed by federal agencies. To show the part now being played by the Federal Government, the development of rural electrification as carried out by private companies will first be reviewed.

Development of Rural Electrification by Private Companies.— The first strictly rural electrification project in the United States was undertaken in 1900 by the Pacific Gas and Electric Company which introduced an electric irrigation pump on a farm in its territory. Its operation was a success, and others were installed. California was favorably situated for the development of rural electrification. Much of the power available in California is generated in hydroelectric plants in the mountains and transmitted across the agricultural valleys to the coastal cities, the large market for irrigation pumping making it profitable to build distribution lines to distribute energy to the farms adjacent to the transmission lines. The electrification of over 50 per cent of all California farms is due largely to this situation,[2] as is the fact that California has the largest consumption of electric energy per rural customer in the United States. Because of this same factor of irrigation pumping, the West South Central, the Mountain, and the Pacific States all have comparatively large consumptions per rural customer, the heavy load from this source promoting an extensive

[1] Federal Power Commission, "Electric Rate Survey—Rural Electric Service," *Rate Series* No. 8, Feb. 1, 1935, p. v.

[2] Coyle, *op. cit.*, pp. 59–60.

development of rural lines in these sections. In general, however, it has been felt by the electrical industry that electricity could be made available to farms only if the lines had to be built for some other purpose; accordingly, the farm market was viewed as an unprofitable one, and the industry did not attempt to develop it, although some effort was made to extend lines to small towns, especially where they were located in compact groups. The rural policy formulated in 1912 by the Middle West Utilities System was of this nature.[1]

The strain on electrical generating capacity during the World War period strengthened the feeling that there was no need to develop the rural market, although about the same time a scarcity of agricultural laborers stimulated the use of agricultural machinery, and there were a few isolated attempts to make use of electric power. A cooperative group in Wisconsin built a distribution line and purchased power wholesale, and a mutual company in Idaho took advantage of the near-by location of a reclamation service plant to buy power at a low wholesale rate. Several cooperative groups in Ohio also built lines and turned them over to power companies to operate.[2]

The utility companies, as a rule, did not look with favor upon requests for the extension of lines into rural areas. The lines were expensive to build in relationship to the few customers and light loads which generally prevailed. Loads were light because the customers usually had to contribute to the construction of the line and therefore would not have funds with which to do extensive wiring and to make purchases of appliances and equipment. Furthermore, there had been but little development of electrical equipment adapted to the special needs encountered on farms. If the lines were to be profitable to the company, it was necessary that high rates be charged, and this further deterred the extensive use of energy and kept loads light.

In such a picture, it seemed that the development of rural electrification could hardly take place. To find a solution to the problem of high costs of rural lines, the National Electric Light Association formed, in 1921, a Rural Lines Committee. This was followed shortly by a Rural Electric Service Committee

[1] *Ibid.*, p. 60.
[2] *Ibid.*, pp. 60–61.

which established many state subcommittees.   In 1923, there was organized a Committee on Relation of Electricity to Agriculture, which was composed of representatives from the National Electric Light Association; the American Farm Bureau Federation; American Society of Agricultural Engineers; and the United States Departments of Agriculture, Interior, and Commerce.   This Committee, generally known as CREA, outlined four steps by which it planned to approach the problem of rural electrification, *viz.:*

(1) A survey of farm power;

(2) A survey of central station and individual plant service to farmers;

(3) An analysis of agricultural uses of electricity in foreign countries; and

(4) A program of experimental and research work on the application of electricity to agriculture.[1]

CREA immediately stimulated interest in rural electrification, and, by 1932, 25 committees had been formed in various states to study the uses of electricity on the farm.   These state committees, as a rule, worked with the state agricultural experiment stations.   The cooperating agencies also set up an experimental project to study the applications of electricity to agriculture. While these developments were taking place, the first investigations made by the National Electric Light Association committees disclosed that the utility companies were hesitant about undertaking rural extensions.   In cases where rural extensions had been made, it was found that rates were high to cover the large investment per customer or that the users were required to pay a substantial part of the construction costs of the distribution lines.   Friction, controversy, and antagonism between the companies and the consumers followed in the wake of either of these policies.

Further studies and analyses of rates, costs, and other problems indicated clearly, however, the need of cooperation between customers and the utilities.   Through the efforts of these committees, the attitude toward rural service changed so that many companies, during the decade of the twenties, started rural services.   Many of these companies established rural

---

[1] *Ibid.*, pp. 62–63.

service departments or placed especially trained men in charge of the rural services.[1] Throughout the industry, there began to develop an attitude that the rural market would offer, if properly developed, a profitable load. Particularly is this true of those companies which established rural service departments. The aim and goal of the rural service work then undertaken were not only an extension of the uses of electricity to agriculture but also an attempt to make the service of value and benefit to the customer. It was general practice for the rural service departments to be given responsibility for developing the rural service. Looking toward this end, these departments engaged in contact and developmental activities which ordinarily involved the following:

1. Visiting customers to get an understanding of their problems and to discuss service, equipment needs, and the like.

2. Preparing and distributing data and information concerning the use of electricity on the farm, farm wiring, and construction of apparatus.

3. Studying present applications and the development of new applications of electricity to farm work.

4. Preparing news articles, supplying speakers for farmers' meetings, and showing exhibits at fairs and other meetings.

5. Surveying the farm territory.[2]

Surveying the farm territory was one of the most essential of the activities of the rural service departments. By this means were collected data and information about the type of farming in the franchise area, actual and potential customers, present equipment and its effect on energy consumption, and possible increases in the use of energy.

---

[1] National Electric Light Association, Rural Electric Service Committee, Report, National Electric Light Association, *Proceedings*, 1927, vol. 84, p. 83. At this time, there were 57 companies with rural service departments and 43 with trained men in charge of rural services.

[2] For specific illustrations of the work of rural service departments, see: "Developing Service for the Farm—Wisconsin Power and Light Company," National Electric Light Association, *Proceedings*, 1929, vol. 86, pp. 225 *ff*.; "Developing Electric Service for the Farm—Alabama Power Company," *ibid.*, pp. 241 *ff*. "Farm Electrification—New York Power and Light Corporation," *ibid.*, 1930, vol. 87, pp. 281 *ff*.; and "Developing Electric Service for the Farm—Organization and Methods of the Puget Sound Power and Light Company," *ibid.*, pp. 261 *ff*.

The crux of the problem of rural electrification encountered by the utility companies centered in stimulating and promoting an extensive use of power by every customer, since a load derived from domestic uses alone could not carry the investment in rural distribution lines. Consequently, much attention was given to the problem of electric power utilization on the farm. In the aggregate, the farming industry of the United States is a potential large user of power, being exceeded only by the transportation industry.[1] The CREA devoted much of its attention to the study of applications of electricity to farm power needs. There are now more than 250 ways in which electricity is actually being used on farms.[2]

From the standpoint of the company, the problem of rural extensions centers in the relationship of the cost of construction to the revenue from the line. The Federal Power Commission, basing its findings on returns from 327 selected utility companies, reports that the average construction cost of a mile of rural line is $1,740.[3] With only a few customers per mile of line, it is necessary to require that the customers contribute toward the building of the line or that they pay relatively high rates. The companies that first undertook to supply rural service usually required a cash contribution from customers for construction purposes, but this policy was soon demonstrated to be unwise because it was inconvenient, if not impossible, for the customer to provide cash for the required contribution, and such an outlay deterred the purchase of equipment. Extension policies later became somewhat liberalized. The Federal Power Commission reports that there are, in general, six groups of plans for making extensions. They are:

Group 1. The construction of a rural line depends upon an average minimum connected load in kilowatts per mile of line and per customer. In case the connected load is less than the

---

[1] For analyses of farm power needs and uses, see: U. S. Department of Agriculture, National Farm Power Survey, *Department Bulletin* 1348, 1925; National Electric Light Association, Rural Electric Service Committee, *Report*, National Electric Light Association, *Proceedings*, 1925, vol. 82, pp. 72 *ff.*; and ZINDER, HANINA, Problems of Rural Electric Service, *Journal of Land and Public Utility Economics*, November, 1928, pp. 340 *ff.*

[2] COYLE, *op. cit.*, p. 63.

[3] Federal Power Commission, "Electric Rate Survey—Rural Electric Service," *Rate Series* No. 8, p. 15.

specified minimum, say 10 kilowatts per mile of line and 1½ kilowatts per customer, the customers are charged for the deficit.

Group 2. Each customer is required to guarantee a fixed monthly payment depending upon the number of customers receiving service per mile of line. Adjustments are made in the guarantees when new customers are added. The minimum monthly guarantees vary throughout the United States from $7 to $37.50 per month per mile of line.

Group 3. This plan calls for an investment by the utility up to a certain fixed amount, say $400, per customer. If the average cost of the line for each customer exceeds this amount, the additional costs are borne by the customers.

Group 4. All rural lines are financed in advance by the prospective customers at an average fixed price per mile, say $1,000. Customers are then refunded a specified amount, say $100, for each customer taking service until the advance is repaid.

Group 5. This plan provides that the utility will bear the entire cost of building rural extensions, and the customers guarantee a minimum annual revenue equal to a certain percentage, varying by companies from 15 to 45 per cent, of the cost of construction.

Group 6. These plans are miscellaneous in character but generally provide for free extensions based upon the number of customers and connected load.[1]

Selected utility companies covered in the Federal Power Commission's survey of rural electric service reported these extension plans. The number of utilities and the number of customers served under each group are given below:

Group number	Number of utilities	Number of customers
1	4	12,203
2	42	132,785
3	30	93,726
4	20	155,262
5	147	486,988
6	102	476,885
Total........	345	1,357,849

[1] *Ibid.*, pp. 7 *ff.*

The rates charged for rural service are directly influenced by extension policies. The greater the contribution by customers toward extension costs, the less can be the rate charged, or, conversely, the amount of the rate increases in proportion to the amount of the investment by the company. If the farm customer aids in financing the line extension, his ability to purchase equipment is affected, and it is likely that but little use can be made of the service at his disposal. The resulting small load practically precludes his receiving the benefits of the lower rate steps accompanying large use of energy. On the other hand, since the rates must be higher when construction costs are borne by the company, the customer is inclined to feel that he is being overcharged. The solution of these difficulties lies in the ability of the company to develop a large load which will permit rates to be on a lower basis. Some companies have recognized that development work must be done in rural areas before a satisfactory load can be obtained and have instituted rates on a basis that looks toward increasing the load. Some loss, of course, is taken during the developmental period, but ultimately the increasing revenue provided by increasing the use is expected to yield a return on the investment. The principle underlying this practice is recognized in many public utility charges. On the whole, the policy has proved to be desirable if the initial rates yield something above the actual operating expenses, on the theory that any new class of service that yields more revenue than the direct expense incurred for it is an advantage to the rest of the business even though it does not furnish so great a contribution to general expenses as does the rest of the business. Urban electric services, to illustrate, would have to pay higher rates in order to give a fair return to the utility if it were not for the contribution to net income, however small it might be, by the rural services.[1]

Progress in rural electrification between 1920 and 1935 was noteworthy, in spite of the obstacles of a heavy investment relative to the possible load on a line and the comparatively high rates that it was necessary to charge in order to make a return on the investment in the rural lines which retarded the use of energy. Furthermore, though many of the power needs of the

[1] Rate Research Committee, *Report*, National Electric Light Association, *Proceedings*, 1925, vol. 82, pp. 31–32.

farm can be supplied economically and satisfactorily by electric motors, other forms of power, particularly for field operations, are necessary, and to have both requires a dual or larger investment in equipment than many farmers can or will make. Construction costs on rural lines were materially reduced as a result of experimentation with various kinds of materials and types of construction; more liberal policies in financing rural line extensions were instituted; rate schedules were revised to stimulate increased consumption and heavier loads; and rural agents were placed in the field to advise and assist in the problems of using electrical power. Machinery and equipment manufacturers designed equipment and appliances adapted to farm needs, and agricultural experiment stations studied and developed ways of effectively using electric power.

The development of rural service by private utilities, however, was confined largely to the more densely populated areas adjacent to the towns and cities and for specialized activities such as poultry and dairy farming and for irrigation. Many believed that the further development of rural electrification would be slow and that the future would witness but little expansion, since the profitable areas already had been electrified. The fact that expansion in rural electrification is again taking place is due to the earlier mentioned cooperation of federal agencies, utility companies, bankers and credit agencies, and electrical manufacturers. The impetus to this development centers in the establishment of the Rural Electrification Administration.

Government Attitude toward Rural Electrification.—Public utterances of Franklin D. Roosevelt, both before and after his election to the Presidency of the United States, indicate his conviction as to the importance of an abundant and widespread use of electricity in modern life, particularly by domestic and rural consumers. The National Resources Board, created by President Roosevelt to study and formulate plans concerning matters of national interest and concern, took cognizance of this problem and in December, 1934, recommended that positive action for rural electrification be undertaken. The Board stated that other industries, in search of reliable and low-cost power, had extensively turned to electricity and that agriculture should also. Because of the limited use of electricity in agriculture, however, it was stated that "It therefore seems necessary

for the Government to stimulate the extension of this [rural]
service in many areas."[1]

In a similar vein, the Mississippi Valley Committee declared:

Having recognized the advantages of rural electric service and
reached the conclusion that only under governmental leadership and
control is any considerable electrification of "dirt farms" possible, we
face the obvious obligation of getting it done . . . an allotment of
$100,000,000 actually to build independent, self liquidating rural pro-
jects would exert a mighty influence in various directions.[2]

Other governmental agencies gave consideration to the
problems of rural electrification. The possibility of including
rural electric lines among its work projects induced the Federal
Emergency Relief Administration to undertake a survey to
obtain information covering the present availability of electric
service to farmers, its use, and the possibilities of extending
service to additional farms; and the Public Works Administration
recognized the construction of rural electric lines as a form of
public works to be undertaken with federal aid. It had prepared
drafts of bills for several types of public agencies which could
make use of PWA funds as sponsors of projects, and several
states passed enabling acts to permit the formation of public
agencies for this purpose.[3]

The Tennessee Valley Authority was directed, in its authorization to sell surplus power, to give special attention to rural
electrification. Its development of rural electrification began

. . . with the study of construction standards for rural electric lines,
with particular emphasis upon the reduction of construction costs
through simplification of structures. At the same time, reconnaissance
surveys were commenced in the Muscle Shoals area, including northeastern Mississippi, and in eastern Tennessee to determine the most
feasible locations for rural electrification projects. The availability of
relief labor in the fall of 1933 stimulated the construction of rural lines,
and at the end of the fiscal year, 220.5 miles of rural line were under
construction. . . . Commercial surveys and engineering had been complete for approximately 568 miles in addition.

Studies were made of the use of electricity on farms, and it was
found, for example, that even in a relatively urban county such as

[1] Quoted in Coyle, *op. cit.*, p. 86.
[2] *Ibid.*, p. 87.
[3] *Ibid.*, p. 90.

Knox County, Tennessee, electric service is now available to fewer than a quarter of the farms of the county outside the corporate limits of the city of Knoxville. A beginning was made on the design of farm electrical equipment based on farm requirements and purchasing power, rather than on preconceived conventional designs. Low-cost electric-wiring systems for homes were considered as a means for facilitating a greater use of electricity.

Retail rates for rural service were studied with care, and it was concluded that the standard residential rates designed for urban use could be applied in rural areas, in conjunction with adjustments on the minimum monthly billing amount based upon the method of financing the rural lines and the number of customers per mile of rural line.[1]

In his message to Congress, January, 1935, President Franklin Roosevelt urged that the Relief Appropriation Act use the program of the National Resources Board as a guide. In this Act, rural electrification was included by Congress as one of the eight categories of projects specifically designated. Acting upon the authority there embodied, there was created by Executive Order, May 11, 1935, the Rural Electrification Administration. Its duties and functions were "To initiate, formulate, administer, and supervise a program of approved projects with respect to the generation, transmission, and distribution of electric energy in rural areas."

The First Year of the Rural Electrification Administration.— The Rural Electrification Administration, aside from the brief statement of duties and functions in the Executive Order, had little to guide it. It believed that, since most of the electrical utility properties in the United States are privately owned, policies looking toward rural electrification must necessarily provide for cooperation with the electric light and power industry. Shortly after the creation of the Rural Electrification Administration, therefore, a conference with utility executives was held. This conference group discussed a tentative program and appointed a committee to act as a connecting link between the Rural Electrification Administration and the industry. Shortly thereafter, a similar conference with municipal system managers was held, and also a third conference with leaders of cooperative organizations. This latter conference discussed the possibilities

[1] Tennessee Valley Authority, *Annual Report*, 1934, pp. **32** *ff.*

of farmers' cooperative groups as agencies to build distribution lines and to distribute power.[1]

The utilities manifested their interest by undertaking a nation-wide survey of proposed rural extensions. This survey disclosed that many new lines would soon be constructed and that, in addition, approximately $250,000,000 would be expended during 1935–1936 to equip and connect 351,000 rural projects, including 247,000 farms. The private utilities stated that the primary problem of the farmer "is not one of rates, but of financing the wiring and purchase of appliances."[2]

The Rural Electrification Administration took exception to this viewpoint and declared, "we hold rate simplification and even rate reductions over large areas to be the heart of the problem of electrifying rural America." In the light of the many suggestions and comments received, the Rural Electrification Administration, through the Administrator, Mr. Morris L. Cooke, announced its program and policies as follows:

The controlling objective of the Rural Electrification Administration is to electrify as many American farms and farm homes as possible and to do this in the shortest possible time. At the same time, the Rural Electrification Administration seeks to put into action fundamentally sound policies upon which rural electrification in the United States may proceed, yield durable results, and achieve its ultimate goal of social welfare.

.   .   .   .

The accomplishment of our program involves the abandonment of practices generally admitted to be outworn, and the adoption of forward-looking policies possible by the favorable 1935 conditions. Some of the new policies suggested, as worked out in cooperation with the Rural Electrification Administration technical staff, follow:

1. *Service charges*, or any demand, transformer, or other fixed charges which do not include current should be avoided in rural rates. Room and area charges are not suitable to ordinary farm service and are out of date.

2. A simple system of *block rates* varying both as to the minimum charge and levels of the blocks provides ample opportunity to recognize varying costs and is easily understood by the customer. These rate schedules should be *promotional*—inducing higher use by having the

[1] COYLE, *op. cit.*, pp. 90–91.

[2] *Ibid.*, pp. 91–92.

price per kilowatt-hour drop sharply in the second and following blocks of the schedule.

3. The *minimum charge* normally should not exceed $3 to $3.50 including 40 to 50 kw.-hr.

4. *Customer contracts* for rural service, that provide for a minimum monthly guarantee, should have a definite termination for such guarantees, normally three years, after which the minimum on the applicable rate should apply.

5. In areas where farms average between three and four to the mile, rural extensions should be built without customer contributions. The rules governing extensions should be simply stated so as to be readily understood.

6. Rules as to *extensions* should apply to an entire district—the cost of providing service should be averaged because individual farmers and groups of farmers are not qualified to dicker as to the cost of building a mile of line or setting a transformer. Preferably the amount the utility will invest *should not be stated in dollars per customer*, but rather *in feet per customer*, varying with load to be obtained.

7. Before authorizing the construction of a rural line the Public Service Commission might well have representatives study the proposal on the ground, consider all possible extensions and confer with residents of the locality to make sure that all entitled to service receive it. Some skimmed milk should normally go with the cream.

8. The Commissions of course recognize that definite distinctions are now made between urban and rural standards for line construction and can protect the farmer by insisting that the less expensive rural standards be adopted. Furthermore, the Public Service Commissions are in a position to check rural line construction costs to insure their reasonableness and can carry on rural cost studies whenever feasible.

9. Experience has demonstrated that *joint committees* of farmers and representatives of electric enterprises are not justified by the results accomplished. The farmers should formulate their needs and then under the leadership and guidance of public officials push for their accomplishment.[1]

The Rural Electrification Administration announced its plans and terms for rural electrification loans in July, 1935. No direct grants are contemplated, though under suitable conditions loans to cover the entire cost of building lines in areas without electric service may be made. Only self-liquidating projects are eligible for loans. Normally, loans are made for

[1] COOKE, M. L., The New Viewpoint, *Rural Electrification News*, vol. I, No. 2, pp. 1 *ff*.

20 years at 3 per cent interest. Preference for loans is given to public agencies and cooperative groups. Loans to private utilities are secured through the general credit of the borrower. In other instances, especially on loans to nonprofit agencies, the line itself is the security for the loans. The erection of lines is directed by contractors, utility companies, states and subdivisions of states, farmers' organizations, and in certain instances by the Federal Government.[1] Later, in recognition of the fact that lack of adequate financing facilities retards the extension of electric service in rural areas, it was announced that wiring of homes and buildings would be financed with Rural Electrification Administration funds.[2] The Electric Home and Farm Authority, as will be described more fully later, contributes to rural electrification by financing the purchase of appliances and equipment.

Initial Results Obtained by the Rural Electrification Administration.—Much of the early planning and work of the Rural Electrification Administration was directed toward reducing the cost of electric service to the rural customer. The attainment of this objective was found to be possible through (1) simplifying and standardizing types of line construction, (2) planning for extensions to serve entire areas so as to effect the economics of mass construction, (3) building lines by contract after competitive bidding, (4) lowering overhead and capital charges, (5) encouraging rates which promote large use of electricity, and (6) making it possible to secure loans for electric appliances on reasonable terms.

Rate simplification and rates based on the principle of increasing consumption, as with block rate forms, were emphasized from the beginning, and many utilities have revised their rural schedules.[3] Marked increases in consumption have occurred in many places. Excluding the irrigation uses in the West, the average farm consumption in 1936 was 941 kw.-hr. The Virginia Electric and Power Company sells an average of nearly 2,200 kw.-hr. a year per farm customer. In Georgia, an aggressive sales campaign resulted in increasing the average farm

[1] *Ibid.*, No. 1, p. 2.
[2] *Ibid.*, No. 4, p. 2.
[3] *Ibid.*, Nos. 5 and 6, pp. 16 *ff.*; and vol. 2, No. 1, pp. 3 *ff.*

consumption from 700 to more than 1,100 kw.-hr. per customer per year.[1]

Decrease in rural line construction costs, considered by the Rural Electrification Administration as necessary for further extensive development of rural electrification has also been notable. The average cost of over $1,400 per mile of line, reported by the *Electrical World* in 1936, had dropped within a year to $1,200, almost a 20 per cent decline. Cooperative borrowers from the Rural Electrification Administration have generally built sturdy, dependable lines for $1,000 or less per mile. Where conditions are especially favorable, lines have been built for much less, a Texas cooperative having constructed a line for an average of $720 per mile; and an Arkansas company, some lines for $600 per mile.[2]

The first line financed with Rural Electrification Administration funds was energized on Dec. 15, 1935. Once underway, the construction of rural lines took place rapidly. As of June 30, 1937, the status of Rural Electrification Administration projects was reported as follows:

Item	Amount	Miles	Customers
Projects under construction, completed or with construction specifications approved........	$30,830,320	26,605.20	110,036
Loan contracts executed........	28,281,751	30,087.97	90,895
Total.....................	$59,112,071	56,693.17	200,931

[1] Source: *Rural Electrification News*, vol. 2, No. 12, pp. 29 *ff*.

The funds with which the Rural Electrification Administration started operation came from earmarked funds for this purpose in the Emergency Relief Appropriation of 1935, approximately $15,000,000 to finance 85 projects coming from this source. The remainder, as above reported, was made available by a later appropriation providing funds for permanently carrying on rural electrification activities.

A Permanent Rural Electrification Administration.—In recognition of the effective work accomplished by the Rural Electrification Administration and the desirability of extensive rural

[1] *Ibid.*, No. 7, p. 9.
[2] *Ibid.*, p. 8.

electrification, Senator Norris and Congressman Rayburn introduced, Jan. 6, 1936, into the United States Senate and House of Representatives, respectively, a proposal to make the Rural Electrification Administration a permanent agency of government. This bill, known as the Norris-Rayburn bill, was enacted into law as the Rural Electrification Act of 1936. It was approved by the President on May 20, 1936.

By this Act, the Rural Electrification Administration became an established agency of the Federal Government. The Act provides for loans for rural electrification in areas not receiving central station service. Two types of loans are specified: (1) for the construction and operation of generating plants or electric transmission and distribution lines or systems; and (2) for wiring, appliances, and equipment. Both electrical and plumbing fixtures were specified for the second type of loan. Borrowers eligible for loans of the first type are persons; corporations; states and political subdivisions and agencies thereof; municipalities; people's utility districts; and cooperative, non-profit, or limited-dividend associations. Preference for loans must be given to borrowers other than persons or corporations. Loans of the second type are to be made to those eligible for loans of the first type as well as to individuals.

Loans of the first type are made on terms and conditions determined by the Rural Electrification Administration but must be self-liquidating within 25 years. Loans of the second type are made on such terms, conditions, and security as to secure repayment. The rate of interest on both types is the same as the average rate paid by the Government on its long-term obligations.

The Reconstruction Finance Corporation was directed to finance the Rural Electrification Administration for loans made during the fiscal year 1937 up to $50,000,000. Thereafter, for a period of nine years, Congress is authorized to appropriate funds up to $40,000,000 a year. Fifty per cent of the annual sums available for loans is allotted yearly in the several states in the proportion that their unelectrified farms bear to the total of such unelectrified farms in the United States. The balance is available for loans without allotment.

The Act contains other provisions relating to the extension of loans, foreclosures, certificates of convenience and necessity, reports, administration, and others. In addition to the extension of loans, the Rural Electrification Administration is authorized and empowered to undertake studies, investigations, and reports concerning rural electrification and to publish and disseminate information with respect thereto.

The Rural Electrification Act of 1936 outlines a very liberal policy toward rural electrification, although the amount appropriated for this work, $50,000,000 for the first year and as much as $40,000,000 per year for nine succeeding years, totaling $410,-000,000, is markedly less than the $1,000,000,000 to be spread over a 10-year period as proposed in the bill when it was introduced. In spite of the reduction in amount, it cannot be contended that the appropriation is niggardly or insufficient. Ample funds are made available to carry forward rural electrification as fast as it is economically feasible to do so.

The liberality of the provisions of the Act indicate that the present Administration is interested in pushing rural electrification even though it may involve losses to the Government or may involve, in the end, subsidization of rural lines. In this connection, it may be pointed out that the Rural Electrification Administration is not restricted in the amounts that it can loan for the construction of generating plants and distribution lines, and the loans will be made, in many cases, to newly organized agencies without past experience in electrical enterprises. Furthermore, since these agencies must rely solely upon earnings from the proposed generating or distribution systems, it is not unreasonable to assume that overestimates of earnings will be made in some cases and that losses to the Government will result. The possibility that losses will occur is further indicated by the fact that many of these agencies will be serving areas in which the farms are somewhat more scattered, and therefore more expensive to reach, than is the case with existing services. Also, it is reported that the estimates of income of these new agencies are based upon expectation of an average consumption of electricity of 1,200 kw.-hr. per year which is about 50 per cent higher than the established record of farm use of electricity throughout the country.[1]

[1] Committee of Utility Executives, "Memorandum, Rural Electrification Act of 1936," mimeograph release submitted to the Committee on Interstate and Foreign Commerce, Mar. 10, 1936.

It should be remembered also that any of the newly created agencies that are financed completely by the Rural Electrification Administration will have to provide out of earnings sums sufficient to cover repayment of the loans within a period of 25 years, the maximum loan period. The operating expenses during this period will have to cover depreciation to permit the replacement of poles and other equipment the normal life of which is less than 25 years. Unless the estimates of earnings are carefully made and unless the obligations of ample reserves for depreciation and retirement of the loan are provided from the beginning, many of the loans may prove to be unsound.[1]

The policy of permitting the Rural Electrification Administration to finance directly the wiring of homes and the purchase of electrical and plumbing equipment represents further liberality in the promotion of rural electrification. If the Rural Electrification Administration follows the practice of making direct loans of this nature to consumers, it is possible that an extensive, nation-wide collection agency will be needed. So far, however, the Rural Electrification Administration has followed the policy of making direct loans only for wiring of farm premises, while the Electric Home and Farm Authority finances the purchase of electrical equipment and appliances, and the Federal Housing Administration's facilities are available for installations of plumbing and for remodeling.[2]

The Electric Home and Farm Authority.—The Electric Home and Farm Authority was incorporated in Delaware on Jan. 17, 1934. The incorporation of this agency had been earlier authorized by President Franklin Roosevelt in an Executive Order based upon a grant of power in the National Industrial Recovery Act.[3] The purposes of the corporation were stated to be "making feasible the increase in the use of electricity in homes and on farms, by seeking to improve the quality, decrease the cost, and finance the consumer purchase of electrical appliances." The agency was reincorporated on July 17, 1935, under the laws of the District of Columbia.

[1] *Ibid.*
[2] Rural Electrification Administration, "Light and Power for the Farm," p. 11; and "What Every Farm Leader Should Know about Rural Electrification," p. 9.
[3] Executive Order, No. 6514.

Originally, the activities of the Electric Home and Farm Authority were limited to the Tennessee Valley Authority area, but it has since extended its basic finance plan to various sections of the country. It operates by purchasing conditional sales contracts or other evidences of indebtedness arising from the retail purchase of electrical appliances. Funds for this purpose are obtained by the Electric Home and Farm Authority from private banks at the standard commercial rate of interest. As a protection of its source of capital, the Electric Home and Farm Authority has an agreement with the Reconstruction Finance Corporation whereby funds may be borrowed from the latter.[1]

Terms and conditions of the conditional sales contracts purchased by the Electric Home and Farm Authority are usually more liberal than those generally available. Small down payments, 5 per cent on most appliances, unusually low monthly payments spread over two to four years, a flat 5 per cent per year financing charge, and the convenience of paying installments along with the electric service bill are the essentials of the Electric Home and Farm Authority plan.[2]

The program has been extended only to those areas where domestic rates are such as to make feasible the use of electrical appliances by families of average income. The plan is available to the customers of the privately and publicly owned electric utilities which enter into an agreement providing that the installment payments on appliances financed through the Electric Home and Farm Authority will be billed and collected by the utility. The utility is paid a compensation for this service. Appliances eligible for financing under this plan must be approved by the Electric Home and Farm Authority. The list of approved appliances manufactured by a large number of manufacturers includes refrigerators, ranges, water heaters, water pumps, dish washers, clothes driers, vacuum cleaners, milk coolers, cream separators, farm motors, clothes washers and ironers, milking machines, and waste disposal units. All appliances financed by the Electric Home and Farm Authority are sold through the regular retail channels. Each cooperating dealer, after approval

[1] MUNGER, G. D., E.H.F.A.—and How It Helps Buyers of Electrical Goods, *Rural Electrification News*, vol. 2, No. 8, p. 9.
[2] *Ibid.*

by the Electric Home and Farm Authority, is eligible to offer customer paper for purchase to the Authority.[1]

The Electric Home and Farm Authority plan has been designed to facilitate and promote the purchase of electrical appliances and equipment by customers. It thus supplements the activities of the Tennessee Valley Authority and the Rural Electrification Administration in promoting the wider use of electricity.

Problems in Rural Electrification.—Some of the major problems connected with rural electrification were pointed out by the Committee of Utility Executives in its analysis of the Norris-Rayburn Farm Electrification bill. These were stated as follows:

First, there is the time element which must be considered in an attempt to change the lifelong habits of any class of people. It required thirty-five years for electricity to supplant gas for house lighting, and fifteen years to connect approximately 11 per cent of our farms to central station service. Merely building distribution lines will not induce sufficient customers, or sufficient use of electricity to justify the expense of the lines. This theory has been tried out on numerous occasions and has proved to be fallacious. Only 75 per cent of the farms located on present lines take service. This low degree of saturation will undoubtedly decrease as the lines are extended into less prosperous territories. The Hydro Commission of Ontario, after an exhaustive study of the problem, has established a rule which requires the signing up of enough customers on long-term contracts to justify the cost of each extension, before the construction of the lines is started.

Second, most of the farms served are located in the most populous rural sections. This group contains a large portion of dairy, poultry, and produce farms, the operation of which will permit the most profitable use of electricity in farm operation. Thus, the most prosperous sections where electricity can be most profitably used are already served. Additional territories served must to a large extent depend upon lighting and household appliances to support the new lines, an almost impossible condition.

Third, the large number of nonfarm homes in many instances have made the present rural lines feasible; future extensions must depend more and more upon the farm load alone. Of the five million nonfarm dwellers in the rural districts, four millions are already served and service is available to the other million. There remain but 1,100,000 nonfarms as future prospects for new lines. A large number of this group will never be able to wire their homes or purchase appliances.

[1] *Ibid.*, p. 10.

Therefore, from now on, rural lines must be supported almost entirely by farm customers alone.

Fourth, past extensions should not be taken as the only criterion for the practicability of constructing new lines. Future extensions should be made with the full realization of the cost of construction, cost of wiring and appliances, the cost of service, and the farmers' financial condition. Eliminating these farms now served, averaging 3.3 per mile, there remain 5,500,000 farms located on 3,000,000 miles of road, a density of 1.8 per mile. The best territories for the next 250,000 prospects average but 2.5 farms per mile, a density so low that carrying charges will not be met for years to come. After these territories have been reached, future lines must be supported by widely scattered farms with a density of only 1 to 2.3 farms per mile. Regardless of how low the interest rate offered, and the length of time allowed for amortization, such a low density simply will not permit of a self-sustaining and self-liquidating extension. Offering terms which will mortgage the farmer's future, which may over-sell rural electric service either to those financially unable to pay for it, or to those who do not desire it, might readily give the movement a black eye, and seriously retard its normal progress.

Fifth, 40 per cent of all farms are tenant operated. Even with the lowest reasonable cost of electric service, and the most liberal financing on the part of the Federal Government for wiring and the purchase of appliances, it will be extremely difficult to induce this group to invest its own money for electric service in temporary homes. A much greater demand for wired tenant farms must be created before this condition will materially improve.

Sixth, almost 50 per cent of all farms are mortgaged. With farm earnings below normal, the saddling of an additional debt burden on this group—unless it increases their earning capacity—is impractical at the present time.

Seventh, the average farm earnings in 1933 were $400; for 1934 they were about $500, while for 1935 they were little better. The appliances to be purchased and the extent of their use must be governed by the amount of money available. If, through the use of electricity, farm productivity could be enhanced sufficiently to offset the investment in appliances, and their cost of operation, the picture would be different, but the number of farms on which this is possible is relatively small.[1]

However, the existence of these obstacles has not kept the Rural Electrification Administration from moving forward with its programs. The way in which some of them have been met

[1] Committee of Utility Executives, "Analysis Norris-Rayburn Farm Electrification Bill," mimeograph release, Feb. 20, 1936, p. 2.

was discussed by Morris L. Cooke, the first Rural Electrification Administrator, as follows:

> When the Federal Government first undertook to help farmers get electric service . . . we received all sorts of advice.   People who should have known better told us it couldn't be done; they outlined all sorts of supposedly insuperable obstacles.
>
> .   .   .   .
>
> The first of these dire warnings was always, "the farmer can't afford it; his annual cash income is only $250, on the average."   This is a widespread misconception of fact.
>
> .   .   .   .
>
> There was just a little truth in the statement that the farmer could not afford electricity.   The farmer could not afford to pay the outrageous charges for individual extensions; the exorbitant rates for electricity which were in effect in some areas. . . . When something approaching a reasonable attitude was adopted by the companies, and the various utility commissions came closer to realizing the importance of electric service to the farmer, these unjustifiable terms were changed. The inevitable result was that the farmers hooked up with the power lines . . . and started using electricity.
>
> .   .   .   .
>
> Another angle of this matter of farm income was disregarded by the earlier prophets.   No matter what the farm income is, electricity properly and generously used will increase it.   Poultrymen who have electricity would hardly get along without lights in the poultry house, without electric brooders—they couldn't afford to.   Dairymen served with electric energy have learned to count on the premium which comes from electrically cooled milk.   Many farmers are learning that electric hotbeds will give them stronger, sturdier plants and let them get their produce to market ahead of the peak, and that irrigation will make them very largely independent of dry spells.   Some farmers have learned that their best vegetable crops can be frozen, and stored for months to command good prices in out-of-season markets.
>
> The final answer to the income bugaboo is that no one ever claimed we could electrify all the farms in the country.   Therefore, national income averages have no significance.
>
> When we examine the figures for average income per farm in a whole county, an entirely different picture is presented.   In a great many counties in which our projects are located—counties where absolutely

no rural-line construction had been undertaken before REA—the average cash income per farm, taking the county as a unit, is more than double the national average of $1,000 a year. . . . I think we are right in assuming that those counties can afford the electricity they so urgently want.

Now about line costs. Rural lines used to be built just like urban lines. In New England there is at least 1 mile of line with 50 poles. The wires are holding the poles up. Such lines cost too much. Lines better suited to the need, better able to withstand the strains and demands placed upon them, can be built for much less money. . . . More recently, the usual price of a mile of line in Pennsylvania—and in many other places too—has been around $2,000. Yet the *Electrical World*, leading journal in its field, recently published an editorial entitled "An Orchid for Somebody," calling attention to the reduction in average cost of line from over $1,400 a mile a year ago to $1,200 now— a drop of nearly 20 per cent in one year.

. . . .

Of course, we think this $1,200 figure is still rather high. Our co-op borrowers have demonstrated that good sturdy lines can be built in most parts of the country for $1,000 or less. Where conditions are especially favorable, the lines cost quite a bit less than that. . . .

This reduction in line costs has a very direct meaning to rural consumers. The prevalent practice among a large number of utilities is to require a monthly guarantee based on the cost of the line. If a line costs $2,000 a mile, the customers must guarantee $30 or $40 a month. If the line costs $1,000, $15 or $20 a month will provide the same percentage.

. . . .

Another one of these misconceptions, another point emphasized by the experts, is the matter of use of electricity by the farmer. The normal farmer, we were told, uses electricity only for lighting—he uses only about 300 kw.-hr. a year. Of course, there are a great many farms where electricity is used only for lighting. But the average per customer consumption of electricity in this country is higher on the farm than in the city—about 700 kw.-hr. per year in the city as against 900 on the farm.

. . . .

Another factor is sometimes overlooked. About three-quarters of REA-financed projects are cooperative in character. The people have come to understand already that the success of the undertaking depends on the use they make of electricity. They realize that it is very much to their own interests for all the customers to use as much electricity as possible. The more they use, the less it costs them.

Another one of the great "obstacles" in our path was the widely held opinion that much farm work could not be done electrically; that the equipment to do it efficiently would cost too much. But the prices are coming down and the efficiency is going up. New machines, better adapted to the task and specifically designed for farm operation, are now coming into the market.

Up to just a few years ago, it was believed impossible to operate a feed grinder, for example, with any motor smaller than 5 horsepower. Now, however, a 1-horsepower motor is known to be adequate in most situations. Even a ½-horsepower motor is known to be efficient for many uses.

.　.　.　.　.　.　.　.　.

Electricity has more than 200 uses on the farm today. No one will hazard a guess as to how many new uses there will be in the future. The little gadget known as the electric eye is doing some very remarkable things. The application of that device to agriculture may have unlimited possibilities. One of the greatest uses of electricity on future farms is almost certain to be for irrigation. Electric motors can pump a great deal of water from shallow or deep wells at low cost, making the truck farmer independent of dry spells. Virginia apple orchard operators have found that a spray system for irrigation not only increases the quantity of the crops but puts a much larger proportion of the crops into the high quality grades.

Just one more example will illustrate why I say we have accomplished rural electrification in spite of the experts. Our new style, long-span construction has been criticized severely as unsafe, by good engineers. We were confident of the quality and durability of the lines, and hopefully awaited a thorough test. The test was provided by the recent sleet storm.[1]

Summary.—The adoption of a liberal governmental policy has resulted in a marked speeding up in the electrification of the rural sections of the United States. Some $30,000,000 has been allotted or spent for projects embracing 26,000 miles of new electric lines to serve more than 100,000 farm homes. In addition, loan contracts for $28,000,000 have been executed for local project sponsors. Altogether, more than $59,000,000 has been

---

[1] COOKE, M. L., Rural Electrification in Spite of the Experts, *Rural Electrification News*, vol. 2, No. 7, pp. 7 *ff*.

lent or earmarked for more that 300 projects in 42 states, embracing 56,000 miles of lines and 200,000 customers. Within two years of operation, the Rural Electrification Administration has provided for the addition of about 25 per cent to the number of rural services that existed at the time of its formation.

The Rural Electrification Administration has lessened the time required to effect a loan and begin construction. While in its formative stage and faced with the problem of perfecting its procedures, the steps involved in bringing a cooperative distribution project into operation took an average of 43 weeks. As practices became standardized and as precedents were established, the time has been shortened to about 22 weeks.

Many of the Rural Electrification Administration loans have been made to privately owned utility companies, and most of the cooperative distribution lines purchase, or plan to purchase, energy from existing private or municipal plants. The policy of rural electrification is thus a cooperative policy and utilizes present facilities to fulfill the objective of rural lines. Continued progress can be expected. Especially is this true since the program of the Rural Electrification Administration has done much to break down the barriers hitherto deterring rural electrification. Experimentation has resulted in the widespread adoption of practices that two years earlier were considered as daring innovations. These changes include long-span construction, elimination of crossarms, abolition of service charges for which no current is furnished, and removal of the requirement that farmers contribute toward the construction of the lines built to serve them. The rapid expansion in rural electrification is concrete evidence of progress toward the objective of the national power policy to make electricity more broadly available at cheaper rates.

References

Committee of Utility Executives: "Analysis of Norris-Rayburn Farm Electrification Bill," Washington, 1936 (mimeographed).
———: "Memorandum, Rural Electrification Act of 1936," Washington (mimeographed).
COYLE, D. C.: "Electric Power on the Farm," Rural Electrification Administration, Washington, 1936.
Edison Electric Institute: "Relations of the Electric Industry to REA," New York, 1936.

Federal Power Commission: "Rural Electric Service," Electric Rate Survey, *Rate Series* No. 8, 1935.

MARLETT, D. L., and W. M. STRICKLER: State Rural Electrification Legislation, *Journal of Land and Public Utility Economics,* vol. 12, No. 3.

National Electric Light Association, *Proceedings,* annual (to 1932).

NORRIS, G. W.: A Finer Life on Nebraska Farms, *Congressional Record,* Jan. 19, 1937.

Pennsylvania Giant Power Board, *Report,* Harrisburg, 1925.

Rural Electrification Administration: *Rural Electrification News,* monthly.

————: "Light and Power for the Farm."

————: "REA Power at a Price the Farmer Can Afford."

————: "REA Guide—An Outline for the Rural Highline."

————: "What Every Farm Leader Should Know about Rural Electrification."

Tennessee Valley Authority, *Annual Reports.*

United States Department of Agriculture, National Farm Power Survey, *Bulletin* 1348, 1925.

WOLFSON, J. D.: "Power Views of Franklin D. Roosevelt," National Power Policy Committee, 1934.

ZINDER, HANINA: Problems of Rural Electric Service, *Journal of Land and Public Utility Economics,* vol. 4, No. 4.

CHAPTER XVIII

FEDERAL REGULATION OF COMMUNICATIONS

BACKGROUND OF THE COMMUNICATIONS ACT OF 1934[1]

Interstate and foreign communications are now subject to regulation by the Federal Communications Commission under the provisions of the Communications Act of 1934. This Act grew out of general dissatisfaction with the existing regulation of communications and widespread recognition in Congress of the need for drastic revamping of the regulatory machinery. The principal defects were the lack of essential powers by regulatory authorities and the absence of coordinated action among those having to do with communications. The Interstate Commerce Commission had been granted jurisdiction over the rates, and a limited jurisdiction over the service, of the interstate and foreign communications of telephone, telegraph, and radio companies by the Mann-Elkins Act, enacted in 1910, and amending appropriately the Interstate Commerce Act. The Interstate Commerce Act was still further amended subsequently, with the result that the Interstate Commerce Commission was given broad powers with respect to communications. These included authority to prescribe the forms of all accounts, records, and memoranda to be kept by the carriers; to prescribe the classes of property for which depreciation charges might be made and the percentages of depreciation to be charged for each such class of property; to fix maximum and minimum rates and charges and to prescribe just and reasonable classifications, regulations, or practices; to investigate, ascertain, and report the value of all the property owed or used by the carriers; and to regulate telephone consolidations and acquisitions of control.

While the powers of the Interstate Commerce Commission with respect to interstate communication were broad and exten-

[1] The material in this chapter is taken largely from J. M. Herring and G. C. Gross, "Telecommunications: Economics and Regulation, "McGraw-Hill Book Company, Inc., New York, 1936.

sive, administration of the law had been desultory and perfunctory.   One reason for this was that the Commission received
few formal complaints concerning the rates and practices of
interstate communication companies.   But the principal reason
was the fact that the Interstate Commerce Commission was so
fully preoccupied with the problems of railroad regulation as to
leave little of the time of its personnel for the consideration of
communication problems, certainly not time for the continuous
watchfulness and supervision that are an essential concomitant of
effective regulation.   The Commission set up no separate departments, bureaus, or divisions to deal exclusively with communication matters, these being handled by the various bureaus
established for railroad regulation.   With the cooperation of
representatives of the telephone companies, the Commission drew
up and prescribed a uniform system of accounts for three classes
of telephone companies which has remained substantially
unchanged until the present; but although directed in the Transportation Act of 1920 to prescribe classes of property of communication companies for which depreciation should be charged,
and the rates of depreciation for each such class of property, it
had failed to do so up to the time when its powers with respect
to communications were transferred to the Federal Communications Commission.   Similarly it failed to determine the value
of the properties of communication companies, although directed
to do so in the Valuation Act of 1914 (Section 19a of the Interstate Commerce Act).   The Commission served tentative valuations on the Western Union Telegraph Company and the Postal
System, but no final reports were made on these properties.   It
did no valuation work on the properties of other communication
companies.

The powers of the Interstate Commerce Commission over
communication rates in many respects were as comprehensive as
those regarding railroad transportation, except that rates for
government telegraph and cable messages were fixed by the
Postmaster General.   However, there were certain defects in
the law.   The communication companies were not required by
law to file, publish, and post rates, charges, rules and regulations,
nor did the Commission have authority to investigate proposed
changes in rates, classifications, and regulations or to suspend
the operation of such changes pending investigation of their

reasonableness. As a consequence, the communication companies could initiate at will new rates and practices which would be operative unless and until upon complaint and after investigation they were set aside as unjust or unreasonable. The Commission had no jurisdiction over through rates, joint rates, divisions of joint rates, physical connections, and security issues.

During the 24-year period of its jurisdiction over the communication companies the Interstate Commerce Commission dealt with telegraph rates in eight, with cable rates in two, and with telephone rates in four formal cases. Most of these concerned matters of local or company importance, only a few having to do with matters of general significance, such as the limitations on liability in the transmission of telegrams. In no case did the Commission deal comprehensively with telephone, telegraph, or cable rates. Nor did the Commission take any action with respect to the rates of commercial radio communication companies, although these were subject to its jurisdiction, undisturbed by separate federal radio legislation. In one case complaint was brought before it against the rates, charges, rules, regulations, and practices of a radio broadcasting company, but the Commission dismissed the complaint for want of jurisdiction, holding that broadcasting stations were not common carriers as defined in the Interstate Commerce Act.[1]

By amendment to the Interstate Commerce Act in 1920, the Interstate Commerce Commission was given jurisdiction over consolidations of telephone companies engaged in interstate commerce. The purpose of this amendment was to make legal, subject to commission control in the public interest, consolidations of telephone companies effected to eliminate the wasteful and uneconomic duplication of facilities that accompanies competition among telephone companies. Its effect was to remove telephone consolidation from the operation of the antitrust laws.

Authority to grant, or to refuse to grant, licenses for the landing of cables on the shores of the United States was given to the President by Act of Congress, approved May 27, 1921. However, this Act merely gave recognition in the law to a practice that had existed for a long time and removed doubts of its legality which were being raised in court proceedings at the time the law was enacted. Executive control of landing licenses

[1] Sta-Shine Products Co. v. Station WGBB, 188 I.C.C. 271.

dates from the action of President Grant, who refused to permit a French cable company, which held an exclusive concession from the French Government for telegraphic communication between France and the United States, to land a cable on our shores until this concession was so modified as to permit American cable companies to enjoy rights in France similar to those enjoyed by French cable companies in the United States. In his annual message to Congress, December, 1875, President Grant laid down certain conditions which he believed should control the granting of cable-landing licenses. These conditions, with later modifications, provided the framework of executive policy until 1921, when they were incorporated in the Submarine Cable Act. Prior to 1921 certain cable licenses were granted by direct action of Congress, but as a general rule the conditions were similar to those laid down by the executive branch of the Government.

Chief among the conditions incorporated in cable-landing licenses was the so-called antimonopoly provision, which was designed to prevent foreign companies from developing cable communication between the United States and foreign countries with which American companies would be unable to connect owing to the possession of exclusive cable concessions by such companies. Its object was to place American companies on an equal footing with foreign companies so far as communication between the United States and other countries was concerned and to foster the development of an American cable system for the diplomatic and consular services free of foreign interference or supervision, whether in times of peace or in times of war. Other conditions controlled the construction, laying, and maintenance of cables, priority of messages, and emergency powers of the President. There was little regulation of the rates and practices of American cable companies either in the licenses or by the Interstate Commerce Commission.

Jurisdiction of radio communication was mostly in the hands of the Federal Radio Commission under a separate law, the Radio Act of 1927. Because of the special conditions surrounding the organization and conduct of radio services, their regulation had been a matter of separate enactment since 1910, the year in which the first regulatory law, the Wireless Ship Act, was passed. This law, as amended in 1912, required the installation of efficient radio apparatus on all vessels above a certain rating leaving American ports and navigating the oceans or the Great Lakes.   Administration was placed under the Secretary of Commerce.

The first law regulating radio communication other than for the protection of life and property at sea was enacted in 1912. Its provisions dealt mostly with marine communication, reflecting the existing development of the radio art, although radio communication was defined in a manner to include both radio-telegraphy and radiotelephony.   Transoceanic radiotelegraph communication was in the developmental stage, and broadcasting, except for some experimental demonstrations of radiotelephony, was unknown.   It is not surprising, therefore, that with the rapidity and the magnitude of radio development after the World War, the regulatory powers of the Secretary of Commerce, to whom had been entrusted the Administration of the Act of 1912, should have proved wholly inadequate.

The breakdown of regulation under the Act of 1912 was occasioned by the astounding development of radio broadcasting. Beginning with the establishment of a few stations in 1921, broadcasting developed by leaps and bounds from a scientific curiosity to a great and important industry.   By the end of 1923 several hundred broadcasting stations had been established, and the number grew rapidly year by year.   To avoid chaos where many stations were using a limited number of frequencies, the Secretary of Commerce, acting upon suggestions made at various National Radio Conferences he had called, set aside a separate band of frequencies for use by each of the radio services, including broadcasting, and assigned frequencies, power, and times for operation to particular broadcasting stations.   These powers were not specifically provided in the Act of 1912, and by implication in a court test they were not upheld.   New stations came into existence in great numbers, the applicants merely being required to satisfy the general requirements of law regarding the issuance of licenses for the operation of radio stations, and new and old stations operated on frequencies and with power and periods of operation of their own choosing.   The result was a display of greed and an utter disregard of the interests of the public by many broadcasters without parallel in the annals of American industry.   Early in 1927 more than 700 stations were in operation in the absence of the restraint, either self-imposed or by regulatory authority, without which interference-free service was impossible.

In this year two events of great importance to the regulation of radio communication took place. The first of these was the enactment by Congress of the Radio Act of 1927, and the second, the adoption of an international agreement with respect to radio regulation by practically all the important nations of the world. The international convention, drawn up by representatives of the various nations at the International Radiotelegraph Conference in Washington, 1927, established the cooperation between nations which is indispensable to efficient radio communication. Radio signals emitted on certain frequencies have a service or an interference range which covers the earth; hence each of these frequencies ordinarily may be used by only one station, regardless of national interests and desires. Others may be used simultaneously by more than one station, but in such cases regional agreements are necessary. Basic to all assignments by any or all nations must be an allocation plan by which the various types of radio communication services are accorded definite portions of the radio spectrum. The Washington Conference, among other things, set up an allocation table which, with slight modifications at the Madrid Conference of 1932, provides the basic framework of international radio regulation to this day. Allocation in the international convention and regulations is by services, any nation being permitted to assign any frequency within the band allotted to the particular service to any station under its jurisdiction, the sole limitation being that no new station shall be licensed if its operation would interfere with the service of an existing station. Since the United States became a signatory to the conventions and radio regulations of the Washington and Madrid conferences, radio regulation in the United States since 1927 has been in conformity with the terms of international agreement. Other international agreements to which the United States is a party are the Executive Agreement with Canada governing broadcasting and the agreement reached at the North and Central American Regional Conference in Mexico City, July, 1933.

The Radio Act of 1927 dealt with all forms of radio communication; a commission of five members, called the Federal

Radio Commission, being established with broad powers. The jurisdiction of this body was not complete, however. The executive branch of the Federal Government retained the right to reserve for, and assign to, strictly governmental agencies bands of radio frequencies and particular frequencies; while jurisdiction over the rates and charges of radio companies engaged in interstate and foreign communication was continued in the Interstate Commerce Commission. Among the powers granted the Federal Radio Commission were authority to grant, or to refuse to grant, licenses for radio communication; to classify stations and prescribe the nature of the service to be rendered by each; to assign frequencies, power, and times for operation; and to make other regulations designed to prevent interference between radio stations. Thus, were incorporated into law the regulatory powers found by the Secretary of Commerce to be indispensable to an orderly development of radio communication.

THE COMMUNICATIONS ACT OF 1934

The Communications Act of 1934 is a broad regulatory measure covering all interstate and foreign communication by wire or radio between points located in the United States and between such points and those in foreign countries. Title I covers general provisions, such as the purposes of the Act, its application, certain definitions, and provisions relating to the commission it creates; Title II, provisions applicable to all common carriers subject to the Act and certain special provisions relating to telephone companies; Title III, special provisions relating to radio; Title IV, procedural and administrative provisions; Title V, penal provisions and those relating to forfeitures; and Title VI, a number of miscellaneous provisions. Our discussion of the Act will be limited to the main regulatory powers, procedural and penal provisions being mostly of legal significance.

The Act creates a commission of six members, called the Federal Communications Commission, to which are transferred all duties, powers, and functions with respect to communications formerly possessed by the Interstate Commerce Commission, as well as those formerly held by the Postmaster General. Thus was achieved one of the main purposes of the Communications Act of 1934, the centralization of all federal control over communications in one body. The only powers now outside the scope of jurisdiction of the Communications Commission are those residing in the executive branch of the Federal Government over cable-landing licenses and radio frequencies for the use of governmental agencies. Paragraph (c) of Section 602 amends the Submarine Cable Act of 1921, to provide that nothing in it shall be construed to limit the power and jurisdiction of the Federal Communications Commission with respect to the transmission of messages.

Provisions Applicable to All Common Carriers.—In Title II are found provisions applicable to all common carriers subject to the terms of the Act. Most of these were taken over bodily or with slight modifications from the Interstate Commerce Act, although certain wholly new provisions were added, and others for the first time were made applicable to communications.

1. *Service and Rates.*—First among the provisions applicable to all common carriers are those relating to the service and charges of communication companies. All common carriers are required to furnish adequate service upon reasonable request therefor, and the Commission is empowered to order physical connections between common carriers when it deems such necessary in the public interest and to establish through routes and charges applicable thereto and the divisions of such charges. All charges, practices, classifications, and regulations must be just and reasonable, the Commission being given full powers with respect to unjust discriminations. Schedules of charges must be filed with the Commission, in such manner as it shall direct, and no charges other than those filed and published shall be made. The Commission is authorized to suspend the operation of new charges pending hearing and investigation to determine their reasonableness and, upon complaint or its own order, may investigate the charges actually made and, where necessary, prescribe just and reasonable charges. These are rate powers commonly granted to modern public service commissions.

The Act requires a carrier to obtain from the Commission a certificate of public convenience and necessity for the construction of a new line or the extension of any line. However, so as to prevent needless delay and expense and unnecessary conflict with state regulation, Congress exempted from the requirements of this provision the construction, acquisition, operation, or extension of (1) a line within a single state unless said line constitutes part of an interstate line; (2) local, branch, or terminal lines not exceeding 10 miles in length; or (3) any lines acquired under the provisions of the Act relating to the consolidation of telephone companies.

2. *Valuation.*—The Commission may from time to time, as may be necessary for the proper administration of the Act, make a valuation of all or any part of the property owned or used by a common carrier subject to the Act. This power is similar to that granted the Interstate Commerce Commission and to the state commissions, either by law or by necessary implication. To reduce its valuation work the law empowers the Commission at any time to require a carrier to file with it an inventory of all or any part of its property together with the estimated cost of reproduction new of each unit and the reproduction cost new less depreciation as of such date as the Commission shall direct; the original cost at the time of dedication to the public use, original cost being defined as the Commission shall prescribe; and the cost to the reporting carrier of acquiring the property where this differs from the original cost at the time of dedication to the public use. Certain controversial points are eliminated by a provision that nothing shall be included in the original cost report on account of any easement, license, or franchise granted by the United States or by any state or political subdivision thereof beyond the reasonable necessary expense lawfully incurred in obtaining the same. The law lays down no rule or formula for valuation; it merely states that in making a valuation the Commission shall be free to adopt any method of valuation that shall be lawful.

Helpful clauses with respect to the valuation of telephone properties authorize the Commission to classify the property of wire telephone carriers to determine what property of a carrier is used in interstate or foreign telephone toll service, and in its discretion to evaluate only that part of the property used in interstate or foreign telephone toll service. These clauses should permit a uniform segregation of interstate and intrastate telephone property, especially for the Bell System, which would remove many of the controversial issues that have been raised before commissions and courts in telephone rate cases.

3. *Consolidation and Competition.*—The Act grants the Commission jurisdiction over consolidation of telephone companies

and provides that no person shall hold the office of director of more than one carrier subject to the Act without the approval of the Commission, but otherwise it has no jurisdiction over consolidation. In general, the policy of the Act is to maintain competition in interstate and foreign communications. By Section 313 the antitrust laws are made specifically applicable to the manufacture and sale of and to trade in radio apparatus and devices entering into or affecting interstate or foreign commerce and to interstate or foreign radio communications; and in suits brought to enforce or review the findings of the Federal Trade Commission or other governmental agency in such matters the court, in addition to other penalties, may revoke the license of the party found guilty. Section 311 instructs the Commission to refuse a license to a person whose license has been revoked under the terms of Section 313 and to any person finally adjudged guilty by a federal court of unlawful monopolizing or attempting unlawfully to monopolize radio communication through the control of the manufacture or sale of radio apparatus, through exclusive traffic arrangements, or by any other means, or to have been using unfair methods of competition. Section 314 prohibits the combination of radio and wire communication companies engaged in interstate and foreign commerce where the purpose is, and/or the effect thereof may be, substantially to lessen competition or to restrain commerce or unlawfully to create monopoly in any line of commerce.

4. *Other Powers with Respect to All Common Carriers.*—The Commission is granted the usual powers with respect to reports, accounts, records, and memoranda of the companies subject to its jurisdiction. It is empowered, also, to prescribe the classes of property for which depreciation charges shall be made and the percentages that shall be charged for each class of property. The Commission is permitted to inquire into the management of the communication companies and is required to keep itself informed as to technical developments and improvements in wire and radio communication to the end that the benefits of new inventions may be made available to the people of the United States. The Act grants no authority to the Commission over transactions between operating companies and affiliated companies involving supplies, research, services, finances, credit, or personnel that have been subjects of recent action in many

states, the Commission merely being instructed to investigate these matters and to report to the Congress whether new legislation regarding such matters would be advisable. Other matters that the Commission was required to investigate and upon which it was to report to the Congress included the extent to which wire telephone companies were furnishing wire telegraph service and wire telegraph companies were furnishing wire telephone service, and all contracts of common carriers subject to the Act that prevented the other party thereto from dealing with another common carrier subject to the Act.

5. *Cooperation with State Commissions.*—The Communications Act recognizes the necessity of, and provides for, cooperation between the federal and state commissions in the regulation of communications. In the case of radio communication this is unnecessary, since the courts have held all radio communication, even though intended only for intrastate transmission, to be interstate commerce, thus practically excluding states from the sphere of radio regulation. Much of the radio legislation enacted by states or local subdivisions, accordingly, is of questionable validity or necessity. Measures that are clearly within the police powers of the states are those which control loud-speaker operation, zoning laws applicable to radio towers and buildings, and those dealing with apparatus construction designed to protect life and property. Clearly invalid or unnecessary because of federal action are those prescribing local licenses or privilege taxes, those restricting hours of transmission, and those dealing with the location of transmitters to avoid interference. On the border line of necessity or validity are those designed to control locally originated interference with radio reception from electric power transmission circuits and from various electrical appliances.[1]

While telegraph communication is largely interstate, a considerable part is intrastate, and telephone communication is preponderantly intrastate, less than 2 per cent of the total number of messages of the Bell System being interstate.[2] In the case of these services, therefore, cooperative action by federal and state regulatory authorities in matters of service, rates, valuation, depreciation, accounting practices, and many others

[1] HERRING and GROSS, *op. cit.*, pp. 356–367.
[2] *Ibid.*, p. 213.

is essential if confusion and wasted effort are to be avoided. The Communications Act establishes the legal basis for such cooperation through joint boards similar to those provided for in Title II of the Public Utility Act of 1935, which were discussed in Chap. XIV.

Special Provisions Relating to Radio.—Title III of the Communications Act of 1934 incorporates bodily most of the provisions of the Radio Act of 1927, as amended, although certain matters no longer applicable are deleted, and new sections added. The declared purpose of the Act with respect to radio communication is to maintain control of the United States over all channels of interstate and foreign radio transmission and to provide for the use of such channels, but not the ownership thereof, by individuals operating under a federal license. No person is permitted to operate a radio station without a license issued by the Commission; the terms of licenses are limited to three years for broadcasting stations and five years for other radio stations; and the license shall be construed to create no right beyond the terms, conditions, and period of the license, the Commission not being empowered to grant a license until the applicant shall have signed a waiver of any claim to the use of a particular frequency or of the ether as against the regulatory power of the United States. To insure American ownership and control of radio stations in the United States the law forbids the issuance of a license to (1) any alien or the representative of any alien; (2) any foreign government or the representative thereof; (3) any corporation organized under the laws of any foreign government; (4) any corporation of which any officer or director is an alien or of which more than one-fifth of the capital stock is owned of record or voted by aliens or their representatives or by a foreign government or representative thereof or by any corporation organized under the laws of a foreign country; or (5) any corporation directly or indirectly controlled by any other corporation of which any officer or more than one-fourth of the directors are aliens or of which more than one-fourth of the capital stock is owned of record or voted, after June 1, 1935, by aliens, their representatives, or a foreign government or representative thereof or by any corporation organized under the laws of a foreign country, if the Commission finds that the public interest will be served by the refusal or the revocation of such license. No license, or rights or privileges thereunder, shall be transferred, assigned, or disposed of without the consent of the Commission.

Commission Powers over Radio Communication.—The powers of the Federal Communications Commission over radio communication under the Act of 1934 consist of those incorporated into the Radio Act of 1927 broadened and expanded as experience has dictated. These include authority over technical matters deemed necessary for the prevention of interference and the improvement of technical operation; and general discretionary powers, involving service standards and the determination and licensing of those applicants for facilities whose past or proposed service would serve the public interest. Among the former are authority to classify stations; to prescribe the nature of the service to be furnished by each class of station; to assign bands of frequencies to various classes of stations and frequencies, power, and times for operation to individual stations; to determine the location of classes of stations or of individual stations; to regulate and inspect transmission apparatus; to make regulations designed to prevent interference; to study new uses of radio and to provide for experimental uses of frequencies; to establish areas or zones to be served by a station; to require the keeping of station records; to prescribe the qualifications of radio station operators and to suspend operators' licenses; and to designate call letters of all stations. Among the latter are authority to pass upon the merits of applications for new stations and, in the case of established stations, to grant, or to refuse to grant, renewals of licenses, as well as to revoke licenses for cause.

Special Provisions Relating to Broadcasting. 1. *Equalization of Broadcasting Facilities.*—The Federal Communications Commission is instructed to establish and maintain an equitable distribution of broadcasting facilities throughout the United States. In the Communications Act of 1934 were carried over the provisions of the Davis Amendment to the Radio Act of 1927, which required equalization by given zones into which the United States was divided and among the states within each zone on the basis of population; but by Act of Congress, approved June 5, 1936, these provisions were repealed. The Act of 1934, as now amended, requires merely that the Commission shall so allocate broadcasting facilities among the several states and communities "as to provide a fair, efficient, and equitable distribution of radio service to each of the same." The principal reason for the original enactment was to prevent the monopolization of broadcasting facilities by any particular section of the United States. It was realized that these facilities were limited and that the use of frequencies, power, and times for operation in one section, owing to natural laws, precluded their simultaneous use in other sections. Broadcasting had developed, quite naturally, mostly in metropolitan areas where large audiences and ample talent and financial resources were available, and Congress feared that unless further development were restrained or directed such regions would monopolize the facilities at the expense of others.

While the Davis Amendment afforded the Commission a fairly efficient means of resisting pressure by applicants from congested areas, it was not well designed to achieve the purposes for which it was intended. The zones, originally created to provide for regional representation on the Federal Radio Commission, were about equal in population but vastly unequal in area, the fifth zone embracing practically 49 per cent of the total area of the United States. Because the service area of a broadcasting station is a geographical area determined by natural laws and having no relation to the distribution of population, the twofold purpose of the Davis Amendment—the equalization of broadcasting facilities as well as of broadcasting service—could not be accomplished. It would result either in further congestion of the small but populous zones or in the denial to the large but less populous zones of facilities that otherwise might be used. The Federal Radio Commission had recommended that the zones be made more nearly to conform to the requirements of natural law or that the requirement of mathematical equalization be stricken from the law, and the Federal Communications Commission made similar recommendations. Eventually Congress made the equalization of facilities a matter of discretionary judgment on the part of the Commission, the emphasis being placed upon the equalization of broadcasting service as between the states and communities of the nation.

2. *Control over Broadcasting Programs.*—As a general rule, the control over broadcasting programs is lodged with the owners and licensees of the stations. Section 315 provides that if any

licensee shall grant the use of his facilities to a legally qualified candidate for public office he shall afford equal opportunities to all other such candidates for that office and that the licensee shall have no power of censorship over the material broadcast by such candidates. Section 316 prohibits the broadcasting of any advertisement of or information concerning any lottery, gift enterprise, or similar scheme offering prizes dependent in whole or in part upon lot or chance; and Section 326 prohibits the utterance of any obscene, indecent, or profane language by means of radio communication. Otherwise, station owners and licensees have complete control of their programs, save that they are answerable to the regulating authority for the quality of their broadcasts. Section 326 provides that nothing in the Act shall be understood or construed to give the Commission the power of censorship over radio communications or signals transmitted by any radio station and that no regulation or condition shall be promulgated or fixed by the Commission that shall interfere with the right of free speech by radio communication.

The clause in Section 315 which denies to broadcasting station licensees authority to censor political speeches has created an uncomfortable situation for the broadcasters. Political speeches, whether of local or national importance, are of interest to listeners, and broadcasters have made available the use of their facilities for such purposes; yet they frequently contain matter that if untrue may constitute actionable defamation for which the station licensee as well as the speaker may be held liable. Such an interpretation of the liability of a station licensee by a lower court was upheld by the Supreme Court of Nebraska,[1] even though it was shown that the licensee had had no advance knowledge of what was to be said and that the announcer paid no attention to the words uttered. Unless this situation is clarified, licensees may be compelled to demand the right to see the manuscript of speeches prior to delivery and to bar statements of a libelous or slanderous nature, or they will be forced to deny the use of their facilities to any but "safe" speakers.

3. *Rebroadcasting; Studios of Foreign Stations.*—Section 325 provides that no broadcasting station shall rebroadcast the program or any part thereof of another broadcasting station without the express authority of the originating station. This

[1] Sorenson v. Wood and KFAB Broadcasting Co., 243 N.W. 82.

section also provides that no person shall be permitted to locate, use, and maintain a radio broadcast studio so located that its transmissions may be received consistently in the United States without first obtaining permission from the Commission. The purpose of the latter provision is to prevent the continuance of the practice that had developed of persons, who had been deprived of broadcasting facilities in the United States because of the character of their programs, setting up and operating stations in foreign countries with programs originated in and designed for audiences in the United States, thus circumventing action of the Commission taken to safeguard the public interest.

ADMINISTRATION OF THE COMMUNICATIONS ACT OF 1934

Organization of the Commission.—In the interest of expediting its work the Federal Communications Commission at first was organized into three divisions: broadcast, telegraph, and telephone, each with three members, the Chairman of the Commission serving with each division. To the Broadcast Division was assigned jurisdiction over all matters relating to or connected with broadcasting; to the Telegraph Division, jurisdiction over all matters relating to or connected with record communication by wire, radio, or cable and all forms and classes of fixed and mobile radiotelegraph services and amateur services; and to the Telephone Division, jurisdiction over all matters relating to or connected with telephone communication (other than broadcasting) by wire, radio, or cable, including all forms of fixed and mobile radiotelephone service. The entire Commission was given jurisdiction over all matters not specifically allocated to a division; over all matters that fall within the jurisdiction of two or more divisions; and over the assignment of bands of frequencies to the various radio services. The technical and administrative work of the Commission was divided among the following departments and sections: the License and Records Section; the Examining Department; the Law Department; the Engineering Department, with Broadcast, Telegraph, Telephone, International, and Field Sections; and the Accounting, Statistical, and Tariff Department. By Order No. 20, effective Nov. 15, 1937, the three divisions were abolished, and all powers and functions vested in the Commission as a whole.

Telegraph Regulation.—The work of the Telegraph Division with respect to wire telegraph communication was mostly routine, consisting largely of the accumulation of factual information regarding the services. However, the Division dealt with many specific matters. One of the first problems it attacked was the abuse of the franking practices of the telegraph companies. Information obtained from the companies showed that telegraph franks were issued quite freely to officers, agents, and employees not only of carriers subject to the Communications Act, as permitted by that law, but of other companies. Taking June, 1934, as a sample month, the total amount of charges that would have accrued on free messages sent under franks issued to others than the officers, agents, and employees of telegraph and telephone companies amounted to about $280,000 a year. The Division considered much of this free service unjustly discriminatory against other users of the service and by order restricted the issuance of franks to others than 10 specified officers, agents, and employees of railroad, steamship, motorbus, air transport, telephone, and telegraph companies not subject to the Communications Act. As a result of its studies of free service the Commission believes the frank holder is without any real justification for existence. It has recommended that Congress make unlawful the issuance or recognition of any frank or the rendering of any free service by carriers subject to the Act except in connection with situations involving the safety of life or property.

A second problem to which the Telegraph Division addressed itself was the establishment of rates of pay for government communications by telegraph. These had been set formerly by the Postmaster General at rates approximately 40 per cent of the full commercial rates and repeatedly had been the subject of complaint by the telegraph companies as unremunerative, the companies holding that government rates should be made the same as commercial rates. The Division set up a new schedule of rates which maintained the 40 per cent ratio on day messages, day letters, night messages, and night letters, but the rates for serial messages and timed-wire service were made 80 per cent of the commercial rates, with minimum charges in all cases. Rates for cable messages were established on a similar basis.

A third matter involved complaints made by the telegraph companies principally against the private wire and teletypewriter services of the American Telephone and Telegraph Company. The telegraph companies charged that these services, which were competitive to telegraph services, were furnished by the telephone company at unreasonable rates and under unfair terms of joint lease, the telephone company being concerned solely with the development of a market for its large reservoir of unused facilities and having no message service to protect as do the telegraph companies. The Telegraph Division ordered the imposition by telephone companies of reasonable monthly minimum guarantees of revenue from such services and reasonable charges for joint-user services, thus eliminating much unfair competition.

On July 1, 1935, the Commission organized a unit to make appraisals and depreciation studies of wire telegraph and radio companies. The work of this unit so far has been mostly the study of recent Supreme Court decisions on valuation, the preparation of indexes for units of material and labor, the study of trends in costs, and the study of the most economical manner of keeping an appraisal current after it has been made. No final valuations of telegraph properties, or of other communication properties, have been made. In July, 1935, the Interstate Commerce Commission transmitted to the Communications Commission a tentative valuation which it had made of the Western Union Telegraph Company as of Dec. 31, 1931, but this has not been made final. The Telegraph Division also has conducted several investigations of the business of the telegraph companies which have led to recommendations by the Commission to Congress as to new legislation.

Telephone Regulation.—The activities of the Communications Commission with respect to telephone communication have involved the accumulation of basic information concerning rates and services and the conduct of a special investigation of the American Telephone and Telegraph Company, provided for by Congress with separate appropriations. This investigation has embraced, or will embrace, inquiry into the rates and practices of the telephone company; its huge patent structure; the license and service contracts between the parent company and the associated operating companies, between the parent company and the Western Electric Company, and between the latter company and the associated companies; the nontelephone activities of the Bell System, such as the production by the Western

Electric Company of a large variety of nontelephonic devices, of which sound-recording equipment for the motion picture industry is an example; and the salary scales and pension system. Since the profits of the American Telephone and Telegraph Company and many of the aforementioned matters have long been subjects of controversy before commissions and courts, it will be in the public interest to have a complete disclosure of the facts as an aid to both state and federal regulation.

Much criticism has been made of this investigation from official and unofficial quarters, but in the absence of an official report to Congress by the Commission no worth-while evaluation of this work may be made at present. The Telephone Division carried on a series of conferences with officials of the various Associated Companies of the Bell System and the American Telephone and Telegraph Company, as a result of which substantial reductions in long-distance telephone rates have been made. Similar conferences between the Telegraph Division and officials of the telegraph companies have resulted in an important change in domestic night letter tariffs. Also, the American Telephone and Telegraph Company recently has revised and adjusted its schedules of charges for furnishing program transmission channels in connection with radio broadcasting, resulting in substantial saving to consumers. These changes in large measure remedy the complaints of broadcasting station licensees concerning the rate practices of the telephone company.

Chief among the achievements in telephone regulation has been the promulgation of a uniform system of accounts for telephone companies. Other matters with which the Commission has been concerned are the routine granting of certificates of public convenience and necessity for the construction and extension of telephone lines, the passing upon applications to consolidate or acquire telephone properties, and the determination of telephone carriers subject to its jurisdiction. Paragraph (*b*) of Section 2 of the Communications Act provides, in part, that the full jurisdiction of the Commission does not apply to "any carrier engaged in interstate or foreign communications solely through physical connection with the facilities of another carrier not directly or indirectly controlling or controlled by, or under direct or indirect common control with, such carrier." These phrases refer to mixed questions of fact and law which must be determined in each case. The Act makes no attempt to define control, and to do so would be difficult without limiting the meaning of the term in an unfortunate manner.

One important matter which came before the Commission was the application of the American Telephone and Telegraph Company for authority to construct a coaxial cable between New York and Philadelphia. The scientific principles of the coaxial cable have been known nearly as long as the electrical communications art, but this cable represents a new commercial application. Its importance to the development of communications is apparent in that this single cable has a capacity of 240 telephone channels and more than 2,000 telegraph channels, thus making available an increase in telephone and telegraph channels at lower cost. Of further significance is the fact that it gives promise of affording a means of visual communication between points, as well as the relaying by wire of television broadcast programs. The jurisdiction of the Communications Commission was questioned, but the Commission held that it had jurisdiction over (1) the proposed construction or installation, (2) the incidental commercial use of the cable during the time the proposed system is substituted for existing transmission facilities, and (3) the ultimate commercial use of the cable system. The application was granted, but in view of the potentialities with respect to the various problems of competition involved between voice and record communication, as well as the problems involved in the ultimate application of television both for person-to-person contact and for general public broadcasting, the Commission granted only an experimental authorization. The grant was made subject to various conditions designed to keep the Commission in touch with developments and ultimately to insure that the cable would be made available upon equal terms to all.

The Communications Commission also was partly instrumental in inducing the American Telephone and Telegraph Company to install a direct radiotelephone circuit to Paris, formally opened to the public Dec. 1, 1936. This is the first direct contact that the Bell System has made with continental Europe, telephone service to France having been theretofore handled through London.

Radio Regulation.—Radio regulation by the Federal Communications Commission has been largely a continuation of the work of the Federal Radio Commission, modifications in practice being made as improvements in the radio art and the demands for service have dictated. As has been pointed out, radio regulation in the United States must first be in conformity with the international allocation of bands of frequencies to various services and regional agreements providing for the exclusive or shared use of frequencies by different governments in order to avoid interference. Within the general pattern of international agreements the Federal Radio Commission established a framework of allocation of frequencies to particular services which has remained substantially unchanged.

Services Other than Broadcasting.—The rules, regulations, and policies of the Federal Radio Commission with respect to radio services other than broadcasting were accepted bodily by the Communications Commission upon its organization. Regulation of these services involves, besides the allocation of frequencies and the licensing of individual stations, the preparation of technical regulations and the examination and licensing of radio operators, the law requiring that operators of radio stations must be licensed by the Commission. The magnitude of this task can be appreciated from the consideration of a few of the more important services. On June 30, 1936, there were licensed 321 stations for point-to-point radiotelegraph fixed public service, 75 stations for fixed public press service, and 7 stations for agriculture service in the United States, subject to the jurisdiction of the Commission. The majority of these stations are licensed and operated primarily for international and overseas communications, although approximately 130 are stations that communicate with similarly licensed stations within continental United States on condition that the use of frequencies above 6,000 kilocycles for domestic service shall not interfere with international service. Except for the agriculture stations, all these licensees may transmit only for the general public pursuant to tariffs filed and approved by the Commission. Other classes of traffic handled as public correspondence in conformity with established tariffs are addressed radio program material to overseas points and one-way transmission of press messages to two or more fixed points and to ships at sea. In addition, 44 point-to-point radiotelephone stations in the continental United States, Puerto Rico, and Hawaii were licensed for international and overseas service in connection with land-wire telephone networks.

In the marine service there were 57 coastal telegraph stations in the public coastal service and 3 in the private coastal service, 42 additional stations for marine relay service, 5 mobile press stations, 6 coastal harbor radiotelephone stations and 3 coastal radiotelephone stations, 6 point-to-point radiotelephone stations to handle telephone calls with ships on the Pacific, and 2,020 licensed ship stations. Coastal stations are licensed for private service only under exceptional circumstances where the required communication cannot be provided efficiently by public service stations. Ship stations are licensed by classes. On June 19, 1936, the United States Senate ratified the International Convention for the Safety of Life at Sea, signed in London in 1929. This Convention requires all cargo ships over 1,600 tons and all passenger ships going on an international voyage to be equipped with radio apparatus and to maintain certain prescribed hours of watch for safety purposes.

In addition to these general public communication services, radio has been adapted to, and stations have been licensed for, many special services. The growth of the aviation industry created such a demand for frequencies that the Federal Radio Commission realized the necessity of developing a comprehensive plan of allocating the frequencies available so as to meet all the radio needs of aviation. This plan, as broadened and amended by the Communications Commission, established seven major chains using 59 frequencies for communication with aircraft and 39 frequencies for point-to-point communication between airports. Many of these frequencies are duplicated in various sections of the United States in order to reduce the ill effects of a shortage of frequencies available for this service. All aircraft desiring to use radio in flying over routes equipped for radio communication are required to use the frequencies and facilities employed on those routes. The Commission cooperates with other governmental agencies in coordinating activities in the interest of safety of life and property in the air, being represented at meetings of the Radio Technical Committee for Aeronautics, organized by the Bureau of Air Commerce and composed of representatives of government departments and commercial organizations interested in aviation.

Similarly, provision has been made for the use of radio in police work in conformity with a general plan. This plan provides a frequency for the use of each state, not exclusive, and the allocation of frequencies to municipalities on a zone basis, all cities within a zone being required to share and cooperate in the use of a single frequency. In addition, recently a nation-wide plan has been developed by the Commission, under which the United States is divided into zones. All licensed radiotelegraph police stations within a zone may communicate with each other under the direction of a control station, known as an interzone police station. This station has control of the operation of other stations within the zone and may communicate with other interzone stations.

Other allocations provide for special emergency stations which operate during emergencies, such as floods, earthquakes, and hurricanes, when wire communications fail; stations for geophysical exploration in the oil industry; marine fire stations for the use of radio on fireboats; stations for use in the motion picture industry; and amateur stations. Amateurs have rendered important services during emergencies, have contributed to the development of the radio art, and together constitute a reserve of experienced radio operators for use in war or other emergency. Radio frequencies are allocated also for many experimental purposes, designed primarily to advance the art. Altogether on June 30, 1936, there were 53,480 radio stations licensed in the United States, of which 46,850 were amateur. There were 656 broadcasting stations.

Regulation of radio communication other than broadcasting in the United States, besides the routine supervision of technical matters, requires the exercise of sound judgment if the maximum use is to be had of this great medium of communication. At any stage in the development of the art the number of available frequencies is limited; hence care must be exercised lest allocations of too many frequencies to certain services deprive other meritorious ones of facilities. Radio is capable of providing services akin to and competitive with those furnished by wire companies, but it has made possible types of communication not before known to man. Therefore, the needs and public benefits of one use of the limited facilities must be balanced against those of other possible uses. The allocations of the Washington and the Madrid conferences must be followed by all nations in the assignment of frequencies to stations capable of causing international interference, although the right of a nation to use any frequency upon the sole condition that no interference to the service of other nations would result is recognized. Similarly, regional agreements among the United States, Canada, and other North American countries, which control allocations to services as well as the exclusive or shared use of channels by the several nations, must be observed. But within these general requirements much opportunity remains for the exercise of discretion by the regulating body, particularly with respect to assignments to individual applicants.

The individual assignments of the Federal Radio Commission reflected the need of making provision for the use of radio for both general public and special purposes. This body first dealt with the transoceanic frequencies because of the urgency, owing to the fact that the use of one of these frequencies by one nation would preclude its use by another since the nation "squatting" on a frequency would preempt its use. Frequencies were granted to the Radio Corporation of America, Mackay Radio and Telegraph Company, Globe Wireless, Inc. (a subsidiary of the Robert Dollar Steamship Company), and Tropical Radio Telegraph Company (a subsidiary of the United Fruit Company) for general public radiotelegraph communications, while special needs were recognized in the grant of separate facilities to the press, to the Firestone Tire and Rubber Company for a circuit to Liberia, Africa, and to the Standard Oil Company of New Jersey for a circuit to South America. The urgency of early assignment in this field is shown by fact that the international frequency list, as compiled by the Berne Bureau, increased from approximately 1,700 stations in 1928 to 17,000 in 1933 and to about 25,000 in 1936, not including ship, aircraft, amateur, and portable stations. It is apparent that further assignments of transoceanic frequencies to American stations will be extremely limited and that those assigned must be utilized fully for maximum service. The Communications Commission has ordered the companies to report upon the use of the frequencies assigned them with a view to ascertaining whether or not they are being employed to the extent of their maximum usefulness.

In the field of domestic radio communication there was no necessity for haste in the appropriation and utilization of channels by American companies, since the frequencies utilized for these services may be duplicated throughout the world, it being necessary only for nations to agree upon their use on a regional or continental basis. The problems of regulation have been greatest in connection with the provision of facilities for special uses, such as for aviation, police, and emergency, as well as for general communication purposes. Owing to the existence of abundant wire telegraph facilities to serve all the larger points, and the uneconomic nature of duplicating such facilities by radiotelegraph communication, no comprehensive radiotelegraph networks for domestic communication have been established. The Federal Commission at one time granted a number of frequencies to the Universal Wireless Communication Company to establish such a system to serve 112 cities, but after setting up a few stations this company became bankrupt, and later the Commission revoked the grant of frequencies. Frequencies for domestic public radiotelegraph communication have been granted to R.C.A. Communications, Inc., and the Mackay Radio and Telegraph Company, both of which furnish service to a limited number of cities; to the Western Radio Telegraph Company, which furnishes service in the mid-continent oil regions where wire facilities are not available; and to the press. Other assignments of the continental frequencies are for the special uses to which reference has already been made.

One of the foremost problems confronting the Communications Commission today is that of providing a frequency allocation plan which will meet the pressing demands of industry for the use of radio in existing types of service, especially aviation and police, and to provide for new services, such as television and facsimile transmission. This problem involves international cooperation, since much of the new development will have to take place in the bands above 30,000 kilocycles not now allocated, owing to the congestion already existing in the frequencies below 30,000 kilocycles. While technical development has not proceeded far enough to justify specific allocations for the new services, it is true that what the Commission does now must be influenced by what it may have to do in the future. For years the Commission has encouraged and provided frequencies for experimentation in these new services, and in June, 1936, it held public hearings to determine the present and future needs of the various classes of service for frequencies above 30,000 kilocycles, to secure a fuller insight into the problems that confront the industry and the Commission, to guide experimentation along more definite lines, to review the existing use of frequencies below 30,000 kilocycles, and to assist the Government in preparing for the International Telecommunication Conference at Cairo in 1938. Evidence produced at these hearings by persons representing every phase of the radio industry and the general public indicated that the frequency spectrum from 10 to 30,000 kilocycles was totally inadequate to accommodate both the established and the developing services, that although the useful spectrum may be expanded greatly in the next few years there would still remain a dearth of facilities in relation to the demand, and that caution must be observed lest premature allocation create a frozen condition inimical to progressive technical development.

Recently the Commission announced that it will allocate frequencies to various classes of service in the radio spectrum from 25,000 to 300,000 kilocycles, bands that technical progress has made available for experimental, and eventually for commercial, use. Among the services to be accommodated in these bands are television; broadcasting; aviation; fixed services, for point-to-point communication; experimental services, to encourage fundamental research; forestry service; mobile press; government; geophysical; motion picture; coastal and harbor communication; marine fire service; special emergency services; and special services not recognized in existing rules. Television channels are to be allocated on an experimental basis until various technical and economic problems have been solved, and standards of transmission and reception have been adopted. This opens up a vast field for the expansion of radio's usefulness.

Broadcasting.—The basic plan of frequency allocation under which broadcasting stations operate in the United States today was formulated by the Federal Radio Commission and promulgated originally on Nov. 11, 1928. This plan was an allocation of frequencies, power, and hours of operation providing for the operation, not simultaneous in many cases, of nearly 700 broadcasting stations on the 90 channels available for the use of the United States in the band of frequencies 550 to 1,500 kilocycles. The basic plan recognized in the main four classes of stations: (1) higher-power or clear-channel stations, each operating alone on a single frequency at night with power of at least 5 kilowatts, designed to provide service over rural areas; (2) regional stations, with power of 500 to 1,000 watts, designed to furnish regional service, two or more stations operating simultaneously on the same frequency at night but so separated as not to cause interference; (3) limited-service stations, with power of 1 or 5 kilowatts, designed to furnish service to urban or metropolitan areas, two or more stations operating simultaneously on the same frequency at night but not free of interference except in their good service areas; and (4) local stations, with power limited to 100 watts, many stations operating simultaneously throughout the United States on the same frequency at night. The frequencies were allocated for the use of such stations, originally providing for the simultaneous operation of 315 stations at night. To provide for the operation of additional stations, some stations were permitted to share frequencies and hours of operation, others to operate during the daytime only, and still others to operate for specified hours when the dominant station on a frequency was not in use or when interference with its operation would not be caused.

Studies of individual situations have resulted in many changes designed to improve the performance of individual stations, and other changes have been made as improvements in transmission and reception devices have dictated, but the basic broadcast allocation pattern has remained substantially unchanged. In October, 1936, the Broadcast Division held hearings on broadcast allocation, after which the Engineering Department made recommendations to the Commission proposing, through evolutionary changes in existing rules and regulations rather than through radical reallocation, to bring the basic allocation plan more nearly into conformity with the developments in technical invention and operating practice that have taken place since its adoption; but so far the Commission has not acted upon these recommendations.

The basic structure of broadcasting having been established by the Federal Radio Commission, the Communications Commission has been concerned with routine matters, such as the formulation and promulgation of rules and regulations governing the technical performance of broadcast stations, the conduct of field inspections, and individual station assignments. Recently the Commission promulgated new rules pertaining to all broadcast stations other than regular broadcast stations in the interest of stabilizing and improving their services. Among these are the international broadcast stations, which broadcast programs for world-wide reception; relay broadcast stations, which originate programs at points where wire facilities are not available; visual broadcast stations, including television and facsimile stations; high-frequency broadcast stations; and experimental stations licensed to carry on the development of research for the advancement of broadcast services.

Broadcasting regulation in the United States has been, and remains, a highly controversial subject. The controversies revolve mostly around the allocation of broadcast facilities as between commercial and cultural and educational groups, and the standards and quality of commercial programs. They arise out of the peculiar nature of the development and organization of the broadcasting industry in the United States. The high cost of broadcasting together with the dependence upon advertising for revenues has created a situation in which the initiative in the establishment of stations comes mostly from persons interested in the service primarily as a source of private profit, and broadcasting stations are located where they will best serve the advertisers. The result is intense competition for stations in areas with large populations and little demand for stations in sparsely settled areas, and the Commission must of necessity consider the possibilities of commercial support in its grants of facilities. It is inevitable, therefore, that commercial stations and commercial programs should dominate the broadcasting picture.

There have long been in the United States, however, groups of people who have felt that the use of broadcasting facilities for commercial purposes represents the prostitution of a medium of great educational and cultural value. Usually inarticulate and unorganized, at times they have brought considerable pressure upon members of Congress for special legislation to safeguard and promote educational broadcasting. Agitation was continued during the hearings on the Communications Act, but Congress refused to set aside by law a fixed proportion of all broadcasting facilities for nonprofit broadcasting, merely requiring the Commission to investigate such a proposal and make recommendations. The Commission held public hearings, as a result of which it recommended that no specific allocation of definite percentages of broadcast facilities to particular types or kinds of nonprofit activities be made but that reliance be placed upon cooperation between the commercial broadcasters and cultural and educational groups for the preparation and broadcasting of educational programs. To foster and promote such cooperation, after a conference held by the Commission in 1935, the Federal Radio Education Committee was established, composed of representative people from many walks of life, as well as of government officials and representatives of the broadcasting industry. Individually, commercial broadcasting stations have cooperated with cultural and educational groups, and the Commission has considered this part of their public service obligation. So far Congress has deemed it inadvisable to allocate broadcasting facilities to specific groups by law.

An important development is the extent to which broadcasting stations have come under the control of newspaper interests. Broadcasting having become a competitor of the newspaper in three fields in which the latter formerly held a dominant position —the dissemination of current news, the control over local advertising, and the formulation of public opinion—it was inevitable that various newspaper organizations should seek facilities or the control of existing stations. How far this development has proceeded was pointed out by former Commissioner Stewart of the Communications Commission in a recent dissenting opinion in which he criticized the Broadcast Division for not paying more attention to this important matter.[1] According to Mr. Stewart there were on Feb. 16, 1937, 200 existing broadcasting stations controlled by newspapers, 8 applications pending to transfer existing stations to newspaper control, and 103 applications pending for new stations to be controlled by newspapers, this compilation not including those forms of indirect control difficult to trace. More than one-half of these had come under newspaper control since Jan. 1, 1934, the greatest rate of increase occurring since the establishment of the Communications Com-

[1] Docket No. 3858.

mission.   There is much to be said for maintaining broadcasting as a separate institution free of newspaper control in the interests of more complete and more accurate reporting of the news and greater freedom of speech.   It is a matter that well might be considered both in the grant of new facilities and in the transfer of existing licenses, particularly where newspaper control of all the broadcasting facilities in a given community is at issue.

It has frequently been charged that the broadcasting industry in the United States is controlled by monopolies.   Recently so much clamor has been raised that in March, 1938, the Communications Commission adopted an order under which it is to undertake an investigation of this matter, particularly with regard to the activities of chain broadcasting systems.

Regulation of the standards of broadcasting programs arouses even more controversy than the specific allocation of facilities. In some respects broadcasting is unlike any other public service. Technical performance is readily amenable to standardization and regulation, but program service cannot, and should not if it could, be standardized because of the varying likes and dislikes of listeners.   Nor can program service be regulated directly, except for glaring abuses, without granting to regulatory authorities intolerable powers of censorship.

In the interpretation and application of the standard of public interest, convenience, or necessity to broadcasting, the Federal Radio Commission and the Communications Commission have at times been criticized by the broadcasters for exercising a forbidden censorship, and by individuals and groups in the listening public, on the other hand, for not maintaining a stricter control over the quality of broadcast programs.   That there is legal basis for broad control over radio programs by the Commission has been well established.   In an appeal from an order of the Federal Radio Commission refusing to renew the license of a broadcasting station chiefly because certain of its programs were deemed by the Commission not to be in the public interest, the Court of Appeals of the District of Columbia held that the Commission must consider the past performance of broadcasting stations in determining whether continued operation would serve the public interest and that, since the Commission made no attempt to subject the licensee's programs to scrutiny prior to their rendition, its action did not constitute censorship.[1] Nor is the Commission's control limited to the deprivation of facilities. Indirectly it may influence the standards of all broadcasting stations by refusing to renew licenses because of objectionable programs or by renewing licenses on the condition that specific programs objected to will not be broadcast in the future and by warning stations that unless programs it deems not to be in the public interest are discontinued the renewal of their licenses will be set for hearing. The latter type of activity in the past few years has resulted in the discontinuance of numerous undesirable programs.

It is true, nevertheless, that vesting so large an amount of control over programs in the hands of station licensees, while necessary if they are to be given full opportunity for the display of ingenuity and showmanship, creates opportunities for abuse and disregard of public obligations most difficult to prevent. Numerous instances are of record in which broadcasters have utilized editorial selection and discretion in a manner heartily to be condemned by fair minded people, while they have put all sorts of sponsored broadcasts on the air. In no other public service is the need so great for the development of adequate standards by the industry itself, for unless this is done the tendency inevitably must be for the Commission or Congress to impose more and more inflexible conditions upon all broadcasting. This scarcely could be done without sacrificing much of the individuality that is so desirable a characteristic of broadcasting in the United States and that has been in no small degree responsible for the development of this great service.

RECOMMENDED AMENDMENTS TO THE COMMUNICATIONS ACT OF 1934

As a result of its investigations, either at the direction of Congress or upon its own motion, the Communications Commission believes that the Communications Act of 1934 is inadequate in certain respects. In some cases the Commission feels that the law should be changed to forbid certain practices; and in others, that its own powers should be amplified. The first of these concerns the existence of exclusive contracts held

[1] KFKB Broadcasting Association v. Federal Radio Comm., 47 F. (2d) 670.

by communication companies which restrain competition, such as exclusive contracts of telegraph companies with railroads, hotels, clubs, etc., and those of American radio and wire companies with foreign communication monopolies. The Commission has recommended that it be made unlawful "for any common carrier subject to the Act to enter into or operate under any contract any provision of which purports to grant an exclusive right of occupancy or any other exclusive right as against any other American-owned and controlled carrier engaged in interstate or foreign communication by wire or radio." The principal reason for this recommendation is that, if competition among American communication companies is to continue, it is manifestly against public policy for one carrier by contract to be able to exclude a competing carrier from places to which the public has general access. Such a provision should be adopted, the Commission has said, whether or not new legislation is enacted authorizing the merger of telegraph companies, since the Commission will still retain the power to license radio stations and to grant certificates for the construction of new telegraph lines.

Recently the Department of Justice has brought suit against the telegraph companies on the ground that many of their activities, especially those with respect to exclusive contracts, are in violation of the antitrust laws. The legality of such contracts has long been a matter of dispute, although no previous official action had been taken. If the suit is prosecuted, this question will be answered completely. It would be a simple matter, however, for Congress to declare such contracts illegal, as the Communications Commission has recommended.

A complex problem in this connection arises from the fact that while it is the policy of the Act and of the Communications Commission, as it was of the Radio Commission, to encourage competition between American radiotelegraph companies, the application of this policy through the grant of facilities to competing companies is handicapped by the existence of exclusive contracts between American companies and foreign monopolies. To remedy this situation, as was stated previously, the Commission has recommended that Congress declare exclusive contracts unlawful. In addition, the Commission has recommended that the law be amended with respect to foreign communications so as to give the Commission jurisdiction over all contracts, agreements, or arrangements for or relating to the establishment of new wire or radio circuits. The reasons for this recommendation are that competition has its worst effects in the field of foreign communication, owing to the fact that almost universally communication services in foreign countries are operated by monopolies. Competition between American companies for the business controlled by a foreign monopoly would enable the latter to drive progressively harder bargains to the detriment of American interests unless controlled by public authority.

A second matter concerns the advisability of new legislation regarding telegraph consolidation. The Communications Act of 1934 did not specifically direct the Commission to investigate this question, but because of its importance and general interest it decided to hold public hearings in order to determine whether or not to recommend new legislation. Influenced by the evidence produced at the hearings, the Commission has recommended that the law be amended so as to grant to the Commission authority to permit consolidations among telegraph companies (including telegraph land lines, cable, or radio) and acquisitions of control, if it finds that such consolidations or acquisitions would be in the public interest. This would extend to telegraph consolidation the jurisdiction that the Commission now possesses over telephone consolidation. In order that there may be no doubt of the Commission's power to protect the interests of rate payers, investors, labor, and national security, the Commission has recommended that the legislative grant of authority be supplemented by contractual obligations imposed upon the carriers as a condition to the Commission's consent to consolidation. These conditions are designed to meet opposition to consolidation by protecting employees of telegraph companies from loss of their jobs or lowered status; by insuring the extension and improvement of service by the consolidated company and preventing the abandonment or diminishing of service without the Commission's consent; by preventing changes in rates without the Commission's consent; by limiting total capitalization; and by restricting foreign ownership of American companies. Consolidation would not be mandatory, initiative resting with the companies.

SUMMARY

In summary it may be said that the Communications Act of 1934 provides a sound legal basis for needed regulation of the interstate and foreign operations of the communication companies. By consolidating all regulation in one commission it empowers this body to deal with communication problems as such, regardless of types or carriers. In this respect the relationship of the Federal Government to communications is more rational than with regard to transportation or power. The powers of the Federal Communications Commission, on the whole, are adequate, although they need to be broadened to cover certain unregulated matters, which have been pointed out previously. The law provides the legal basis for cooperation between the federal and state commissions, cooperation that is indispensable if regulation is to be effective where intrastate and interstate property and operations are inextricably intermingled. Whether or not the recent reorganization of the Commission will make for more efficient administration remains to be seen. The former organization of the Commission into divisions was based upon the theory that efficiency would be promoted through division of labor and specialization. Chairman McNinch gives as reasons for the abandonment of the divisions that the subdivision of a small commission has a "divisive effect and tends away from cooperation and mutual understanding." Furthermore, an unnecessary burden of responsibility is placed upon each group of commissioners without "opportunity to exchange views with and profit by free discussion and expression of opinion by the other commissioners."

The most controversial problems that face the Commission, and perhaps the most difficult, concern the regulation of broadcasting. In their technical aspects these problems are not particularly perplexing owing to the development of radio science, but the social and economic aspects of broadcasting regulation are involved, and the consequences far reaching. There is first the fundamental task of seeing to it that the broadcast medium is used by commercial stations primarily for the performance of a public service, whatever the wishes of the advertisers whose sponsorship makes broadcasting in the United States possible. To place restraints upon the quantity and quality of advertising matter appearing in radio programs is necessary, but to do so without exercising forbidden, and undesirable, powers of censorship, and without killing the "goose that lays the golden egg," requires tact and ingenuity.

In the second place, unchangeable physical laws make of the Commission a dispenser of favors. In order that many stations may operate simultaneously some must be limited in power, and if still more stations are to be accommodated there must be sharing of time for operation. Such limitations represent handicaps to those who must compete with more favored stations for the public ear and for advertising revenues; yet it is upon competition between stations, rather than upon stringent regulation, that we in the United States rely for high-quality programs, believing that listeners in turning their dials will decide which stations and which programs are to survive the struggle. Granting the better assignments to certain commercial groups leads inevitably to charges of corruption and favoritism by those less highly favored, charges that have been echoed in the halls of Congress. Furthermore, it is unfortunate that, in the very nature of things, the Commission through its assignments determines the status and to a large extent the future prospects of the various licensees. Local stations may, as many have, become important factors in their communities, but so long as those with better assignments operate in accordance with the Commission's ideas of what is in the public interest, the local stations can expect no further reward simply because of the fact that there are only a limited number of the better assignments. Advertisers are interested in radio coverage, just as they are in newspaper circulation, and for this they pay. Local stations with limited coverage, therefore, have little to offer other than local advertisers; their resources accordingly are limited, and the competition is at best a very unequal one. How to equalize this competition is a problem that the Commission so far has done little to solve.

Finally, there remains for solution the problem of providing more adequately for noncommercial educational and cultural broadcasting. While commercial stations have made exceptionally fine broadcasts available in considerable number, advertising, because it supplies the essential revenues, has controlled the types of programs and, as a general rule, has dictated that they have mass appeal, to the neglect of numerous

minority groups. The specific allocation by law of broadcasting facilities for educational stations has been frowned upon
repeatedly by Congress, and with the meager resources that
such stations have at their disposal their fields of usefulness are
too limited to warrant the establishment of more of them.
The only practical solution, therefore, short of a publicly sponsored broadcasting service, is cooperation between the established
commercially sponsored broadcasting system and the noncommercial interests. The Federal Radio Education Committee was created to effect such cooperation, but this Committee
has remained largely inactive. Recently, serious attempts
have been made to increase the number of agencies and to
broaden the range of interests represented in cooperative efforts
by setting up regional organizations, such as the Rocky Mountain
Radio Council to serve the states of Colorado and Wyoming
and the Texas Radio Council to serve the State of Texas. The
purpose of each of these organizations is to inventory all the
resources in a given region that may be employed for educational
broadcasting and upon the basis of the information obtained to
set up integrating machinery consisting of an administrative
organization and a technical staff to assist the cooperating
agencies in the preparation of programs. These experiments
will be watched closely by those interested in educational
broadcasting.

References

Commercial Radio Advertising, Sen. Doc. 137, 72d Cong., 1st Sess.
Federal Communications Commission, *Annual Reports.* 1935–1936.
Federal Radio Commission, *Annual Reports*, 1927–1934.
Hearings, S. 6, 71st Cong., 1st and 2d Sess.
Hearings, S. 2910, 73d Cong., 2d Sess.
HERRING, J. M., and G. C. GROSS: "Telecommunications: Economics and
    Regulation," McGraw-Hill Book Company, Inc., New York, 1936.
MOSHER, W. E., and F. G. CRAWFORD: "Public Utility Regulation," Harper
    & Brothers, New York, 1933, Chap. XXV.
Preliminary Report on Communications Companies, House Report 1273,
    73d Cong., 1st Sess.

CHAPTER XIX

GOVERNMENT OWNERSHIP

In approaching the matter of the public ownership of utilities we shall give attention first to certain general considerations. It has been argued, on the one hand, that public ownership and operation of utilities are not proper functions of government, being foreign to American ideals and incompatible with American institutions. On the other hand, government ownership and operation have been adopted as a matter of principle and party policy by socialists and communists, mostly as a step in the direction of ultimate common ownership of all means of production. That these two contrasting viewpoints are based for the most part upon traditional, even emotional, rather than scientific attitudes no student familiar with the facts will deny. Branding public ownership and operation of public utilities as "socialistic" is a scheme commonly employed by those with vested interests at stake to arouse irrational attitudes and to close minds to a realization of the fact that while the bulk of productive enterprise in the United States is conducted under private ownership, the American people have accepted the socialization of certain activities that formerly have been, and could now be, given over to private enterprise. Outstanding illustrations are parks, highways and bridges, schools, fire protection, postal service, and water supply.

On the other hand, to imply that because government enterprise has been successful in the conduct of such undertakings it is to be preferred over private enterprise in the supplying of all utility service is to overlook the vast amount of corruption and inefficiency that too often in American history have characterized the conduct of public affairs. In these opening paragraphs the authors stress the need for a consideration of this controversial issue on its merits. There are examples of efficiently operated government enterprises just as there are examples of inefficiently operated ones, and there are many illustrations of good and bad governments. Social, economic, and political conditions vary so widely as between municipalities and states and as between the United States and other countries that the generalization of unique experience is but to disseminate and to perpetuate error. A scientific viewpoint calls for a consideration of this problem in individual cases solely in the light of relevant facts and the adoption of the system that in this light will provide the best service at the lowest cost.

The matter of public ownership and operation of public utilities may be considered as a distinct and separate problem from that of public ownership in general. The industries we call public utilities make up a group that are commonly regarded as, and the courts have declared to be, "affected with a public interest." While these industries do not constitute a fixed category, and our ideas with respect to the public nature of any industry vary, it is nevertheless the common feeling that public service industries, because of the nature of their services or some peculiar relationship to the public, cannot be left solely to private enterprise. They are regulated in the public interest, and regulation as time has passed has become detailed and intrusive. Farther and farther has the sphere of regulation encroached upon that of management, and to this extent these industries have already been socialized. Whether or not ownership and management should be made completely governmental, therefore, raises problems of a more immediate and practical nature in the case of the public service industries than would the application of a similar policy to other industries.

The problem of public ownership and operation must be considered from still another viewpoint which will have a marked bearing upon the success that may be anticipated. The late President Hadley of Yale University distinguished two types of industries—the "standardized" and the "progressive"—which present vastly different types of management problems. In the standardized type, such as the post office and water supply, a large part of management is merely routine. The capital invested is either small in proportion to the year's business or subject to easily calculated depreciation charges, and necessity rarely arises for making radical changes of method to keep abreast of the times or for scrapping plant that has become obsolescent before it has worn out. In the progressive industries, on the other hand, such as transportation, communication, electric light and power, and gas, success depends upon more than mere routine performance of duties. New inventions and new methods come frequently to render plants obsolete so that depreciation is an unknown factor. Where such changes take place, the year's budget does not and cannot accurately reflect the year's actual conditions, since delay in scrapping obsolescent plant may convert a real loss into an apparent profit, or an experiment that will be successful in the long run may create present losses to be repaid in the profit of future years. It was his opinion that the history of the nineteenth century showed government enterprises to be fairly successful in the standardized industries but habitually unsuccessful in the progressive ones.[1]

Various other writers on economics and public finance have distinguished features of business that make an undertaking appropriate or inappropriate for government operation. Taussig points to maturity and monopoly as the "strictly economic earmarks for state-managed industries,"[2] and Seligman enumerates three conditions that must be carefully weighed: (1) the simplicity or complexity of the enterprise, (2) the amount of capital invested, and (3) the effectiveness or ineffectiveness of social control.[3] While there are differences of opinion as to the precise economic characteristics of industries appropriate for public enterprise, there is general agreement that the degree of success to be anticipated will depend upon the efficiency of governmental administration. Because of the difficulties of obtaining and maintaining efficiency in representative governments where political patronage plays so persistent and so pernicious a role, H. C. Adams has said that "government should avoid those industries which invite favoritism on the part of officials, or in which the charge of favoritism from customers will naturally arise."[4] It is clear, therefore, that certain

[1] HADLEY, A. T., State versus Private Management of Power Plants, First World Power Conference, *Transactions*, London, 1924, vol. 4, pp. 1569–1571.

[2] TAUSSIG, F. W., "Principles of Economics," The Macmillan Company, New York, 1911, vol. 2, p. 407.

[3] SELIGMAN, E. R. A., "Principles of Economics," Longmans, Green & Company, New York, 1905, p. 556.

[4] ADAMS, H. C., "The Science of Finance," Henry Holt & Company, New York, 1912, pp. 266–267.

public enterprises are more likely to be successful than others and that it does not follow that because a measure of success has been achieved by public ownership in one industry a like degree of success may be anticipated in others.

The term "government" has been used so far in a generic sense, although obviously the governmental unit involved in public ownership will vary with circumstances. Questions concerning public ownership of water supply systems, urban transportation systems, and gas and electric distribution systems involve mostly local units, whereas those of public ownership of railroads and communication systems necessarily involve the Federal Government. These facts hold important implications with respect to the success that may attend government enterprise, since the efficiency with which the affairs of different governmental units are conducted varies, but to discuss them fully would take us too far afield. Principal interest today is centered in municipal ownership, and to this we shall largely confine our attention.

Before 1860 strict construction of the Federal Constitution militated against broad programs of internal improvement by the Federal Government, but since the Civil War the Federal Government has engaged in various business ventures, a few of which are of interest to us here. During the period of great railroad construction the Federal Government extended financial and other aid to railroad companies for the purpose of opening up the undeveloped regions of the West and to achieve more perfect political and economic union; just before our entry into the World War it undertook the rehabilitation and extension of the railroad system in Alaska which had been constructed and operated by private companies that had failed; and during the World War it operated the railroads of the United States. Since 1902 the Federal Government has been engaged in the reclamation of tillable land as a self-supporting and self-liquidating venture, and for some time, especially during recent years, it has been engaged in various banking activities.

These activities of the Federal Government have been undertaken largely for the accomplishment of political and social purposes, however, and they throw little light upon the advisability of public ownership as an economic policy. Of a somewhat different type are the conduct of shipping operations following the World War by the United States Shipping Board and the Emergency Fleet Corporation; the activities of the Inland Waterways Corporation, created in 1924 to operate vessels on the Mississippi and Warrior rivers; and the recently inaugurated power projects of the Federal Government. With respect to such projects, the advisability of the Federal Government engaging in business ventures in lieu of, or in competition with, its citizens is at issue, not primarily the achievement of political and social objectives which are more generally thought to be the proper prerogatives of government.

Legally a state may engage in almost any form of business ordinarily considered private in character, unless restrained by the constitution of the state;[1] and before the Civil War many states did engage in business ventures, such as turnpikes, toll roads and bridges, canals, railroads, and banking. However, maladministration, inefficiency, and political corruption led generally to dismal failure and the saddling of needless debt burdens upon the citizens. The result was increased taxation and in many cases actual repudiation of state debts. Opposition to state enterprise became so general that state governments retired almost entirely from business enterprise. In many instances amendments to state constitutions were adopted forbidding the state to engage in works of internal improvement. Since the World War the states of North Dakota and South Dakota have engaged in various types of business enterprise but without any marked success, and recently some attempts have been made to revive state development and ownership of electric power systems in the establishment of power authorities and rural electrification authorities, but, on the whole, state ownership of public utilities is not a live issue. The immediate practical problem of public ownership in the utilities with which we are here concerned is that of municipal ownership, except in so far as the power projects of the Federal Government are involved.

Extent of Municipal Ownership.—The extent of municipal ownership of utilities in cities of 10,000 population and over is shown in the following summary from the "Municipal Yearbook" of 1936.[2]

[1] Wolff Packing Co., v. Court of Industrial Relations, 262 U.S. 522.
[2] "Municipal Yearbook," 1936, pp. 169–170.

MUNICIPAL OWNERSHIP OF UTILITIES

Type of utilities	All cities over 10,000	Over 500,000	200,000 to 500,000	100,000 to 200,000	30,000 to 100,000	10,000 to 30,000
Abattoir..........	36	1	0	3	14	18
Airport...........	261	12	22	27	59	141
Electric distribution............	13	1	0	0	3	9
Electric light......	131	3	2	5	26	95
Gas..............	30	1	3	3	3	20
Gas distribution...	4	0	0	0	1	3
Market...........	108	7	14	12	36	39
Port..............	60	5	10	13	15	17
Street railway.....	14	3	3	2	2	4
Waterworks.......	658	12	25	42	153	426
No utilities........	187	0	0	4	31	152
Not reporting......	30	0	0	2	9	19

Water Companies.—The preceding compilation shows that 70 per cent of the cities of over 10,000 population own water plants. Estimates for the country as a whole indicate an even greater percentage of public ownership, and the tendency is toward an increase, thus bearing out a trend that has been marked in this industry since the beginning of the nineteenth century when only 16 central water supply systems were municipally owned. Probably the principal explanations for this trend are the economic necessity of a water supply, the need for fire protection, and sanitary and hygienic considerations.

Electric Utilities.—Next in importance to water in the number of municipal establishments are the electrical utilities. Municipal ownership in this field is as old as the industry itself. Four municipal plants for street lighting were established in 1882, and the number of municipal plants increased year by year to a peak of 3,077 in 1923. From 1923 to 1932 the number of municipal plants declined to 1,849. The decrease, however, was confined to the smaller plants, since the number over 500 horsepower in size increased steadily from 60 in 1903 to 536 in 1930, and the average size of municipal generating plants increased from 231 horsepower in 1903 to 2,799 horsepower in

1930. Of the 1,849 municipal plants in existence in 1932, 905 generated all or part of their own power supply, while 944 purchased the total supply from privately owned utilities.

From 1923 to 1928 the municipal plants generating all or part of their output declined 45 per cent, whereas the number of plants purchasing all of their energy declined less than 8 per cent, thus indicating a distinct trend away from isolated generating municipal plants to the purchasing type. However, from 1928 to the close of 1930 an opposite trend is noted, the decline being 8 per cent for generating plants and 15 per cent for purchasing establishments.[1] Since 1932 there has been a slight reversal in the trend of municipal ownership of electric plants, the number having increased 21 to a total of 1,870 at the end of 1935. Of a total of 3,938 municipal plants established at one time or another since 1882, 2,068 have been sold or abandoned.[2]

The principal explanation for the decline in the number of municipal electric plants has been the revolution in technological processes. The development and improvement of interconnections between generating plants have made for more economic operation and for more dependable, more continuous service. Small isolated generating plants, except in situations where the Diesel engine is an economical installation, have become obsolete, and the tendency has been for municipalities to scrap them and to purchase power from private companies or to sell their entire systems to private interests. The decline also has been due in part to the activities of holding companies in seeking markets for the power generated in huge interconnected systems, as well as in discouraging the growth of sentiment favoring public ownership and operation. Often high prices have been offered for municipal plants in order to round out a private system. The recent upward trend in the number of municipal plants is attributable in part to the assistance offered municipalities by the Public Works Administration of the Federal Government in the form of loans and grants to enable them to construct or purchase electric systems of their own. Important in this connection also are the power enterprises of the Federal Government in the Tennessee Valley, at Boulder Dam, in the Columbia Basin, and the actual or contemplated projects in other regions,

[1] RAVER, P. J., Is Municipal Ownership at the Crossroads? *Journal of Land and Public Utility Economics*, vol. 10, pp. 61–66.

[2] *Edison Electric Institute, Records.*

which have been discussed. Those responsible for this power development have already sought, and to a greater extent in the future will seek, outlets for the power generated by encouraging municipalities to establish their own distribution systems and to purchase power at wholesale rates from the generating systems of the Federal Government. Whether the trend will be toward isolated generating plants or municipal establishments purchasing the power they retail remains to be seen.

Seventeen cities in the Tennessee Valley are using TVA power, and 75 other communities have expressed willingness to enter into contracts with the Authority. In some instances the Tennessee Valley Authority itself has constructed or bought city distributing plants and is operating them until the municipalities have amortized the costs by a "surcharge" on consumers of electric energy.[1]

The relative importance of municipal establishments to the industry as a whole is shown in the following table composed of items selected from the Bureau of Census report on Central Electric Light and Power Stations in 1932:

Item	Commercial	Municipal	Total United States
Number of establishments..	1,627	1,802	3,429
Generated output, 1,000 kw.-hr.	75,692,668	3,964,798	79,657,466
Number of customers......	21,630,662	2,227,749	23,858,411
Current sold, 1,000 kw.-hr..	62,417,695	3,748,280	65,895,975
Revenue from electric service..	$1,703,303,728	$117,801,796	$1,821,105,524

Gas Plants.—Public ownership of gas plants has never been a prominent feature of the industry. The peak of municipal ownership was reached in 1914 with 138 plants, but the number has steadily declined since then. Most of the existing public plants are in smaller communities, only 30 of the cities of over 10,000 population owning gas plants, and only 4, gas distribution systems. Philadelphia is the only city with a population over 500,000 that owns a gas plant and it is operated by a private company.

[1] "Municipal Yearbook," 1936, p. 161.

Street Railways.—Municipally owned street railways constitute a very small proportion of this industry. Only 14 of the cities of over 10,000 population report municipally owned street railways, and the number for the whole country probably does not exceed 20. The three largest cities that own street railways are New York, Detroit, and San Francisco. Subways are publicly owned in New York, Boston, and Philadelphia.

Comparison of Public and Private Electric Plants.—Attempts to measure the relative efficiency of public and private operation by making comparisons of rates paid by ultimate consumers are not very satisfactory and often lead to erroneous conclusions. There are few cases where public and private utilities serve the same community, and where comparisons are made between utilities operating in different communities multitudes of variables operate to invalidate them. As one economist put it with respect to electric utilities, rates vary with geographical location; accessibility to water and fuel; and numerous other conditions affecting costs of plant operation, transmission, and distribution of energy.[1] Thus, the rates of a particular municipal plant are not a suitable yardstick for measuring the reasonableness of the rates of another municipal plant or of a private plant; yet the familiar practice of propagandists is to argue the merits of public or private ownership from specially selected cases, the unrepresentative nature of which even a superficial examination will disclose. In the second place, unless the accounts of a municipal utility are completely segregated and kept in accordance with sound practice, with adequate provision for maintenance and the replacement of capital, it is not possible to determine whether or not the rates charged are remunerative.

Comparisons on a broad scale are faulty enough, but they do present a more satisfactory total picture. Recently, the Federal Power Commission made a nation-wide survey of the rates charged for electricity through the United States by both private companies and publicly owned systems, including irrigation districts and mutual companies. This survey embraced bills for residential service in 25,387 communities of all sizes, bills for commercial light and incidental power service in 3,447 communi-

[1] PERSONS, W. M., "Comparison of Net Monthly Bills and Rates for Specific Domestic Service of Municipal and Private Plants in the United States," published by the author, February, 1935.

ties of 2,500 population and over, bills for commercial power and incidental light service in 3,444 communities of 2,500 population and over, and bills for large commercial and industrial power service in 381 communities of 25,000 population and over. Comparisons of rates charged by private and publicly owned utilities for each class of service were made for each state on the basis of the average charges for electric service in communities of similar size, determined by weighting the bills of each community on the basis of its population, for specified quantities of electric energy. On this basis in most states the rates charged by publicly owned plants were shown to be lower than those charged by privately owned plants.

The Commission gave as reasons for making the comparisons of rate levels on the basis of the average bills in communities of similar size, instead of on the basis of over-all state averages, the following: (1) It is true generally that smaller communities have higher rate levels than do larger communities; and (2) in practically all the states there is a decided lack of uniformity in the distribution of the publicly owned and privately owned utilities in regard to the size of the communities that they serve. In some states municipal utilities serve only a few small communities, while in others they serve communities of all sizes, including some of the largest cities. Privately owned utilities, on the other hand, serve communities ranging from the smallest to the largest in each of the states.

These differences are reflected also in the volume of business done by municipal plants in the various states. In Montana and West Virginia, only 0.4 and 0.5 per cent, respectively, of the ultimate consumers are served by publicly owned utilities as compared with 29.9 and 32.5 per cent, respectively, in Kansas and Washington. Over-all state averages, the Federal Power Commission believes, do not properly reflect the influence of these factors. Thus, in the State of Iowa the Commission's compilation showed lower municipal average bills in five of the six community-size groups in which they were represented, yet a 3.1 per cent lower over-all state average bill for the private utilities, this resulting from the fact that 42.9 per cent of the population of the State served by private utilities was found in cities of 25,000 population and over, whereas all the municipal systems of that State were located in smaller towns and cities.

If the comparisons for the State of Iowa were confined to communities within the classifications which both types of utilities served, the Commission found that the average bill for private utilities would be 11.3 per cent higher, instead of 3.1 per cent lower, than for public plants.[1]

Comparisons of the rates charged by public and private plants have been attacked by representatives of the private industry as presenting an unfair picture owing to the fact that municipal plants have many advantages not possessed by private plants. Where municipalities have developed their own enterprises they have financed them through the sale of tax-exempt bonds, and in many cases they have had the advantage of being able to conduct their engineering, inspection, bookkeeping, billing, and collection activities through other departments of the city government. It has been argued, further, that private utilities bear a much heavier tax burden than public plants, the effect of this factor being very great upon the net amounts received for service. Thus, in the year 1933 the municipal utilities received an average of 2.58 cents per kilowatt-hour from all classes of customers, as against 2.62 cents collected by private companies, but if the taxes paid in the same year by both types of utilities are deducted from their gross revenues the net amount received by private utilities was 2.27 cents per kilowatt-hour, as against 2.55 cents by municipal plants.[2]

Because of the necessity, in comparing rates charged by public and private utilities, of considering amounts paid in taxes by private utilities and taxes paid, cash contributions, and free services rendered by publicly owned utilities, the Federal Power Commission in its survey made a study of these factors. It found that in 1933 taxes paid by the reporting private utilities amounted to $206,988,870, which was 11.6 per cent of their total gross revenues and 12.5 per cent of their total base revenues (excluding sales for resale to private utilities). In 1934 the total taxes paid by these utilities amounted to $237,773,260 or 12.5 per cent of their gross revenues and 14.1 per cent of their base revenues. However, in 1933 taxes and cash contributions of

[1] Federal Power Commission, Electric Rate Survey, *Rate Series* No. 5, p. 3.
[2] CARLISLE, F. L., "National Power and Resources Policies," a paper presented at the Third World Power Conference, Washington, D.C., Sept. 7 to 12, 1936.

1,618 reporting public plants aggregated $957,629 and $14,973,-872, respectively, or 0.9 and 14.2 per cent, respectively, together 15.1 per cent, of their operating revenues.

The Commission found that cash contributions by a municipal plant to the city were made for various purposes, such as payments to the municipal general fund, payments on the interest or principal of the municipal debt not contracted for the benefit of the utility, and payments to special city funds. For individual states the taxes paid varied from 0 to 6.2 per cent, and cash contributions from 0 to 56.6 per cent of operating revenues, with the municipal utilities in the three southern census divisions of the United States making the largest contributions. In view of the fact that taxes and cash contributions during 1933 might have been unusually high owing to the general financial difficulties of municipalities, the Commission requested the municipal utilities to furnish data concerning such payments for the year 1934. Compilation of the replies from 518 municipal utilities revealed their tax payments to be 1 per cent, and their cash contributions 14.9 per cent, of their operating revenues in 1934, as against 1.1 and 13.9 per cent, respectively, for the same utilities in 1933.

Services supplied cities by municipal electric plants free or at a nominal charge consist of street and park lighting; water and sewage pumping; light and power for municipal buildings; and energy for traffic lights, fire alarm systems, and other miscellaneous uses. On the other hand, municipalities often render free services to municipal utilities, such as free office space, joint superintendence, meter reading, and bill collection. That the furnishing of free services affects the cost of the service of a municipal plant is obvious, but the task of measuring this effect quantitatively is a well-nigh insuperable one. The Federal Power Commission, from a study of the free service of 689 municipal utilities, estimated that the average value of net free service furnished by publicly owned utilities in 1933 amounted to 7.4 per cent of the adjusted operating revenues, the percentages ranging from 4 per cent in the Pacific division to 13.9 per cent in the East South Central division. From its study of taxes and cash contributions, the Federal Power Commission concluded that there is little difference between the over-all totals for the United States of amounts paid by private utilities in the form of taxes and the amounts paid by municipal utilities in the form of taxes and cash contributions, when expressed as percentages of base revenue. In addition the municipal utilities have been burdened by free services to the extent previously indicated.[1]

This survey of the Federal Power Commission has done much to throw light into formerly dark corners. On the whole, and considering the facts brought to light concerning taxes, cash contributions, and free services of municipal utilities, the showing for municipal plants is more favorable than propagandists for the private industry contend, but there are wide ranges in average bills for service rendered. These variations are so striking as to warrant the citing of a few specific illustrations from the residential service. For 25 kw.-hr. of consumption, average monthly bills varied from $1 to $2.96 in communities under 250 population; from $1.19 to $2.98 in communities from 250 to 999 population; from $1.73 to $2.54 in communities from 1,000 to 2,499 population; from $1.59 to $2.40 in communities from 2,500 to 4,999 population; from $1.46 to $2.29 in communities from 5,000 to 9,999 population; and from $1.32 to $2.23 in communities from 10,000 to 24,999. For the same community-size groups, respectively, average monthly bills for 100 kw.-hr. varied from $3.50 to $10, from $3.66 to $7.65, from $4.16 to $6.32, from $4.28 to $6.21, from $3.93 to $5.80, and from $3.61 to $5.31; and for 250 kw.-hr., from $6 to $25, from $6.34 to $15.36, from $7.97 to $12.19, from $6.99 to $11.82, from $6.70 to $10.97, and from $6.14 to $9.86.

Such variations in charges, which are much wider than those of private companies operating in the same territories, reflect not alone differences in the natural or artificial conditions under which municipal utilities must operate but varying degrees of efficiency and economy. If municipal operation is to be used as a yardstick by which to measure the efficiency and the reasonableness of the rates of private companies, there is here a yardstick to suit any purpose.

The obvious conclusion from these rate comparisons is that there are municipal plants that compare in efficiency with the best of private plants and that there are poorly managed ones. However, as has been stated previously, comparisons of rates are faulty and, at best, tell but a part of the story. To judge

[1] *Rate Series* No. 5, p. 31.

the relative efficiency of public and private plants the quality and dependability of service would need to be considered, since these factors are as important as the rates themselves in determining the reasonableness of charges for electric service. Isolated municipal plants have been notoriously deficient in these respects. It has been pointed out that for the most part the successful municipal plants are those that have been in operation for long periods of time during which they have paid off all or large parts of their bonded indebtedness and have accumulated substantial reserves, making it possible for them to operate at present at relatively low cost;[1] but these are commendable practices which attest to the ability and integrity of the managements. Nevertheless, it would be mere delusion to believe that a new public plant, particularly a small isolated one, could be installed and begin operation at rates comparable to those charged by such plants without facing bankruptcy.

Restrictions upon Municipal Ownership.—There are in most states legal and other restrictions upon municipal ownership and operation of utilities which militate against the spread of this movement. Of these, three are of outstanding importance: (1) general economic and legal restrictions, (2) debt limitations, and (3) restrictions upon sales outside municipalities.

Economic and Legal Restrictions.—The right of a municipality to construct and operate a public utility, even in competition with a private utility, where there are no restrictions upon this in its charter powers or in the constitution of the state, was upheld by the Supreme Court of the United States as long ago as 1913. In a case brought to restrain a city from proceeding with the construction of a water plant in competition with a private plant, the Court held that if the constitution of the state authorized municipalities to construct utility plants, it can be done as well after, as before, such plants have been built by private parties, and one constructing such a plant takes the risk of what might happen and cannot invoke the Fourteenth Amendment to protect him against loss by the erection of a municipal plant.[2]

This case was followed and the principles amplified in a recent case involving a municipal license or excise tax imposed upon

[1] RIGGS, H. E., Facts about Public Ownership of Electric Utilities, *Public Utilities Fortnightly*, Nov. 22, 1934.
[2] Madera Water Works v. Madera, 228 U.S. 454 (1913).

privately owned utilities in the State of Washington, but from which municipally owned utilities were exempt. Mr. Justice Stone, writing the opinion in this case, held that the city and the private corporation were clearly to be classed in different categories and that "the equal protection clause does not forbid discrimination with respect to things that are different." In this opinion the following significant statements were made:

> In conducting the business by state authority the city is exercising a part of the sovereign power of the state which the Constitution has not curtailed. The decisions of this Court leave no doubt that a state may, in the public interest, constitutionally engage in a business commonly carried on by private enterprise, levy a tax to support it [cases cited], and compete with private interests engaged in like activity [the Madera and other cases cited].
>
> . . . .
>
> The injury, which appellant fears may result, is the consequence of competition by the city, and not necessarily of the imposition of the tax. Even without the tax the possibility of injury would remain, for the city is not bound to conduct the business at a profit. The argument that some way must be found to interpret the due process clause so as to preclude the danger of such an injury fails to point the way. Legislation may protect from the consequences of competition, but the Constitution does not. . . . It does not preclude competition, however drastic, between private enterprises or prevent unequal taxation of competitors which are different. Those were risks which appellant took when it entered the field. No articulate principle is suggested calling for the conclusion that the appellant is not subject to the same risks because the competing business is carried on by the state in the exercise of a power which has been constitutionally reserved to it from the beginning.[1]

Although the right of a municipality to construct and operate a utility, in the absence of constitutional, legislative, or charter restrictions, is clear, in a number of states municipalities must first secure a certificate of public convenience and necessity from the public service commission. In such cases, as in cases where municipalities may engage in public utility enterprise regardless of the existence of private companies, the question involves the economic advisability of establishing a competitive

[1] Puget Sound Power and Light Co. v. Seattle, 291 U.S. 619, 624, 625–626.

system with the attendant uneconomic duplication of facilities and personnel. This requirement has been justified on the ground that although the right of the citizens of a municipality to decide this matter for themselves free of restraint by state law or commission decision is a fundamental concomitant of self-government, it is nevertheless true that uneconomic duplication in industries that are natural monopolies is a policy the soundness of which at best is questionable, and one that the average citizen is not well qualified to decide for himself. In some cases, because of the incompetence and inefficiency of private managements, municipal plants have been constructed as the only means of furnishing reasonably good service at fair rates.[1]

The construction, extension, and operation of public power projects in the United States have frequently been obstructed by restraining orders and injunctions. The Federal Power Commission, in a recent study of this matter, found that from 1888, the year in which the first suit was filed, until Dec. 1, 1935, 278 petitions for injunctions had been filed against 195 public authorities in the United States, including municipalities or divisions or agencies of state or federal governments. The delay caused by 246 of these suits totaled 289 years, 8 months, and 22 days, or an average delay caused per case of 1 year, 2 months, and 4 days. A total of $376,233 of direct expense resulted from 198 cases, or an average of $1,900 per case; and $11,920,207 of indirect expense from 162 cases, or $73,582 per case. These cases affected public authorities in 35 different states, there being only 13 states in which no public authority had been petitioned against.

According to the records of the Federal Power Commission, the number of suits brought have increased greatly in recent years. During the 40 years from 1881 to 1921 only 26 injunction suits were instituted against 17 authorities; but from 1931 to December, 1935, 127 cases were filed involving 86 public authorities, excluding those suits filed against the operations of the Public Works Administration and of the Tennessee Valley Authority and those in which funds of either of these two agencies were involved. The creation of the Public Works Administration, and the proposal of the Federal Government to finance, by

[1] *Re* Village of Hustisford, 2 P.U.R. (N.S.) 485; and other cases.

loans and grants, the construction of municipal and other public electric plants, brought a veritable flood of injunction suits. Up to December, 1935, 75 cases were filed against PWA proposals to finance 52 public electric projects. Many suits have been brought also to enjoin municipalities from contracting for electric energy from the Tennessee Valley Authority. As of Dec. 1, 1935, injunctions had been granted in 53 cases against 46 public authorities. Forty of these cases were directed at proposals to construct or purchase an electric plant, 11 at proposals to extend facilities already owned, and 2 at proposals to operate such facilities. However, only 17 of the authorities were completely restrained from proceeding, the remainder resorting to other measures in order to achieve the proposed end or finding ways to evade the terms of the injunction.

With respect to existing plants, the Federal Power Commission found that 55 public authorities now owning and operating electric plants were interfered with by means of suits for injunction in the course of construction of their facilities, 47 in connection with the extension of existing facilities, and 17 concerning the operation of their facilities. Also, 91 public authorities that had proposed, but not yet built, an electric plant reported 119 suits for injunction brought against such proposals.[1] In so far as injunctive suits represent legitimate attempts to protect existing property rights they are above criticism, but too often they have constituted obstructive tactics designed to circumvent the will of the people and as such cannot be too severely condemned.

Debt Limitations.—In all but 18 states there are constitutional provisions limiting the debt-incurring power of local units. In six others the legislature is specifically permitted to restrict local borrowing powers, so that in only 12 states is the constitution completely silent on this matter. In addition, in 28 states a majority popular vote is required for most issues. Debts are usually limited to a certain percentage of assessed valuation of taxable property, although practically all states allow certain exemptions from the percentage limitation. The exemptions most frequently permitted are for refunding issues, special assessment debts, and debts for self-liquidating utilities. Forty-

[1] Restraining Orders and Injunctions Instituted against Public Electric Projects, Sen. Doc. 182, 74th Cong., 2d Sess.

four states have provisions, usually statutory, limiting the term for which debts may run; and in 28 states the maximum rate of interest permitted by law is 6 per cent, in 2 states it is 5 per cent, and in 1 it is 8 per cent.[1] Debt limitations present insuperable obstacles to municipal ownership where borrowing capacity is already used up, except in states that exempt debts incurred for the construction or purchase of utilities. Various devices have been employed to circumvent this limitation, such as a lease with an option to purchase or a conditional sales contract, but these devices must run the gamut of legality and have little popular appeal.

Service outside Municipalities.—Restrictions upon municipal sales beyond city limits are most serious in the case of electrical utilities. In most states restrictions are placed upon the furnishing of electric service by municipalities outside the corporate limits, only 11 states (Alabama, Arizona, California, Kansas, Louisiana, Mississippi, Montana, New Jersey, Oregon, Texas, and Washington), granting them an unconditional right to do so. In 4 states (Missouri, New Mexico, North Dakota, and Oklahoma) municipalities have no legal rights to serve customers outside the corporate limits. In 3 states they may serve outside with approval of the state commission if the area is not already served and if the private utilities able to serve waive the right to do so; in 3 other states, with commission approval if the territory is not already served; in 5 other states, with commission approval; and in 6 other states if there is a special charter provision, one of these requiring also commission approval and that the territory be not already served. In Connecticut, commission approval is not required, but private utilities must waive the right to serve the territory in question. In South Carolina, municipalities may not serve territories already served, and territory to be served must be contiguous for municipalities of less than 50,000 population, although it need not be so for larger cities. In still other states municipalities may sell excess power outside the corporate limits or up to a certain proportion of the sales within the municipality, or within a restricted outside area or when permission of local authorities has been obtained.[2]

[1] "Municipal Yearbook," 1936, pp. 312–327.

[2] Federal Power Commission, State Commission Jurisdiction and Regulation of Electrical Rates and Service, *Rate Series* No. 6.

These restrictions create needless obstacles to the normal expansion and development of municipal enterprise, since they prevent the development of larger operating units in order to reap the economies of large-scale operation and to take advantage of technological improvements. Of importance in this connection are the recent acts of several state legislatures which permit the establishment of power districts by popular referendum. These districts usually need not correspond with political boundaries, and in many cases, especially in California, Washington, and Oregon, their purposes include irrigation and water supply as well as the generation or distribution of electric power.

State Commission Regulation of Municipal Utilities.— Although it is not true for all, in many states municipal utilities are not subject to the jurisdiction of state commissions. The commissions in 12 states (Indiana, Kentucky, Maine, Maryland, Montana, Nevada, New York, Rhode Island, Vermont, West Virginia, Wisconsin, and Wyoming) have jurisdiction over rates charged by municipal electric utilities both within and outside the corporate limits of the municipality, and in 9 states (Arkansas, Colorado, Georgia, Louisiana, Nebraska, New Hampshire, New Jersey, Oklahoma, and Utah) they have such jurisdiction only outside the corporate limits. This authority has not been tested in the courts, however, with respect to the commissions in Louisiana, Oklahoma, and Utah. Recent legislation in Indiana, Oregon, and South Carolina exempts municipal utilities from commission regulation, although in the case of Indiana this applies only to plants acquired after Mar. 2, 1933.[1]

In 17 states contracts for the sale of power by private utilities to municipal utilities do not require the approval of the state commission. In other states these contracts are controlled through the authority granted the commissions to regulate rates paid by ultimate consumers. In Utah, commission approval is not required, but such contracts may be investigated, and amendment ordered on complaint or on motion of the commission. Ten of the states that do not require commission approval require the filing of power contracts between private and municipal utilities.[2]

The commissions in 35 states have authority to require rural extensions by private electric utilities, a power generally derived

[1] *Ibid.*, pp. 3–4.
[2] *Ibid.*, pp. 6–7.

from provisions in the law requiring adequate service. In 20 of these states, however, the commissions do not have similar jurisdiction over municipal electric utilities. In Maryland and Utah, commission authority over rural extensions by municipal utilities has not been judicially determined. In Vermont such authority by the commission is conditioned upon the scope of the municipal charter. In West Virginia the commission may require rural extensions where the municipality "holds itself out to serve beyond the corporate limits."[1]

PWA Allotments for Public Electric and Gas Projects.— During the past few years departments of the Federal Government have done much to encourage the establishment of municipal electric and gas plants. The Public Works Administration early declared that it was receptive to applications for loans with which municipalities might construct their own electric plants as yardsticks to determine whether or not they could satisfy themselves and charge lower rates for electricity than those charged by private companies. In most cases funds have been advanced by the PWA to a municipality under a contract providing that 30 or 45 per cent of the amount to be spent for materials and labor is to be in the form of a grant and the balance a loan. In some cases only the grant has been allotted, the municipality obtaining the balance of the funds elsewhere. These contracts impose many conditions on municipalities with respect to the expenditure of the funds, the method and manner of construction, wages and hours, persons to be employed, etc. Practical financial difficulties due to debt limitations were often circumvented by revenue-bond plans, under which the city would pledge for the repayment of loans incurred as a result of such construction or acquisition only the revenues accruing from the utility operations. The validity of this federal financing of municipal plants has been challenged in the courts, but no final decision has been rendered so far by the United States Supreme Court.

The PWA also has promoted enabling legislation in states where the legal powers of municipalities otherwise would render them ineligible for such loans. This Administration drafted and had presented to many of the state legislatures a series of measures providing for the creation of local authorities or cor-

[1] *Ibid.*, p. 9.

porations empowered to acquire, construct, and operate electric plants and transmission systems, to make contracts with the Federal Government or its agencies, and to issue revenue bonds. In order to qualify for PWA loans, many state legislatures enacted appropriate measures. These consisted of laws validating proceedings taken and bonds issued in connection with PWA loans; laws authorizing the creation of power districts, state rural electrification authorities, or nonprofit electric membership corporations; laws varying from local acts authorizing particular municipalities to acquire and operate utilities to general laws authorizing countries, cities, and incorporated towns to engage in municipal utility operations; and laws approving contracts with federal agencies regarding the financing of public works.

On Feb. 15, 1936, there were 269 allotments of funds from the Public Works Administration outstanding to public bodies, other than the Federal Government, for electric power projects. Of these, 81 were under construction, 59 were in litigation, and 60 completed. Ninety-three allotments were for new generating plants and/or distribution systems where none was publicly owned at the time of the allotment; 117 were for additional facilities for existing public plants; 3 were for transmission systems; and 56 for institutions. In addition, there were 48 allotments for federal electric projects. On the same date there were 29 allotments for gas projects, of which 12 were for new public natural gas plants, 2 for additional facilities to existing public natural gas plants, 11 for new public manufactured gas plants, and 4 for additional facilities to existing public manufactured gas plants. There were allotments outstanding also for two federal gas projects. Estimates of the amounts of funds thus allotted were $151,240,482 for the federal electric projects, $76,091,446 for the nonfederal electric projects, $49,500 for the federal gas projects, and $2,088,216 for the nonfederal gas projects. There was no litigation on the federal projects, and none on the nonfederal gas projects, obstructive litigation being confined almost entirely to electric generating plants or distribution systems in places where these facilities were not publicly owned at the time of the allotment.[1]

[1] Report of the Federal Emergency Administration of Public Works on Electric and Gas Projects, Sen. Doc. 184, 74th Cong., 2d Sess.

Advantages and Disadvantages of Public Ownership.—In this section we shall summarize the principal advantages and disadvantages of public ownership as related specifically to municipal ownership, although many of the points will have more general application. These will be discussed under two main headings: economy and efficiency in operation, and public ownership as a substitute for regulation.

Economy and Efficiency in Operation.—Relative economy and efficiency in supplying public utility service are for most people the crux of the question as to whether public utilities should be privately or publicly owned. The first advantage municipal utilities enjoy in this respect is the lower cost of capital, a material advantage because of the large amounts of fixed capital in any utility enterprise. As a general rule, municipalities can borrow at lower rates than private utilities, owing largely to the fact that municipal bonds are tax exempt. The differential is not the same for all municipalities, however, and as obligations accumulate the rate at which any municipality may borrow is bound to rise. This is an important consideration, since the construction or purchase of utilities would add greatly to the debt burden of a municipality, except where interest and amortization were payable only out of utility earnings. A further advantage in this connection is that a municipal enterprise need not be operated for profit. Thus, part of the funds that private companies must pay out in dividends on preferred or common stocks may be utilized for the retirement of debt. Such a policy has been adopted by certain well-managed municipal plants with consequent reduction in the total costs of operation and savings to consumers. As a whole, municipal utilities enjoy an advantage of lower capital costs, although this is influenced by the efficiency with which the plant is originally constructed or the price at which it is purchased.

In the case of municipal electric plants, savings due to lower capital costs may be more than counterbalanced by higher costs of operating isolated plants. Except in the larger cities, isolated generating plants are not large enough to reap the full advantages of large-scale operation, and the cost of stand-by and reserve equipment necessary to insure continuous dependable service would be disproportionately large as compared with that of large interconnected private systems. Where power is purchased, savings through lower capital costs would accrue only with respect to the investment in distribution equipment and facilities.

A second saving claimed for municipal operation follows from the possibility of consolidating certain operations of different utilities owned and operated by a municipality, or of a utility with other departments of the city government. Economies can be achieved through the common use of buildings and structures; joint billing, meter reading, inspection, etc; and common use of personnel. Also, if a city were to own its gas and electric systems the costs of competitive development, including much commercial and advertising expense, could be eliminated. In answer to this claim it is pointed out that similar economies are achieved by private companies that supply more than one type of utility service, or whose operations cover wide areas. In fact, in certain cases municipal ownership would increase the number of separate operations over consolidated companies and thus more than counterbalance such economies. There is also a real objection to the consolidation of administrative activities of different utilities, especially with other city departments, because of certain unavoidable wastes which would accompany the addition of new and unfamiliar tasks to the personnel of departments already bearing a full burden. Furthermore, in fairness to consumers and the public generally, utility operations should be self-supporting, yet under the intermingling of administrative activities the problems of cost allocation would render such determinations difficult, if not impossible to make.

The argument that since municipal corporations are free from the usual forms of taxation and their bonds are tax free, whereas private corporations and their securities are subject to taxation, savings could be effected which would be passed on to ultimate consumers in the form of lower rates for utility service will stand further examination. It has been shown previously that municipal electric utilities today have burdens of taxes, cash contributions, and free services furnished to cities which are quite comparable to the tax burdens of private utilities; and other municipal utilities have similar burdens; hence, in some cases the saving would not be appreciable. Moreover, financing municipal plants through the use of tax-exempt bonds would not constitute a net saving to the state or the nation. To destroy sources of tax revenue is not to eliminate costs of government but merely to shift them to other taxable property or income. While one community might enjoy a temporary advantage in this respect, all communities could not do so, and the more universal municipal ownership became the more completely any such advantage would tend to disappear. Real saving results only where municipal credit is superior to that of private companies, not by shifting tax burdens from one group of citizens to another.

Akin to this argument is that based upon the existence of so-called "taxless" cities, in which the profits of municipal utilities are utilized to meet the costs of government. That such cities are not taxless is obvious. Whatever the costs of government, whether low or high, they are being met by the ultimate consumers in the rates for utility service. This may be an inexpensive method of raising taxes, and one calculated to encounter less public opposition than other methods, but the citizens should not be deluded into thinking that in this way the burden of taxation is being evaded. Also, there are many valid objections to methods of taxation which in the last analysis employ modified sales taxes. In any community, taxpayers and utility consumers are not necessarily identical groups, and taxation in proportion to consumption of utility service places disproportionate burdens upon consumers with small incomes who nevertheless utilize relatively large quantities of utility service. Analysis of the consumers of electric, and especially gas, service shows clearly that the small consumer is often not the "poor man" but the professional office, the small store, the lodge hall, or the tenant of an apartment with high rental.[1] Also, with the commingling of utility and other governmental operations it is difficult, if not impossible, to determine or to place adequate checks upon the degree of efficiency and economy with which the utility services are performed or governmental departments are conducted. The arguments for "taxless" cities involve mostly methods of taxation. They have little relationship to the relative costs of public and private ownership and operation of utilities.

Opponents of public ownership and operation generally concede that certain of the savings mentioned above can be effected

---

[1] See WILSON, G. L., J. M. HERRING and R. B. EUTSLER, "Public Utility Industries," McGraw-Hill Book Company, Inc., New York, 1936, p. 49.

through public ownership, but they hold that private operation is more economical. This contention is usually based principally on the following points: (1) that a management responsible to stockholders having a financial stake in the enterprise is likely to be more efficient than a management responsible to an electorate through a commission or board serving with or without compensation; (2) that political selection, promotion, and discharge of personnel make for inefficiency and corruption; (3) that public managements are subject to political influences in the awarding of contracts and the purchasing of supplies which result in waste and extravagance; and (4) that owing to the absence of a profit motive public managements are lacking in initiative and fail to carry on the research that is essential to technical improvement.

These arguments against public ownership are based upon conditions which too frequently have characterized public enterprise, but they are not conclusive. In the first place, as has been pointed out, there are many instances of successful municipal ownership and operation, and what has been done in such cases at least indicates the possibility of its being done elsewhere if the same attention is given to avoidance of practices that make for inefficiency and high-cost operation. Certainly awareness of the historical defects in public operation should enable communities better to avoid such pitfalls in the future. In the second place, private managements are not wholly free of the defects that are pointed out as characteristic of public managements. Control of a private utility corporation by stockholders is in many respects a remote control. Too often the controlling stock of operating electric and gas utilities is owned by a holding company which in turn is controlled by individuals interested in the operating company primarily as a source of private income. Economies achieved by the industry and ingenuity of private managements of operating companies instead of being passed on to the consumers may merely go to swell the incomes of the dominant interests in a holding-company organization. Moreover, while private managements have a distinct advantage in the selection, and discharge of employees on the basis of merit, they are often subject to influences as deleterious as political ones in the awarding of contracts and the purchase of supplies. In Chap. XI it was shown conclusively that many construction, engineering, accounting, legal, purchasing, and supervision services have been supplied operating companies through servicing companies controlled by the dominant interests in a holding-company group at prices out of proportion to the costs of furnishing them and that the economies in consolidating and centralizing such services have not been passed on to consumers.

In the third place, in answer to the claim that government management would be inefficient, corrupt, and guided by political expediency rather than sound business principles, proponents of government ownership urge that here are services that touch more directly the consumer than do many other functions of government. Were government to undertake the supplying of public utility services, it is believed, there would be widespread and insistent demand for administration in accord with sound business principles, and demand for efficiency and economy in the conduct of these services might well be a spur to similar demands for efficiency and economy in the conduct of other governmental activities. Broadening the sphere of governmental activity, especially in this direction, might do much to educate the mass of citizens with respect to their collective responsibilities for good government. Political control of personnel, it is contended, could be reduced in importance through extension of the civil service.

Public Ownership as a Substitute for Regulation.—Advocates of public ownership, including many who recognize its deficiencies, hold that it would be superior to the existing system of regulated private ownership and operation. It is pointed out, in the first place, that regulatory machinery adequate to protect the interests of consumers does not exist. In one state (Delaware) there is no public service commission at all, and in many other states, as we have seen, the jurisdiction of the commissions does not embrace certain utilities or does not include powers essential to effective regulation.

In the second place, it is contended that men with sufficient ability to regulate public utilities efficiently are not attracted to regulatory commissions in great number and that many of those who display marked ability use the office of commissioner as a stepping stone to something else or are drawn into private employment where standards of compensation are much higher. In addition, the special knowledge required of an able commissioner must be attained usually after he has assumed office, and this is often of fleeting value to the commission as a body, since the personnel of a commission, under the system of political appointment for a limited period of years, is subject to frequent change. This turnover makes for inefficient personnel and lack of continuity in policy. Moreover, commissions must obtain the information upon which they act, not as executives who follow the details of operation but through the processes of hearings with opposing experts disagreeing, and in court proceedings where relief from their orders has been sought.

In the third place, the powers of commissions are restricted by legislative and constitutional limitations, the courts being final arbiters as to their scope. Thus, the courts become a factor having to do, at least indirectly, with management. Such a divided administration, it is held, makes it difficult to fix responsibility, places a premium upon the adoption of dilatory and obstructive tactics by utility executives, and runs counter to principles of sound administration.[1]

In the fourth place, regulatory action to be effective must be prompt and immediate, since conditions change continually and rapidly, yet the slowness with which final determinations are arrived at in cases involving the larger utilities is an outstanding characteristic of regulation today. In each of two recent telephone cases, involving the rates of the New York Telephone Company and the Illinois Bell Telephone Company, settlement was reached only after 10 years or more of litigation; and in the latter case, decided against the company, the court required the restitution of some $20,000,000 paid in by the consumers. Such procedure not only results in delay, but by the time decision is rendered conditions have changed, new values have been created which must be adjudicated, and the order is largely inapplicable. The Johnson Act, referred to in Chap. III, is designed to speed up the process of court review, although the various qualifications of this act give rise to numerous questions requiring of themselves judicial interpretation.

Conclusion.—In conclusion it may be said that as a substitute for regulation public ownership and operation would at a single

[1] EASTMAN, J. B., A Plan for Public Ownership and Operation, *Annals of the American Academy of Political and Social Science*, vol. 159, Part I, pp. 112–114.

stroke eliminate many of the serious defects in the present administration of public utility services. It would do away with the divided responsibility for efficiency and economy which now exists among managements, commissions, and courts; it would eliminate the troublesome, time-consuming question of valuation; and it would reduce cumbersome judicial procedure in connection with questions of management to a minimum. It would greatly simplify financing, removing the incentive to financial manipulation which has been carried to varying extremes in the case of many large utility systems; and it would enable the handling in ordinary normal administrative routine of such matters as service, accounting, and new construction. Economies could be realized, but it is an open question as to whether or not they would overbalance the incompetence and inefficiency that too often accompany municipal enterprise.

Our position in this highly controversial matter is that the advisability of municipal ownership is a question to be settled in individual cases, the integrity and efficiency with which the affairs of a particular municipality are conducted being an important, if not the decisive factor. To advocate universal municipal ownership in view of the existing inefficiency and corruption in many municipal governments is in such cases to court disaster. That the economies of public operation are uniformly not achieved is evidenced by the wide variations in the performance of existing publicly owned utilities. If public ownership of utilities were to become the accepted policy, the transition from private ownership should be gradual and should be preceded by reform in municipal affairs. Where graft, incompetence, bureaucracy, and patronage are such realities in American political life, it can scarcely be said that we are ready for the immediate adoption of public ownership on a broad scale. It has been argued that public ownership of utilities, apart from considerations of economy and efficiency, would be more democratic and would lead to cleaner politics and better government, but in our opinion the wise procedure would be to clean up existing municipal administration before assuming additional functions, especially those of a highly technical character.

That municipalities should have the unconditional right to engage in utility enterprise is undeniable in a democracy. Self-government demands that the voters be empowered to decide this matter for themselves free of legal restraints of the types previously discussed and unrestrained by the vested interests of state officials or of private parties. Restrictions in state laws should be removed, and state commissions, which in the very nature of things are committed to private ownership, should not be permitted to frustrate the will of the people. On the other hand, unwise encouragement of municipal ownership through the use of federal funds, unless adequate safeguards are provided, may result in the saddling upon some communities of technical and financial burdens that they are poorly prepared to bear.

In recent years many states have taken action designed to remove disabilities of municipalities that in the past have prevented them from exercising freedom of choice in the matter of public ownership. These new statutes vary with the states and reflect the diversity of conditions prevailing, so that generalization is impossible. In individual cases they enable municipalities to decide this matter for themselves and grant freedom to negotiate for purchase of or condemn existing utility plants or construct new facilities; permit municipal plants to serve territories beyond municipal limits; empower municipalities to issue bonds for self-liquidating utility projects; and grant various other powers without which municipalities could not undertake the ownership and operation of utilities with reasonable prospects of success.

The most significant experiment in public ownership in the entire history of the electrical utilities is today being carried on in the Tennessee Valley. Here for the first time a governmental authority is engaging in the generation and transmission of electric energy on a scale comparable to private interconnected systems covering wide areas. The Tennessee Valley Authority has relied upon municipalities and power districts to purchase its power, and it must do so to an increasing extent in the future. Thus, there has been established a system of public generation, transmission, and distribution of electric energy sufficiently far reaching to enable the working out of effective methods on a proper scale. The objections to isolated municipal electric plants do not apply to this system, and if the experiment is carried on in its pristine form many claims for or against public ownership of electrical utilities that today are mere guesses may be transformed into certainties.

Finally, the nature of the utility service has an important bearing upon the success that may be anticipated under government ownership. The problems of managing a water utility are not so complex, nor do they change so rapidly or continuously as those of the management of a gas or electric utility or a street railway system. Public ownership of the communication utilities, which would of necessity involve the Federal Government because of the interstate character of their operations, obviously would raise a different set of problems than municipal ownership of local utilities. This illustrates further the point we have made that the question of public ownership is not to be solved satisfactorily by generalizations but by the consideration of individual utilities and governmental units.

The question has frequently been raised as to whether the public ownership movement could be stopped with the industries ordinarily considered to be public utilities. If government were to take over these industries, it is asked, would not the impetus created extend government ownership to other industries clearly affected with a public interest but not of this group, and would not government be forced into the business of supplying its needs, and thus government ownership ultimately become universal throughout industry? The first of these points deals with public attitudes and reactions impossible to predict. Success of government ownership in one industry would no doubt raise the question of the desirability of extending the same policy to other industries, but wise heads would need to prevail here as in all other matters of public policy. The part of wisdom would be to recognize that all industries are not equally suited for public enterprise. As to the government being forced into industries not even remotely related to the public utilities in order to supply its needs, there is nothing inherent in the situation to require it, and in any case relative efficiency and economy should determine the policy. While vertical integration is rather common in industry generally, that it is not essential to profitable operation is evidenced by the fact that often in the same industry, *e.g.*, the automobile industry, success has been attained with or without such integration. Moreover, public enterprises today purchase supplies from private industry. Discussions of public ownership of all industry in the United States, in view of the complexity and variety of the problems of industrial organization, are for the most part fruitless. It is a question of individual industries and, in most cases, of individual governmental divisions.

References

EASTMAN, J. B.: A Plan for Public Ownership and Operation, *Annals of the American Academy of Political and Social Science*, vol. 159, Part I.

Federal Power Commission: Electric Rate Survey, *Rate Series* No. 5, 1936.

————: State Commission Jurisdiction and Regulation of Electric Rates and Service, *Rate Series* No. 6, 1936.

FERGUSON, SAMUEL: A Defense of Private Ownership, *Annals of the American Academy of Political and Social Science*, vol. 159, Part I.

HADLEY, A. T.: State versus Private Management of Power Plants, First World Power Conference, *Transactions*, London, 1924.

JONES, ELIOT, and T. C. BIGHAM: "Principles of Public Utilities," The Macmillan Company, New York, 1931, Chap. XV.

MOSHER, W. E., and F. G. CRAWFORD: "Public Utility Regulation," Harper & Brothers, New York, 1933, Chaps. XXXII–XXXIII.

"Municipal Yearbook," 1934–1936.

PERSONS, W. M.: "Comparison of Net Monthly Bills and Rates for Specific Domestic Service of Municipal and Private Plants in the United States," published by the author, 1935.

RAVER, P. J.: Is Municipal Ownership at the Crossroads? *Journal of Land and Public Utilities Economics*, vol. 10.

Report of the Federal Emergency Administration of Public Works on Electric and Gas Projects, Sen. Doc. 184, 74th Cong., 2d Sess.

Restraining Orders and Injunctions Instituted against Public Electric Projects, Sen. Doc. 182, 74th Cong., 2d Sess.

RIGGS, H. E.: Facts about Public Ownership of Electric Utilities, *Public Utilities Fortnightly*, vol. 14.

ALPHABETICAL LIST OF CASES

INDEX

A

Abandonment of service, 212

Accidents, report of, 349

Accounting, commission control of, 71

  conflict between state and federal regulation of, 385

  limits to commission control of, 80

  needed revisions in uniform classifications, 82

  objectives of regulation of, 79

  regulation by Federal Power Commission, 383

  relationship to regulation, 74

Accounting services of holding companies, 263

Accounts, audit of, 84

  as evidence, 78

  regulation of holding company, 293

  uniform classification of, 73

Act to regulate commerce (*see* Interstate Commerce Act)

Adams, H. C., views on conditions necessary to public ownership, 519

Advertising services of holding companies, 263

Advisory commissions, 13

Air Commerce Act, 1926; 304

Air mail, contracts for, 302

Air Mail Act, 1934; 305

Air transportation, Air Commerce Act, 1926, 304

  growth of, 301

  National Advisory Committee for Aeronautics, 302

  regulation of, 304

    federal, 301

    lack of coordination in, 305

Air transportation, regulation of, state, 308

  trend toward uniformity in state, 310

  Uniform Air Licensing Act, 309

  Uniform Airport Act, 310

  Uniform State Aeronautics Act, 309

All-America Canal, 444

American Association of State Highway Officials, recommendations, speed and safety regulations, 334

  vehicle size and weights, 331

American Bar Association, Aeronautical Committee, 309

  Uniform Public Utilities Act, 53

American Farm Bureau Federation, views on operation of Muscle Shoals, 417

American Gas Association, standards laboratory, 205

American Telephone and Telegraph Company, investigation by Federal Communications Commission, 499

  request for coaxial cable, 500

Annual reports, 88

Antimerchandising laws, 88

Antistockwatering laws, 241

Appliance sales, accounting for, 85

  controversy concerning, 85

  holding-company services, 263

Appliances, gas input rating, 217

Asset inflation, by holding companies, 270

Atwill, H. C., statement on achievement of security control in Massachusetts, 251

  Massachusetts plan of security control, 249

555

National Electric Light Association, Rural Electric Service Committee, 457
Rural Lines Committee, 457
uniform classification of accounts, 73
National Electric Safety Code, 222
National planning, need for, in public works, 317
National Planning Board, 316
National power policy, possibilities of, 449
and rural electrification, 453
(*See also* Water power policy)
National Power Policy Committee, 411
and coordination in power policy, 414
recommendations for operation of Bonneville Dam, 442
National Radio Conference, and allocations of broadcast channels, 485
National Resources Board, recommendations concerning rural electrification, 463
views on benefits of water resources, 390
National Resources Committee, 313
evaluation of Colorado River Compact, 374
Natural gas, interstate movements, need for federal regulation, 387
problems in regulating, 388
problems concerning relations between wholesalers and retailers, 369
Navigable streams, limitations on placing structures thereon, 393
Navigation, activities of Tennessee Valley Authority, 420
New York Commission on Revision of Public Service Commissions Law, on accounting control, 82
on contract valuation, 149
on funding short-term debt, 239

New York Commission on Revision of Public Service Commissions Law, on rate of return and efficiency of management, 168
New York plan of valuation, 149
New York Public Service Commission, establishment of, 15
New York Telephone Company, valuation of, 116
Nonconfiscatory rates, 114
No-par value stock, 241
Norris, Senator George W., advocacy of government operation of Muscle Shoals, 417
Conservation Authorities bill introduced by, 446
North and Central American Regional Conference, 486

O

Observation method for determining depreciation, 188
Ohio Bell Telephone Company, valuation of, 116
Original cost basis of valuation, 122
advantages and disadvantages of, 124
Overcapitalization, defined, 232
and financial abuses, 228
and no-par value stock, 241
and rate base, 236
and rates, 235
regulatory policies concerning, 238
regulatory problems of, 235
and service, 235
watered stock, 232
Overhead values, valuation of, 135

P

Peak load, effect on rate making, 106
Pennsylvania Public Service Commission, organization of, 68
Pipe lines, subject to Interstate Commerce Commission, 299
Port Authority of New York, 373
Port-of-entry laws, 336